JUN 2 8 2012

Fodor's

BAHAMAS

28th Edition

Fodor's Travel Publications   New York, Toronto, London, Sydney, Auckland
www.fodors.com

Eugene Fodor:
The Spy Who Loved Travel

As Fodor's celebrates our 75th anniversary, we are honoring the colorful and adventurous life of Eugene Fodor, who revolutionized guidebook publishing in 1936 with his first book, *On the Continent, The Entertaining Travel Annual.*

Eugene Fodor's life seemed to leap off the pages of a great spy novel. Born in Hungary, he spoke six languages and graduated from the Sorbonne and the London School of Economics. During World War II he joined the Office of Strategic Services, the budding spy agency for the United States. He commanded the team that went behind enemy lines to liberate Prague, and recommended to Generals Eisenhower, Bradley, and Patton that Allied troops move to the capital city. After the war, Fodor worked as a spy in Austria, posing as a U.S. diplomat.

In 1949 Eugene Fodor—with the help of the CIA—established Fodor's Modern Guides. He was passionate about travel and wanted to bring his insider's knowledge of Europe to a new generation of sophisticated Americans who wanted to explore and seek out experiences beyond their borders. Among his innovations were annual updates, consulting local experts, and including cultural and historical perspectives and an emphasis on people—not just sites. As Fodor described it, "The main interest and enjoyment of foreign travel lies not only in 'the sites,' ... but in contact with people whose customs, habits, and general outlook are different from your own."

Eugene Fodor died in 1991, but his legacy, Fodor's Travel, continues. It is now one of the world's largest and most trusted brands in travel information, covering more than 600 destinations worldwide in guidebooks, on Fodors.com, and in ebooks and iPhone apps. Technology and the accessibility of travel may be changing, but Eugene Fodor's unique storytelling skills and reporting style are behind every word of today's Fodor's guides.

Our editors and writers continue to embrace Eugene Fodor's vision of building personal relationships through travel. We invite you to join the Fodor's community at fodors.com/community and share your experiences with like-minded travelers. Tell us when we're right. Tell us when we're wrong. And share fantastic travel secrets that aren't yet in Fodor's. Together, we will continue to deepen our understanding of our world.

Happy 75th Anniversary, Fodor's! Here's to many more.

Tim Jarrell, Publisher

FODOR'S BAHAMAS

Editor: Molly Moker

Writers: Cheryl Blackerby, Chelle Koster Walton, Justin Higgs, Julianne Hoell, Kevin Kwan, Jessica Robertson, Patricia Rodriguez Terrell, Ramona Settle, Sharon Williams

Production Editor: Carrie Parker
Maps & Illustrations: Mark Stroud and Henry Colomb, Moon Street Cartography; David Lindroth, Inc., *cartographers;* Bob Blake, Rebecca Baer, *map editors;* William Wu, *information graphics*
Design: Fabrizio La Rocca, *creative director;* Guido Caroti, *art director;* Tina Malaney, Nora Rosansky, Chie Ushio, Jessica Walsh, *designers;* Melanie Marin, *associate director of photography*
Cover Photo: (Harbour Island): Nina Buesing/Stone/Getty Images
Production Manager: Angela L. McLean

28th Edition

ISBN 978–0–679–00937–5

ISSN 1524-7945

SPECIAL SALES

This book is available at special discounts for bulk purchases for sales promotions or premiums. Special editions, including personalized covers, excerpts of existing books, and corporate imprints, can be created in large quantities for special needs. For more information, write to Special Markets/Premium Sales, 1745 Broadway, MD 3-2, New York, NY 10019, or e-mail specialmarkets@randomhouse.com.

AN IMPORTANT TIP & AN INVITATION

Although all prices, opening times, and other details in this book are based on information supplied to us at press time, changes occur all the time in the travel world, and Fodor's cannot accept responsibility for facts that become outdated or for inadvertent errors or omissions. So **always confirm information when it matters,** especially if you're making a detour to visit a specific place. Your experiences—positive and negative—matter to us. If we have missed or misstated something, **please write to us.** Share your opinion instantly through our online feedback center at fodors.com/contact-us.

PRINTED IN CHINA

10 9 8 7 6 5 4 3 2 1

CONTENTS

Fodor's Features

MAPS

ABOUT THIS BOOK

Our Ratings

At Fodor's, we spend considerable time choosing the best places in a destination so you don't have to. By default, anything we recommend in this book is worth visiting. But some sights, properties, and experiences are so great that we've recognized them with additional accolades. Orange **Fodor's Choice** stars indicate our top recommendations; black stars highlight places we deem **Highly Recommended**; and **Best Bets** call attention to top properties in various categories. Disagree with any of our choices? Care to nominate a new place? Visit our feedback center at www.fodors.com/feedback.

Hotels

Hotels have private bath, phone, TV, and air-conditioning, and do not offer meals unless we specify that in the review. We always list facilities but not whether you'll be charged an extra fee to use them.

Restaurants

Unless we state otherwise, restaurants are open for lunch and dinner daily. We mention dress only when there's a specific requirement and reservations only when they're essential or not accepted—it's always best to book ahead.

Credit Cards

We assume that restaurants and hotels accept credit cards. If not, we'll note it in the review.

Budget Well

Hotel and restaurant price categories from ¢ to $$$$ are defined in the opening pages of the respective chapters. For attractions, we always give standard adult admission fees; reductions are usually available for children, students, and senior citizens.

Listings
- ★ Fodor's Choice
- ★ Highly recommended
- ⊠ Physical address
- ✛ Directions or Map coordinates
- ⌖ Mailing address
- ☎ Telephone
- 🖷 Fax
- ⊕ On the Web
- ✐ E-mail
- ⛛ Admission fee
- ☉ Open/closed times
- Ⓜ Metro stations
- ⊟ No credit cards

Hotels & Restaurants
- 🗏 Hotel
- ⤵ Number of rooms
- ⚲ Facilities
- ⅧⅪ Meal plans
- ✕ Restaurant
- ⚲ Reservations
- ⚲ Dress code
- ↘ Smoking

Outdoors
- 🏌 Golf
- ⛺ Camping

Other
- ☺ Family-friendly
- ⇨ See also
- ⊠ Branch address
- ☞ Take note

1

Experience the Bahamas

WHAT'S WHERE

Numbers refer to chapter numbers.

2 New Providence and Paradise islands. Nassau and nearby Paradise Island are the most action-packed places in the Bahamas. From flashy megaresort Atlantis to fine dining and high-end shopping, development here is unrivaled on any of the other islands.

3 Grand Bahama Island. Urban and deserted vibes mix to create a quieter alternative to fast-paced Nassau. Lucaya has great shopping, gambling, golfing, and beach parties, but old-island fishing settlements and vast expanses of untouched nature appeal to adventurous travelers.

4 The Abacos. Shallow, translucent waters, top-notch marinas, and idyllic, historic settlements spread over 120 mi of cays (some uninhabited) give the Abacos the apt title of "Sailing Capital of the Bahamas."

5 Andros, Bimini, and the Berry Islands. In the northwest corner of the Bahamas, these islands share many characteristics, most notably their reputation for excellent fishing and diving. Each exudes a casual, old-island atmosphere and abundant natural beauty.

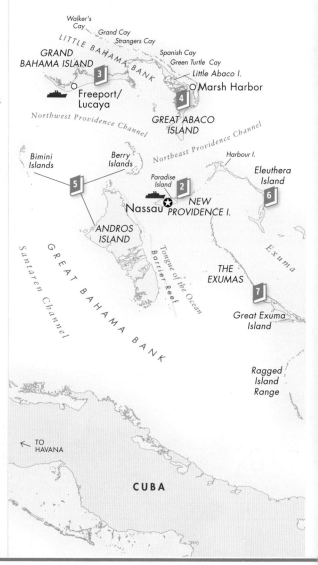

6 Eleuthera and Harbour Island. The Nantucket of the Bahamas, Harbour Island—rimmed by its legendary pink-sand beach—is the most chic Out Island. Eleuthera is the opposite, with historic churches and pretty fishing villages, unpretentious inns, and a few upscale, intimate beach resorts.

7 The Exumas. Hundreds of islands skip like stones across the Tropic of Cancer, all with gorgeous white beaches and the most beautiful water in the Bahamas. Mainland Great Exuma has friendly locals and great beach parties.

8 The Southern Out Islands. The Bahamas' southernmost islands have so few visitors and so many natural wonders. These islands are also known as the Family Islands, since many Bahamians have roots on these smaller and less populated cays.

9 Turks and Caicos. Just south of the Bahamas, miles of white-sand beaches surround this tiny chain of islands, only eight of which are inhabited. Go for deserted beaches and excellent diving on one of the world's largest coral reefs.

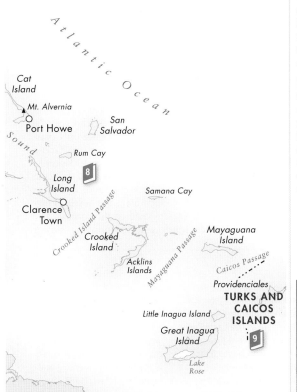

BAHAMAS TODAY

Like much of the world, the Bahamas has had to put big development plans on the back burner as the country rides out the economic recession. The largest project, the Baha Mar overhaul of the Cable Beach strip, is finally underway, but is years behind schedule. Bahamians have used this situation as an opportunity to spruce up existing properties and improve an infrastructure that was starting to show signs of age and neglect. Once the tide turns and tourism picks back up, the Bahamas will be better than ever.

Today's Bahamas

. . . is still very British. From driving on the left side of the road (albeit mostly in left-hand drive cars) to tea parties to wig-wearing lawyers strolling into court, the Bahamas still has a decidedly British air about it. The country gained independence from England in 1973, but old colonial habits die hard. Bahamians learn British spelling in school, and the country still uses the Westminster style of government. That said, a constant diet of American media has had an impact on the country. Bahamians measure temperature in Fahrenheit instead of Celsius, and although the English gentleman's cricket is the national sport, you'll be hard-pressed to find a local who understands the game, much less plays it.

. . . is a playground for the rich and famous. With its near-perfect year-round weather, modern infrastructure and amenities, and proximity to the United States, it's no wonder that the Bahamas is a home away from Hollywood for many celebrities. Sean Connery lives behind the gates of the exclusive Lyford Cay community on New Providence Island. Johnny Depp owns his own private island in the Exumas, as do Tim McGraw and Faith Hill, David Copperfield, and Nicolas Cage, who also owns a home on Paradise Island. Mariah Carey and Nick Cannon got hitched on the grounds of her private Eleuthera estate; the island is also home to Lenny Kravitz, whose mother, actress Roxie Roker, grew up there.

. . . is many different destinations. The majority of the 4 million tourists who visit the Bahamas each year experience only Nassau, Paradise Island, or perhaps Grand Bahama. But with more than 700 islands, there's so much more to see and do. Each island offers a different flavor and none of them have the hustle and bustle of big-city life experienced in the capital. The farther south you venture, the slower

WHAT WE'RE TALKING ABOUT

Bahamians are passionate about their politics, and with a general election scheduled to be called in 2012, you'll be sure to hear opinions about which party will win, what the issues will be, and scandals that may or may not sway voters. The Bahamas adopted the democratic parliamentary Westminster system of government from England. As elsewhere in the Commonwealth, there is a Governor General who serves as the Queen's representative. A Prime Minister leads the government made up of two levels of legislature. The upper chamber is called the Senate, with senators appointed by the Prime Minister in consultation with the leader of the official opposition. The lower chamber is the House of Assembly, and members are elected by the people. Hubert Ingraham and

the pace. Locals have distinct looks, dialects, and surnames on each island. White Americans and British settled in the Abacos and north Eleuthera, and their strong accents—putting an 'h' where there isn't one and omitting one where there should be—help tell them apart from expats. Long Island is home to a large "conchy joe" population, white Bahamians who might have had a black great grandpa. Tell someone you're a Knowles and they'll want to know if you're a Long Island Knowles or an Eleuthera Knowles.

. . . is getting spruced up. After 10 years of temporary tent quarters, the Nassau straw market's magnificent $11 million new home opened in 2011. Bay Street, once Nassau's Madison Avenue, is on the road to recovery after years of neglect. The Lynden Pindling International Airport is now a modern gateway that truly welcomes visitors. And following a number of false starts, the multibillion dollar Baha Mar transformation of the Cable Beach strip is well underway. As Nassau continues to develop, the Out Islands remain untouched, preserving the quaint nature that attracts adventure travelers each year.

. . . is not part of the Caribbean. Even though the country gets lumped in with the Caribbean in glossy travel brochures and on cruise itineraries, it is not geographically a part of it. Rather than being situated in the Caribbean Sea, the islands of the Bahamas are in the Atlantic Ocean. In fact, more Bahamians have traveled to nearby South Florida than to the Caribbean. But from a cultural and political point of view, the Bahamas is aligned with the neighboring islands. The country is a full member of the Caribbean Community (CARICOM) and Bahamians will cheer on their Caribbean brothers and sisters in any sporting match.

. . . is worried about the environment. Thankfully, the 2010 Deepwater Horizon oil spill did not affect the Bahamas, but Bahamians now have become much more aware of the need to protect the 'sun, sand, and sea' that puts food on so many tables. The government works closely with the Bahamas National Trust to identify and develop protected green spaces and any developer interested in putting up a sizeable or potentially environmentally sensitive project anywhere in the country is required to pay for and submit an Environmental Impact Assessment before consideration is granted.

the Free National Movement Party are currently in a third nonconsecutive term. The Progressive Liberal Party is the main opposition; Bahamians have never given fringe parties a second glance.

Even the most patriotic Bahamian will admit that the country's jewel—downtown Nassau—had lost its luster. Sidewalks and building facades were grimy with soot from nonstop traffic, and with the recent global economic slump, once spectacular stores had given way to tacky T-shirt shops or were left vacant. In 2009 the Downtown Nassau Partnership was formed to revitalize the historic city. The first initiative was a new home for the straw market that was destroyed by fire in September 2001. Also on tap are plans to make the roads that connect Shirley Street, Bay Street, and the wharf pedestrian-only.

BAHAMAS TOP EXPERIENCES

Junkanoo

(A) The Bahamas' answer to Rio de Janeiro's Carnaval and New Orleans' Mardi Gras, Junkanoo is a festival of parades and parties held on Boxing Day (the day after Christmas) and New Year's Day. Groups compete with elaborate, colorful costumes and choreographed routines to distinctly Bahamian music created by goatskin drums, clanging cowbells, conch-shell horns, shrieking whistles, and brass bands.

Pink Sand

(B) Head to Eleuthera, Harbour Island, or Cat Island to experience pink-sand beaches. The pink hue comes from the shell of a microscopic sea creature living on the coral reefs offshore. Waves crush the pink and red shells and wash them onto the beach. The most famous pink beach is on the northern side of Harbour Island.

Coral Reefs

(C) The Bahamas is home to the world's third-largest barrier reef. If diving along the Andros Barrier Reef is too advanced for you, no worries, there are many opportunities to explore the magnificent undersea world surrounding the Bahamas. Colorful coral, sea fans, and marine creatures abound; take an underwater camera, since the only things you're allowed to bring back to the surface are photographs and memories.

Fish Fry

No matter which island you're visiting, there's bound to be a fish fry in full swing at least one night of the week. Clusters of wooden shacks and stalls fry up snapper, goggle eye, or jack fish, served with fries or a thick chunk of sweet island bread. Each stall plays its own music, creating a cacophony of sound; groups gather around wooden tables to play dominoes or to catch up on the local sip-sip (gossip).

The fish fry at Arawak Cay in Nassau is open daily, but on the other islands they can be a once-a-week occurrence.

Conch

(D) Conch, pronounced "konk," is popular for more than just its distinctive, spiral-shape shells; this sea creature, essentially a giant snail, is one of the mainstays of Bahamian cuisine. Firm white conch meat is tenderized, then turned into a variety of dishes. There's cracked conch, conch salad, conch chowder, and the popular appetizer, conch fritters. Islanders often claim that conch has two other magical powers—as a hangover cure (when eaten straight from the shell with hot peppers, salt, and lime) and as an especially tasty aphrodisiac.

Rake 'n' Scrape

(E) Generations ago, many Bahamians didn't have the money to buy instruments, so they made music using whatever was at hand. Someone played a saw, someone else made a bass out of string and a tin tub, and another musician kept the beat by shaking a plastic jug filled with rocks or dried beans, or beating a goat-skin drum. Today the best place to hear authentic Rake 'n' Scrape is on Cat Island, where the style is said to have been born.

Rum Drinks

(F) The Bahamas has a long history with rum, dating back to the days of bootlegging during the United States Prohibition. Rum consumption is perfectly legal nowadays, and Bahamian bartenders have mixed up some rum-infused concoctions that have become synonymous with tropical vacations: Bahama Mama, Yellow Bird, and the Hurricane. If you're in Green Turtle Cay in Abaco, pop into Miss Emily's Blue Bee Bar, where the Goombay Smash was born.

ISLAND FINDER

	NEW PROVIDENCE AND PARADISE ISLANDS	GRAND BAHAMA ISLAND	THE ABACOS	ELEUTHERA	HARBOUR ISLAND	THE EXUMAS	THE OTHER OUT ISLANDS
BEACHES							
Activities and Sports	●	●	●	◖	◖	◖	◖
Deserted	○	●	●	●	○	◖	●
Party Scene	●	◖	◖	○	●	◖	○
Pink Sand	○	○	○	●	●	○	◖
CITY LIFE							
Crowds	●	◖	○	○	◖	○	○
Urban Development	●	◖	◖	○	○	○	○
ENTERTAINMENT							
Bahamian Cultural Events and Sights	●	◖	●	○	◖	○	◖
Hot Restaurant Scene	●	◖	○	◖	●	○	○
Nightlife	●	◖	○	○	◖	○	○
Shopping	●	◖	◖	○	◖	◖	○
Spas	●	◖	○	○	○	◖	○
Casinos	●	◖	○	○	○	○	○
LODGING							
Luxury Hotels and Resorts	●	●	◖	◖	●	◖	◖
Condos	●	◖	◖	◖	◖	◖	◖
NATURE							
Wildlife	◖	●	●	◖	○	●	●
Ecotourism	◖	●	●	◖	○	●	●
SPORTS							
Golf	●	●	◖	○	○	●	○
Scuba and Snorkeling	●	●	●	●	●	●	●
Fishing	●	●	●	●	●	●	●

● : noteworthy; ◖ some; ○ : little or none

THE BAHAMAS' BEST BEACHES

by Jessica Robertson

There's no feeling as invigorating as putting the first footprints on a powdery sand beach. With 800 miles of beachfront across the Bahamas, you could be the first to leave your mark even if you head out at sunset. But if your idea of a perfect beach day includes tropical drinks, water sports, and pulsating music, most islands have those, too.

pictured: Gold Rock Beach, Grand Bahama

BEACH PLANNING

With so many spectacular stretches of sand in the Bahamas, how do you increase your odds of stumbling upon the best ones?

Decide whether you want a deserted island experience or a beach with lots of amenities. For beaches with bathrooms, water sport activities, and pick-up volleyball games, you'll find the most options on New Providence, Paradise Island, and Grand Bahama. The Exumas, Harbour Island, Bimini, and the Abacos have a good mix of secluded sand and beach parties. The farther south you travel, the more deserted the beaches become. You might have the sand entirely to yourself on Eleuthera or any of the southern Out Islands.

Waters in the Bahamas are calm, for the most part. But when weather picks up, so do the waves. That said, most of the Atlantic-side beaches are protected by coral reefs offshore, so waves are broken up before they reach you. More good news: these natural barriers break up shells, creating powder-fine white—and in some cases pink—sand. Most of the noteworthy beaches that don't face the Atlantic are in bays and coves where you'll rarely find a ripple in the water. These are the beaches to visit with small children and if you're a serious shell seeker.

If you're traveling with children, shade is a must. When you venture away from the hotel, head for a beach lined with tall casuarinas trees. Although considered invasive nuisances by locals because the carpet of needles they shed prevent any other native foliage to grow, they do provide the best shade from the relentless Bahamian sunshine.

Pink Sands Beach, Harbour Island

PINK SAND

❶ **Club Med Beach, Eleuthera.** The island's less famous (and less crowded) pink sand beach got its name from the European resort that once overlooked it. The Atlantic-side beach has baby's-bottom-soft pink sand and lots of shady casuarinas pines.

❷ **Fine Beach, Cat Island.** Twelve miles of fine, powdery pink sand lie just north of Greenwood Beach. Despite the pristine beauty of this Atlantic-side beach, you'll likely be the only one here on any given day.

❸ **Greenwood Beach, Cat Island.** Eight miles of pink sand stretch along the Atlantic Ocean at the southeast tip of Cat Island. This remote beach is never crowded, so even on a busy beach day you'll find your own spot for swimming, strolling, or sunbathing.

❹ **Lighthouse Beach, Eleuthera.** Ask any Eleutheran to point you to his or her favorite beach, and you'll probably end up on a long drive south to Bannerman Town on roads with more potholes than asphalt. But when you get to Lighthouse Beach, you'll know you weren't led astray. Caves, cliffs, and a long-abandoned, centuries-old lighthouse make for fun exploring on the 3 mi of pink sand that curve around the island's southern point.

❺ **Pink Sands Beach, Harbour Island.** Finely crushed shells give this 3-mi stretch of sand its spectacular hue, and the wide, flat topography is ideal for sunbathing or galloping along on horseback.

Chat 'N' Chill, Stocking Island, the Exumas

Great Exuma

BEACH PARTIES

❶ **Cabbage Beach, Paradise Island.** The fun and activities from the Bahamas' largest resort, Atlantis, spill over onto 3-mi Cabbage Beach. This is the best spot on Paradise Island for Jet Skis, banana boats, or parasailing. Dreadlocked men carrying cardboard boxes of fresh coconuts will crack one open and create your very own intoxicating concoction. If you're not staying at one of the resorts lining the beach, you can access it just east of the Riu Palace.

❷ **Guana Cay Beach, the Abacos.** On Sunday afternoon, head to Nippers, on the north side of the beach, and wonder at all the people. Locals and tourists alike come out for the legendary all-day pig roast. Grab a drink and find a perch at the bar, beach, or bi-level pool.

❸ **Lucaya Beach, Grand Bahama.** If you're looking for water sports, tropical music, and drinks served beachside, this 7.5-mi stretch of white sand is a good place to lay your towel. The most action is right in front of the Our Lucaya resort, but if you head west, you can barhop at the hotels, restaurants, and beach bars lining the strip.

❹ **Stocking Island, the Exumas.** On Sunday, everyone heads to Stocking Island for the pig roast at Chat 'N' Chill. The music is good, the food is spectacular, and the drinks flow. Play volleyball, go snorkeling just offshore, or sit under a tree with a fresh bowl of conch salad and an infamous Goombay Smash.

WORTH THE TREK

❶ **Gold Rock Beach, Grand Bahama.** This seemingly endless stretch of sand near the Lucayan National Park is extraordinarily peaceful. As the tide goes out, wide, rippled sand banks pop out of the water, giving the illusion that you could walk out to the horizon. To access the beach, leave your car at the park and walk about a half hour over a low bridge crossing the mangrove swamps. Note, however, that there are planks missing in some parts of the bridge.

❷ **Sandy Cay, the Exumas.** The southernmost Exuma cay only gets more spectacular as the tide goes out. The main beach is exquisite, but it's the sand bar that emerges at low tide that makes this location well worth the short boat ride from William's Town, the southernmost settlement on Little Exuma. Starfish, sand dollars, and shells usually dot the tidal beach, and the kaleidoscopic crystal-clear water surrounding it is breathtaking. It's no wonder scenes from *Pirates of the Caribbean* were filmed here.

❸ **Surfer's Beach, Eleuthera.** The Bahamas aren't known as a surfer's paradise, but Surfer's Beach near Gregory Town, Eleuthera, is one of the sport's best-kept secrets. Even if you don't hang ten, this beautiful beach makes the treacherous journey worthwhile. Unless you're in an off-road vehicle, you'll probably have to abandon your car halfway down rough-and-bumpy Ocean Boulevard and walk nearly a mile up and over cliffs to the beach.

FODOR'S CHOICE BEST BEACHES

❶ Fernandez Bay Beach, Cat Island

Why: The odds of being the only one on this sparsely populated island's most amazing beach are definitely stacked in your favor, even though it's home to a small resort. White sand lines the crescent-shaped cove from end to end.

Claim to fame: Nothing yet. It's just waiting for you to come and discover beach perfection.

Don't miss: The beach faces west, so sundown here is spectacular.

❷ Cape Santa Maria Beach, Long Island

Why: The sand on Cape Santa Maria Beach is shimmering white and powder fine, and goes on for more than 4 mi. Lined with swaying palms, this flat beach on the northwest coast of Long Island is postcard-perfect.

Claim to fame: Christopher Columbus named this cape after one of three ships he used to sail from Spain.

Don't miss: The chance to catch dinner when the tidal flats rise out of the turquoise water at low tide.

❸ Pink Sands Beach, Harbour Island

Why: The vibrant 3-mi pink sand beach and extraordinary palette of blues and aquamarines in the ocean make a stunning backdrop for a sunrise or sunset stroll.

Claim to fame: Martha Stewart, Nicole Kidman, and Brooke Shields have stayed at the beach's posh Pink Sands resort.

Don't miss: A chance for a seaside canter. Just look for the dreadlocked man with the horses, and pick your mount.

❹ Treasure Cay Beach, the Abacos

Why: One of the widest stretches of powdery white sand in the Bahamas, the beach at Treasure Cay is 3½ mi long and borders a shallow aquamarine bay that's perfect for swimming. Activities and a restaurant are on one end, and a deserted oasis on the other.

Claim to fame: Voted the Best Beach in the Caribbean in 2004 by readers of *Caribbean Travel and Life* magazine.

Don't miss: The sand dollars that line the sand as the tide gently rolls out.

LIKE A LOCAL

If you want to experience more of the Bahamas than just the sand at your resort's beach, make like a local and try one of the following.

Enjoy a Boil' Fish Breakfast

Pass on the eggs and pancakes and try a real Bahamian breakfast of boil' fish. Fillets of grouper, turbot, or muttonfish are cooked up in a delicious peppery lime-based broth with onions and potatoes. It's served with grits or a chunk of johnnycake. Alternatives on the Bahamian breakfast menu include stew' fish or conch—similar to boil' fish but cooked in thick brown gravy—chicken, pig-feet, or sheep-tongue souse. Even though all of these dishes are soups and stews, they're never served for lunch or dinner.

Worship at a Jumper Church

Religion plays a central role in the lives of many Bahamians, and there's a church on just about every corner of every island. While there is an array of traditional Anglican, Catholic, Presbyterian, and Lutheran churches, the Jumper Baptist services are often the liveliest and most unusual. Think fire-and-brimstone sermons, boisterous singing and dancing, and choruses of "hallelujah" and "amen." Congregations welcome out-of-town guests, but expect to stand up and introduce yourself. Bahamians put on their Sunday best for church, but won't turn away a visitor who isn't dressed the part; please be respectful.

Speak Bahamian

To the untrained ear fresh off a cruise ship or plane, it could seem as if Bahamians are speaking a foreign language. English is the native tongue, but get a group of locals engaged in hot debate and you won't be able to keep up. Words are strung together, the letter 'g' is dropped from the ends of most words, and quite a few slang words are thrown in for good measure. If a club is too crowded, a Bahamian might leave, saying "it's too jam up in dere"; your taxi driver might warn you that he needs to "back back" the car; a rude child might get a "cut hip" from his mother; the word "dead" is used to intensify any adjective as in "dead ugly"; and ask someone when they're going to do something or go somewhere, and they'll likely respond "terreckly," which means soon. Despite what you may see printed on T-shirts, Bahamians don't say "Hey mon!" If you don't understand, just ask the Bahamian to slow down and they'll quickly start speaking the queen's English.

Play Dominoes

Just about anywhere you see a group of men gathered around a makeshift table, you'll find a dominoes game in progress. Usually games are played for bragging rights and not money, and matches can get loud and raucous, as it's customary for anyone making a big play to slam the plastic tile down on the table. Ask if you can get in on a game (the same rules as American dominoes apply), but don't expect any mercy.

Eat a Fish Top to Tail

Order a fried, grilled, or steamed snapper at any local restaurant or fish fry and be prepared to have your meal looking up at you from the plate. In the Bahamas, this tasty dish is served up whole, from head to tail. Take a look at a Bahamian's plate at the end of his meal and you'll never guess it once held a fish; all that's left is a pile of sucked-clean bones. If you don't think you can stomach the whole fish, ask your waiter to remove the head before bringing it to the table. Just be warned, the sweetest meat is found in the cheeks.

FAMILY TRAVEL

It might not be an exaggeration to say that the Bahamas is a playground for children—or anyone else who likes building castles in the sand, searching for the perfect seashell, and playing tag with ocean waves.

While water-related activities are the most obvious enticements, these relaxed and friendly islands also offer a variety of land-based options, particularly in Nassau and on adjacent Paradise Island. For tales of the high seas, **Pirates of Nassau** has artifacts and interactive exhibits of the original pirates of the Caribbean.

The **Ardastra Gardens, Zoo and Conservation Center** is home to a variety of animals. Some you'd expect to find in the Bahamas—like the world-famous marching flamingos—and others are endangered creatures from faraway places like the pair of jaguars and Madagascar lemurs.

Let the kids pick out their favorite straw-hat-wearing pony at the **Surrey Horse Pavilion** on Prince George Wharf and take a leisurely clip-clopping ride through the old city of Nassau. For a few extra dollars, most guides will extend your tour beyond the typical route to include other sites. Keep your guidebook handy to verify facts; guides are trained but often add their own twist on history, which can be entertaining to say the least.

Of course, megaresort **Atlantis** is always a crowd pleaser, with everything from pottery painting to remote-control car making and racing, to an 8,000-square-foot, state-of-the-art kids camp and the Bahamas' and Caribbean's largest casino and water park.

Both Nassau and Freeport, on Grand Bahama Island, offer the chance to have close encounters of the dolphin kind. **Blue Lagoon Island Dolphin Encounter,** off Paradise Island, lets you stand waist deep in a protected pool of water and interact with trained dolphins, or put on snorkeling gear and swim with them. In Freeport, **UNEXSO** (one of whose founders was Jacques Cousteau) has a similar program at Sanctuary Bay, a refuge for dolphins. After a performance of back flips and other tricks, these intelligent creatures literally snuggle up to be petted. Older children and adults also can spend a day learning how these remarkable creatures are trained.

For water-sports enthusiasts, snorkeling, parasailing, and boating opportunities abound. In the Exumas, rent a powerboat and take the kids to Big Major's Cay to see the famous **swimming pigs.** Don't forget some scraps! Kids will also get a kick out of the hundreds of **iguanas** on nearby Allan's Cay and the **giant starfish** near mainland Great Exuma.

Much of the Bahamas' most incredible scenery is underwater, but kids of all ages can enjoy the scenes beneath the sea without even getting wet. At **Stuart Cove's Dive Bahamas** in Nassau, kids 12 and up can go 15 feet under with a SUB (Scenic Underwater Bubble) and zoom around the reefs. **Seaworld Tours'** semisubmarine explores Nassau Harbour and Paradise Island for an hour and a half with sightseeing above and below water.

WEDDINGS AND HONEYMOONS

With easy access from the United States and plenty of secluded beaches to make your own, the Bahamas is a no-brainer destination wedding location. Follow in Mariah Carey's footsteps and start planning your dream ceremony or celebration.

The Big Day

Find a Wedding Planner. Contact the **Ministry of Tourism's Weddings and Honeymoon Unit** (☎ *888/NUPTIAL or 242/356–0435* ✎ *romance@bahamas.com*) for recommended planners or the **Bahamas Bridal Association** (☎ *888/777–6794* ✎ *info@bahamas-bridal-association.com*). If you choose to get married at one of the larger resorts, most have their own planners in-house.

Get Your License. The only government requirement to get married in the Bahamas is that the couple must be in the country at least 24 hours before they apply for a license. Licenses will be processed that day and cost $120. No blood test is required.

Scout the Perfect Backdrop. The obvious choice for a Bahamas destination wedding is right on the beach, with waves rolling in, guests wiggling their toes in powdery white sand, and the sun setting over the turquoise ocean. Many hotels have gazebos on the beachfront to make ceremonies more private. One of the most beautiful settings for a Bahamas wedding is the **Cloisters** on Paradise Island. The stone remnants of a 14th century French Monastery and steps leading down to the water's edge create a truly magical location.

What to Wear. Bahamian weddings tend to be formal affairs, but a simple dress with no shoes is a popular choice for out-of-town brides, and most grooms tend to shun the jacket and tie in lieu of white linen shirts and khakis. Classy sundresses for ladies and linen or cotton shirts and pants for men are acceptable wear for guests. If you plan on having a church wedding, respect local culture and dress a bit more conservatively (no bare shoulders).

The Honeymoon

Many resorts offer honeymoon suites and special packages for newlyweds, so be sure to inquire when booking your stay. The following hotels are our top honeymoon picks.

Cape Santa Maria, Long Island. The resort has a special honeymoon package for newlyweds (which includes massages), and a beautiful beachfront gazebo makes the perfect wedding backdrop.

Hope Town Harbour Lodge, the Abacos. Secluded cottage-style rooms overlook the beach at the edge of town. This is where the TV show *Scrubs* filmed the janitor's wedding episode.

Kamalame Cay, Andros. This 96-acre all-inclusive resort sits on a private cay laced with white-sand beaches and coconut palms. Ask for a beachfront cottage or villa.

One & Only Ocean Club, Paradise Island. This exclusive resort on magnificent Cabbage Beach's quietest stretch also has the romantic Versailles Gardens, including 35 acres of terraced serenity and an imported French cloister.

Pink Sands, Harbour Island. Harbour Island's famed beachfront resort has long been praised by honeymooners for its 25 private cottages scattered over 20 secluded acres, including the renowned Pink Sands Beach.

ECOTOURISM IN THE BAHAMAS

The word ecotourism is believed to have been coined by Mexican environmentalist Héctor Ceballos-Lascuráin in 1983. According to Ceballos-Lascuráin, ecotourism "involves traveling to relatively undisturbed natural areas with the specific object of studying, admiring, and enjoying the scenery and its wild plants and animals." His original definition seemed a bit too general, so in 1993 he amended it with a line that stressed that "ecotourism is environmentally responsible travel."

Natural beauty abounds in the Bahamas, so eco-friendly tourists will have no problem finding national parks to explore, birds to watch, or virgin reefs to snorkel, especially in the Out Islands. There's a concerted effort to make development more sustainable here, too. Time and money are being spent to ensure that as the more remote islands develop, it is done responsibly. The Bahamian government now requires that an independent **Environmental Impact Assessment** be conducted before approval is given for any major development project on any islands. Inagua was also selected for a pilot program sponsored by the **Inter-American Development Bank** to design a regional plan for sustainable development.

Accommodations

Although there's certainly a long way to go before most properties can call themselves eco-friendly, many of the small resorts, particularly those on the Out Islands, are independently doing what they can to reduce their footprint and impact on the environment. Some have installed their own reverse osmosis systems to generate potable water, solar energy is becoming more popular, restaurants use local fishermen and farmers for

food sourcing, and ecotour options have increased due to visitor demand.

The **Tiamo Resort** in Andros sets the standard for eco-resorts in the Bahamas and the Caribbean. The cottages were built of sustainable local pine and thatch. While many developers completely clear their properties in order to build, Tiamo cut down as few mature trees as possible. Energy on property is generated by solar panels, and hot showers come courtesy of the sun. An organic garden ensures meals are made from the freshest fruits and vegetables. Guests can indulge in a plethora of eco-activities including bonefishing, snorkeling, biologist-led nature walks, and ocean kayaking.

Hotel Higgins Landing on Stocking Island in the Exumas is completely solar powered, uses cisterns that collect rainwater, and has a renowned biological composting toilet system. No cars are allowed on the island.

Few large Bahamas resorts are considered eco-friendly, but the mega **Atlantis** has coined its own phrase and concept: Blue Tourism. They've teamed up with local dive operator Stuart Cove's to provide marine-based activities, and a portion of revenue from the Reef Atlantis complex will go toward the restoration of a nearby coral reef.

Bird-Watching

With birds migrating north and south for warmer or cooler climates, there's good bird-watching all year-round. More than 300 bird species live in the Bahamas, 28 of them found only here and in the Caribbean.

The endangered Bahama parrot is found only on Abaco and Inagua, and conservation efforts are underway to reverse the

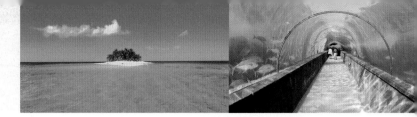

population decline. Inagua is also home to the West Indian pink flamingo. Other unique bird species include the Bahamas swallow, the Bahama woodstar humming-bird, and the Bahama yellowthroat.

Grand Bahama Nature Tours (☎ *242/373-2485*) offers single or multiday birding tours. **Bahamas Outdoors Ltd** (☎ *242/362-1574*) offers daily expeditions in Nassau starting early morning or midday and also organizes multiday trips to Andros, Eleuthera, Cat, San Salvador, Crooked and Acklins, and Inagua. Bird enthusiasts should not miss the unique opportunity to tour **Inagua National Park** (☎ *242/393-1317*), home to the world's largest breeding colony of West Indian flamingos. Birding guides are certified by the Ministry of Tourism; contact them for more options.

National Parks

The Bahamas boasts 25 national parks spanning more than 700,000 protected acres. *We've highlighted four exceptional parks at the start of Chapters 3, 4, 7, and 8.* For more information on visiting parks, contact the **Bahamas National Trust** (☎ *242/393-1317* ⊕ *www.bnt.bs*).

Resources

The **Bahamas Ministry of Tourism's sustainable tourism department** (☎ *242/356-6963* ⊕ *www.bahamas.com*) is developing eco-friendly programs for visitors. Visit their Web site for information on green travel and ecotours.

The **International Ecotourism Society** (⊕ *www.ecotourism.org*) has a database of tour companies, hotels, and other travel services that are committed to sustainable practices.

TIPS FOR BEING ENVIRONMENTALLY CONSCIOUS

■ Buy locally made souvenirs.

■ Eat locally provided seafood and produce.

■ Bring a washable water bottle rather than using small disposable bottles.

■ Obey Bahamian fishing seasons for grouper and crawfish.

■ Open windows and turn on fans rather than blast the air-conditioning.

■ Use hotel towels more than once.

■ Ask your hotel to recycle.

■ Don't disturb animals and plant life.

CRUISING TO THE BAHAMAS

More tourists cruise into Nassau and Freeport than anywhere else in the Caribbean region. The islands are just a couple of hundred miles off the coast of Florida and its large cruise-ship ports, so cruise lines are able to schedule short excursions over, or make it the first or last port of call on longer trips venturing into the eastern or western Caribbean. In late 2009 the Bahamian government completed an extensive dredging project to make Nassau Harbour deep enough to accommodate the new supersize cruise ships. The first to hit the high seas, Royal Caribbean's *Oasis of the Seas*, made its inaugural voyage to the Bahamas in December 2009.

With Bay Street and historic sights just steps away from the cruise docks, Nassau is a great place to disembark for even just a few hours. Your first stop is **Festival Place**, a vibrant marketplace right on the wharf, complete with live Bahamian music and a variety of small shops designed to look like clapboard houses. You can get around downtown on foot or you can take a taxi, scooter, or horse-drawn surrey. If you have a full day, buy an **Atlantis** day pass and enjoy the waterslides, casino, walk-through aquarium, and beaches.

Freeport's cruise-ship port is a bit farther from town and the beaches, so you'll need to take a taxi or tour bus to explore. **Port Lucaya** is the no-brainer stop for shopping and a bite to eat. If you have a longer stopover, book an organized tour or take a taxi to **Lucayan National Park** and explore caves and Gold Rock Creek beach across the road.

Your cruise ship will likely offer tours and excursions that can be booked in advance. Unless you're dead set on doing something in particular and are concerned there might not be space, you might consider waiting until you disembark to book something with a local operator. Many times this is a cheaper option.

In addition to Nassau and Freeport, some cruise lines have leased private islands in the Bahamas. All have stunning beaches lined with lounge chairs and umbrellas, motorized and nonmotorized water sports, casual waterfront bars and restaurants, live entertainment, nature trails, and pricey souvenir shops. Disney Cruise Line stops off at **Castaway Cay** in the Abacos, Holland America visits the 45-acre **Half Moon Cay** between Cat Island and Eleuthera, Norwegian Cruise Lines has **Great Stirrup Cay** in the Berry Islands, and Royal Caribbean stops off at **Coco Cay** between Nassau and Freeport.

Most cruise ships offer just one or two stops within the Bahamas as part of a wider Caribbean itinerary, but there are a few smaller lines that offer cruises through the Bahamas chain. **Pearl Seas Cruises'** (☎ *800/983–7462* ⊕ *www.pearlseascruises.com*) eight-day Bahamas cruise on board a 335-foot, 210-passenger ship stops in Grand Bahama, the Abacos, Harbour Island, the Exumas, and San Salvador. The **American Canadian Caribbean Line's** (☎ *800/556–7450* ⊕ *www.blountsmallshipadventures.com*) 183-foot, 100-passenger *Grande Caribe* has an 11-night tour through the Bahamas, stopping in Nassau, north Eleuthera, and the Exuma Cays.

LODGING PRIMER

With almost 16,000 hotel rooms across the country, you're bound to find a home away from home in the Bahamas. Unfortunately this is not an inexpensive destination, but almost all islands offer a mix of low-key lodges and sparkling resorts. Room prices come down significantly in the off season (mid-April through mid-December), and many hotels and resorts offer special deals on their room rates or throw in extras during peak hurricane season, late August and early September.

Splashy Resorts

Mostly in Nassau, Paradise Island, and on Grand Bahama, these resorts are big enough and fancy enough to rival the major resorts found anywhere in the world. Casinos, amazing swimming pools, countless dining options, and rooms that make you wish you didn't have to go home are what set these properties apart. The downside—with thousands of rooms, the staff will provide top service, but aren't likely to remember your name. ⇨ *Atlantis, Paradise Island; Our Lucaya, Grand Bahama.*

All-Inclusives

For the budget-conscious traveler, an all-inclusive resort is a good option. Rates cover the room, all meals, most activities, and usually your bar tab. Most guests tend to spend most of their vacation on property, since it's been paid for up front, so there are lots of activities to keep you entertained. Be sure to do your homework, as these resorts vary in terms of quality. ⇨ *Club Med, San Salvador; Riu Palace, Paradise Island; Sandals Emerald Bay, the Exumas.*

Boutique Resorts

These properties are small and don't often have a lot of amenities, but they've created a high-end luxury experience that makes

that irrelevant. There may be just one restaurant on property, but it's guaranteed to be top of the line. Staff-to-guest ratios are higher than at any other property type and they are there to cater to your every whim and fancy. Of course, be prepared to pay for such special treatment. ⇨ *A Stone's Throw Away, New Providence; Cocodimama Resort, Eleuthera; Rock House, Harbour Island; Sammy T's Beach Resort, Cat Island.*

Budget Hotels

The Bahamas is not known for being a cheap destination, but throughout the country there are no-frills budget hotels if you're really just looking for a clean safe place to get a shower and grab a good night's sleep. If you plan on spending full days exploring the islands or lounging on a beach and are happy to do without extras like pay-per-view TV, in room minibars, room service, and high-thread-count sheets, this accommodation type is for you. ⇨ *Castaways Resort and Suites, Grand Bahama; Tingum Village, Harbour Island.*

Homey Guesthouses and Cottages

Out Island accommodations tend to be more like a home away from home. Small, and often family owned and operated, these guesthouses and cottages are usually simply decorated, but have all you need to make your stay comfortable. Guests often gather in common areas for drinks, meals, and conversation, and the staff take a personal interest in making your stay perfect. On-site activities and amenities will likely be basic, but you'll feel right at home. ⇨ *The Cove, Eleuthera; Fernandez Bay Village, Cat Island; Orange Hill Beach Inn, New Providence; Seascape Inn, Andros.*

FLAVORS OF THE BAHAMAS

You'll find food from all over the world in Nassau and Freeport restaurants, but you'll be missing out if you don't try the local cuisine. There's nothing fancy about Bahamian food, just fresh ingredients and peppery spices you'll remember long after your trip is over.

Breakfasts include hearty eggs, bacon, and pancakes, or Bahamian favorites such as chicken souse, boil' fish, or stew' fish, served with grits and johnnycake. At lunch you'll likely find variations on a few standards: fresh fish, conch, or chicken sandwiches, or hamburgers sided with french fries, coleslaw, or local favorites like peas 'n' rice or baked macaroni and cheese with jalapeño peppers. At dinner you'll find fish, fried chicken, and pasta.

"Steamed" fish means cooked with tomatoes, peppers, and onions. Order any fish "Bahamian style;" baked and smothered in tomatoes and spices.

Conch

(A) You'll find conch, the unofficial dish of the Bahamas, prepared in a variety of ways, on nearly every menu. The sea snail has a mild flavor and taste and texture similar to calamari. The safest way to ease into conch is conch fritters, tasty fried dough balls packed with chunks of conch. Conch chowder is tomato based; cracked conch is battered and fried; grilled conch is wrapped in a foil packet with lime juice, pepper, onion, tomato, and a bit of butter and cooked on top of the barbecue; and, perhaps the most popular entrée, conch salad is akin to ceviche. Fresh-caught conch is diced and mixed with chopped onions and red or green bell peppers. The mix is drizzled with fresh lime and sour orange juices, and spiced with either homemade hot sauce or finely minced local hot peppers.

Guava Duff

This local favorite is similar to English pudding. A guava fruit compote is folded into a sweet dough and wrapped up in aluminum foil, and then steamed or boiled for as long as three hours. It's topped with a sweet rum or brandy sauce.

Johnnycake

(B) Despite its name, johnnycake is not actually a dessert but a thick, heavy, slightly sweet bread that's typically served alongside souses, soups, and stews.

Mac 'n' Cheese

If you order a side of macaroni, don't expect anything resembling Kraft mac and cheese. Bahamians bake their macaroni noodles in a mixture of cream, daisy cheese, and butter.

Peas 'n' Rice

This popular side dish is made of white rice cooked with salt pork, thyme, a dab of tomato paste, and fresh or canned pigeon peas.

Rum Cake

(C) Given Bahamians' long-standing love affair with rum, it's no surprise that rum cake is an all-time favorite in the islands. Rum is mixed into the batter and then poured in a syrupy glaze over the fresh-out-of-the-oven cake. Don't worry about getting drunk; the alcohol cooks off when it bakes.

Souse, Boil', or Stew'

(D) A peppery bowl of chicken souse or boil' fish—the clear broth has a lime-and-goat-pepper base with pieces of chicken or meaty fish, onions, and potatoes—is an authentic breakfast dish. Variations include pig-feet and sheep-tongue souse, which are more of an acquired taste. You'll also find stew' fish or conch on most menus. The soup in bowls of stew is a Bahamian variation on the traditional French roux made with flour, water, and browning sauce, and seasoned with pepper and fresh thyme.

IT'S 5 O'CLOCK SOMEWHERE

Whether you like it straight up, mixed into a colorful fruity concoction, or prefer a cold local beer, you'll find the perfect beverage to wet your whistle in the Bahamas. Rum, in particular, has played an interesting part in Bahamian history since the days of the U.S. Prohibition. Entrepreneurial Bahamians got rich smuggling liquor across the Atlantic from Britain; when the U.S. government put a ban on alcohol consumption, a ready supply less than 50 mi away made the island nation a key trans-shipment point for contraband.

In 1962 Bacardi and Company, the world's largest rum producer, opened a distillery in Nassau, which closed in 2009. The Bahamas does have two of its own breweries, and one rum distillery. **Kalik**, brewed on the southwestern end of New Providence at Commonwealth Brewery is a nice, light ale and comes in regular, Kalik Lite, and, for the serious drinker, the stronger Kalik Gold. The beer was awarded four Monde Selection Gold Medals. Commonwealth also has a distillery, turning out **Ole Nassau** and **Ron Ricardo** rums. Brewery and distillery tours are not available. The newer **Sands Beer**, brewed on Grand Bahama, comes in regular and light. The line recently expanded to include stouts and lagers. Tours are available at this 20-acre brewery (☎ 242/352–4070).

Bahamian Cocktails

Bahama Mama. Light rum, coconut rum, vanilla-infused rum, orange and pineapple juices.

(A) Goombay Smash. Light rum, coconut rum, pineapple juice, a dash of Galliano, grenadine. Created at Miss Emily's Blue Bee Bar on Green Turtle Cay, where her daughter and granddaughter still serve them daily.

Rum Punch. Campari, light rum, coconut rum, orange and pineapple juices.

Sky Juice. Gin, fresh coconut water, condensed milk, a sprinkle of nutmeg. Served over crushed ice.

Best Beach Bars

(B) Chat 'N' Chill, the Exumas. The restaurant and 9-acre playground—an amazing white-sand beach—is the Exumas' party central, particularly for the famous all-day Sunday pig roasts and the Friday-night bonfire beach bash. Play volleyball in the powdery sand, slam the notorious Goombay Smash, order what's cooking on the outdoor grill—fresh fish, ribs—or chat and chill.

Mackey's Sand Bar and Tiki Bar, South Bimini. Boat in or take the shuttle from Bimini Sands Resort to this party place where you can get sand between your toes just as easily inside—where sand carpets the floor—as well as outside. Play a little volleyball, take a dip in the pool, or snorkel right off the beach between cold Kaliks.

(C) Nippers, the Abacos. Guana Cay's infamous party spot is a lively bar with spectacular views of the Abaco Great Barrier Reef. The Frozen Nipper—a slushy rum-and-fruit-juice beverage—goes down well on a hot day. Don't miss the Sunday pig roasts, which draw everyone on the island.

Pete's Pub, Abaco. This beachside tiki hut in Little Harbour is jumping from 11 am to sunset. Take a dip in the shallow harbor or luxuriate on the beach with a cup of their special rum punch—the Blaster.

Tony Macaroni's, Grand Bahama. Follow up Tony's famous roasted conch with a Gully Wash (green coconut milk and gin) on Taino Beach, arguably the island's most spectacular. There's usually great live music at this thatch-roof shack.

WHEN TO GO

The Bahamas enjoys sunny days, refreshing breezes, and moderate-to-warm temperatures with little change from season to season. That said, the most pleasant time to visit is from December through May, when temperatures average 70°F–75°F. It stands to reason that hotel prices during this period are at their highest—around 30% higher than during the less popular times. The rest of the year is hot and humid and prone to tropical storms; temperatures hover around 80°F–85°F.

Whether you want to join it or avoid it, be advised that spring break takes place between the end of February and mid-April. This means a lot of vacationing college students, beach parties, sports events, and entertainment.

Hurricane Season

Hurricane season is from June 1 through November 30, with greatest risk of a storm from August through October. Meteorology being what it is, you generally know days in advance if the area you're traveling to will be affected. Check with your hotel if a storm is on the horizon—the islands are so spread out that, just as most of the United States was unaffected when Katrina hit New Orleans, one island could be experiencing hurricane-force winds while it's nice and sunny in another.

The Bahamas has been relatively lucky when it comes to hurricanes. Nassau, the capital and central hub of the country, has not had a direct devastating hit in many decades. A glancing blow from a storm can result in some downed trees and power lines as well as localized flooding, but Bahamians have learned how to prepare for these situations and within days manage to get things pretty much back to normal. The country enforces strict building codes to guard against major structural damage from the 100-mi-an-hour winds a hurricane can bring with it. Even in the Out Islands, where more storms have come aground, the worst damage is caused by tidal flooding, which washes away quickly.

Most hotels have meticulously detailed hurricane plans that are put into action once a major storm is headed toward the country. If the storm is a major category system, extra flights are lined up to help evacuate tourists, and some hotels have hurricane policies that offer guests free stays at a later date if their vacation is interrupted by Mother Nature.

Climate

What follows are average daily maximum and minimum temperatures for Nassau. Freeport's temperatures are nearly the same: a degree or two cooler in spring and fall, and a degree or two warmer in summer. As you head down to the more southern islands, expect temperatures to be about a degree or two warmer than the capital year-round.

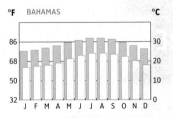

GREAT WATER ADVENTURES

In an archipelago nation named for shallow seas that amaze even astronauts in space, don't miss having a close marine encounter. Water adventures range from a splash at the beach to shark diving. Or stay between the extremes with fishing and snorkeling.

by Justin Higgs

WHERE TO DIVE AND SNORKEL IN THE BAHAMAS

Although most water in the Bahamas is clear enough to see to the bottom from your boat, snorkeling or diving gets you that much closer to the country's true natives. Coral reefs, blue holes, drop-offs, and sea gardens abound.

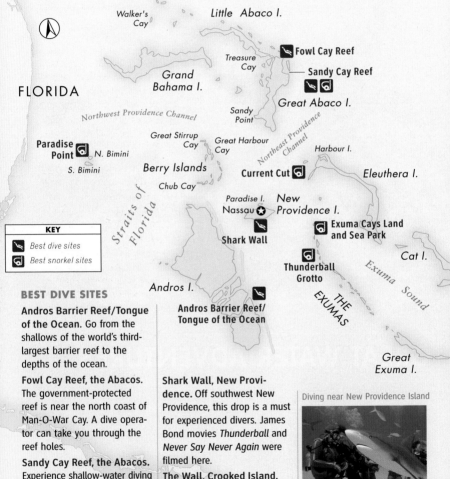

Walker's Cay

Little Abaco I.

FLORIDA

Treasure Cay

Fowl Cay Reef

Sandy Cay Reef

Grand Bahama I.

Great Abaco I.

Northwest Providence Channel

Sandy Point

Paradise Point

N. Bimini

S. Bimini

Great Stirrup Cay

Great Harbour Cay

Berry Islands

Chub Cay

Northeast Providence Channel

Harbour I.

Current Cut

Eleuthera I.

Paradise I.

Nassau ✪

New Providence I.

Straits of Florida

Shark Wall

Exuma Cays Land and Sea Park

Thunderball Grotto

Cat I.

Exuma Sound

Andros I.

Andros Barrier Reef/ Tongue of the Ocean

THE EXUMAS

Great Exuma I.

KEY

🐋 *Best dive sites*

🐚 *Best snorkel sites*

BEST DIVE SITES

Andros Barrier Reef/Tongue of the Ocean. Go from the shallows of the world's third-largest barrier reef to the depths of the ocean.

Fowl Cay Reef, the Abacos. The government-protected reef is near the north coast of Man-O-War Cay. A dive operator can take you through the reef holes.

Sandy Cay Reef, the Abacos. Experience shallow-water diving in Pelican Cays National Park. The reef is full of life (turtles, spotted eagle rays, tarpon), thanks to its protected status.

Shark Wall, New Providence. Off southwest New Providence, this drop is a must for experienced divers. James Bond movies *Thunderball* and *Never Say Never Again* were filmed here.

The Wall, Crooked Island. The famed dive site about 50 yards off Crooked Island's coast drops from 45 feet to thousands.

Diving near New Providence Island

BEST SNORKEL SITES

Current Cut, Eleuthera. Near the Current settlement in North Eleuthera there is great drift snorkel with the right tide.

Exuma Cays Land and Sea Park. This 176-sq-mi park was the first of its kind. Since the park is protected and its waters have essentially never been fished, you can see what the ocean looked like before humanity.

Paradise Point, Bimini. Off northern Bimini, this area is rich in sea life and is famous for the underwater stone path some believe marks the road to the lost city of Atlantis. Dolphins and black coral gardens are just offshore.

Sandy Cay Reef, the Abacos. The water surrounding this reef is just 25-feet deep, making it great for snorkeling or diving.

Thunderball Grotto, the Exumas. This three-story limestone-ceiling cave at the northern end of the Exumas chain was featured in the James Bond movie of the same name.

Diving near Bimini

EXTREME DIVING ADVENTURES

Various outfitters on Grand Bahama and New Providence offer shark dives. With **Caribbean Divers** (☎ 242/373–9111 ⊕ www.bellchannelinn.com) and **UNEXSO** in Grand Bahama and **Stuart Cove's** in New Providence, you'll watch dive masters feed reef sharks which brush by you—no cage included. Dive masters control the ferocity and location of the frenzy, so the sharks' attention is on the food.

Incredible Adventures (☎ 800/644–7382 ⊕ www.incredible-adventures.com) in Grand Bahama offers cage diving with tiger sharks. You'll sit in the water as giant sharks come breathtakingly close, the only thing between you a few strips of metal.

Feeding sharks when humans are present make these dives controversial, especially when multiple sharks are involved and there's the possibility of a frenzy. Dive operators doing these extreme adventures are experienced and knowledgeable about shark-feeding patterns and signs of aggression, but partake in these dives at your own risk.

San Salvador

Rum Cay

Crooked Island Passage

Samana Cay

Long I.

The Wall 🐚
Crooked I.

Mayaguana Passage

Mayaguana I.

Acklins I.

0   50 mi

0   50 km

Little Inagua I.

Great Inagua I.

French Angelfish

Four-Eyed Butterflyfish

Grunt

Nassau Grouper

Parrotfish

Queen Triggerfish

Sergeant Major

Snapper

Tang

Barracuda*

Lionfish*

Shark*

* dangerous fish

WHAT YOU'LL SEE UNDER THE SEA

Reefs in the Bahamas are alive with colorful life. Vibrant hard corals—such as star, brain, staghorn, and elk—and waving purple sea fans are home to schools of myraid fish, some pictured above. Be on the lookout for lionfish; a prick from the fins of this poisonous fish is painful and could send you to the hospital. The most common sharks in the Bahamas are nurse sharks (typically non-threatening to humans) and Caribbean reef sharks. The deeper you dive, the bigger and more varied shark species get.

Generally, the further the reef is from a developed area the more abundant the marine life, but even sites around developed islands might surprise you.

ISLAND-HOPPING

The Bahamas is a boater's paradise, with shallow protected waters and secluded, safe harbors. In small island groups, travel takes just a few hours, even minutes. The Abacos archipelago and the Exuma Cays are the best and most convenient islands to hop.

THE ABACOS

If you're cruising from Florida, clear customs in West End, Grand Bahama; the Abaco Cays start just north.

Grand Cay, at the northern end of the chain, has a small community of 200 people. Most yachters find the anchorage off the community dock adequate, and the docks at Rosie's Place can take boats up to 80 feet. Double anchors are advised to handle the harbor's tidal current.

Fox Town, on the "mainland" of Little Abaco, is a good fuel stop, the first if you're traveling east from West End. Farther south, stock up on provisions in **Coopers Town,** Little Abaco's largest community. Just northeast is an 80-slip marina at **Spanish Cay.**

Cruising south, **Green Turtle Cay** has excellent yachting facilities. The Green Turtle Club dominates White Sound's northern end, whereas Bluff

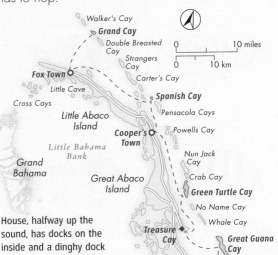

Fishing near Green Turtle Cay

House, halfway up the sound, has docks on the inside and a dinghy dock below the club on the Sea of Abaco side.

South of Green Turtle, back on mainland Great Abaco, **Treasure Cay** Hotel Resort and Marina is one of the largest marinas on the island. Here you can play golf, dine, or relax on a beautiful beach.

Straight back out in the Sea of Abaco is **Great Guana Cay** and its gorgeous 7-mi strip of pristine sand. On Sunday don't miss the famous pig roast at Nippers Bar. Just south is New England–style charmer **Man-O-War Cay,** a boatbuilding settlement with deserted beaches and 28-slip Man-O-War Marina. Fowl Cay

Park offers great snorkeling and diving just to the north.

Back on Great Abaco, **Marsh Harbour** is the capital and most populated settlement in the Abacos. Boaters consider it one of the easiest harbors to enter. It has several full-service marinas, including the 190-slip Boat Harbour Marina and the 80-slip Conch Inn Marina. This is the stop to catch up on banking and business needs. There are great restaurants and shops, too.

Exuma Cays Land and Sea Park

THE EXUMA CAYS

To really get off the beaten path, the Exuma Cays are where it's at. This 120-mi archipelago is made up of small cays, many of which are still uninhabited or privately owned, and interspersed with sand banks and spits. Throughout is excellent diving and snorkeling. Boaters usually stock up and clear customs in Nassau, cross the yellow banks to the north of the chain, and slowly make their way south.

BOAT TOURS

If you don't have your own boat, these outfitters will take you on island-hopping adventures.

Captain Plug. ☎ 242/577–0273 ⊕ www.captplug.com. $200 for a full day of island hopping in the Abacos.

Four C's Adventures. ☎ 242/464–1720 ⊕ www.exumawatertours. com. $1400 for a full day excursion to the Exuma Cays from Great Exuma.

High Seas Private Excursions. ☎ 242/363–4183 ⊕ www.highseasbahamas. com. $2500 for a full day excursion to the Exuma Cays from Nassau.

Highbourne Cay at the chain's northern end has a marina and food store. You can explore many of the surrounding cays by tender if you prefer to dock here. Nearby, **Allan's Cay** is home to hundreds of iguanas that readily accept food.

Norman's Cay has an airstrip and Norman's Cay Beach Club has a fantastic restaurant and bar. Just south is the 176-sq-mi **Exuma Cays Land and Sea Park.** It has some of the country's best snorkeling and diving. Warderick Wells Cay houses the park headquarters, which has nature trail maps and a gift shop. Just below, **Compass Cay** has a marina known for its friendly nurse sharks and a small convenience store. **Pipe Creek,** which winds between Compass and Staniel Cays, has great shelling, snorkeling, diving, and bonefishing. **Staniel Cay** is the hub of activity in these parts and a favorite destination of yachters. That's thanks to the Staniel Cay Yacht Club, the only full-service marina in the cays. It makes a good base for visiting **Big Major's Cay,** where wild pigs swim out to meet you,

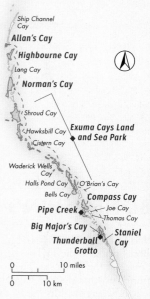

and **Thunderball Grotto,** a beautiful marine cave that snorkelers (at low tide) and experienced scuba divers can explore.

BONEFISHING

WHAT IS BONEFISHING?

Bonefishing is the fly-fishing sport of choice in the Bahamas. The country is full of pristine shallow flats and mangroves where stealthy "gray ghosts"— silvery white, sleek fish—school in large groups. Hooking one is a challenge, as the fish are fast, strong, and perfectly camouflaged to the sand and water.

To catch bonefish you need the right mix of knowledge, instinct, and patience. Guides are the best way to go, as their knowledge of the area and schooling patterns gives them an uncanny ability to find bonefish quickly.

EQUIPMENT

Basics include a fly-fishing rod and reel and the right lure. Experienced anglers, guides, and fishing-supply dealers can help you gear up with the best and latest technology. Bonefishing is catch and release, so always use barbless hooks and work quickly when removing them to avoid stressing the fish. Wear comfortable, light clothing that protects much of your body from the sun, as you'll be out for hours without shade.

In many places you can just walk offshore onto the flats. Some anglers use shallow draft boats with a raised platform in the back, where they pole into extremely shallow areas.

BEST PLACES TO BONEFISH

Bonefish hang out in shallow flats and mangrove areas. Andros, Bimini, and the Exumas have the best bonefishing; Abaco, Eleuthera, and Long Island also provide excellent adventures. If you have the time, visit the southernmost islands, like Crooked, Acklins, or Inagua, where these gray ghosts are "uneducated" to anglers.

WHERE TO STAY

Bonefishing lodges are common in the Bahamas and often include top-notch guides. Accommodations are usually basic. Here are our top bonefishing lodges:

- Andros Island Bonefishing Club

- Bishop's Bonefish Resort, Grand Bahama

- Crooked Island Lodge

- Peace and Plenty Bonefish Lodge, the Exumas

- Rickmon Bonefish Lodge, the Abacos

- Small Hope Bay Lodge, Andros

(left pg) Bonefishing in Andros.
(right) A prize catch.

OTHER TYPES OF FISHING

Make sure you are familiar with fishing regulations before you begin your adventure. Visit ⊕ *www.bahamas-travel.info.*

DEEP-SEA FISHING

Deep water is just a few miles off most islands, where anglers try for large ocean fish—tuna, wahoo, mahi mahi, shark, and marlin. Like bonefishing, the fight is what most anglers are after; however, a day on the ocean can provide a great meal. The Abacos has great deep-sea fishing, and many tournaments are held there each year.

REEF/SHOAL FISHING

Fishing with a rod, or Bahamian "handlining" can be a great family fishing adventure. Anchoring near a shoal or reef, or even trolling with a lure, can be relaxing. The Out Islands are home to shoals, reefs, and wrecks that are less visited by fishing enthusiasts.

SPEARFISHING

Most reefs are okay for free-dive spear fishing, but spear guns (guns that fire spears) are illegal in the Bahamas. Spear is the traditional Bahamian fishing method, so reefs close to more developed islands tend to have fewer fish. The Out Islands still have lesser-known spots good for spearfishing.

New Providence and Paradise Islands

WORD OF MOUTH

"A short walk from Atlantis will get you to the Potter's Cay (dock area) where they will prepare a fresh conch salad before your eyes. I mean pull the conch out of the shell, dice it up with veggies, and then squeeze the fresh lime over the top. It was a cheap lunch with some built in entertainment. VERY casual and very 'local.'"

—Michaelpl

WELCOME TO NEW PROVIDENCE AND PARADISE ISLANDS

TOP REASONS TO GO

★ **Beach hop:** New Providence beaches, though less secluded than those on the Out Islands, still tempt travelers with their balmy breezes and aquamarine water. Choose between the more remote beaches on the island's western end, action-packed strips on Cable Beach, or public beaches in downtown Nassau.

★ **Dine with the best of 'em:** New Providence is the country's culinary capital. Eat at a grungy local dive for one meal, then feast in a celebrity-chef restaurant for the next.

★ **Experience Atlantis:** Explore the world's largest outdoor aquarium, splash around in the something-for-everyone water park, or dine at one of 40+ restaurants, all while never leaving the resort property.

★ **Celebrate Junkanoo:** This uniquely Bahamian carnival takes place the day after Christmas and New Year's Day. If you miss it, there are smaller parades in Marina Village on Paradise Island each Wednesday and Saturday at 9:30 pm.

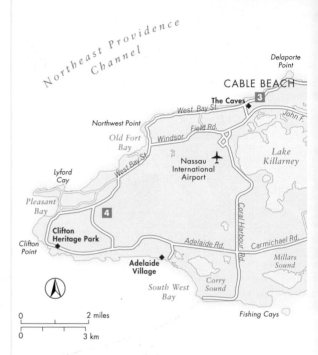

1 Nassau. Pink buildings dating back to the colonial era are interspersed with modern-day office complexes; horses pull their wooden carriages alongside stretch limousines; and tourists can browse the local craft-centric straw market or shop for luxurious handbags at Gucci, all in this historic capital city.

2 Paradise Island. P.I. (as locals call the island) is connected to downtown Nassau's east end by a pair of bridges. Atlantis, the tallest building in the Bahamas, is a beachfront resort complete with a gamut of dining options, the country's largest casino, and some of the region's fanciest shops. Most memorable, however, are the water-based activities, slides, and aquariums. Love it or despise it, it's today's face of Paradise.

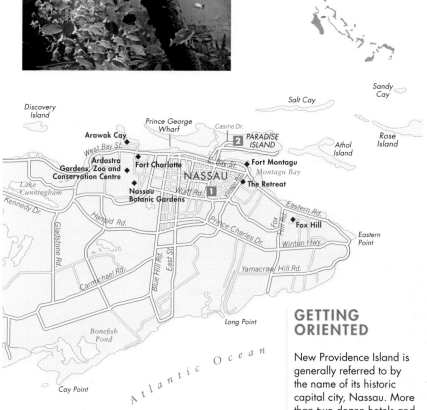

2

GETTING ORIENTED

New Providence Island is generally referred to by the name of its historic capital city, Nassau. More than two dozen hotels and at least double as many restaurants lure more than 2 million tourists to the city—and nearby Paradise Island and Cable Beach—annually. The heart of commerce and government and the bulk of the country's 300,000 people are crammed onto the 21-mi-by-7-mi island, less than 200 mi from Miami. Venturing outside the three main tourist areas will give you a better idea of true Bahamian life, and a glimpse at some less-visited but worth-the-trek attractions.

3 **Cable Beach.** The crescent-shape stretch of sand west of Nassau is in the midst of a major face-lift, transforming into a destination to rival Paradise Island. Beyond the resorts' casinos, restaurants, bars, and pretty beaches, there's not a whole lot to do here. A short walk west are a small straw market and a smattering of restaurants, cafés, and bars that cater mostly to locals.

4 **Western New Providence.** West of Cable Beach's high-rise hotels, New Providence becomes primarily residential, with small restaurants and bars along the way. West Bay Street hugs the coastline, providing spectacular ocean views. This part of the island is the least developed, so it's the perfect spot to find a secluded beach or go bird-watching.

NEW PROVIDENCE AND PARADISE ISLANDS PLANNER

When to Go

With the warm Gulf Stream currents swirling and balmy trade winds blowing, New Providence is an appealing year-round destination. Temperatures usually hover in the 70s and 80s and rarely get above 90°F on a mid-summer's day or below 60°F on a winter's night. June to October tend to be the hottest and wettest months, although rain is often limited to periodic afternoon showers.

The best time to visit the island is December to May, especially if you're escaping the cold. Don't mind the locals, who'll likely tell you it's too chilly to hit the beach in winter, but you may want to pack a light sweater if you plan on dining outdoors. Visitors from colder climates may find the humid summer days and nights a bit stifling. Be aware that tropical depressions, tropical storms, and hurricanes are a possibility in New Providence during the Atlantic hurricane season from early June to late November. Expect to pay between 15% and 30% less off-season at most resorts.

Getting Here

Lynden Pindling International Airport (NAS) (☎ 242/702–1000) is 8 mi west of Nassau. There is no public bus service from the airport to hotels. Major car-rental companies are represented at the airport. A taxi ride for two people from the airport to downtown Nassau costs $27; to Paradise Island, $42 (this includes the $1 bridge toll); and to Cable Beach $25. Each additional passenger is $3, and excess baggage costs $2 a bag.

Nassau is a port of call for several cruise lines. Ships dock at Prince George Wharf in downtown Nassau. (⇨ *see Cruises in Travel Smart, at the back of the book.*)

Getting Around

By Boat Water taxis travel between Prince George Wharf and Paradise Island during daylight hours at half-hour intervals. The one-way cost is $3 per person, and the trip takes 12 minutes.

By Bus The frequent jitneys are the cheapest choice on routes such as Cable Beach to downtown Nassau. Fare is $1.50 each way, and exact change is required. Hail one at a bus stop, hotel, or public beach. In downtown Nassau jitneys wait on Frederick Street and along the the middle of Bay Street. Bus service runs throughout the day until 7 pm.

By Car Rent a car if you plan to explore the whole island. Rentals are available at the airport, downtown, on Paradise Island, and at some resorts for $40–$120 per day. Gasoline costs between $5 and $6 a gallon. Remember to drive on the left.

By Moped Two people can ride a motor scooter for about $65 for a half day, $85 for a full day.

By Taxi Unless you plan to jump all over the island, taxis are the most convenient way to get around. The fare is $9 plus $1 bridge toll between downtown Nassau and Paradise Island, $20 from Cable Beach to Paradise Island (plus $1 toll), and $18 from Cable Beach to Nassau. Fares are for two passengers; each additional passenger is $3. It's customary to tip taxi drivers 15%.

About the Restaurants

Foodies will delight in New Providence's restaurant range, from shabby shacks serving up the kind of food you'd find in any Bahamian's kitchen, to elegant eateries where jackets are required and the food rivals that found in any major city. You'll recognize celebrity chef names like Bobby Flay, Jean-Georges Vongerichten, and Nobu Matsuhisa, all of whom have restaurants on Paradise Island.

Eating out can get expensive, particularly in resort restaurants, so a budget-friendly strategy is having brunch at one of the myriad all-you-can-eat buffets at the larger hotels on Paradise Island and Cable Beach, then a light snack to hold you over until dinnertime.

Note: A gratuity (15%) is often added to the bill automatically. Many all-inclusive hotels offer meal plans for non-guests.

About the Hotels

If you want to mix with locals and experience a little more of Bahamian culture, choose a hotel in downtown Nassau. Its beaches are not dazzling; if you want to be beachfront on a gorgeous white strand, stay on Cable Beach or Paradise Island's Cabbage Beach. Reasons to stay in Nassau include proximity to shopping and affordability (although the cost of taxis to and from the better beaches can add up).

The plush Cable Beach and Paradise Island resorts are big and beautiful, glittering and splashy, and have the best beaches, but they can be overwhelming. In any case, these big, top-dollar properties generally have more amenities than you could possibly make use of, a selection of dining choices, and a full roster of sports and entertainment options. Stay in Cable Beach if you don't plan to visit Nassau and Paradise Island often; you need to take a cab, and the costs add up.

WHAT IT COSTS IN DOLLARS

	¢	$	$$	$$$	$$$$
Restaurants	under $10	$10–$20	$20–$30	$30–$40	over $40
Hotels		under $100	$100–$200	$200–$300	$300–$400	over $400

Restaurant prices are based on the median main course price at dinner, excluding gratuity, typically 15%, which is often automatically added to the bill. Hotel prices are for two people in a standard double room in high season, excluding service and 6%–12% tax.

Essentials

Banks Banks are open Monday through Thursday from 9:30 to 3 and Friday from 9:30 to 5. International ATMs are scattered throughout the island.

Car Rentals Orange Creek Car Rentals ☎ 242/323–4967. **Virgo Car Rental** ☎ 242/377–1275.

Embassy U.S. Embassy ✉ Queen St. across from British Colonial Hilton, Nassau, New Providence Island ☎ 242/322–1181.

Emergencies Ambulance ☎ 911, 919, 242/322–2881. **Doctors Hospital** ✉ Collins Ave. and Shirley St., Nassau, New Providence Island ☎ 242/302–4600. **Police** ☎ 911, 919, 242/322–4444. **Princess Margaret Hospital** ✉ Shirley St., Nassau, New Providence Island ☎ 242/322–2861.

Taxis Bahamas Transport ☎ 242/323–5111. **Taxi Cab Union** ☎ 242/323–5818.

Visitor Information The Ministry of Tourism operates tourist information booths at the airport, open daily from 8:30 am to 11:30 pm, and at the Welcome Center (Festival Place) adjacent to Prince George Wharf, open daily from 9 am to 5 pm. The Ministry of Tourism's People-to-People Program sets you up with a Bahamian family with similar interests to show you local culture firsthand. **Ministry of Tourism** ☎ 242/322–7500 ⊕ www.bahamas.com. **People-to-People Program** ☎ 242/324–9772 ⊕ www.bahamas.com/peopletopeople.

NEW PROVIDENCE AND PARADISE ISLAND BEACHES

New Providence is the Bahamas' most urban island, but that doesn't mean you won't find beautiful beaches. Powdery white sand, aquamarine waves, and shade-bearing palm trees are easy to come by, regardless how populated you like your beach to be. Whether you crave solitude or want to be in the middle of the action, there's a sand spot that's just right for you.

(above) Cable Beach (upper right) Blue Lagoon Island (lower right) Love Beach

Cable Beach and the beaches near Atlantis are where you'll typically find loud music, bars serving tropical drinks, and vendors peddling everything from parasailing and Jet Ski rides to T-shirts and hair braiding. Downtown Nassau only has man-made beaches, the best being Junkanoo Beach just west of the British Colonial Hilton. But the capital city's beaches can't compare to the real thing. For a more relaxed environment, drive out of the main tourist areas. You'll likely find stretches of sand populated by locals only, or, chances are, no one at all.

OFFSHORE ADVENTURES

For a true beach getaway, head to one of the tiny islands just off the coast of Paradise Island. A 20-minute boat ride from Nassau, Blue Lagoon Island has a number of beaches, including one in a tranquil cove lined with hammocks suspended by palm trees. Enjoy a grilled lunch and then rent a kayak or water bike if you're feeling ambitious.

NEW PROVIDENCE AND PARADISE ISLAND'S BEST BEACHES

ADELAIDE BEACH

Time your visit to this far-flung beach on the island's southwestern shore to catch low tide, when the ocean recedes, leaving behind sandbanks and seashells. It's a perfect place to take the kids for a shallow-water dip in the sea, or for a truly private rendezvous. Popular with locals, you'll likely have the miles-long stretch all to yourself unless it's a public holiday.

CABBAGE BEACH

Cabbage Beach is 3 mi of white sand lined with shady casuarina trees, sand dunes, and sun worshippers. This is the place to go to rent Jet Skis or get a bird's-eye view of Paradise Island while parasailing. Hair braiders and T-shirt vendors stroll the beach, and hotel guests crowd the areas surrounding the resorts, including Atlantis. For peace and quiet, stroll east.

CABLE BEACH

Hotels dot the length of this 3-mi beach, so don't expect isolation. Music from the hotel pool decks wafts out onto the sand, Jet Skis race up and down the waves, and vendors sell everything from shell jewelry to coconut drinks right from the shell. If you get tired of lounging around, join a game of beach volleyball.

JAWS BEACH

Rent a car or scooter and head southwest towards Clifton Heritage Park. As you approach you'll see a sign for beach access. This is where you will find Jaws Beach—so called because it's where the much-panned final installment in the *Jaws* series, *Jaws The Revenge*, was filmed. Contrary to what happens in the movie, the shallow-water, tree-lined beach is a great place for kids. Make sure to pack drinks and snacks, as it is a long drive to any store. To the left you can get a long-distance view of some of the multi-million dollar homes in exclusive Lyford Cay.

JUNKANOO BEACH

Right in downtown Nassau, this beach is spring-break central from late February through April. The man-made beach isn't the prettiest on the island, but it's conveniently located if you only have a few quick hours to catch a tan. Music is provided by everything from bands and DJs to guys with boom boxes; a few bars keep the drinks flowing.

LOVE BEACH

If you're looking for great snorkeling and some privacy, drive about 20 minutes west of town. White sand shimmers in the sun and the azure waves gently roll ashore. About a mile offshore is 40 acres of coral reef known as the Sea Gardens. Access is not marked, just look for a vacant lot.

Updated by Jessica Robertson

An incongruous mix of glitzy casinos and quiet shady lanes; splashy megaresorts and tiny settlements that recall a distant simpler age; land development unrivaled elsewhere in the Bahamas, and vast stretches of untrammeled territory. This is New Providence Island, a grab-bag destination. The island, home to two-thirds of all Bahamians, provides fast-paced living, nightlife that goes on until dawn, and high-end shopping strips. And when all the hustle and bustle becomes too much, it's easy to find quiet stretches of sandy white beach where the only noise is the waves rolling in.

In the course of its history, the island has weathered the comings and goings of lawless pirates, Spanish invaders, slave-holding British Loyalists who fled the United States after the Revolutionary War, Civil War–era Confederate blockade runners, and Prohibition rumrunners. Nevertheless, New Providence remains most influenced by England, which sent its first royal governor to the island in 1718. Although Bahamians won government control in 1967 and independence six years later, British influence is felt to this day.

Nassau is the nation's capital and transportation hub, as well as the banking and commercial center. The fortuitous combination of tourist-friendly enterprise, tropical weather, and island flavor with a European overlay has not gone unnoticed: each year nearly 2 million cruise-ship passengers arrive at Nassau's Prince George Wharf.

There's a definite hustle and bustle in this capital city that's not found elsewhere in the country, but that doesn't mean you have to follow suit. From shark diving and snorkeling to bicycle tours, horseback riding, tennis, and golf, active pursuits abound in New Providence. Avid water-sports fans will find a range of possibilities, including waterskiing, sailing, windsurfing, and deep-sea fishing. Or simply cruise the clear Bahamian waters for a day trip or an evening ride.

2

GREAT ITINERARIES

Numbers in the text correspond to numbers on the Nassau and Paradise Island map.

IF YOU HAVE 3 DAYS

We're guessing you came to the Bahamas to get some sun, so don't waste any time. Decide whether you'd prefer a secluded stretch of sand or a beach right in the middle of the action, such as **Cable Beach**—New Providence has both. After relaxing on the beach, catch a show at the Rainforest Theatre or check out the downtown bar-and-club scene. Spend Day 2 taking in the markets, gardens, and historic sites of **Nassau**. A good starting point is **Rawson Square ❶**, in the heart of the commercial area. Do your shopping in the morning, hitting **Bay Street,** the capital's main street, and Festival Place at **Prince George Wharf ❷**. To avoid the afternoon heat, visit the **National Art Gallery ❾**, checking out the colonial architecture along the way. Head to Arawak Cay (the Fish Fry to locals) for dinner; pick a shack and order an

authentic Bahamian meal of grilled snapper (served whole) washed down with a cold Kalik or Sands beer. On your third day, tour Paradise Island. Try your luck at the **Atlantis** casino or explore the giant aquariums (nonresort guests will have to pay a hefty $39 for adults or $29 for kids under 12). For your final night, book reservations at one of Atlantis's fancier restaurants; Nobu, Mesa Grill, or Café Martinique will serve up a last supper to remember.

IF YOU HAVE 5 DAYS

On Day 4, consider a day trip to one of the Out Islands. Quaint Harbour Island is just two hours away on the Bohengy ferry (📠 *242/323–2166* 🌐 *www.bahamasferries.com*), or book seats on one of the large speedboats that will take you to a private island in the Exumas. For your final day, rent a car or scooters and head to **Western New Providence**, stopping for lunch at Goodfellow Farms on your way to the **Clifton Heritage Park**.

EXPLORING

NASSAU

Nassau's sheltered harbor bustles with cruise-ship activity, while a block away Bay Street's sidewalks are crowded with shoppers who duck into air-conditioned boutiques and relax on benches in the shade of mahogany and lignum vitae trees. Shops angle for tourist dollars with fine imported goods at duty-free prices, yet you'll find a handful of stores overflowing with authentic Bahamian crafts, food supplies, and other delights.

With a revitalization of downtown ongoing—the revamped British Colonial Hilton leading the way—Nassau is recapturing some of its past glamour. Nevertheless, modern influences are completely apparent: fancy restaurants, suave clubs, and trendy coffeehouses have popped up everywhere. These changes have come partly in response to the growing number of upper-crust crowds that now supplement the spring

The Royal Bahamas Police Force Band performs in front of Government House.

breakers and cruise passengers who have traditionally flocked to Nassau. Of course, you can still find a wild club or a rowdy bar, but you can also sip cappuccino while viewing contemporary Bahamian art or dine by candlelight beneath prints of old Nassau, serenaded by soft, island-inspired calypso music.

A trip to Nassau wouldn't be complete without a stop at some of the island's well-preserved historic buildings. The large, pink colonial-style edifices house Parliament and some of the courts, while others, like Fort Charlotte, date back to the days when pirates ruled the town. Take a tour via horse-drawn carriage for the full effect.

TOP ATTRACTIONS

Fodor's Choice ★ **National Art Gallery of the Bahamas.** Opened in July 2003, the museum houses the works of esteemed Bahamian artists such as Max Taylor, Amos Ferguson, Brent Malone, John Cox, and Antonius Roberts. The glorious Italianate-colonial mansion, built in 1860 and restored in the 1990s, has double-tiered verandas with elegant columns. It was the residence of Sir William Doyle, the first chief justice of the Bahamas. Join locals on the lawn for movie night under the stars; call for the schedule. Don't miss the museum's gift shop, where you'll find books about the Bahamas and Bahamian quilts, prints, ceramics, jewelry, and crafts. ☒ *West and W. Hill Sts., across from St. Francis Xavier Cathedral* ☎ *242/328–5800* ⊕ *www.nagb.org.bs* ☒ *$5* ☉ *Tue.–Sat. 10–4.*

☪ **Pirates of Nassau.** Take a journey through Nassau's pirate days in this interactive museum devoted to such notorious members of the city's past as Blackbeard, Mary Read, and Anne Bonney. Board a pirate ship, see dioramas of intrigue on the high seas, hear historical narration, and

2

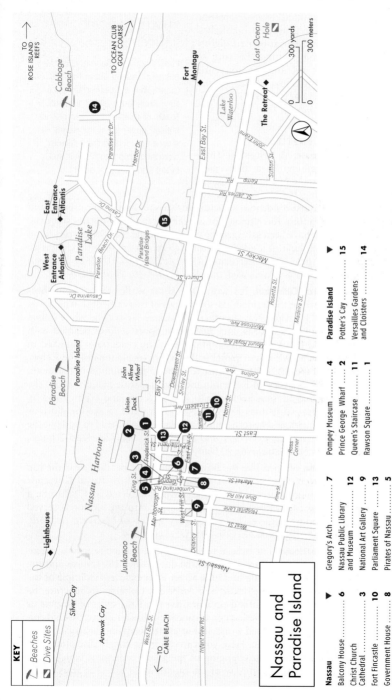

Nassau and Paradise Island

KEY

⊿ *Beaches*

⊿ *Dive Sites*

TO ROSE ISLAND REEFS

Cabbage Beach

TO OCEAN CLUB GOLF COURSE

Fort Montagu ♦

Lost Ocean Hole ⊿

Paradise Hts. Dr.

Harbour Dr.

East Bay St.

Lake Waterloo

John Evans

Kemp Rd

St. James Rd

The Retreat ♦

Sutton St.

0   300 yards

0   300 meters

East Entrance Atlantis ♦

Casino Dr.

Paradise Lake

Paradise Island Bridges

West Entrance Atlantis ♦

Paradise Beach Dr.

Casuarina Dr.

Paradise Dr.

Mackey St.

Church St.

Rosetta St.

Madeira St.

Montrose Ave.

Mount Royal Ave.

Collins Ave.

Paradise Island

Paradise Beach

John Alfred Wharf

Union Dock

Bay St.

Dowdeswell St.

Shirley St.

Elizabeth Ave.

North St.

East St.

Ross Corner

⑮

② ① ⑬ ⑫ ⑪ ⑩

③ ⑥ ⑦

④ ⑤ ⑧

⑨

Frederick St.

St. Parliament St.

East Hill St.

George St.

Market St.

Blue Hill Rd.

Hospital Lane

Nassau Harbour

King St.

Cumberland Rd.

Marlborough St.

West Hill St.

Delancy St.

West St.

Nassau St.

Lighthouse ♦

Junkanoo Beach

Silver Cay

Arawak Cay

West Bay St.

TO CABLE BEACH

Infant View Rd.

Nassau   ▶

Balcony House **6**

Christ Church Cathedral ... **3**

Fort Fincastle **10**

Government House **8**

Gregory's Arch **7**

Nassau Public Library and Museum **12**

National Art Gallery **9**

Parliament Square **13**

Pirates of Nassau **5**

Pompey Museum **4**

Prince George Wharf **2**

Queen's Staircase **11**

Rawson Square **1**

Paradise Island   ▶

Potter's Cay **15**

Versailles Gardens and Cloisters **14**

experience sound effects re-creating some of the gruesome highlights. It's a fun and educational (if slightly scary) family outing. Be sure to check out the offbeat souvenirs in the Pirate Shop. ⊠ *George and King Sts.* ☎ *242/356–3759* ⊕ *www. pirates-of-nassau.com* 🎫 *$12* ⊙ *Mon.–Sat. 9–6, Sun. 9–12:30.*

WORTH NOTING

Balcony House. A delightful 18th-century landmark—a pink two-story house named aptly for its overhanging balcony—this is the oldest wooden residential structure in Nassau, and its furnishings and design recapture the elegance of a bygone era. A mahogany staircase, believed to have been salvaged from a ship during the 19th century, is an interior highlight. A guided tour through this fascinating building is an hour well spent. ⊠ *Market St. and Trinity Pl.* ☎ *242/302–2621* 🎫 *Donations accepted* ⊙ *Mon.–Wed. and Fri. 9:30–4:30, Thurs. 9:30–1.*

Christ Church Cathedral. It's worth the short walk off the main thoroughfare to see the stained-glass windows of this cathedral, which was built in 1837, when Nassau officially became a city. The white pillars of the church's spacious, airy interior support ceilings beamed with dark wood handcrafted by shipbuilders. The crucifixion depicted in the east window's center panel is flanked by depictions of the Empty Tomb and the Ascension. Be sure to spend a few minutes in the small, flower-filled Garden of Remembrance, where stone plaques adorn the walls. Sunday mass is held at 7:30, 9, 11:15 am, and 6 pm. Drop by the cathedral Christmas Eve and New Year's Eve to see the glorious church at night, and hear the music and choir. Call ahead to find out the time of the service. ⊠ *George and King Sts.* ☎ *242/322–4186* ⊕ *www. christchurchcathedral.com* ⊙ *Daily 8–5.*

Fort Fincastle. Shaped like the bow of a ship and perched near the top of the Queen's Staircase, Fort Fincastle—named for Royal Governor Lord Dunmore (Viscount Fincastle)—was completed in 1793 to be a lookout post for marauders trying to sneak into the harbor. It served as a lighthouse in the early 19th century. ⊠ *Top of Elizabeth Ave. hill, south of Shirley St.* ☎ *242/356–9085* ⊙ *Daily 8–4.*

Government House. The official residence of the Bahamas governor-general, the personal representative of the queen since 1801, this imposing pink-and-white building on Duke Street is an excellent example of the mingling of Bahamian-British and American Colonial architecture. Its graceful columns and broad circular drive recall the styles of Virginia or the Carolinas. But its pink color, distinctive white quoins (cross-laid cornerstones), and louvered wooden shutters (to keep out the tropical sun) are typically Bahamian. Here you can catch the crisply disciplined but beautifully flamboyant changing of the guard ceremony, which takes place every second Saturday of the month at 11 am. The stars of the

PIRATES OF THE BAHAMAS

Pirates roamed the waters of the Bahamas, hiding out in the 700 islands, but they especially liked New Providence Island. Edward Teach, or Blackbeard, even named himself governor of the island. He scared enemy and crew alike by weaving hemp into his hair and beard and setting it on fire.

pomp and pageantry are members of the Royal Bahamas Police Force Band, who are decked out in white tunics, red-stripe navy trousers, and spiked, white pith helmets with red bands. The drummers sport leopard skins. The governor's wife hosts a tea party open to the public from 3 to 4 pm on the last Friday of the month January–June as part of the People-to-People program. Dress is casual but elegant—no shorts, jeans, or tennis shoes. Musicians, poets, and storytellers provide entertainment. ⊠ *Duke and George Sts.* ☎ *242/356–5415 ceremony schedule, 242/328–7810 tea party, 242/322–2020 Government House.*

SAFETY FIRST

Crime is up in Nassau, so be mindful of your surroundings, especially near the cruise-ship dock and in areas less visited by tourists. Police force has increased on the streets of downtown Nassau for added security. See Travel Smart, at the end of this book for more information on safety.

Gregory's Arch. Named for John Gregory (royal governor 1849–54), this arch, at the intersection of Market and Duke streets, separates downtown from the "over-the-hill" neighborhood of **Grant's Town,** where much of Nassau's population lives. Grant's Town was laid out in the 1820s by Governor Lewis Grant as a settlement for freed slaves. Visitors once enjoyed late-night mingling with the locals in the small, dimly lighted bars; nowadays you should exhibit the same caution you would if you were visiting the commercial areas of a large city. Nevertheless, it's a vibrant section of town where you can rub shoulders with Bahamians at a funky take-out food stand or down-home restaurant.

Nassau Public Library and Museum. The octagonal building near Parliament Square was the Nassau Gaol (the old British spelling for jail), circa 1797. You're welcome to pop in and browse. The small prison cells are now lined with books. The museum has an interesting collection of historic prints and old colonial documents. Computers with Internet access are available for rent—$1.25 for 15 minutes, $5 for an hour. ⊠ *Shirley St. between Parliament St. and Bank La.* ☎ *242/322–4907* ⊕ *bahamaslibraries.org* ☞ *Free* ⊗ *Mon.–Thurs. 10–7, Fri. 10–5, Sat. 10–4.*

Parliament Square. Nassau is the seat of the national government. The Bahamian Parliament comprises two houses—a 16-member Senate (Upper House) and a 41-member House of Assembly (Lower House)—and a ministerial cabinet headed by a prime minister. If the House is in session, sit in to watch lawmakers debate. Parliament Square's pink, colonnaded government buildings were constructed in the late 1700s and early 1800s by Loyalists who came to the Bahamas from North Carolina. The square is dominated by a statue of a slim young Queen Victoria that was erected on her birthday, May 24, in 1905. In the immediate area are a handful of magistrates' courts. Behind the House of Assembly is the **Supreme Court.** Its four-times-a-year opening ceremonies (held the first weeks of January, April, July, and October) recall the wigs and mace-bearing pageantry of the Houses of Parliament in London. The Royal Bahamas Police Force Band is usually on hand for the event. ⊠ *Bay St.* ☎ *242/322–2041* ☞ *Free* ⊗ *Weekdays 10–4.*

The Cloisters in Versailles Gardens is possibly the most peaceful spot on the island.

Pompey Museum. The building, where slave auctions were held in the 1700s, is named for a rebel slave who lived on the Out Island of Exuma in 1830. Exhibits focus on the issues of slavery and emancipation and highlight the works of local artists. A knowledgeable, enthusiastic young staff is on hand to answer questions. ⊠ *Bay and George Sts.* ☎ *242/356–0495* ⊕ *www.antiquitiescorp.com* ✉ *$3 adults, $1 children under 14 and $2 seniors* ☉ *Mon.–Wed., Fri., and Sat. 9:30–4:30, Thurs. 9:30–1.*

Prince George Wharf. The wharf that leads into Rawson Square is the first view that cruise passengers encounter after they tumble off their ships. Up to a dozen gigantic cruise ships call on Nassau at any one time, and passengers spill out onto downtown, giving Nassau an instant, and constantly replenished, surge of life. Even if you're not visiting via cruise ship, it's worth heading to Festival Place, a Bahamian village–style shopping emporium. Here you'll find booths for 45 Bahamian artisans; Internet kiosks; vendors selling diving, fishing, and day trips; scooter rentals; and an information desk offering maps, directions, and suggestions for sightseeing. You can also arrange walking tours of historic Nassau here. ⊠ *Waterfront at Rawson Sq.*

Queen's Staircase. A popular early-morning exercise regime for locals, the "66 Steps" (as Bahamians call them) are thought to have been carved out of a solid limestone cliff by slaves in the 1790s. The staircase was later named to honor Queen Victoria's reign. Pick up some souvenirs at the ad hoc straw market along the narrow road that leads to the site. ⊠ *Top of Elizabeth Ave. hill, south of Shirley St.*

Rawson Square. This shady square connects Bay Street to Prince George Wharf. As you enter off Bay Street, note the statue of Sir Milo Butler, the first postindependence (and first native Bahamian) governor general. Horse-drawn surreys wait for passengers along Prince George Wharf (expect to pay about $30 for a half-hour ride through Nassau's streets). Between Rawson Square and Festival Place, check out (or perhaps stop inside) the open-air **hair-braiding pavilion,** where women work

DID YOU KNOW?

Judges and barristers still wear wigs in court. Each Supreme Court judge has two wigs—one for the courtroom and one for formal occasions that require pomp and pageantry.

their magic at prices ranging from $2 for a single strand to $100 for an elaborate do. An often overlooked pleasure near the pavilion is Randolph W. Johnston's lovely bronze statue, *Tribute to Bahamian Women.* ⊠ *Bay St.*

PARADISE ISLAND

The graceful, arched Paradise Island bridges ($1 round-trip toll for cars and motorbikes; free for bicyclists and pedestrians) lead to and from the extravagant world of Paradise Island. Until 1962 the island was largely undeveloped and known as Hog Island. A&P heir Huntington Hartford changed the name when he built the island's first resort complex. In 1994 South African developer Sol Kerzner transformed the existing high-rise hotel into the first phase of Atlantis. Many years, a number of new hotels, a water park, and more than $1 billion later, Atlantis has taken over the island. From the ultraexclusive Cove hotel to the acclaimed golf course, it's easy to forget there's more to Paradise Island. It's home to multimillion-dollar homes and condominiums and a handful of independent resort properties. Despite the hustle and bustle of the megaresorts, you can still find yourself a quiet spot on Cabbage Beach, which lines the northern side of the island, or on the more secluded Paradise Beach west of Atlantis. Aptly renamed, the island *is* a paradise for beach lovers, boaters, and fun seekers.

WORTH NOTING

Potter's Cay. Walk the road beneath the Paradise Island bridges to Potter's Cay to watch sloops bringing in and selling loads of fish and conch— pronounced *konk*. Along the road to the cay are dozens of stands where you can watch the conch, straight from the sea, being extracted from its glistening pink shell. If you don't have the know-how to handle the tasty conch's preparation—getting the diffident creature out of its shell requires boring a hole at the right spot to sever the muscle that keeps it entrenched—you can enjoy a conch salad on the spot, as fresh as it comes, and take notes for future attempts. Empty shells are sold as souvenirs. Many locals and hotel chefs come here to purchase the fresh catches; you can also find vegetables, herbs, and such condiments as fiery Bahamian peppers preserved in lime juice, and locally grown pineapples, papayas, and bananas. Join in on a raucous game of dominoes outside many of the stalls. Some stalls are closed on Sunday. There's also a police station and dockmaster's office, where you can book an inexpensive trip on a mail boat headed to the Out Islands. Be aware that

Continued on page 63

LIVING LARGE AT
ATLANTIS

by Jessica Robertson

The unmistakable sight of this peach fantasia comes into view long before you cross the Paradise Island Bridge. With a glitzy shopping mall, the biggest casino and water park in the country, and seemingly unlimited choices for dining and drinking (40 restaurants and bars), the Bahamas' largest resort is as much a tourist attraction as a hotel.

Royal Towers entrance

Water Paradise

Aura Nightclub

Atlantis at night

Poseidon's Kids Pool

✉ Casino Dr., Paradise Island ☎ 888/528-7155 or 242/363-3000 🎫 Discover Atlantis tour $35; Aquaventure day pass $120; beach day pass $69; casino admission free ⏰ Tours daily 9–4:45, casino daily 24 hrs.

CUTTING-EDGE EXPERIENCES

As kid friendly as Atlantis is, the resort has recently upped its sophistication levels. Trendy clubs and private pool areas ensure adults have their own space. Below are our top picks for family and adult activities.

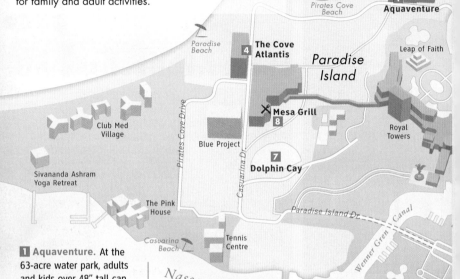

Pirates Cove

Pirates Cove Beach

1 Aquaventure

Leap of Faith

Paradise Beach

4 The Cove Atlantis

Paradise Island

Royal Towers

Club Med Village

Pirates Cove Drive

Blue Project

✕ Mesa Grill **8**

Casuarina Dr.

7 Dolphin Cay

Sivananda Ashram Yoga Retreat

The Pink House

Paradise Island Dr.

Wenner Gren Canal

Casuarina Beach

Tennis Centre

Nassau Harbour

1 Aquaventure. At the 63-acre water park, adults and kids over 48" tall can take the **Leap of Faith**, meander along a lazy river, or paddle in fun-filled themed pools like Poseidon and Splasher's Island. ☾

2 Atlantis Kids Adventures. Check the kids into this 8,000-sq-foot wonderland, and they might not come out until it's time to head back to the airport. Interactive activities include a **gaming center, Lego room, performance stage, and cooking classes.** ☾

Miss USA and Miss Universe DJing at Cain

☾ Great for families
🍸 Perfect for adults

3 Aura. Hot tunes, sexy people, and top-shelf drinks are all at the country's trendiest (and most expensive) nightclub. If you're really a big spender, invest in a VIP table with bottle service. 🍸

4 Cain at the Cove. A DJ orchestrates the mood from morning 'til night at this adults-only pool lounge, while concierges keep the food and drinks coming. For a totally decadent experience, book a private cabana, and have it stocked with whatever your heart desires. 🍸

5 Casino. The largest casino in the Bahamas and the Caribbean never closes. Test your luck on one of the 850 slot machines, play a hand of blackjack or Caribbean stud poker, or place a bet on major sporting events at Pegasus Race and Sports Book. 🍸

6 The Dig. You don't have to get wet to get up close and personal with some of the ocean's most incredible creatures. The Dig houses everything from spiny lobster to lionfish, seahorses, and even piranha in a 2½ million gallon habitat, the world's largest aquarium. ☾

Casino

Dolphin Cay

Aquaventure

Atlantis Beach

Paradise Lagoon

The Dig **6**

Beach Tower

Sheraton Grand Res

Casino Dr.

3 **5**
Aura Night Club
Casino Coral Towers
Nobu

✕ **Bahamian Club**
✕ Casa d'Angelo
✕ Chop Stix
Atlantis Kids Adventure **2**

Casino Drive

Paradise Lake
Café Martinique

✕

Comfort Suites Paradise Island

Paradise Island Dr.

Atlantis Marina
Harborside Resort

Marina Village

◆ **Bahamacraft Centre**

Bridge toll

Ferry Terminal

Harbour Road

Bridge from Paradise Island
Hurricane Hole

0 ─── 220 yards
0 ─── 200 meters

Leap of Faith

7 Dolphin Cay. Dolphins rescued from a Louisiana aquarium destroyed by Hurricane Katrina now call Atlantis home. Don a wet suit and join them for a swim, be a trainer for a day, or just lounge on **Dolphin Cay Beach** and watch them play. ☕

8 Mesa Grill. Chef Bobby Flay's first restaurant outside the United States serves up his signature southwestern dishes, many with a Bahamian twist. ☕

SAVE VS. SPLURGE

Save at Paradise Lagoon

Splurge at the casino

ACTIVITY	SAVE	SPLURGE
Dining	So long as everyone in your group can settle on a dish or two, **Carmine's** (242/363–3000 Ext. 29) is a great deal. Italian food is served up family style, which means portions large enough to share. Desserts like the chocolate cannoli and the tiramisu are wonderful, so save room and order your own.	For the ultimate in fine dining, try **Café Martinique**. Select your courses from the exquisite menu, which includes a market-price mixed-seafood appetizer and Chateaubriand for two. Or order the chef's tasting menu for $145 per person.
Underwater Adventures	Pack your mask, snorkel, and swimsuit, and hit the 7-acre **Paradise Lagoon** or the reefs just off **Cove Beach.**	Sign up to be an **Aquarist for a Day** and get hands-on experience helping care for the thousands of marine animals that call Atlantis home. Prices start at $179, and it's limited to 12 people.
A Night Out	Take a leisurely stroll through **Marina Village** for some great people watching, "ooh" and "ahh" at the luxurious yachts docked there, and grab a seat across from Bimini Road to listen to live music.	**Aura Nightclub**, upstairs from the casino, is one of the hottest nightspots in the country. Admission can range from nothing to $100, drinks cost a pretty penny, and tables are only available to groups buying a bottle of top-shelf liquor.
Entertain the Kids	The **Atlantis Theater** shows recent Hollywood blockbusters and is free for resort guests. Make it a family affair, or the kids can catch a flick while you dine at a nearby restaurant.	The newly overhauled **Atlantis Kids Adventures** offers kids ages 3–12 more activities than they could ever take advantage of. It costs $40–$65 per session.
Souvenirs	Head over to the **Bahama Craft Centre** and pick up a locally made straw bag or a T-shirt to remind you of your time in Paradise. Bartering is the norm in the markets.	**Marina Village** and the main shopping court at Atlantis are lined with stores selling many of the world's most exclusive brands. A duty-free regime ensures that even when splurging, you'll often land a deal.

Off the Beaten Path: Eastern New Providence

New Providence Island's eastern end is residential, although there are some interesting historic sites and fortifications here. From East Bay Street, just beyond the Paradise Island bridges, it's a 20-minute scenic drive to Eastern Point. Take Eastern Road, lined with gracious homes (and during the early summer months, the red and deep orange blooms of the Royal Poinciana tree). The following are worthy sights to see.

Fort Montagu. The oldest of the island's three forts, Montagu was built of local limestone in 1741 to repel Spanish invaders. The only action it saw was when it was occupied for two weeks by rebel American troops—among them a lieutenant named John Paul Jones—seeking arms and ammunition during the Revolutionary War. The small fortification is quite simple, but displays a lovely elevated view of Nassau Harbour. The second level has a number of weathered cannons. A narrow public beach, which disappears at high tide, looks out upon Montagu Bay, where many international yacht regattas and Bahamian sloop races are held annually. ⊠ *East of Bay St. on Eastern Rd., Paradise Island* ⟳ *Free.*

The Retreat. Nearly 200 species of exotic palm trees grace the 11 verdant acres appropriately known as The Retreat, which serves as the headquarters of the Bahamas National Trust. Stroll in blessed silence through the lush grounds, past smiling Buddhas, and under stone arbors overhung with vines. It's a perfect break on a steamy Nassau day. The Retreat hosts the Jollification—the unofficial start to the Christmas season—the third weekend in November. Carols, festive food and drinks, a kids' holiday craft center, and local artisans selling native and Christmas crafts make this a must-do event. ⊠ *Village Rd., Paradise Island* ☎ *242/393–1317* ⟳ *$2* ⟳ *Weekdays 9–5.*

these boats are built for cargo, not passenger comfort, and it's a rough ride even on calm seas.

Versailles Gardens. Fountains and statues of luminaries and legends (such as Napoléon and Josephine, Franklin Delano Roosevelt, David Livingstone, Hercules, and Mephistopheles) adorn Versailles Gardens, the terraced lawn at the One & Only Ocean Club, once the private hideaway of Huntington Hartford. At the top of the gardens stand the **Cloisters,** the remains of a stone monastery built by Augustinian monks in France in the 13th century. They were imported to the United States in the 1920s by newspaper baron William Randolph Hearst. (The cloister is one of four to have ever been removed from French soil.) Forty years later, Hartford bought the Cloisters and had them rebuilt on their present commanding site. At the center is a graceful, contemporary white-marble statue called *Silence,* by U.S. sculptor Dick Reid. Nearly every day tourists take or renew wedding vows under the delicately wrought gazebo overlooking Nassau Harbour. Although the garden is owned by the One & Only Ocean Club, visitors are welcome so long as they check in at the security gate. ⊠ *One & Only Ocean Club, Paradise Island Dr.* ☎ *242/363–2501.*

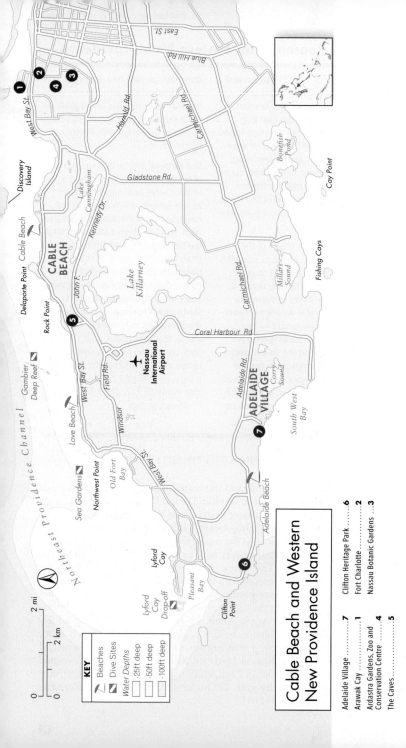

Cable Beach and Western New Providence Island

KEY

/ Beaches

/ Dive Sites

Water Depths

-25ft deep

-50ft deep

-100ft deep

CABLE BEACH AND WESTERN NEW PROVIDENCE

From downtown Nassau, West Bay Street follows the coast west past Arawak Cay to the Cable Beach strip. If you're not driving, catch the #10 jitney for a direct ride from downtown. This main drag is lined with hotels and is being completely transformed by the Baha Mar group. A small straw market and a roadside daiquiri stall round out the area's offerings, outside of the resort and beaches.

Immediately west, the hotel strip gives way to residential neighborhoods interspersed with shops, restaurants, and cafés. Homes become more and more posh the farther west you go; Lyford Cay—the island's original gated community—is home to the original 007, Sean Connery. Hang a left at the Lyford Cay roundabout and eventually you'll come across the historic Clifton Heritage Park, the local brewery where Kalik and Heineken are brewed and bottled, a new upscale resort development whose financiers include golfers Ernie Els and Tiger Woods, and eventually the sleepy settlement of Adelaide.

The loop around the island's west and south coasts can be done in a couple of hours by car or scooter, but take some time for lunch and a swim along the way. Unless you're being taken around by a taxi or local, it's best to return to Cable Beach along the same route, as internal roads can get confusing.

TOP ATTRACTIONS

Arawak Cay. Known to Nassau residents as "The Fish Fry," Arawak Cay is one of the best places to knock back a Kalik beer, chat with locals, watch or join in a fast-paced game of dominoes, or sample traditional Bahamian fare. You can get small dishes such as conch fritters or full meals at one of the pastel-color waterside shacks. Order a fried snapper served up with a sweet homemade roll, or fresh conch salad (a spicy mixture of chopped conch—just watching the expert chopping is a show as good as any in town—mixed with diced onions, cucumbers, tomatoes, and hot peppers in a lime marinade). The two-story Twin Brothers and Goldie's Enterprises are two of the most popular places. Try their fried "cracked conch" and Goldie's famous Sky Juice (a sweet but potent gin, coconut-water, and sweet-milk concoction sprinkled with nutmeg). There's usually a live band on the outdoor stage Friday and Saturday nights. ⊠ *W. Bay St. and Chippingham Rd.*

Ardastra Gardens, Zoo, and Conservation Centre. Marching flamingos? These national birds give a parading performance at Ardastra daily at 10:30, 2:10, and 4:10. The brilliant pink birds are a delight—especially for children, who can walk among the flamingos after the show. The zoo, with more than 5 acres of tropical greenery and ponds, also has an aviary of rare tropical birds including the bright green Bahama parrot, native Bahamian creatures such as rock iguanas and the little (and harmless) Bahamian boa constrictors, and a global collection of small animals. ⊠ *Chippingham Rd. south of W. Bay St.* ☎ *242/323–5806* ⊕ *www.ardastra.com* 🖃 *$15 adults, $7.50 children* ☉ *Daily 9–5 except Christmas Day, Boxing Day, and New Years Day.*

🕚 **Fort Charlotte.** Built in 1788, this imposing fort comes complete with a waterless moat, drawbridge, ramparts, and a dungeon, where children love to see the torture device where prisoners were "stretched." Young local guides bring the fort to life. (Tips are expected.) Lord Dunmore, who built it, named the massive structure in honor of George III's wife. At the time, some called it Dunmore's Folly because of the staggering expense of its construction. It cost eight times more than was originally planned. (Dunmore's superiors in London were less than ecstatic with the high costs, but he

> **SNAKES ALIVE!**
>
> The Bahamas has five types of snakes, none poisonous, but the most interesting is the Bahamian boa constrictor, threatened with extinction because Bahamians kill them on sight. The Bahamian boa is extremely unusual in that it has remnants of legs, called spurs. The male uses his spurs to tickle the female. Ask one of the trainers at Ardastra Gardens and Zoo to show you the boa, so you can see the tiny legs.

managed to survive unscathed.) Ironically, no shots were ever fired in battle from the fort. The fort and its surrounding 100 acres offer a wonderful view of the cricket grounds, the beach, and the ocean beyond. Inquire about Segway tours. ⊠ *W. Bay St. at Chippingham Rd.* 📧 *$5* ☉ *Tours daily 8–4.*

WORTH NOTING

Adelaide Village. The small community on New Providence's southwestern coast sits placidly, like a remnant of another era, between busy Adelaide Road and the ocean. It was first settled during the early 1830s by Africans who had been captured and loaded aboard slave ships bound for the New World. They were rescued on the high seas by the British Royal Navy and the first group of liberated slaves reached Nassau in 1832. Today there are two sides to Adelaide—the few dozen families who grow vegetables, raise chickens, and inhabit well-worn, pastel-painted wooden houses, shaded by casuarina, mahogany, and palm trees; and the more upscale beach cottages that are mostly used as weekend getaways. The village has a primary school, some little grocery stores, and the popular **Avery's Restaurant and Bar** (*Adelaide Village Rd.; 242/362–1547*), serving delicious native dishes daily, 11 am–11 pm.

The Caves. These large limestone caverns that the waves sculpted over the aeons are said to have sheltered the early Arawak Indians. An oddity perched right beside the road, they're worth a glance—although in truth, there's not much to see, as the dark interior doesn't lend itself to exploration. A daiquiri bar is situated just alongside the caves, providing a nice place for a break, and across the street is a concrete viewing platform overlooking the ocean. Just a short drive beyond the caves, on an island between traffic lanes, is **Conference Corner,** where U.S. President John F. Kennedy, Canadian Prime Minister John Diefenbaker, and British Prime Minister Harold Macmillan planted trees on the occasion of their 1962 summit in Nassau. ⊠ *W. Bay St. and Blake Rd.*

Clifton Heritage Park. It's quite a distance from just about any hotel you could stay at, but for history and nature buffs, this national park,

Cable Beach

rescued from the hands of developers, is worth the drive. Situated on a prehistoric Lucayan Village dating back to AD 1000–1500, Clifton Heritage Park allows you to walk through the ruins of slave quarters from an 18th-century plantation. There's still much work to be done to really develop this site; call ahead to arrange a tour guide for the best experience. Be sure to walk the path from the main parking lot toward the west, where you can enjoy the peace and quiet of the Sacred Space and admire the African women carved out of dead casuarinas trees by local artist Antonius Roberts. Naturalists will enjoy walking along the paths lined with native flora and fauna that lead to wooden decks overlooking mangrove swamps. ⊠ *Clifton Pier, West Bay St.* ☎ *242/362–5360* ⊕ *www.bahamascliftonheritagepark.org* ☉ *Mon.–Fri. 9–5, weekends and holidays by appointment only.*

Nassau Botanic Gardens. Six hundred species of flowering trees and shrubs, a small cactus garden, and two freshwater ponds with lilies, water plants, and tropical fish cover 18 acres. The many trails that wind through the gardens are perfect for leisurely strolls. Various events are held here each year, including the International Food Festival the third weekend in October, when the many cultural groups living on the island cook and sell their native dishes and perform traditional songs and dances. The Botanic Gardens are across the street from the Ardastra Gardens and Conservation Centre, home of Nassau's zoo. Note that although the gardens have set hours, gates sometimes still remain locked. ⊠ *Chippingham Rd. south of W. Bay St.* ☎ *242/323–5975* ⊠ *$1* ☉ *Weekdays 8–4, weekends 9–4.*

WHERE TO EAT

Note: A gratuity (15%) is often added to the bill. Many all-inclusive hotels offer meal plans for nonguests.

NASSAU

$
GREEK

✕ **Athena Café and Bar.** A mainstay since 1960, this Greek restaurant provides a break from the Nassau culinary routine. Sit on the second floor among Grecian statuary, or on the balcony overlooking the action below. Enjoy souvlaki, moussaka, or a hearty Greek gyro in a relaxed and friendly establishment. Gregarious owner Peter Mousis and his family serve tasty fare at moderate prices seven days a week. ⊠ *Bay St. at Charlotte St.* ☎ *242/326–1296* ⊘ *No dinner Sun.*

$$
ECLECTIC
Fodor's Choice
★

✕ **Café Matisse.** Low-slung settees, stucco arches, and reproductions of the eponymous artist's works set a casually refined tone at this restaurant owned by a husband-and-wife team—he's Bahamian, she's northern Italian. Sit in the ground-floor garden under large white umbrellas or dine inside the century-old house for lunch or dinner. Start with beef carpaccio, then dive into freshly made pasta such as duck-filled ravioli and shrimp in a spicy red-curry sauce, or such delights as pizza frutti di mar (topped with fresh local seafood). ⊠ *Bank La. and Bay St., behind Parliament Sq.* ☎ *242/356–7012* ⊕ *www.cafe-matisse.com* ⊘ *Closed Sun., Mon., and Aug.*

$
BAHAMIAN

✕ **Double D's.** Don't let the dark-tinted windows and green lighting over the doorway put you off. Inside you'll find a simply decorated bar offering friendly service and good native food. This is a popular spot with locals for its Bahamian cuisine and 23-hour service in a town where most kitchens are closed at 10 pm. Try boil' fish—a peppery lime-based broth filled with chunks of boiled potatoes, onions, and grouper—or be adventurous and order a bowl of pig-feet or sheep-tongue souse. Although souplike, these Bahamian delicacies are typically served only for breakfast. All come with a chunk of johnnycake or a bowl of steaming white grits. ⊠ *E. Bay St. at the foot of the bridges from Paradise Island* ☎ *242/393–2771.*

$$$
CHINESE

✕ **East Villa Restaurant and Lounge.** In a converted Bahamian home, this is one of the most popular Chinese restaurants in town. The Chinese-continental menu includes entrées such as conch with black-bean sauce, *hung shew* (walnut chicken), and steak *kew* (cubed prime fillet served with baby corn, snow peas, water chestnuts, and vegetables). The New York strip steak is nirvana. A short taxi ride from Paradise Island or downtown Nassau, this is the perfect spot if you're seeking something a little different from the typical area restaurants. Dress is casual elegance. ⊠ *E. Bay St. near Nassau Yacht Club* ☎ *242/393–3377* ⊘ *Lunch and dinner weekdays, dinner only weekends.*

$$$$
CONTINENTAL
Fodor's Choice
★

✕ **Graycliff.** A meal at this hillside mansion begins in the elegant parlor, where, over live piano music, drinks are served and orders are taken. It's a rarefied world, where waiters wear tuxedos and Cuban cigars and cognac are served after dinner. Graycliff's signature dishes include Kobe beef, Kurobuta pork, and Nassau grouper. The wine cellar contains more than 200,000 bottles that have been handpicked

2

by owner Enrico Garzaroli, some running into the tens of thousands of dollars. You can even buy the world's oldest bottle of wine, a German vintage 1727, for $200,000. ✉ *W. Hill St. at Cumberland Rd., across from Government House* ☎ *242/322–2796* ⊕ *www.graycliff. com* ⌂ *Reservations essential.*

$ ✕**Green Parrot.** Sip a green-color Parrot Crush while tackling the large Works Burger as you sit and enjoy the cool breeze and lovely Nassau Harbour scenery. This casual, all-outdoor restaurant and bar is popular with locals. The menu includes burgers, wraps, quesadillas, and other simple but tasty dishes. The conch po'boy is a new favourite. Happy hour from 5–9 and a DJ on Friday nights mean the huge bar is lively and packed. ✉ *E. Bay St. west of the bridges to Paradise Island* ☎ *242/322–9248* ⊕ *www. greenparrotbar.com.*

AMERICAN

$$$$ ✕**Humidor Churrascaria Restaurant.** The salad bar at this casual restaurant offers everything from simple salad fixings to scrumptious seafood salads and soups. And that is just the start. Each table setting includes a coaster that's red on one side and green on the other. Just like a stoplight, green means go and red means stop. Waiters serve a never-ending selection of delicious skewered meats and fresh fish until you turn your coaster to red and declare uncle. When you're done, stop by the smoking lounge to see the cigar rollers in action or stroll along the garden terraces and fountains out back. ✉ *W. Hill St. off Cumberland Rd., next to Graycliff Hotel* ☎ *242/328–7050* ☽ *Dinner only.*

BRAZILIAN

$$$ ✕**Luciano's.** Green Roofs, the sprawling former residence of the late Sir Roland Symonette (the country's first premier), houses this harborside restaurant. The mansion's mahogany woodwork, gardens, and terraces create a romantic setting for dining on Tuscan fare, including escarole, white bean, and sausage soup; osso buco; grouper; and homemade pastas—including a delicious frutti di mar over linguine. The sweeping view of Paradise Island and the towers of Atlantis is particularly lovely at sunset. Reservations are essential for waterside tables. ✉ *E. Bay St., 2 blocks west of Paradise Island bridges* ☎ *242/323–7770* ⊕ *www. lucianosnassau.com* ☽ *lunch weekdays; dinner daily.*

ITALIAN

$$ ✕**Montagu Gardens.** Angus beef and fresh native seafood—flame-grilled and seasoned with home-mixed spices—are the specialties at this romantic restaurant in an old Bahamian mansion on Lake Waterloo. The dining room opens to a walled courtyard niched with Roman-style statues and gardens that lead to a waterside balustrade. Besides seafood and steak (carnivores should try the filet mignon smothered in mushrooms), menu selections include chicken, lamb, pasta, ribs, and several Bahamian-inspired dishes such as conch fritters and stuffed grouper. A favorite dessert is Fort Montagu Mud Pie. ✉ *E. Bay St.* ☎ *242/394–6347* ☽ *Closed Sun.*

CONTINENTAL

$$$
BAHAMIAN
★

✕ **The Poop Deck.** Just east of the bridges from Paradise Island and a quick cab ride from the center of town is this favorite local haunt. There's usually a wait for a table, and it's worth waiting a little longer for one overlooking the marina and Nassau Harbour. The restaurant's popularity has resulted in a second Poop Deck on Cable Beach's west end, but for residents, this is still the place. Expect spicy dishes with names such as Mama Mary's Steamed Fish; there's also an extensive wine list. Start with Paula's Conch Fritters and then select a fresh, whole-hog snapper for the chef to fry up. It's usually served head to tail, so if you're squeamish, ask your waiter to have the head cut off before it comes out on your plate. Save room for guava duff and a calypso coffee spiked with secret ingredients. ⊠ *E. Bay St. at Nassau Yacht Haven Marina, east of bridges from Paradise Island* ☎ *242/393–8175* ⊕ *www.thepoopdeckrestaurants.com.*

PARADISE ISLAND

$$
BAHAMIAN

✕ **Anthony's Grill.** Color is the standout feature at Anthony's: bright red, yellow, and blue tablecloths spiked with multihued squiggles; yellow-and-green walls with jaunty cloths hanging from the ceilings; booths printed with bright sea themes; and buoyant striped curtains. The lively spirit is reflected in the cheery service you'll receive at breakfast, lunch, or dinner. The extensive menu (68 items to choose from) includes seafood pasta, grilled-to-order shrimp, grouper and salmon brochettes, steaks, burgers, ribs, and salads. ⊠ *Paradise Village Shopping Plaza* ☎ *242/363–3152* ⊕ *www.anthonysgrillparadiseisland.com.*

$$$$
CONTINENTAL

✕ **Bahamian Club.** Reminiscent of a British country club, this handsome restaurant has walls lined with dark oak, overstuffed chairs, and leather banquettes. Meat is the house specialty—rib-eye steak, veal chop, herb roasted rack of lamb, and chateaubriand for two—but grilled swordfish steak, Bahamian lobster, salmon fillet, and other fresh seafood dishes are all prepared with finesse. ⊠ *Atlantis* ☎ *242/363–3000* ⟁ *Reservations essential* ☾ *No lunch.*

$$$
SEAFOOD

✕ **Blue Lagoon Seafood Restaurant.** The interior tends toward the nautical, with hurricane lamps and brass rails, in this narrow third-floor dining room looking out to Nassau on one side and Atlantis to the other. Choose from simply prepared dishes such as stuffed grouper au gratin, the roast Long Island duckling a l'orange, or the Tour of the Bahamas—Long Island minced lobster, Bimini steamed grouper, Exuma cracked conch, pigeon-peas soup, and steamed rice. ⊠ *Club Land'O* ☎ *242/363–2400* ⊕ *www.clublandor.com* ⟁ *Reservations essential* ☾ *No lunch.*

$$$$
FRENCH
Fodor's Choice
★

✕ **Café Martinique.** The original restaurant made famous in the 1965 James Bond film *Thunderball* has long been bulldozed, but with the help of renowned international chef Jean-Georges Vongerichten and New York designer Adam D. Tihany, Atlantis resurrected a classic. Nestled in the center of Marina Village on Paradise Island, Café Martinique is the height of sophistication in design, service, and cuisine. The decor includes a wrought-iron birdcage elevator and a mahogany staircase; a grand piano helps create a refined experience. The classic French gourmet menu offers simple classic dishes made spectacular

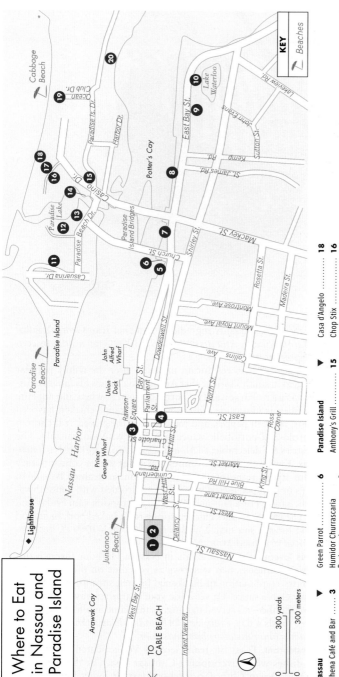

Where to Eat in Nassau and Paradise Island

KEY

↗ *Beaches*

0 ——— 300 yards
0 ——— 300 meters

→ TO CABLE BEACH

Nassau

▶

Athena Café and Bar	**3**
Café Matisse	**4**
Double D's	**7**
East Villa Restaurant and Lounge	**9**
Graycliff	**2**
Green Parrot	**6**
Humidor Churrascaria Restaurant	**1**
Luciano's	**5**
Montagu Gardens	**10**
The Poop Deck	**8**

Paradise Island

▶

Anthony's Grill	**15**
Bahamian Club	**17**
Blue Lagoon Seafood Restaurant	**13**
Café Martinique	**14**
Casa d'Angelo	**18**
Chop Stix	**16**
Columbus Tavern	**20**
Dune Restaurant	**19**
Mesa Grill	**11**
Nobu	**12**

Tuna tartare at Café Martinique

thanks to the highest quality ingredients and chef Jean-George's influence. ✉ *Marina Village, Atlantis* ☎ *242/363–3000* ⊕ *www.atlantis.com* ⌖ *Reservations essential.*

$$$$
ITALIAN

✕ **Casa D'Angelo.** At this restaurant modeled after the wildly popular Casa d'Angelo in south Florida, chef Angelo Elia brings his famous Tuscan-style cuisine to Paradise. The antipasti display whets the appetite for such dishes as fettuccine with lobster; free-range chicken flavored with onions, red bell pepper, and pancetta; or the grilled veal chop in a dark Barolo-and-portobello sauce sprinkled with Gorgonzola. The dessert pastries are delectable. ✉ *Atlantis* ☎ *242/363–3000* ⊗ *No lunch.*

$$$
CHINESE

✕ **Chop Stix.** Expect traditional Chinese favorites with a contemporary twist at this stylish restaurant. Try the Cantonese steamed Bahamian lobster tails or grouper seared in a wok and drizzled with a mouthwatering garlic sauce. For a late-night bite, pop in for dim sum Friday and Saturday. The menu includes chicken spring rolls, baked pork buns, and shrimp and lobster shu mai. ✉ *Atlantis* ☎ *242/363–3000* ⌖ *Reservations essential* ⊗ *Closed Mon. No lunch.*

$$$
SEAFOOD

✕ **Columbus Tavern.** Watch the boats in Nassau Harbour through this restaurant's enormous open windows as you dine on the fisherman's fiesta—a tasty combination of blackened lobster, shrimp, and scallops with a spicy creole sauce. Or set aside your seafaring ways and try the steak Diane flambé—it's served flaming, as the name implies. The tavern serves three meals a day, every day. ✉ *Paradise Island Dr.* ☎ *242/363–5923* ⊕ *www.columbustavernbahamas.com.*

$$$$
BAHAMIAN
★

✕ **Dune Restaurant.** Feast on Jean-Georges Vongerichten's intricately prepared dishes while overlooking Cabbage Beach at the renowned One & Only Ocean Club. Go for breakfast or lunch for the most reasonable prices. For breakfast, try the smoked salmon with potato pancake and chive sour cream or the egg-white omelet with fresh herbs. Dinner entrées include roasted grouper, rack of lamb, and sirloin steak. It's a great place to unwind amid ocean breezes. ⊠ *One & Only Ocean Club, Ocean Club Dr.* ☎ *242/363–3000* ⊕ *www. oneandonlyresort.com* ⚓ *Reservations essential.*

$$$$ ✕ **Mesa Grill.** Bobby Flay is the latest
ECLECTIC celebrity chef to lend his name and
★ expertise to the restaurant lineup at Atlantis. In the Cove hotel, Mesa Grill (his first international outpost) serves the Southwestern cuisine he is known for, but with a Bahamian twist. The menu features unique dishes such as shrimp-and-grouper ceviche with serrano chilies, tomatoes, mango, and plantain crisp, and grilled red snapper with red-chili tomato sauce, crushed avocado, and barbequed red onion. More traditional Flay-inspired dishes like blue-corn pancake with barbecued duck and New Mexican spice-rubbed pork tenderloin are also available. ⊠ *The Cove Atlantis* ☎ *242/363– 3000* ⊕ *www.atlantis.com* ⚓ *Reservations essential.*

$$ ✕ **Nobu.** Sushi connoisseurs, celebrities, and tourists pack this Atlantis
ECLECTIC restaurant night after night. The rock shrimp and tomato ceviche and
★ the yellowtail sashimi with jalapeño are Nobu favorites, but this restaurant also takes advantage of fresh Bahamian seafood—try the lobster shiitake salad or the cold conch shabu-shabu with Nobu sauces. The central dining room is surrounded by a Japanese pagoda, and guests seated at a long, communal sushi bar can watch chefs work. ⊠ *Royal Towers, Atlantis* ☎ *242/363–3000 Jacket required* ⊗ *No lunch.*

QUICK BITES

A quick snack or light lunch on the go can be picked up at most gas stations or bakeries on the island. Grab a hot patty—peppery chicken or beef is most popular—or a yellow pastry pocket filled with conch. One of these with a "coke soda"—the generic name for all brands of soft drink—will tide you over until your next real meal.

CABLE BEACH

$$$ ✕ **Amici A Trattoria.** Savor delicious Italian cuisine in a casual setting over-
ITALIAN looking the ocean. The menu features hearty pasta dishes like fettuccine with Italian sausage, mushrooms, roasted peppers, and broccoli tossed in a garlic cream, or baked penne with zucchini and four cheeses. For a special treat order the spiny lobster tail drizzled with a tomato-basil cream served up with asparagus and lobster ravioli. ⊠ *Sheraton Nassau Beach Resort* ☎ *242/327–6000* ⊗ *No lunch.*

$$$ ✕ **Androsia Bahamian Cuisine Steak & Seafood Restaurant.** Tucked away in
BAHAMIAN the back of a small shopping plaza, this restaurant is simply decorated, but a great place to get Bahamian cuisine. Seafood takes top billing on the menu. Try the seafood platter—a delectable mixture of whatever's fresh and available, or the Bimini snapper, stuffed with sautéed onions, tomatoes, and fresh herbs. They also serve up traditional Bahamian breakfast including boil' fish and chicken souse daily. ⊠ *W. Bay St. in Shoppers Haven Plaza* ☎ *242/327–7805* ⚓ *Reservations essential.*

$$$
STEAK
★

✕ **Black Angus Grille.** This steak house offers some of the best certified Angus beef on the island. Bring your appetite if you're going to try the double porterhouse which is carved right in front of you. It's not all about the beef, though. The skewered shrimp, ahi tuna, and seared-scallops gnocchi are delightful alternatives. Finish up with the Cay lime pie made with Bahamian instead of the traditional Florida citrus. ⌧ *Wyndham Nassau Resort, W. Bay St.* ☎ *242/327–6200* ⊘ *Closed Sun. and Mon.*

$$
ASIAN

✕ **Indigo.** This eclectic restaurant doubles as an art gallery—walls are lined with Bahamian originals, many of them painted by the owner's late father Brent Malone. Bahamian ingredients are transformed into international dishes with a decidedly Asian flair. Fresh salads are a big hit, and the coconut curried conch chowder is not to be missed. The funky inside bar is a popular local predinner hangout, and reservations are recommended most nights and definitely on Fridays. ⌧ *W. Bay St. at Sandals roundabout* ☎ *242/327–2524* ⊘ *Closed Sun.*

$$
ASIAN

✕ **Moso.** The restaurant has Asian appeal from the moment you walk in. Vibrant red-and-black furnishings and elegant orchids accent the space; a wall of windows offers pool- and ocean-view dining. Try the steamed snapper fillet, the fillet blue moon, or the succulent braised short ribs in oyster sauce. Finish up your meal with a cinnamon-banana spring roll. ⌧ *Wyndham Nassau Resort, W. Bay St.* ☎ *242/327–6200* ⌂ *Reservations essential* ⊘ *Closed Tues. No lunch.*

$$$
SEAFOOD

✕ **The Poop Deck at Sandyport.** A more upscale version of the other Poop Deck, this waterside restaurant has soaring ceilings, a cool-pink-and-aqua color scheme, and a dazzling view of the ocean. Start with grilled shrimp and Brie before diving into the fresh catch of the day paired with a selection from the extensive wine list. There's a smattering of choices for the seafood-phobic. ⌧ *W. Bay St.* ☎ *242/327–3325* ⊕ *www.thepoopdeck.com* ⊘ *Closed Mon.*

$$$
MEDITERRANEAN

✕ **Provence.** The chef bills his fare as *cuisine du soleil*—you can see why with the fiery, grilled rib-eye steak in peppercorn sauce, and the Seafood Ultimate—yellowfin tuna, sea scallops, and prawns pan-seared and drizzled with a rich lobster sauce. Twenty-four-hour notice is requested if you'd like the Moroccan lamb–and-chicken tagine or the restaurant's famous paella. The tapas plate for two people starts at $20 and is a great light-bite option. ⌧ *Old Town Sandyport* ☎ *242/327–0985* ⊕ *www.provencerestaurant.net* ⊘ *Closed Sun. No lunch Sat.*

WESTERN NEW PROVIDENCE

$$$
AMERICAN

✕ **Compass Point.** This friendly restaurant and bar has one of the best sunsets on the island. Sit indoors or out on the terrace overlooking the ocean and enjoy their simple but tasty Bahamian and island-style American fare for breakfast, lunch, and dinner. The kitchen is open daily until midnight, so it's a great stop for a late-night meal or snack. The long outdoor bar stays open until the last guest leaves, and there's live music on Saturdays. ⌧ *W. Bay St. near Gambier Village* ☎ *242/327–4500* ⊕ *www.compasspointbeachresort.com* ⊘ *Serves breakfast, lunch, dinner, and bar snacks until midnight.*

$ ✕**Goodfellow Farms.** This unique
ECLECTIC   treat is well worth the long drive
to the western end of the island.
The vegetable farm has a country
store and small restaurant with
outdoor dining under shady trees
and umbrellas. Lunch is simple
but delicious—cranberry-almond
chicken salad wraps, flank steak,
or Bahamian crawfish pasta salad
served over greens picked from
the farm earlier in the day. ⊠ *W.
Bay St., Mount Pleasant Village.
Take left at Lyford Cay roundabout, go over the hill, entrance
to farm road is signposted* ☎ *242/
377–5000* ⊕ *www.goodfellowfarms.
com* ⊙ *Lunch daily.*

$$ ✕**Traveller's Rest.** A scenic 10-mi
BAHAMIAN   drive along the coast from down-
town Nassau brings you to this
relaxed family restaurant, which
has a great ocean view. The food is
delicious, but service tends to be slow, so sit and enjoy the view or chal-
lenge your tablemate to a game of Connect Four. The fresh seafood din-
ner served just steps from the beach is a real treat—conch, grouper, and
crawfish are the heavy hitters. Try the "smudder groupre"—a tasty local
fish literally smothered in onions, peppers, and other vegetables. Dine
outside or in, and toast the sunset with a fresh-fruit banana daiquiri—
a house specialty. ⊠ *W. Bay St., Gambier* ☎ *242/327–7633* ⊕ *www.
bahamastravellersrest.com.*

> **THE PALM BEACH CONNECTION**
>
> Palm Beach, Florida, and Nassau shared Standard Oil cofounder Henry Flagler. He built the Break-ers Hotel in Palm Beach, which had ferries that traveled to his other hotel, the luxurious British Colonial in Nassau. Flagler lived in the two-story house on Parlia-ment Street in Nassau that was, for many years after his death, the Green Shutters restaurant, across the street from the legendary Victoria Hotel, one of the world's most luxurious resorts. In the mid-1990s the hotel was torn down, but the name remains on a column at the driveway entrance, which now leads to an empty lot.

WHERE TO STAY

NASSAU

$$$ ⬚ **British Colonial Hilton Nassau.** The first Colonial Hotel, built by Stan-
★   dard Oil cofounder Henry Flagler in 1899, attracted socialites, royals,
and industrialists at the turn of the 20th century and during the boom
years of Prohibition. That building was destroyed by fire in 1921, and
the present Mediterranean-style British Colonial—an exact replica—
opened a year later, featuring a lustrous saffron facade, gleaming marble floors, and soaring arched ceilings. This landmark building is the
social heart of Nassau, the setting for political meetings and the city's
most important events. Guest rooms have dark mahogany furniture and
marble baths; some have harbor views, others offer a wonderful view
of old Nassau. The resort sits on 8 lush acres with spectacular views
of Nassau Harbour. It's the best business choice in the Bahamas, and is
also a popular spot for weddings. Watch for brides descending the grand
staircase in the lobby on Saturday and Sunday afternoons. **Pros:** right

Humidor Churrascaria Restaurant at the Graycliff Hotel

on Bay Street; quiet beach and pool area; centrally located. **Cons:** busy with local meetings and events; man-made beach; hard to access at peak traffic times. ⊠ *1 Bay St.* ☎ *242/322–3301* ⊕ *www.hiltoncaribbean. com/nassau* ⇌ *288 rooms, 23 suites* ⌂ *In-room: safe, Internet. In-hotel: restaurant, bar, pool, gym, beach, water sports, business center, parking.*

$ 🖼 **El Greco Hotel.** A pleasant Greek owner and a friendly staff make it a point to get to know their guests and ensure they have a nice stay. Although the decorations are not elaborate, the rooms are large, quiet, and have soothing earth tones. Rooms surround a small pool tucked within a bougainvillea-filled courtyard. El Greco is directly across the street from the public Western Esplanade beach. The hotel appeals primarily to a European crowd, and for those on a budget who want to be in Nassau, it's a pleasant find. You are allowed to use the lobby phone to make free (!!!) calls to the United States. **Pros:** close to downtown; friendly staff; free overseas calls. **Cons:** no on-site restaurant; public beach is across busy street. ⊠ *W. Bay St.* ☎ *242/325–1121* ⊕ *www.hotels-nassau-bahamas. com* ⇌ *27 rooms* ⌂ *In-room: Internet, Wi-Fi. In-hotel: pool.*

$$$ 🖼 **Graycliff.** The old-world flavor of this Georgian colonial landmark—
Fodor's Choice built in the 1720s by ship captain Howard Graysmith—has made it a
★ perennial favorite with the upscale crowd. Past guests have included the Duke and Duchess of Windsor, Winston Churchill, Aristotle Onassis, and the Beatles. Al Capone stayed here when his sweetie, Polly Leach, owned it during the Roaring '20s, and Lord Mountbatten visited when Lord and Lady Dudley were the proprietors. It's easy to forget that you're steps from downtown Nassau when you stay here. Thick foliage envelops a series of garden villas and cottages, amid limestone court-yards with ponds and fountains. Rooms have been recently renovated,

NEW PROVIDENCE ISLAND SPAS

Mandara Spa. Located at Atlantis but open to the public, the Indonesian-inspired Mandara Spa has treatments utilizing traditions from around the world. ⊠ *Atlantis, Casino Dr.* ☎ *242/363–3000* ⊕ *www. mandaraspa.com.*

Relaxation Zone. Relaxation Zone is a true escape from the hustle and bustle of Bay Street. Book ahead for Swedish massages and facial and manicure package, but just pop

in for a soothing chair massage. Five minutes costs $7.50. ⊠ *Bay St. upstairs in the International Bazaar* ☎ *242/323–5774.*

Windermere Day Spa at Harbour Bay. This spa has a variety of ultramodern spa treatments—such as hydrotherapy and salt glows—as well as top-quality facials, massages, manicures, and pedicures. ⊠ *E. Bay St.* ☎ *242/393–8788.*

giving life to the plush, old-world, upscale interiors. They each bear a Bahamian name—Hibiscus, Yellowbird, Baillou (for the name of the road it overlooks). For refined continental fare, the hotel's namesake restaurant is one of the island's premier places to dine. **Pros:** one of the most luxurious accommodations on the island; lush tropical gardens; large rooms. **Cons:** centered around the busy restaurant and bar area; not easily accessible for handicapped; no beach access. ⊠ *W. Hill St.* ☎ *242/322–2796, 800/476–0446* ⊕ *www.graycliff.com* ⤳ *7 rooms, 13 suites* ⚭ *In-room: safe, Wi-Fi. In-hotel: restaurant, bar, pool, gym, spa, business center, parking.*

$ 📺 **Quality Inn Junkanoo Beach.** This simple and quiet six-floor hotel is a welcome addition to the New Providence budget-lodging market. It's clean and well kept, with pleasantly decorated rooms. Ask for a room with an ocean view, as many rooms have only a partial view or none at all. In fact, the rooms vary wildly in size, with a few just barely bigger than the bed. Front-desk staff will generally show you what's available and let you take your pick if you ask. Sliding-glass doors open to false balconies, but allow nice cool breezes in. Be aware that each guest must pay a daily service charge of $11.50. **Pros:** walking distance from downtown; continental breakfast on-site. **Cons:** on two busy streets; popular with spring breakers; public beach is across the street. ⊠ *W. Bay St. and Nassau St.* ☎ *242/322–1515* ⊕ *www.qualityinn.com* ⤳ *63 rooms* ⚭ *In-room: safe, Wi-Fi. In-hotel: restaurant, bar, parking.*

PARADISE ISLAND

$$$$ 📺 **Atlantis, Paradise Island.** A bustling fantasy world—part water park,
Ⓒ entertainment complex, megaresort, and beach oasis—this is by far the
★ biggest and boldest resort in the country. The overriding theme here is water—for swimming, snorkeling, and observing marine life, as well as for mood and effect, in lagoons, caves, waterfalls, and several walk-through aquariums (touted as the largest artificial marine habitat in the world). The public areas are lavish, with fountains, glass sculptures, and gleaming shopping arcades. Numerous sporting activities are available,

and there is plenty of nightlife on the premises; the casino, ringed by restaurants, is the largest in the Bahamas and the Caribbean. In high season (winter) expect long lines at restaurants. Despite the large number of guests on the property, the pool and beach area is so expansive that you'll be sure to find a secluded spot just for you. Be aware, some Fodors.com users have complained about the resort's poor service. The most expensive rooms are in the glamorous, high-rise Royal Towers, but the Coral Towers and Beach Towers rooms are nice and still offer access to all the fun and activities. **The Cove Atlantis** is worlds away from its sister property Atlantis in terms of overall look, experience, and sophistication. The 600-suite hotel has step-down living areas and luxurious modern furnishings. The resort is home to Bobby Flay's Mesa Grill and Cain, an überexclusive adults-only pool area. This haven has private poolside cabanas stocked with everything from gourmet treats to en suite spa treatments. Families are welcome—there is a separate pool for kids—but it's a hike to the fun-filled Aquaventure. Atlantis, Paradise Island is the newest addition to the Atlantis megaresort. The 497-suite tower has exquisitely outfitted studios or one and two-bedroom condominium-style accommodations. Each unit has a stainless-steel kitchen or kitchenette (some have washers and dryers), which makes this setup perfect for self-sufficient families or those trying to stretch their dollar. There's no restaurant in the tower, so unless you plan to cook, be prepared for a bit of a walk or a shuttle for meals. **Pros:** never run out of things to do; kid-friendly with some adult-only areas; incredible resort experience. **Cons:** resort is expansive and requires lots of walking; thousands of guests; food and drinks are expensive. ⊠ *Casino Dr.* ☎ *242/363–3000, 800/285–2684* ⊕ *www.atlantis.com* ⇥ *2,156 rooms, 1,258 suites* ⚬ *In-room: safe, kitchen, Wi-Fi. In-hotel: restaurant, bar, golf course, pool, tennis court, gym, spa, beach, water sports, children's programs, business center, parking, some pets allowed* ¶⊙*Some meals.*

$$ 🏨 **Best Western Bay View Suites.** This 4-acre condominium resort has a lush, intimate character. Guests socialize around three pools (two for general use, one reserved for the villas) that are surrounded by tropical plants, including several hibiscus and bougainvillea varieties. Choose between one- or two-bedroom suites, villas, and town houses, all of which are spacious and have enough closet space for a long visit. All rooms have private balconies or garden terraces. Cabbage Beach is a 10-minute walk away. **Pros:** children under 12 stay free; private "at home" vibe; free Wi-Fi in pool area. **Cons:** long walk from beach; no restaurant serving dinner on property; no organized activities on-site. ⊠ *Bay View Dr.* ☎ *242/363–2555, 800/757–1357* ⊕ *www. bwbayviewsuites.com* ⇥ *25 suites, 2 villas, 3 town houses* ⚬ *In-room: safe, kitchen, Wi-Fi. In-hotel: bar, pool, tennis court, gym, laundry facilities, business center, parking.*

$$$ 🏨 **Club Land'Or.** In Atlantis's shadow just over the bridges from Nassau, this friendly time-share property has one-bedroom villas with full kitchens, bathrooms, living rooms, desks, and patios or balconies that overlook the lagoon, the gardens, or the pool. The units are described as accommodating four people, but they seem better suited for couples. The Blue Lagoon Seafood Restaurant is a favorite of locals and

guests. Many activities are planned throughout the week. **Pros:** everything you need for an extended vacation; walking distance to Marina Village and Atlantis. **Cons:** surrounded by Atlantis resort; beach is quite a walk away. ⊠ *Paradise Beach Dr.* ☎ *242/363–2400* ⊕ *www.clublandor.com* ↵ *72 villas* ♿ *In-room: safe, kitchen. In-hotel: restaurant, bar, pool, gym, laundry facilities* ⦿*Some meals.*

$$ ⚅ **Comfort Suites.** This all-suites, three-story pink-and-white hotel has an arrangement with Atlantis that allows you to use the megaresort's facilities. Kids can also enroll at Atlantis's Kids Camp. For many, that's reason enough to stay here, in the middle of the Paradise Island action. If you'd rather stay on the grounds, try a poolside lunch and a drink at the swim-up bar. Cozy rooms have sitting areas with sofa beds. Cabbage Beach is just a hop, skip, and a jump away. Rates include breakfast. **Pros:** access to Atlantis amenities; near shops and restaurants. **Cons:** not located on a beach; in the midst of busy traffic. ⊠ *Paradise Island Dr.* ☎ *242/363–3680, 800/228–5150* ⊕ *www.comfortsuites.com* ↵ *229 suites* ♿ *In-room: safe, Wi-Fi. In-hotel: restaurant, bar, pool* ⦿*Breakfast.*

$$$$ ⚅ **One & Only Ocean Club.** Once the private hideaway of A&P heir Huntington Hartford, this exclusive resort on magnificent Cabbage Beach's quietest stretch provides the ultimate in understated—and decidedly posh—elegance. Its Versailles Gardens include 35 acres of terraced serenity and an imported French cloister. Set amid private gardens, the spacious colonial-style rooms have intricately carved furniture, marble bathrooms, and private butlers. The open-air restaurant, Dune, is perched over the beach. **Pros:** ultraexclusive; lovely beach; top-rated amenities. **Cons:** not within walking distance of Atlantis and its myriad restaurant and nightlife choices. ⊠ *Ocean Club Dr.* ☎ *242/363–2501, 800/321–3000* ⊕ *www.oneandonlyresorts.com* ↵ *86 rooms, 14 suites, 6 villas* ♿ *In-room: safe, Wi-Fi. In-hotel: restaurant, bar, golf course, pool, tennis court, gym, spa, beach, water sports, children's programs, business center, parking, some pets allowed.*

Fodor's Choice
★

$$ ⚅ **Paradise Harbour Club & Marina.** With a marina and an enviable location, this collection of oversize, comfortable apartments is a great choice for those who want the freedom of a private residence with the facilities of a large resort. Full kitchens (complete with refrigerator, minibar, and dishwasher) lend a homey mood to these somewhat characterless but extremely cushy lodgings. Commodious closet and sink spaces are among the extras. If you prefer a view, opt for the top-floor digs. **Pros:** quiet location; cooking facilities. **Cons:** need to walk or be shuttled to and from the beach; condo built nearby towers over property. ⊠ *Paradise Island Dr.* ☎ *242/363–2992* ⊕ *www.phc-bahamas.com* ↵ *23 units* ♿ *In-room: kitchen, Wi-Fi. In-hotel: bar, pool, laundry facilities.*

WORD OF MOUTH

We went (to Atlantis) a few years ago and stayed in the Royal Towers. We had very nice rooms. My brother was trying to save money and stayed at the Beach Tower. He said it was like a Motel 6 and he overlooked the parking lot. It was a long walk to the slides. He moved over to the Royal Towers on day 3 and said it was worth it to pay more money. —girlonthego

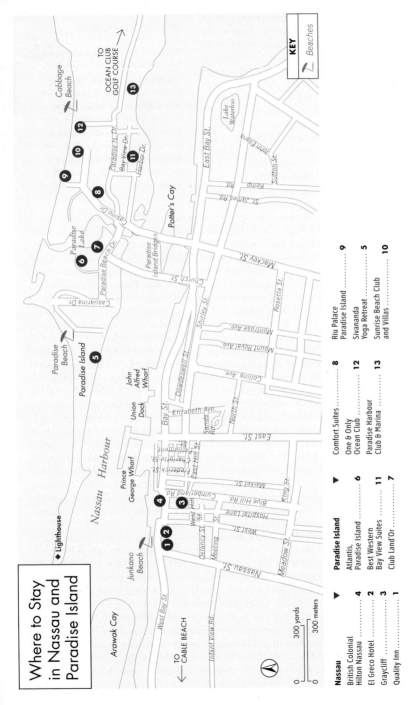

Where to Stay in Nassau and Paradise Island

KEY
↗ Beaches

0 ——— 300 yards
0 ——— 300 meters

Nassau

British Colonial
Hilton Nassau **4**
El Greco Hotel **2**
Graycliff **3**
Quality Inn **1**

Paradise Island

▶

Atlantis,
Paradise Island **6**
Best Western
Bay View Suites **11**
Club Land'Or **7**

Comfort Suites **8**
One & Only
Ocean Club **12**
Paradise Harbour
Club & Marina **13**

Riu Palace
Paradise Island **9**
Sivananda
Yoga Retreat **5**
Sunrise Beach Club
and Villas **10**

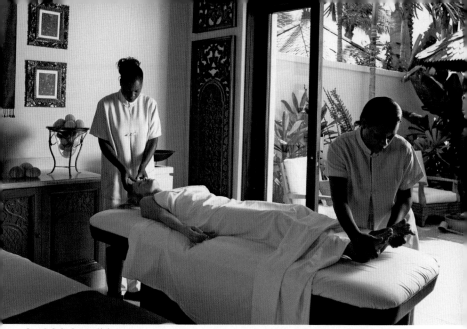

One & Only Ocean Club

▥ Riu Palace Paradise Island. This all-inclusive resort sits on gorgeous Cabbage Beach, and no matter which of the wonderfully decorated suites you end up in, you'll wake up to a view of the ocean. The hotel was gutted and completely renovated in 2009, going from dated '80s to old-world opulence with crystal chandeliers, marble, and mahogany everywhere. With five restaurants, including Japanese and a steak house, a large buffet, and a sports bar that's always stocked with light snacks, you'll never go hungry. An entertainment team and a small cabaret-style theater with a different show each night of the week ensures that you won't get bored, either. **Pros:** all rooms have an ocean view; large selection of restaurants. **Cons:** no water sports included. ⊠ *6307 Casino Dr.* ☎ *242/363–3500, 888/666–8816* ⊕ *www.riu.com* ⤳ *379 suites* △ *In-room: safe. In-hotel: restaurant, bar, pool, gym, spa, beach, parking* ❖❘ *All-inclusive.*

▥ Sivananda Yoga Retreat. Accessible only by boat, this resort is the antithesis of the high-rollers' Atlantis down the road. Guest rooms in the main house and tiny one-room bungalows overlook a gorgeous white-sand beach in a 5-acre compound that stretches from Nassau Harbour to the ocean; air-conditioning is an additional $10 per day. Tent sites are available for $59 per day. This retreat is for those who are serious about yoga and good health: the community gathers morning and evening for meditation and yoga. However, during free time from 10 am to 4 pm the retreat's shuttle boat will take you to Nassau for shopping and sightseeing, or there's massage therapy in the Well-Being Center on-site. Yoga decks are next to the beach and harbor, and there are also meditation rooms, frequent guest lecturers, and special classes for advanced teacher certification. The per-person price includes two

CLOSE UP

Bond in the Bahamas

In *Casino Royale,* the 21st James Bond installment, Bond took on the bad guys at an embassy, which was, in reality, the lovely Buena Vista Restaurant and Hotel in Nassau, which closed shortly after filming. The ruggedly handsome new Bond, Daniel Craig, also had the glamorous background of the One & Only Ocean Club resort on Paradise Island, where another Bond, Pierce Brosnan, frequently stays.

Bond and the Bahamas have a long relationship. Six Bond films have used the Bahamas as a backdrop, including *Thunderball,* filmed in 1965 with the original 007, Sean Connery. Connery loved the Bahamas so much he has chosen to live here year-around in the luxury gated community of Lyford Cay.

Thunderball was filmed at the Café Martinique, which, after being closed for more than a decade, reopened at Atlantis resort on Paradise Island in 2006. Scenes were also shot at the Mediterranean Renaissance–style British Colonial, built in the 1920s. The hotel pays tribute to its illustrious Bond history with a Double-O Suite, which is filled with Bond memorabilia including posters, books, and Bond films.

You can swim and snorkel in Thunderball Cave in the Exumas, site of the pivotal chase scene in the 1965 Sean Connery film. The ceiling of this huge, dome-shape cave is about 30 feet above the water, which is filled with yellowtails, parrots, blue chromes, and yellow-and-black striped sergeant majors. Swimming into the cave is the easy part—the tide draws you in—but paddling back out can be strenuous, especially because if you stop moving, the tide will pull you back.

The Rock Point house, better known to 007 fans as Palmyra, the villain Emilio Largo's estate, was another Bond location, and Bay Street where Bond and his beautiful sidekick Domino attended a Junkanoo carnival, is still the location of Junkanoo twice a year. The *Thunderball* remake, *Never Say Never Again,* was also shot in the Bahamas, using many of the same locations as the original.

Underwater shots for many of the Bond flicks were filmed in the Bahamas, including Thunderball Grotto, while Nassau's offshore reefs were the underwater locations for the 1983 film *Never Say Never Again,* the 1967 film *You Only Live Twice,* the 1977 film *The Spy Who Loved Me,* and *For Your Eyes Only,* released in 1981.

—Cheryl Blackerby

vegetarian meals each day. Rooms are austere, and you are expected to spend an hour a day helping to clean communal bathrooms or doing other chores. Alcohol, coffee, tea, meat, fish, cigarettes, radios, and TVs are not allowed. **Pros:** ideal for peace and quiet; inexpensive accommodations; free shuttle to and from Nassau. **Cons:** strict regulations; basic accommodations; no road access. ⊠ *Paradise Island* ☎ *242/363–2902, 800/441–2096* ⊕ *www.sivanandabahamas.org* ⇝ *48 rooms, 36 dorm beds, 16 tent huts, 90 tent sites* ⚲ *In-room: no a/c, no TV. In-hotel: restaurant, spa, beach* ⧖ *All-inclusive.*

2

$$$$ 🖻 **Sunrise Beach Club and Villas.** Lushly landscaped with crotons, coconut palms, bougainvillea, and hibiscus, this low-rise, family-run resort on Cabbage Beach has a tropical wonderland feel. Two pools sustain the aura with statuary and tropical plantings, and the beach is accessible via a long flight of wooden stairs built right into the cliff. Paths wind through the floral arcadia, past trickling fountains,

archways, and terra-cotta tiles with color insets. Choose from one-bedroom town houses with spiral staircases that lead to an upstairs bedroom, two-bedroom apartments, or three-bedroom villas. All have fully equipped kitchens, king-size beds, and patios. **Pros:** on one of the best beaches on the island; lively bar on property; great for families. **Cons:** no activities. ⊠ *Casino Dr.* ☎ *242/363–2234, 800/451–6078* ⊕ *www.sunrisebeachclub.com* ⤴ *16 rooms, 10 suites, 1 villa* ⌂ *In-room: kitchen, Internet. In-hotel: bar, pool, beach, laundry facilities.*

CABLE BEACH

$$$ 🖻 **Bluewater Resorts.** These newly renovated time-share and short-term rental accommodations are perfect for young families or groups of friends traveling together. The stucco units are spread across landscaped grounds. Tiled three-bedroom luxury villas, oceanfront or garden-side, sleep six comfortably—up to eight using roll-aways (so the price is really quite reasonable when shared by several people). Each unit has oversize rooms, delightful secluded patios, a fully equipped kitchen, a washer and dryer, and a dishwasher. The pool and some units overlook the ocean. **Pros:** spring breakers not allowed; great for families; tennis courts. **Cons:** no major activities; need car to go into town; housekeeping costs extra. ⊠ *W. Bay St.* ☎ *242/327–7568* ⊕ *www.bluewaterresortnassau.com* ⤴ *35 units* ⌂ *In-room: safe, kitchen, Wi-Fi. In-hotel: restaurant, bar, pool, tennis court, beach, children's programs, laundry facilities, parking.*

🖻 **Marley Resort & Spa.** Fans of legendary reggae icon Bob Marley are not the only ones who will love this resort and spa, opened by his wife and children. The Marleys have transformed their vacation home of 20 years into an all-around appealing two-story boutique hotel just west of the Cable Beach strip. All of the rooms are named after famous Bob Marley songs. One Love is the honeymoon suite, complete with a private Jacuzzi for two overlooking the beach. Royal Rita, also with an ocean view, is the room where his widow, Rita Marley, used to sleep. Some rooms, including Three Little Birds, which is big enough to sleep a family, are in the courtyard building and are without pool or ocean views. The Simmer Down Restaurant serves gourmet Caribbean cuisine and the jerk fish is divine. You can chill out poolside, in the tropical gardens of hibiscus and banana plants, or at Stir It Up, the on-site bar. A visit to the Natural Mystic Spa is a must, where the foot-washing

CLOSE UP

Changes at Cable Beach

Cable Beach, a string of resorts on a white-sand beach west of Nassau, is getting a makeover so massive that it's expected to rival Las Vegas when everything is completed in 2014, although numerous setbacks and delays make this date questionable. A mammoth $3.4-billion resort called Baha Mar will include eight hotels—the already-in-place Sheraton and Wyndham, as well as a Westin, W, St. Regis, Hyatt, Rosewoods, and Morgans and a 1,000-room luxury casino-hotel. The 3,600-room beachside complex is the single largest investment in the history of the Bahamas.

Cable Beach's two current resorts—the Sheraton Nassau Beach Resort and the Wyndham Nassau Resort & Crystal Palace Casino—are open and operating as Cable Beach Resorts during the building of Baha Mar. The company has already spent more than $150 million renovating these two hotels and casino. Updates at the Wyndham include flat-screen TVs and refrigerators in all guest rooms, and two bars are being added to the casino. The Sheraton Nassau Beach Resort was completely overhauled and now presents a sophisticated lobby and brand-new room furnishings. Together, the current resorts offer 1,250 guest rooms and suites (most with ocean views), 13 restaurants and lounges, more than a half mile of gorgeous white-sand beach, and a variety of water-sport activities. Headliners continue to perform at the Rainforest Theatre, and a cabaret show is in the works.

When finished, Baha Mar's attractions will include a 100,000-square-foot casino, the Caribbean's largest freestanding spa, 200,000 square feet of combined meeting space, the West Bay Village shopping-and-entertainment complex—all connected by a series of canals and wide pedestrian paths—as well as an 18-hole Jack Nicklaus Signature golf course.

Michael Hong, known for his work on the $1.6 billion Bellagio Resort and Wynn Resort in Las Vegas, is leading the design team for Baha Mar, which will sprawl across 1,000 acres. The reconstruction of the landscape and the development of the hotels will be extensive, but the Baha Mar Group says it will all be done in a way that does not disturb guest experience.

For more information on Baha Mar, visit ⊕ www.bahamar.com or ⊕ www.crystalpalacevacations.com, or call ☎ 800/222–7466.

ritual and outdoor herbal baths help you relax. **Pros:** one-of-a-kind, customizable resort experience; 200 feet of private beach. **Cons:** located on busy main road (though peaceful and quiet); must drive to nearby attractions; no activities for children. ⊠ *West Bay St.* ☎ *242/702–2800* ⊕ *www.marleyresort.com* ⤴ *11 suites, 5 rooms* ⌣ *In-room: safe, Wi-Fi. In-hotel: restaurant, bar, pool, spa, beach.*

$$$$
ALL-INCLUSIVE
🏨 **Sandals Royal Bahamian Resort & Spa.** Cable Beach's most expensive spot has elegantly furnished rooms with views of the ocean, pool, or grounds replete with pillars and faux-Roman statuary. There's a state-of-the-art fitness club, and a multilingual concierge service that assists foreign guests. Nine restaurants offer cuisines ranging from Caribbean to Japanese (make reservations well in advance), and nightly

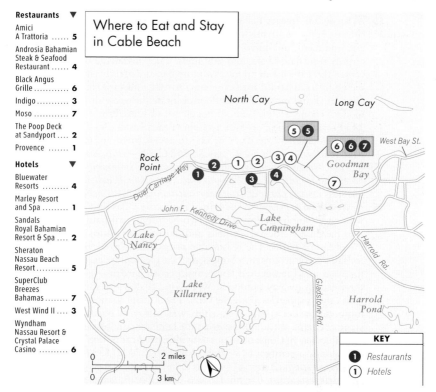

Restaurants ▼

Amici
A Trattoria **5**

Androsia Bahamian
Steak & Seafood
Restaurant **4**

Black Angus
Grille **6**

Indigo **3**

Moso **7**

The Poop Deck
at Sandyport **2**

Provence **1**

Hotels ▼

Bluewater
Resorts **4**

Marley Resort
and Spa **1**

Sandals
Royal Bahamian
Resort & Spa **2**

Sheraton
Nassau Beach
Resort **5**

SuperClub
Breezes
Bahamas **7**

West Wind II **3**

Wyndham
Nassau Resort &
Crystal Palace
Casino **6**

Where to Eat and Stay
in Cable Beach

entertainment takes place in the resort's amphitheater. **Pros:** no children; lovely setting; private offshore cay. **Cons:** no children; need car or taxi to go into town; convention center popular for local functions. ⊠ *W. Bay St.* ☎ *242/327–6400, 800/726–3257* ⊕ *www.sandals.com* ⇌ *403 rooms* ♿ *In-room: Wi-Fi. In-hotel: restaurant, bar, pool, tennis court, gym, spa, beach, water sports, laundry facilities, some age restrictions* ⏀ *All-inclusive.*

$$ ⬚ **Sheraton Nassau Beach Resort.** Situated on 7 acres of prime beachfront property, the Sheraton has a modern, grown-up feel. But the hotel caters to kids, too, with three pools, a kids' center complete with computers, and arts and crafts. Almost all of the expertly decorated rooms have a pool or beach view, and all include 32-inch flat-screen TVs. The hotel is connected by a shopping arcade to the Crystal Palace Casino, and you can use amenities at the Wyndham next door. **Pros:** excellent ocean views and beach access; newly renovated; many activities, including beach volleyball and live music on the weekends. **Cons:** will be undergoing major renovations as part of the Baha Mar complex; walls somewhat thin. ⊠ *W. Bay St.* ☎ *242/327–6000* ⊕ *www.bahamar.com* ⇌ *694 rooms* ♿ *In-room: safe, Internet. In-hotel: restaurant, bar, pool, gym, beach, water sports, children's programs, business center, parking* ⏀ *Multiple meal plans.*

$$
ALL-INCLUSIVE **SuperClub Breezes Bahamas.** Right on Cable Beach, this property offers couples and singles an all-inclusive rate that covers lodging, entertainment, unlimited food and beverages, land and water sports, airport transfers, taxes, and gratuities. Take advantage of the fitness center, three freshwater pools, swim-up bar, and nightly entertainment, including local bands, toga or pajama parties, and karaoke. A huge fish chandelier and multicolor tile floor decorate the open-air lobby. Large modern rooms are pleasant, although not striking. **Pros:** no one under 14 allowed; walking distance to Cable Beach casino; lots of activities. **Cons:** no children; need car or taxi to access town; in midst of Baha Mar renovation area. ⊠ *W. Bay St.* ☎ *242/327–5356, 800/467–8737* ⊕ *www.breezesbahamas.com* ⌇ *400 rooms* ⟁ *In-room: kitchen. In-hotel: restaurant, bar, pool, tennis court, gym, spa, beach, water sports, business center, parking, some age restrictions* �‖ *All-inclusive.*

$$ **West Wind II.** Privacy is the lure of these cozy villas on Cable Beach's west end, 6 mi from downtown. Two-bedroom, two-bath condominiums have fully stocked kitchens and balconies or patios overlooking the ocean or pools. The reasonable prices and relaxed vibe are ideal for families or groups on a budget, and the pleasant quiet location—off the road amid manicured lawns and pruned gardens—gives children the freedom to play outdoors. West Wind II shares a stunning beach with other properties along the Cable Beach strip, so more activity and motorized water sports are a short walk away. A bus stop and taxi stand are right outside. **Pros:** great for families; condos sleep six; right on Cable Beach. **Cons:** no major activities; need car or taxi to go downtown; basic amenities. ⊠ *W. Bay St.* ☎ *242/327–7211, 242/327–7019* ⊕ *www.westwind2.com* ⌇ *54 villas* ⟁ *In-room: safe, kitchen, Internet. In-hotel: restaurant, bar, pool, tennis court, beach, water sports, laundry facilities, parking.*

$$ **Wyndham Nassau Resort & Crystal Palace Casino.** Part of the Baha Mar project, this resort's large pool area includes a twisting waterslide, and the attached casino goes all night long. There's a fully equipped fitness center with stunning beach views for guests only. High rollers can opt to stay in the Casino Tower with 30 high-end executive suites. The Rainforest Theatre hosts headliners of yesterday and today. **Pros:** casino on-site; variety of restaurants; great pool and beach area. **Cons:** sprawling layout means lots of walking; in the midst of Baha Mar renovation site. ⊠ *W. Bay St.* ☎ *242/327–6200, 800/222–7466* ⊕ *www.wyndhamnassauresort.com* ⌇ *559 rooms, 30 suites* ⟁ *In-room: safe, Wi-Fi. In-hotel: restaurant, bar, golf course, pool, gym, spa, beach, water sports, business center, parking.*

WESTERN NEW PROVIDENCE

$$
★ **A Stone's Throw Away.** Featuring seaside comfort in fashionable surroundings, this "gourmet bed-and-breakfast"—as the French and Belgian owners describe it—is a luxurious hideaway. The three-story colonial-style inn with wraparound verandas is perched on a limestone cliff overlooking the beach, 13 mi west of Nassau. The public rooms and guest rooms have the character of a century-old manor house with pickled-wood ceilings, pine plank floors, Oriental rugs, leather

Compass Point cottages

plantation chairs, mahogany antiques, and a dining room that serves breakfast, lunch, and dinner. You can read on the porch, walk to the beach, or relax by a small pool and waterfall. **Pros:** serene; secluded public-beach access; friendly staff. **Cons:** in flight path; long distance from anything else; hotel access up a steep staircase cut out of the limestone hill. ⊠ *Tropical Garden Rd. and W. Bay St., Gambier* ☎ *242/327-7030* ⊕ *www.astonesthrowaway.com* ↪ *8 rooms, 2 suites* ⚭ *In-room: Wi-Fi. In-hotel: restaurant, bar, pool.*

$$$ ⌂ **Compass Point.** This whimsical-looking hotel made up of brightly colored one- and two-story cottages offers a relaxing alternative to many of the area's major resorts. Built by Island Records founder Chris Blackwell, oceanfront rooms include a private downstairs deck complete with a kitchenette for entertaining. Windows on all sides of the rooms open to allow a cool breeze in. Sit on the dock and enjoy one of the most stunning sunset views the island has to offer. There's Internet access throughout, but for those who don't bring a laptop, a closet has been converted into Hut.com, complete with a computer and printer for guests. **Pros:** best view on the island; access to incredible private beach. **Cons:** in flight path; not ideal for children; expensive taxi ride to town. ⊠ *W. Bay St., Gambier* ☎ *242/327-4500* ⊕ *www.compasspointbeachresort. com* ↪ *18 cottages* ⚭ *In-room: kitchen, Wi-Fi. In-hotel: restaurant, bar, pool, spa, water sports.*

$ ⌂ **Orange Hill Beach Inn.** If you prefer down-home coziness over slick glamour, then this adorable inn—on the site of a former orange plantation perched on a hilltop overlooking the ocean—is the place to stay. Irish transplant Judy Lowe, who's owned the inn for more than 30 years, and her son Brendan treat guests like family. The inn is a half-hour drive from town, 15 minutes from the casino, and 300 feet from a pleasant roadside beach. Rooms and apartments vary considerably in size, and are all decorated with simple pine furniture and tropical bedding. Some of the larger poolside rooms lack an ocean view, so be sure to state your preference when booking. There's a restaurant on-site serving Bahamian and continental fare, and you can help yourself at an honor bar set up in the cozy living room. The inn provides daily trips to a nearby grocery store for guests who want to stock up their in-room refrigerator. **Pros:** across the road from a nice beach; small; family-style service. **Cons:** long distance from town; not much by way of activities. ⊠ *W. Bay St.* ☏ *242/327–5184* ⊕ *www.orangehill.com* ⤵ *30 rooms, 2 cottages* ♿ *In-room: safe, kitchen. In-hotel: restaurant, bar, pool, laundry facilities, business center, parking, some pets allowed.*

NIGHTLIFE

NASSAU

NIGHTCLUBS

Bambu. Pop into this open-air club overlooking Nassau Harbour and you may find the DJ playing the latest Top 40 dance tunes. Wait a few moments and Europe's sexiest house beats will change the vibe entirely. Popular with hip young locals and cruise passengers and staff. ⊠ *Upstairs Prince George Plaza, Bay St.* ⊕ *www.bambunassau.com* 🎫 *$20* 🕑 *Thurs., Fri., and Sat. 9 pm–5 am.*

Club Waterloo. Claiming to be Nassau's largest indoor-outdoor nightclub, this club has five bars and nonstop dancing Monday through Saturday, and live bands on the weekend. Try the spring-break-special Green Lizard, a tropical mixture of rums and punches. ⊠ *E. Bay St.* ☏ *242/393–7324* ⊕ *www.clubwaterloo.com* 🕑 *Daily 8 pm–4 am.*

Fluid Lounge. The hottest nightclub in Nassau is also the hardest to find. Look for the sign on downtown Bay Street in the Kings Court building. You'll walk downstairs to two bars and two dance floors, where a well-dressed crowd moves to Top 40 hits and R&B. Ladies get in free Friday and Saturday before 11 pm. ⊠ *W. Bay St. between Market and Frederick* 🎫 *$20, with taxi pass $5 (buy one for $5 from any taxi driver)* 🕑 *Tues. and Thurs.–Sun. 9 pm–4 am.*

PARADISE ISLAND

CASINOS

Atlantis Casino. At 50,000 square feet (100,000 if you include the dining and drinking areas), this is the largest casino in the Bahamas. Featuring a spectacularly open and airy design, the casino is ringed with restaurants and offers more than 1,100 slot machines, baccarat, blackjack, roulette, craps tables, and such local specialties as Caribbean stud poker. There's also a high-limit table area, and most of the eateries have additional games. ⊠ *Atlantis* ☏ *242/363–3000* ⊕ *www.atlantis.com* 🕑 *Main casino 24 hrs daily, tables open 10 am–4 am daily.*

2

NIGHTCLUBS

Aura. This is the country's hottest nightclub, located upstairs at the Atlantis Casino. It's the place to see and be seen, though many of the celebrities that frequent the club opt for the ultraexclusive private lounge. Dancing goes on all night, and the handsome bartenders dazzle the crowd with their mixing techniques. Music varies, depending on the crowd. ⊠ *Atlantis* ☎ *242/363–3000* ⊕ *www.atlantis.com* ▭ *$20–$100; free for Atlantis guests Tues.–Thurs.* ☉ *Tues.–Sat. 9:30 pm–4 am.*

Oasis Lounge. There's live piano or vocal music here every night except Sunday from 7:30 to midnight. Go early to get a good seat and take advantage of one of the best drink deals on Paradise Island—buy one, get one free and complimentary hors d'oeuvres 5–7 pm. ⊠ *Club Land'Or* ☎ *242/363–2400* ⊕ *www.clublandor.com* ☉ *Daily 4 pm–midnight.*

CABLE BEACH

CASINOS

Crystal Palace Casino. Four hundred slot machines, craps, baccarat, blackjack, roulette, Big Six, and face-up 21 are among the games in this 35,000-square-foot space. There's a Sportsbook facility equipped with big-screen TVs that air live sporting events. Both VIPs and low-limit bettors have their own areas. Casino gaming lessons are available for beginners. ⊠ *Wyndham Nassau Resort & Crystal Palace Casino, W. Bay St.* ☎ *242/327–6200* ⊕ *www.wyndhamnassauresort.com* ☉ *24 hrs.*

THE ARTS

THEATER

Dundas Centre for the Performing Arts. Plays, concerts, ballets, and musicals by local and out-of-town artists are staged here throughout the year. The box office is open from 10 am to 4 pm. ⊠ *Mackey St., Nassau* ☎ *242/393–3728.*

Rainforest Theatre. The redesigned theater, which now has surroundings true to its name, presents lavish shows. Some of the headliners who've performed here include Michael Bolton, Patti LaBelle, Boyz II Men, and the Pointer Sisters. Check with the resort for the latest offerings. ⊠ *Wyndham Nassau Resort & Crystal Palace Casino, Cable Beach* ☎ *242/327–6200.*

SHOPPING

Most of Nassau's shops are on Bay Street between Rawson Square and the British Colonial Hotel, and on the side streets leading off Bay Street. Some stores are popping up on the main shopping thoroughfare's eastern end and just west of the Cable Beach strip. Bargains abound between Bay Street and the waterfront. Upscale stores can also be found in Marina Village and the Crystal Court at Atlantis and in the arcade joining the Sheraton Nassau Beach and the Wyndham on Cable Beach.

You'll find duty-free prices—generally 25%–50% less than U.S. prices—on imported items such as crystal, linens, watches, cameras, jewelry, leather goods, and perfumes.

NASSAU

ANTIQUES, ARTS, AND CRAFTS

Balmain Antiques and Gallery. Balmain Antiques and Gallery collects Bahamian artwork as well as antique maps, prints, bottles, and small furniture. ⊠ *Bay St. near Charlotte St.* ☎ *242/323–7421.*

BAKED GOODS

Bahamas Rum Cake Factory. At the Bahamas Rum Cake Factory, delicious Bahamian rum-soaked cakes are made and packaged in tins right on the premises (peek into the bakery) and make a great souvenir. Just make sure you take one home for yourself! ⊠ *E. Bay St.* ☎ *242/328–3750.*

Model Bakery. Be sure to try the cinnamon twists or the gingerbread sticks at this great local bakery in the east end. ⊠ *Dowdeswell St.* ☎ *242/322–2595.*

Mortimer's Candies. Mortimer's Candies whips up batches of uniquely Bahamian sweet treats daily. Pop in for a sno-cone on a hot day or buy some bags of bennie cake, coconut-cream candy, or their signature Paradise Sweets in a swirl of the Bahamian flag colors. ⊠ *East St. Hill* ☎ *242/322–5230* ⊕ *www.mortimercandies.com.*

CIGARS

Be aware that some merchants on Bay Street and elsewhere in the islands are selling counterfeit Cuban cigars—sometimes unwittingly. If the price seems too good to be true, chances are it is. Check the wrappers and feel to ensure that there's a consistent fill before you make your purchase.

Graycliff. Graycliff carries one of Nassau's finest selections of hand-rolled cigars, featuring leaves from throughout Central and South America. Graycliff's operation is so popular that it has expanded the hotel to include an entire cigar factory, which is open to the public for tours and purchases. A dozen Cuban men and women roll the cigars; they live on the premises and work here through a special arrangement with the Cuban government. True cigar buffs will seek out Graycliff's owner, Enrico Garzaroli. ⊠ *W. Hill St., and departure lounge at Lynden Pindling International Airport* ☎ *242/302–9150* ⊕ *www.graycliff.com.*

FASHION

Brass and Leather. Here you can find leather goods for men and women, including bags, shoes, and belts. ⊠ *Charlotte St. off Bay St.* ☎ *242/ 322–3806.*

Cole's of Nassau. This is a top choice for designer fashions, sportswear, bathing suits, shoes, and accessories. ⊠ *Parliament St.* ☎ *242/322–8393.*

La Casita. This cute boutique offers high-end straw bags and purses, as well as costume jewelry. ⊠ *Bay St. near the Straw Market* ☎ *242/356–7302* ☉ *Closed Sun.*

Continued on page 96

IT'S PARTY TIME IN THE BAHAMAS!
by Jessica Robertson

It's after midnight, and the only noise in downtown Nassau is a steady buzz of anticipation. Suddenly the streets erupt in a kaleidoscope of sights and sounds—Junkanoo groups are parading down Bay Street. Vibrant costumes sparkle in the light of the street lamps, and the revelers bang on goatskin drums and clang cowbells, hammering out a steady celebratory beat. It's Junkanoo time!

Junkanoo is an important part of the Bahamas' Christmas season. Parades begin after midnight and last until midday on Boxing Day (December 26), and there are more on New Year's Day. What appears to be a random, wild expression of joy is actually a well-choreographed event. Large groups (often as many as 500 to 1,000 people) compete for prize money and bragging rights. Teams choose a different theme each year and keep it a closely guarded secret until they hit Bay Street. They spend most of the year preparing for the big day at their "shacks," which are tucked away in neighborhoods across the island. They practice dance steps and music, and they design intricate costumes. During the parade, judges award prizes for best music, best costumes, and best overall presentation.

Junkanoo costume, Grand Bahama

JUNKANOO HISTORY

Junkanoo holds an important place in the history and culture of the Bahamas, but the origin of the word *junkanoo* remains a mystery. Many believe it comes from John Canoe, an African tribal chief who was brought to the West Indies as a slave and then fought for the right to celebrate with his people. Others believe the word stems from the French *gens inconnus*, which means "the unknown people"—significant because Junkanoo revelers wear costumes that mask their identities.

The origin of the festival itself is more certain. Though its roots can be traced back to West Africa, it began in the Bahamas during the 16TH or 17TH century when Bahamian slaves were given a few days off around Christmas to celebrate with their families. They left the plantations and had elaborate costume parties at which they danced and played homemade musical instruments. They wore large, often scary-looking masks, which gave them the freedom of anonymity, so they could let loose without inhibition.

Over the years, Junkanoo has evolved. Costumes once decorated with shredded newspaper are now elaborate, vibrant creations incorporating imported crepe paper, glitter, gemstones, and feathers.

MUSIC'S ROLE

There's something mesmerizing about the simple yet powerful beat of the goatskin drum. Couple that steady pounding with the "kalik-kalik" clanging of thousands of cowbells and a hundreds-strong brass band, and Junkanoo music becomes downright infectious.

Music is the foundation of Junkanoo. It provides a rhythm for both the costumed revelers and crowds of spectators who jump up and down on rickety bleacher seats. The heavy percussion sound is created by metal cowbells, whistles, and oil barrel drums with fiery sternos inside to keep the animal skin coverings pliant. In the late 1970s, Junkanoo music evolved with the addition of brass instruments, adding melodies from Christmas carols, sacred religious hymns, and contemporary hits.

If you're in Nassau anytime from September through the actual festival, stand out on your hotel balcony and listen carefully. Somewhere, someone is bound to be beating out a rhythm as groups practice for the big parade.

DRESS TO IMPRESS

Each year, talented artists and builders transform chicken wire, cardboard, Styrofoam, and crepe paper into magnificent costumes that are worn, pushed, or carried along the Junkanoo parade route. Dancers and musicians tend to wear elaborate head dresses or off-the-shoulder pieces and cardboard skirts completely covered in finely fringed, brightly colored crepe paper—applied a single strip at a time until every inch is covered. Gemstones, referred to as "tricks" in the Junkanoo world, are painstakingly glued onto costumes to add sparkle. In recent years, feathers have been incorporated, giving the cardboard covered creations an added level of movement and flair.

In order to wow the crowd, and more importantly, win the competition, every member of the group must be in full costume when they hit Bay Street. Even their shoes are completely decorated. Massive banner pieces so big they graze the power lines and take up the entire width of the street are carried along the route by men who take turns. Every element, from the smallest costume to the lead banner, as well as the entire color scheme, is meticulously planned out months in advance.

EXPERIENCE JUNKANOO

SECURE YOUR SEATS

■ Junkanoo bleacher seat tickets ($10–$50) can be hard to come by as the parade date approaches. Contact your hotel concierge ahead of time to arrange for tickets or visit ⊕ www.tajiz.com, the official online retailer.

■ Rawson Square bleachers are the best seats. This is where groups perform the longest and put on their best show.

■ If you don't mind standing, make your way to Shirley Street or the eastern end of Bay Street, where the route is lined with barricades. Judges are positioned all along the way so you'll see a good performance no matter where you end up.

■ Junkanoo groups make two laps around the parade route. Each lap can take a few hours to complete, and there are many groups in the lineup, so most spectators stay only for the first round. Head to Bay Street just before dawn, and you'll be sure to score a vacant seat.

BEHIND THE SCENES

■ During the parade, head east along Bay Street and turn onto Elizabeth Avenue to the rest area. Groups take a break in the parking lot here before they start round two. Costume builders frantically repair any pieces damaged during the first rush (Bahamian slang for parading), revelers refuel at barbeque stands, goatskin drums are placed next to a giant bonfire to keep them supple,

and in the midst of all the noise and hubbub, you'll find any number of people taking a nap to ensure they make it through a long and physically demanding night.

■ If star-stalking is your thing, scour the crowds in the VIP section in Parliament Square or look across the street on the balcony of the Scotiabank building. This is where celebrities usually watch the parades. Some who've been spotted include Michael Jordan, Rick Fox, and former New York City mayor Rudy Giuliani.

■ When the parade ends, wander along the route and surrounding streets to score a one-of-a-kind souvenir. Despite the many hours Junkanoo participants spend slaving over their costumes, by the time they're done rushing the last thing they want to do is carry it home. Finders keepers.

■ If you're in Nassau in early December, watch the Junior Junkanoo parade. School groups compete for prizes in various age categories. The littlest ones are usually offbeat and egged on by teachers and parents, but are oh-so-cute in their costumes. The high school groups put on a show just as impressive as the groups in the senior parade.

JUNKANOO TRIVIA

■ Kalik beer, brewed in the Bahamas, gets its name from the sound of clanking cowbells.

■ An average costume requires 3,000 to 5,000 strips of fringed crepe paper to completely cover its cardboard frame.

■ Junkanoo widows are women whose husbands spend every waking moment working on their costumes or practicing music routines the weeks before the parade.

■ During the height of sponge farming in the Bahamas, a major industry in the early 1900s, many Junkanoo participants used natural sponge to create their costumes.

Junkanoo parade in Nassau

JUNKANOO ON OTHER ISLANDS

Nassau's Junkanoo parade is by far the biggest and most elaborate, but most other islands hold their own celebrations on New Year's Day. Nassau's parades are strictly a spectator sport unless you are officially in a group, but Out Island parades are more relaxed and allow visitors to join the rush.

JUNKANOO YEAR-ROUND

Not satisfied with limiting Junkanoo to Christmastime, the Bahamas Ministry of Tourism hosts an annual **Junkanoo Summer Festival**. Smaller scale parades are held on alternating weekends in June and July on most major islands, including Nassau. In addition to the traditional Junkanoo rush, these festivals offer arts and crafts demonstrations, conch cracking, crab catching, coconut-husking competitions, concerts featuring top Bahamian artists, and of course, lots of good Bahamian food. ☎ 242/302–2000 ✉ tourism@bahamas.com.

Marina Village on Paradise Island hosts **Junkanoo rushouts** on Wednesday (9 pm) and Saturday (9:30 pm). There are no big stand-alone pieces, but dancers and

musicians wear color-coordinated costumes and headpieces. The parade is much less formal, so feel free to jump in and dance along.

The **Educulture Museum and Workshop** in Nassau gives a behind-the-scenes look at Junkanoo. Some of each year's best costumes are on display, as well as costumes from years gone by when newspaper and sponges were used as decoration. The diehard Junkanoo staff will help you make your own Junkanoo creations. Be sure to arrange your visit ahead of time. ☎ 242/328–3786 ✉ info@educulturebahamas.com.

Tempo Paris. Tempo Paris offers men's clothing by major designers, including Ralph Lauren, Polo, and Lacoste. ⊠ *Bay St.* ☎ *242/323–6112.*

GIFT SHOPS

Bahama Handprints. Bahama Handprints fabrics emphasize local artists' sophisticated tropical prints in an array of colors. Also look for leather handbags, a wide range of women's clothing, housewares, and bolts of fabric. Ask for a free tour of the factory in back. ⊠ *Island Traders Bldg. Annex, off Mackey St.* ☎ *242/394–4111* ⊕ *www.bahamahandprints. com* ☽ *Closed Sun.*

Linen Shop. This shop sells fine embroidered Irish linens and lace and has a delightful Christmas corner. ⊠ *Bay St.* ☎ *242/322–4266.*

My Ocean. Here you can find candles, soaps, salt scrubs, and lotions in island- and ocean-inspired scents and colors, all locally made. The store also sells an eclectic mix of international home accents and gifts. ⊠ *Charlotte St. south of Bay St.* ☎ *242/325–3050* ☽ *Closed Sun.*

JEWELRY, WATCHES, AND CLOCKS

Coin of the Realm. Coin of the Realm has Bahamian coins, stamps, native conch pearls, tanzanite, and semiprecious stone jewelry. ⊠ *Charlotte St. off Bay St.* ☎ *242/322–4862, 242/322–4497.*

Colombian Emeralds International. Colombian Emeralds International is the local branch of this well-known jeweler; its stores carry a variety of fine jewelry in addition to its signature gem. ⊠ *Bay St. near Rawson Sq* ☎ *242/326–1661.*

John Bull. Established in 1929 and magnificently decorated in its Bay Street incarnation behind a Georgian-style facade, John Bull fills its complex with wares from Tiffany & Co., Cartier, Mikimoto, Nina Ricci, and Yves Saint Laurent. The company has 12 locations throughout Nassau. ⊠ *284 Bay St.* ☎ *242/302–2800.*

MARKETS AND ARCADES

International Bazaar. This collection of shops under a huge, spreading bougainvillea, sells linens, jewelry, souvenirs, and offbeat items. There's usually a small band playing all sort of music along this funky shopping row on Bay Street at Charlotte Street in Nassau.

Prince George Plaza. Prince George Plaza, which leads from Bay Street to Woodes Rogers Walk near the dock, just east of the International Bazaar, has about two dozen shops with varied wares.

Straw Market. More than 10 years after the "world famous strawmarket" burned to the ground, vendors finally have a new permanent structure from which to sell their wares, set to open in fall 2011. Situated on the original site on Bay Street is a towering colonial-style marketplace housing hundreds of straw vendors selling straw bags, T-shirts and other native souvenirs.

The Straw Market is one place in the Bahamas where bartering is accepted, so it's best to wander around and price similar items at different stalls before sealing a deal.

2

PERFUMES AND COSMETICS

The Cosmetic Boutique. This shop has beauty experts on hand to demonstrate the latest cosmetics offerings, including M.A.C., Clinique, Bobby Brown, and La Mer. ⊠ *Bay St. near Charlotte St.* ☎ *242/323–2731.*

Perfume Bar. Perfume Bar carries the best-selling French fragrance Boucheron and the Clarins line of skin-care products, as well as scents by Givenchy, Fendi, and other well-known designers. ⊠ *Bay St.* ☎ *242/325–1258.*

The Perfume Shop & The Beauty Spot. This is a landmark perfumery that has the broadest selection of imported perfumes and fragrances in the Bahamas. Experienced makeup artists are on hand to help pick out the perfect foundation or blush from a wide array of lines, including Lancôme, Clinique, and Chanel. ⊠ *Bay and Frederick Sts.* ☎ *242/322–2375.*

PARADISE ISLAND

ANTIQUES, ARTS, AND CRAFTS

Bahamacraft Centre. Bahamacraft Centre offers some top-level Bahamian crafts, including a selection of authentic straw work. Dozens of vendors sell everything from baskets to shell collages inside this vibrantly colored building. You can catch a shuttle bus from Atlantis to the center. ⊠ *Paradise Island Dr.*

Doongalik Art Gallery. This gallery showcases the artwork of more than 70 local artists. ⊠ *Marina Village* ☎ *242/363–1313.*

CIGARS

Havana Humidor. Havana Humidor has the largest selection of authentic Cuban cigars in the Bahamas. Watch cigars being made or browse through the cigar and pipe accessories. ⊠ *Crystal Court at Atlantis* ☎ *242/363–5809.*

FASHION

Bahama Sol. Bahama Sol sells brightly designed batik cotton Androsia fabric by the yard ($16.95) or sewn into sarongs, dresses, blouses, and men's shirts. ⊠ *Paradise Island Shopping Center* ☎ *242/363–0605.*

SPORTS AND THE OUTDOORS

BOATING

From Chub Cay—one of the Berry Islands 35 mi north of New Providence—to Nassau, the sailing route goes across the mile-deep Tongue of the Ocean. The Paradise Island Lighthouse welcomes yachters to Nassau Harbour, which is open at both ends. The harbor can handle the world's largest cruise liners; sometimes as many as eight tie up at one time. Two looming bridges bisect the harbor connecting Paradise Island to Nassau. Sailboats with masts taller than the high-water clearance of 72 feet must enter the harbor from the east end to reach marinas east of the bridges.

TOP FESTIVALS

WINTER

Bahamas International Film Festival. In early December the Bahamas International Film Festival in Nassau celebrates cinema in paradise, with screenings, receptions, and movie-industry panels.

Authentically Bahamian Christmas Trade Show. The Authentically Bahamian Christmas Trade Show on Cable Beach showcases conch-shell jewelry, straw handbags, batiks, and other island-made crafts the first weekend of December.

Christmas Jollification. This ongoing arts-and-crafts fair with Bahamian Christmas crafts, food, and music is held at the Retreat in Nassau.

Junior Junkanoo Parade. The island's schoolchildren compete for bragging rights in the Junior Junkanoo Parade in mid-December. The parade starts at 6 pm, and kids in preschool through high school rush down Bay Street, putting on an exciting show.

Junkanoo. Once Christmas dinner is over, the focus shifts to Junkanoo. The first major parade of the season starts just after midnight in downtown Nassau. There's a second parade on New Year's Day.

SPRING

International Dog Show & Obedience Trials. In Nassau, watchdogs of all classes compete at the International Dog Show & Obedience Trials, held late March. Check www.bahamaskennelclub.org for location.

SUMMER

Junkanoo Summer Festival. Woodes Rodgers Walk is transformed during the annual Junkanoo Summer Festival held weekends during the month of July. Listen to Rake 'n' Scrape bands, watch a Junkanoo rush-out, and sample local foods.

Fox Hill Festival. The Nassau Fox Hill Festival in early August pays tribute to Emancipation with church services, Junkanoo parades, music, cookouts, games, and other festivities.

FALL

International Cultural Weekend. Eat and drink your way around the world at the International Cultural Weekend, hosted at the Botanic Gardens the third weekend of October.

Nassau Yacht Haven. On the Nassau side of the harbor, Nassau Yacht Haven is a 150-berth marina—the largest in the Bahamas—that also arranges fishing charters. ☏ 242/393–8173 ⊕ www.nassauyachthaven.com.

Hurricane Hole Marina. Sixty-five-slip Hurricane Hole Marina is on the Paradise Island side of the harbor. ☏ 242/363–3600 ⊕ www.hurricaneholemarina.com.

Atlantis. The marina at Atlantis has 63 megayacht slips. ☏ 242/363–3000.

Brown's Boat Basin. On the Nassau side, Brown's Boat Basin offers a place to tie up your boat, as well as on-site engine repairs. ☏ 242/393–3331.

Lyford Cay. At the western end of New Providence, Lyford Cay, a posh development for the rich and famous, has an excellent marina, but there is limited availability for the humble masses. ☎ *242/362–4271.*

A number of outfitters rent Jet Skis in front of Atlantis and the Riu Palace Paradise Island on Cabbage Beach.

Premier Watersports. If your children would enjoy sitting in a row on a rubber banana and bouncing along behind a motorboat, ride the big banana at Premier Watersports, at the beach at the Riu and Atlantis. ☎ *242/324–1475, 242/427–0939 cellular.*

FISHING

The waters here are generally smooth and alive with many species of game fish, which is one of the reasons why the Bahamas has more than 20 fishing tournaments open to visitors every year. A favorite spot just west of Nassau is the Tongue of the Ocean, so called because it looks like that part of the body when viewed from the air. The channel stretches for 100 mi. For boat rental, parties of two to six will pay $600 or so for a half day, $1,600 for a full day.

Born Free Charters. This charter company has three boats and guarantees a catch on full-day charters—if you don't get a fish, you don't pay. ☎ *242/393–4144* ⊕ *www.bornfreefishing.com.*

Brown's Charters. Brown's Charters specializes in 24-hour shark-fishing trips, as well as reef and deep-sea fishing. ☎ *242/324–2061* ⊕ *www. brownscharters.com.*

Charter Boat Association. The Charter Boat Association has 15 boats available for fishing charters. ☎ *242/393–3739.*

Chubasco Charters. This charter company has four boats for sportfishing and shark-fishing charters. ☎ *242/324–3474* ⊕ *www.chubascocharters. com.*

Nassau Yacht Haven. Nassau Yacht Haven runs fishing charters out of its 150-slip marina. ☎ *242/393–8173* ⊕ *www.nassauyachthaven.com.*

GOLF

Cable Beach Golf Club. The oldest golf course in the Bahamas, Cable Beach Golf Club (7,040 yards, par 72), will be completely overhauled when Baha Mar gets on with its Cable Beach transformation. In 2011 the course was reduced to 9 holes as construction got underway, and at some point the existing course will be closed entirely. Best to inquire when booking your vacation if nearby golf is a must. ⊠ *W. Bay St., SE end of Cable Beach strip* ☎ *242/327–6000* ⛳ *18 holes $95, 9 holes $70; carts included. Clubs $25* ☉ *Daily 7–5:30; last tee off at 5:15.*

One & Only Ocean Club Golf Course. Designed by Tom Weiskopf, One & Only Ocean Club Golf Course (6,805 yards, par 72) is a championship course surrounded by the ocean on three sides, which means that winds can get stiff. Call to check on current availability and up-to-date prices

DID YOU KNOW?

Marina Village, an open-air marketplace at Atlantis, is a popular tourist destination. The bazaar features five restaurants, a craft market, and upscale stores.

Golfing in paradise

(those not staying at Atlantis or the One & Only Ocean Club may find themselves shut out completely). ⊠ *Paradise Island Dr. next to airport, Paradise Island* ☎ *242/363–3925, 800/321–3000 in U.S.* ⛳ *18 holes $260. Clubs $70* ☉ *Daily 6 am–sundown.*

HORSEBACK RIDING

Happy Trails Stables. Happy Trails Stables gives guided 90-minute trail rides, including basic riding instruction, through remote wooded areas and beaches on New Providence's southwestern coast. Two morning group rides are offered, but private rides can be arranged at any time. Courtesy round-trip bus transportation from hotels is provided (about an hour each way). Tours are limited to eight people. There's a 200-pound weight limit, and children must be at least 12 years old. Reservations are required. ⊠ *Coral Harbour, Western New Providence* ☎ *242/362–1820* ⊕ *www.bahamahorse.com* ⛳ *$150 per person* ☉ *Mon.–Sat. by appointment.*

PARASAILING

Premier Watersports. Premier Watersports gives you the chance to be lifted into the skies for five to eight minutes—at $70 a pop. Ask for Captain Tim or his crew on Cabbage Beach in front of the large hotels. You must be at least eight years old. ☎ *242/324–1475, 242/427–0939 cellular.*

SCUBA DIVING AND SNORKELING

SITES

Lost Ocean Hole. The elusive (and thus exclusive) Lost Ocean Hole (east of Nassau, 40–195 feet) is aptly named because it's difficult to find. The rim of the 80-foot opening in 40 feet of water is studded with coral heads and teeming with small fish—grunts, margate, and jacks—as well as larger pompano, amberjack, and sometimes nurse sharks. Divers will find a thermocline at 80 feet, a large cave at 100 feet, and a sand ledge at 185 feet that slopes down to 195 feet.

Rose Island Reefs. The series of shallow reefs along the 14 mi of Rose Island is known as Rose Island Reefs (Nassau, 5–35 feet). The coral is varied, although the reefs are showing the effects of the heavy traffic. Still, plenty of tropical fish live here, and the wreck of the steel-hulled ship *Mahoney* is just outside the harbor.

Gambier Deep Reef. Gambier Deep Reef, off Gambier Village about 15 minutes west of Cable Beach, goes to a depth of 80 feet.

Sea Gardens. This site is off Love Beach on the northwestern shore beyond Gambier.

Lyford Cay Drop-Off. Lyford Cay Drop-Off (west of Nassau, 40–200-plus feet) is a cliff that plummets from a 40-foot plateau almost straight into the inky blue mile-deep Tongue of the Ocean. The wall has endless varieties of sponges, black coral, and wire coral. Along the wall, grunts, grouper, hogfish, snapper, and rockfish abound. Off the wall are pelagic game fish such as tuna, bonito, wahoo, and kingfish.

OPERATORS

All dive shops listed below are Professional Association of Diving Instructors (PADI) facilities. Expect to pay about $65–$99 for a two-tank dive or beginner's course. Shark dives run $100–$125, and certification costs $450 and up.

Bahama Divers Ltd. The largest and most experienced dive operation in the country offers twice-a-day dive safaris as well as half-day snorkeling trips. PADI certification courses are available for $550 a person, and there's a full line of scuba equipment. Destinations are drop-off sites, wrecks, coral reefs and gardens, and an ocean blue hole. For Paradise Island guests, Bahama Divers has opened a small dive operation (which also carries snorkel equipment for rent) in the Paradise Island Harbour Resort. ☎ *242/393–1466, 800/398–3483* ⊕ *www.bahamadivers.com.*

GET INTO THE GAME!

If you happen to be in Nassau on a Saturday or Sunday afternoon, drop by Haynes Oval cricket field and watch the Bahamas Cricket Club members play the country's national sport. You don't have to follow what the men in white are doing, just enjoy the game from the balcony of the Cricket Club Pub over a dinner of bangers and mash, kidney pie, and a Murphy's or Guinness. The field is wedged between Fort Charlotte and a beach—all the ingredients for a great afternoon.

TOUR OPERATORS

Cruises **Barefoot Sailing Cruises** ☎ 242/393–0820 ⊕ www.barefootsailingcruises.com. **Flying Cloud** ☎ 242/394-5067 ⊕ www.flyingcloud.info.

Out Islands Trips Bahamas Fast Ferries ☎ 242/323–2166 ⊕ www.bahamasferries.com. **Exuma Powerboat Adventures** ☎ 242/363–2265 ⊕ www.powerboatadventures.com. **High Seas Private Excursions** ☎ 242/363–4183 ⊕ www.highseasbahamas.com. **Island World Adventures** ☎ 242/363–3333 ⊕ www.islandworldadventures.com.

Special-Interest Tours Bahamas Outdoors Ecoventures ☎ 242/362–1574 ⊕ www.bahamasoutdoors.com. **Dolphin Encounters** ☎ 242/363–1003 ⊕ www.dolphinencounters.com. **Seaworld Explorer** ☎ 242/356–2548 ⊕ www.seaworldtours.com.

Walking Tours Historic Nassau ☎ 242/356–4625 ⊕ www.bahamasupclose.com.

Stuart Cove's Dive South Ocean. This shop, on the island's south shore, is considered by aficionados to be the island's leading dive shop. Although they're pros at teaching beginners (scuba instruction and guided snorkel tours are available), experienced thrill-seekers flock to Stuart Cove's for the famous shark dives. Also popular are his Out Island "Wilderness Safaris," and "Wall Flying Adventures," in which you ride an underwater scooter across the ocean wall. Check out the collection of celebrity photos. The shop runs dive trips to the south-shore reefs twice a day. The mini-sub adventure, which requires no experience, is $119; snorkeling expeditions cost $65 for adults and $30 for kids 11 and under. The shark dives are $150 for a three-hour dive. ☎ 242/362–4171, 800/879–9832 ⊕ www.stuartcove.com.

Grand Bahama Island

WORD OF MOUTH

"Rent a scooter and head out to Gold Rock Beach, a really fun day trip, and the beach is superb. There are many beaches along the way that were totally empty of people, really nice."

—soboyle

WELCOME TO GRAND BAHAMA ISLAND

TOP REASONS TO GO

★ **Get your green on.** Rare birds and stretches of undisturbed wilderness attract nature lovers to the island's "bush." Take in a variety of habitats—from secluded beaches to bat caves.

★ **Party at a fish fry.** Head to Smith's Point every Wednesday night to feast and party with locals on the beach. On Thursday night the festivities move to Eight Mile Rock's Sunset Village. Friday and Saturday it's at Port Lucaya Marketplace.

★ **Golf in paradise.** Grand Bahama has the most golf courses of any island in the Bahamas. Try your swing at one of four greens.

★ **Shop for local crafts at Port Lucaya Marketplace.** The liveliest spot on the island features a cute Bahamian-style cluster of shops, cafés, and bars.

★ **Go down under.** Between the shipwrecks, caves, and coral reefs, Grand Bahama offers some of the country's most varied and vivid snorkeling and diving.

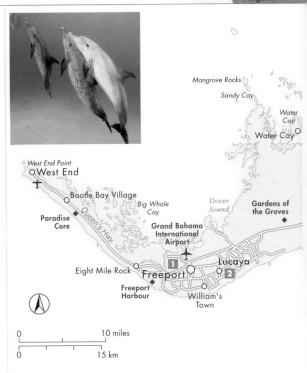

1 Freeport. The working end of Grand Bahama, Freeport is convenient to the airport and harbor for visitors in transit. Rand Nature Centre and Xanadu Beach make the area worth a visit, although downtown looks a bit forlorn as developers await economic recovery before starting massive renovations.

2 Lucaya. Freeport's newer beachfront counterpart is more tourism-oriented, dominated by Our Lucaya Beach and Golf Resort and Port Lucaya Marketplace, the island's best shopping. It also currently claims the island's only casino and the finest concentration of restaurants. The beach can get crowded, but sublime Taino Beach is nearby for those who prefer more space and privacy.

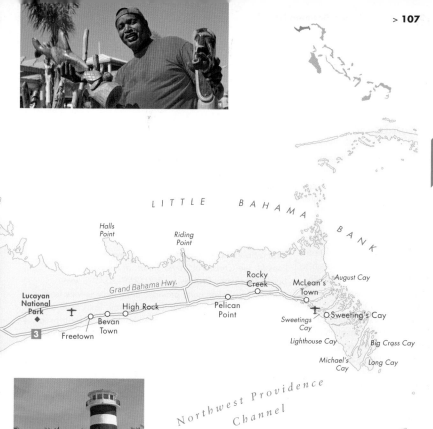

3 Greater Grand Bahama. The bulk of the island lies on either side of the neighboring metropolitan duo of Freeport and Lucaya. Escaping town means discovering treasures such as Lucayan National Park's caves, remote beaches, time-stilled fishing villages, and pristine wooded land the locals refer to as the "bush."

GETTING ORIENTED

Only 52 mi off Palm Beach, Florida, 96-mi-long Grand Bahama is one of the chain's northernmost islands. Freeport and Lucaya, which more or less melt into one another, are its main cities, comprising the second-largest metropolitan area in the Bahamas. Lucaya sees the most action these days, as Freeport struggles to regain ground

lost in the hurricanes and financial setbacks of the last decade. The town of West End is a quiet, colorful fishing village that gets lively with a Sunday-night street party. Its upscale Old Bahama Bay resort, marina, and residential development are the extent of tourism on this end of the island. East of Freeport-Lucaya small fishing settlements and undeveloped forest stretch for 60 mi.

GRAND BAHAMA ISLAND PLANNER

When to Go

As one of the northernmost Bahama Islands, Grand Bahama experiences temperatures dipping into the 60s with highs in the mid-70s in January and February, so you may need a jacket and wet suit. On the upside, the migrant bird population swells and diversifies during that time of year. The other timing considerations are seasonal crowds and the subsequent increase in room rates. High tourist season runs from Christmas to Easter, peaking during spring break (late February to mid-April), when the weather is the most agreeable.

Summers can get oppressively hot (into the mid and high 90s) and muggy, however; unless you're planning on doing a lot of snorkeling, diving, and other water sports, you may want to schedule your trip for cooler months. Afternoon thunderstorms and occasional tropical storms and hurricanes also make summer less attractive weather-wise. The island averages around 20 days of rain per month from June to September, but it usually falls briefly in the afternoon. The good news is that hotel rates plummet and diving and fishing conditions are great.

To avoid the crowds, high prices, heat, and cold, visit from October through mid-December.

Getting Here

By Air Grand Bahama International Airport (FPO) (☎ 242/352–2205) is about 6 minutes from downtown Freeport and about 10 minutes from Port Lucaya. No bus service is available between the airport and hotels. Metered taxis meet all incoming flights. Rides cost about $17 for two to Freeport, $22 to Lucaya. The price drops to $4 per person with larger groups.

Grand Bahama is the port of call for several cruise lines (⇨ *see Cruises in Travel Smart, at the back of the book*). **Discovery Cruises** (☎ *800/259–1579* ⊕ *www.discoverycruiseline.com*) provides daily ferry service from Fort Lauderdale, a five-hour trip each way. Taxis meet all cruise ships. Passengers (two) are charged $16 for trips to Freeport and $24 to Lucaya. The price drops to $4–$5 per person with larger groups.

Getting Around

By Bus Buses are an inexpensive way to travel the 4 mi between downtown Freeport and Port Lucaya Marketplace daily until 8 pm. The fare is $1. Buses from Freeport to the West End cost $5 each way; to the East End, $15. Exact change is required.

By Car If you plan to drive around the island, it's cheaper to rent a car than to hire a taxi. You can rent vehicles from the major agencies at the airport. Cars start at $75 for one day.

By Taxi Taxi fares are fixed (but generally you're charged a flat fee for routine trips) at $3 for the first ¼ mi and 40¢ for each additional ¼ mi. Additional passengers over two are $3 each. There's a taxi waiting area outside the Our Lucaya Resort or you can call the Grand Bahama Taxi Union for pickup.

About the Restaurants

The Grand Bahama dining scene stretches well beyond traditional Bahamian cuisine. The resorts and shopping centers have eateries that serve up everything from Italian to fine continental and creative Pacific Rim specialties. For a true Bahamian dining experience, look for restaurants named after the owner or cook—such as Becky's, Geneva's Place, and Billy Joe's.

A native fish fry takes place on Wednesday evening at Smith's Point, east of Lucaya (taxi drivers know the way). Here you can sample fresh fish, sweet-potato bread, conch salad, and all the fixings cooked outdoors at the beach. It's a great opportunity to meet local residents and taste real Bahamian cuisine—and there's no better place than seaside under the pines and palms.

Note: A gratuity (15%) is often added to the bill automatically.

About the Hotels

Grand Bahama accommodations remain some of the Bahamas' most affordable, especially those away from the beach. The majority of these provide free shuttle service to the nearest stretch of sand. The island's most extravagant hotels are beachfront, with the exception of Pelican Bay. These include the sprawling Our Lucaya Beach and Golf Resort; Viva Wyndham Fortuna Beach, an all-inclusive east of Lucaya; and the West End's elegant Old Bahama Bay Resort & Yacht Harbour. Small apartment complexes and time-share rentals are economical alternatives, especially if you're planning to stay for more than a few days.

Rates post-Easter through December 14 tend to be 25%–30% lower than those charged during the rest of the year.

WHAT IT COSTS IN DOLLARS

	¢	$	$$	$$$	$$$$
Restaurants	under $10	$10–$20	$20–$30	$30–$40	over $40
Hotels	under $100	$100–$200	$200–$300	$300–$400	over $400

Restaurant prices are based on the median main course price at dinner, excluding gratuity, typically 15%, which is often automatically added to the bill. Hotel prices are for two people in a standard double room in high season, excluding service and 6%–12% tax.

Essentials

Banks Banks are generally open Monday–Thursday 9:30–3 and Friday 9:30–4:30.

Car Rentals Bahama Buggies ☎ 242/351–7285, 242/359–5438 ⊕ www.bahamabuggies.com. **Cartwright's Rent-A-Car** ☎ 242/351–3002 ⊕ www.cartwrightsrentacar.com. **Island Jeep and Car Rentals** ☎ 242/373–4001. **KSR Car Rental** ☎ 242/351–5737 ⊕ www.ksrrentacar.com.

Emergencies Ambulance ☎ 242/352–2689. **Bahamas Air Sea Rescue** ☎ 242/352–2772. **Fire Department** ☎ 242/352–8888, 911. **Police** ☎ 911. **Rand Memorial Hospital** ⊠ E. Atlantic Dr., Freeport, Grand Bahama Island ☎ 242/352–6735.

Taxis Grand Bahama Taxi Union ☎ 242/352–7101.

Visitor Information Tourist information centers are open Monday–Friday at the Fidelity Financial Center in Freeport (9–5), the Grand Bahama International Airport (9–5), Lucayan Harbour (according to cruise ship arrivals), and Port Lucaya Marketplace (10–6). The People-to-People Program matches your family with hospitable locals who share like interests. **Ministry of Tourism Grand Bahama Office** ☎ 242/352–8044, 800/448–3386 ⊕ www.grandbahama.bahamas.com. **People-to-People Program** ☎ 242/352–8045 ⊕ www.peopletopeople.bahamas.com/bahamas/people-people.

3

GRAND BAHAMA ISLAND BEACHES

(above and upper right) Lucaya Beach

Fluffy white sand carpets in-your-dream beaches, where water sparkles like sapphires, lapis, tanzanite, emeralds, aquamarines . . . you get the picture. Grand Bahama Island has more than its share of beautiful beaches fringing the south coast of its 96-mi length. Some are bustling with water-sports activity, while others lie so far off the beaten path it takes a four-wheel-drive vehicle and local knowledge to find them.

Lucaya, Taino, and Xanadu beaches are the most accessible to the general public. Farther off the beaten path, some 60 mi of magnificent stretches of sand extend between Freeport-Lucaya and McLean's Town, the island's isolated eastern end. Most are used only by people who live in adjacent settlements along the way. The outlying beaches have no public facilities, so beachgoers often headquarter at one of the local beach bars. Some, such as Paradise Cove on the island's West End, have vans that will pick you up at your hotel.

BEACH-SHACKING

A dozen open-air, no-need-for-shoes shacks dot the island's sandy shores, with the largest concentration in the Freeport-Lucaya–Taino Beach area. Here locals cook up beach eats and dispense cold beer and Bahama Mama rum cocktails. Grand Bahama has more beach shacks than any other island; Billy Joe's on Lucaya Beach and Tony Macaroni's on Taino Beach are our favorites.

GRAND BAHAMA ISLAND'S BEST BEACHES

DEADMAN'S REEF BEACH
The spectacular swim-to reef is the best asset of this beach, a 15-minute drive from Freeport. It's part of Paradise Cove, a small native-owned resort that will bus you out if you call ahead. The beach is short but wide, with scrubby vegetation and swaying palm trees. Snorkel equipment and kayaks are available to rent, and refreshments flow at the Red Bar. This beach will give you a taste of what the Out Islands are like; come here when the crowds in Lucaya become too much.

LUCAYA BEACH
Although somewhat monopolized by the broad spread of Our Lucaya Resort, this beach is accessible to the public and a good place to visit if you like lots of options for drinking, dining, and water sports. Cruise-ship excursions add to the resort's crowds. The white-sand beach is interrupted by rocky protrusions, so it's not great for strolling. Instead, spend the day people-watching at one of the beach bars, swimming pools, or the famous Billy Joe's beach shack.

TAINO BEACH
Arguably the most marvelous beach on the island, Taino is just far enough removed from Lucaya to thin the crowds some, although cruise-ship passengers

often make their way here en groupe. Junkanoo Beach Club has a small food menu (compared to its long menu of 34 different drinks) and water-sports operators are on hand. With lapping water that puts gemstones to shame, this fluffy-sand beach begs for explorations. A short walk down the long, gently coved beach takes you to Tony Macaroni's Conch Experience.

WILLIAM'S TOWN BEACH
When the tide is high, this slice of relatively hidden beach (off East Sunrise Highway and down Beachway Drive) can get a little narrow, but there's a wide area at its east end, where a pig roast–jerk pit stand does business. Across the road a number of beach shacks have names such as Bikini Bottom and Toad's on the Bay. Island Seas Resort, next to the pig roast stand, has its own modern interpretation of the local beach shack, called CoCoNuts Grog & Grub.

XANADU BEACH
The old Xanadu Resort of Howard Hughes fame has now morphed into a time-share vacation club, but the beach club on wide powdery sands remains vibrant with guests from other Freeport resorts that bus them here. The scent of grilling burgers in the open-air kitchen and restaurant is as luring as the mile-long, fluffy stretch of beach itself.

LUCAYAN NATIONAL PARK

In this extraordinary 40-acre seaside land preserve, trails and elevated walkways wind through a natural forest of wild tamarind and gumbo-limbo trees, past an observation platform, a mangrove swamp, sheltered pools, and one of the largest explored underwater cave systems in the world (more than 6 mi long).

(above) Creek Trail (upper right) Ben's Cave

You can enter the caves at two access points; one is closed in June and July, the bat-nursing season. Twenty miles east of Lucaya, the park contains examples of the island's five ecosystems: beach, hardwood forest, mangroves, rocky coppice, and pine forest. Across the road from the caves, two trails form a loop. Creek Trail's boardwalk showcases impressive interpretive signage, and crosses a mangrove-clotted tidal creek to Gold Rock Beach, a narrow, lightly visited strand of white sand edged by some of the island's highest dunes and jewel-tone sea. ⊠ *Grand Bahama Hwy., Grand Bahama Island* ☎ *242/352–5438* ⊕ *www.bnt.bs/parks_lucayan. php* ⊡ *$3* ⊘ *Daily 8:30–4:30.*

BEST TIME TO GO

Visitors will find subtle treasures no matter what time of year they explore. Summer can be overbearingly hot for walking, plus one of the caves closes June and July for bat season. However, that's also when certain orchids and other plants flower. Migrating birds and cooler temperatures make October–April optimal, especially mornings and low tide, when birds are most plentiful.

BEST WAYS TO EXPLORE

KAYAK

A kayak launch, near a beach where parts of the *Pirates of the Caribbean* movies were filmed, lies about 3 mi east of the park entrance on the south side at a chain-link fence. From here paddlers can work their way through mangrove forest to the park and its beach. Kayaking to Peterson Cay National Park, an offshore island and coral reef, is the easiest way to get there to snorkel and picnic.

SNORKEL AND DIVE

Snorkeling around Gold Rock Beach and its eponymous offshore Gold Rock is good. Certified cave divers can explore the intricate underwater network with Underwater Explorers Society (UNEXSO).

WALK

Trails come in two parts. On the north side of the road at the parking lot, one trail takes you into Ben's Cave and the Burial Mound Cave, where ancient Lucayan remains and artifacts have been discovered. A tricky spiral staircase descends into the dark depths (a flashlight comes in handy) of the former, and an easier wooden staircase to the latter. At both, observation platforms accommodate visitors who want to peer into the caves' clear depths. Across the road, two flat, easy trails form a loop to the beach. Creek Trail (0.2 mi) is the easiest because its boardwalk is newer. Birds are more abundant here in the tidal creek with its low forest of mangroves at your feet. Mangrove Swamp Trail (0.3 mi) tends to be wet, and its boardwalk more difficult to negotiate (especially for small feet). Take one to the beach and the other to return to see the full range of environment here.

FUN FACT

A species of crustacean labeled *Speleonectes lucayensis* was discovered here and exists exclusively in the caverns of Lucayan National Park, where its population is protected. The rare, cave-dwelling Remipedia has no eyes or pigmentation.

PETERSON CAY NATIONAL PARK

Only accessible by boat or swimming, Peterson Cay National Park, one of the Bahamas' smallest national parks, takes up 1½ acres 1 mi offshore from Barbary Beach. Its gorgeous, usually deserted beach and lively marine life make it worth the effort of snorkeling the reef to the west or enjoying a quiet picnic. However, vegetation on the cay is salt-stunted and scrubby, so shade is scarce.

All wildlife is protected in the park, including a quarter mile of surrounding marine environment. Local ecotour operators lead kayak and snorkel excursions.

Updated by
Chelle Koster
Walton

Natural beauty conspires with resort vitality to make Grand Bahama Island one of the Bahamas' most well-rounded, diverse destinations. In its two main towns, Freeport and Lucaya, visitors can find much of what bustling Nassau has to offer: resort hotels, a variety of restaurants, golfing, duty-free shopping, and gambling. But unlike New Providence, the touristy spots take up only a small portion of an island that, on the whole, consists of uninhabited stretches of sand and forest.

Once the epicenter of the Bahamas' logging industry and a playground for the wealthy in the 1920s, the fate of Grand Bahama changed in the 1950s when American financier Wallace Groves envisioned Grand Bahama's grandiose future as a tax-free shipping port. The Bahamian government signed an agreement that set in motion the development of a planned city, an airport, roads, waterways, and utilities as well as the port. From that agreement, the city of Freeport—and later, Lucaya—evolved. The past decade's hurricanes and economic downfall have tarnished Freeport's resort glamour, and the tourism center has shifted to Lucaya, home of the island's largest resort.

Not much else on the island has changed since the early days, however. Outside of the Freeport-Lucaya commercial-and-resort area, fishing settlements remain, albeit now with electricity and good roads. The East End is Grand Bahama's "back-to-nature" side, where Caribbean yellow pine–and-palmetto forest stretches for 60 mi, interrupted by the occasional small settlement. Little seaside villages with white churches and concrete-block houses painted in bright blue and pastel yellow fill in the landscape between Freeport and West End. Many of these settlements are more than 100 years old.

GREAT ITINERARIES

IF YOU HAVE 3 DAYS

Begin in the morning with a shopping binge at **Port Lucaya Marketplace ❹**. Stop at **UNEXSO ❸** next door to make reservations for tomorrow's swim with dolphins, resort dive course, or excursion. Have lunch at the marketplace before heading to the beach across the street for an afternoon of sunning and water sports. Hit the restaurants and bars at the marketplace for the evening's entertainment. On Day 2, after your dolphin experience, get a quick taste of Bahamian nature at **Bahamas National Trust Rand Nature Centre ❷**. Catch a fish fry or beach bonfire for your evening's entertainment. On Day 3, head west to **Taino Beach** for great beach action, lunch, and sunning. Catch an evening dinner cruise and show with **Bahama Mama Cruises**.

IF YOU HAVE 5 DAYS

Spend the morning of Day 4 exploring the caves, trails, and beach at **Lucayan National Park**. Stop at Garden of the Groves for lunch and a

tour. Have dinner in Lucaya and test your luck at the casino. The next day, rent a car for an excursion to **West End** for snorkeling at Paradise Cove and an eyeful of local culture. Stop at Pier One restaurant for dinner and shark feedings

IF YOU HAVE 7 DAYS

A week allows you to explore in greater depth the island's environmental treasures. On Day 6, visit the William's Town beach and have lunch at one of the local eateries. In the afternoon, do a snorkel or fishing excursion and eat dinner at one of the restaurants at Our Lucaya. Spend your last morning wandering, shopping, and lunching at Garden of the Groves. In the afternoon, go on a semisubmarine or glass-bottom boat tour.

■TIP→ Club Grand Bahama packages several dining and activity experiences into all-island inclusive vacations. Participants use a special card to pay at each outlet. (*wwww.clubgrandbahama.com*)

EXPLORING

FREEPORT

Freeport, once an attractive, planned city of modern shopping centers, resorts, and other convenient tourist facilities, took a bad hit from the 2004 and 2005 hurricanes; its main resort and casino have not reopened. An Irish firm has purchased International Bazaar—currently a ghost town with a few crafts vendors, shops, and clubs—and has plans to revive the area once the American economy improves. In the meantime, Freeport's native restaurants, Rand Nature Centre, and beaches make it worth the visit. It's close to Lucaya (a 15-minute drive), and the airport and harbor are just a few minutes from downtown.

★ **Bahamas National Trust Rand Nature Centre.** On 100 acres just minutes from downtown Freeport, a half mile of self-guided botanical trails shows off 130 types of native plants, including many orchid species. The center is the island's birding hot spot, where you might spy a

More than 300 bird species call the Bahamas home, including this Bananaquit.

red-tailed hawk or a Cuban emerald hummingbird. Visit the caged one-eyed Bahama parrot the center has adopted and a Bahama boa, a species that inhabits most Bahamian islands, but not Grand Bahama. On Tuesday and Thursday free (with admission) guided tours depart at 10:30 am. The visitor center hosts changing local art exhibits. ⊠ *E. Settlers Way* ☎ *242/352–5438* ☒ *$5* ⊙ *Weekdays 9–4; guided nature walk by advance reservation.*

Perfume Factory. Behind the now nearly defunct International Bazaar, the quiet and elegant Perfume Factory occupies a replica 19th-century Bahamian mansion—the kind built by Loyalists who settled in the Bahamas after the American Revolution. The interior resembles a tasteful drawing room. This is the home of Fragrance of the Bahamas, a company that produces perfumes, colognes, and lotions using the scents of jasmine, cinnamon, gardenia, spice, and ginger. Take a free five-minute tour of the mixology laboratory and get a free sample. For $30 an ounce you can blend your own perfume using any of the 35 scents ($15 for 1½ ounces of blend-it-yourself body lotion). Sniff mixtures until they hit the right combination, then bottle, name, and take home the personalized potion. ⊠ *Behind International Bazaar, W. Sunrise Hwy. and Mall Dr., on access road* ☎ *242/352–9391* ⊕ *www.perfumefactory.com* ☒ *Free* ⊙ *Weekdays 9:30–5, Sat. 11–3.*

3

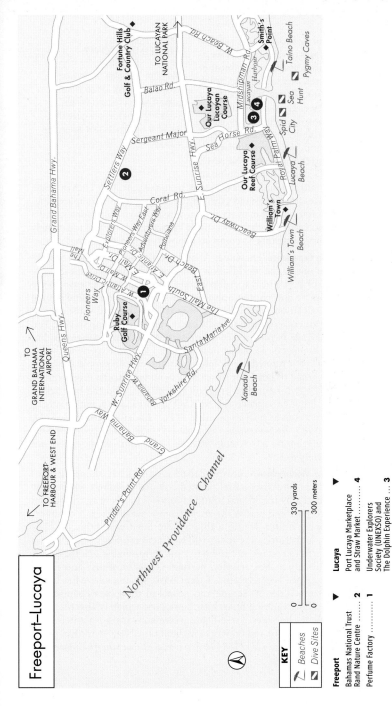

Freeport–Lucaya

KEY

↗ Beaches

▨ Dive Sites

▶ **Freeport**

Bahamas National Trust
Rand Nature Centre **2**

Perfume Factory **1**

▶ **Lucaya**

Port Lucaya Marketplace
and Straw Market **4**

Underwater Explorers
Society (UNEXSO) and
The Dolphin Experience ... **3**

LUCAYA

Lucaya, on Grand Bahama's southern coast, was developed after western neighbor Freeport as another resort center, this one on the beach and harbor. Pretty Port Lucaya Marketplace grew up along the safe harbor, known for its duty-free shops, clubs, restaurants, straw market, and outdoor bandstand. This is also the home of UNEXSO, the island's star diving and dolphin-encounter attraction. Across the street from the port, Our Lucaya Beach and Golf Resort is the island's thriving beach megaresort complex, complete with restaurants in every flavor, a casino, two golf courses, and a water park. Currently the resort's Reef Village hotel is closed indefinitely until tourism warrants its complete renovation and reopening.

☾ **The Dolphin Experience.** Encounter Atlantic bottlenose dolphins in Sanctuary Bay at one of the world's first and largest dolphin facilities, about 2 mi east of Port Lucaya. A ferry takes you from Port Lucaya to the bay to observe and photograph the animals. If you don't mind getting wet, you can sit on a partially submerged dock or stand waist deep in the water and one of these friendly creatures will swim up to you. You can also engage in one of two swim-with-the-dolphins programs, but participants must be 55 inches or taller. The Dolphin Experience began in 1987, when it trained five dolphins to interact with people. Later the animals learned to head out to sea and swim with scuba divers on the open reef. A two-hour dive program is available. You can buy tickets for the Dolphin Experience at UNEXSO in Port Lucaya, but be sure to make reservations as early as possible. ⊠ *Port Lucaya* ☎ *242/373–1244, 800/992–3483* ⊕ *www.unexso.com* ✉ *2-hr interaction program $82, 2-hr swim program $169, dolphin dive $219, open-ocean experience $199* ⊙ *Daily 8–5.*

★ **Port Lucaya Marketplace.** Lucaya's capacious and lively shopping complex—a dozen low-rise, pastel-painted colonial buildings whose style was influenced by traditional island homes—is on the waterfront 4 mi east of Freeport and across the street from a massive resort complex. The shopping center, whose walkways are lined with hibiscus, bougainvillea, and croton, has about 100 well-kept establishments, among them waterfront restaurants and bars, and shops that sell clothes, crystal and china, watches, jewelry, perfumes, and local arts and crafts. The marketplace's centerpiece is **Count Basie Square,** where live bands often perform Rake 'n' Scrape and gospel in the gazebo bandstand. Lively outdoor watering holes line the square, which is also *the* place to celebrate the holidays: a tree-lighting ceremony takes place in the festively decorated spot and fireworks highlight the New Year's Eve party. ⊠ *Sea Horse Rd.* ☎ *242/373–8446* ⊕ *www.portlucayamarketplace.com* ⊙ *Daily 10–6.*

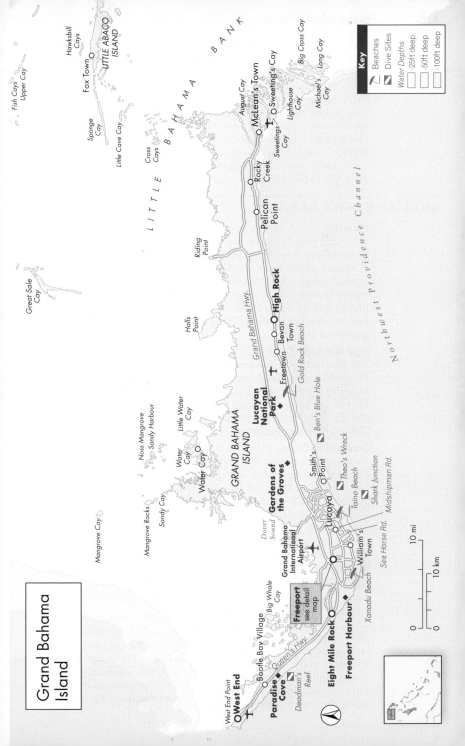

Fodor's Choice
★

Underwater Explorers Society (UNEXSO). One of the world's most respected diving facilities, UNEXSO welcomes more than 50,000 individuals each year and trains hundreds of them in scuba diving. Facilities include a 17-foot-deep training pool with windows that look out on the harbor, changing rooms and showers, docks, equipment rental, an outdoor cafe, and an air-tank filling station. Daily dive excursions range from one-day discovery courses and dives to specialty shark, dolphin, and cave diving. ⊠ *On wharf at Port Lucaya Marketplace* ☎ *242/373–1244, 800/992–3483* ⊕ *www.unexso.com* 🖃 *One-tank reef dives $59, Discover Scuba course $109, night dives $79, dolphin dives $219, shark dives $99* ⊙ *Daily 8–5.*

GREATER GRAND BAHAMA

On either side of the Freeport–Lucaya development, the island reverts to natural pine forest, fishing settlements, and undiscovered beaches. Heading west from Freeport, travelers pass the harbor area, a cluster of shacks selling fresh conch and seafood at Fishing Hole, a series of small villages, and Deadman's Reef at Paradise Cove before reaching the historic fishing town of West End and its upscale resort at the island's very tip. East of Lucaya lies Taino Beach, Garden of the Groves, Lucayan National Park, and long stretches of forest interrupted by the occasional small town.

Eight Mile Rock. You have to get off the main road to get to the heart and soul of Grand Bahama Island. This settlement, only 10 mi from Freeport Harbour, holds some pleasant surprises along its seaside road, including a historic church and cemetery and a string of brightly painted food shacks known as Sunset Village, where home cooking, rum punch, and Thursday-night live music make for a fun, old-island experience. ⊠ *Western Grand Bahama.*

Garden of the Groves. This vibrant 12-acre garden, featuring a trademark chapel and waterfalls, is filled with native Bahamian flora, butterflies, and birds. Interpretative signage identifies plant and animal species. First opened in 1973, the park was renovated and reopened in 2008; additions include a labyrinth modeled after the one at France's Chartres Cathedral, colorful shops and galleries, a playground, and a multideck outdoor café. Explore on your own or take a guided tour at 10 or 2 (except Sunday). ⊠ *Midshipman Rd. and Churchill Dr., Eastern Grand Bahama* ☎ *242/374–7778* ⊕ *www.thegardenofthegroves.com* 🖃 *$15* ⊙ *Daily 9–5; guided tours at 10 and 2 Mon.–Sat.*

High Rock. About 45 mi east of Lucaya and 8 mi from Lucaya National Park, it's worth the extra drive to visit an authentic, old-time island settlement affected only lightly by tourism. Its beach spreads a lovely white blanket of plump sand, with two beach clubs for food and drink. Take a walk along the beach and its parallel

RUN DOGGIE RUN

Island dogs, known as "potcakes"—a reference to the bottom of the rice pans they clean up—run wild, so be careful when driving. Efforts in recent years have raised awareness of the need for neutering and spaying.

Ecotourism on Grand Bahama

3

Beyond the 6-mi strip that comprises Grand Bahama Island's metropolis lies another 90 mi of unadulterated wilderness. The balance of the island is given to natural and uncrowded beaches, old-island settlements, and untamed "bush," as locals call the wilds.

The emphasis on the island's natural attributes begins below the water line with **UNEXSO** diving and the **Dolphin Experience.** UNEXSO's preoccupation with extreme diving led to the exploration of the island's unique cave system and the 1977 opening of **Lucayan National Park,** a portal to the underground labyrinth accessible to the public. One of the caves holds a cemetery of the island's aboriginals, the Lucayans. The park also gives intrepid visitors a taste of the beauty and seclusion of out-of-town beaches.

Kayaking, biking, snorkeling, boating, jeeping, and cultural safaris provide ways for visitors to take in Grand Bahama Island's most precious treasures.

Grand Bahama Nature Tours, a topnotch operation, follows backwater kayaking trails to Lucayan National Park and other off-the-beaten-path destinations. Knowledgeable native guides give lessons on island ecology en route.

Right in downtown Freeport, the **Bahamas National Trust Rand Nature Centre** was one of the precursors to ecotourism on Grand Bahama Island. It still provides an oasis for rare birds as well as residents and visitors. On the island's other extreme, close to West End, **Paradise Cove** takes you below the waves. Here you can rent snorkeling equipment or kayaks to experience the island's best swim-to reef—Deadman's Reef.

Ecotourism promises to be a fixture on Grand Bahama Island, attracting a different brand of island vacationer, one more adventurous and ready to experience the less-touted and richer offerings of Grand Bahama's great outback. For more information, contact the **Ecotourism Association of Grand Bahama** (☎ *242/352-8044, 800/448-3386 in the U.S.*).

DID YOU KNOW?

Eat up! Fried specialties abound in the Bahamas, including sautéed plantains and conch fritters.

road (rock outcroppings interrupt the sand in places) past the cemetery to the faux lighthouse that makes a nice photographic punctuation. Although the welcome sign identifies the village as "Home of Hospitality," it holds just two small lodges. ⊠ *Eastern Grand Bahama.*

Paradise Cove. For the island's best from-shore snorkeling, drive to this outpost near West End or call for a pickup and spend the day beaching, exploring Deadman's Reef, kayaking, and lunching at Red Bar, a classic island beach shack. Two modern, stilted cottages provide one- or two-bedroom accommodations. ⊠ *Deadman's Reef, 8 mi east of West End turnoff, Western Grand Bahama* ☎ *242/349–2677* ⊕ *www.deadmansreef.com.*

West End. Once a rowdy, good-time resort area, West End still attracts party folk every Sunday night for street feting. Today's reputation, however, rests more firmly on its charter fishing. Day visitors stop at one of the bayfront conch shacks for conch salad straight from the shell or at one of the other tiny eateries along the way. Overnighters stay at Old Bahama Bay Resort & Yacht Harbour, a gated resort. If you come for breakfast or lunch at its beach bar, you are allowed use of its small but pretty sand beach and water-sports opportunities. ⊠ *Western Grand Bahama.*

WHERE TO EAT

FREEPORT

$ ✕ **Geneva's Place.** Geneva's sets the standard for home-cooked Bahamian
BAHAMIAN food. Cook and owner Geneva Munroe will prepare your grouper or
★ pork chops broiled, steamed, or fried; your conch cracked (fried light and flaky), or, for breakfast, stewed. Everything comes with a choice of comfort side dishes such as peas 'n' rice or baked macaroni and cheese. For lunch, salads and sandwiches provide lighter options. The simple dining room oozes cheerfulness in shades of yellow. ⊠ *E. Mall Dr. and Kipling La., across from Wendy's* ☎ *242/352–5085.*

$$ ✕ **Ruby Swiss European Restaurant.** The extensive Continental menu has
CONTINENTAL options for every budget, with burgers, fried chicken, and fine seafood, steak, and veal. Specialties include steak Diana (flamed with cognac), Wiener schnitzel, lobster Alfredo, and peach melba. The wine list's 60-odd varieties represent five countries. Dinnertime guitar music adds a romantic touch to the dining-hall scene. A smaller but complete menu is served into the wee hours (4 am weekdays, 5 am weekends). ⊠ *W. Sunrise Hwy.* ☎ *242/352–8507* ☉ *Closed Sun. and Mon. No lunch Sat.*

LUCAYA

$
BAHAMIAN
★
× Billy Joe's on the Beach. Eating fresh conch salad and drinking Kalik beer with your toes in the sand: it doesn't get any better or more Bahamian. Billy Joe was such a fixture on the beach, selling his freshly made-on-the-spot (watch it being prepared!) conch salad, cracked conch, and grilled conch (minced and cooked with tomatoes,

onions, and bell peppers in an aluminum packet on the barbecue), that when Our Lucaya opened, the owners allowed him to stay on the property. This is where resort guests go "slumming" without having to travel farther than the edge of the resort's beach. Fried lobster, cheeseburgers, and cracked conch are other specialties. ⊠ *Lucaya Beach* ☎ *242/373–1333* ▭ *No credit cards.*

$$
ASIAN
★
× China Beach. For fine Pacific Rim dining with a view of the ocean, have dinner here, where the menu covers the various culinary regions of China plus Thailand and Japan, with a nod to the Bahamas. Feast on sushi rolls, Japanese dumplings, stir-fried conch, Szechuan prawns, and other Asian specialties. ⊠ *Our Lucaya Beach and Golf Resort* ☎ *242/373–1333* ⊕ *www.ourlucaya.com/resorts/radisson-our-lucaya-resort/dining/china-beach/* ⊘ *Days of operation vary according to season. No lunch.*

$$$
STEAK
× Churchill's Chophouse. Unwind in the handsome wood piano bar before enjoying a top-quality meal in the dining room, surrounded by white wainscoting and French windows. The atrium ceiling over the circular room illuminates Bahamian life with mural scenes and heavy chandeliers, and the character evokes the plantation era. In this elegant environment the menu focuses on beef, but escapes single-mindedness with lamb chops, salmon, and shrimp and lobster scampi. ⊠ *Our Lucaya Beach and Golf Resort* ☎ *242/373–1333* ⊕ *www.ourlucaya. com/resorts/radisson-our-lucaya-resort/dining/churchhill-s-chop-house-and-bar/* ⌛ *Reservations essential* ⊘ *Days of operation vary according to season. No lunch.*

$
ITALIAN
× Giovanni's Cafe. Tucked away under the bougainvillea at Port Lucaya Marketplace, this corner café evokes a bit of Italy. As you relax on the patio or study the giant mural of an Italian waterway inside the café, treat yourself to local seafood such as lobster in white-wine cream sauce and panfried grouper in lemon-wine sauce. Full-flavored, classic Italian dishes include spaghetti carbonara and chicken marsala. If you're on a budget, come between 4 and 6 for $12 early-bird pasta dinners (including a glass of wine). ⊠ *Port Lucaya Marketplace* ☎ *242/373–9107* ⊘ *Closed Sun.*

$
MEDITERRANEAN
× "Le Med" Mediterranean. Enjoy a taste of Europe while gazing upon yachts bobbing in the harbor. Outdoors is the best spot for breakfast, lunch, or dinner, but there's also spacious indoor dining around a European-style bakery. Under the same management as Luciano's, it goes a more casual route with tapas, crepes, pasta, seafood, sandwiches,

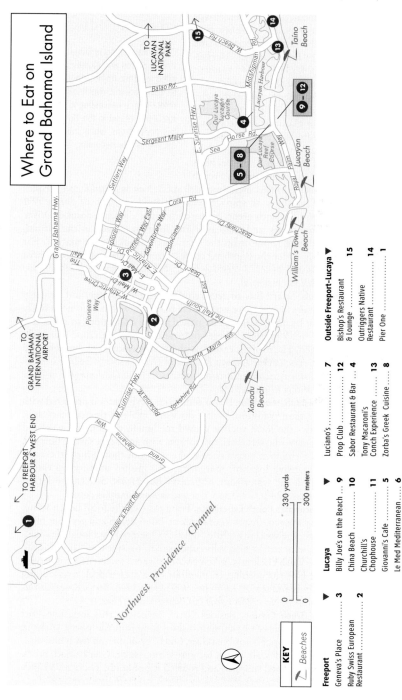

Where to Eat on Grand Bahama Island

KEY

Beaches

0 ⊢——⊣ 330 yards
0 ⊢——⊣ 300 meters

Freeport ▶

Geneva's Place **3**
Ruby Swiss European
Restaurant **2**

Lucaya ▶

Billy Joe's on the Beach ... **9**
China Beach **10**
Churchill's
Chophouse **11**
Giovanni's Cafe **5**
Le Med Mediterranean **6**

Luciano's **7**
Prop Club **12**
Sabor Restaurant & Bar ... **4**
Tony Macaroni's
Conch Experience **13**
Zorba's Greek Cuisine **8**

Outside Freeport-Lucaya ▶

Bishop's Restaurant
& Lounge **15**
Outriggers Native
Restaurant **14**
Pier One **1**

3

grilled meat, and homemade French pastries. At breakfast time there are Bahamian specialties and omelets. ✉ *Port Lucaya Market-place* ☎ *242/374–2804* ⊕ *www.thebahamasguide.com/lemed.*

$$$ ✕ **Luciano's.** Linens, soft candlelight,
FRENCH and a twinkling view of the harbor
Fodor'sChoice add to the glamour and romance
★ of this sophisticated, second-story Port Lucaya restaurant with a dedicated following of yachters and locals. Its menu speaks French with English subtitles, including such specialties as *coquilles St. Jacques florentine* (scallops on spinach with hollandaise), *filet au poivre vert* (tenderloin fillet with green peppercorn sauce), scampi flambé, Dover sole, stuffed quail, and chateaubriand for two, served in the formal, subdued dining room or on the veranda overlooking the marina. For a big finish, order the flambéed crêpes suzette for two. ✉ *Port Lucaya Marketplace* ☎ *242/373–9100* ⊕ *www.thebahamasguide.com/lucianos* ॐ *Reservations essential.*

$ ✕ **Prop Club.** Spare bits of recovered aircraft wreckage and brightly
AMERICAN painted chairs accent this casual resort hangout, which becomes a lively
☾ dance floor by night. Giant glass-paned garage doors open to make this an indoor-outdoor place where young and old come to dine and party on the beach. The menu is casual, with offerings like pizza, burgers, and baby back ribs. ✉ *Our Lucaya Beach and Golf Resort* ☎ *242/373–1333* ⊕ *www.ourlucaya.com/resorts/our-lucaya-reef-village/dining/prop-club/* ॐ *Reservations not accepted.*

$ ✕ **Sabor Restaurant and Bar.** If you want your fresh seafood prepared with
ECLECTIC more dare than tradition, pick a dockside table at this culinary star.
Fodor'sChoice Sabor draws the local yachtie crowd for lunch, dinner, and weekend
★ brunch. Curry mussels, shrimp wonton with jalapeño sauce, burgers, broiled hog snapper, guava cheesecake with bourbon whipped cream, and an extensive martini, margarita, and mojito menu keep things mixed up on the waterfront. ✉ *Pelican Bay Hotel, Sea Horse Rd. at Port Lucaya* ☎ *242/373–5588* ⊕ *www.sabor-bahamas.com.*

$ ✕ **Tony Macaroni's Conch Experience.** For a taste of the local beach scene,
BAHAMIAN find this weathered, thatch-roof shack at Taino Beach and get your fill of roast conch, the specialty of the "house." Operated by a local personality, the popular eatery also sells conch salad, roast lobster and shrimp, and Gully Wash cocktails (green coconut water, sweetened condensed milk, and gin) for noshing en plein air on a stilted deck overlooking pristine sands and sea. ✉ *Taino Beach* ☎ *242/533–6766* ॐ *Reservations not accepted* ⊟ *No credit cards* ☾ *Closed Mon.–Tues.*

$ ✕ **Zorba's Greek Cuisine.** Besides Greek favorites, this longtime Port
GREEK Lucaya tenant serves Bahamian dishes, too. Join the port's yacht-in clientele and shoppers for breakfast, lunch, or dinner on the white-and-blue-trimmed sidewalk porch for gyros, moussaka, Greek salad, pizza, conch fritters, fried snapper, and roasted leg of lamb. There's a $15 fee

CONCHING OUT

Conch harvesting is illegal in the United States and closely regulated in other tropical locations to guard against overfishing. Currently, conch harvesting is limited to six per vessel in the Bahamas, but populations, while still plentiful, are slowly becoming depleted.

Sailing near Our Lucaya Beach and Golf Resort

for using a credit card. ⊠ *Port Lucaya Marketplace* ☎ *242/373–6137* ⊕ *zorbasfreeport.com* ⌂ *Reservations not accepted.*

GREATER GRAND BAHAMA

¢ ✗**Bishop's Beach Club & Bar.** A longtime favorite of locals and visitors
BAHAMIAN who venture out to Lucayan National Park (about 6 mi away) and into
★ the East End's settlements, Bishop's serves all the Bahamian favorites
with homemade goodness and a view of the sea. Come for lunch and
stay for the beach. The cracked conch is light and crunchy, the peas 'n'
rice full-flavored. There are also barbecued ribs, broiled lobster, burgers, and sandwiches. Breakfast is a simple choice of bacon or ham with
your fried eggs and toast. A $30 minimum for credit-card use applies.
⊠ *High Rock* ☎ *242/353–5485* ⊕ *bishopsresort.net/restaurant.html.*

$ ✗**Outriggers Native Restaurant.** For Bahamian food fixed by Bahamians,
BAHAMIAN head east to the generational property of an old island family, just
beyond Taino Beach. When you stop at Gretchen Wilson's place for
cracked conch, lobster tail, fried grouper, and barbecue chicken down-
home style, you'll feel as though you're dining in someone's spotlessly
clean home. On Wednesday nights the quiet little settlement comes to
life when Outriggers throws its famous weekly fish fry. Tuesday and
Thursday nights there are beach bonfires in season. ⊠ *Smith's Point*
☎ *242/373–4811* ▭ *No credit cards* ⊙ *Closed Sun. No lunch.*

$$ ✗**Pier One.** Blown down in the 2004 hurricanes, Pier One is back with
SEAFOOD a sturdier building decorated with the old trademark nautical para-
phernalia. Diners have their choice of picnic tables around the balcony
or inside the spacious dining and bar area. Popular with cruise-ship

passengers because of its location at the port entrance, the restaurant also hosts shark feedings nightly at 7, 8, and 9. To go with this activity, order specialties such as smoked shark, shark fritters, blackened lemon shark fillet, or shark curry with bananas. The extensive menus also offer mussels, panfried mahi, grouper cordon bleu, lobster and mushrooms with cream, chicken curry, fettuccini with seafood, and steaks. ⊠ *Freeport Harbour* ☎ *242/352–6674* ⊕ *www.pieronebahamas.com* ⌲ *Reservations essential.*

WHERE TO STAY

FREEPORT

$ ⚅ **Castaways Resort and Suites.** In Freeport, this property is one of the
★ nicer budget options in the area. The coral rock–accented lobby introduces four stories of rooms in rattan and earth-and-floral tones. Family friendliness is underscored by a playground next to the pool, and a beach shuttle is provided. The restaurant is open for dinner and its famous breakfast. **Pros:** reputable restaurant; nice array of services and facilities, close to airport. **Cons:** the neighborhood is currently in a slump; lacking character. ⊠ *E. Mall Dr.* ☎ *242/352–6682* ⊕ *www. castaways-resort.com* ⌲ *97 rooms, 21 suites* ⌂ *In-room: safe, Wi-Fi. In-hotel: restaurant, bar, pool, laundry facilities, business center.*

$$ ⚅ **Island Seas Resort.** This time-share property accommodates nonmembers looking for fun on the beach away from urban traffic. Balconies overlook the flowery courtyard, where thatch-roof CoCoNuts Grog & Grub and a free-form pool with waterfalls and swim-up bar are the centerpiece. The beach, used also by guests from other nonbeachside resorts, is busy with water-sports activity. One- and two-bedroom rooms are done in bright, modern island style. A new beachfront restaurant serves breakfast and dinner. **Pros:** fun pool and bar area; great beach; free Port Lucaya shuttle. **Cons:** fitness center is below par; other resort guests use property. ⊠ *123 Silver Point Dr., William's Town* ☎ *242/373–1271, 800/801–6884* ⊕ *www.islandseas.com* ⌲ *90 rooms* ⌂ *In-room: kitchen, Wi-Fi. In-hotel: restaurant, bar, pool, gym, spa, beach, laundry facilities, business center.*

¢ ⚅ **Royal Islander.** Amenities without the sticker shock: this two-story, tin-roof, motel-style property provides free scheduled shuttle service to Xanadu Beach. The rooms have light-wood and rattan furnishings, lively tropical fabrics, framed pastel prints, and tile floors on the lower level. You'll find carpeted floors upstairs, where no-smoking rooms are available. An inviting white-and-floral lobby faces the spacious pool area. **Pros:** affordable; convenient to airport. **Cons:** no beach on property; low on character. ⊠ *E. Mall Dr.* ☎ *242/351–6000* ⊕ *www.royalislanderhotel.com* ⌲ *100 rooms* ⌂ *In-room: Wi-Fi. In-hotel: restaurant, bar, pool.*

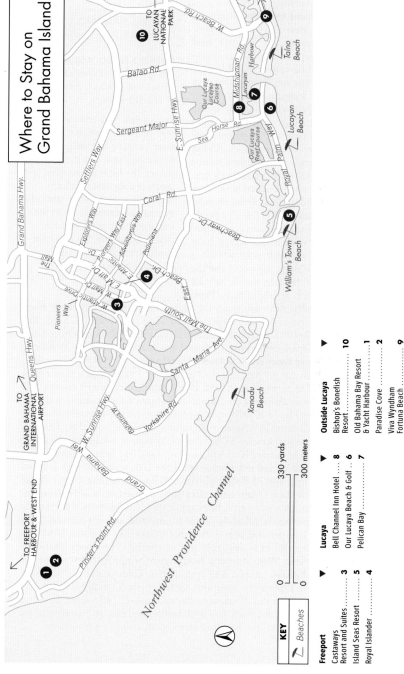

Where to Stay on Grand Bahama Island

KEY

Beaches

0 ——— 330 yards

0 ——— 300 meters

Freeport ▶

Castaways
Resort and Suites **3**

Island Seas Resort **5**

Royal Islander **4**

Lucaya ▶

Bell Channel Inn Hotel **8**

Our Lucaya Beach & Golf .. **6**

Pelican Bay **7**

Outside Lucaya ▶

Bishop's Bonefish
Resort **10**

Old Bahama Bay Resort
& Yacht Harbour **1**

Paradise Cove **2**

Viva Wyndham
Fortuna Beach **9**

LUCAYA

¢ 🕮 **Bell Channel Inn Hotel.** Right on the water near Port Lucaya with easy access to the island's best down-under sites, this hotel is perfect for scuba-oriented and budget travelers. The inn has its own dive shop and lodging-dive packages. The dive boat conveniently leaves from behind the hotel, and the shop is full-service with equipment rentals and certification courses. All but two of the simply furnished rooms are equipped with a small refrigerator; all have a kitchen sink, cupboards, and a view of the channel or Port Lucaya. The hotel's convivial restaurant-bar serves seafood and good spirit, come happy hour each day. A small pool sits on a wood deck along the water and the hotel provides free shuttle service to the beach at Island Seas. **Pros:** diver-friendly; affordable; on the water. **Cons:** no beach; away from shopping and restaurant scene; slightly rundown rooms. ⊠ *Kings Rd.* ☎ *242/373–1053* ⊕ *www.bellchannelinn.com* ↪ *32 rooms* ☐ *In-room: Wi-Fi. In-hotel: restaurant, bar, pool, water sports, laundry facilities.*

$ 🕮 **Our Lucaya Beach and Golf Resort.** Here's where it's always happening, from beach fun to nightlife and gambling. Lucaya's grandest resort

Fodor's Choice includes 7½ acres of soft-sand beach (the entire resort covers 372 ★ acres). The focus here is on dramatic play-area water features and golf. The property has a 17,000-square-foot casino, six restaurants, lounges, a children's camp, a first-rate spa, and a shopping complex. The section of the resort known as Breaker's Cay is now a Radisson-branded property. (The former Reef Village closed in 2011 for renovations and has remained closed indefinitely until the U.S. economy and demand pick back up.) The 10-floor high-rise building curves like a wavy cruise ship with oversize rooms and suites done with art deco interpretation. In addition, two-story structures replicate Caribbean-style plantation manors and house all-water-view rooms and suites removed from the resort's hustle and bustle. Another manor-like building holds the lobby, where Wi-Fi is available free-of-charge. The resort offers all-inclusive plans. **Pros:** stunning beach; great water features; variety of accommodations, casino, and restaurants. **Cons:** currently not fully operational; expensive restaurants. ⊠ *Sea Horse Rd.* ☎ *242/373–1333, 866/870–7148 in U.S.* ⊕ *www.ourlucaya.com* ↪ *540 rooms, 26 suites* ☐ *In-room: safe, Internet. In-hotel: restaurant, bar, golf course, pool, tennis court, gym, spa, beach, water sports, children's programs.*

GRAND BAHAMA ISLAND SPAS

Amanda's Facials 'n Spa. This spa features a chocolate facial. ⊠ *16 Lillian Ct., Freeport* ☎ *242/373–6734.*

Senses Spa. Here you can find state-of-the-art exercise equipment, including free weights, a spinning studio, and fitness classes. The fee is $25 for non-guests per day, which includes use of the sauna facilities. Many of the spa treatments use local bush ingredients, and range from massage to hydrobaths. ⊠ *Our Lucaya Beach and Golf Resort, Lucaya* ☎ *242/350–5281.*

$ 🏨 **Pelican Bay.** Close to the beach
Fodor'sChoice and situated on the harbor, Pelican
★ Bay has a tidy modern appeal, and
some of its newer suites overflow
with character and decorative elements collected from around the
world. Building exteriors are fanci-
fully trimmed in West Indian lat-
ticework and red barrel-tile roofs.
Smartly furnished rooms and suites
overlook the pool and whirlpool,
the channel, and the marina. The
waterfront suites have extras like
rain showers, espresso machines,
and boxes built into the doors

into which fresh pastries are delivered each morning (a full continental breakfast is also available). Pelican Bay is next door to UNEXSO,
which makes it popular with divers. It's also only steps away from
Port Lucaya Marketplace. The resort provides a ferry shuttle to Taino
Beach. Lucaya Beach access is a five-minute walk away. **Pros:** stylish and comfortable; water views; great restaurants. **Cons:** no beach;
no water sports; corporate focus. ⊠ *Sea Horse Rd. at Port Lucaya*
☎ *242/373–9550, 800/600–9192* ⊕ *www.pelicanbayhotel.com* ⤻ *89
rooms, 93 suites* ⚹ *In-room: safe, Wi-Fi. In-hotel: restaurant, bar, pool,
laundry facilities, business center* ❧❘ *Breakfast.*

GREATER GRAND BAHAMA

¢   🏨 **Bishop's Bonefish Resort.** Stay on the beach in a small community east
★ of the cities, without the hefty price tags and bustle of Lucaya. Owned
by Bahamian Ruben "Bishop" Roberts, the property comprises seven
white-tile, spacious rooms. Bishop will arrange bonefishing excursions
to the East End, feed you at his landmark restaurant, and talk politics with you at the beach bar. **Pros:** gorgeous beach; in touch with
local community; near Lucayan National Park. **Cons:** far from other
restaurants and shopping; spartan accommodations. ⊠ *High Rock*
☎ *242/353–5485* ⊕ *www.bishopsresort.net* ⤻ *7 rooms* ⚹ *In-hotel:
restaurant, bar, beach.*

$$ 🏨 **Old Bahama Bay Resort & Yacht Harbour.** Relax and luxuriate in rela-
☽ tive seclusion at this hotel designed for boating vacationers as well as
Fodor'sChoice fly-in guests looking to get away from it all. Waterfront suites, one and
★ two bedrooms, have heavy wood furnishings and restful views of the
beach through French doors. All suites contain wet bars, bathrobes,
cooking utensils, and DVD/CD players (with a complimentary on-site
library). Premium suites include jetted bathtubs and in-room laundry
facilities. Bike, kayak, and snorkel equipment use is complimentary.
Although endearingly intimate and individual, Old Bahama Bay has all
the amenities of a full-grown, self-contained resort, including a casual
beach bar, a fine restaurant, and a customs office, making it one of the
Bahamas' top small marina properties. **Pros:** peace and serenity; top-
shelf marina; close to local color. **Cons:** limited dining choices; far from

DID YOU KNOW?

Grand Bahama is one of the most eco-oriented islands in the Bahamas. Kayaks are readily available across the island.

TIME-SHARING

For information about other time-share houses, apartments, and condominiums, check with the Grand Bahama Ministry of Tourism (☎ 242/352–8044, 800/448–3386 in U.S. ⊕ www.bahamas.com).

Freeport Resort & Club. Freeport Resort & Club has 50 suites in a garden setting. ✉ Near International Bazaar, Rum Cay Dr., Freeport ☎ 242/352–5371, 877/699–9474 ⊕ www.freeportresort.com.

Mayfield Beach and Tennis Club. These 10 town houses share a pool, small beach, and tennis court. ✉ Port-of-Call Dr. at Xanadu Beach, Freeport ☎ 242/352–9776.

Ocean Reef Yacht Club & Resort. Ocean Reef Yacht Club & Resort has 60 one- to three-bedroom apartments about 2 mi from Port Lucaya. The resort has a marina, restaurant, tennis courts, and pools. ✉ Bahama Reef Blvd., Freeport ☎ 242/373–4661 ⊕ www.oryc.com.

airport and shopping. ✉ West End ☎ 242/350–6500, 888/800–8959 ⊕ www.oldbahamabay.com ⇌ 67 rooms, 6 suites ⊜ In-room: safe, kitchen. In-hotel: restaurant, bar, pool, gym, beach, water sports, children's programs.

$ ⊡ **Paradise Cove.** Devoted snorkelers and peace-lovers seek out this offbeat location. Owned by a local family, Paradise Cove has rebuilt two two-bedroom stilted cottages damaged in the 2005 hurricane demise. (Lower rates are available for those wanting to rent the cottages as a one-bedroom with the other room locked off.) The two-bedroom units hold up to six, but there's a $50 fee per person over two. The small property is the only lodging on Deadman's Reef, quiet and far removed from the resort world. By day, activity mounts as snorkelers arrive by bus. The comfortable, nicely decorated accommodations have full kitchens. There's a protected stretch of beach, and snorkeling gear is available for a fee. Kayaks are available for your use. **Pros:** superb snorkeling; quiet in the off-hours; run by local family. **Cons:** far from restaurants and shopping; at times swarmed with bused-in visitors during the day. ✉ Deadman's Reef, 8 mi east of West End turnoff ☎ 242/349–2677 ⊕ www.deadmansreef.com ⇌ 2 cottages ⊜ In-room: kitchen. In-hotel: bar, beach, water sports.

$$ ⊡ **Viva Wyndham Fortuna Beach.** Popular with couples and families, this
ALL-INCLUSIVE secluded resort provides a casual, low-stress, all-inclusive getaway. One
⟳ price covers meals, drinks, tips, nonmotorized water sports, and nightly entertainment. A 1,200-foot private beach bustles with activity. Meals are served buffet style in the huge, gazebolike dining pavilion named Junkanoo or table-side at guest-only Italian La Trattoria and Asian Bambu. Viva Circus affords an opportunity to experience trapeze flying; professional circus people perform and give interactive lessons. Kids under age 12 stay free with adults and can take advantage of the kids' club, family shows, and children's pool. **Pros:** family-friendly; dining variety; secluded beach. **Cons:** sequestered feel; rooms are small; resort bustles. ✉ Churchill Dr. and Doubloon Rd. ☎ 242/373–4000,

TOP FESTIVALS

WINTER

Festival Noel, an annual holiday fest featuring music, crafts, wine tastings, and food at the Rand Nature Centre, takes place in early December.

Bacardi Rum Billfish Tournament. The weeklong Bacardi Rum Billfish Tournament is held at Port Lucaya in conjunction with the Bahamas Wahoo Championship. Both rotate around Grand Bahama and the Out Islands December through March.

SPRING

Coconut Festival. The Coconut Festival in Pelican Point includes live music, coconut food sampling, coconut bowling, and other contests and activities in late April.

SUMMER

Grand Bahama Sailing Regatta. Sailing sloops from throughout the country meet at June's Grand Bahama Sailing Regatta, in the exciting "Championship of the Seas." Onshore festivities take place at Taino Beach and include Junkanoo parades, dancing, music, and food.

FALL

McLean's Town Conch Cracking Contest. The annual McLean's Town Conch Cracking Contest, which includes 20 days of conch-cracking competitions, games, Junkanoo parades, and good eating, takes place in October, as it has for more than 30 years.

Conchman Triathlon. The annual Conchman Triathlon in November is a swimming-running-bicycling competition for amateurs that raises funds for local charities. ⊕ *www.conchman.com.*

800/996–3426 in U.S. ⊕ www.vivaresorts.com ⌇276 rooms ⌂ In-room: safe. In-hotel: restaurant, bar, pool, tennis court, gym, beach, water sports, children's programs, business center ⎡⊙⎤ All-inclusive.

NIGHTLIFE

For evening and late-night entertainment, Port Lucaya is filled with restaurants and bars, and there's usually live entertainment in the middle square. Other options include finding a bonfire beach party or fish fry or taking a cruise on a sunset party boat. On Sunday nights the party takes to the main drag in West End and the bar-crawling lasts into the wee hours. You can also find nightclubs near International Bazaar; they're generally open from 8 until 3.

FREEPORT

NIGHTCLUB

Club Amnesia. This is one of the hot spots around International Bazaar; it rocks weekend nights with live entertainment (including international recording artists in season), a huge dance floor, and a youthful crowd. Sports fans crowd around the bar on game days. ⊠ *Across from International Bazaar on E. Mall Dr.* ☏ *242/351–2582.*

Hand-woven souvenirs at Port Lucaya Marketplace

LUCAYA

CASINO

★ **Treasure Bay Casino.** This 17,000-square-foot, bright, tropically decorated playland has more than 320 slot machines and 33 game tables consisting of minibaccarat, Caribbean stud and three-card poker, craps, blackjack, and roulette. The Cove restaurant serves salads and sandwiches. The casino is open from 9 am until 2 am Sunday through Thursday and 9 am to 4 am Saturday and Sunday (or at the manager's discretion) and hosts live entertainment in the evening; slot machines are open 24 hours on weekends. Bathing suits and bare feet are not permitted. ⊠ *Our Lucaya Beach and Golf Resort* ☎ *242/350–2000, 866/273–3860* ⊕ *www.tblucaya.com.*

NIGHTCLUBS

★ **Bahama Mama Cruises.** Bahama Mama Cruises has some of the best nightlife in Grand Bahama. In addition to sunset "booze cruises," Bahama Mama offers a surf-and-turf dinner with a colorful "native" show (a local term used to indicate entertainment with a traditional cultural flair); it's $79 for adults, $45 for children (ages 2–12). The Sunset Cruise and Show is $45 and adults only. Reservations are essential. Both cruises are offered Monday, Wednesday, and Friday 6–9 (April–September) or 6:30–9:30 (October–March). ⊠ *Superior Watersports at Port Lucaya* ☎ *242/373–7863* ⊕ *www.superiorwatersports.com.*

Prop Club Sports Bar & Dance Club. This club hosts live music that propels you out to the giant dance floor on weekends, plus karaoke on certain evenings, and sports-TV Sundays. Seating is indoors as well as outdoors on the beach. Open daily for lunch and dinner and nightly entertainment. ⊠ *Our Lucaya Beach and Golf Resort* ☎ *242/373–1333* ⊕ *www. ourlucaya.com/resorts/our-lucaya-reef-village/dining/prop-club/.*

Rumrunners. This outdoor pub in Count Basie Square specializes in keeping young barhoppers supplied with tropical frozen drinks and punches, Kalik beers, burgers, and conch fritters. ⊠ *Port Lucaya Marketplace* ☎ *242/373–7233.*

THE ARTS

THEATER

Freeport Players' Guild. A nonprofit repertory company, Freeport Players' Guild produces American comedies, musicals, and dramas in the 300-seat Regency Theatre during its September–June season. ☎ *242/352–5533.*

Grand Bahama Players. Grand Bahama Players perform at Regency Theatre, staging cultural productions by Bahamian, West Indian, and North American playwrights. ☎ *242/352–5533.*

Port Lucaya Marketplace. The stage at Port Lucaya Marketplace becomes lively after dark, with live or piped-in calypso music and other performances at Count Basie Square (ringed by three popular hangouts: the Corner Bar, the Daiquiri Bar, and Rumrunners). ⊠ *Sea Horse Rd.* ☎ *242/373–8446* ⊕ *www.portlucayamarketplace.com.*

SHOPPING

In the stores, shops, and boutiques in Port Lucaya Marketplace you can find duty-free goods costing up to 40% less than what you might pay back home. At the numerous perfume shops, fragrances are often sold at a sweet-smelling 25% below U.S. prices. Be sure to limit your haggling to the straw markets.

Shops in Lucaya are open Monday–Saturday from 9 or 10 to 6. Stores may stay open later in Port Lucaya. Straw markets, grocery stores, some boutiques, and drugstores are open on Sunday.

FREEPORT

ART

The Glassblower Shop. The Glassblower Shop features the work of Sidney Pratt, who demonstrates his craft in the shop's front window. ⊠ *International Arcade* ☎ *242/352–8585.*

PERFUMES

★ **Perfume Factory.** Here you can find a large variety of perfumes, lotions, and colognes by Fragrance of the Bahamas, all under $21. Its biggest-selling Pink Pearl cologne actually contains conch pearls, and Sand cologne for men has a little sterilized island sand in each bottle. You can also create your own scent and brand-name and register it. ⊠ *In-*

ternational Bazaar, W. Sunrise Hwy. and Mall Dr. ☎*242/352–9391* ⊕ *www.perfumefactory.com.*

LUCAYA

ART

Hoyte's Art & Nature. Hoyte's Art & Nature sells a higher quality of handicrafts than the straw markets and souvenir shops. Look for painted canvases and handbags, and quality wood carvings. ⊠ *Port Lucaya Marketplace* ☎ *242/373–8326.*

Leo's Art Gallery. This gallery showcases the expressive Haitian-style paintings of local artist Leo Brown. ⊠ *Port Lucaya Marketplace* ☎ *242/373–1758* ⊕ *www.bahamasvacationguide.com/leobrown.*

CHINA AND CRYSTAL

Island Galleria. Here you can find china and crystal by Waterford, Wedgwood, Aynsley, Swarovski, and Coalport, as well as Lladró figurines. ⊠ *Port Lucaya Marketplace* ☎ *242/373–5274.*

CIGARS

Note: it's illegal to bring Cuban cigars into the United States.

FASHION

Animale. This shop is known for the wild appeal of its fine ladies' clothing and jewelry. ⊠ *Port Lucaya Marketplace* ☎ *242/374–2066.*

Bandolera. Bandolera sells European-style women's fashions, bags, and jewelry for the young and flirty. ⊠ *Port Lucaya Marketplace* ☎ *242/373–7691* ⊕ *www.bandolera.com.*

JEWELRY AND WATCHES

Colombian Emeralds. Colombian Emeralds purveys a line of Colombia's famed gems plus other jewelry and crystal. ⊠ *Port Lucaya Marketplace* ☎ *242/373–8400.*

Freeport Jewellers. This jeweller caters to locals and visitors with watches, heavy gold and silver chains, gemstones, and sea charms. It also sells cigars, crystal, and Fossil brand watches. ⊠ *Port Lucaya Marketplace* ☎ *242/373–2776.*

LEATHER GOODS

Unusual Center. Unusual Center carries eel-skin leather, peacock-feather goods, high-end bags, luggage, and jewelry. ⊠ *Port Lucaya Marketplace* ☎ *242/373–7333.*

MARKETS AND ARCADES

★ **Port Lucaya Marketplace.** This marketplace has more than 100 boutiques and restaurants in 13 pastel-color buildings in a harborside locale, plus an extensive straw market. Local musicians often perform at the bandstand in the afternoons and evenings. ⊠ *Sea Horse Rd.* ☎ *242/373–8446* ⊕ *www. portlucayamarketplace.com.*

GET TWISTED

One of tourists' favorite Bahamian souvenirs is braided hair. Licensed braiders, found wherever visitors shop, generally charge $2 per braid up to 15 and $120 for a full head. For the best of the best, head to Port Lucaya Marketplace.

Port Lucaya Straw Market. Port Lucaya Straw Market is a collection of wooden stalls at the Port Lucaya complex's east and west ends. Vendors will expect you to bargain for straw goods, T-shirts, and souvenirs. ⊠ *Sea Horse Rd.* ☎ *No phone.*

MISCELLANEOUS

Photo Specialist. Photo Specialist carries photo and video equipment. ⊠ *Port Lucaya Marketplace* ☎ *242/373–7858.*

★ **Sun & Sea Outfitters.** This store sells everything water-related, from snorkel equipment and marine animal T-shirts to dolphin jewelry, toys, and swimsuits. ⊠ *UNEXSO, Port Lucaya Marketplac* ☎ *242/373–1244.*

SPORTS AND THE OUTDOORS

BIKING

By virtue of its flat terrain, broad avenues, and long straight stretches of highway, Grand Bahama is perfect for bicycling. There's a designated biking lane on Midshipman Road.

When biking, wear sunblock, carry a bottle of water, and keep left when riding on the road. Inexpensive bicycle rentals (about $20 a day plus deposit) are available from some resorts, and the Viva Wyndham Fortuna Beach allows guests free use of bicycles.

Grand Bahama Nature Tours. For a biking tour that takes you sightseeing from a native settlement to Garden of the Groves, contact Grand Bahama Nature Tours. The 10-mile, five-hour tour includes beachside lunch for $79 per person. ⊠ *Lucaya* ☎ *866/440–4542, 242/373–2485* ⊕ *www.grandbahamanaturetours.com.*

BOATING AND FISHING

CHARTERS

Private boat charters for up to four people cost $100 per person and up for a half day. Bahamian law limits the catching of game fish to six each of dolphinfish, kingfish, tuna, or wahoo per vessel.

★ **Bonefish Folley & Sons.** Bonefish Folley & Sons can take you deep-sea fishing or flats fishing. "Bonefish," now almost 90 years old and a legend in these parts, makes fewer trips than his two sons. Rates are negotiable. ⊠ *West End* ☎ *242/646–9504* ⊕ *www.web-wrx.com/sites/tommy.*

Capt. Phil & Mel's Bonefishing Guide Services. Capt. Phil & Mel's Bonefishing Guide Services provides a colorful and expert foray into the specialized world of bonefishing. A whole day (eight hours) for up to two people will run you $450, transportation included; a half day costs $350. ⊠ *McLean's Town* ☎ *242/441–0863, 877/613–2454* ⊕ *www.bahamasbonefishing.net.*

Reef Tours Ltd. This company offers deep-sea fishing for four to six people on custom boats. Equipment and bait are provided free. All vessels are licensed, inspected, and insured. Trips run from 8:30 to 12:15 and from 1 to 4:45, weather permitting ($130 per angler, $60 per spectator).

DID YOU KNOW?

Most dive operations in the Bahamas offer certification programs. If you are simply looking to scuba on your vacation, opt for a resort course that provides enough instruction to get you into the water for a few dives. If you find scuba is your new favorite adventure, get full open-water certification. Initial certification in the Bahamas costs about $600. To save valuable vacation and bottom time, you can often begin your instruction at home.

TOUR OPERATORS

CRUISES

Reef Tours Ltd. ☎ *242/373–5880* ⊕ *www.bahamasvacationguide.com/ reeftours.*

Seaworld Explorer ☎ *242/373– 7863* ⊕ *www.superiorwatersports. com.*

Smiling Pat's Adventures ☎ *242/533–2946* ⊕ *www.smilingpat. com.*

Superior Watersports ☎ *242/373– 7863* ⊕ *www.superiorwatersports. com.*

ECOTOURS

Calabash Eco Adventures ☎ *242/727–1974* ⊕ *www. calabashecoadventures.com.*

Grand Bahama Nature Tours ☎ *242/373–2485, 866/440–4542* ⊕ *www.grandbahamanaturetours. com.*

ISLAND TOURS

Executive Tours ☎ *242/373–7863* ⊕ *www.superiorwatersports.com/ executive.*

H.Forbes Charter & Tours ☎ *242/352–9311* ⊕ *www. forbescharter.com.*

Full-day trips are also available, as are bottom-fishing excursions, glass-bottom boat tours, snorkeling trips, and sailing–snorkeling cruises. Reservations are essential. ⊠ *Port Lucaya Marketplace* ☎ *242/373–5880* ⊕ *www.bahamasvacationguide.com/reeftours.*

MARINAS

Grand Bahama Yacht Club at Lucayan Marina Village. Grand Bahama Yacht Club at Lucayan Marina Village offers guests complimentary ferry service to Port Lucaya; the marina has 125 slips accommodating boats up to 175 feet long, a fuel dock, swimming pools, a bar and grill, transportation to customs and immigrations, and a clubhouse. ⊠ *Midshipman Rd., Port Lucaya* ☎ *242/373–8888* ⊕ *www.lucayanmarina.com.*

★ **Old Bahama Bay Resort & Yacht Harbour.** Old Bahama Bay has 72 slips to accommodate yachts up to 120 feet long. Facilities include a customs and immigration office, fuel, showers, laundry, and electric, cable, and water hookups. ⊠ *West End* ☎ *242/350–6500.*

Port Lucaya Marina. Here you can find a broad range of water sports, free wireless Internet access, and a pump-out station; the marina has 106 slips for vessels no longer than 190 feet. Customs and immigrations officials are on-site full-time. ⊠ *Port Lucaya Marketplace* ☎ *242/373–9090* ⊕ *www.portlucayamarina.com.*

CRICKET

Lucaya Cricket Club. For a taste of true Bahamian sports, visit the Lucaya Cricket Club. If you feel like joining in, go to training sessions on Tuesday, Thursday, or Sunday. Visitors can use equipment free of charge. The clubhouse has a bar, gym, and changing rooms. Tournaments take place at Easter and Thanksgiving times. ⊠ *Baloa Rd., Lucaya* ☎ *242/373–1460* ⊕ *www.lucayacricketclub.com.*

GOLF

Fortune Hills Golf & Country Club. Fortune Hills Golf & Country Club is a 3,453-yard, 9-hole, par-36 course—a Dick Wilson and Joe Lee design—with a restaurant, bar, and pro shop. ⊠ *E. Sunrise Hwy.* ☎ *242/373–2222* 🖃 *$50 for 9 holes, $64 for 18 holes, cart included. Club rental $16 for 9 holes, $20 for 18 holes* ☻ *Restaurant closed Mon.*

Fodor's Choice ★ **Our Lucaya Beach and Golf Resort Lucayan Course.** This golf course, designed by Dick Wilson, is a dramatic 6,824-yard, par-72, 18-hole course featuring a balanced six straight holes, six classic left-turning doglegs, and six right-turning holes. The 18th hole has a double lake, towering limestone structure, and a clubhouse nearby. Its state-of-the-art instruction facilities include a practice putting green with bunker and chipping areas, covered teaching bays, and a teaching seminar area. A shared electric cart is included in greens fees. Ask about special "twilight" fees that are as low as $55 for 9 holes. ⊠ *Our Lucaya Beach and Golf Resort* ☎ *242/373–2002, 866/870–7148* ⊕ *www.ourlucaya.com/golf/the-lucayan-course* 🖃 *Resort guests $120, nonguests $130.*

Our Lucaya Beach and Golf Resort Reef Course. Our Lucaya Beach and Golf Resort Reef Course is a par-72, 6,930-yard course designed by Robert Trent Jones Jr., with lots of water (on 13 of the holes), wide fairways flanked by strategically placed bunkers, and a tricky dogleg left on the 18th hole. ⊠ *Our Lucaya Beach and Golf Resort* ☎ *242/373–2002* ⊕ *www.ourlucaya.com/golf/the-reef-course* 🖃 *Resort guests $120, nonguests $130.*

Ruby Golf Course. This course reopened in 2008 with renovated landscaping but basically the same 18-hole, par-72 Jim Fazio design—a lot of sand traps and challenges on holes 7, 9, 10, and 18—especially playing from the blue tees. Hole 10 requires a tee shot onto a dogleg right fairway around a pond. There's a small restaurant-bar and pro shop at the 18th hole. ⊠ *West Sunrise Hwy. and Wentworth Ave., Freeport* ☎ *242/352–1851* 🖃 *$65–$90.*

FLYING TEETH

Known in some parts as no-see-ums, what the Bahamians call the practically invisible sand flies are a force to be reckoned with, especially at the West End. At and after sunset they come out in force on still nights, and their bites can result in itchy red welts. Dress in long sleeves and pants or apply a repellent. Avon's Skin-So-Soft lotion is the generally accepted deterrent, and Old Bahama Bay resort considerately stocks its rooms with a bottle.

HORSEBACK RIDING

Pinetree Stables. Pinetree Stables runs eco-trail and beach rides twice a day. All two-hour trail rides are accompanied by a guide—no previous riding experience is necessary, but riders must be at least eight years old. Reservations are essential. ⊠ *Freeport* ☎ *242/373–3600, 305/433–4809* ⊕ *www.pinetree-stables.com* 🖃 *$99 for a 2-hr beach ride.*

Horseback riding on the beach

KAYAKING

★ **Grand Bahama Nature Tours.** Grand Bahama Nature Tours leads group kayaking tours of Lucayan National Park and other custom tours. ✉ *Lucaya* ☎ *242/373–2485, 866/440–4542* ⊕ *www.grandbahama-naturetours.com.*

Ocean Motion Watersports. Here you can rent one- and two-person sea kayaks for $20–$25 per hour. ✉ *Our Lucaya Beach and Golf Resort, Freeport* ☎ *242/374–2425, 242/373–2139* ⊕ *www.oceanmotionbahamas.com.*

PARASAILING

Ocean Motion Watersports. Ocean Motion Watersports charges $70 for its flights from Lucaya Beach. It also has Hobie Cat and WaveRunner rentals, waterskiing and banana-boat rides, and a water trampoline. ✉ *Our Lucaya Beach and Golf Resort, Freeport* ☎ *242/374–2425, 242/373–9603* ⊕ *www.oceanmotionbahamas.com.*

Paradise Watersports. Paradise Watersports has parasailing towboats and offers five-minute flights for $70. ✉ *Island Seas Resort, Freeport* ☎ *242/373–4001, 954/237-6660 US* ⊕ *www.the-bahamas-watersports.com/paradisewatersports.*

PERSONAL WATERCRAFT

Ocean Motion Watersports. You can rent WaveRunners for $75 per half hour and conducts one-hour guided tours for $150 per one- to two-person craft. ✉ *Our Lucaya Beach and Golf Resort, Freeport* ☎ *242/374–2425, 242/373–2139* ⊕ *www.oceanmotionbahamas.com.*

SCUBA DIVING

An extensive reef system runs along Little Bahama Bank's edge; sea gardens, caves, and colorful reefs rim the bank all the way from the West End to Freeport–Lucaya and beyond. The variety of dive sites suits everyone from the novice to the advanced diver, and ranges from 10 to 100-plus feet deep. Many dive operators offer a "discover" or "resort" course where first-timers can try out open-water scuba diving with a short pool course and an instructor at their side.

SITES

Ben's Blue Hole. This horseshoe-shape ledge overlooks a blue hole in 40 to 60 feet of water.

Pygmy Caves. Pygmy Caves, for moderately experienced divers, provides a formation of overgrown ledges that cut into the reef.

Sea Hunt. This shallow dive is named for the *Sea Hunt* television show, portions of which were filmed here.

Shark Junction. One of Grand Bahama Island's signature dive sites, made famous by the UNEXSO dive operation, Shark Junction is a 45-foot dive where 4- to 6-foot reef sharks hang out, along with moray eels, stingrays, nurse sharks, and grouper. UNEXSO provides orientation and a shark feeding with its dives here.

Spid City. Spid City has an aircraft wreck, dramatic coral formations, blue parrot fish, and an occasional shark. You'll dive about 40 to 60 feet down.

Theo's Wreck. For divers with some experience, Theo's Wreck, a 228-foot cement hauler, was sunk in 1982 in 100 feet of water.

OPERATORS

Caribbean Divers. This dive operator offers guided tours; NAUI, PADI, and SSI instruction; and equipment rental. A resort course allows you to use equipment in a pool and then in a closely supervised open dive for $120. A one-tank dive costs $45. Shark-feeding (two-tank) dives are $105. The boat resides right on the channel leading out to the sea, so rides to most major sites are about five minutes. Lodging packages with Bell Channel Inn are available.

HERE'S WHERE

The last time locals spotted pirates on Grand Bahama Island was in 2005 when Johnny Depp and his crew were filming the second and third movies in the *Pirates of the Caribbean* series. They used a special device in Gold Rock Creek at one of the world's largest open-water filming tanks to give the illusion that the pirate ship was pitching and yawing. You can view the set at the new Gold Rock Beach access about 3 mi past Lucayan National Park.

✉ *Bell Channel Inn, opposite Port Lucaya* ☎ *242/373–9111* ⊕ *www. bellchannelinn.com.*

Fodor's Choice   **UNEXSO (Underwater Explorers Society).** This world-renowned scuba-div-
★   ing facility with its own 17-foot dive pool, provides rental equipment, guides, and boats. A wide variety of dives is available for beginners and experienced divers, starting at $109 for a Discover Scuba Reef Diving resort course. UNEXSO and its sister company, the Dolphin Experience, are known for their work with Atlantic bottlenose dolphins. ✉ *Port Lucaya Marketplace* ☎ *242/373–1244, 800/992–3483* ⊕ *www.unexso.com.*

SNORKELING

☺   **Paradise Cove.** Here you can snorkel right offshore at Deadman's Reef,
★   a two-system reef with water ranging from extremely shallow to 35 feet deep. It's considered the island's best spot for snorkeling off the beach—you're likely to see lots of angelfish, barracudas, rays, and the occasional sea turtle. There is an access fee of $3 per person; snorkel equipment rentals are available for $15 a day, $5 an hour extra for wet suits or $3 for ski belts. Try the battery-operated Seascooters, which pull you through the water, for $25 an hour. For $41, a snorkel tour includes a briefing, narrated transportation, equipment, and lunch ($35 without lunch). It's a great deal, especially if you go early and stay late. ✉ *Deadman's Reef, 8 mi east of West End turnoff* ☎ *242/349–2677* ⊕ *www.deadmansreef.com.*

Paradise Watersports. Paradise Watersports offers a 90-minute reef snorkeling cruise for $40. ✉ *Island Seas Resort, Freeport* ☎ *242/373–4001* ⊕ *www.the-bahamas-watersports.com/paradisewatersports.*

☺   **Pat & Diane Fantasia Tours.** Pat & Diane Fantasia Tours takes snorkelers to a shallow reef on cruises aboard a fun-boat catamaran with a 30-foot rock-climbing wall and slide into the water. The fee is $40 ($25 for children ages 6–13) for the two-hour trip. ✉ *Port Lucaya Marina* ☎ *242/373–8681, 888/275–3603* ⊕ *www.snorkelingbahamas.com.*

TENNIS

★   **Our Lucaya Beach and Golf Resort Tennis Center.** Here there are four lighted courts: grass, rebound, French red clay, and deco-turf. Wimbledon-white tennis attire is required on the grass court. Racquet rental and stringing, lessons, and clinics are available. ✉ *Our Lucaya Beach and Golf Resort* ☎ *242/373–1333* ▭ *$25–$100 per hr.*

The Abacos

WORD OF MOUTH

"If you are looking for simple, laid back, peaceful, and casual, then the Abacos are a good place to start. Before my first trip there, a friend and travel agent told me that "getting dressed for dinner in the Abacos meant putting on earrings" and I think that is still true— shorts, flip flops, bathing suit, and you are ready to go."

—ishkribbl

WELCOME TO THE ABACOS

TOP REASONS TO GO

★ **Bonefish the Marls:** One of the most spectacular bonefishing flats anywhere, the Marls is an endless maze of lush mangrove creeks, hidden bays, and sandy cays. Hire a professional guide to show you the best spots.

★ **Cay-hop:** Rent a boat and spend a day (or more) skipping among 150 cays. Settle onto your own private strip of beach and enjoy.

★ **Beach bash:** When the Gully Roosters play on Green Turtle Cay, the island rocks. Stop in at Miss Emily's Blue Bee Bar first for a mind-altering rum, pineapple juice, and apricot brandy Goombay Smash; it's where the popular drink was born. On Great Guana Cay, Nippers' Sunday pig roast is the best beach party of the year—and it happens every week.

★ **Swim with the fishies:** With clear shallow waters and a series of colorful coral reefs extending for miles, the Abacos provide both the novice and the experienced underwater explorer plenty of visual stimulation.

GETTING ORIENTED

The Abacos, 200 mi east of Palm Beach, Florida, are the northernmost chain of cays in the Bahamas. Covering 120 mi, this miniarchipelago offers both historic settlements and uninhabited islands. Great Abaco is the main island, the chain's largest and its most populated. Here you'll find rugged stretches of white limestone bluffs, miles of kelp-strewn beaches devoid of footprints, landlocked lakes, pine forests where wild horses and boar roam, and the Bahamas' third-largest community: the thriving commercial center of Marsh Harbour. Up north on Little Abaco, a smaller cay connected by bridge, tourism is less prominent and locals live as they have for the last hundred years. Running parallel 5 mi off the west coast of these islands are the Abaco Cays, including Green Turtle, Great Guana, Man-O-War, and Elbow, all of which offer full services for boaters and just the right sprinkling of small resorts and enchanting settlements. The majority of the other 146 cays are uninhabited.

1 Great Abaco Island. The Abacos' commercial center still boasts fishing and farming communities, blue holes, caves, wild parrots, and pine forests. Marsh Harbour, the island's main hub, has great restaurants and bustling nightlife. Treasure Cay has a large marina, the only public golf course, and one of the best beaches in the world. Other communities are quiet and tucked away, each with its own personality that makes them worthy day trips.

2 Elbow Cay. Home of the famous candy cane–striped Hope Town Lighthouse, this cay balances a historic getaway with modern conveniences. Hope Town, the main settlement, is known for neat clapboard cottages painted in pastel hues.

3 Man-O-War Cay. Proud of its stance as a dry island (no liquor sold), this community holds fast to its history. It's famous for its boatbuilding, which can still be seen here daily on the waterfront, where men work by hand.

4 Great Guana Cay. A real getaway island, here you'll find modern luxuries or empty beaches. Guana also has Nippers, a restaurant-bar with the best party scene in Abaco.

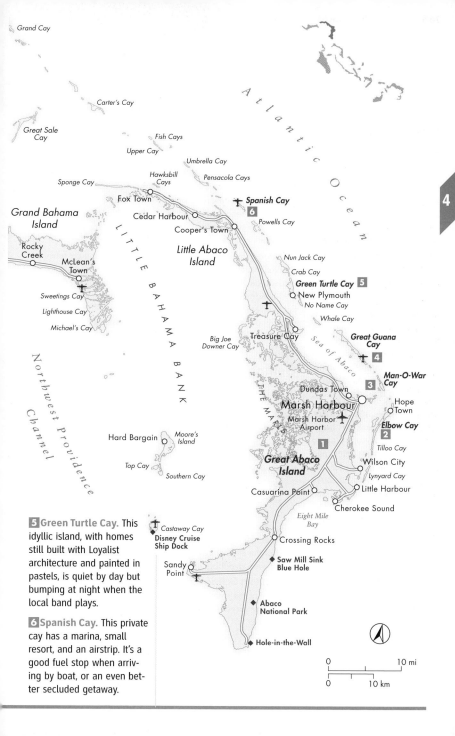

Grand Cay

Atlantic Ocean

Carter's Cay

Great Sale Cay

Fish Cays

Upper Cay

Umbrella Cay

Sponge Cay

Hawksbill Cays

Pensacola Cays

Fox Town

✝ *Spanish Cay* **6**

Grand Bahama Island

Cedar Harbour

Powells Cay

Cooper's Town

Rocky Creek

McLean's Town

Little Abaco Island

Nun Jack Cay

Crab Cay

Green Turtle Cay **5**

Sweetings Cay

New Plymouth

No Name Cay

Lighthouse Cay

Whale Cay

Michael's Cay

Big Joe Downer Cay

✝

Treasure Cay

Sea of Abaco

Great Guana Cay

✝ **4**

Man-O-War Cay

3

Dundas Town

Hope Town

Marsh Harbour

Marsh Harbor Airport

Elbow Cay **2**

Northwest Providence Channel

Hard Bargain

Moore's Island

Tilloo Cay

Top Cay

Southern Cay

1

Great Abaco Island

Wilson City

Lynyard Cay

Casuarina Point

Little Harbour

Cherokee Sound

5 Green Turtle Cay. This idyllic island, with homes still built with Loyalist architecture and painted in pastels, is quiet by day but bumping at night when the local band plays.

Eight Mile Bay

✝ Castaway Cay
Disney Cruise Ship Dock

Crossing Rocks

Sandy Point

◆ Saw Mill Sink Blue Hole

6 Spanish Cay. This private cay has a marina, small resort, and an airstrip. It's a good fuel stop when arriving by boat, or an even better secluded getaway.

✝

◆ Abaco National Park

◆ Hole-in-the-Wall

0   10 mi

0   10 km

4

THE ABACOS PLANNER

When to Go

June, July, and early August are the best months for sailing, boating, and swimming, precisely why the most popular regatta and fishing tournaments are held during this time. Afternoon thunderstorms are common but usually clear quickly. Temperatures can reach the 90s.

December through May is a pleasant time to visit, with temperatures in the 70s and 80s, though sometimes dropping into the 50s at night when cold fronts blow through. Fishing, particularly deep-sea fishing, is good during this time of year.

In September and October, typically the peak of hurricane season, visitors drop to a trickle and many hotels and restaurants shut down for two weeks to two months. If you're willing to take a chance on getting hit by a storm, this can still be a great time to explore, with discounts of as much as 50% at the hotels that remain open.

Getting Here

Most flights land at the international airports in **Marsh Harbour (MHH)** (☎ 242/367–5500) or **Treasure Cay (TCB)** (☎ 242/225–2047). Taxis wait at the main airports, and the fare to most resorts is between $15 and $30 for the first two passengers and $3 for each additional person. Cab fare between Marsh Harbour and Treasure Cay or the ferry dock is $85.

The *Legacy* mail boat leaves Potter's Cay, Nassau on Tuesday for Marsh Harbour and Green Turtle Cay, returning to Nassau on Thursday. The *Sealink* leaves Nassau on Friday and Sunday mornings for Sandy Point, at the southern tip of Great Abaco, and returns to Nassau on Fridays and Sundays. For details, call the **Dockmaster's Office** (☎ 242/393–1064).

Getting Around

By Boat A good system of public ferries allows you to reach even the most remote cays. (⇨ *See Getting Here and Around within the island sections.*)

If you don't want to be bound by the somewhat limited ferry schedule, rent a small boat. The best selections are at Marsh Harbour, Treasure Cay, Hope Town, and Green Turtle Cay.

By Car On Great Abaco, renting a car is the best option if you plan on exploring outside Marsh Harbour or Treasure Cay. Rentals start at $70 a day, and gasoline costs between $5 and $6 per gallon. Cars are not necessary on most of the smaller cays in the Abacos; in fact, rental cars aren't even available in most locations.

By Golf Cart Golf carts are the vehicle of choice on the majority of the smaller cays, including Elbow Cay, Green Turtle Cay, Great Guana Cay, and Man-O-War Cay. Rates are $40 to $50 per day, or $245 per week. Reservations are essential from April to July.

By Taxi Taxi service is available on Great Abaco in Marsh Harbour and Treasure Cay. Hotels will arrange for taxis to take you on short trips and to the airport. Fares are generally $1.50 per mile. A 15% tip is customary.

About the Restaurants

Fish, conch, land crabs, and rock lobster—called crawfish by the locals—have long been the bedrock of local cuisine. Although a few menus, mostly in upscale resorts, feature dishes with international influences, most restaurants in the Abacos still serve simple Bahamian fare, with a few nods to American tastes. There are some fancier restaurants in Marsh Harbour, Treasure Cay, and Hope Town, but most restaurants are relaxed about attire and reasonably priced. Some offer live music, and shape the nightlife scene on weekends.

Lunch usually costs about $15 per person, and you can easily spend upward of $30 apiece at dinner, without drinks.

About the Hotels

Intimate hotels, cottage-style resorts, and rental homes are the rule in the Abacos. There are a few full-scale resorts in Marsh Harbour, Treasure Cay, Green Turtle Cay, and Hope Town—with multiple restaurants, bars, pools, and activities—but most accommodations are more homey. What you might give up in modern amenities you'll gain in privacy and beauty. Many hotels have water views, and with a cottage or private house you may even get your own stretch of beach. Air-conditioning is a standard feature, and more places are adding luxuries like satellite TV and wireless Internet. Small and remote doesn't equate with inexpensive, however; it's difficult to find lodging for less than $100 a night, and not uncommon to pay more than $300 a night for beachside accommodations with all the conveniences. Still, the Abacos remains affordable when compared to other islands.

WHAT IT COSTS IN DOLLARS

	¢	$	$$	$$$	$$$$
Restaurants	under $10	$10–$20	$20–$30	$30–$40	over $40
Hotels	under $100	$100–$200	$200–$300	$300–$400	over $400

Restaurant prices are based on the median main course price at dinner, excluding gratuity, typically 15%, which is often automatically added to the bill. Hotel prices are for two people in a standard double room in high season, excluding service and 6%–12% tax.

Essentials

Banks Banks are generally open Monday–Thursday 9:30–3 and Friday until 4:30. They are sometimes closed on Wednesday. ATMs are available in Marsh Harbour at all banks.

Car Rentals A & P Rentals ⊠ *Marsh Harbour* ☎ *242/367-2655.* **Rental Wheels of Abaco** ⊠ *Marsh Harbour* ☎ *242/367-4643.*

Emergencies Green Turtle Cay Government Clinic ☎ *242/365-4028.* **Hope Town Government Clinic** ☎ *242/366-0108.* **Marsh Harbour Government Clinic** ☎ *242/367-2510.* **Police or Fire Emergencies** ☎ *919.*

Golf Cart Rentals Blue Marlin Rentals ⊠ *Treasure Cay* ☎ *242/365-8687.* **D & P Rentals** ⊠ *Green Turtle Cay* ☎ *242/365-4655.* **Hope Town Cart Rentals** ⊠ *Hope Town* ☎ *242/366-0064.* **Island Cart Rentals** ⊠ *Hope Town* ☎ *242/366-0448.* **Man-O-War Marina** ⊠ *Man-O-War Cay* ☎ *242/365-6008.* **T&N Cart Rentals** ⊠ *Hope Town* ☎ *242/366-0069.*

Visitor Information Abaco Tourist Office ⊠ *Marsh Harbour* ☎ *242/367-3067* ⊕ *www. bahamas.com.*

ABACO BEACHES

(above and lower right)
Treasure Cay Beach

From island-long stretches to strips as short as your boat, with powder-white to warm-cream sand, the roar of the surf or the silence of a slow rising tide, the Abacos have a beach suited to everyone's liking. And most likely, you'll find a secluded spot to call your own.

Oceanside beaches are long expanses of white powder that change their form throughout the year depending on the surge brought in by weather. Beaches sheltered from strong winds, on the lee sides of islands, are small, narrow, and stable. Trees are taller on the lee sides of the islands and provide shaded areas for picnics. On the outer cays beaches make popular surf spots and snorkel sites, with the barrier reef running along the shore. Most Abaco beaches are secluded, but if you're looking for a beach party, head to Great Guana Cay for the Sunday pig roast.

RED BAYS

Just north of Marsh Harbour eroded rocks offshore give the beaches a distinct red-brown color. Some people think this is the result of ancient deposits of windblown soil from the Sahara. These beaches are smaller than the more popular beaches, and run along the shore in a series of small scalloped curves. They are only accessible through old logging trails, but are secluded and unique to the area.

THE ABACOS' BEST BEACHES

GUANA CAY BEACH

The beaches on Guana Cay stretch along much of the island's ocean side and are often only separated by rocky outcroppings. The sand here is slightly courser and is more cream-color, with speckles of pink from wave-ground corals. Surfing is popular here, too, especially on the northern beaches. The North Side Beach, as it is known by locals, offers both long quiet walks and Sunday pig roasts at Nippers restaurant, one of the best beach parties in the Bahamas.

PELICAN CAY BEACH

In a protected park, this is a great spot for snorkeling and diving on nearby Sandy Cay reef. The cay is small and between two ocean cuts, so the water drops off quickly but its location is also what nurtures the beach's pure white sand. If you get restless, ruins of an old house are hidden in overgrowth at the top of the cay, and offers fantastic views of the park.

SANDY POINT BEACH

If shelling and solitude are your thing, venture 50 miles southwest of Marsh Harbour to the sleepy fishing village of Sandy Point. Large shells wash up on the sandy beaches, making it great for a stroll and shelling. The best spot for picking up one of nature's souvenirs is between the picnic site and Rocky Point.

Well offshore is the private island Castaway Cay, where Disney Cruise Line guests spend a day.

TAHITI BEACH

This small beach at the southern tip of Elbow Cay is a popular boater's stop. The soft white sand is well protected from the close ocean cut by thick vegetation, a few barrier cays, and shallow water. This shallow area is popular for shelling, and of course simply relaxing and watching the tide rise. At low tide the true beauty of this beach is revealed when a long sand spit emerges, perfect for picnics. It's great for young children, as the water on one side of the spit is ankle deep, stays calm, and remains warm. During peak season the beach can become a bit crowded.

TREASURE CAY BEACH

This beach is world famous for its expanse of truly powderlike sand and turquoise water. On the beach's southern end is a bar and grill with a couple of shade-bearing huts. The rest of the beach is clear from development, since the land is privately owned, and almost clear of footprints. With a top-notch marina across the road and lunch a short stroll away, you have luxury; a walk farther down the beach gives you a quiet escape.

ABACO NATIONAL PARK

The Abaco National Park was established in 1994 as a sanctuary for the endangered Abaco parrot, of which there are fewer than 3,000. Many other birds call the park home, including the Bahama yellowthroat and pine warbler.

(above) Abaco Parrot (lower right) Hole-in-the-Wall Lighthouse

A 15-mi dirt track passes through the 20,500 protected acres, ending at the Hole-in-the-Wall lighthouse, a starkly beautiful and desolate location overlooking the ocean. The drive from the paved highway all the way to the lighthouse takes about 1½ hours, and can only be done in a 4X4 vehicle. The lighthouse is not technically open to visitors, but people still do climb the rickety stairs to the top where views of the island and the sea are mesmerizing. ⊠ *South end of Great Abaco Island, before you make the final turn on the main road leading to Sandy Point* ☎ *242/367–3067.*

BEST TIME TO GO

Berries ripen in fall and spring, and the parrots become active. The best time to spot the birds is early morning, when they move out of the forest to feed. Temperatures then are also ideal, in the 70s and 80s. The annual bird counts in North and South Abaco held at the beginning of each year are a good opportunity to work with other bird-watchers to gather information on the parrots, which is sent to the Audobon Society.

BEST WAYS TO EXPLORE

DRIVE TO HOLE-IN-THE-WALL LIGHTHOUSE

Take the 15-mi, 1½-hour drive along a dirt trail out to the lighthouse. This is the only part of the park you can drive. This lighthouse has spectacular views of the coast. Take a packed lunch and have a picnic on a ledge overlooking the ocean.

GUIDED TOUR

For the best experience, arrange a guided tour with the tourist office. A knowledgeable guide will walk or drive you through the park, pointing out plant and animal species. If you're an early riser, join a bird-watching tour to find the endangered Abaco parrot, as well as other avian beauties that reside here. Walking the park alone is not recommended, as poisonous wood saplings are a problem if you don't know how to identify them.

Note: Friends of the Environment (☎ 242/367–2721) is a local education organization that offers more information on the park and the parrots.

FUN FACT

The park's pine forest is prone to summer lightning fires, but the Abaco pine is extremely resistant and actually depends on the fires to remove dense underbrush that would otherwise smother it. The Abaco parrots nest in holes in the limestone floor to escape the flames. Unfortunately, this makes them vulnerable to feral cats and raccoons that threaten their population.

FOWL CAY NATIONAL RESERVE

This quarter-mile reef located on the ocean side of Fowl Cay is a great snorkeling and dive spot. It's well known among divers for its tunnels and wide variety of fish. On the opposite side of Fowl Cay is a small sand spit, which makes a great spot to reconvene for a sun-soaked picnic.

PELICAN CAYS LAND AND SEA PARK

This 2,000-acre land and marine park is protected and maintained by the Bahamas National Trust. The park's preserved reef is only 25 feet under water, making it an easy snorkel excursion. It's also a great dive site, as the variety of life here is astounding. Nearby is an incredibly soft beach, great for a post-swim picnic.

Updated by
Justin Higgs

The attitude of the Abacos might best be expressed by the sign posted in the window of Vernon's Grocery in Hope Town: "If you're looking for Wal-Mart—it's 200 miles to the right." In other words, the residents of this chain of more than 100 islands know that there's another world out there, but don't necessarily care to abandon theirs, which is a little more traditional, slow-paced, and out of the way than most alternatives.

Here you'll feel content in an uncrowded environment, yet still have access to whatever level of accommodations and services you desire. Ecotourism is popular, and aficionados have revitalized exploration of Abacos' Caribbean pine forests, which are home to wild boar, wild horses, the rare Abaco parrot, and myriad other bird and plant life. Hiking and biking through these forests and along abandoned beaches at the forest's edges are popular activities. Sea kayaking in pristine protected areas also provides a rewarding sense of adventure, and more conventional activities such as golf, tennis, and beach volleyball are available, too. But if you don't feel like doing anything at all, that's also a highly rated activity.

Of course, this is the Bahamas, so you shouldn't neglect activities happening in one of its most magnificent assets—the water. Snorkeling and diving have long been staple activities for visitors. Abaconians are proud of their marine environment and have worked with the government to protect some of the more vibrant reefs. The islands' calm, naturally protected waters, long admired for their beauty, have also helped the area become the Bahamas' sailing capital. Man-O-War Cay remains the Bahamas' boatbuilding center; its residents turn out traditionally crafted wood dinghies as well as high-tech fiberglass craft. The Abacos play host annually to internationally famous regattas and to a half dozen game-fish tournaments.

GREAT ITINERARIES

IF YOU HAVE 3 DAYS

Make your base in **Marsh Harbour**, the largest settlement in the Abacos, and where you'll most likely fly in. Spend the first day exploring the city or a nearby beach, then have a leisurely dinner at one of the local restaurants overlooking the busy harbor. If you arrive on a weekend you can probably find a bar with live island music. On Day 2, get up early and take the 20-minute ferry to **Hope Town**, the **Elbow Cay** settlement often considered the most lovely in the Abacos. Here you can rent a boat and take a snorkel trip out to the reefs, take a historical walk, kayak, stroll the beach, or rent a golf cart and explore outside the settlement. Day 3 brings a choice: for another dose of Loyalist history, take the ferry again, this time to **Man-O-War Cay**, the boatbuilding capital of the region; or stay put and book a diving or fishing trip out of one of the Marsh Harbour marinas.

IF YOU HAVE 5 DAYS

On Day 4, drive to **Treasure Cay** and hit the links, where the 18-hole course is considered one of the finest in the Bahamas and Caribbean. Afterward, catch the ferry to **Green Turtle Cay**, your base for the next two days. Stroll through **New Plymouth**, wandering through the sculpture garden and the **Albert Lowe Museum**. After lunch, spend the afternoon at a beach, then dress up for a fancy dinner at one of the two fine resorts on **White Sound**. On your last day, rent a small boat and visit some of the uninhabited nearby cays, where the snorkeling and deserted white-sand beaches are sublime.

IF YOU HAVE 7 DAYS

On Day 6, head back to Marsh Harbour and take a ferry to **Great Guana Cay**, which has some of the most gorgeous beaches in the Abacos and one of the best party-scene restaurants, **Nippers**. On your last day, back in Marsh Harbour, rent a car and explore the southern reaches of **Great Abaco Island**, perhaps searching for the endangered Bahama parrot at the **Bahamas National Trust Sanctuary**, or checking out the bronze sculptures at **Pete Johnston's Foundry** in **Little Harbour**.

If all that sounds like too much work, consider experiencing life like a local: bring some books, sunblock, and a few swimsuits; rent a cottage, a dinghy, and a golf cart, perhaps on **Elbow Cay** or **Great Guana Cay**; and learn to practice the fine art of relaxation.

4

GREAT ABACO ISLAND

If arriving by air, your trip will most likely begin on Great Abaco, the main island. It's bordered on its eastern side by a chain of cays that extend from the north to about midway down the island, and on the western side by a fishing flat called the Marls, a shallow-water area of mangrove creeks and islands. Great Abaco was once logged for its pine trees, and traveling by car allows you to access many old logging trails that will lead you to secluded beaches along the coast. The island is home to wild horses, cows, and boars, and the endangered Abaco parrots, who make their homes in the pine forests.

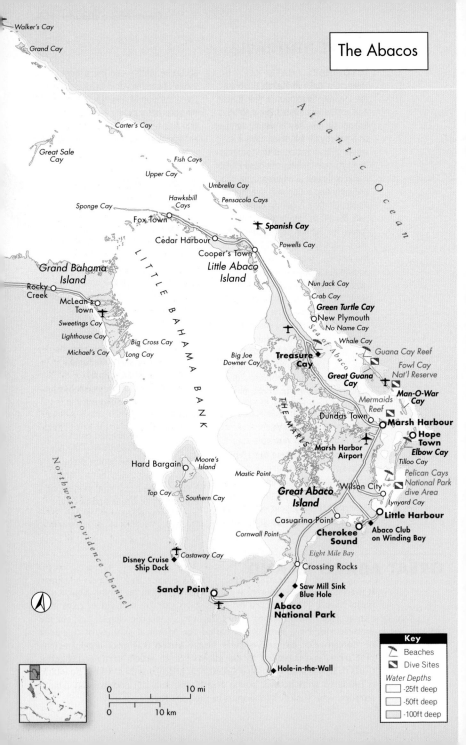

The Abacos

Walker's Cay

Grand Cay

Carter's Cay

Great Sale Cay

Fish Cays

Upper Cay

Umbrella Cay

Hawksbill Cays

Pensacola Cays

Sponge Cay

Fox Town

Spanish Cay

Cedar Harbour

Powells Cay

Cooper's Town

Little Abaco Island

Grand Bahama Island

Rocky Creek

McLean's Town

Nun Jack Cay

Crab Cay

Green Turtle Cay

New Plymouth

No Name Cay

Sweetings Cay

Lighthouse Cay

Big Cross Cay

Michael's Cay

Long Cay

Whale Cay

Sea of Abaco

Guana Cay Reef

Big Joe Downer Cay

Treasure Cay

Great Guana Cay

Fowl Cay Nat'l Reserve

Man-O-War Cay

Mermaids Reef

Dundas Town

Marsh Harbour

Hard Bargain

Moore's Island

Mastic Point

Marsh Harbor Airport

Hope Town

Elbow Cay

Tilloo Cay

Top Cay

Southern Cay

Great Abaco Island

Wilson City

Pelican Cays National Park dive Area

Lynyard Cay

Casuarina Point

Little Harbour

Cornwall Point

Cherokee Sound

Abaco Club on Winding Bay

Disney Cruise Ship Dock

Castaway Cay

Eight Mile Bay

Crossing Rocks

Sandy Point

Saw Mill Sink Blue Hole

Abaco National Park

Hole-in-the-Wall

Atlantic Ocean

Northwest Providence Channel

LITTLE BAHAMA BANK

THE MARLS

Key

Beaches

Dive Sites

Water Depths

-25ft deep

-50ft deep

-100ft deep

0   10 mi

0   10 km

TOP FESTIVALS

WINTER

Many Abaco communities have their own **Junkanoo** celebrations; Hope Town has a New Year's Eve children's rushout for locals and visitors to join in. Parades in the Abacos are much smaller and more intimate than in Nassau, and far less competitive.

SPRING

Hope Town's annual **Heritage Day** in April celebrates the Loyalist settlement's history with traditional songs, speeches and exhibits on historical topics, and a boat parade.

The **Island Roots Festival** celebrates Bahamian traditions with an outdoor party on tiny Green Turtle Cay the first weekend in May.

SUMMER

Junkanoo Summer Festival— traditional summertime parties with dance troupes and musical groups— take place throughout summer in Marsh Harbour.

There are big cash prizes that increase with the number of registered boats at the Treasure Cay Billfish Championship in June. The final day includes a Lionfish Tournament designed to help save the Bahamas indigenous marine life from this relatively new predator.

Regatta Time in Abaco, the first week of July, stretches over several islands, with races and plenty of onshore parties.

Marsh Harbour is the main hub of activity on the island, and where most visitors stay. Heading north on the S.C. Bootle Highway will take you to **Treasure Cay** peninsula, a resort development. There's another, smaller, airport here. Farther north are **Cooper's Town** and the small communities of **Little Abaco**, which don't provide much for visitors besides nearly total seclusion. South of Marsh Harbour on the Ernest Dean Highway are artists' retreat **Little Harbour** and **Cherokee Sound** and **Sandy Point**, both small fishing communities.

GETTING HERE AND AROUND

To travel around Great Abaco you'll need a vehicle. Renting a car is the most convenient and economical option. If you plan on staying in one town or only making short, one-time, or one-way trips you can hire a taxi. Taxis will take you all over the island, but the farther you travel from Marsh Harbour, the more extreme rates get, sometimes in excess of a hundred dollars. The closest settlement worth a visit out of Marsh Harbour is Little Harbour, about 30 minutes away.

Golf carts are used locally in Treasure Cay and Cherokee Sound. From Marsh Harbour you can boat to Little Harbour and Cherokee Sound to the south and Treasure Cay in the north.

MARSH HARBOUR

Most visitors to the Abacos make their first stop in Marsh Harbour, the Bahamas' third-largest city and the Abacos' commercial center. Besides having the Abacos' largest international airport, it offers what boaters consider to be one of the easiest harbors to enter. It has several full-service marinas, including the 190-slip Boat Harbour Marina and the 80-slip Conch Inn Marina.

Marsh Harbour has a more diverse variety of restaurants, shops, and grocery items than other communities. Stock up on groceries and supplies on the way to other settlements or islands. The downtown area has several supermarkets with a decent selection, as well as a few department and hardware stores. If you need cash, this is the place to get it; banks here are open every day and have ATMs, neither of which you will find on the smaller, more remote settlements or cays.

> **DID YOU KNOW?**
>
> Bahamian currency includes a $3 bill. There's also a half-dollar bill and a 15-cent piece, which is square and decorated with a hibiscus. These three currencies are not frequently seen now, and make great souvenirs if you come across one. All Bahamian banknotes feature a prominent Bahamian political figure and a watermark thereof, as well as a see-through sand dollar. The colorful banknotes are printed in England, while all coins are minted in Canada.

WHERE TO EAT

$$$
BAHAMIAN
Fodor's Choice
★
✕ **Angler's Restaurant.** Dine on roasted rack of lamb with garlic mashed potatoes or a broiled lobster tail while overlooking gleaming rows of yachts moored in the Boat Harbour Marina at the Abaco Beach Resort. White tablecloths with fresh orchid arrangements and sea-blue napkins folded like seashells create an experience a step up from typical island dining. It's not uncommon to see guests dressed in sports coats and cocktail dresses fresh off a stunning megayacht alongside other guests in shorts and T-shirts with kids in tow. Everyone can enjoy fresh grilled catch of the day—don't pass up the grilled wahoo—seafood pastas, Bahamian chicken, or charbroiled steaks. For dessert, try the calorie-drenched guava duff. ✉ *Abaco Beach Resort, off Bay St.* ☎ *242/367–2158, 800/468–4799* ⊕ *www.abacoresort.com.*

¢
DELI
✕ **Bahamas Family Market.** At lunchtime the best bargains in town are at the lunch counter inside this small grocery. Jamaican meat pies stuffed with curried beef or chicken go for $4.50. A sandwich and bag of chips is just $5. At breakfast, go for a hearty Bahamian breakfast for $6 or snag a fresh-baked pastry and coffee for $3. There's no eating area, but they'll heat up your order if you'd like. It's also the perfect spot to pack your boat or car cooler for a picnic. ✉ *Queen Elizabeth Dr. at stoplight* ☎ *242/367–3714.*

$$
BAHAMIAN
✕ **Curly Tails Restaurant and Bar.** Enjoy kick-back harborside dining for lunch and dinner at the Conch Inn Hotel and Marina. Savor your meal outside on the open-air deck. At lunch, salads, burgers, cracked conch, and grouper fillets go great with a cold Kalik. Try dinner in the air-conditioned dining room. Fresh grilled snapper and mahimahi can be prepared with an Asian flair, while broiled lobster and tomato-smothered chicken are traditional favorites. If you're into sunsets, don't miss the daily happy hour. Sample a frozen Tail Curler or a Curlytini to go with your conch fritters. There's also live music every weekend. ✉ *Conch Inn Hotel and Marina, Bay St.* ☎ *242/367–4444* ⊕ *www.abacocurlytails. com* ☾ *Closed Tues.*

Mangoes waterfront restaurant on Marsh Harbour

$ ✕ **Jamie's Place.** There's nothing fancy about this clean, bright, diner-
BAHAMIAN style eatery, but the welcome is warm, the Bahamian dishes are well
executed, and the prices are right, with most meals clocking in under
$15. Choose fried chicken, cracked conch, or fresh-caught dolphin (also
called mahimahi), with a side of mashed or roasted potatoes, peas 'n'
rice, macaroni and cheese, or coleslaw. Jamie's is also an ice-cream
parlor, with a dozen flavors. Locals love this place, and it has stayed
one of Great Abaco Island's best-kept secrets. ✉ *Queen Elizabeth Dr.*
☎ *242/367–2880* ▭ *No credit cards.*

$$ ✕ **Jib Room.** Expect casual lunches of hot wings, conch burgers, fish nug-
BAHAMIAN gets, and steak wraps in this harbor-view restaurant and bar, located
inside the Marsh Harbour Marina. Dinner is served twice a week, and
these "barbecue nights" are especially popular; on Wednesday it's baby
back ribs, fish, chicken, potato salad, slaw, and baked beans. On Sat-
urday it's grilled steak, featuring New York strip, with fish and chicken
as options along with baked potatoes and salad. If you're dying for a
steak after a steady fish diet, these are the best in the Abacos. ✉ *Pelican
Shores* ☎ *242/367–2700* ⊕ *www.jibroom.com* ⌕ *Reservations essential*
☽ *Closed Sun.–Tues. No dinner Thurs. and Fri.*

$$ ✕ **Mangoes.** An open-air deck makes Mangoes a great place for water-
ECLECTIC side dining. Enjoy a traditional Bahamian breakfast; cracked conch and
★ zesty salads at lunch; at dinner try house specialties like smudder grouper, fried and seasoned with tomato, thyme, and pepper sauce; grilled
rack of lamb; or the catch of the day grilled, fried, or blackened. If it's
wahoo, order it grilled with lots of extra lime. The restaurant is housed
in a complex that contains a boutique selling resort wear and fine jewelry from around the world, and a 31-slip marina—which means you

can sail in from the offshore cays, tie up in front, enjoy a meal, and do some shopping. They also offer free Wi-Fi so you can check your emails while grabbing a bite to eat. ⊠ *Queen Elizabeth Dr.* ☎ *242/367–2366.*

¢   ✕**Show-Boo's Conch Salad Stand.** "Just be nice" implores the hand-let-
BAHAMIAN tered sign on this ramshackle stand between the Harbour View and Conch Inn marinas. Follow the instructions, and you'll be rewarded with what the proprietor claims to be "the world's best conch salad," often diced and mixed while you watch. Hours are erratic, especially during the September–November off-season. To find out if Show-Boo showed up for business, just swing by around lunchtime and see if there's a line forming in front of his stand. ⊠ *Queen Elizabeth Dr.* ☎ *No phone* ▭ *No credit cards* ⊘ *No dinner.*

$$ ✕**Snappas Grill and Chill.** Savvy boat people and in-the-know locals
BAHAMIAN hang out here in the Harbour View Marina. The polished-wood bar is the center of gravity around which the dining room sprawls outward toward the open-air waterside deck. Killer appetizers include grilled shrimp, chicken kebabs, and sizzling onion rings. For lunch the grilled-fish Caesar salad and the Snappa Filly are hard to beat. Fresh grilled catch of the day and grilled conch are crossover items that always hit the spot. When the sun goes down—the sunsets are dazzling—order a New York steak or grilled lobster with a garden salad. Want more? Party on with live music Wednesday and Saturday nights. ⊠ *Harbour View Marina, Bay St.* ☎ *242/367–2278* ⊕ *www.snappasbar.com.*

$$$ ✕**Wally's.** This two-story, pink colonial villa sits across Bay Street from
BAHAMIAN the marina, fronted by green lawns, hibiscus, and white-railed verandas.
★   This is the Abacos' most popular restaurant—*the* place to go for good food, potent rum cocktails, and serious people-watching. Lunch is a scene, especially if you sit outside, where you'll find a mix of locals, tourists, and boat people munching on Greek or Caesar salads, spicy grouper, and mahimahi burgers. Inside are a stylish bar, a boutique, and three dining rooms, all adorned with Haitian-style paintings. Dinner is served Friday and Saturday only, and the menu includes tarragon chicken, grilled wahoo, and tender lamb chops. Save room for the irresistible key lime pie. ⊠ *E. Bay St.* ☎ *242/367–2074* ⊿ *Reservations essential* ⊘ *Closed Sun. and Sept. and Oct. No dinner Mon.–Thurs.*

WHERE TO STAY

$$ 🖼 **Abaco Beach Resort and Boat Harbour.** One of the liveliest party spots
☾   on the island, this place rocks during the half-dozen fishing tourna-
Fodor'sChoice ments it hosts every year in spring and early summer. The boating
★   crowd keeps the place hopping the rest of the year as well, with a slight slowdown in August and September. The resort is set on 52 manicured acres overlooking the Sea of Abaco, just five minutes from the Marsh Harbour airport or a short ferry ride away from Hope Town on Elbow Cay. The spacious ocean-view rooms have natural-stone floors, white-wicker furnishings, marble wet bars, built-in hair dryers, and in-room satellite TVs. Dine on roasted rack of lamb with garlic mashed pota-toes or a broiled lobster tail at Angler's Restaurant, which overlooks gleaming rows of yachts moored in the marina. The resort's dive shop will arrange fishing charters and boat rentals; use of small sailboats and kayaks is complimentary. Lounge poolside and enjoy fruity rum drinks

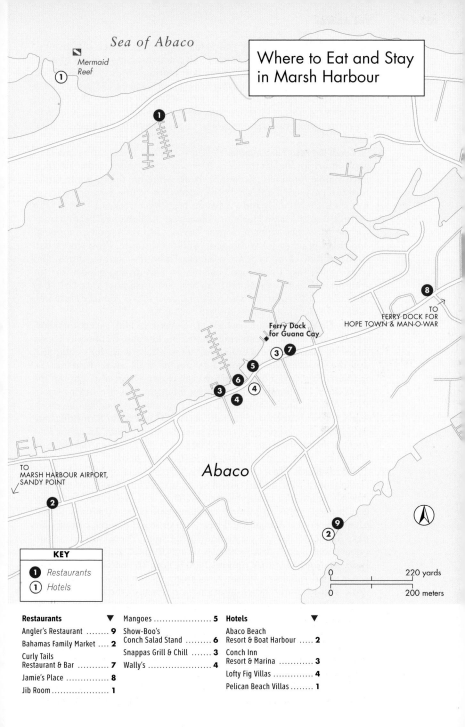

Sea of Abaco

Mermaid
Reef

①

①

**Where to Eat and Stay
in Marsh Harbour**

Ferry Dock
for Guana Cay

⑧

TO
FERRY DOCK FOR
HOPE TOWN & MAN-O-WAR

③ **⑦**

⑤

⑥

④

③

④

TO
MARSH HARBOUR AIRPORT,
SANDY POINT

Abaco

②

⑨

②

KEY	
①	*Restaurants*
①	*Hotels*

0   220 yards

0   200 meters

at the swim-up bar while your kids explore the beach playground. **Pros:** ideal location for all water-related activities; easy access to town shops and restaurants; one of the best marinas in the Abacos. **Cons:** can be crowded and noisy during fishing tournaments. ⊠ *East of Conch Sound Marina* ☏ *242/367–2158, 800/468–4799* ⊕ *www.abacoresort. com* ☞ *82 rooms* ⅃ *In-room: safe. In-hotel: restaurant, bar, pool, tennis court, gym, beach, water sports, laundry facilities* ⅋⊙⅋ *Multiple meal plans.*

$ 🛏 **Conch Inn Resort and Marina.** This low-key, one-level marina hotel is a good choice for budget travelers, but make reservations well in advance. Each simple room has two double beds, white-tile floors, white-rattan furniture, and color-splashed bedspreads. Curly Tails restaurant serves lunch and dinner daily and a delicious brunch on weekends. The 80-slip marina, one of Marsh Harbour's busiest, is the Bahamas' headquarters for the Moorings sailboat charter service. Top restaurants, shopping, and small beaches are within easy walking distance. **Pros:** smack dab in the middle of everything in Marsh Habour—marina, shops, and restaurants; easy to arrange boat rentals and diving; good value for comfortable rooms. **Cons:** far from beaches; small pool area. ⊠ *E. Bay St.* ☏ *242/367–4000* ⊕ *www.conchinn.com* ☞ *10 rooms* ⅃ *In-hotel: restaurant, bar, pool, water sports.*

$ 🛏 **Lofty Fig Villas.** The hotel owners envelop guests with exceptional hospitality, as does the superfriendly staff. The intimate compound has six spacious villas with pool or harbor views. Kitchens are fully equipped, and the supermarket is about a 10-minute walk away. Restaurants, marinas, bars, and a dive shop are even closer—basically right out the front door. For families or groups on a budget, this is a super option. **Pros:** location, location, location; good pool area for hanging out; excellent value with warm and friendly service. **Cons:** room furnishings are dated; no place to tie up a rental boat. ⊠ *Across from Mangoes Restaurant and Conch Inn Resort* ☏ *242/367–2681* ⊕ *www.loftyfig.com* ☞ *6 villas* ⅃ *In-room: kitchen, Wi-Fi. In-hotel: pool.*

$$ 🛏 **Pelican Beach Villas.** On a quiet private peninsula opposite the main settlement of Marsh Harbour sit seven waterfront clapboard cottages cheerily painted in pale pink, yellow, blue, and green. Inside the air-conditioned rooms are rattan furnishings with pastel cushions and porcelain tile floors. A small sand beach is out front, and the cottages are near Mermaid Reef, a primo snorkeling spot. There's no restaurant on-site, but there's food within walking distance at the Marsh Harbour Marina; for other options, you'll need to rent a car or, better yet, a small runabout, which you can tie up for free at the 100-foot dock. **Pros:** tranquil beach location; near some of the best snorkeling in the Abacos; many repeat guests. **Cons:** no restaurant; need to rent a car or boat; on the expensive side for less than full-service accommodations. ⊠ *Northwest of Marsh Harbour Marina* ☏ *877/326–3180* ⊕ *www.pelicanbeachvillas.com* ☞ *7 cottages* ⅃ *In-room: kitchen. In-hotel: beach, laundry facilities.*

NIGHTLIFE

Curly Tails. Stop by for live music on weekends. ⊠ *Conch Inn Hotel and Marina, Bay St.* ☎ *242/367–4444* ⊕ *www.abacocurlytails.com* ⊘ *Closed Tues.*

Snappa's Grill and Chill. Wednesday through Saturday nights feature live music. ⊠ *Harbour View Marina, Bay St.* ☎ *242/367–2278* ⊕ *www.snappasbar.com.*

PLAN AHEAD

Even though you're going to the laid-back islands, you need to reserve your boats, cars, and golf carts in advance. You can save time and money by having your boat-rental company meet you at the airport or the ferry dock nearest to your offshore cay.

SHOPPING

Abaco Treasures. At Marsh Harbour's traffic light, look for the turquoise-and-white stripe awnings of Abaco Treasures, purveyors of fine china, crystal, perfumes, and gifts. ☎ *242/367–3460.*

Iggy Biggy. This store, inside a bright peach-and-turquoise building, is your best bet for hats, sandals, tropical jewelry, sportswear, and souvenirs. If you are looking for gifts to take back home, you should be able to find something cool here. ⊠ *E. Bay St.* ☎ *242/367–3596.*

Java in Abaco. Sip an iced latte or a strong mug of joe while admiring the ceramics, quilts, pillows, carved wooden boats, and other locally produced artwork at Java in Abaco. ⊠ *Royal Harbour Village* ☎ *242/367–5523.*

John Bull. On the water across from the entrance to the Abaco Beach Resort, John Bull sells Rolex and other brand-name watches, fine jewelry by designers such as David Yurman and Yvel, and makeup and perfume from Chanel, Christian Dior, Clinique, and Lancôme. Fine leather goods, silk ties and scarves, and cool sunglasses are also on hand. ⊠ *E. Bay St.* ☎ *242/367–2473* ⊕ *www.johnbull.com.*

Sand Dollar Shoppe. This shop sells resort wear and jewelry, featuring locally made Abaco gold necklaces and earrings. ⊠ *Royal Harbour Village* ☎ *242/367–4405.*

SPORTS AND THE OUTDOORS

BICYCLING **Rental Wheels of Abaco.** You can rent bicycles for $10 a day here; it also has Suzuki and Yamaha mopeds. It's located on the main strip between Conch Inn Marina and the turnoff to Boat Harbour Marina. ⊠ *E. Bay St.* ☎ *242/367–4643* ⊕ *www.rentalwheels.com.*

BOATING **Boat Harbour Marina.** The marina has 190 fully protected slips and a slew of amenities, including accommodations at the Abaco Beach Resort. ☎ *242/367–2158* ⊕ *www.abacobeachresort.com.*

Conch Inn Marina. This is one of the busiest marinas and has 80 slips, with accommodations available at the Conch Inn. ☎ *242/367–4000* ⊕ *www.conchinn.com.*

Harbour View Marina. The first marina on the west end of Bay Street, across from Wally's Restaurant, has extra-wide slips and 100-foot piers to accommodate boats with unlimited beam size, a private pool, wireless Internet, and Snappas Restaurant. ☎ *242/367–3910* ⊕ *www.harbourviewmarina.com.*

The Abacos are the sailing capital of the Bahamas.

Mangoes Marina. This marina has 29 slips and a full range of amenities, including onshore showers, a pool, and a popular restaurant of the same name. ☎ *242/367–4255.*

Marsh Harbour Marina. Marsh Harbour Marina has 68 slips and is the only full-service marina on the left side of the harbor, near Pelican Shores. It is a 10-minute drive from most shops and restaurants. ☎ *242/367–2700* ⊕ *www.jibroom.com.*

Boat Rentals The Moorings ☎ *242/367–4000* ⊕ *www.moorings.com.* **Rainbow Rentals** ☎ *242/367–4602.* **Rich's Rentals** ☎ *242/367–2742.* **Sea Horse Boat Rentals** ☎ *242/367–2513.*

FISHING   You can find bonefish on the flats, yellowtail and grouper on the reefs, or marlin and tuna in the deeps of the Abacos.

Justin Sands. Premier fly-fishing guide Justin Sands works out of a state-of-the-art Hell's Bay flats skiff that will put you on tailing bones in the skinniest water. Justin was the Abacos bonefish champ for two years running, and he will guide you in the Marls or around Snake Cay, Little Harbour, and Cherokee Sound. Advance reservations are a must. ☎ *242/367–3526* ⊕ *www.bahamasvacationguide.com/justfish.html.*

Pinder's Bone Fishing. Buddy Pinder has 20 years' experience in the local waters, and professional Pinder's Bone Fishing provides year-round excursions in the Marls, a maze of mangroves and flats on the western side of Abaco. Advance reservations are essential. ☎ *561/202–8575, 242/366–2163.*

SCUBA DIVING AND SNORKELING There's excellent diving throughout the Abacos. Many sites are clustered around Marsh Harbour, including the reef behind **Guana Cay,** which is filled with little cavelike catacombs, and **Fowl Cay National Reserve,** which contains wide tunnels and a variety of fish. **Pelican Cays National Park** is a popular dive area south of Marsh Harbour. This shallow, 25-foot dive is filled with sea life; turtles are often sighted, as are spotted eagle rays and tarpon. The park is a 2,000-acre land and marine park protected and maintained by the Bahamas National Trust. Hook up your own boat to one of the moorings, or check with the local dive shops to see when trips to the park are scheduled. All of these sights can be easily snorkeled. Snorkelers will also want to visit **Mermaid Beach,** just off Pelican Shores Road in Marsh Harbour, where live reefs and green moray eels make for some of the Abacos' best snorkeling.

> **PLAY THE TIDES**
>
> If you're going bonefishing, tide pooling, or snorkeling, you'll want up-to-date tide information for the best results. A low incoming tide is usually best for bonefishing, though the last of the falling is good, too. Low tides are best for beachcombing and tide pools, although higher tides can give better coverage to your favorite reef. Ask at your hotel or a local dive shop for current tide information.

Dive Abaco. Located at the Conch Inn, Dive Abaco offers scuba and snorkeling trips on custom dive boats. Sites explored include reefs, tunnels, caverns, and wreck dives. Dive Abaco also maintains a boat and office at Abaco Beach Resort. ☎ *800/247–5338* ⊕ *www.diveabaco.com.*

Rainbow Rentals. Rainbow Rentals rents catamarans and snorkeling gear. ☎ *242/367–4602.*

Sea Horse Boat Rentals. Sea Horse Boat Rentals rents snorkeling gear. ☎ *242/367–2513.*

TENNIS **Abaco Beach Resort.** The two lighted courts here are open to visitors. A tennis pro is on hand for clinics and private lessons for adults and children, and there are round-robin tournaments for guests. ☎ *242/367–2158.*

WINDSURFING **Abaco Beach Resort.** Windsurfing equipment and sea kayaks are available free of charge to hotel and marina guests at the Abaco Beach Resort. ☎ *242/367–2158.*

TREASURE CAY

Twenty miles north of Marsh Harbour is Treasure Cay, technically not an island but a large peninsula connected to Great Abaco by a narrow spit of land. This was once the site of the first Loyalist settlement in Abaco, called Carlton.

While Treasure Cay is a large-scale real-estate development project, it's also a wonderful small community where expatriate residents share the laid-back, sun-and-sea vibe with longtime locals. The development's centerpiece is the Treasure Cay Hotel Resort and Marina, with its Dick Wilson–designed golf course and a 150-slip marina that has boat rentals, a dive shop, pool, restaurant, and lively bar. Despite its name, there is no hotel at the resort, only a large grouping of condominiums and villas around the marina. Treasure Cay's commercial center consists of two rows of shops near the resort as well as a post office, laundromat, ice-cream parlor, a couple of well-stocked grocery stores, and BaTelCo, the Bahamian telephone company. You'll also find car-, scooter-, and bicycle-rental offices here.

EXPLORING

Carleton Settlement Ruins. Tucked away toward the northwestern end of the Treasure Cay development are the ruins of the very first settlement in Abaco, founded by the Loyalists that left the Carolinas during the American Revolutionary War. The sight is not well marked, but ask a local for directions.

WHERE TO EAT AND STAY

$$ ✕ **Spinnaker Restaurant and Lounge.** Ceramic-tile floors, rattan furniture,
BAHAMIAN and floral-print tablecloths accent this large resort restaurant—250
★ guests fit in the air-conditioned main dining area and the adjacent screened-in outdoor patio—and bar at the Treasure Cay Marina. Locals and tourists mix in an often-rowdy scene, though things quiet down in the off-season. Conch fritters, salads, burgers, and grilled grouper are the usual lunch fare. Dinner boasts an international flair with grilled steaks and lamb chops, along with seafood pasta, grilled mahimahi, broiled lobster, and a salad bar. Even with reservations you often have to wait, but you can relax in the lounge and enjoy an array of cocktails and frozen rum drinks. ⊠ *Treasure Cay Marina* ☎ *242/365–8801* ⌣ *Reservations essential.*

$$ ✕ **Touch of Class.** Ten minutes north of Treasure Cay, this locals'-favorite,
BAHAMIAN no-frills restaurant serves traditional Bahamian dishes such as grilled freshly caught grouper and minced local lobster stewed with tomatoes, onions, and spices. Reasonably priced appetizers, such as conch chowder and conch fritters, and a full bar make this a nice option for a night out. Free shuttle service is available from the parking lot in front of the Treasure Cay Marina. ⊠ *Queen's Hwy. at Treasure Cay Rd.* ☎ *242/365–8195* ⊗ *No lunch.*

$$$ ⌂ **Bahama Beach Club.** Ideal for families and small groups, these two-
★ to four-bedroom condos are right off the famous Treasure Cay beach. Interiors vary, but each unit has ceramic-tile floors and stylish rattan furniture with colorful accents, as well as a fully equipped kitchen and a large living room. All also have a patio or balcony overlooking the water and the grounds, which are landscaped with tropical palms. These are some of the nicest condos in the Abacos, and they are within a few minutes' walk of the Treasure Cay Hotel Resort and Marina. **Pros:** luxury accommodations on one of the most sublime beaches in the world; large pool area with Jacuzzi; walking distance to the marina, restaurants, and shops. **Cons:** check-in can be slow. ⊠ *Treasure Cay* ☎ *800/284–0382, 242/365–8500* ⊕ *www.bahamabeachclub. com* ⇱ *88 condos* ⌂ *In-room: kitchen, Wi-Fi. In-hotel: pool, beach, laundry facilities.*

$ ⓣ **Treasure Cay Hotel Resort & Marina.** Treasure Cay is best known for its
☾   18-hole golf course, which *Golf Digest* frequently rates as the Bahamas'
Fodor'sChoice best, and its first-class 150-slip marina. The property has suites and
★   town house–style accommodations set along the marina's boardwalk.
Suites have full-size refrigerators, toaster ovens, and small dining coun-
ters; town houses have vaulted ceilings, spacious living–dining areas,
modern kitchens, full and loft bedrooms, and balconies. The indoor-
outdoor Spinnaker restaurant serves Bahamian and continental cuisine.
A more casual, kid-friendly option is Thursday-night pizza at the Tipsy
Seagull poolside bar and grill, also a popular happy-hour destination,
and there's live music and dancing three times a week. The resort can
arrange fishing, diving, and island excursions. **Pros:** most convenient
location in Treasure Cay; good on-site restaurants and bar; Dick Wilson
championship golf course. **Cons:** if you forget to make a dinner reservation in the main season you could be out of luck at the restaurant;
pool area can get crowded with boat people and happy-hour patrons
at the Tipsy Seagull Bar. ⊠ *Treasure Cay Marina* 🕿 *242/365–8801,
800/327–1584* ⊕ *www.treasurecay.com* ⇶ *32 suites, 32 town houses*
⌂ *In-room: kitchen. In-hotel: restaurant, bar, golf course, pool, tennis
court, beach, water sports* ⦿ *Multiple meal plans.*

NIGHTLIFE
Tipsy Seagull. This outside bar and grill is a fun happy-hour spot.
There's usually live music on the weekend. ⊠ *Treasure Cay Marina*
🕿 *242/365–8801.*

SHOPPING
Abaco Ceramics. Near Treasure Cay Resort is Abaco Ceramics, which
offers its signature white-clay pottery with blue fish designs. 🕿 *242/365–
8489* ☽ *Closed weekends.*

SPORTS AND THE OUTDOORS
BICYCLING **Wendell's Bicycle Rentals.** Wendell's Bicycle Rentals rents mountain bikes
by the half day, day, or week. 🕿 *242/365–8687.*

BOATING Treasure Cay marina has 150 slips and can accommodate large yachts.
It's a great base for jaunting to outer uninhabited cays for day fishing
or diving trips, or to Green Turtle Cay.

Boat Rentals J.I.C. Boat Rentals 🕿 *242/365–8582.*

FISHING **Justin Sands.** Reservations are a must to fish with Justin Sands,
the Abacos' two-time bonefish champ. 🕿 *242/367–3526* ⊕ *www.
bahamasvacationguide.com/justfish.html.*

O'Donald Macintosh. Top professional bonefish guide O'Donald Macintosh meets clients each day at the Treasure Cay Marina for full or half
days of guided bonefishing in the northern Marls or outside Coopers
Town. In more than 20 years of guiding, O'D has built up a large loyal
base of repeat clients, so you'll need to book him well in advance—especially in the prime months of April, May, and June. 🕿 *242/365–0126.*

Treasure Cay Hotel Resort & Marina. Arrange for local deep-sea fishing
or bonefishing guides through Treasure Cay Hotel Resort & Marina.
🕿 *242/365–8250.*

GOLF   **Treasure Cay Hotel Resort & Marina.** A half mile from the Treasure Cay
★   Hotel Resort & Marina is the property's par-72, Dick Wilson–designed
course, with carts available. There's no need to reserve tee times, and the
course is usually delightfully uncrowded—ideal for a leisurely round.
A driving range, putting green, and small pro shop are also on-site.
☎ *800/327–1584, 954/525–7711* ⊕ *www.golfbahamas.com.*

SCUBA   **No Name Cay, Whale Cay,** and the **Fowl Cay Preserve** are popular marine-
DIVING AND   life sites. The 1865 wreck of the steamship freighter *San Jacinto* also
SNORKELING   affords scenic diving and a chance to feed the resident green moray eel.

Treasure Divers. Treasure Divers, in the Treasure Cay Marina, rents
equipment and takes divers and snorkelers out to a variety of sites.
☎ *242/357–6796* ⊕ *www.treasure-divers.com.*

TENNIS   **Treasure Cay Hotel Resort & Marina.** The tennis courts here are six of the
best courts in the Abacos, four of which are lighted for night play.
☎ *800/327–1584, 242/365–8801.*

WINDSURFING   **Treasure Cay Hotel Resort & Marina.** Windsurfers and a complete line of
nonmotorized watercraft are available for rent at the Treasure Cay
Hotel Resort & Marina. ☎ *242/365–8250.*

SOUTH OF MARSH HARBOUR

Thirty minutes south of Marsh Harbour, the small, eclectic artists'
colony of **Little Harbour** was settled by the Johnston family more than
50 years ago. Randolph Johnston moved his family here to escape the
consumerist, hectic lifestyle he felt in the United States and to pursue a
simple life where he and his wife could focus on their art. The family is
well known for their bronze sculptures, some commissioned nationally.

Just to the south of Little Harbour is the seaside settlement of **Cherokee Sound,** home to fewer than 100 families. Most of the residents
make their living catching crawfish or working in the growing tourism
industry; many lead offshore fishing and bonefishing expeditions. The
deserted Atlantic beaches and serene salt marshes in this area are breathtaking, and though development at Winding Bay and Little Harbour
are progressing, the slow-paced, tranquil feel of daily life here hasn't
changed. **Sandy Point,** a "takin' it easy, mon" fishing village with miles
of beckoning beaches and a couple of bonefishing lodges, is slightly
more than 50 mi southwest of Marsh Harbour, about a 40-minute
drive from Cherokee.

EXPLORING

Abaco Club on Winding Bay. Twenty-five minutes south of Marsh Harbour this glamorous private golf and sporting club is set on 534 acres
of stunning oceanfront property. The clubhouse, restaurant, and pool,
which sit on 65-foot-high white limestone bluffs, offer guests and members a mesmerizing view of the purple-blue Atlantic Ocean, and the
bay has more than 2 mi of sugar-sand beaches. Amenities and activities
at the club include an 18-hole tropical links golf course, a luxurious
European-style spa and fitness center, scuba diving, snorkeling, tennis,
bonefishing, and offshore fishing. This is a private club whose members
have bought property; nonmembers can stay in the hotel-style cabanas

and cottages and use all facilities one time while evaluating membership and real-estate options. The Ritz-Carlton manages the property. ✉ *Cherokee Sound turnoff* ☏ *242/367–0077, 800/593–8613* ⊕ *www. theabacoclub.com.*

Hole-in-the-Wall. Off the Great Abaco Highway at the turn in the road that takes you to Sandy Point, a rugged, single-lane dirt track leads you to this navigational lighthouse that stands on Great Abaco's southern tip. The lighthouse was constructed in 1838 against local opposition from islanders who depended on salvaging shipwrecks for their livelihood. Over the years the lighthouse has survived sabotage and hurricanes, and was automated in 1995 to continue serving maritime interests. The Bahamas Marine Mammal Research Organisation has leased the site to monitor whale movements and conduct other ocean studies. ✉ *South of Sandy Point.*

Johnston Studios Art Gallery and Foundry. Sculptor Johnston and his sons and acolytes cast magnificent lifelike bronze figures using the age-old lost-wax method at the only bronze foundry in the Bahamas. You can purchase the art in the gallery. ✉ *Little Harbour* ☏ *242/577–5487.*

Sawmill Sink Blue Hole. A half-hour drive south of Marsh Harbour is a crudely marked electric pole directing you to turn right onto an old logging trail. A short drive down this road takes you to an incredible blue hole. It was featured by *National Geographic* in 2010 for the fossils found deep within in. Though you cannot dive this hole, as scientists are still exploring the bottom, you can swim in it. ✉ *40 mins south of Marsh Harbour.*

WHERE TO EAT AND STAY

$
BAHAMIAN

✕ **Pete's Pub.** Next door to Pete's Gallery is an outdoor tiki-hut restaurant and bar where you can wiggle your toes in the sand while you chow down on fresh seafood, burgers, and cold tropical drinks. Try the mango-glazed grouper, lemon-pepper mahimahi, or coconut cracked conch while you kick back and enjoy the view of the harbor. If you want to be part of the local scene, don't miss the wild-pig roasts, which happen whenever big events take place. ✉ *Little Harbour* ☏ *242/577–5487* ⊕ *www.petespubabdgallery.com* ☾ *Closed August through Oct. No dinner Mon.*

$$$$
ALL-INCLUSIVE

🛏 **Rickmon Bonefish Lodge.** Well-regarded fishing guide Ricardo Burrows operates this comfortable waterside lodge at the end of the road in Sandy Point. The whitewashed, plantation-style building has 11 modern rooms, each with air-conditioning and satellite TV; 5 overlook the ocean through sliding French doors. Fishing packages—which include top private guides, all meals, and accommodations—are the most popular option here, but nonfishing guests can fill their time beachcombing, bird-watching, snorkeling, and boating. The location is ideal for accessing the flats around Castaway Cay, Moore's Island, and the southern Marls. **Pros:** perfect location for bonefishing; some of the best professional fly-fishing guides in the Abacos; comfortable for nonfishing companions. **Cons:** average restaurant; intermittent Internet. ✉ *Sandy Point* ☏ *800/211–8530* ⊕ *www.anglingdestinations.com* ⇆ *11 rooms* ⌂ *In-hotel: restaurant, bar, beach* ⊟ *No credit cards* ⬚ *All-inclusive.*

St. James Methodist Church in Hope Town

SHOPPING

Johnston Studios Art Gallery. The gallery displays original bronzes by the Johnstons, as well as unique gold jewelry, prints, and gifts. ⊠ *Little Harbour* ☎ *242/577–5487* ⊕ *www.petespubandgallery.com.*

SPORTS AND THE OUTDOORS

FISHING   This is a great bonefishing location, given that Cherokee Sound is a large shallow bank ideal for the sport.

ELBOW CAY

Five-mile-long Elbow Cay's main attraction is the charming village of **Hope Town**. The saltbox cottages—painted in bright colors—with their white picket fences, flowering gardens, and porches and sills decorated with conch shells, will remind you of a New England seaside community, Bahamian style. Most of the 300-odd residents' families have lived here for several generations, in some cases as many as 10. For an interesting walking or bicycling tour of Hope Town, follow the two narrow lanes that circle the village and harbor. (Most of the village is closed to motor vehicles.)

Although modern conveniences like high-speed Internet and satellite TV are becoming more common, they are a relatively new development. In fact, most residents remember the day the island first got telephone service—back in 1988. Before that, everyone called each other the way many still do here and in the other Out Islands: by VHF, the party line for boaters. If you are boating, want to communicate with the locals, or would like to make a dinner reservation on one of the cays, you should carry a VHF radio and have it tuned to channel 16.

GETTING HERE AND AROUND

Elbow Cay is 4 mi southeast of Marsh Harbour. Every day except Sunday and holidays, **Albury's Ferry Service** (☎ *242/367–0290* ⊕ *www. alburysferry.com*) leaves Marsh Harbour for the 20-minute ride to Hope Town at 7:15, 9, 10:30, 12:15, 2, 4, and 5:45; ferries make the return trip at 8, 9:45, 11:30, 1:30, 3, 4, 5, and 6:30. A same-day round-trip costs $27. One-way tickets cost $17.

Once in Hope Town you can walk everywhere. In fact, only local work vehicles are permitted through town. To visit other areas you can rent a bicycle or a golf cart.

EXPLORING

Hope Town Lighthouse. Upon arrival in Hope Town Harbour you'll first see a much-photographed Bahamas landmark, a 120-foot-tall, peppermint-stripe lighthouse built in 1838. The light's construction was delayed for several years by acts of vandalism; then-residents feared it would end their profitable wrecking practice. Today the lighthouse is one of the Bahamas' last three hand-turned, kerosene-fueled beacons. Weekdays 10–4 the lighthouse keeper will welcome you at the top for a superb view of the sea and the nearby cays. There's no road between the lighthouse and the town proper. You can use your own boat to cross the harbor or catch a ride on the ferry before it leaves to go back to Marsh Harbour, but if you take a ferry it probably won't be back for at least an hour.

Wyannie Malone Historical Museum. This volunteer-run museum houses Hope Town memorabilia and photographs. Exhibits highlight Lucayan and pirate artifacts found on the island. Many descendants of Mrs. Malone, who settled here with her children in 1875, still live on Elbow Cay. ⊠ *Queen's Hwy., Hope Town* ☎ *242/366–0293* 💲 *$3 adults, $1 children* ☉ *Closed Sept. and Oct.*

WHERE TO EAT

$$
BAHAMIAN
Fodor'sChoice
★

✕ **Abaco Inn Restaurant.** Set in the country-club-style main lodge splashed with lively Bahamian colors, the restaurant serves breakfast, lunch, and dinner to guests and visitors in classic island style. Attentive friendly service and expansive ocean views are appetite enhancers. Fresh-baked bread, fruit, and egg dishes are breakfast highlights. But where the restaurant really shines is in its servings of the freshest seafood on the island. At lunch, sample the grilled grouper or spicy cracked conch. For dinner, grilled wahoo, hog snapper, or mahimahi can be prepared to your liking. When you make your reservation, ask for a table on the enclosed patio overlooking the ocean. ⊠ *2 mi south of Hope Town, Hope Town* ☎ *242/366–0133* ⚓ *Reservations essential.*

$
BAHAMIAN

✕ **Cap'n Jack's.** There are a handful of booths and a small rowdy bar, but most of this casual eatery's seating is out on the pink-and-white-striped dock–patio. Locals, boat people, and land-based tourists gather here every day for value-priced eats and drinks. The menu is nothing fancy, but provides reliable grouper burgers, pork chops, fresh fish catch-of-the-day, and cracked conch. When it's in season, there's sometimes

CLOSE UP

A Living History

Though the Abacos may be most famous for beaches, sailing, and fishing, you'd be missing the boat, so to speak, if you didn't explore the area's rich history. And that doesn't mean spending all those sunny days inside a museum, although there are fine, small museums in Hope Town and New Plymouth, each worth a visit to learn about the boatbuilding and seafaring traditions of the Loyalists who settled these islands.

Because the original settlements have been so well preserved, it's possible to absorb history just by wandering through them. In Hope Town, look for the gingerbread cottages with white picket fences, built 100 or more years ago but still lived in today. In New Plymouth, check out the sculpture garden depicting the accomplishments of famous Bahamians. While you're there, observe the architecture: the neat clapboard homes, shops, and churches, many with carefully tended flower boxes and airy front porches, have survived hurricanes and tropical storms and still look much as they did when they were built a century ago. On Man-O-War Cay, witness boatbuilding as it's been done for generations, or see women carefully crafting modern bags out of the same cloth their ancestors used for sails. And everywhere in the Abacos, simply try engaging the local residents in conversation. Nearly all of them, but especially those over 60, have some great tales to tell of what it's like to live on an island where many grew up without cars, TVs, telephones, or daily mail service.

a lobster special. Cap'n Jack's serves three meals a day, offers a full bar, and has live music Friday nights and a DJ Wednesday and Saturday nights. There are nightly drink specials and a different event each night, from trivia to sushi. ⊠ *Hope Town* ☎ *242/366–0247* ⏱ *Closed mid-Aug.–Sept.*

$$$
BAHAMIAN
✕ **Great Harbour Room.** Warm up with a key-lime martini rimmed with graham-cracker crumbs, or any of a fine selection of wines, before tackling steak, crispy duck, or grilled mahimahi with creamy butter and lime. While casual attire is fine, the restaurant feels like an upscale establishment with dimmed lighting, quiet music, and especially attentive service. ⊠ *Upper Rd., Hope Town* ☎ *242/366–0095* ⊕ *www.hopetownlodge.com.*

$$
BAHAMIAN
★
✕ **Harbour's Edge.** Hope Town's happening hangout for locals and tourists, this bar and restaurant's deck is the best place to watch the goings-on in the busy harbor; you can tie your boat up right in front. Kick back and have an icy Kalik, or for extra punch, try a Kalik Gold—just make sure someone else drives your golf cart or boat afterward. For lunch, try the tender conch burgers, white caps, or lobster salad. For dinner, the fresh grilled seafood and pasta dishes are some of the best in the islands. Authentic Bahamian breakfasts are served on Sunday. A band plays on Thursday and Saturday nights during high season. ⊠ *Lower Rd., Hope Town* ☎ *242/366–0087* ⏱ *Closed Tues.*

¢
CAFÉ
✕ **Hope Town Coffee House.** Overlooking Hope Town Harbour, this upscale coffee house, bakery, boutique, and hot-spot café features

coffees roasted right in the historic settlement, the first and only roastery in the Bahamas. It's a must for java drinks, smoothies, homemade pastries and ice cream, quiches, and tapas-size savories. ⊠ *Queen's Hwy., Hope Town* ☎ *242/366–0760* ⊕ *www.hopetowncoffeehouse.com.*

$ ✕ **On the Beach Bar and Grill.** Burgers, sandwiches, conch, fish, and icy
BAHAMIAN rum drinks are served up with a terrific Atlantic view at this open-air bar and grill perched high on the beach dunes across the road from the small Turtle Hill resort. It closes at sunset because all seating is open to the elements, and a gully washer of a storm can shut the place down. Go in your bathing suit and enjoy the beach and snorkeling right out front. ⊠ *Queens Hwy. between Hope Town and White Sound, Hope Town* ☎ *242/366–0557* ⚑ *Reservations not accepted* ⊗ *Closed Mon.*

¢ ✕ **Sugar Shack.** This cute shack is an ice-cream parlor (14 flavors!), deli,
DELI and T-shirt shop all tied into one. Located about 1½ mi south of Hope Town, it's a worthwhile ride for a cool treat or a fresh sandwich. Unique gift items such as Bahama Bee pepper jelly are available, too. ⊠ *Centerline Rd., White Sound, Hope Town* ☎ *242/366–0788* ⊗ *Closed Sun. in Sept. and Oct.*

WHERE TO STAY

$$ 🏠 **Abaco Inn.** The motto here is "Tan your toes in the Abacos," making
★ this beachfront resort the ideal place for a getaway. The cozy rooms—seven with Atlantic Ocean views and seven overlooking the harbor and the Sea of Abaco—have simple comfortable furnishings and individual hammocks. Luxury villas have kitchenettes, small living areas, and sunrise and sunset water views. After your complimentary pick-up in Hope Town, rent your own boat so you can zoom into town or to the smaller neighboring cays. Excellent reefs for surfing, snorkeling, and diving are nearby. The bar is a lively spot for guests and locals to mingle, and for couples to watch the magenta sunsets. The restaurant, which serves some of the freshest seafood on the island, is outstanding. Ask for a table on the enclosed patio overlooking the ocean. The lounge has satellite TV and live music on occasion. **Pros:** self-contained resort with the best restaurant on the island; easy access to beaches, surfing, and fishing; hypnotic ocean views. **Cons:** 10-min golf-cart or boat ride to Hope Town. ⊠ *2 mi south of Hope Town, Hope Town* ☎ *242/366–0133* ⊕ *www.abacoinn.com* ⟿ *14 rooms, 8 villas* ⚑ *In-room: kitchen, no TV. In-hotel: restaurant, bar, pool, beach.*

$$$$ 🏠 **Elbow Cay Properties.** Besides being the most cost-efficient way for a family to stay a week or longer on Elbow Cay, a private house or villa is also likely to be the most comfortable. This longstanding rental agency handles a variety of properties, from cozy two-bedroom, one-bath

4

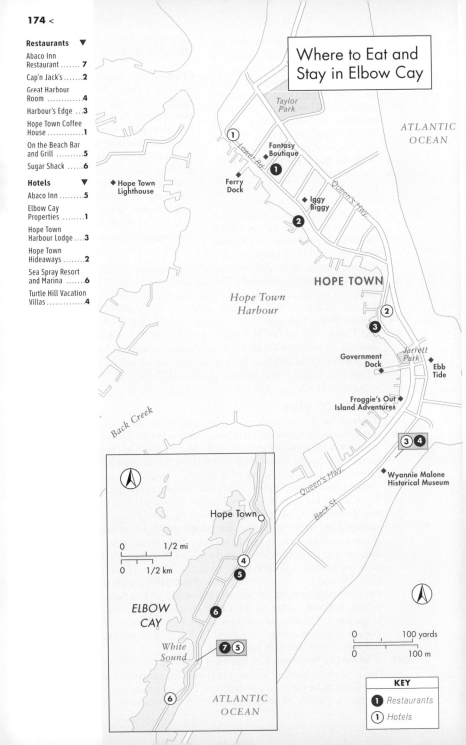

Restaurants ▼

Abaco Inn Restaurant **7**

Cap'n Jack's **2**

Great Harbour Room **4**

Harbour's Edge ... **3**

Hope Town Coffee House **1**

On the Beach Bar and Grill **5**

Sugar Shack **6**

Hotels ▼

Abaco Inn **5**

Elbow Cay Properties **1**

Hope Town Harbour Lodge ... **3**

Hope Town Hideaways **2**

Sea Spray Resort and Marina **6**

Turtle Hill Vacation Villas **4**

Where to Eat and Stay in Elbow Cay

Taylor Park

ATLANTIC OCEAN

Fantasy Boutique

Ferry Dock

◆ Hope Town Lighthouse

◆ Iggy Biggy

HOPE TOWN

Hope Town Harbour

Jarrett Park

◆ Ebb Tide

Government Dock ◆

Froggie's Out ◆ Island Adventures

◆ Wyannie Malone Historical Museum

Back Creek

Queen's Hwy

Back St.

Hope Town ○

0 ____ 1/2 mi

0 ____ 1/2 km

ELBOW CAY

White Sound

ATLANTIC OCEAN

0 ____ 100 yards

0 ____ 100 m

KEY
❶ *Restaurants*
① *Hotels*

cottages to a six-bedroom, six-bath villa better described as a mansion. Many of the rental homes are on the water, with a dock or a sandy beach right out front. The owners are set on finding you a place to match your wishes and budget. There are no Sunday check-ins, as the agency is closed. **Pros:** variety of accommodation options in all price

> **SURFS UP, DUDE!**
>
> Though it's not well known, there is good surfing off Elbow Cay. If you want to wake up to the waves, stay at the Abaco Inn or at the Sea Spray Resort, or rent a house at Tahiti Beach.

4

ranges; style choices from beachy casual to ultraluxurious; close to town but still remote and private. **Cons:** no Sunday check-in; do-it-your-self vacation. ⊠ *Western Harborfront, Hope Town* ☎ *242/366–0569* ⊕ *www.elbowcayrentals.com* ⌁ *78 units.*

$ 🖼 **Hope Town Harbour Lodge.** You can have it all at this casually classy
Fodor's Choice resort—spectacular views of the Atlantic Ocean and the beach, quality
★ amenities, and a location steps away from the town and harbor. Pleasant rooms are decorated island style, but for a splurge, treat yourself to one of the ocean-view or oceanfront cottages, with light pine paneling, terra-cotta-tile floors, full kitchenettes, and French doors opening onto private decks. Breakfast and lunch are poolside, with views of the ocean. Dinner is served in the Great Harbour Room, with views of the harbor. Book early, as reservations are essential for both the restaurant and the lodge. Discounted rates are available September 5 to October 31. **Pros:** best lodging location on Elbow Cay for views, beach, and access to town; casual patio restaurant for lunch overlooking the ocean; romantic. **Cons:** Internet access can be sporadic. ⊠ *Upper Rd., Hope Town* ☎ *242/366–0095, 866/611–9791* ⊕ *www.hopetownlodge.com* ⌁ *12 rooms, 6 cabanas, 6 cottages, 1 private house* ⚭ *In-room: kitchen, no TV, Wi-Fi. In-hotel: restaurant, bar, pool, beach.*

$$$ 🖼 **Hope Town Hideaways.** Choose one of four comfy island villas scat-
★ tered on 11 acres of gardens, with access to the harbor and the beach, or go more upscale with a West Indies–style Flamingo Villa, perfectly situated across from the lighthouse at the entrance to the harbor. The spacious two-bedroom, two-bath villas have large kitchens, satellite TV, Internet access, deluxe bedrooms with balconies, and wraparound decks with pools and barbecues. Owners Peggy and Chris Thompson also run a property-management company that rents more than 75 private cottages and houses, including spectacular beachfront retreats at Tahiti Beach on the south end of the cay. Most of these units sleep four or more, and some of the more upscale properties can accurately be described as mansions. Peggy and Chris can also arrange for everything from kayak, boat, and golf-cart rentals to island excursions and fishing guides. All rentals have a 4-night minimum stay. **Pros:** variety of accommodation and style options in all price ranges; convenient locations. **Cons:** check-in can take a while for first-time guest; do-it-yourself vacation. ⊠ *1 Purple Porpoise Pl., Hope Town* ☎ *242/366–0224* ⊕ *www.hopetown.com* ⌁ *75 units.*

$$ 🖼 **Sea Spray Resort and Marina.** Consider this resort if you're planning to catch any waves, or you just want to get away from it all. The

accommodations are just off Garbanzo Beach, which is popular with surfers. One-, two-, and three-bedroom villas have full kitchens, satellite TVs, air-conditioning, and large decks with outdoor grills. You can rent snorkeling gear. The on-site store sells everything from charcoal to surfboard wax. There are also a 60-slip full-service marina, swimming pool with ample deck chairs for catching rays, and a swinging bar that rocks at happy hour and after dinner. The bar also has a wide-screen TV for taking in sporting events, and a restaurant where you can enjoy the ocean view while feasting on steamed lobster or grilled, freshly caught grouper. Free shuttle service is available to Hope Town, about a 10-minute drive. **Pros:** the Atlantic beach is on one side of the resort, and the leeward-side marina on the other; self-contained relaxing retreat near the Abaco Inn; full-service marina for boaters and guests. **Cons:** restaurant food is just OK; 10-min golf cart or boat ride to Hope Town. ✉ *South end of White Sound, Hope Town* ☎ *242/366–0065* ⊕ *www. seasprayresort.com* ⤳ *7 villas* ♿ *In-room: kitchen. In-hotel: restaurant, bar, pool, water sports, business center.*

$$$ 🏨 **Turtle Hill Vacation Villas.** Bougainvillea- and hibiscus-lined walkways encircle the central swimming pools of this cluster of six villas, each with its own private patio. Inside, villas have central air-conditioning, full kitchens that open into the spacious dining–living room, light-wood paneling, tile floors, and rattan furnishings, as well as sleeper sofas. A mile-long crescent beach is steps away, as is the On the Beach Bar and Grill. Each villa comes with a golf cart for jaunts into town. Choose an upper villa for views of the ocean. **Pros:** comfortable accommodations for families and small groups; steps away from the beach. **Cons:** you have to golf cart out to restaurants for dinner if you don't want to cook in; extra charge for daily maid service. ✉ *Off Queens Hwy. between Hope Town and White Sound* ☎ *242/366–0557* ⊕ *www.turtlehill.com* ⤳ *6 villas* ♿ *In-room: kitchen. In-hotel: pool.*

NIGHTLIFE

Cap'n Jacks. Each evening Cap'n Jacks offers a different event, including bingo and trivia and drink specials. After nine on Wednesday and Friday nights there is DJ music. This is a popular spot for young adults. ✉ *Hope Town* ☎ *242/366–0247* ⊗ *Closed Sept.*

Harbour's Edge. After nine every Saturday night Harbour's Edge has local bands playing Bahamian and reggae music. They also play Thursday nights during peak seasons. This is a favorite spot for locals. ✉ *Lower Rd., Hope Town* ☎ *242/366–0087* ⊗ *Closed Tues.*

Sea Spray Resort. Local bands perform here every Saturday night. This is a popular stop, where locals and visitors can mingle and dance to classic rock-and-roll and Bahamian tunes. ✉ *South end of White Sound* ☎ *242/366–0065.*

Wine Down and Sip Sip. Featuring a selection of 50 properly cellared wines, Wine Down and Sip Sip is a classy hangout with a high-end liquor bar, draft beer, and weekly flights and pairings. The aura is sophisticated, and complimented by a lend-and-exchange selection of books. ✉ *Queen's Hwy.* ☎ *242/366–0399.*

Tahiti Beach on Elbow Cay

SHOPPING

Ebbtide. This shop is on the upper-path road in a renovated Loyalist home. Come here for such Bahamian gifts as batik clothes, original driftwood carvings and prints, and nautical jewelry. Browse through the extensive Bahamian book collection. ⊠ *Hope Town* ☎ *242/366–0088.*

Fantasy Boutique. Here you can find a nice selection of souvenirs, beach wraps, T-shirts, arts and crafts, and Cuban cigars. ⊠ *Front Rd., Hope Town* ☎ *242/366–0537.*

★ **Iggy Biggy.** This is the only shop in Hope Town that carries the lovely Abaco ceramics handmade in Treasure Cay. It also sells home decorations, handmade dishware and glasses, wind chimes, sandals, resort wear, jewelry, and island music. ⊠ *Front Rd., Hope Town* ☎ *242/366–0354.*

SPORTS AND THE OUTDOORS

BOATING **Hope Town Hideaways.** Hope Town Hideaways has 12 slips, mostly used for guests staying in its rental cottages and houses. Call well in advance to reserve yours. ☎ *242/366–0224.*

Sea Spray Resort and Marina. This full-service marina has 60 slips and boat rentals. ☎ *242/366–0065.*

Boat Rentals Island Marine ☎ *242/366–0282* ⊕ *www.islandmarine.com.* **Sea Horse Boat Rentals** ☎ *242/367–2513.*

FISHING **Local Boy.** Local Boy is recommended for deep-sea charters. ☎ *242/366–0528.*

Maitland Lowe. Maitland Lowe will guide you around Snake Cay or Little Harbour, but you need to book him well in advance. ☎ *242/366–0234.*

Seagull Charters. Seagull Charters sets up guided deep-sea excursions with Captain Robert Lowe, who has more than 35 years' experience in local waters. ☎ *242/366–0266.*

KAYAKING   **Abaco Eco.** This company offers tours and rentals of the local area and Snake Cay. ☎ *242/475–9616, 954/889–7117* ⊕ *www.abacoeco.com.*

SCUBA   **Froggies Out Island Adventures.** Froggies has snorkel and dive trips, scuba
DIVING AND   and resort courses, full-day adventure tours, island excursions, and
SNORKELING   dolphin encounters. You can also rent snorkeling and diving gear to
★   venture out on your own. Professional and friendly service has earned Froggies many repeat customers. You need to book your excursions as far in advance as possible. ☎ *242/366–0431* ⊕ *www.froggiesabaco. com.*

MAN-O-WAR CAY

Fewer than 300 people live on skinny, 2½-mi-long Man-O-War Cay, many of them descendants of early Loyalist settlers who started the tradition of handcrafting boats more than two centuries ago. These residents remain proud of their heritage and continue to build their famous fiberglass boats today. The island is secluded, and the old-fashioned, family-oriented roots show in the local policy toward liquor: it isn't sold anywhere on the island. (But most folks won't mind if you bring your own.) Three churches, a one-room schoolhouse, several shops, grocery stores, and restaurants that cater largely to visitors round out the tiny island's offerings.

A mile north of the island you can dive to the wreck of the USS *Adirondack,* which sank after hitting a reef in 1862. It lies among a host of cannons in 20 feet of water.

GETTING HERE AND AROUND

Man-O-War Cay is an easy 45-minute ride from Marsh Harbour by water taxi or aboard a small rented outboard runabout. The island has a 28-slip marina. No cars are allowed on the island, but you'll have no problem walking it, or you can rent a golf cart. The two main roads, Queen's Highway and Sea Road, run parallel.

WHERE TO STAY

$$ ⛵ **Schooner's Landing.** Perched on a rocky promontory overlooking a long, isolated beach, this small, Mediterranean-style resort has four two-bedroom town-house condos with ocean views; two of these units include lofts for children or extra friends. Rooms are airy, with wicker furniture and ceramic-tile floors, and include fully equipped kitchens, ceiling fans, TVs, and stereos with CD players. Gaze out to sea from the freshwater swimming pool's wraparound deck, or lounge in the gazebo, which has a barbecue and wet bar. There's no restaurant, but you can easily walk to almost every establishment, eating or otherwise, on the cay. The resort also has golf carts for rent, and the nearby grocery store delivers. **Pros:** spectacular surroundings on a bluff overlooking the Atlantic Ocean; easy access to deserted beaches; stress-melting environment. **Cons:** not much to do; island restaurants are just OK; groceries can be scarce at times. ⊠ *Oceanside Beach* ☎ *242/365–6143*

⊕ *www.schoonerslanding.com* ⤙ *4 condominiums* ⚘ *In-room: kitchen. In-hotel: pool, beach.*

SHOPPING

★ **Albury's Sail Shop.** This shop is popular with boaters, who stock up on duffel bags, briefcases, hats, and purses, all made from duck, a colorful, sturdy canvas fabric traditionally used for sails. ⊠ *Front Rd.* ☎ *242/365–6014.*

Joe's Studio. This store sells paintings by local artists, books, clothing, and other nautically oriented gifts, but the most interesting souvenirs are the half models of sailing dinghies. These mahogany models, which are cut in half and mounted on boards, are meant to be displayed as wall hangings. Artist Joe Albury, one of the store's owners, also crafts full, 3-D boat models. ⊠ *Front Rd.* ☎ *242/365–6082.*

SPORTS AND THE OUTDOORS

BOATING **Man-O-War Marina.** This marina has 26 slips and also rents golf carts. For people coming from Marsh Harbour or other cays, the Albury Ferry dock is adjacent. ⊠ *Front Rd.* ☎ *242/365–6008.*

SCUBA DIVING **The Painted Fish.** You can rent snorkeling equipment here. Fowl Cay Undersea Park, located just north of Man-O-War Cay, is a good place for snorkeling. ⊠ *Man-O-War Marina* ☎ *242/365–6013.*

GREAT GUANA CAY

The essence of Great Guana Cay can be summed up by its unofficial motto, painted on a hand-lettered sign: "It's better in the Bahamas, but it's gooder in Guana." This sliver of an islet just off Great Abaco, accessible by ferry from Marsh Harbour or by private boat, is the kind of place people picture when they dream of running off to disappear on an exotic island, complete with alluring deserted beaches and grassy dunes. Only 100 full-time residents live on 7-mi-long Great Guana Cay, where you're more likely to run into a rooster than a car during your stroll around the tranquil village. Still, there are just enough luxuries here to make your stay comfortable, including a couple of small, laid-back resorts and a restaurant–bar with one of the best party scenes in the Abacos. The island also has easy access to bonefishing flats you can explore on your own.

GETTING HERE AND AROUND

The ferry to Great Guana Cay leaves from the Conch Inn Marina in Marsh Harbour. The ride is about 30 minutes. Golf carts are available for rent in Great Guana Cay, though most places are within walking distance.

WHERE TO EAT AND STAY

$$
BAHAMIAN
Fodor's Choice
★

✕ **Nippers Beach Bar & Grill.** With awesome ocean views and a snorkeling reef just 10 yards off its perfect beach, this cool bar and restaurant is a must-visit hangout. Linger over a lunch of burgers and sandwiches or a dinner of steak and lobster, then chill out in the double pool, one for families and one with a swim-up bar just for adults. Nurse a "Nipper Tripper"—a frozen concoction of five rums and two juices. If you

Dolphin Beach Resort, Great Guana Cay

down more than one or two of these, you'll be happy to take advantage of the Nippermobile, which provides free transport to and from the cay's public dock. Every Sunday, everybody who is anybody, or not, revels in the all-day party disguised as a pig roast. ⊠ *Great Guana Cay* ☎ *242/365–5111* ⊕ *www.nippersbar.com.*

$$ 🏨 **Dolphin Beach Resort.** You'll be tempted to stay forever at this upscale
Fodor's Choice island haven. Spacious, uniquely designed rooms and larger cottages—
★ handcrafted of Abaco pine by Guana Cay shipwrights—are all painted in bright Junkanoo colors. Each island-style cottage is individually furnished and includes a private deck or terrace. Two cottages are set away from the resort, ideal for honeymooners. Outside, secluded showers are surrounded by bougainvillea and sea grape trees. Boardwalk nature trails winding through the carefully tended 15-acre property lead to miles of secluded beach. Prime fishing, diving, and snorkeling are nearby, and guided tours can be arranged by the accommodating resort staff. **Pros:** beachfront location with casually luxurious accommodations; personalized service. **Cons:** if you are looking for nightlife, shopping, lots of people, this is not the place for you; no Internet service. ⊠ *Fisher's Bay* ☎ *800/222–2646, 242/365–5137* ⊕ *www. dolphinbeachresort.com* ⟿ *9 cottages, 4 rooms* ⚴ *In-room: kitchen. In-hotel: pool, tennis court, beach, water sports* ⊙ *Closed Sept.–mid-Oct.*

$$$ 🏨 **Flip Flops on the Beach.** Reserve one of the four one- or two-bedroom beachside bungalows at this casually elegant boutique and you can melt into the island lifestyle of sun, sand, serenity, and ocean breezes on arrival. Bungalows are bright, fresh, and furnished with white wicker, mahogany four-poster beds with 1,000-thread-count sheets, and an array of modern kitchen appliances. Additional amenities are satellite flat-screen TV, patio furnishings, charcoal grill, beach chairs, and umbrellas. A private beach pavilion is ideal for picnicking or enjoying a sunset cocktail. Guests may use the pool, tennis court, and other facilities at the adjacent Dolphin Beach Resort. Restaurants and shops are a short walk or golf-cart ride away. **Pros:** beachfront location; the essence of tranquillity; quality accommodations and in-room amenities. **Cons:** remote location means there is no nightlife, shopping, or larger resort-style activities; no Internet service. ⊠ *Great Guana Cay* ☎ *800/222–2646, 242/365–5137* ⊕ *www.flipflopsonthebeach.com* ⇄ *4 bungalows* ⚴ *In-room: kitchen. In-hotel: beach* ☯ *Closed Sept.–mid-Oct.*

> **CELEBRATE GOOD TIMES!**
>
> All-day pig roasts are a common weekend event, from Nippers on Great Guana Cay to Pete's Pub in Little Harbour. These events are a fun and inexpensive way to enjoy a day on the beach with lots of tasty Bahamian chow, live music, dancing, and island camaraderie. Ask at your hotel for a schedule of events.

NIGHTLIFE

Grabbers Bar and Grill. This is a popular local spot on weekend nights. There's music and the Guana Grabber, a potent drink designed to lighten any mood. ☎ *242/365–5133.*

Nippers. Not only is this the best spot on a Sunday, but weekend nights Nippers continues to rock. ☎ *242/365–5143.*

SPORTS AND THE OUTDOORS

BOATING **Baker's Bay Golf & Ocean Club.** At the northwestern end of the island, Baker's Bay Golf & Ocean Club has 158 slips. ☎ *242/367–0612* ⊕ *www. discoverylandco.com.*

Orchid Bay Yacht Club and Marina. Orchid Bay Yacht Club and Marina has 66 deepwater slips and full services for boaters at the entrance to the main settlement bay, across from the public docks. The club office rents luxury apartments, cottages, and homes, and prime real estate is for sale. There's also a swimming pool and a restaurant that serves fresh seafood, steaks, and healthy salads on an outdoor deck overlooking the marina. ☎ *242/365–5175* ⊕ *www.orchidbay.net.*

SCUBA DIVING **Dive Guana.** This dive shop, on the grounds of Dolphin Beach Resort, organizes scuba and snorkeling trips and island tours. The shop also rents boats, kayaks, and bicycles. Renting a boat, at least for a day, is the best way to get around and enjoy other nearby cays. ☎ *242/365–5178* ⊕ *www.diveguana.com.*

GREEN TURTLE CAY

This tiny 3-mi-by-½-mi island is steeped in Loyalist history; some residents can trace their heritage back more than 200 years. Dotted with ancestral New England–style cottage homes, the cay is surrounded by several deep bays, sounds, bonefish flats, and irresistible beaches. **New Plymouth,** first settled in 1783, is Green Turtle's main community. Many of its approximately 550 residents earn a living by diving for conch or

Nippers Beach Bar and Grill, Great Guana Cay

selling lobster and fish. There are a few grocery and hardware stores, several gift shops, a post office, a bank, a handful of restaurants, and several offices.

GETTING HERE AND AROUND

The **Green Turtle Cay Ferry** (☎ *242/365–4166*) leaves the Treasure Cay airport dock at 8:30, 10:30, 11:30, 1:30, 2:30, 3:30, 4:30, and 5, and returns from Green Turtle Cay at 8, 9, 11, 12:15, 1:30, 3, and 4:30. The trip takes 10 minutes, and one-way fares are $11, same-day round-trip fare is $16. The ferry makes several stops in Green Turtle, including New Plymouth, the Green Turtle Club, and the Bluff House Beach Hotel.

Many hotels provide an occasional shuttle from the main ferry dock in Green Turtle Cay to their property, and there are a couple of taxis on the island. Most people travel via golf cart or boat. Don't worry, you won't miss having a car; even in the slowest golf cart you can get from one end of the island to the other in 20 minutes or less.

EXPLORING

Albert Lowe Museum. New Plymouth's most frequently visited attraction is the Bahamas' oldest historical museum, dedicated to a model-ship builder and direct descendant of the island's original European-American settlers. You can learn island history through local memorabilia from the 1700s, Lowe's model schooners, and old photographs, including one of the aftermath of the 1932 hurricane that nearly flattened New Plymouth. One of the galleries displays paintings of typical Out Island scenes by acclaimed artist Alton Lowe, Albert's son. Mrs. Ivy Roberts, the museum's director, enjoys showing visitors around and sharing stories of life in the Out Islands before the days of high-speed Internet and daily airline flights. ⊠ *Parliament St., New Plymouth* ☎ *242/365–4094* ⌖ *$5 adults, $3 children* ⊙ *Mon.–Sat. 9–11:45 and 1–4.*

Memorial Sculpture Garden. The past is present in this garden across the street from the New Plymouth Inn. (Note that it's laid out in the pattern of the British flag.) Immortalized in busts perched on pedestals are local residents who have made important contributions to the Bahamas. Plaques detail the accomplishments of British Loyalists, their descendants, and the descendants of those brought as slaves, such as Jeanne I. Thompson, a contemporary playwright and the country's second woman to practice law. This is an open garden, free to the public. ⊠ *Parliament St., New Plymouth.*

WHERE TO EAT

$$$ ✕ **Captain's Table.** The colonial-style dining room serves memorable
BAHAMIAN Bahamian-style dinners with a continental touch. The menu changes nightly, though there is always a choice of seafood, meat, or chicken. When it's available, don't pass up the hog snapper. The nightly fresh fish is always well prepared, and meat lovers can enjoy roasts, steaks, and chops. For dessert, don't miss the key lime pie. ⊠ *New Plymouth Inn, Parliament St., New Plymouth* ☎ *242/365–4161* ⌖ *Reservations essential.*

$$ ✕ **Green Turtle Club Dining.** Breakfast and lunch are served harborside on
CONTINENTAL a covered, screened-in patio. At lunch, treat yourself to a lobster salad,
★ lobster corn chowder, cheeseburger, or grilled grouper sandwich. Dinner is where the club really shines, transporting you back to the 1920s with elegant dining beneath antique chandeliers. Reservations must be made by 5 pm each day, and there are two seatings, at 7 and 7:30. Shrimp cocktail, raspberry-glazed Cornish game hens, medallions of lobster in ginger beurre blanc, seared tuna Mediterranean, and grilled New York strip steaks are just a few of the temptations. For dessert, guava crème brûlée will finish you off. For those who prefer a casual environment, you can eat from an à la carte menu outside on the enclosed patio. ⊠ *Green Turtle Club, north end of White Sound, New Plymouth* ☎ *242/365–4271* ⌖ *Reservations essential* ⊙ *Closed Sept. and Oct.*

$ ✕ **Jolly Roger Bar and Bistro.** This casual eatery on the water in the Bluff
AMERICAN House Marina offers tasty lunches and, in the evening, a less formal alternative to the reservations-only fine dining in the Clubhouse restaurant. Sitting under a canvas umbrella on the deck is the best way to enjoy the view of the sailboat-filled harbor, but you can also eat in the air-conditioned pub-style dining room. Menu choices range from standard Bahamian (conch fritters and burgers) to new American (roasted pork tenderloin with salsa, salads with goat cheese and roasted vegetables, and even, on occasion, sushi). Another fun option is to enjoy a rum drink from the bar while catching some rays at the pool. ⊠ *Between Abaco Sea and White Sound, at Bluff House Beach Hotel Marina, New Plymouth* ☎ *242/365–4247.*

$ ✕ **McIntosh Restaurant and Bakery.** At this simple, diner-style restaurant,
BAHAMIAN lunch means excellent renditions of local favorites, such as fried grouper and cracked conch, and sandwiches made with thick slices of slightly sweet Bahamian bread. At dinner, large portions of pork chops, lobster,

fish, and shrimp are served with rib-sticking sides like baked macaroni and cheese, peas 'n' rice, and coleslaw. Save room for a piece of pound cake or coconut cream pie, baked fresh daily and displayed in the glass case up front. ⊠ *Parliament St., New Plymouth* ☎ *242/365–4625.*

$ ✕ **Pineapples Bar & Grill.** Hang out, take a dip in the freshwater pool,
BAHAMIAN   and enjoy Bahamian fare with a flair. In Black Sound, at the entrance to the Other Shore Club and Marina, you'll find this simple open-air restaurant with a canopy-shaded bar and picnic tables next to the pool. Some of the best conch fritters in the islands are served from noon on. At lunch, try a fresh salad or spicy jerk chicken; for dinner, grilled daily-caught fish. The jerk-spiced grouper is sensational. Specialty drinks include a Pineapple Smash and a Yellowbird, both capable of mellowing your mood. ⊠ *Black Sound, New Plymouth* ☎ *242/365–4039* ⊕ *www. othershoreclub.com* ▭ *No credit cards* ⊗ *Closed Sun.*

$ ✕ **The Wrecking Tree.** The wooden deck at this casual restaurant was
BAHAMIAN   built around the wrecking tree, a place where 19th-century wrecking vessels brought their salvage. Today it's a cool place to linger over a cold Kalik and a hearty lunch of cracked conch, fish-and-chips, or zesty conch salad. It has great pastries, too—take some back to your hotel. Dinner is served during "the season." ⊠ *Bay St., New Plymouth* ☎ *242/365–4263* ▭ *No credit cards* ⊗ *Closed Sun. Dinner served in the busy season only.*

WHERE TO STAY

$$ ⊞ **Barefoot Homes.** From its perch on a rocky bluff overlooking White
★   Sound, this romantic hilltop hideaway provides sweeping views of the sheltered harbor or the Sea of Abaco. The split-level suites have tropical-style wicker furniture, parquet-inlay floors, and double doors opening onto balconies with sensational ocean vistas. Even more spacious are the two- and three-bedroom villas, with huge screened-in verandas overlooking the marina. Or go for the ultimate decadence with the three-bedroom Yachtsman's Cottage, which is ideal for families or couples traveling together. Formal dinners are still served by reservation only in the dining room, although hours are irregular. The open-air, natural pine cocktail lounge and library is a tranquil spot for an afternoon or predinner cocktail. **Pros:** inspiring views; spacious luxury accommodations; tranquil and romantic. **Cons:** 20-minute golf-cart ride or 10-minute boat ride to New Plymouth; no reliable Internet service. ⊠ *Between Abaco Sea and White Sound, New Plymouth* ☎ *242/365–4092* ⊕ *www.barefoothomesbahamas.com* ⇦ *4 suites, 4 villas, 5 cottages.* △ *In-room: kitchen. In-hotel: restaurant, bar, pool, tennis court, beach, water sports, laundry facilities* |○| *Some meals.*

$$ ⊞ **Coco Bay Cottages.** Sandwiched between one beach on the Atlantic and another calmer, sandy stretch on the bay are six spacious cottages—including two three-bedroom cottages added in 2006 and a four-bedroom cottage completed in July 2009—that all have views of the water. Each has lovely rattan furniture and a modern kitchen with utensils. Conch Shell and Conch Pearl, the three-bedroom cottages, each have a master suite with king bed and walk-in closet, washer and dryer, satellite TV, and DVD player. Snorkeling and diving are excellent around the reef that protects the Atlantic beach. The bay, where sunset

views are fabulous, is prime territory for shell or sea-glass collecting and bonefishing. A separate building holds a library with games and books and satellite TV. If you rent a boat—it's recommended—you can tie up at the property's bay-side dock. There is a four night minimum stay. **Pros:** spacious, well-located do-it-yourself accommodations; awesome beaches; Wi-Fi for those who can't totally get away. **Cons:** renting a boat and/or golf cart is essential; if you don't like silence, the peace and quiet will kill you. ✉ *Coco Bay, north of Green Turtle Club, New Plymouth* ☎ *561/202–8149, 800/752–0166* ⊕ *www.cocobaycottages. com* ☞ *6 cottages* ⚭ *In-room: kitchen, Internet, Wi-Fi. In-hotel: beach, water sports, laundry facilities.*

$ ⛤ **Green Turtle Club.** The longstanding colonial tradition and tone of
★ casual refinement continues at this well-known resort. Cheerful yellow cottages are scattered up a hillside amid lush trees and shrubs. Villa accommodations have decks overlooking the water and docks for rental boats; poolside rooms are more formal, furnished with mahogany Queen Anne–style furniture, gleaming hardwood floors, and Oriental rugs. Breakfasts and lunches are served on a screened, terra-cotta-tile patio, but it's dinner under the harbor-view dining room's chandeliers that makes the club shine. Choose from an ever-changing menu that might include fresh grilled lobster, sautéed lemon grouper, or rack of lamb, accompanied by the best selection of wines in the Abacos. The modern 40-slip marina makes it easy to dock your boat out front, and in a 10-minute walk you can be bonefishing in Coco Bay or lying on the secluded Atlantic Ocean beach. If you need anything else, the accommodating hotel staff can arrange it. **Pros:** excellent on-site restaurants for casual or fine dining; easy access to great beaches; personalized service. **Cons:** if you're looking for Bahamian casual, this isn't it. ✉ *North end of White Sound, New Plymouth* ☎ *242/365–4271, 866/528–0539* ⊕ *www.greenturtleclub.com* ☞ *24 rooms, 2 suites, 8 villas* ⚭ *In-room: no TV, Wi-Fi. In-hotel: restaurant, bar, pool, beach, laundry facilities* ⊙ *Closed Sept. and Oct.* ⫾⊙⫿ *Some meals.*

$$$$ ⛤ **Island Property Management.** A five-bedroom, oceanfront mansion with wraparound veranda, full-time staff, and a marble fireplace could be yours. Or rent a two-bedroom cottage in the heart of New Plymouth. This agency has more than 50 cottages and houses for rent to meet different budgets and needs. It can also help arrange excursions and boat and golf-cart rentals. Most homes have water views, and some have docks for your rental boat. The offices in New Plymouth are in a blue two-story building along with Green Turtle Real Estate, just down from the ferry dock. **Pros:** do-it-yourself flexibility in spacious accommodations; prime beachfront locations; good value for families and small groups. **Cons:** you pay extra for daily maid service; not all units have Internet; if something is not working in the unit, maintenance can be slow. ✉ *Various Green Turtle Cay locations, New Plymouth* ☎ *242/365–4047* ⊕ *www.abacoislandrentals.com* ☞ *50 units.*

$$ ⛤ **Linton's Beach and Harbour Cottages.** These three classic Bahamian-style cottages are ideally placed on 22 private acres between Long Bay and Black Sound. Two beachside cottages are on a rise overlooking Pelican Cay and the Atlantic. Each has two comfortable bedrooms,

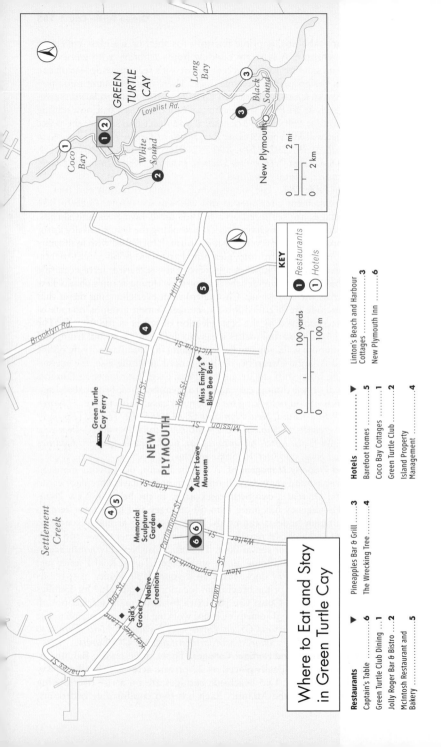

Where to Eat and Stay in Green Turtle Cay

Restaurants ▼

Captain's Table **6**
Green Turtle Club Dining ...**1**
Jolly Roger Bar & Bistro **2**
McIntosh Restaurant and
Bakery **5**
Pineapples Bar & Grill **3**
The Wrecking Tree **4**

Hotels ▼

Barefoot Homes **5**
Coco Bay Cottages **1**
Green Turtle Club **2**
Island Property
Management **4**
Linton's Beach and Harbour
Cottages **3**
New Plymouth Inn **6**

KEY

① Restaurants
① Hotels

a screened-in porch, a combination living–dining room with built-in settees, a well-stocked library, and a fully equipped kitchen. The Harbour Cottage, with one air-conditioned bedroom, is on Black Sound, steps away from the dock. If you're renting a boat, you can tie it up right out front. Families, groups of friends, and couples looking for an escape will enjoy this location. Three night minimum stay. **Pros:** well-located do-it-yourself cottages; value priced for families and groups. **Cons:** gathering groceries and supplies can be an adventure; some beach cottages don't have phones or TV. ⊠ *S. Loyalist Rd., Black Sound, New Plymouth* ☎ *772/538–4680* ⊕ *www.lintoncottages.com* ↘ *3 cottages* ⌂ *In-room: no a/c, kitchen, no TV. In-hotel: beach, business center* ⊟ *No credit cards.*

$ ⛫ **New Plymouth Inn.** This charming, two-story historic hotel with white balconies and a turn-of-the-20th-century-style lobby and drawing-room bar is conveniently located in New Plymouth's center. Originally built in 1830, the hotel reopened in November 2007 with fresh paint, linens, and upgrades to some furniture. A patio pool is nestled in well-manicured tropical gardens, and the cozy rooms have comfortable beds with handmade quilts and terra-cotta-tile baths. The rates are among the most affordable options on the cay and include breakfast. **Pros:** central New Plymouth location; good value for Green Turtle Cay; excellent restaurant for dinner. **Cons:** rooms are small, so don't bring a lot of luggage; no public Internet service. ⊠ *Parliament St., New Plymouth* ☎ *242/365–4161* ⊕ *www.newplymouthinn.com* ↘ *9 rooms* ⌂ *In-room: no TV. In-hotel: restaurant, bar, pool.*

NIGHTLIFE

Gully Roosters. At night, Green Turtle can be deader than dead or surprisingly lively. Bet on the latter if the local favorites, the Gully Roosters, are playing anywhere on the island. Known locally as just the Roosters, this reggae-calypso band is the most popular in the Abacos. Its mix of original tunes and covers can coax even the most reluctant reveler onto the dance floor. The band's schedule is erratic, but they play every Wednesday at 9 pm under the Buttonwood tree at the **Green Turtle Club** during the high season (*242/365–4271*).

★ **Miss Emily's Blue Bee Bar.** Other nighttime options include a visit to Miss Emily's Blue Bee Bar, where you might find a singing, carousing crowd knocking back the world-famous Goombay Smash. (Or not—many Goombay novices underestimate the drink's potency, and end up making it an early night.) Mrs. Emily Cooper, creator of the popular Goombay Smash drink, passed away in 1997, but her daughter Violet continues to serve up the famous rum, pineapple juice, and apricot brandy concoction. The actual recipe is top secret, and in spite of many imitators throughout the islands, you'll never taste a Goombay this good anywhere else. It's worth a special trip to try one. ☎ *242/365–4181.*

Pineapples Bar & Grill. On the water in front of the Other Shore Club and Marina, this bar has a hopping happy hour from 4to 6 daily and live music every Friday at 8. ☎ *242/365–4039* ⊕ *www.pineapplesbar.com.*

Sundowner's. Locals hang out at Sundowner's, a waterside bar and grill where attractions include a pool table and, on weekend nights, a DJ spinning dance music on the deck under the stars. ☎ *242/365–4060.*

SHOPPING

Native Creations. Colorful Abaco Ceramics, handmade in Treasure Cay, are the best bet at Native Creations. The shop also sells beaded jewelry, picture frames, candles, postcards, and books. ✉ *Parliament St., New Plymouth* ☎ *242/365–4206.*

Plymouth Rock Liquors and Café. Plymouth Rock Liquors and Café sells Cuban cigars and more than 60 kinds of rum. ✉ *Parliament St., New Plymouth* ☎ *242/365–4234.*

Sid's Grocery. This store has the most complete line of groceries on the island, plus a gift section that includes books on local Bahamian subjects—great for souvenirs or for replenishing your stock of reading material. ✉ *Upper Rd., New Plymouth* ☎ *242/365–4055.*

Vert's Model Ship Shop. This shop has Vert Lowe's handcrafted two-mast schooners and sloops. Model prices range anywhere from $100 to $1,200. If Vert's shop door is locked—and it often is—knock at the white house with bright pink shutters next door. If you're still unsuccessful, inquire at the Green Turtle Club, where Vert has worked for more than 30 years. ✉ *Corner of Bay St. and Gully Alley, New Plymouth* ☎ *242/365–4170.*

SPORTS AND THE OUTDOORS

BICYCLING　**D&P Rentals.** The flat roads of Green Turtle Cay are perfect for getting around by bicycle. D&P Rentals rents mountain bikes for $10 a day from their location at the Green Turtle Club. ☎ *242/365–4655.*

BOATING　It's highly recommended that you reserve your boat rental at the same time you book your hotel or cottage. If you're unable to rent a boat on Green Turtle Cay, try nearby Treasure Cay or Marsh Harbour.

Bluff House Beach Hotel. Here you can find a marina with 40 slips, and a full range of services—everything from Texaco fuel to laundry facilities. ☎ *242/365–4247.*

Green Turtle Club. Green Turtle Club has 40 slips and offers cable TV and Wi-Fi as well as a full stocked commissary. ☎ *242/365–4271.*

The Other Shore Club Marina and Cottages. The Other Shore Club Marina and Cottages, tucked into quiet and protected Black Sound, is an ideal place to keep your small cay-hopping boat if you are staying in one of Green Turtle's many rental houses and cottages. The club has its own rental cottages and can arrange fishing, diving, and snorkeling trips. ☎ *242/365–4226* ⊕ *www.othershoreclub.com.*

Boat Rentals Donnie's Boat Rentals ☎ *242/365–4119.* **Reef Rentals** ☎ *242/365–4145.*

FISHING　**Captain Rick Sawyer.** Captain Rick Sawyer is one of Abaco's best guides, and the top recommendation on Green Turtle Cay. Rick's company, Abaco Flyfish Connection and Charters, offers bonefishing on 17-foot Maverick flats skiffs, and reef and offshore fishing aboard his 33-foot

Tiara sportfisher. Book as far in advance as you can. ☎ *242/365–4261* ⊕ *www.abacoflyfish.com.*

Ronnie Sawyer. Ronnie Sawyer works with Rick and on his own. ☎ *242/365–4070.*

SCUBA DIVING AND SNORKELING

★

Brendal's Dive Center. Brendal's Dive Center leads snorkeling and scuba trips, plus wild dolphin encounters, glass-bottom boat cruises, and more. Personable owner Brendal Stevens has been featured on the Discovery Channel and CNN, and he knows the surrounding reefs so well that he's named some of the groupers, stingrays, and moray eels that you'll have a chance to hand-feed. Trips can include a seafood lunch, grilled on the beach, and complimentary rum punch. Kayak and canoe rentals are available. ☎ *242/365–4411* ⊕ *www.brendal.com.*

Lincoln Jones. Rent some snorkel gear or bring your own, and call Lincoln Jones, known affectionately as "the Daniel Boone of the Bahamas," for an unforgettable snorkeling adventure. Lincoln will dive for conch and lobster (in season) or catch fish, then grill a sumptuous lunch on a deserted beach. ☎ *242/365–4223.*

TENNIS

Bluff House Beach Hotel. There is one hard-surface court, and rackets and balls are provided. ☎ *242/365–4247.*

SPANISH CAY

Only 3 mi long, this privately owned island was once the exclusive retreat of millionaires, and many visitors still arrive by yacht or private plane. Although several private upscale homes dot the coast, a small resort also rents rooms and condos. A well-equipped marina, great fishing, and some fine beaches are among the attractions here.

GETTING HERE AND AROUND

There is no ferry service from Great Abaco, so you'll need a boat to get to the cay. There is also a small private airstrip. The only facility here is the resort and marina, so no transportation on the island is needed.

WHERE TO STAY

$$ 🏨 **Spanish Cay Resort and Marina.** Take your pick here—either a beachfront room or a two-room hotel suite tucked away on a hill overlooking the marina and the Sea of Abaco. Decisions, decisions. Regardless of location, all rooms have tile floors, pastel draperies and bedspreads, private porches, king or double beds, and desks. Two- to four-bedroom condos and luxury villas are also available. The Pointe House restaurant serves three meals daily; locally caught fish is your best bet for dinner. The adjacent bar has a game room and outdoor deck for enjoying a sunset cocktail. The 80-slip marina can handle yachts up to 200 feet. **Pros:** totally off-the-beaten-path location; lots of privacy on remote beaches; full-service marina. **Cons:** for entertainment you need to rely on yourself; accommodations are dated. ✉ *Spanish Cay,* ☎ *242/365–0083* ⊕ *www.spanishcay.com* ⇲ *18 rooms, 5 condos, 12 villas* ♿ *In-room: Wi-Fi. In-hotel: restaurant, bar, pool, tennis court, beach, laundry facilities.*

Andros, Bimini, and the Berry Islands

WORD OF MOUTH

"Our experiences in these islands proved that while each of the Out Islands is different from the others, they share a common denominator of welcoming and interesting islanders and visitors. It's not for everyone, but once you find yourself at home with the Out Island experience, nothing else is quite as satisfying."

—Callaloo

WELCOME TO ANDROS, BIMINI, AND THE BERRY ISLANDS

TOP REASONS TO GO

★ **Bonefish:** Andros has a reputation for the best bonefishing in the world, and Bimini comes in a close second. Hire a fishing guide to teach you how to fly-fish, then cruise the West Side flats of Andros Island or Bimini's North Sound Lagoon in pursuit of the elusive "gray ghost."

★ **Charter a boat:** Explore the necklace of islands that comprise Bimini and the Berries. Start in Bimini and end up in Chub Cay. It's quite possible that you may choose not to come back.

★ **Dive Andros Island:** Go with the diving experts at Small Hope Bay and drop "over the wall" or explore some of Andros's magnificent reefs.

Alice Town — North Bimini — South Bimini — Turtle Rocks — Holm Cay — North Cat Cay — South Cat Cay — *Bimini* **2** — Ocean Cay

1 Andros. Incredible blue holes, vibrant reefs (including the third-largest barrier reef in the world), and the Tongue of the Ocean wall make diving and snorkeling some of the main reasons adventurers travel to Andros year-round. Legendary bonefishing on its West Side flats and in its creeks and bights is the other. The island is mostly flat, lush with mangroves, rimmed with white-sand beaches, and laced with miles of creeks and lakes. Exploring is best done by boat, not car, though taxis are available.

2 Bimini. In spring and summer, boaters from south Florida attack nearby Bimini looking for fish and fun. Most go to North Bimini and its big modern resort or one of its older, smaller fishing lodges. South Bimini, a short ferry ride away and home to the islands' only airport,

also boasts a major resort, but appeals more to the nature-minded visitor looking for peace and beach. Uninhabited East Bimini is a maze of mangrove islands, some with beaches and the Healing Hole springs.

3 The Berry Islands. For the ultimate remote island getaway, choose a Berry, any Berry island, which range from the main hub of Great Harbour Cay to private resorts such as Chub Cay. (Royal Caribbean and Norwegian cruise lines also own two private islands in the 30-cay chain.) Plan to spend your days lolling on the secluded, low-key beaches or in pursuit of game and bonefish. Chub Cay, at the Tongue of the Ocean, attracts derring-do divers.

Great Stirrup Cay

Great Harbour Cay

Hoffman's Cay

Berry Islands Comfort Cay

Bond's Cay

Chub Cay · Whale Cay

Joulters Cays

Lowe Sound · Morgan's Bluff

Red Bays · Nicholl's Town

Mastic Point

San Andros · *Barrier Reef*

Staniard Creek

Fresh Creek

Captain Bill's Blue Hole · Andros Town

Andros Island

Behring Point · Cargill Creek

Barrier Reef

Big Wood Cay

Moxey Town

Lisbon Creek

Yellow Cay · Mangrove Cay · Driggs Hill

Congo Town

South Bight · The Bluff

Kemps Bay

Barrier Reef

Deep Creek

Mars Bay

Water Cays · Curley Cut Cays

GRAND BAHAMA BANK

NASSAU

New Providence I.

Tongue of the Ocean

GETTING ORIENTED

The northern islands of Andros, Bimini, and Berry lie just off the east coast of Florida. Bimini, which consists of three main islands—North, South, and East Bimini—is only 50 mi from Miami. The Berry Islands are a 30-cay chain about 100 mi east of Bimini. South of Chub Cay—Berry's southernmost island—Andros comprises the Bahamas' largest land-mass—about half of all the Bahamas' land in total. North and Central Andros occupy the largest of the three major islands, while South Andros is separated from it by North and Middle Bight. South Bight splits South Andros into two parts. On their eastern shores, magnificent remote beaches stretch along most of these northern islands. Vast mangrove estuaries and swamps characterize their western leeward coasts.

ANDROS, BIMINI, AND THE BERRY ISLANDS PLANNER

When to Go

Andros, Bimini, and the Berries have a slightly different high season than most of the other Bahamas islands. Because of their close proximity to Florida, boaters make the crossing in droves from spring break through summer, especially to Bimini. Andros and the Berries, because of their famed fishing and diving, experience traffic also in the winter season (mid-December through Easter), but not as much as elsewhere. Fishing and diving are good throughout the year, although cold fronts December through February can cause rough seas. Temperatures usually remain steady enough to enjoy the beaches year-round, but occasionally drop into the 60s. At many resorts rates remain steady throughout the year, except in Bimini and at fishing lodges on the other islands, where they are generally higher in spring and summer. Hurricane season technically runs from June through November; August and September (the most likely months for hurricanes) can be hot and steamy, and many resorts and restaurants are closed.

Top Festivals

Winter Junkanoo Celebrations take place in Nicholl's Town, North Andros, on New Year's Day, including a traditional Junkanoo parade, music, dancing, and food. Bimini hosts a series of fishing tournaments and boating events throughout the year, including the **Bahamas Wahoo Challenge** (November and February).

Spring April fishing tournaments in Bimini include **Bahamas Billfish Championship, Bimini Women in Fishing,** and the **Ocean Reef Rendezvous**. Bimini also hosts an annual **Homecoming** (formerly the Bimini Regatta), which takes place Easter weekend.

Summer In June, five days of crab races, cook-offs, live Rake 'n' Scrape music, and national musical artists comprise the **All Andros Crab Fest** in Fresh Creek. The **North Andros–Berry Islands Regatta** takes place the second weekend in July, featuring A and B Class Bahamian sailing sloops, local cuisine, and entertainment at Regatta Village in Morgan's Bluff. **Goombay Festivals**—traditional summertime parties with dance troupes and musical groups—take place throughout summer in Andros. The Berry Islands kick off a month of cultural celebrations the first weekend in July with **Conch Fest/Junkanoo Summer Festival.** The Berries' **Lobster Festival** early in August includes cooking contests and music. Bimini holds its **Sail Race** in June, its **Annual Bimini Native Tournament** in August, and the **Bahamas Boating Flings** (formerly the Bimini Open Angling Tournament) in July and August.

Tour Operators

Cruises Bimini Sands Resort ☎ 242/347–3500 ⊕ www.biminisands.com.

Eco Tours Surf Watersport ✉ Bimini ☎ 242/554–4450.

Island Tours Ashley Saunders ✉ Bimini ☎ 242/347–3201. **Small Hope Bay Lodge** ✉ Andros ☎ 242/368–2014, 800/223–6961 ⊕ www.smallhope.com.

Special-Interest Tours Small Hope Bay Lodge can customize tours, focusing on folklore, blue holes, history, and birding.

About the Restaurants

Dining in these parts is a casual experience and rarely involves anything fancy. Restaurants, lodges, and inns serve traditional Bahamian fare—fresh seafood, grilled chicken, johnnycake, cracked (deep-fried) conch, and barbecued pork with all the fixings (potato salad, coleslaw, peas 'n' rice, and macaroni and cheese). Call ahead to make sure a restaurant is open; some require you to order your dinner ahead of time. Resort restaurants are often the most dependable source of sit-down meals and most welcome nonguests. Many of the favored food outlets are take-out places. Thatched conch stands and colorful roadside bars are a treat—and a cool way to mingle with the locals.

About the Hotels

Andros, Bimini, and the Berry Islands have accommodations to suit most tastes, from a handful of luxury properties on private cays and remote beaches to simple fishing lodges and funky hotels with swinging nightlife on weekends. Figure out what you want—service, amenities, activities—then do your homework. Comfortable motel-style accommodations are most common, and usually have a restaurant and bar. Some fishing lodges are not well suited to overall vacationing or for families with small children. Some lodges don't have air-conditioning, in-room telephones and TVs, or Internet. Most do have a phone for guest use on the property, and some will have a computer with Internet in the lobby area. Often you must pay your hotel bill in cash. If these issues are important to you, check with the hotel before you book. And remember, even places that say they have Internet service may not have it all the time, as connections can go on the blink without warning.

Rates typically stay constant throughout the year in Andros and the Berry Islands. In Bimini, spring and summer are high season, and rates reflect that.

WHAT IT COSTS IN DOLLARS					
	¢	$	$$	$$$	$$$$
Restaurants	under $10	$10–$20	$20–$30	$30–$40	over $40
Hotels	under $100	$100–$200	$200–$300	$300–$400	over $400

Restaurant prices are based on the median main course price at dinner, excluding gratuity, typically 15%, which is often automatically added to the bill. Hotel prices are for two people in a standard double room in high season, excluding service and 6%–12% tax.

Essentials

Banks Andros and Bimini banks are open Monday through Friday 9:30–3. All have ATMs. There are no banks on the Berry Islands.

Emergencies AAPI Air Ambulance Professionals provides aero-medical services out of Fort Lauderdale. **AAPI Air Ambulance Professionals** ☎ 954/491–0555, 800/752–4195. **Andros Medical Clinics** ☎ 242/329–2055 Nicholl's Town/North Andros, 242/368–2038 Fresh Creek, 242/369–0089 Mangrove Cay, 242/369–4849 Kemp's Bay/South Andros. **Andros Police** ☎ 242/329–2003 North Andros, 242/368–2626 Fresh Creek/Central Andros, 242/369–4733 Kemp's Bay/South Andros. **Great Harbour Cay Medical Clinic, Berry Islands** ☎ 242/367–8400. **Berry Islands Police** ☎ 242/367–8344. **North Bimini Medical Clinic** ☎ 242/347–2210. **Bimini Police** ☎ 919, 242/347–3144.

Visitor Information Andros Tourism Office ✉ Fresh Creek and South Andros ☎ 242/368–2286 Central Andros, 242/369–1688 South Andros ⊕ www.bahamas.com/out-islands/andros. **Berry Islands Tourism Board** ✉ Bullock's Harbour ☎ 242/367–8291 ⊕ www.berryislands.bahamas.com/out-islands/berry-islands. **Bimini Tourism Office** ✉ Alice Town ☎ 242/347–3529 ⊕ www.bahamas.com/out-islands/bimini. **Bahama Out Islands Promotion Board** ☎ 954/759–2210 ⊕ www.myoutislands.com.

5

ANDROS, BIMINI, AND THE BERRY ISLANDS' BEACHES

Because they're famous for their off-the-chart fishing and diving, the islands of Andros, Berry, and Bimini often get shorted when talk turns to beaches. This is a great injustice, especially in the case of the abandoned way-white sand beaches of South Andros, Great Harbour Cay (in the Berry Islands), and South Bimini.

(above) North Bimini beach (upper right) Coco Cay Beach, Berry Islands (lower right) Berry Island sandbars

Seclusion is these islands' forte, with the exception of North Bimini, which spring breakers and weekend warriors swarm with their coolers of Kalik beer. South Bimini, because of its convenient boat docks right at the beach, also grabs a party crowd, but there's more room to spread out here. Andros beaches as a whole are, like Berry's, ungroomed and wild. Some take a bit of searching to find, others front resorts and lodges.

BLUE HOLES

Mystical and mesmerizing, blue holes pock Andros's marine landscape in greater concentration than anywhere else on Earth— an estimated 160-plus— and provide entry into the islands' network of coral-rock caves. Offshore, some holes drop off to 200 feet or more. Inland blue holes reach depths of 120 feet, layered with fresh, brackish, and salt water. They make cool spots for swimming and snorkeling.

ANDROS, BIMINI, AND THE BERRY ISLANDS' BEST BEACHES

BIMINI SANDS BEACH, SOUTH BIMINI

South Bimini claims Bimini's prettiest beaches, with some of the best from-shore snorkeling around. Beachgoers can set up headquarters at the Bimini Sands Beach Club, where public boat docks, volleyball, tiki umbrellas, restaurants, and bars provide convenience and action. It's so popular that vacationers on North Bimini often take the quick ferry ride over for the day.

GREAT HARBOUR CAY BEACH, THE BERRY ISLANDS

One of two crescent beaches that scoop the coastline of Great Harbour Cay is within walking distance of the airport and town. The 5-mi sweep appeals to beachgoers who like the conveniences of food, drink, and hotel with their sand. Beach Villa, the Beach Club restaurant, and houses line its length.

MORGAN'S BLUFF BEACH, ANDROS

At the north end of North Andros near Nicholl's Town, this wide, lovely beach is normally quiet except around regatta time. Otherwise, it's an entirely natural stretch with no facilities and sparkling gem-colored waters. It's adjacent to the harbor, so boaters sometimes make use of the beach. Australian pines and palms provide a bit of shade inland at its edges.

SHELL BEACH, SOUTH BIMINI

Head here for seclusion, around the point from Bimini Sands Resort's beach on the island's west side. The beach stretches long and natural, and calm waters typically prevail. The snorkeling is also good here. A small picnic shelter is the only concession to facilities, but Bimini Sands' restaurants and bars are a short walk away.

SMALL HOPE BAY BEACH, ANDROS

Small Hope Bay Lodge is planted squarely on this coved beach where from-shore snorkeling is excellent, the sand is white, and tidal limestone pools make for fun tiny sea creature exploration at low tide. It's a good, long walking beach, and you can also sign up for a resort course or diving excursion at the resort, or simply enjoy a beachside lunch buffet.

SUGAR BEACH, THE BERRY ISLANDS

For more seclusion than the island's main beach offers, move to the second beach 5 mi north, where rock bluffs divide the gorgeous, fine white sand into "private" beaches roughly 1 mi in length. Exploring the caves is an added attraction. The calm waters along these coved beaches make them great for snorkeling.

5

Updated by
Chelle Koster
Walton

Legends loom large (and small) on these northwestern Bahamas islands. On Bimini, you'll hear about the lost underwater city of Atlantis, Ernest Hemingway's visits, and the Fountain of Youth. Tiny birdlike creatures known as chickcharnies are said to inhabit the pine forests of Andros Island. On both islands, along with the Berry Islands, bonefishing has made legends of mere men.

Despite the legends, Andros, Bimini, and the Berries remain a secret mostly known to avid divers, boaters, and fishermen. These islands stash their reputation for superlative bonefishing, diving, blue holes, and other natural phenomena away from the glitter-focused eyes of visitors to nearby Nassau, just minutes away by plane but a world apart. Bimini is probably best known, for its Hemingway connection and because it's an easy boat ride from Miami, which means a brisk spring and summer trade. Yet the island has virtually no cars (and only one gas station). Andros weighs in as the largest Bahamas island, accounting for more than half of the nation's landmass. Still, much of it is uninhabitable and largely undiscovered. In fact, no resort has more than 30 rooms. The 30-some cays of the Berry Islands are less known still, in spite of gorgeous beaches and destination resorts. None of the islands have traffic lights, movie theaters, or fast-food outlets—let alone water parks, shopping centers, or golf courses.

So, with that in mind, plan your trip here as an adventurer. If you're not into diving, snorkeling, fishing, kayaking, hiking, biking, or secluded beach-vegetating, these are not the islands for you. If you are into any of the above, you will be thrilled and endlessly entertained. All three islands are spoken of synonymously with bonefishing, and commercial fishing—focused on lobster, grouper, and snapper—and recreational guide fishing drive the economies of many of these communities. Andros thrives also on its harvest of land crabs, fruit and vegetable crops, and fresh water; it exports all of these products to Nassau.

GREAT ITINERARIES

IF YOU HAVE 3 DAYS

Fly into **Andros Town** and spend the first day relaxing at one of the island's beaches and making plans for your snorkeling, diving, or fishing excursion the next day. Have dinner at one of the local resorts before turning in early. On Day 2, divers and snorkelers should head to **Small Hope Bay Lodge** for a day-long excursion. Fishermen will find a wealth of knowledgeable bonefish guides in the **Cargill Creek-Behring Point** area who will take you into the Northern Bight and West Side for the world's best bonefishing. On Day 3, stop at the **Androsia Batik Works Factory** and **Androsia Outlet Store** in Andros Town. Spend the afternoon windsurfing, snorkeling, fishing, or kayaking, or soaking in some last rays on the beach.

IF YOU HAVE 5 DAYS

On Day 4, rent a car or hire a tour guide and visit North Andros's Morgan's Bluff, Nicholl's Town, **Conch Sound**, and **Red Bays** to explore the beaches and visit Red Bays' basket weavers. On Day 5, join a guided tour from Small Hope Bay Lodge to **Rainbow Blue Hole,** where you can enjoy a leisurely picnic and a cooling swim. Stay at the lodge for cocktail hour on the deck and buffet dinner.

IF YOU HAVE 7 DAYS

Fly or charter a boat to **Bimini**. Spend Day 6 deep-sea fishing or diving the famous **Road to Atlantis** site. On your final day, hop the ferry to **South Bimini** to wander the white-sand beaches, snorkel, and swim. Top the day off with a romantic beachside dinner at **the Bimini Sands Resort's Beach Club Restaurant,** then return to **North Bimini** for live music at **Big John's Conch Shell Bar**.

ANDROS

The Bahamas' largest island (100 mi long and 40 mi wide) and one of the least explored, Andros's landmass is carved up by myriad channels, creeks, lakes, and mangrove-covered cays. The natural **Northern, Middle,** and **South Bights** cut through the width of the island, creating boating access between both coasts. Andros is best known for its bonefishing and diving, and is also a glorious ecotourism spot with snorkeling, blue-hole exploration, sea kayaking, and nature hikes.

The Spaniards who came here in the 16th century called Andros *La Isla del Espíritu Santo*—the Island of the Holy Spirit—and it has retained its eerie mystique. The descendants of Seminole Indians and runaway slaves who left Florida in the mid-19th century settled in the North Andros settlement of **Red Bays** and remained hidden until a few decades ago. They continue to live as a tribal society, making a living by weaving straw goods. The Seminoles originated the myth of the island's legendary (and elusive) chickcharnies—red-eyed, bearded, green-feathered creatures with three fingers and three toes that hang upside down by their tails from pine trees. These mythical characters supposedly wait deep in the forests to wish good luck to the friendly passerby and vent their mischief on the hostile trespasser. The rest of Andros's roughly

8,000 residents live in a dozen settlements on the eastern shore. Farming and commercial fishing sustain the economy, and the island is the country's largest source of fresh water.

Andros's undeveloped **West Side** adjoins the Great Bahama Bank, a vast shallow-water haven for lobster, bonefish, and tarpon. Wild orchids and dense pine and mahogany forests cover the island's lush green interior. The marine life–rich **Andros Barrier Reef**—the world's third largest— is within a mile of the eastern shore and runs for 140 mi. Sheltered waters within the reef average 6 to 15 feet, but on the other side ("over the wall") they plunge to more than 6,000 feet at the **Tongue of the Ocean**.

GETTING HERE

There are four airports on Andros. The San Andros airport (SAQ) is in North Andros; the Andros Town airport (ASD) is in Central Andros; the South Andros airport (TZN) is in Congo Town; and the Mangrove Cay airport (MAY) is on Mangrove Cay. Several small airlines and charter companies have flights from Nassau. Daily charter service is also available from Fort Lauderdale and Freeport.

Taxis meet airplanes and ferries and are available for transporting and touring around the islands. They can also be arranged ahead of time through hotels. Rates are around $1.50 a mile, though most fares are set. You should always agree on a fare before your ride begins. Cab drivers will charge $80 to $120 for a half-day tour of the island.

Airport Information Andros Town ☎ *242/368–2030.* **Congo Town, Andros** ☎ *242/369–2640.* **Mangrove Cay, Andros** ☎ *242/369–0083.* **San Andros** ☎ *242/329–4224.*

From Potter's Cay Dock in Nassau, the M/V *Lisa J.* sails to Morgan's Bluff, Mastic Point, and Nicholl's Town in North Andros every Wednesday, returning to Nassau the following Tuesday. The one-way trip takes five hours and costs $30. The M/V *Lady D* sails to Fresh Creek in Central Andros on Tuesday (with stops at Stafford Creek, Blanket Sound, and Behring Point) and returns to Nassau on Sunday. The trip takes five hours, and the fare is $30. The M/V *Mal Jack* sails to Kemp's Bay, Long Bay Cays, and the Bluff, in South Andros on Monday at 11 pm. It returns to Nassau on Wednesday. The trip takes 7 hours; the fare is $30. The M/V *Lady Gloria* departs from Nassau on Tuesday for Mangrove Cay and Cargill Creek (with two other stops) and returns on Sunday. The five-hour trip costs $30. Schedules are subject to change due to weather conditions or occasional dry-docking. Call 242/369–0667 for the latest information.

Bahamas Ferries sails seasonally (mostly in summer) from Potters Cay to Morgan's Bluff and Fresh Creek. Check ⊕ *www.bahamasferries.com* or call ☎ *242/323–2166* for current schedule and fares.

A free government ferry makes the half-hour trip between Mangrove Cay and South Andros twice daily. It departs from South Andros at 8 am and 4 pm and from Mangrove Cay at 8:30 am and 4:30 pm, but schedules are subject to change. Call the Commissioner's Office for information. There's no public transportation from Central Andros to Mangrove Cay.

Boat and Ferry Information Commissioner's Office ☎ *242/369–0331.* **Dockmaster's Office** ☎ *242/393–1064.*

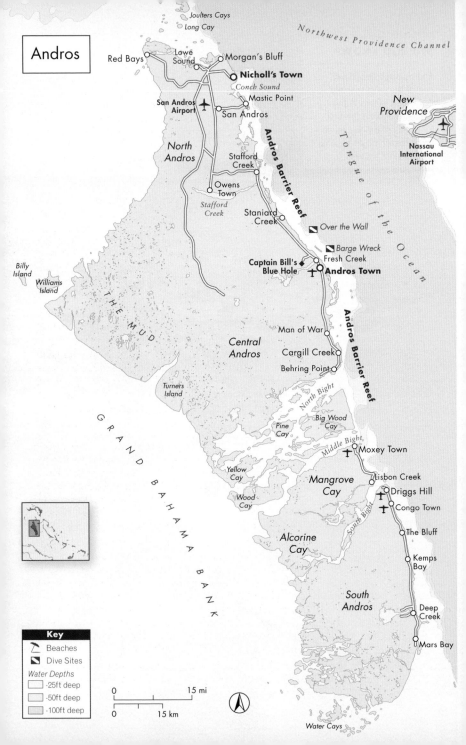

Andros

Joulters Cays
Long Cay

Northwest Providence Channel

Red Bays
Lowe Sound
Morgan's Bluff
Nicholl's Town
Conch Sound
Mastic Point

San Andros Airport
San Andros

New Providence

Nassau International Airport

North Andros

Stafford Creek

Owens Town
Stafford Creek

Staniard Creek

Andros Barrier Reef

Over the Wall

Barge Wreck
Fresh Creek

Captain Bill's Blue Hole
Andros Town

Tongue of the Ocean

Billy Island

Williams Island

THE MUD

Central Andros

Man of War

Cargill Creek

Behring Point

Andros Barrier Reef

Turners Island

North Bight

Big Wood Cay

Pine Cay

Middle Bight
Moxey Town

G R A N D   B A H A M A   B A N K

Yellow Cay

Wood Cay

Mangrove Cay

Lisbon Creek
Driggs Hill
Congo Town

Alcorine Cay

South Bight

The Bluff

Kemps Bay

South Andros

Deep Creek

Mars Bay

Key
- Beaches
- Dive Sites

Water Depths
- -25ft deep
- -50ft deep
- -100ft deep

0   15 mi
0   15 km

Water Cays

NORTH ANDROS

The northern part of Andros spreads from the settlements of **Morgan's Bluff**, **Nicholl's Town**, and **Red Bays** and ends at **Stafford Creek**. North Andros is not only geographically removed from Central Andros, but essentially different in makeup: it consists of long stretches of pine forests, limestone bluffs, and fields and gardens of ground crops. Seminole Indians, American slaves, and Mennonites settled this land along with the West Indian population. White-sand beaches, mostly deserted, line the island's eastern face, interrupted by creeks, inlets, and rock outcroppings. Logging supported North Andros in the '40s and '50s, and laid the foundation for its roads.

San Andros is home to North Andros's airport, but **Nicholl's Town** is the largest settlement here and in all of Andros. Once home to a vogue resort in the 1960s, today it is mostly residential, inhabited in part by snowbirds who own the adorable Bahamian-style, brightly painted cottages that were once part of Andros Beach Hotel. Visitors will find lots to explore in this area, from caves to funky beach bars. Offshore to the north, Joulters Cays are a popular bonefishing spot; low tide reveals a duneslike bottom.

GETTING HERE AND AROUND

The San Andros airport (SAQ) has flights from Nassau via Performance Air and Western Air. Taxis meet incoming flights.

You can get around on foot in Nicholl's Town; car rentals are available for exploring the island's 65 mi of Queen's Highway and feeder roads in the north. They run about $70 to $85 a day. Main roads are in good shape, but watch out for potholes on the north end of North Andros.

Car Rentals Executive Car Rental ⊠ *Nicholl's Town* ☎ *242/329–2636.*

EXPLORING

Conch Sound. South of Nicholl's Town, Conch Sound is a wide protected bay with strands of white sand and tranquil waters. Swimmers and bonefishers can wade on their own on the easily accessible flats. Commercial fishermen bring their catches to a little beach park where you can buy what's fresh if your timing is right (ask around to find out what time they usually come in from fishing). A small offshore blue hole beckons snorkelers a short way off the beach.

Morgan's Bluff. A few miles north of Nicholl's Town is a crescent beach and a headland known as Morgan's Bluff, named after the 17th-century pirate Henry Morgan, who allegedly dropped off some of his stolen loot in the area. Morgan's Bluff is the site of Regatta Village, a colorful collection of stands and stalls that open in July when the North Andros–Berry Islands Regatta takes place. Tourism officials have plans to turn it into a year-round site for craftspeople and farmers in the North Andros area. It is adjacent to Government Dock and a safe harbor, meaning it sees a fair amount of boater and ferry day-trip traffic.

Nicholl's Town. Nicholl's Town, at Andros's northeastern corner, is the island's largest village, with a population of about 600. This friendly community with its agriculturally based economy has stores for supplies and groceries, a few motels, a public medical clinic, a telephone station, shops, small restaurants, and a fun strip of beach bars on the waterfront. Adorable cottages, a throwback from the town's big resort era of the '60s, house the island's wintering population from the States and Europe.

WHERE TO EAT AND STAY

$ ✕**Conch Sound Resort Inn Restaurant and Bar.** This diner-style restaurant
BAHAMIAN   serves hearty Bahamian and traditional dishes indoors and on the pool terrace. Scrambled eggs, bacon, grits, home fries, and pancakes will fill you up at breakfast. For lunch, conch salad, burgers, fried conch, and grouper with slaw are menu mainstays. Fresh fish, usually fried (though you can request grilled or pan-sautéed), and broiled lobster dominate the dinner choices, but often you can order Bahamian chicken, pork chops, or a steak to go with a garden salad, peas 'n' rice, or macaroni and cheese. The convivial staff creates a snappy aura, and on weekends the outdoor bar is a party spot for locals and guests alike. ⊠ *Conch Sound Resort Inn, Conch Sound Hwy. between Nicholl's Town and Conch Sound* ☎ *242/329–2060* ▭ *No credit cards* ⊘ *Hrs vary; call ahead.*

¢   ⬚**Conch Sound Resort Inn.** This secluded, ground-level inn several miles northeast of Nicholl's Town on the road to Conch Sound has six simple but clean and spacious motel-style rooms with carpeting, mahogany furniture, handmade quilts, soft-cushioned chairs, and cable TV. There are also four two-bedroom suites with modern furnishings, kitchens, and an overindulgence of pink. If you'd prefer not to cook, go to the restaurant for basic Bahamian fare. The beach is a two-minute walk away, but the hotel will provide transportation when it can. The staff is extremely welcoming and friendly, and will make you feel like family. Bonefishing, diving, deep-sea fishing, and even wild-boar hunting can be arranged. **Pros:** excellent location for anglers to fish the north end of the island; restaurant and bar on-site; friendly people. **Cons:** you need to rent a car to stay here or use taxis, which are expensive; rooms are small. ⊠ *Conch Sound Hwy. between Nicholl's Town and Conch Sound,* ☎ *242/329–2060* ↵*6 rooms, 4 suites* ⌂ *In-room: kitchen, Wi-Fi. In-hotel: restaurant, bar, pool, gym* ▭ *No credit cards.*

NIGHTLIFE

Big Shop. This place is liveliest on the weekends; it's a popular hangout for young locals. ⊠ *Nicholl's Town* ☎ *242/329–2047.*

SHOPPING

West of Nicholl's Town, the settlement of **Red Bays** was settled by Seminole Indians and runaway African slaves escaping Florida pre–Civil War. Their descendants are known for their craftsmanship, particularly basketry and wood carving. The tightly plaited baskets, some woven with scraps of colorful Androsia batik, have become a signature craft of Andros. Artisans have their wares on display in front of their homes, so be on the lookout as you approach the tiny town.

CENTRAL ANDROS

The bulk of Andros's resort scene centers here around the neighboring towns of **Fresh Creek** and **Andros Town,** north to **Stafford Creek** and down to Queen's Highway's southernmost reaches at **Cargill Creek** and **Behring Point.** Andros Town is the transportation and governmental hub midisland. Andros's largest resorts are here and at nearby **Small Hope Bay.** They are dedicated to boaters and divers, whereas the southern settlements cater exclusively to bonefishermen with small lodges. Central Andros accounts for 60% of the island's resort rooms.

As you head south in Central Andros, pine forests and later scrubby vegetation give way to hardwood hammocks. Coved beaches scallop the eastern shoreline, while the famed West Side is riddled with mangrove estuaries rich with marine life, including lobster and bonefish. Pleasing Behring Point, at the end of Queen's Highway, fronts Northern Bight, another bonefish sweet-spot. Nice homes with flowering gardens, palm trees, and sea grapes overlook the bight along Coakley Street. Several fishing guides in this area have started up their own small fishing lodges. Guesthouse-style, they often include all-day fishing and meals.

GETTING HERE AND AROUND

The Andros Town airport (ASD) sees the most traffic on the island. Besides Western Air and Performance Air, which fly from Nassau into all four Andros airports daily, LeAir flies only to Andros Town twice a day. Continental Connection flies in Saturdays from Fort Lauderdale. Taxis meet airplanes and ferries. The fare from the airport to Fish Creek is $15; to Cargill Creek area, some 20 mi south of the airport, about $40.

A number of car-rental operators are available (rentals start at $70 a day), but if you're staying in the Cargill Creek area, you'll probably be doing most of your traveling by boat. In Andros Town you can easily get around to the local restaurants, beaches, and blue holes by bike and on foot.

Car Rentals Adderley's Car Rental ⊠ *Fresh Creek* ☎ *242/357–2149.*

EXPLORING

Androsia Batik Works Factory. Brilliantly colored batik fabric called Androsia is designed and dyed at the Androsia Batik Works Factory, a 3-mi drive from Andros Town airport. The Small Hope Bay Lodge family started the enterprise in 1973 to provide employment for local women. Today it has been declared the official fabric of the Bahamas. You can visit the factory and see how the material is made, plus take lessons in the art of batik ($25, which includes the piece of fabric you decorate). Batik fabric is turned into wall hangings and clothing for men and women, which are sold throughout the Bahamas and the Caribbean, and are quite popular with the locals. You can stock up at the outlet next door. ⊠ *Andros Town* ☎ *242/368–2080* ⊕ *www.androsia. com* ☉ *Weekdays 8:30–4:30, Sat. 8:30–2:30.*

Fresh Creek. Near the Andros Town airport in Central Andros and on the north side of a creek that shares the same name and separates it from Andros Town, is the small hamlet of Fresh Creek. A few restaurants,

Andros has the third-largest barrier reef in the world (behind those of Australia and Belize).

including Hank's Place, line the waterfront, along with several boat docks and a small hotel with a convenience store. A few blocks in from the creek are a couple of markets, shops, and offices. The creek itself cuts over 16 mi into the island, creating tranquil bonefishing flats and welcoming mangrove-lined bays that boaters and sea kayakers can explore.

Staniard Creek. Sand banks that turn gold at low tide lie off the northern tip of Staniard Creek, a small island settlement 9 mi north of Fresh Creek, accessed by a bridge off the main highway. Coconut palms and casuarinas shade the ocean-side beaches, and offshore breezes are pleasantly cooling. **Kamalame Cove** and its nearby private cay are at the northern end of the settlement. Three creeks snake into the mainland, forming extensive mangrove-lined back bays and flats. The surrounding areas are good for wading and bonefishing.

WHERE TO EAT

$ ✕ **Hank's Place Restaurant and Bar.** On the north side of Fresh Creek, a

BAHAMIAN block or so east of the bridge, this restaurant and bar is shaded by coco-

★ nut palms and graced with clear views of the water. Eat inside, where plastic chairs and flowered tablecloths define the vibe, or outside on the spacious deck. Bahamian specialties—steamed, fried, or baked fish or chicken; ribs; shrimp; and pork chops—make it a favorite hangout for locals and visitors, especially for the Saturday-night parties. Fresh lobster, prepared to your liking, is available in season (August–March). Hank's signature cocktail, aptly named "Hanky Panky," is a dynamite frozen rum–and–fruit juice concoction. If you're looking for a cheap stay, Hank has four air-conditioned guest rooms for rent. He also rents flats boats and can arrange fishing guides. ⊠ *Fresh Creek* ☎ *242/368–2447* ⌲ *Reservations not accepted.*

¢   ✕ **Kristina's Café.** New and clean, this small eatery with a vaulted ceiling
BAHAMIAN   along Queen's Highway is a good stop for lunch; it also serves breakfast and dinner. Like many local restaurants, selections come from a "human menu," meaning there's no set listing but a few choices that change daily and usually include cracked conch and a chicken dish, whether fried or baked. Meals come with peas 'n' rice and a choice of coleslaw and potato salad. Deck seating is available. ⊠ *Andros Town* ☎ *242/368–2182.*

WHERE TO STAY

$$$$ ⊡ **Andros Island Bonefishing Club.** If you're a hard-core bonefisher, AIBC
ALL-INCLUSIVE   is the place for you. Guests have access to 100 square mi of lightly fished flats, including wadable (at low tide) flats right out front. Owner Captain Rupert Leadon is a gregarious, attention-grabbing legend with many stories of the elusive bonefish and his role in pioneering the sport of fly-fishing. His three sons and team of professional guides are highly regarded. The 20-acre waterfront property is laced with palm trees, well-tended gardens and lawns, and even some ruins from the island's sisal plantation era of the 1800s. Rooms are comfortable, with queen-size beds, mini-refrigerators, and ceiling fans. The dining room–lounges have satellite TV and fly-tying tables. Meals are hearty, with Bahamian fare such as fresh grilled seafood and peas 'n' rice served up family style. Package rates include room, meals, guided fishing, and laundry service. **Pros:** one of the best bonefishing lodges in the Bahamas; prime location on Cargill Creek. **Cons:** not much for nonanglers other than relaxing pool- or water-side. ⊠ *Cargill Creek* ☎ *242/368–5167* ⊕ *www.androsbonefishing.com* ⤢ *29 rooms* ⌂ *In-room: no TV. In-hotel: restaurant, bar, pool, water sports, business center* ⍣ *All-inclusive.*

$$$ ⊡ **Kamalame Cay.** This 96-acre all-inclusive resort sits on a private cay
★   laced with white-sand beaches and coconut palms. Gleaming, airy accommodations have plush furnishings, linens, and towels. Cottages and one- to four-bedroom villas are on the beach, with sitting areas, soaking tubs, and private terraces. Meals and cocktails are served in the veranda-wrapped plantation-style great house, which is adorned with oversize furniture and antiques. Guests feast on fresh fruits, prime beef, homemade breads and soups, and innovative seafood dishes. You can fish, dive, snorkel, lounge by the pool, or head to the deluxe spa facility. House rates include breakfast (all-inclusive plans available), use of pool, tennis court, snorkeling gear, and sea kayaks. **Pros:** discreet pampering; delicious innovative food; many daily activities, including outstanding bonefishing. **Cons:** no nightlife or shopping; you'll need insect repellent when the breeze is down; round-trip airport transfer costs $65 per person from nearest airport. ⊠ *At the north end of Staniard Creek, Central Andros* ☎ *242/368–6281, 800/790–7971* ⊕ *www.kamalame.com* ⤢ *6 rooms, 5 cottages, 5 villas* ⌂ *In-room: kitchen, no TV. In-hotel: restaurant, bar, pool, tennis court, spa, beach, water sports.*

$ ⊡ **Lighthouse Yacht Club and Marina.** This is the best place on Andros
to park your boat, though if you have a full-time captain there are a number of anchorages around the island. You're sure to meet an

ever-changing parade of people in the cocktail lounge and restaurant, which overlook the Fish Creek marina, and the bar has its lively moments on the weekends. The spacious rooms are comfortable, but in need of renovation (four are newer). Boat rentals, dive excursions, and fishing guides can be arranged. It's a five-minute walk across the bridge to Hank's Place Restaurant and Bar and convenience stores. The beach is a couple of minutes away by foot. The 31-space full-service marina can take boats up to 100 feet in length. **Pros:** best location on Andros to safely park your boat; easy access to town, shops, restaurants. **Cons:** facility is in need of renovation; service at check-in and in the restaurant can be slow. ⊠ *Andros Town* ☎ *242/368–2305* ⊕ *www.androslighthouse.com* 🖙 *20 rooms* ⌂ *In-room: Wi-Fi. In-hotel: restaurant, bar, pool, beach, laundry facilities.*

$ 🛏 **Love at First Sight.** At the mouth of Stafford Creek, self-sufficient anglers and do-it-yourself vacationers can sit on the sundeck, sip a cold Kalik, and contemplate the vast bonefish flats of Central Andros (or take a wilderness hike through the pine forests to a remote landlocked lake). Bright motel-style rooms are comfortable, with double beds and private bath. The restaurant, overlooking the lovely waters known as the "giddy hole," serves traditional Bahamian seafood, steaks, chicken, and pork, and at the bar you can enjoy an array of fruity rum drinks. Bonefishing and diving excursions can be arranged. Most guests arrive at Andros Town airport, but San Andros is an equal distance away. **Pros:** on-site restaurant and bar; economical location for exploring both Central and North Andros. **Cons:** if you want to explore, you'll need to rent a car. ⊠ *On the main highway at the mouth of Stafford Creek, Central Andros* ☎ *242/368–6082* ⊕ *www.loveatfirstsights.com* 🖙 *10 rooms* ⌂ *In-room: no TV. In-hotel: restaurant, bar, pool, business center.*

$$$$ 🛏 **Mount Pleasant Fishing Lodge.** Typical of the small bonefishing lodges that have cropped up in the southern part of Central Andros, Mount Pleasant caters to fishermen who care about nothing more than being out on the water all day. Guests can charter boat-fishing excursions or can cast from the flats that stretch into the bay. A gorgeous, sea-breeze cooled beach fronts the property, which holds one building with two two-bedroom apartments, another with two traditional rooms, and a restaurant–bar with satellite TV. The accommodations look brand-new and shiny, and have either full kitchens or a mini-refrigerator, but no phones or televisions. The restaurant serves breakfast and dinner, which consist mostly of seafood. There are kayaks for guest use. Fishing packages are available, which include a packed lunch. **Pros:** great beach; from-shore fishing. **Cons:** off-the-beaten-path; far from other restaurants. ⊠ *Cargill Creek* ☎ *242/368–5171* ⊕ *www.mtpleasantfish.com* 🖙 *2 rooms, 2 apartments* ⌂ *In-room: kitchen, no TV, Wi-Fi. In-hotel: restaurant, bar, beach, water sports, laundry facilities.*

$$$$ 🛏 **Small Hope Bay Lodge.** This casual, palm-shaded oceanfront property—
ALL-INCLUSIVE   which celebrated 50 years in 2010—has a devoted following of div-
ⓒ   ers, snorkelers, eco-adventurers, anglers, couples, and families. Rooms
Fodor'sChoice   with Androsia batik prints and straw work are in rustic beachside cot-
★   tages made of coral rock and Andros pine. Hammocks hang between

trees in plentitude. The homey main lodge—with a dining room, bar–lounge, game room (containing the only guest TV and a Ping-Pong table), reading area, and outdoor bar—is the center of activity. Tasty meals include Bahamian luncheon buffets and dinner buffets with international flair. Guests quickly get to know and bond with one another and the staff, who share meals with them. Children ages two

to seven eat dinner separately with a complimentary babysitter. For an additional charge you can select bonefishing and specialty diving packages, such as guided explorations of blue holes, diving instruction and certification, and "over-the-wall" dives. Rates include meals, beverages, and taxes. **Pros:** best dive operation on Andros; laid-back natural character and warm and welcoming service; free Wi-Fi and long-distance calls to the United States and Canada. **Cons:** limited nightlife; you'll need insect repellent against the sand flies that bite at sunrise and sunset; no pool. ⊠ *Small Hope Bay, Fresh Creek* ☎ *242/368–2014, 800/223–6961* ⊕ *www.smallhope.com* ⟿ *20 cottages* ⧖ *In-room: no a/c, no TV. In-hotel: restaurant, bar, beach, water sports, children's programs, business center, some pets allowed* ☉ *Closed Labor Day to mid-Aug.* ⑩ *All-inclusive.*

NIGHTLIFE

Hank's Place Restaurant and Bar. This is the place to be on Saturday nights for disco. ⊠ *Fresh Creek, Central Andros* ☎ *242/368–2447.*

SHOPPING

Androsia Outlet Store. Adjacent to the factory is the Androsia Outlet Store, where you can buy original fabrics, clothing, stuffed toys, Bahamian carvings and straw baskets, maps, CDs, and books. ☎ *242/368–2080* ⊕ *www.androsia.com* ☉ *Closed Sun.*

SPORTS AND THE OUTDOORS

BOATING AND FISHING   Andros fishermen claim the island is the best bonefishing location, and legends at Central Andros's south end are famed for pioneering the field of fly-fishing and island fishing lodges. The four main charter fishing regions include the hard-to-reach West Side flats, the creeks (particularly Fresh Creek), Joulters Cays north of North Andros, and the bights between Central and South Andros. There are also many areas where fishermen can wade-fish for the elusive "gray ghost." Full-day fishing excursions cost about $600. Bonefishing–lodging–dining packages run about $500 per person per day at the half dozen lodges in the area.

Reef and deep-sea fishing excursions are also available, but are secondary and not as spectacular as on other islands, although you can catch mahi-mahi, wahoo, and tuna in certain seasons.

★ **Andy Smith.** Andy Smith is highly recommended for guiding anglers through the bights and on the West Side. ☎ *242/368–4261.*

★ **Charlie Neymour.** Contact Big Charlie's Lodge to hire Charlie Neymour. He is a respected bonefishing and tarpon guide. ☎ *242/368–4297* ⊕ *www.bigcharlieandros.net.*

Small Hope Bay Lodge. Small Hope Bay Lodge has bone-, deep-sea, fly-, and reef fishing, as well as a "west side overnight"—a two-night camping and bone- and tarpon-fishing trip to the island's uninhabited western end. Rates run $290–$400 for a half day and $425–$550 for a full day (full-day trips include all gear and lunch). Book in advance. ☎ *242/368–2014, 800/223–6961.*

Tranquility Hill Fishing Lodge. Call Tranquility Hill Fishing Lodge at Behring Point to book Barry Neymour, Frankie Neymour, Deon Neymour, Dwain Neymour, Ray Mackey, and Ricardo Mackey, all recommended guides. ☎ *242/368–4132* ⊕ *www.tranquilityhill.com.*

HIKING **Small Hope Bay Lodge.** Small Hope Bay Lodge gives a number of self-guided and guided nature and cultural tours to the beach, mangroves, and blue holes, and into Fresh Creek by bike or on foot. The Bush Medicine walk takes you to Rainbow Blue Hole. ⊠ *Small Hope Bay, Central Andros* ☎ *242/368–2014, 800/223–6961* ⊕ *www.smallhope.com.*

SCUBA **Andros Barrier Reef.** Divers can't get enough of the sprawling Andros DIVING AND Barrier Reef, just off Fresh Creek–Andros Town. Snorkelers can explore SNORKELING such reefs as the Trumpet Reef, where visibility is clear 15 feet to the sandy floor and jungles of elkhorn coral snake up to the surface. Divers can delve into the 60-foot-deep coral caves of the Black Forest, beyond which the wall slopes down to depths of 6,000 feet. Anglers can charter boats to fish offshore or over the reef, and bonefishers can wade the flats on their own in Fresh Creek.

Small Hope Bay Lodge. Andros's main dive center is full-service, with resort dives, certification courses, one- and two-tank dives, specialty dives such as shark and night, and snorkeling. One-tank dives are $80. Rental equipment is available for Small Hope Bay Lodge excursions only. Lodging-dive packages are offered. ⊠ *Small Hope Bay, Central Andros* ☎ *242/368–2014, 800/223–6961* ⊕ *www.smallhope.com.*

MANGROVE CAY

Remote Mangrove Cay is sandwiched between two sea-green bights, separating it from Central and South Andros and creating an island of shorelines strewn with washed-up black coral, gleaming deserted beaches, and dense pine forests. **Moxey Town,** known locally as Little Harbour, rests on the northeast corner in a coconut grove. Pink piles of conch shells and mounds of porous sponges dot the small harbor of this commercial fishing and sponging community. Anglers come on a mission, in search of giant bonefish on flats called "the promised land" and "land of the giants." A five-minute boat ride takes fly-fishers to Gibson Cay to wade hard sand flats sprinkled with starfish.

GETTING HERE AND AROUND

Mangrove Cay Airport (MAY) has flights from Nassau via Performance Air, Western Air, or private charter. Western Air accepts cash only. Taxis meet incoming flights.

The cay's main road runs south from Moxey Town, past the airport, then along coconut-tree-shaded beaches to the settlement of Lisbon Creek. Car rentals are available for exploring Mangrove Cay's 8 mi of roads. They run about $70 to $85 a day. Taxis meet airplanes and ferries and are available for transporting and touring around the islands.

A free government ferry makes the half-hour trip between Mangrove Cay and South Andros twice daily. It departs from South Andros at 9 am and 5 pm and from Mangrove Cay at 8:30 am and 4:30 pm, but schedules are subject to change. Call the Commissioner's Office for information. There's no public transportation from Central Andros to Mangrove Cay.

WHERE TO EAT AND STAY

$ ✕ **Barefoot Bar and Grill.** Every table has a perfect ocean view at this
BAHAMIAN warm and friendly beachfront restaurant and bar at the Seascape Inn.
★ Owners Mickey and Joan McGowan do the baking and cooking themselves. Enjoy the sunrise over coffee with steaming scones, cinnamon buns, orange-walnut bread, and fresh fruit. Grilled chicken salad, burgers, sandwiches on kaiser rolls, and at times, quesadillas, are ample lunch temptations. Lunch items can also be prepared to take along as picnics on a daily outing. Chicken in white wine–lime sauce, roast pork loin, grilled steaks, and fresh fish of the day are a few dinner sensations. Call ahead at lunchtime to order your entrée. Even if you're full, the chocolate ganache, Grand Marnier–chocolate cloud, and homemade ice creams should not be missed. ⊠ *Seascape Inn* ☎☎ *242/369–0342* ⊕ *www.seascapeinn.com* ⌘ *Reservations essential.*

$ 🏠 **Mangrove Cay Inn.** In a coconut grove with wild orchid and hibiscus gardens, the inn caters to island aficionados and anglers alike. The rooms are decorated in peach and green with light Andros pine walls. Enjoy your favorite fresh seafood dish or a cold Kalik while relaxing in the restaurant and bar. Rent a bicycle to explore the cay, roam miles of nearby beach, or hire a fishing guide. Two cottages are also available for rent—a one-bedroom and a three-bedroom, with full kitchens and satellite TV, overlooking a saltwater lake filled with baby tarpon and snappers. Rates include taxes and gratuity. **Pros:** on-site restaurant and bar; quiet location near the beach; friendly staff. **Cons:** this isn't for you if you are not an angler or are high maintenance; you need insect repellent on calm humid days. ⊠ *5 mins south of the Mangrove Cay Airport on the island's main road* ☎ *242/369–0069* ⊕ *www.mangrovecayinn. net* 🔑 *12 rooms, 2 cottages* ⌂ *In-room: kitchen, no TV. In-hotel: restaurant, bar* ▭ *No credit cards.*

$ 🏠 **Seascape Inn.** Five individual, impeccably maintained cottages with
★ private decks overlook the glass-clear ocean. Many repeat guests say this is the most relaxing place in the world, and they take advantage of it by vacationing here two or three times a year. The elevated restaurant and beachfront bar is *the* place to relax, swap stories, and enjoy cocktails with the locals. Breakfasts, included in the room rate, consist of homemade banana bread, cinnamon buns, assorted muffins, and fresh fruit. On-site owners Mickey and Joan McGowan make guests feel like family. Mickey can arrange fishing guides or point you in the right direction to explore land and sea on your own. **Pros:** perfect beachfront

CLOSE UP

Undersea Adventures in Andros

Andros probably has the largest number of dive sites in the country. With the third-longest barrier reef in the world (behind those of Australia and Belize), the island offers about 100 mi of drop-off diving into the Tongue of the Ocean.

Uncounted numbers of **blue holes** are forming in the area. In some places these constitute vast submarine networks that can extend more than 200 feet down into the coral (Fresh Creek, 40–100 feet; North Andros, 40–200-plus feet; South Bight, 40–200 feet). Blue holes are named for their inky-blue aura when viewed from above and for the light-blue filtered sunlight that is visible from many feet below. Some of the holes have vast cathedral-like interior chambers with stalactites and stalagmites, offshoot tunnels, and seemingly endless corridors. Others have distinct thermoclines (temperature changes) between layers of water and are subject to tidal flow.

The dramatic Fresh Creek site provides an insight into the complex Andros cave system. There isn't much coral growth, but there are plenty of midnight parrot fish, big southern stingrays, and some blacktip sharks. Similar blue holes are all along the barrier reef, including several at Mastic Point in the north and the ones explored and filmed off South Bight.

Undersea adventurers also have the opportunity to investigate wrecks such as the *Potomac,* a steel-hulled freighter that sank in 1952 and lies in 40 feet of water off Nicholl's Town. And off the waters of Fresh Creek, at 70 feet, lies the deteriorated 56-foot-long World War II LCM (landing craft mechanized) known only as the

Barge Wreck, which was sunk in 1963 to create an artificial reef. Newer and more intact, the *Marian* wreck lies in 70 feet. Both are encrusted with coral and are home to a school of groupers and a blizzard of tiny silverfish. You'll find fish-cleaning stations where miniature cleaning shrimp and yellow gobies clean grouper and rockfish by swimming into their mouths and out their gills, picking up food particles. It's an excellent subject matter for close-up photography.

The multilevel **Over the Wall** dive at Fresh Creek takes novices to depths of 65–80 feet and experienced divers to 120–185 feet. The wall is covered with black coral and all kinds of tube sponges. **Small Hope Bay Lodge** is the most respected dive resort on Andros. It's a friendly, informal place where the only thing taken seriously is diving. There's a fully equipped dive center with a wide variety of specialty dives, including customized family-dive trips with a private dive boat and dive master. If you're not certified, check out the lodge's morning resort course and be ready to explore the depths by afternoon. If you are certified, don't forget to bring your C card.

If you are leery of diving but want to view the spectacular undersea world, try a snorkeling excursion. Shallow reefs, beginning in 6 feet of water, and extending down to 60 feet or more, are ideal locations for spotting myriad brightly colored fish, sea urchins, and starfish. Don't forget your underwater camera!

Winter water temperatures average about 74°F. In summer, water temperatures average about 84°F.

Tiamo Resort, South Andros

location for a do-it-yourself vacation; outstanding food; guests are treated like family. **Cons:** no a/c or TV; you need insect repellent when the wind is down. ⊠ *About 5 mins south of the Mangrove Cay Airport on the island's main road* ☏ *242/369–0342* ⊕ *www.seascapeinn.com* ⊷ *5 cottages* ⸖ *In-room: no a/c, no TV, Wi-Fi. In-hotel: restaurant, bar, beach, water sports* ⦿ *Breakfast.*

SOUTH ANDROS

South Andros's road stretches 25 mi from **Drigg's Hill**—a small settlement of pastel houses, a tiny church, a grocery store, the government dock, and the Emerald Palms Resort—to Mars Bay. Eight miles farther south, the Bluff settlement sprawls atop a hill overlooking miles of golden beaches, lush cays, and the Tongue of the Ocean. Here skeletons of Arawak natives were found huddled together. A local resident attests that another skeleton was found—this one of a 4-foot-tall, one-eyed owl, which may have given rise to the legend of the mythical, elflike chickcharnie.

GETTING HERE AND AROUND

The Congo Town Airport (TZN) is a mile south of Drigg's Hill and receives daily flights from Nassau via Performance Air and Western Air. Taxis meet incoming flights.

A free government ferry makes the half-hour trip between Mangrove Cay and South Andros twice daily. It departs from South Andros at 9 am and 5 pm and from Mangrove Cay at 8:30 am and 4:30 pm, but schedules are subject to change. Call the Commissioner's Office for information. There's no public transportation from Central Andros to Mangrove Cay.

Car Rentals Lenglo Car Rental ✉ *Congo Town* ☎ *242/369–1702.*

WHERE TO EAT AND STAY

$$
BAHAMIAN

✕ **Emerald Palms Clubhouse Restaurant.** The breakfast buffet in the Clubhouse Restaurant at the Emerald Palms Resort is a pleasant way to energize your day. You can choose from fresh fruits and cereals or scrambled eggs and bacon. The brightly colored dining room overlooks the resort's pool and beach. At lunch, burgers, conch salad (when available), panfried grouper, and club sandwiches are served on the terrace by the pool. The adjacent bar is a relaxing spot for a predinner cocktail. Nightly dining specialties are broiled lobster, grilled fresh mahimahi, steaks, chops, and chicken prepared Bahamian style. A children's menu is available. ✉ *Emerald Palms Resort, Driggs Hill* ☎ *242/369–2713.*

$
☍

⌕ **Emerald Palms Resort of South Andros.** This boutique ocean-side property has clubhouses and villas with marble floors, mahogany furniture, king-size or double beds, individual gardens, and private decks surrounded by palm trees. Phones reach other rooms and the front desk but not outside the resort. The spacious clubhouse rooms run along the blue-tile pool and out to the glimmering beach. Ask for one of the beachfront rooms or villas. Hearty Bahamian breakfasts, light zesty lunches, and theme-night four-course dinners are served in the poolside restaurant. A cabana bar overlooks the gin-clear sea. The resort is family-friendly, and island excursions and guided fishing can be arranged. Wi-Fi is accessible in the lobby and dining room. **Pros:** spacious villa accommodations are ideal for families and small groups; pristine beachfront location; good access to prime diving and fishing. **Cons:** need to create your own nightlife; service can be slow in the restaurant. ✉ *Driggs Hil* ☎ *242/369–2713* ⊕ *www.emerald-palms.com* ⇱ *18 rooms, 22 villas* ☍ *In-room: kitchen. In-hotel: restaurant, bar, pool, beach, water sports, business center.*

$$$$
ALL-INCLUSIVE
Fodor'sChoice
★

⌕ **Tiamo.** You arrive at this low-key yet sophisticated South Bight eco-resort via private launch. Over-the-top service awaits, along with a cold drink in the Great Room—a stress-free gathering place with wood-beam ceilings that naturally combines bar and library. Individual cottages with wraparound porches are strung out along the powdery beach, shaded by coconut palms. Commodious bedrooms with soft linens are positioned to receive the cooling ocean breeze. Cool Cottages and the Pool Cottage are air-conditioned with enormous bathrooms and a minibar. Island Breeze Cottages are the top eco option, without air-conditioning. Leisurely meals, exquisitely prepared with the freshest ingredients, include seafood delights, homemade breads, and luscious desserts. All meals, snacks, and nonalcoholic beverages are included in the room rate. To explore the wilds of sea and land, guided snorkeling, sea kayaking, nature hikes, and fishing excursions can be arranged at your whim. **Pros:** 1.5-to-1 staff-to-guest ratio; spectacular private beachfront location; great food. **Cons:** you'll need insect repellent on calm humid days. ✉ *South Bight, accessible only by boat, Driggs Hill* ☎ *242/359–2330* ⊕ *www.tiamoresorts.com* ⇱ *10 cottages* ☍ *In-room: no a/c, no TV.*

In-hotel: restaurant, bar, pool, gym, spa, beach, water sports, business center, some age restrictions ⊗ *Closed Sept.* ⱺ *All-inclusive.*

NIGHTLIFE

Cabana. This hole-in-the-wall island spot is a local hangout, with reggae music and cheap drinks on the beach. ⊠ *Drigg's Hill* ☎ *No phone.*

Conch Stand. Get fresh conch salad, hang with locals, and play dominoes or backgammon on the beach to a reggae-and-calypso soundtrack at Conch Stand. ⊠ *Mangrove Cay* ☎ *No phone.*

SPORTS AND THE OUTDOORS

FISHING **Emerald Palms Resort of South Andros.** Emerald Palms Resort of South Andros can arrange boat rentals and schedule guides for bonefishing, reef fishing, or deep-sea fishing. ☎ *242/369–2711.*

Reel Tight Charters. This charter company offers a variety of services on South Andros and throughout the Bahamas, including deep-sea and reef fishing, plus diving, snorkeling, and spearfishing. ⊠ *Drigg's Hill Marina, Driggs Hill, Andros Island* ☎ *242/554–0031.*

5

BIMINI

Bimini has long been known as the Bahamas' big game-fishing capital. Unlike most other Bahamian islands, Bimini's strong tourist season falls from spring through summer, when calmer seas mean the arrival of fishing and pleasure boats from south Florida. The nearest of the Bahamian islands to the U.S. mainland, Bimini consists of a handful of islands and cays just 50 mi east of Miami, across the Gulf Stream that sweeps the area's western shores. Most visitors spend their time on bustling North Bimini; South Bimini is quieter and more eco-oriented. Most of the hotels, restaurants, churches, and stores in Bimini are in capital **Alice Town** along North Bimini's King's and Queen's highways, which run parallel to each other. Everything on **North Bimini**, where most of the islands' 2,000 inhabitants reside, is so close that you do not need a car to get around. The largest resort, Bimini Bay, takes up the northern quarter of the island, with a huge upscale marina development that continues to grow, with a casino slated to open in late 2012.

Sparsely populated **South Bimini** is where Juan Ponce de León allegedly looked for the Fountain of Youth in 1513, and a site with a well and natural trail memorialize it. More engaging, however, is the island's biological field station, known as the Sharklab for its study of lemon-shark behavior, among other things. The main resort on this island, Bimini Sands, is as equally marina-oriented as Bimini Bay, but much more low-key.

Salvagers, gunrunners, rumrunners, and the legendary Ernest Hemingway peopled the history of Bimini. Hemingway wrote much of *To Have and Have Not* and *Islands in the Stream* here between fishing forays and street brawls. Today spring breakers who cruise over from Fort Lauderdale continue North Bimini's reputation as a party island.

Boat and Ferry Information Commissioner's Office ☎ *242/369-0331.* **Dockmaster's Office** ☎ *242/393-1064.*

Bimini at sunset

GETTING HERE

South Bimini (BIM) has a teensy airport, but blessedly with air-conditioning. It services flights from Fort Lauderdale (Gulfstream International and Island Air Charters), Nassau (Western Air and Sky Bahamas), and Grand Bahama Island (Regional Air). A short taxi ride ($3) from the airport delivers you to the ferry to North Bimini, a five-minute crossing that costs $2 each way.

For information on traveling to Bimini from Nassau by mailboat, call ☎ 242/323–2166. *Bimini Mack* leaves Potter's Cay, Nassau, Thursday afternoon for North Bimini and Cat Cay. The trip takes about 12 hours and costs $45 one-way. Return is Monday morning.

Boaters often travel from Florida to Bimini, mostly from West Palm Beach, Fort Lauderdale, and Miami. Crossing the Gulf Stream, however, should only be done by skippers who can plot a course using charts for that purpose. The distance is 48 nautical mi. Customs and Immigrations offices are located in Alice Town next to the straw market and at Bimini Bay and Bimini Sands resorts.

NORTH BIMINI

Bimini's main community, **Alice Town,** is at North Bimini's southern end. It's colorful, painted in happy Caribbean pastels, but has lately taken on a glory-gone look. In a prominent location stand the ruins of the Compleat Angler Hotel, Ernest Hemingway's famous haunt, which burned down in 2006. A short walk away is the Bimini Native Straw and Craft Market, which bustles on weekends and during fishing tournaments.

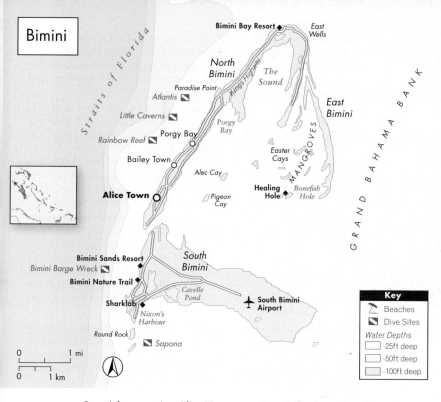

Bimini

In quick succession Alice Town turns into **Bailey Town**, then **Porgy Bay**—these three towns are separated only by signs heralding the change. Toward King's Highway's north end, north of Alice Town, you'll see bars, grocery shops, clothing stores, the pink medical center, and a group of colorful fruit stalls. This part of the island, from Bailey Town to the Bimini Bay Resort, is clean, fresh, and lively.

GETTING HERE AND AROUND

Catch a taxi in South Bimini at the South Bimini Airport for transportation to the ferry service between South Dock and North Dock. The entire process costs $5. Once there, walk or take one of the waiting taxis to your accommodations. Ferries cannot take you directly to your hotel or marina—to Bimini Bay Resort for example—because government regulations protect the taxi union.

Most people get around North Bimini on gas-powered golf carts, and they are available for rent from various vendors and resorts for $70 to $90 per day, or $20 for the first hour, and $10 for each additional hour.

Rentals Capt. Pat's ✉ *Alice Town* ☎ *242/347–3477.*

The Bimini Tram regularly runs the length of North Bimini to Bimini Bay for $3 per person. It picks up at a number of stops along King's Highway.

Contact Bimini Tram ☎ *242/473-2055.*

EXPLORING

Bailey Town. Most of the island's residents live in Bailey Town in small, pastel-color concrete houses. Bailey Town lies on King's Highway, north of the Bimini Big Game Club and before Porgy Bay and the Bimini Bay Resort. It's also a good place to find a home-cooked meal or conch salad from shacks along the waterfront.

Bimini Museum. The Bimini Museum, sheltered in the restored (1921) two-story original post office and jail—a two-minute walk from the ferry dock, across from the native straw market—showcases varied artifacts, including Adam Clayton Powell's domino set, Prohibition photos, rum kegs, Martin Luther King Jr.'s immigration card from 1964, and a fishing log and rare fishing films of Papa Hemingway. The exhibit includes film shot on the island as early as 1922. ⊠ *King's Hwy., Alice Town* ☎ *242/347–3038* 🎫 *$2* ⊙ *Mon.–Sat. 9–9, Sun. noon–9.*

Dolphin House. Bimini historian and poet laureate Ashley Saunders has spent 18 years constructing this sturdy home and guesthouse from materials salvaged from local construction sites and the sea. Mr. Saunders will take you on a tour of the still-in-progress structure—named for the 27 mosaic, sculpted, and painted dolphins throughout—then continue through Alice Town to tell the island's history. ⊠ *Alice Town between King's and Queen's Hwys.* ☎ *242/347–3201* 🎫 *Tours $20/hr* ⊙ *By appointment.*

OFF THE
BEATEN
PATH

Healing Hole. Locals recommend a trip here for curing what ails you—gout and rheumatism are among the supposedly treatable afflictions. Ask your hotel to arrange a trip out to this natural clearing in North Bimini's mangrove flats. Surf Watersport at Bimini Bay organizes three-hour kayak excursions. You can take a leap of faith into the water and, if nothing else, enjoy a refreshing dip.

Road to Atlantis. Road to Atlantis, a curious rock formation under about 20 feet of water, 500 yards offshore at Bimini Bay, is shaped like a backward letter J, some 600 feet long at the longest end. It's the shorter 300-foot extension that piques the interest of scientists and visitors. The precision patchwork of large, curved-edge stones forms a perfect rectangle measuring about 30 feet across. A few of the stones are 16 feet square. It's purported to be the "lost city" whose discovery was predicted by Edgar Cayce (1877–1945), a psychic with an interest in prehistoric civilizations. Archaeologists estimate the formation to be between 5,000 and 10,000 years old. Carvings in the rock appear to some scientists to resemble a network of highways. Skeptics have pooh-poohed the theory, conjecturing that they are merely turtle pens built considerably more recently.

WHERE TO EAT

$ ✕ **Captain Bob's.** Across from the Sea Crest Marina, centrally located in
BAHAMIAN Alice Town, this casual joint starts serving rib-sticking American and Bahamian breakfasts (try the conch or lobster omelet) at 6:30 am seven days a week. This is an ideal place for anglers to start their day before heading out to the flats or the blue water. Lunches of burgers, conch, soups, salads, and fresh fish are served until 2 pm Monday through Saturday and until 1 pm on Sunday. After a long day on the sea, step

Mangrove flats, North Bimini

in for a hearty dinner (summer only) of stuffed lobster or the popular seafood platter. If you call ahead, fishing lunches to take out on your boat can be prepared. ✉ *Queen's Hwy., Alice Town* ☎ *242/347–3260* ⊕ *www.captainbobsbimini.com.*

$$ ✕ **Sabor.** Enjoy the view of the bay or the display kitchen while nosh-
BAHAMIAN ing on artistic yet simple island dishes from the freshest ingredients.
★ Breakfast is hot baked breads, eggs any style, fresh fruit, and juices. Dinner—the most formal on the island—includes starters of conch frit-ters, ceviche, and Caesar salad. For your entrée, try the steak frites, paella, mojo-glazed chicken or sesame-crusted yellowfin tuna. For des-sert, order the guava duff for a local treat when it's offered. ✉ *Bimini Bay Resort, King's Hwy.* ☎ *242/347–2900, 866/344–8759* ⊕ *www. biminibayresort.com.*

WHERE TO STAY

$ 🏨 **Big John's Hotel.** Seven deluxe hotel rooms—five with ocean views, two with town views—are perfect for the traveler who wants to get away from the megaresort scene but still stay in style. Amenities include flat-screen TVs, antique nautical furniture, high-thread-count sheets, soft oversize towels, and boutique soaps. Downstairs, the casual, popu-lar outdoor lounge serves icy rum drinks along with a full array of international cocktails. There's even a small beach. The Hypnotics, Bimini's favorite band for 20 years, plays live music Thursday through Saturday. **Pros:** central Alice Town location; great value for extremely pleasant accommodations on the bay; can park your boat at Brown's Marina, in front of the hotel. **Cons:** lively bar can make getting to sleep a challenge if you turn in early; no pool, but the beach is in walking distance. ⊠ *King's Hwy. across from Gateway Gallery, Alice Town* ☎ *242/347–3117* ⊕ *www.bigjohnshotel.com* ⇋ *7 rooms* ♿ *In-hotel: bar* ▭ *No credit cards.*

$ ⊡ **Bimini Bay Resort and Marina.** You can choose an ocean view, a bay ☾ view, or both at this luxury resort that includes spacious suites, condo-★ miniums, and town houses with island art, seashell accents, hardwood and rattan furnishings, lavish bedrooms and baths, and ultramodern kitchens (some units have no stoves). There are also larger single-family beach houses, with up to four bedrooms, that make it hard for some guests to return to their own permanent homes. Why leave such posh digs in paradise? The pastel-painted wooden structures, landscaping, fountains, and road systems blend with the natural terrain of beaches, palms, and the two bay-side marinas. At the biggest marina there's a saltwater beach-entry pool and windowed Sabor restaurant. A casino is scheduled to open in 2012. Enjoy your lunch at the infinity-pool grill, Aqua, overlooking the ocean. **Pros:** luxury accommodations and amenities on the beach; top-quality marinas with all services; shuttle service around the property. **Cons:** additional construction is still in progress; the north-end units are a long walk from town. ⊠ *King's Hwy. north of Bailey Town* ☎ *242/347–2900, 866/344–8759* ⊕ *www. biminibayresort.com* ⇋ *350 units* ♿ *In-room: kitchen, Wi-Fi. In-hotel: restaurant, bar, pool, tennis court, beach, water sports, children's programs, laundry facilities.*

¢ ⊡ **Bimini Blue Water Resort.** You can still rent three-bedroom Marlin Cottage, the place where Hemingway wrote parts of *Islands in the Steam,* and knock back daiquiris in the wood-paneled bar. Rooms in the main building are well worn but comfortable. Additional rooms and suites, which have large windows and private patios, have a circa-1960 south Florida theme. The Anchorage restaurant, overlooking the ocean, serves excellent fresh seafood and has satellite TV. Situated in the middle of town, the resort gives access to other places to eat, as well. The 32-slip marina and dockside pool are across the road on the lee side of the island. **Pros:** good restaurant; close to the local scene. **Cons:** can be noisy and bustling. ⊠ *King's Hwy., Alice Town* ☎ *242/347–3166* ⇋ *9 rooms, 1 cottage* ♿ *In-hotel: restaurant, bar, pool, beach.*

¢ ⊡ **Sea Crest Hotel and Marina.** Tucked between the beach and the marina, this three-story hotel has comfortable, simply furnished rooms with tile floors, cable TV, balconies, and one of the island's friendliest owner–management teams. Pick a room or suite on the third floor; they have lofty, open-beam ceilings and lovely sea or marina views. The marina is across the street (King's Highway). Diving, snorkeling, and fishing charters can be arranged. **Pros:** economical and comfortable; central location; welcoming service. **Cons:** rooms could use renovation; credit-card fee. ⊠ *King's Hwy., Alice Town* ☎ *242/347–3071* ⊕ *www. seacrestbimini.com* ⇋ *25 rooms, 2 suites* ♿ *In-hotel: restaurant.*

NIGHTLIFE

Big John's Conch Shell Bar & Lounge. Catch the Hypnotics at Big John's Conch Shell Bar & Lounge Thursday through Saturday nights. ⊠ *King's Hwy.* ☎ *239/347–3117.*

★ **End of the World Saloon.** The back door of the small, noisy End of the World Saloon, better known by locals as "Sand Bar," is always open to the harbor. This place—with a sandy floor and visitors' graffiti, business cards, and other surprises on every surface—is a good spot to meet local folks over a beer and a lobster-and-conch pizza, while playing a game of ringtoss. The bar is 100 yards from the Compleat Angler ruins, and just down the way from Brown's Marina and Big John's Conch Shell Bar and Hotel. ⊠ *King's Hwy.* ☎ *No phone* ⊙ *Closed in winter until spring break.*

SHOPPING

Bimini Native Straw and Craft Market. Bimini Native Straw and Craft Market has almost 20 vendors, including Nathalie's Native Bread stand. ⊠ *Next door to Bahamas Customs Bldg.* ☎ *No phone.*

SPORTS AND THE OUTDOORS

BOATING AND FISHING

Capt. Jerome. Capt. Jerome, with 32 modern slips, charges from $1,300 a day, and from $750 a half day for deep-sea fishing, with captain, mate, and gear included. ☎ *242/347–2081, 242/359–8082.*

Fisherman's Village Marina. This 136-slip full-service marina has blue-water boats for charter fishing, a liquor store, ice-cream shop, gourmet pizza restaurant, and customs and immigration offices. ☎ *242/347–2900* ⊕ *www.biminibayresort.com.*

Weech's Bimini Dock. Weech's Bimini Dock has 15 slips. ☎ *242/347–3028.*

The following are highly recommended bonefish guides, and they must be booked in advance:

Bonefish Ansil. Also a local boatbuilder, Bonefish Ansil holds the world's record for the biggest bonefish ever caught. ☎ *242/347–2178.*

Bonefish Ebbie ☎ *242/347–2053, 242/359–8273.*

Bonefish Tommy ☎ *242/347–3234.*

SCUBA DIVING AND SNORKELING

The **Bimini Barge Wreck** (a World War II landing craft) rests in 100 feet of water. **Little Caverns** is a medium-depth dive with scattered coral heads, small tunnels, and swim-throughs. **Rainbow Reef** is a shallow dive popular for fish gazing. And, of course, there's **Bimini Road to Atlantis,** thought to be the famous "lost city." Dive packages are available through most Bimini hotels. You can also check out the best diving options through the **Bahamas Diving Association** (☎ *954/236–9292 or 800/866–DIVE* ⊕ *www.bahamasdiving.com*).

Bill and Nowdla Keefe's Bimini Undersea. Bill and Nowdla Keefe's Bimini Undersea, headquartered at Bimini Bay Resort, lets you snorkel near a delightful pod of Atlantic spotted dolphins for $129 per person. You can also rent or buy snorkel and diving gear. It offers two two-tank dives a day for $99 per person and introductory scuba lessons. Dive packages with accommodations at Bimini Bay Resort are available. ☎ *242/347–3089, 800/348–4644* ⊕ *www.biminiundersea.com.*

A large bonefish caught on Bimini's shallow flats

SOUTH BIMINI

Bigger, with better beaches and higher elevation than low-lying North Bimini, South Bimini is nonetheless the quieter of the two islands. Home to the island's only airport, it has a smattering of shops near the ferry landing, where boats make regular crossings between the two islands, a short five-minute ride. Bimini Sands Resort occupies the bulk of the island with its safe-harbor marina, condos, beach club, and nature trail. It helps preserve the island's eco-focus by staying low-key and keeping much of its land undeveloped. It helps maintain the little Fountain of Youth Park, the Sharklab, and beaches.

GETTING AROUND

Visitors do not need a car on Bimini, and there are no car-rental agencies. A taxi from the airport to Bimini Sands Resort is $3.

EXPLORING

★ **Bimini Biological Field Station Sharklab.** Showcased often on the Discovery Channel and other TV shows, the Sharklab was founded some 20 years ago by Dr. Samuel Gruber, a shark biologist at the University of Miami. Important research on the lemon and other shark species has furthered awareness and understanding of the misunderstood creatures. Visitors can tour the lab at low tide. The highlight is wading into the bay where the lab keeps several lemon sharks, rotating them on a regular basis. The tour leader gets in the pen with the sharks, captures one in a net, and speaks about its behaviors and common misconceptions people have of the lemon. ⊠ *South Bimini* ☎ *242/347–4538* ✈ *Free* ☉ *Call ahead for tour time.*

Bimini Nature Trail. Developed by Bimini Sands Resort on undeveloped property, this mile-loop trail is one of the best of its kind in the Bahamas. Its slight rise in elevation means a lovely shaded walk under hardwood trees such as gumbo-limbos, poisonwood (marked with "Don't Touch" signs), and buttonwood. Check out the ruins of the historic Conch House, a great place for sunset-gazing. The resort also recently added a pirate's well exhibit devoted to the island's swashbuckling history. Excellent signage guides you through the island's fauna and flora, but for the best interpretation and learning experience, book a guided tour with Grant Johnson. Don't miss petting an indigenous Bimini boa. Johnson always keeps one in a cage and rotates specimens. ⊠ *South Bimini* ☎ *242/347–3500* ☜ *Free, tours $12* ⊗ *Daily sunrise–sunset.*

WHERE TO EAT AND STAY

$
SEAFOOD
Fodor'sChoice
★
✕ Bimini Twist. One of the top two dining spots in Bimini, Bimini Twist at the Bimini Sands' Beach Club has an exceptional sushi bar and an elegant dining room. Time dinner for the sunset show if possible. If you'd rather not do sushi, start with conch, shrimp, lobster, or tomato ceviche. The chef is at the top of his game, and will prepare special requests with panache. Entrées provide good variety from pasta pomodoro and conch linguine to chicken sautéed with mushroom and onions, and sirloin steak. ⊠ *Bimini Sands Resort* ☎ *242/347–4500* ⊕ *www.biminisands. com* ⚓ *Reservations essential.*

$
★
⊡ Bimini Big Game Club. In July 2010 this lodging fixture since 1936 reopened after two years of being closed. Under the auspices of Guy Harvey Outpost, named for the famed Jamaican artist and conservationist who has taken over the operation, it is a prototype for more resorts planned throughout the Caribbean. Here the resort property will hold 51 rooms, a 75-slip marina, a dive shop, pool hall, deli, and the Bimini Big Game Bar & Grill, serving casual Bahamian and American fare. **Pros:** newly renovated, excellent marina for fishing boats. **Cons:** can be wild and noisy during fishing tournaments (though this might be a pro for some). ⊠ *King's Hwy., at pink wall* ☎ *242/347–3391, 800/867–4764* ⊕ *www.biggameclubbimini.com* ⇆ *35 rooms, 12 cottages, 4 penthouses* ⚐ *In-room: kitchen. In-hotel: restaurant, bar, pool, children's programs, business center.*

$$
☺
Fodor'sChoice
★
⊡ Bimini Sands Resort and Marina. Overlooking the Straits of Florida, this well-designed property rents one- to three-bedroom condominiums with direct beach access. The bright, nicely decorated condos have balconies and patios with views of the tropical surroundings, the marina, or the beach. The Petite Conch restaurant serves three meals a day, blending Bahamian staples with American favorites. There's a 60-slip marina, ship's store, and a convenient customs office, so guests with boats can tie up and clear their paperwork without venturing to North Bimini. The beach club with pool, bars, and a dinner restaurant is a short drive away; a colorful shuttle bus provides complimentary transportation in the evening hours. An all-night (until 2 am or later depending upon demand) water taxi shuttles you to North Bimini to shop, dine, and party. Boat and golf-cart rentals are available. **Pros:** two good restaurants (including a sushi bar); great nature trail on property; good tour operations; full-service marina with customs clearance. **Cons:**

5

South Bimini location is away from the "action" on North Bimini. ⊠ *South Bimini* ☎ *242/347–3500* ⊕ *www.biminisands.com* ⇒ *206 condominiums* ⅃ *In-room: kitchen, Wi-Fi. In-hotel: restaurant, bar, pool, tennis court, beach, water sports, children's programs, laundry facilities.*

PLAN AHEAD

Even though you're going to the laid-back islands, you need to reserve your guides, boats, cars, and golf carts in advance. And if you ask, these friendly islanders might include an airport greeting and transfer to your hotel.

NIGHTLIFE

Mackey's Sand Bar. With its beachfront location, sand floor, sports TVs, and Wednesday-night karaoke (and live music during the spring and summer season), Mackey's Sand Bar is South Bimini's one and only hot spot. Folks often make the water-taxi ride from North Bimini for dinner and cocktailing. ☎ *242/347–4500* ⊕ *www.biminisands.com.*

SPORTS AND THE OUTDOORS

BOATING AND FISHING **Bimini Sands Marina.** Bimini Sands Marina, on South Bimini, is a top-notch 60-slip marina capable of accommodating vessels up to 100 feet. Convenient customs clearance for guests is at the marina. Rent a 20- to 22-foot Twin Vee for $125 (plus fuel) for a half day, $250 per day. Rental fishing gear (flats and blue water) is also available. The Bimini Sands Resort has a variety of eco and other boat excursions including snorkeling and a shark-feeding tour. ☎ *242/347–3500* ⊕ *www.biminisands.com.*

SCUBA DIVING AND SNORKELING Bimini has excellent diving opportunities, particularly for watching marine life. Off the shore of South Bimini the concrete wreck of the S.S. *Sapona* attracts snorkelers as well as partiers.

Bimini Sands Resort. This resort has an excellent recreation program that includes snorkeling excursions to reefs, wrecks, and the Bimini Road to Atlantis. It also offers kayaking trips, boat tours, shark encounters, tours of the Bimini Nature Trail, and Kid's Club activities. ☎ *242/347–3500* ⊕ *www.biminisands.com.*

THE BERRY ISLANDS

Remote, undiscovered, and pristine in beauty, the Berry Islands consist of more than two dozen small islands and almost a hundred tiny cays stretching in a sliver moon–like curve north of Andros and New Providence Island. Although a few of the islands are privately owned, most of them are uninhabited—except by rare birds who use the territory as their nesting grounds, or by visiting yachters dropping anchor in secluded havens. The Berry Islands start in the north at **Great Stirrup Cay**, where a lighthouse guides passing ships, and they end in the south at **Chub Cay**, only 35 mi north of Nassau.

Most of the islands' 700 residents live on **Great Harbour Cay**, which is 10 mi long and 1½ mi wide. Great Harbour, the largest of the Berry Islands, is sedate, self-contained, and oriented toward family beach and water-sport vacationing. Its main settlement, **Bullock's Harbour**, more commonly known as "the Village," has a couple of good restaurants near the marina, plus a grocery store and some small shops. The Great Harbour Cay resort and beach area, a few miles away from Bullock's Harbour, was developed in the early 1970s. More homes have been built since then, and many of the older beach villas and cottages have been remodeled.

Although the area has long been geared toward offshore fishing, in recent years family vacations and bonefishing have become more popular. Both Chub and Great Harbour cays are close to the Tongue of the Ocean, where big-game fish roam. Remote flats south of Great Harbour, from Anderson Cay to Money Cay, are excellent bonefish habitats, as are the flats around Chub Cay. Deeper water flats hold permit and tarpon.

GETTING HERE AND AROUND

In the Berry Islands the government airport in Great Harbour Cay (GHC) receives regular flights from Nassau (Cat Air), Fort Lauderdale (Gulfstream International), and Grand Bahama (Flamingo Air) plus private charters from south Florida and other Bahamas islands. Chub Cay (CCZ) has a private airport with regular flights from Nassau (Pineapple Air) and Fort Lauderdale (Gulfstream). There's another private airport on Big Whale Cay.

The Great Harbour Cay airport is within walking distance of resorts, but taxis are available at the airport, as are car, golf-cart, and boat rentals, but you can get around the main settlement of Bullock's Harbour on foot. Car rentals run about $60 per day.

On Great Harbour Cay you can get most places on foot, but you can also rent a bike, car, or golf cart. Golf-cart rentals go for about $50 a day. They are the most common and convenient source of transportation off the water.

Rentals Happy People's Rental ✉ *Great Harbour Cay* ☎ *242/367–8117.*

WHERE TO EAT

$ ✕ **The Beach Club.** This is the island's cool locale for breakfast and lunch,
BAHAMIAN across the road from the airport, overlooking the beach and turquoise water. At breakfast, go for the eggs and ham with home grits. At lunch, have a grilled cheeseburger or whatever fresh fish is available. Takeout is available, including fishing lunches. Dinner is available on request, but if you eat at the open-air tables, be sure to have insect repellent, especially if the wind is down and especially at sunset. Hours and days are irregular, so talk to the locals or go by to see if it's open. ✉ *Across from Great Harbour Airport, Great Harbour Cay* ☎ *242/367–8108* ⊟ *No credit cards.*

$$ ✕ **Coolie Mae's.** Expats, locals, and visitors rate Mae's food as the best
BAHAMIAN on the island. Her bright sign makes the casual 60-seat restaurant in
★ the Village, on the north side of the marina entrance, easy to find. Mae's secret is simple: she uses the best and freshest ingredients available each day to serve up wonderful home-style chow. Midday, try the conch salad, panfried grouper, or a tasty burger. Broiled lobster, steaks, pork chops, and fried conch along with peas 'n' rice and macaroni and cheese are dinner specialties. The menu changes daily. Conch fritters

and cocktails are often served at sunset, and island art exhibits are on display throughout the year. ⊠ *The Village, Great Harbour Cay* ☎ *242/367–8730* ▭ *No credit cards* ⊘ *Closed Sun. and after 9 pm (kitchen closes at 8).*

$$$ ✗ **Tamboo Dinner Club.** A tradition
BAHAMIAN   at the Great Harbour Marina, this supper club is open Saturday, and other nights with reservations depending on the season. There is usually a lively crowd enjoying grilled seafood, rack of lamb, beef tenderloin, pork loin, baked duck, Cornish hen, and Bahamian specialties like smothered chicken with macaroni and cheese. The bar has satellite TV and backgammon. ⊠ *Great Harbour Marina, Great Harbour Cay* ☎ *242/367–8203* ▭ *No credit cards* ⊘ *Sometimes closed in Aug. and Sept.; call ahead.*

WHERE TO STAY

$ ⊞ **Berry Islands Vacation Rental.** There are two convenient marina location
★   options—the Anglers Roost one-bedroom apartment, and the Seaside Cottage, a lovely four-bedroom house with huge decks, a freshwater pool, an outside bar, and a dock that can take boats up to 58 feet long—plus a Seaside Villa. The villas are ideal for one couple, or two guys on a fishing trip. The house works for families and groups of friends. The minimum rental on the Seaside Cottage is one week; two days for Anglers Roost. Four sea kayaks are included with the cottage, ideal for exploring and flats fishing. You must book well in advance for these prime rentals. **Pros:** ideal off-the-beaten-path location for couples or families; easy access to beaches and bonefish flats; economical. **Cons:** you need to rent a golf cart to get around and gather supplies. ⊠ *Located on a private peninsula opposite Great Harbour Marina about 5 mins by boat, 10 mins by golf cart* ☎ *561/313–4760 U.S., 242/367–8155* ⊕ *www.berryislands.com* ⤶ *2 villas, 1 house* ⚉ *In-room: kitchen, Wi-Fi. In-hotel: pool, laundry facilities* ▭ *No credit cards.*

¢   ⊞ **Great Harbour Inn.** Perched at the water's edge on the marina in Great Harbour, this inn has convenient access to the area's restaurants, shops, and activities. The suites, clean and neat but in need of renovation, range in size from 450 to 900 square feet, and have private baths, minikitchens, and laundry facilities. The larger water-view suites have decks and porches. To make a reservation you must be persistent, as the owners don't always answer the phone. But hey, this laid-back style is a main reason people go to Great Harbour, and of course there are the fabulous beaches and fishing. **Pros:** good choice for a no-frills economical getaway; easy access to nearby beaches and fishing. **Cons:** no TV or Internet service; can be hot and buggy when the wind is down. ⊠ *On the waterfront at Great Harbour Marina, Great Harbour Cay* ☎ *242/367–8370* ⤶ *5 suites* ⚉ *In-room: kitchen, Wi-Fi. In-hotel: laundry facilities.*

Kayaks on the beach at Little Stirrup Cay, Berry Islands

$ ⊡ **Tat's Rental.** In the Beach Villas, just northeast of the airport, this property-management company rents spacious marina town houses, beach villas, and beach homes. The 1,600-square-foot town houses, for couples or groups of up to eight guests, include a private dock on the marina for boats up to 30 feet. Beach villas range in size from studios to three bedrooms, and are situated on the 8-mi-long crescent beach just to the east of the airport. Custom homes on this same beach, some brand new, range in size from three to five bedrooms and can include satellite TV. Tat's also rents cars and jeeps. **Pros:** best selection of beach-front rentals on the island; airport greeting and check-in service; other activities and rentals can be arranged. **Cons:** no phones or Internet service; most units don't have TV. ⊠ *Beach Villas, Great Harbour Cay* ☎ *242/464–4361* ⊃ *Rentals vary* ⚄ *In-room: kitchen, no TV. In-hotel: laundry facilities.*

SPORTS AND THE OUTDOORS

BOATING The clarity of Bahamian waters is particularly evident when you cross the Great Bahama Bank from Bimini, then cruise along the Berry Islands on the way to Nassau. The water's depth is seldom more than 20 feet here. Grass patches and an occasional coral head or flat coral patch dot the light-sand bottom. Starfish abound, and you can often catch a glimpse of a gliding stingray or eagle ray. You might spot the odd turtle, and if you care to jump over the boat's side with a mask, you might also pick up a conch or two in the grass. Especially good snorkeling and bonefishing, and peaceful anchorages, can be found on the lee shores of the Hoffmans and Little Harbour cays. When it's open, **Flo's Conch Bar,** at the southern end of Little Harbour Cay, serves fresh conch prepared every way you can imagine.

Great Harbour Cay Marina. In the upper Berry Islands the full-service Great Harbour Cay Marina has 80 slips that can handle boats up to 150 feet. Accessible through an 80-foot-wide channel from the bank side, the marina has one of the Bahamas' most pristine beaches running along its east side. The marina is also one of the best hurricane holes in the Bahamas. ☎ 242/367–8005.

Happy People's. Happy People's has boats available for exploring the island. It also rents golf carts and jeeps. ☎ 242/367–8117.

STOCK UP

Planning to rent a private house? Be sure to take all essentials with you, including food, toiletries, insect repellent, and medicine, and check with local island providers in advance to see when the supply boats arrive. Then dash down to the local store the minute the supply boat docks to be sure food, drink, and other items are available. Fresh produce, eggs, milk, meat, and cheese are the most commonly out-of-stock food items.

FISHING **Percy Darville.** Percy Darville knows the flats of the Berries better than anyone, and two of his brothers are now guiding with him. Call him as far in advance as possible to book a guide. ☎ 242/464–4149, 242/367–8119.

Eleuthera and Harbour Island

WORD OF MOUTH

"Spend your days finding the next pink sand beach and snorkeling off those beaches. Eleuthera also has just offshore Harbour Island, the hot new destination small enough to explore on foot, with several resorts. The kids would love the golf cart transportation on this island; it is becoming more 'upscale' by the minute though."

—joan

WELCOME TO ELEUTHERA AND HARBOUR ISLAND

TOP REASONS TO GO

★ **Play in pink sand:** Glorious, soft pink sand, the ethereal shade of the first blush of dawn, draws beach connoisseurs to Harbour Island, which boasts a world-famous 3-mi stretch. Plenty of pretty pink beaches also dot Eleuthera's east and north coasts.

★ **Ogle island architecture:** Lovely 18th- and 19th-century homes with storybook gables and gingerbread verandas are the norm on Harbour Island and Spanish Wells. Picturesque Victorian houses overlook Governor's Harbour in Eleuthera.

★ **Savor soulful sounds:** Nights here rock with the hot new Bahamian group Afro Band, the hip hop of TaDa, the traditional sound of Jaynell Ingraham, the calypso of Dr. Sea Breeze, the soul music of Ronnie Butler, and the impromptu performances of local resident Lenny Kravitz (who built a recording studio in Gregory Town).

1 **Gregory Town and North Eleuthera.** Eleuthera's undeveloped, serene north holds some of the island's most iconic natural wonders: the Glass Window Bridge, a heart-racing span between 80-foot cliffs often buffeted by a raging Atlantic; the 17th-century Preacher's Cave; and the thrilling waves of Surfer's Beach.

2 **Hatchet Bay.** "The Country's Safest Harbour" is Hatchet Bay's claim to fame. The naturally protected harbor is a popular place to anchor sailboats and fishing vessels, and is mid-Eleuthera's only marina.

3 **Governor's Harbour.** The pretty Victorian town, with a lively harbor that's a frequent stop for mail boats, ferries, and yachts, offers upscale restaurants and down-home conch cafés; boutique inns and inexpensive apartments.

4 **Rock Sound and South Eleuthera.** Rock Sound, the original capital of Eleuthera, is a quaint seaside settlement with 19th-century homes. Thirty miles away, yachties stop at Cape Eleuthera peninsula for a few nights of luxury in elegant town houses. Environmentalists also come here from around the world to learn about the self-sustaining Island School.

5 **Harbour Island.** Dunmore Town, the first capital of the Bahamas, may be the country's loveliest place, with its historic Loyalists' houses. White picket fences, some with cutouts of pineapples and boats, are festooned with red bougainvillea and tumbling purple morning glories. Luxurious inns, renowned restaurants, and the magnificent pink beach attract a parade of celebrities.

6 **Spanish Wells.** A quaint town of tidy clapboard white houses is on windswept St. George's Cay, a destination for those who don't want to bump elbows with other tourists. Idyllic white- and pink-sand beaches are the main attractions.

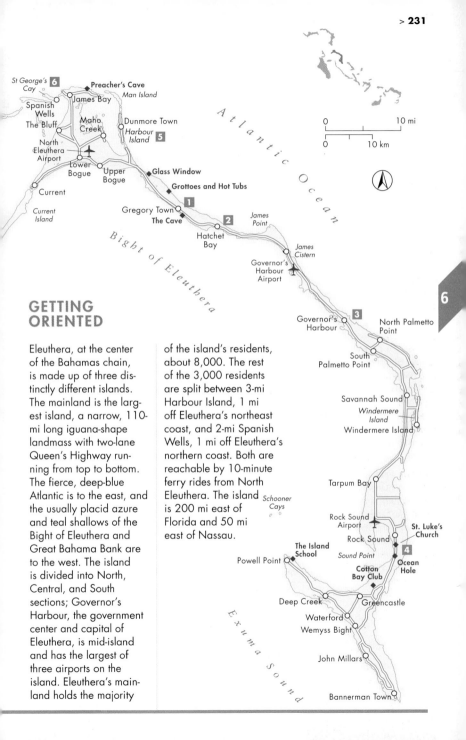

St George's Cay **6**

Preacher's Cave

Man Island

James Bay

Spanish Wells

The Bluff

Maho Creek

Dunmore Town

Harbour Island **5**

North Eleuthera Airport

Lower Bogue

Upper Bogue

Current

Current Island

Glass Window

Grottoes and Hot Tubs

Gregory Town

The Cave **2**

Hatchet Bay

James Point

James Cistern

Governor's Harbour Airport

Governor's Harbour

3

North Palmetto Point

South Palmetto Point

Savannah Sound

Windermere Island

Windermere Island

Tarpum Bay

Schooner Cays

Rock Sound Airport

Rock Sound

St. Luke's Church

The Island School

Powell Point

Sound Point

Cotton Bay Club

4

Ocean Hole

Deep Creek

Greencastle

Waterford

Wemyss Bight

John Millars

Bannerman Town

Atlantic Ocean

Bight of Eleuthera

Exuma Sound

0 ___ 10 mi

0 ___ 10 km

6

GETTING ORIENTED

Eleuthera, at the center of the Bahamas chain, is made up of three distinctly different islands. The mainland is the largest island, a narrow, 110-mi long iguana-shape landmass with two-lane Queen's Highway running from top to bottom. The fierce, deep-blue Atlantic is to the east, and the usually placid azure and teal shallows of the Bight of Eleuthera and Great Bahama Bank are to the west. The island is divided into North, Central, and South sections; Governor's Harbour, the government center and capital of Eleuthera, is mid-island and has the largest of three airports on the island. Eleuthera's mainland holds the majority of the island's residents, about 8,000. The rest of the 3,000 residents are split between 3-mi Harbour Island, 1 mi off Eleuthera's northeast coast, and 2-mi Spanish Wells, 1 mi off Eleuthera's northern coast. Both are reachable by 10-minute ferry rides from North Eleuthera. The island is 200 mi east of Florida and 50 mi east of Nassau.

ELEUTHERA AND HARBOUR ISLAND PLANNER

When to Go

High season in Eleuthera runs December through April, when residents of cold-weather climates head to the Bahamas to defrost and soak up some rays. Low temperatures might dip into the 60s, and the water can be chilly. Bring a sweater and a jacket, especially if you are boating. Expect to pay higher rates for rooms, boat rentals, and airfare during this time. For the cheapest hotel rates and some of the best deals on water-sports packages, visit in summer or fall, when the ocean is generally calm and warm. But beware, hurricane season runs June through November, with most risk of storms from August to October. During this time weather can be steamy and rainy.

For those who want to catch some action, the liveliest times to visit Eleuthera are Christmas during the annual Junkanoo celebration, the Pineapple Festival and Conch Fest in June, and the North Eleuthera Sailing Regatta in October. Reserve hotel rooms early.

Getting Here

Eleuthera has three airports: **North Eleuthera (ELH)** (☎ 242/335–1242), mid-island **Governor's Harbour (GHB)** (☎ 242/332–2321), and **Rock Sound (RSD)** (☎ 242/334–2177) in the south. Taxis usually wait for scheduled flights at the airports. Taxi service for two people from North Eleuthera Airport to the Cove is $35 ($60 from Governor's Harbour Airport); from Governor's Harbour to Pineapple Fields, $35; from Rock Sound airport to Cape Eleuthera, $80. Visitors going to Harbour Island and Spanish Wells should fly into North Eleuthera Airport.

Mail boats leave from Nassau's Potter's Cay for the five-hour trip to Eleuthera. One-way tickets cost $35. M/V *Current Pride* sails to Current Island, Hatchet Bay, the Bluff, and James Cistern on Thursday, returning Tuesday to Nassau. M/V *Bahamas Daybreak III* leaves Nassau on Monday and Wednesday for Harbour Island, Rock Sound, and Davis Harbour, returning to Nassau Tuesday and Friday. The *Eleuthera Express* sails for Governor's Harbour, Rock Sound, Spanish Wells, and Harbour Island on Monday and Thursday, returning to Nassau on Tuesday and Sunday. Contact the **Dockmaster's Office** (☎ 242/393–1064). **Bahamas Ferries** (☎ 242/323–2166 ⊕ www.bahamasferries.com), high-speed catamarans, connect Nassau to Harbour Island, Governor's Harbour, and Spanish Wells. The trip takes two hours and costs $125 round-trip.

Getting Around

By Car Rent a car if you plan to travel around Eleuthera. North to south is about a three-hour drive. Daily rentals run about $70. Request a four-wheel drive if you plan to visit Preacher's Cave or Surfer's Beach.

By Golf Cart You'll want a golf cart if you spend more than a couple of days on Harbour Island or Spanish Wells. Four-seater carts start at about $50 a day. Carts can be rented at most hotels and at the docks.

By Taxi Taxis are almost always waiting at airports and at the North Eleuthera and Harbour Island water taxi docks. Your hotel can call a taxi for you; let them know a half hour before you need it.

About the Restaurants

Don't let the outdoor dining on rustic wood tables fool you—Harbour Island and Eleuthera offer sophisticated cuisine that rivals that of any restaurants in Nassau. Although the place is usually casual and you never have to wear a tie, food is taken seriously. Of course, island specialties such as cracked conch, barbecued pork or chicken, and the succulent Bahamian lobster most locals call crawfish still abound, but you'll also find cappuccinos, steak, and lobster ravioli. Stop by Harbour Island's conch shacks on Bay Street north of Government Dock, where you can eat fresh conch salad on decks next to the water.

Most eateries are closed Sunday. Many restaurants have entertainment on regular nights so plan your dining schedule accordingly.

About the Hotels

Harbour Island, more than any other Out Island, is where the cognoscenti come to bask in ultraluxurious inns and atmospheric small resorts. Follow the celebrities to $600-a-night cottages with views of the pink-sand beach or ultraelegant rooms in Dunmore Town. Eleuthera offers elegant intimate resorts next to pink- and white-sand beaches happily empty of crowds. Those on tight budgets have a range of friendly, tidy, and affordable inns, a few on the beach, for around $100 a night. For urbanites who want all-out American luxury, there are modern town houses with stainless-steel appliances and granite in the kitchens, and bedrooms for the entire family. Whether you spend a lot or a little, the staff on this friendly island will know your name after a day. Many hotels are closed in September and October.

WHAT IT COSTS IN DOLLARS

	¢	$	$$	$$$	$$$$
Restaurants	under $10	$10–$20	$20–$30	$30–$40	over $40
Hotels		under $100	$100–$200	$200–$300	$300–$400	over $400

Restaurant prices are based on the median main course price at dinner, excluding gratuity, typically 15%, which is often automatically added to the bill. Hotel prices are for two people in a standard double room in high season, excluding service and 6%–12% tax.

Essentials

Banks Banks are open Monday through Thursday from 9:30 to 3, Friday from 9:30 to 4:30. ATMs are available at most banks.

Car Rentals Dingle Motor Service ☎ 242/334–2031. Gardiner's Automobile Rentals ☎ 242/332–2665.

Emergencies Medical Clinics ☎ 242/332–2774 *Governor's Harbour, 242/333–2227 Harbour Island, 242/334–2226 Rock Sound, 242/333–4064 Spanish Wells.* **Police** ☎ *242/332–2117 Governor's Harbour, 242/335–5322 Gregory Town, 242/333–2111 Harbour Island, 242/334–2244 Rock Sound.*

Golf Cart Rentals Abner's Rentals ☎ 242/333–4090. Baretta's Golf Cart ✉ *Harbour Island* ☎ 242/333–2361. Dunmore Rentals ✉ *Harbour Island* ☎ 242/333–2372. Johnson's Rentals ✉ *Harbour Island* ☎ 242/333–2376. Kam Kourts ✉ *Harbour Island* ☎ 242/333–2248.

Taxis Amos at Your Service ☎ 242/422–9130. **Neville Major Taxi** ✉ *Harbour Island* ☎ 242/333–2361. **Stanton Cooper** ☎ 242/359–7007.

Visitor Information Eleuthera Tourist Office ✉ *Governor's Harbour* ☎ 242/332–2142. **Harbour Island Tourist Office** ✉ *Dunmore Street, Harbour Island* ☎ 242/333–2621. **Out Islands Promotion Board** ⊕ www.myoutislands.com.

6

ELEUTHERA AND HARBOUR ISLAND BEACHES

Eleuthera and Harbour Island beaches are some of the best in the world, thanks to their pristine beauty and dazzling variety. Deep-blue ocean fading to aqua shallows makes gorgeous backdrops for gourmet restaurants and the wooden decks of fishing shacks. The sand is for bonfires, celebrity-watching, Friday-night fish fries, dancing, and music, as much as it is for afternoon naps and stargazing.

(above and upper right) Pink Sands Beach, Harbour Island.

Tranquil coves' sparkling white sand are as calm as a pool on the west side of Eleuthera, while the Atlantic's winter waves challenge skilled surfers on the east side, which has long stretches of pink sand. On Harbour Island, pink sand is on the ocean side and the white-sand coves face the calm channel. Home to shells that tumble in with every wave and starfish resting just offshore, the island's occasional glitz can't compete with the beaches' natural beauty.

BLUSHING BEACHES

Contrary to popular opinion, pink sand comes primarily from the crushed pink and red shells of microscopic insects called foraminifera, not coral. Foraminifer live on the underside of reefs and the sea floor. After the insects die, the waves smash the shells, which wash ashore along with sand and bits of pink coral. The intensity of the rosy hues depends on the slant of the sun.

ELEUTHERA'S AND HARBOUR ISLAND'S BEST BEACHES

CLUB MED BEACH

This stretch of pink sand was Club Med's famed beach before the resort was destroyed by a hurricane in 1999. But the gorgeous Atlantic-side beach remains, anchored by fantastic bistros like the Beach House and Tippy's. The wide expanse, ringed by casuarina trees, is often deserted, and makes a great outpost for romantics.

COCODIMAMA BEACH

Many necklaces and shell decorations come from Cocodimama, which, along with Ten Bay Beach at South Palmetto Point, is well known for perfect small shells. The water at Cocodimama, a secluded beach 6 mi north of Governor's Harbour, has the aqua and sky-blue shades you see on Bahamas posters, and is shallow and calm, perfect for children and sand castles. The Cocodimama Resort is next to the beach, and makes a perfect lunchtime respite for pasta and wine.

GAULDING'S CAY BEACH

Snorkelers and divers will want to spend time at this beach, 3 mi north of Gregory Town. You'll most likely have the long stretch of white sand and shallow aqua water all to yourself, and it's great for shelling. At low tide, you can walk or swim to Gaulding's Cay, a tiny

rock island with a few casuarina trees. There's great snorkeling around the island; you'll see a concentration of sea anemones so spectacular it dazzled even Jacques Cousteau's biologists.

PINK SANDS BEACH, HARBOUR ISLAND

This is the fairest pink beach of them all: 3 mi of pale-pink sand behind some of the most expensive and posh inns in the Bahamas. Its sand is of such a fine consistency that it's almost as soft as talcum powder, and the gentle slope of the shore makes small waves break hundreds of yards offshore; you have to walk out quite a distance to get past your waist. This is the place to see the rich and famous in designer resort wear or ride a horse bareback across the sand and into the sea.

SURFER'S BEACH

This is Gregory Town's claim to fame and one of the few beaches in the Bahamas known for surfing. Serious surfers have gathered here since the 1960s for decent waves from December to April. If you don't have a jeep, you can walk the ¾ mi to this Atlantic-side beach—follow rough-and-bumpy Ocean Boulevard at Eleuthera Island Shores just south of town. Look for a young crowd sitting around bonfires at night.

THE HARBOUR ISLAND LIFESTYLE

There are Out Islands and then there are "In" Islands (think fashionable St. Bart's), where the person at the next beachside table could be a film star, supermodel, or Grammy-winning musician. Harbour Island is both, an island where celebrities and billionaires gallivant freely, wearing flip-flops and driving old four-seater golf carts.

There are no megamansions or gated estates (only one electronic gate on the island, actually), no high-rise condos, no luxurious spas, but plenty of fresh fish and lobster, one of the world's most magnificent beaches, elegant intimate inns, bakeries that rival any in Paris, good weather, and good cheer. When you're here you don't have to live the pampered life of the rich and famous; go fishing (regulars develop relationships with their fishing guides that last longer than some of their marriages), diving, and kayaking—or just sit back on the beach and watch how the beautiful people do it.

CLAIMS TO FAME

Movies (filmed in Eleuthera): *Tyler Perry's Why Did I Get Married, Too?* with Janet Jackson and Jill Scott; *Fool's Gold* with Matthew McConaughey and Kate Hudson; *Mysterious* starring James Brolin and Antonio Sabato Jr.; *Three* with Billy Zane and Kelly Brook.

Photo Shoots: 2006 swimsuit issue of *Sports Illustrated; Vogue* fashion spreads.

TV: *International House Hunter* episodes on the Home & Garden Channel (the real-estate agent on both episodes was Robert Arthur, co-owner with his wife of Arthur's Bakery).

HOW-TO IN HARBOUR ISLAND

KNOW YOUR GOLF CART ETIQUETTE
A friendly hello and wave separate the insiders from the visitors. Use hand signals to indicate turns— another thing newcomers don't do which causes some confusion on the narrow lanes. And drive on the left, for goodness sake! Americans have a habit of drifting toward the right, especially when they're looking at the scenery.

PLAN YOUR SUNSETS
The hallowed daily ritual of watching the sun set is best complemented by food and a libation: a glass of Italian wine and crab cakes at Acquapazza, tequila shrimp on the deck of Harbour Lounge, lobster dumplings on the porch of the Landing, refreshing gazpacho on the terrace of the posh Rock House, conch fritters at Sunsets Bar and Grille, or cold Kaliks at Valentine's Marina. So many choices, so few vacation days.

WHO'S HERE?
Bahamians are famously unimpressed with celebrities, but ask the staff at shops and restaurants, and they usually don't mind telling you who's in town. It's nice to know what famous musician is on the island, just in case there's an impromptu bonfire sing-along.

PRONOUNCE IT LIKE A LOCAL
Islanders have a shorthand name for their island: Briland. But say it right: BRI (rhymes with dry)-land.

BRING YOUR POOCH
To really blend in with the locals, you should take your dog— everywhere. You will look right at home with your furry best friend riding in the golf cart, frolicking on the beach, sharing a table on the terrace of a café, and going on long walks down the narrow lanes. There's no quarantine, just an import permit available at ⊕ *www.bahamas.com*, a $10 fee, and your vet's health certificate.

WHO'S WHO OF HARBOUR ISLAND

Homeowners include **Wayne Huizenga**, former owner of the Miami Dolphins; Revlon Chairman **Ron Perelman**; media mogul **Barry Diller** and his fashion designer wife **Diane von Furstenberg**; duty-free tycoon **Robert Miller**; J. Crew CEO **Mickey Drexler**; supermodel **Elle Macpherson**; and **India Hicks**, English model and goddaughter of Prince Charles.

Island Records founder **Chris Blackwell** started the influx of the ultra-wealthy when he bought Pink Sands Resort in 1992; guests include **Martha Stewart** and the **Duchess of York**.

Dave Mathews, Tyra Banks, Jimmy Buffett, and **Mick Jagger** all rent homes in Harbour Island. Just next door, **Mariah Carey** and **Patti LaBelle** own homes on the mainland of Eleuthera, as well as **Lenny Kravitz**, who amuses residents by living in a modest wooden house and walking around in bare feet.

6

Updated by Cheryl Blackerby

You haven't experienced a real escape until you've vacationed in Eleuthera. Simple luxury resorts are the norm, deserted expanses of white- or pink-sand beaches are your playground, and islanders are genuinely friendly. Although the low-key, relax-and-relax-some-more island vacation isn't for everyone, Eleuthera is the place to go when you need to recharge your batteries. Seclusion, sun, and starry skies—just what the doctor ordered.

Eleuthera was founded in 1648 by a British group fleeing religious persecution; the name is taken from the Greek word for freedom. These settlers, who called themselves the Eleutheran Adventurers, gave the Bahamas its first written constitution. "Adventurers" has taken on new meaning as a clarion call to sailors, tourists, and, more recently, retirees looking for adventures of their own.

Largely undeveloped rolling green hills and untrammeled sandy coves, along with sleepy 19th-century towns, offer an authentic Bahamas experience that is quickly disappearing. Try not to notice the ubiquitous HG Christie and Sotheby's "For Sale" signs unless, of course, you're so smitten you want to stay. Rent a car—or even better, an SUV—for washboard back roads, and explore the island's secluded beaches and sandy coves fringing turquoise and aqua water that rivals anything in the Caribbean. The island is among the prettiest in the Bahamas, with gentle hills, unspoiled "bush" (backwoods), and gardens of tumbling purple lantana and sky-blue plumbago. Hotels and inns are painted in the shades of Bahamian bays and sunset, which is best watched from the comfort of inviting verandas and seaside decks.

If you're looking for all of this and a bit more action, ferry over to Harbour Island, Eleuthera's chic neighbor. With its uninterrupted 3-mi pink-sand beach, top-notch dining, and sumptuous inns, the island has long been a favorite hideaway for jet-setters and celebrities. For splendid beaches with few, if any, tourists, head to Spanish Wells, a quiet private island.

GREAT ITINERARIES

IF YOU HAVE 3 DAYS

Fly into North Eleuthera and take the ferry to **Harbour Island**. Base yourself at a hotel near the famous 3-mi pink-sand beach or in historic Dunmore Town. Relax on the beach and have lunch at an ocean-side restaurant. Stroll through **Dunmore Town** in the afternoon, stopping at crafts stands and fashionable shops, admiring colonial houses along Bay Street, and visiting historic churches. At night, dine at one of the island's fine restaurants, such as the Landing, Rock House, Pink Sands, or Acquapazza. On Day 2, go scuba diving or snorkeling, or hire a guide and try to snag a canny bonefish. Visit the conch shacks on Bay Street for a low-key beachside dinner. On Day 3 get some last-minute color on the beach or some in-room spa pampering; stop by Vic-Hum Club or Gusty's for late-night music.

IF YOU HAVE 5 DAYS

Head back to **Eleuthera** for the next two days. Rent a car at the North Eleuthera Airport (reserve in advance) and drive south past the **Glass Window Bridge**, where you can stand in one spot and see the brilliant-blue and often-fierce Atlantic Ocean to the east and the placid Bight of Eleuthera to the west. Continue to **Governor's Harbour**, the island's largest town, and grab lunch at Tippy's or the Beach House, upscale, laid-back beach bistros overlooking the Atlantic Ocean. Stay at one of the beach resorts and enjoy the incredible water views. Head into town if you're looking for some nightlife or dining options.

IF YOU HAVE 7 DAYS

On your last two days, drive back to **North Eleuthera**, base yourself at the Cove, and relax on the resort's two beaches. If you're there on a Tuesday or Friday night, head to Elvina's in Gregory Town and see the local bands. On your final day take the ferry to **Spanish Wells**, where you can rent a golf cart and spend a half day exploring the tiny town and relaxing on a white-sand beach with no tourists. Or stay put and explore Surfer's Beach.

6

GREGORY TOWN AND NORTH ELEUTHERA

Gregory Town is a sleepy community, except on Friday nights when people are looking for music, whether that is speakers blasting reggae or a local musician playing Rake 'n' Scrape at a roadside barbecue. There's action, too, at Surfer's Beach, where winter waves bring surfers from around the world. They hang their surfboards from the ceiling at Elvina's Bar for free summer storage. The famous Glass Window Bridge is north of town, and Preacher's Cave, landing of the earliest settlers, is on the northern tip of the island. Gregory Town is home to a little more than 400 people, residing in small houses on a hillside that slides down to the sea. The town's annual Pineapple Festival begins on the Thursday evening of the Bahamian Labor Day weekend, at the beginning of June, with live music continuing into the wee hours.

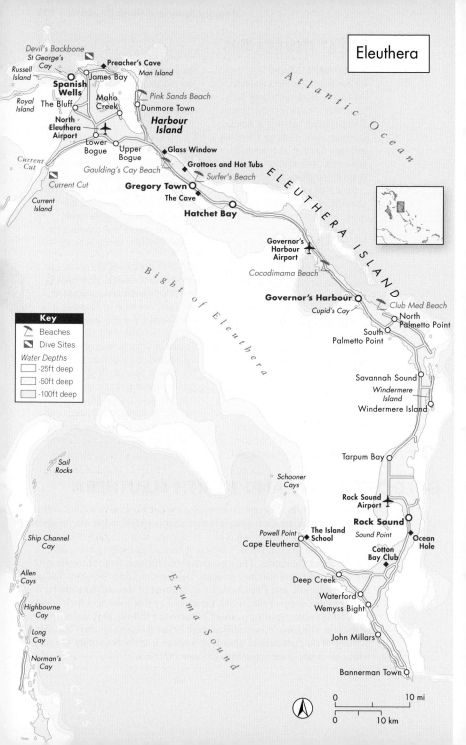

Eleuthera

Atlantic Ocean

Devil's Backbone
St George's Cay
Russell Island
Preacher's Cave
Man Island
Royal Island
James Bay
Spanish Wells
The Bluff
Maho Creek
Pink Sands Beach
North Eleuthera Airport
Dunmore Town
Harbour Island
Lower Bogue
Upper Bogue
Glass Window
Current Cut
Grottoes and Hot Tubs
Current Cut
Gaulding's Cay Beach
Gregory Town
Surfer's Beach
Current Island
The Cave

ELEUTHERA ISLAND

Hatchet Bay

Governor's Harbour Airport

Cocodimama Beach

Bight of Eleuthera

Governor's Harbour
Club Med Beach
Cupid's Cay
North Palmetto Point
South Palmetto Point

Savannah Sound

Windermere Island
Windermere Island

Key
- Beaches
- Dive Sites

Water Depths
- -25ft deep
- -50ft deep
- -100ft deep

Sail Rocks

Tarpum Bay

Schooner Cays

Rock Sound Airport

Rock Sound
Sound Point
Ocean Hole

Ship Channel Cay

The Island School
Powell Point
Cape Eleuthera

Cotton Bay Club

Allen Cays

Deep Creek
Waterford
Wemyss Bight

Highbourne Cay

Long Cay

John Millars

Exuma Sound

Norman's Cay

EXUMA CAYS

Bannerman Town

0   10 mi
0   10 km

GETTING HERE AND AROUND

The North Eleuthera Airport is closer to Gregory Town hotels than the airport in Governor's Harbour. The taxi fare from the North Eleuthera Airport to the Cove Eleuthera, the area's most upscale inn, is $35 for two people. Rent a car at the airport unless you plan to stay at a resort for most of your visit.

EXPLORING

★ **Glass Window Bridge.** At a narrow point of the island a few miles north of Gregory Town, a slender concrete bridge links two sea-battered bluffs that separate the island's Central and North districts. Sailors going south in the waters between New Providence and Eleuthera supposedly named this area the Glass Window because they could see through the natural limestone arch to the Atlantic on the other side. Stop to watch the northeasterly deep-azure Atlantic swirl together under the bridge with the southwesterly turquoise Bight of Eleuthera, producing a brilliant aquamarine froth. Artist Winslow Homer found the site stunning, and painted *Glass Window* in 1885. The original stone arch, created by Mother Nature, was destroyed by a combination of storms in the 1940s. Subsequent concrete bridges were destroyed by hurricanes in 1992 and 1999. Drive carefully, because there is frequent maintenance work going on. ⊠ *North of Gregory Town.*

6

Grottoes and Hot Tubs. If you're too lulled by the ebb and flow of lapping waves and prefer your shores crashing with dramatic white sprays, a visit here will revive you. The sun warms these tidal pools—which the locals call "moon pools"—making them a markedly more temperate soak than the sometimes chilly ocean. Be careful, and ask locals about high seas before you enjoy. On most days refreshing sprays and rivulets tumble into the tubs, but on some it can turn dangerous; if the waves are crashing over the top of the cove's centerpiece mesa, pick another day to stop here. ✛ *5 mi north of Gregory Town on the right (Atlantic) side of Queen's Hwy., across the road from two thin tree stumps. If you reach the one-lane Glass Window Bridge, you've gone too far.*

Preacher's Cave. At the island's northern tip is where the Eleutheran Adventurers (the island's founders) took refuge and held services when their ship wrecked in 1648. Note the original stone altar inside the cave. The last 2 mi of the road to Preacher's Cave is a hilly, rocky dirt road, but passable if you go slowly. Ask locals about the condition of the road before you head out. Across from the cave is a long succession of deserted pink-sand beaches.

PINEAPPLE EXPRESS

Pineapples remain Eleuthera's most famous product, even though the industry has been greatly reduced since the late 1800s, when the island dominated the world's pineapple market. These intensely sweet fruits are still grown on family farms, primarily in northern Eleuthera. Don't miss Gregory Town's Pineapple Festival in June.

WHERE TO EAT AND STAY

$$ ✗ **The Cove Eleuthera Restaurant.**
CONTINENTAL   The spacious, window-lined dining room serves three meals a day, blending classic continental with Bahamian to produce delights such as conch burgers for lunch, and for dinner grilled chicken breast with papaya sauce, prawn skewers, lobster tail with lime and thyme beurre blanc, and potato-crusted sea bass. It's one of the nicest restaurants on the island. Order the key lime pie—you won't be disappointed. ⊠ *Queen's Hwy., Gregory Town* ☎ *242/335–5142.*

> ### GREGORY TOWN SOUND
>
> In 2009, Grammy Award–winning musician Lenny Kravitz built a multimillion-dollar recording studio called Gregory Town Sound, and he and his band often slip into Elvina's Bar down the road for inspiration. Kravitz, who lives in Gregory Town part-time, has said, "This is the place I love being the most. Some of the nicest people I've ever met in my life are here."

¢ ✗ **Thompson Bakery.** Located appropriately at the top of Sugar Hill
CAFÉ   Street, Daisy Thompson bakes the island's best banana muffins; cinnamon rolls; pineapple bread; pizza; and pineapple, coconut, and lemon tarts in a tiny hilltop enclave. Her family reputedly developed the recipe for pineapple rum. ⊠ *Sugar Hill St., Gregory Town* ☎ *242/335–5053* ▭ *No credit cards* ☉ *Closed Sun.*

$$ ▦ **The Cove Eleuthera.** Twenty-eight secluded acres studded with scenic
Fodor's Choice   beach cottages set the tone for this relaxing island escape. A rocky
★   promontory separates two coves: one has a small sandy beach with palapa huts, lounge chairs, and kayaks, the other is rocky and ideal for snorkeling. The poolside patio is a good place for breakfast or relaxing cocktails, but sitting at the bar and chatting with resident bartender Wallace will become one of your favorite activities. Clustered cottages have ocean or garden views, tile floors, high slanted ceilings, 600-thread-count sheets, and white rattan furnishings. MP3 players and alarm clocks are available on request, otherwise the point is to forget the time. Take in both the sunrise and the sunset from one of two suites in the Point House; it's built on the promontory with a 180-degree view of the coves and the sea. **Pros:** private sandy beaches; friendly staff; great island flavor. **Cons:** need a car if you want to do anything outside the property. ⊠ *1½ mi north of Gregory Town, Gregory Town* ☎ *242/335–5142, 800/552–5960* ⊕ *www.thecoveeleuthera.com* ⇱ *12 rooms, 12 suites* ⚭ *In-room: no TV. In-hotel: restaurant, bar, pool, tennis court, gym, water sports, laundry facilities* ☉ *Sept.–Oct.*

NIGHTLIFE

★   **Elvina's Bar and Restaurant.** A one-room bar with a small stage and dance floor, Elvina's has been a music and social institution for 30 years. It's owned and run by local Elvina Watkins and her Baton Rouge–born husband Ed. You can't miss Tuesday and Friday open-mike nights, where you never know who will walk in the door and sing—Kid Rock, Mariah Carey, the Black Crows, or Lenny Kravitz, who lives nearby. The place

TOP FESTIVALS

WINTER

Junkanoo is celebrated in Tarpum Bay on Christmas Day, and in Rock Sound and Harbour Island on December 26. Celebrations start around 7 pm.

SPRING

Cyclists from around the globe come in April to ride the 100-mi **Ride for Hope**, an event that benefits cancer care and research. Riders of all ages and skill levels can ride 10 mi or 100. The route starts at Governor's Harbour. ⊕ *www. riodeforhopebahamas.com.*

SUMMER

Conch Fest. Deep Creek's annual Conch Fest in June has lots of conch, Rake 'n' Scrape, and arts and crafts.

Eleuthera Pineapple Festival. In June Gregory Town hosts the four-day Eleuthera Pineapple Festival, with a Junkanoo parade, crafts displays, tours of pineapple farms, the

annual 40-mi Continental Airlines Cycling Race—as well as an opportunity to sample what Eleuthera natives proclaim to be the sweetest pineapple in the world.

FALL

Softball Playoff Games. Softball is the top sport in Eleuthera, and you can't beat Softball Playoff Games in September for excitement and camaraderie with locals. The winner competes in the national tournament. Games are held in Palmetto Point, Rock Sound, Governor's Harbour, and James Cistern.

North Eleuthera/Harbour Island Sailing Regatta. The North Eleuthera/Harbour Island Sailing Regatta in October provides five days of exciting competition of Bahamian Class A, B, and C boats. Onshore activities based on Harbour Island include live bands, Bahamian music, cultural shows, food, and drink.

is open every day of the year but doesn't really get hopping until after 9 pm. ⊠ *Queens Hwy., Gregory Town* ☎ *242/335–5032.*

SHOPPING

Island Made Shop. This shop, run by Pam and Greg Thompson, is a good place to shop for Bahamian arts and crafts, including Androsia batik (made on Andros Island), driftwood paintings, Abaco ceramics, and prints. Look for the old foam buoys which have been carved and painted into fun faces. ⊠ *Queen's Hwy., Gregory Town* ☎ *242/335–5369.*

SPORTS AND THE OUTDOORS

SCUBA DIVING AND SNORKELING

Current Cut. This narrow passage between North Eleuthera and Current Island is loaded with marine life, and provides a roller-coaster ride on the currents.

Devil's Backbone. Devil's Backbone, in North Eleuthera, offers a tricky reef area with a nearly infinite number of dive sites and a large number of wrecks.

Dr. Sea Breeze performing at the Rainbow Inn

SURFING **Rebecca's Beach Shop.** In Gregory Town, stop by Rebecca's Beach Shop, a general store, crafts shop, and, most importantly, surf shop, where local surf guru "Ponytail Pete" rents surfboards, snorkel gear, and more. A chalkboard lists surf conditions and tidal reports. He also gives surf lessons. ⊠ *Queen's Hwy., Gregory Town* ☎ *242/335-5436.*

HATCHET BAY

Hatchet Bay, which has mid-Eleuthera's only marina, is a good place to find a fishing guide and friendly locals. Take note of the town's side roads, which have such colorful names as Lazy Road, Happy Hill Road, and Smile Lane. Just south of town, the Rainbow Inn and Restaurant is the hub of activity for this stretch of the island. Bay Inn Estates Bed and Breakfast opened in late 2009, and has been busy since the first day.

"The Country's Safest Harbour" is Hatchet Bay's claim to fame. The naturally protected harbor is a popular place to anchor sailboats and fishing vessels when storms are coming. One of the most memorable days for the harbor, however, wasn't a storm but the day years ago when Jackie Kennedy Onassis came in on a friend's yacht.

The pastoral scenery outside of Hatchet Bay is some of the island's most memorable—towering, long-empty grain silos, windswept green hillsides, and wild cotton, remnants of the old cotton plantations. Don't miss James Cistern, a seaside settlement to the south. Time your visit for a Friday or Saturday so you can drop by Billy and Brenda Stubbs' weekly barbecue (from 11 to 3 pm) under a tamarind tree next to the Queen's Highway. Chicken and ribs are cooked on the grill, and you can eat on picnic tables in the shade or take your lunch across the street to the side of the bay.

GETTING HERE AND AROUND

Hatchet Bay is equidistant between the Governor's Harbour and North Eleuthera airports. The taxi fare from either airport is about $50 for two people. Rent a car at the airport unless you plan to stay at a resort for most of your visit.

EXPLORING

The Cave. North of Hatchet Bay lies a subterranean, bat-populated tunnel complete with stalagmites and stalactites. Pirates supposedly once used it to hide their loot. An underground path leads for more than a mile to the sea, ending in a lofty, cathedral-like cavern. Within its depths, fish swim in total darkness. The adventurous may wish to explore this area with a flashlight (follow the length of guide string along the cavern's floor), but it's best to inquire first at one of the local stores or the Rainbow Inn for a guide. ⊠ *North of Hatchet Bay, take a left after the vine-covered silo on Queen's Hwy's north side.*

WHERE TO EAT AND STAY

$$ ✕ **The Rainbow Inn Steakhouse.** With a classy but no-fuss aura and exhi-
CONTINENTAL bition windows that face gorgeous sunsets, this restaurant is well
★ known for its steaks, including 14-ounce New York strip, 8-ounce filet mignon, and 20-ounce rib eye, which are flown in daily. Grouper, conch, mahimahi, and cobia are also fresh, caught daily. Diners have 180-degree views of the ocean from the screened patio or inside. Dr. Sea Breeze plays here on Wednesday night (in high season). The restaurant is open for breakfast. ⊠ *Queen's Hwy., 2½ mi south of Hatchet Bay* ☎ *242/335-0294* ⊘ *Closed Sun. and end of Aug.–mid-Oct.*

¢ 🏠 **Bay Inn Estates Bed and Breakfast.**
You can't miss the lime-green, yel-
low, and pink clapboard buildings
and lush landscaping at this bed-
and-breakfast, which opened in
June 2009. Spacious rooms have
mahogany beds and desks, modern
bathrooms, and kitchens. All have
balconies or terraces. A friendly
young staff can help with sightsee-
ing and can arrange fishing trips,
especially bonefishing. Continental
breakfast and coffee are served in
a separate building; you can eat
outside under shady almond trees.
The inn is exceptionally bright and
cheery. **Pros:** Continental break-
fast; relaxing outdoor space; help-
ful staff. **Cons:** not on the beach or
bay; no water views; not close to

TOUR OPERATORS

ADVENTURE TOURS
**Bahamas Out-Islands
Adventures.** Bahamas
Out-Islands Adventures gives
overnight kayaking and surfing
lessons. ☎ 242/335-0349
⊕ www.bahamasadventures.com.

ISLAND TOURS
Arthur Nixon Tours
☎ 242/332-2052, 242/359-7879.

Eleuthera Adventure Tours
☎ 242/334-2203 ⊕ www.
eleutheraadventuretours.com.

Freedom Tours ☎ 242/335-1700.

shops. ⊠ *West off Queen's Hwy.* 📠 *242/335–0730* ↴ *12 rooms* ᐃ *In-room: a/c, kitchen, Wi-Fi. In-hotel: laundry facilities, business center.*

$ 🏨 **Rainbow Inn.** Immaculate, generously sized cottages, some octago-
★ nal—all with large private porches—have sweeping views of the ocean.
The resort was renovated in 2009 by new Canadian owners. The restaurant is one of the island's best, and islanders drive great distances
for a meal here, especially when the famed Dr. Sea Breeze strums away
and sings island tunes on Wednesday and Friday nights (in high season). The Nautical Bar, hung with authentic ships' wheels salvaged
from wrecks, attracts British and American expats as well as locals. A
sublime beach is a long walk down the paved road; rent a car or use
the on-property swimming dock. The helpful staff will arrange fishing
trips and adventure tours. **Pros:** superspacious cottages at reasonable
prices; great water views; friendly service. **Cons:** not on the beach; not
close to a town or shops. ⊠ *Queen's Hwy., 2½ mi south of Hatchet
Bay* 📠 *242/335–0294* ⊕ *www.rainbowinn.com* ↴ *4 cottages, 2 villas*
ᐃ *In-room: kitchen, Wi-Fi. In-hotel: restaurant, bar, pool, tennis court,
water sports* ⦿ *Some meals.*

NIGHTLIFE

Dr. Sea Breeze. The debonair Cebric Bethel, better known as Dr. Sea
Breeze, strums his acoustic guitar while singing island songs Wednesday
and Friday nights at the Rainbow Inn, and Saturday nights at Unique
Village in Governor's Harbour. To be sure you don't miss him, check
with the resorts beforehand to confirm his schedule.

GOVERNOR'S HARBOUR

Governor's Harbour, the capital of Eleuthera and home to government
offices, is the largest town on the island and one of the prettiest. Vic-
torian-era houses were built on Buccaneer Hill, which overlooks the
harbor, bordered on the south by a narrow peninsula and Cupid's Cay
at the tip. To fully understand its appeal, you have to settle in for a
few days and explore on foot—if you don't mind the steep climb up
the narrow lanes. The town is a step into a gentler, more genteel time.
Everyone says hello, and entertainment means wading into the harbor
to cast a line, or taking a painting class taught by Martha's Vineyard
artist Donna Allen at the 19th-century pink library on Monday mornings. You can see a current movie at the balconied Globe Princess, the
only theater on the island, which also serves the best hamburgers in
town. Or swim at the gorgeous beaches on either side of town, which
stretch from the pink sands of the ocean to the white sands of the Bight
of Eleuthera. There are three banks, a few grocery stores, and some of
the island's wealthiest residents, who prefer the quiet of Eleuthera to
the fashionable party scene of Harbour Island.

GETTING HERE AND AROUND

Fly into Governor's Harbour Airport north of town, or arrive by mail
boat from Nassau. You will want to rent a car at the airport, even if
you plan to stay in Governor's Harbour, to best explore the beaches

A Governor's Harbour home

and restaurants. If you stay at Duck Inn or Laughing Bird Apartments, you'll be able to walk to nearby restaurants.

EXPLORING

★ **Haynes Library.** The heart of the community, this 19th-century building offers art classes and morning coffee hours for visitors and residents. The library has a wide selection of books and Internet terminals, with gorgeous views of the harbor. ⊠ *Cupid's Cay Rd.* ⊕ *www.hayneslibrary. org.*

EN ROUTE **Windermere Island.** About halfway between Governor's Harbour and Rock Sound, distinguished Windermere Island, 5 mi long with a lovely pink-sand beach, is the site of vacation homes of the rich and famous, including Mariah Carey and members of the British royal family. Don't plan on any drive-by ogling of these million-dollar homes, though; the security gate prevents sightseers from passing.

WHERE TO EAT

$$ ✕ **The Beach House Tapas Restaurant.** On a gorgeous pink-sand beach, this
CONTINENTAL outdoor restaurant offers stunning views and exquisite Spanish appetiz-
★ ers and entrées such as shrimp-stuffed goat cheese with prosciutto and jumbo crab–and–lobster ravioli. Often, there is entertainment such as live music on Thursday nights and an outside movie on Wednesday. ⊠ *Banks Rd.* ☎ *242/332–3387.*

$ ✕ **Buccaneer Club.** On the top of Buccaneer Hill overlooking the town
BAHAMIAN and the harbor, this mid-19th-century farmhouse is now a restaurant

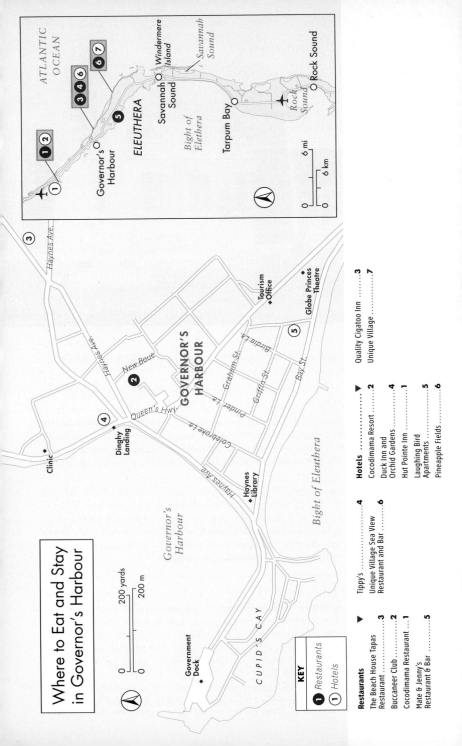

Where to Eat and Stay in Governor's Harbour

KEY
▶ Restaurants
① Hotels

ATLANTIC OCEAN

ELEUTHERA

Windermere Island

Savannah Sound

Savannah Sound

Bight of Eleuthera

Governor's Harbour

Tarpum Bay

Rock Sound

Rock Sound

6 mi
6 km

Haynes Ave.

Clinic

Haynes Ave.

New Bove

Dinghy Landing

Queen's Hwy

Governor's Harbour

GOVERNOR'S HARBOUR

Colebrooke La.

Pinder La.

Graham St.

Birdie La.

Griffin St.

Bay St.

Haynes Ave.

Haynes Library

Tourism Office

Globe Princes Theatre

Bight of Eleuthera

CUPID'S CAY

Government Dock

200 yards
200 m

Restaurants ▶

The Beach House Tapas Restaurant 4
Buccaneer Club 2
Cocodimama Restaurant ... 1
Mate & Jenny's Restaurant & Bar 5
Tippy's 4
Unique Village Sea View Restaurant and Bar 6

Hotels ①

Cocodimama Resort 2
Duck Inn and Orchid Gardens 4
Hut Pointe Inn 1
Laughing Bird Apartments 5
Pineapple Fields 6
Quality Cigatoo Inn 3
Unique Village 7

serving three meals a day, with an outdoor dining area surrounded by a garden of bougainvillea, hibiscus, and coconut palms. The beach is a leisurely five-minute stroll away, and the harbor, where you can also swim, is within shouting distance. Sample such native specialties as grouper, conch, and crawfish. ⊠ *Haynes Ave.* ☎ *242/332–2000.*

$$ ✕ **Cocodimama Restaurant.** Overlooking spectacular Cocodimama Beach
ITALIAN and gorgeous sunsets, this Italian restaurant is run by Francesco Scar-
Fodor's Choice pulla from Palermo, Italy. Specialties include a salad with local greens
★ and seared sesame tuna; and homemade spaghetti sautéed with shrimp and calamari. ⊠ *Queen's Hwy.* ☎ *242/332–3150.*

$$ ✕ **Mate & Jenny's Restaurant & Bar.** A few miles south of Governor's Har-
BAHAMIAN bour, this casual neighborhood restaurant specializes in pizza; try one topped with conch. Sandwiches, Bahamian specialties, and ice-cream sundaes are also served. The walls are painted with tropical sunset scenes and decorated with photos and random memorabilia, and the jukebox and pool table add to the joint's local color. Pizza pie prices range from $10 to $25, depending on the toppings. ⊠ *S. Palmetto Point* ☎ *242/332–1504* ◷ *Closed Tues.*

$$ ✕ **Tippy's.** Despite its barefoot-casual environment (old window shutters
ECLECTIC used as tabletops, sand in the floor's crevices), the menu at this open-air
★ beach bistro is a sophisticated mix of Bahamian and European, with a menu that changes daily based on the fresh local products available. Expect things like lobster salad, specialty pizzas, and fresh fish pre-pared with some sort of delectable twist. This place may look like a beach shack, but everything has been well planned—it even imported a French chef to satisfy discriminating palates. Try to grab a table on the outdoor deck, which has a fantastic view of the beach. Locals and visitors keep this place hopping year-round, and there's live music on Saturday nights. ⊠ *Banks Rd.* ☎ *242/332–3331* ⚓ *Reservations essen-tial* ◷ *Closed Oct.*

$$ ✕ **Unique Village Sea View Restaurant and Bar.** Bahamas home cooking is
BAHAMIAN the reason to come to the octagonal restaurant, with its pagoda-style natural-wood ceiling, wraparound covered deck, and panoramic view of the beach. The restaurant–bar is a popular spot for locals and visi-tors, especially when Dr. Sea Breeze sings. Specialties include cracked conch, the chef's snapper special with peas 'n' rice, homemade bread, and coconut tarts for dessert. ⊠ *Banks Rd., North Palmetto Point* ☎ *242/332–1830.*

WHERE TO STAY

$$ 🏨 **Cocodimama Resort.** This upscale boutique resort with a Mediter-
★ ranean vibe was renovated top-to-bottom by the Urgo Hotel Group in 2009. The resort has 12 spacious rooms in two-story island-style buildings painted in playful Junkanoo colors. All rooms have great views of the gorgeous white sand of Cocodimama Beach and the calm azure water of Alabaster Bay. Sammy Delancey, one of the island's most popular bartenders, mans the bar. The open-air lobby and deck also have great water views and loungy sofas for socializing. The res-taurant, one of the island's best, has an Italian chef. Rates include con-tinental breakfast. **Pros:** great rooms; great beach; great restaurant.

Cons: not within walking distance of town; you will need a car to go sightseeing or to Governor's Harbour ⊠ *Queen's Hwy., 6 mi north of Governor's Harbour* ☎ *242/332–3150* ⊕ *www.cocodimama.com* ⤣ *12 rooms* ⌂ *In-room: Wi-Fi. In-hotel: restaurant, bar, beach, water sports, parking* ⊙ *Sept.–Oct.*

$ ⊡ **Duck Inn and Orchid Gardens.** Facing west into the sunset, overlooking beautiful Governor's Harbour, two colonial cottages and a two-story home built in the 1850s are surrounded by a tropical garden with a superb orchid collection. John and Kay Duckworth bought the compound from a Canadian timber baron and restyled the houses. With one bedroom each, the cottages are perfect for couples, whereas the four-bedroom, two-bath house can sleep eight. Each dwelling has a full kitchen (there are grocery stores just a block away) and a veranda. A full-time gardener tends to tropical fruit trees including plums, papayas, figs, dates, and carambolas; you are welcome to pick and eat. **Pros:** historic buildings; harbor views; lush orchid gardens. **Cons:** not on the beach; only a few restaurants and shops within walking distance. ⊠ *Queen's Hwy.* ☎ *242/332–2608* ⊕ *www.theduckinn.com* ⤣ *2 cottages, 1 house* ⌂ *In-room: kitchen, Wi-Fi.*

$ ⊡ **Hut Pointe Inn.** Those looking for history and luxury will find much to like about the historic building constructed in 1944 by the first premier of the Bahamas, Sir Roland Symonette. The two-story limestone building had a fabulous renovation in 2009 with full kitchens, stone walls, and mahogany decks. It's a short walk to the beach, and a pool is in the works. **Pros:** historic building; wonderfully landscaped grounds; upscale amenities. **Cons:** within a few feet of the Queen's Highway; not on beach; 10 minutes from town. ⊠ *Queen's Hwy.* ☎ *760/908–6700* ⊕ *www.hutpointe.com* ⤣ *7 suites* ⌂ *In-room: a/c, kitchen, Wi-Fi. In-hotel: parking.*

$ ⊡ **Laughing Bird Apartments.** Jean Davies and her son Pierre own these four tidy apartments on an acre of land across the street from Laughing Bird Beach. It's a scenic walk from here to the bank, restaurants, library, and two Internet cafes on Cupid's Cay. Linens and crockery (including an English teapot and china cups) are furnished. You can stock your kitchen with produce from local stores. This is a quiet, on-your-own kind of place, where relaxing and fishing are the name of the game. **Pros:** nice view of beach through garden foliage; roomy guest rooms with full kitchens. **Cons:** needs refurbishing and redecorating. ⊠ *Off Queen's Hwy. between Haynes Ave. and Gibson La.* ☎ *242/332–2012* ⤣ *4 apartments* ⌂ *In-room: kitchen. In-hotel: beach.*

$$ ⊡ **Pineapple Fields.** Set back on 80 acres of manicured wilderness, and
★ across the street from a pink-sand Atlantic beach, Pineapple Fields is the perfect base for a disappearing act. Hole up in one of 32 condo units, each with front and back verandas, a full kitchen, and a living room with pull-out queen sofa. Washers and dryers in each unit are especially handy for families and visitors who aren't planning to leave any time soon. Next door to the hotel is the new 25 acre Leon Levy Native Plant Preserve, opened in March 2011. Guests also love Tippy's, the beach bistro across the street that serves a changing menu of sophisticated European-influenced fare. When you've had enough seclusion, Governor's Harbour,

The beach at Governor's Harbour

Eleuthera's liveliest town, is just 4 mi down the road. **Pros:** modern facilities and amenities; large units; secluded beach and Tippy's across the street. **Cons:** Sterile American-style condo; will need to drive to town. ✉ *Banks Rd.* ☎ *242/332–2221, 877/677–9539* ⊕ *www.pineapplefields.com* ⟳ *32 condo units* ⟳ *In-room: safe, kitchen, Wi-Fi. In-hotel: restaurant, bar, pool, beach, laundry facilities, parking, some pets allowed.*

$ **Quality Cigatoo Inn.** Surrounded by a white picket fence, this resort sits high on Buccaneer Hill in a 19th-century neighborhood. It has crisp white buildings trimmed in vibrant hues, surrounded by tropical gardens. Rooms are decorated in an island theme and have private patios or balconies. Ask for one of the second-floor rooms, which have views of the ocean in the distance. The resort is a long walk from a pink-sand beach, so you'll need to rent a car. The guest-services department arranges bonefishing or deep-sea fishing trips, day trips to other islands, and car or bike rentals. The restaurant serves full American breakfast. **Pros:** friendly bar and hotel staff; nice landscaping and pool; walking distance to town. **Cons:** not on beach; will need a car to go to restaurants; on-site restaurant only serves breakfast. ✉ *Haynes Ave.* ☎ *242/332–3060* ⊕ *www.choicehotels.com* ⟳ *22 rooms* ⟳ *In-room: Wi-Fi. In-hotel: restaurant, bar, pool, tennis court.*

$ ★ **Unique Village.** Just south of Governor's Harbour, near North Palmetto Point on marvelous pink Poponi Beach, this resort has large, refurbished rooms with French doors opening to private balconies. Second-floor rooms have better views of the ocean. The Unique is probably the best bargain on the beach, with a great Bahamian restaurant and large pool steps away. At night you can hear the lapping waves and watch a full moon rise over the ocean. The resort is efficiently run with a friendly staff who will be happy to organize fishing trips and tours. **Pros:** on a gorgeous pink beach; steps to large pool and restaurant. **Cons:** must go down many wood stairs to access beach; a 10-minute drive to Governor's Harbour. ⊠ *Banks Rd., North Palmetto Point* ☎ *242/332–1830* ⊕ *www.uniquevillage.com* ⇨ *10 rooms, 4 villas* ⚒ *In-room: kitchen, Wi-Fi. In-hotel: restaurant, bar, pool, tennis court, beach, water sports, laundry facilities.*

NIGHTLIFE

Dr. Sea Breeze. Dr. Sea Breeze plays calypso at Unique Village resort at Palmetto Point Saturday nights. Be sure to check with the hotel first to make sure he's scheduled.

Globe Princess. The Globe Princess shows current movies, one show each night at 8 pm. Movies change weekly. The concession serves the best hamburgers in town. ⊠ *Queen's Hwy., Governor's Harbour, Eleuthera Island* ☎ *242/332–2735* ⊡ *$5* ⊙ *Closed Thurs.*

ROCK SOUND AND SOUTH ELEUTHERA

One of Eleuthera's largest settlements, the village of **Rock Sound** has a small airport serving the island's southern part. Front Street, the main thoroughfare, runs along the seashore, where fishing boats are tied up. If you walk down the street, you'll eventually come to the pretty, white-washed St. Luke's Anglican Church, a contrast to the deep blue and green houses nearby, with their colorful gardens full of poinsettia, hibiscus, and marigolds. If you pass the church on a Sunday, you'll surely hear fervent hymn singing through the open windows. Rock Sound has the island's largest supermarket shopping center, where locals stock up on groceries and supplies.

The tiny settlement of **Bannerman Town** (population 40) is 25 mi from Rock Sound at the island's southern tip, which is punctuated by an old cliff-top lighthouse. Rent an SUV if you plan to drive out to it; the rutted sand road is often barely passable. The pink-sand beach here is gorgeous, and on a clear day you can see the Bahamas' highest point, Mt. Alvernia (elevation 206 feet), on distant Cat Island. The town lies about 30 mi from the residential Cotton Bay Club, past the quiet little fishing villages of Wemyss Bight (named after Lord Gordon Wemyss, a 17th-century Scottish slave owner) and John Millars (population 15), barely touched

LEARNING IN PARADISE

The Island School is a pioneering 14-week program for high-school students that's a model of sustainability—students and teachers work together to run a campus where rainwater is captured for use, solar and wind energy is harnessed, food comes from its own small farm, wastewater is filtered and reused to irrigate landscaping, and biofuel is made from cruise ships' restaurant grease to power vehicles and generators. This "mind, body, and spirit experience" aims to inspire students to be responsible, caring global citizens. Call the school and see if someone's available to give a tour. ☎ *242/334–8551.*

over the years. Visitors will want to check out Cape Eleuthera Resort and Yacht Club. Plan to have lunch here and enjoy the ocean views. If you're in the mood for adventure, rent a Hobie Cat, a 16-foot Carolina skiff, water skis, a Windsurfer, or a kayak. Better yet, stay in the resort's luxury town houses so you have time to explore the 4,500 wooded acres and miles of beaches.

GETTING HERE AND AROUND

Fly into Rock Sound Airport and rent a car. It's 22 mi to Cape Eleuthera Resort and Yacht Club, the main resort in South Eleuthera. If you are arriving by private boat, you can dock at Cape Eleuthera Resort and Yacht Club Marina. If you fly into Governor's Harbour, plan to rent a car at the airport—Cape Eleuthera is 56 mi from the airport. Taxis are available at both airports, but can be expensive: the fare for two people to Cape Eleuthera Resort and Yacht Club is $80 from Rock Sound Airport and $130 from Governor's Harbour Airport.

> ### A SWINGING TIME
>
> In Eleuthera the game that brings the crowds is fast-pitch softball. The Eleuthera Twin City Destroyers were the men's champions of the 2006 Bahamas Softball Federation tournament. On most any weekend afternoon from March to November you can find the team playing at Rock Sound or Palmetto baseball parks on the island, known as the Softball Capital of the Bahamas. Eleuthera pitchers and brothers Edney and Edmond Bethel are both players for the Bahamas National Team, which has been consistently in the top 10 in the world.

EXPLORING

Ocean Hole. A small inland saltwater lake a mile southeast of Rock Sound is connected by tunnels to the sea. Steps have been cut into the coral on the shore so visitors can climb down to the lake's edge. Bring a piece of bread or some fries and watch the fish emerge for their hors d'oeuvres, swimming their way in from the sea. A local diver estimates the hole is about 75 feet. He reports that there are a couple of cars at the bottom, too. Local children learn to swim here.

St. Luke's Anglican Church. The idyllic seaside church on Front Street, which runs along the shore, has a pretty belfry and a garden of poinsettia, hibiscus, and marigolds.

WHERE TO EAT AND STAY

$
BAHAMIAN

✕ **Sammy's Place.** This spotless stop is owned by Sammy Culmer and managed by his friendly daughter Margarita. It serves conch fritters, fried chicken, lobster and fish, and peas 'n' rice. When it's available in season, don't miss the guava duff dessert, sweet bread with swirls of creamy guava. It's open for breakfast, too. ⊠ *Albury La., Rock Sound* ☎ *242/334–2121* ▭ *No credit cards.*

$$
Fodor's Choice
★

⊞ **Cape Eleuthera Resort and Yacht Club.** How many times can you say Wow in one vacation? Let us count the ways at Cape Eleuthera Resort and Yacht Club. Nestled between the aquamarine and emerald waters

DID YOU KNOW?

Deserted Island: It's not difficult to find an empty cay to call your own. Schooner Cays are just off the island's southern coast.

Strolling through Dunmore Town, Harbour Island

of Rock and Exuma sounds, gigantic town homes have two bright bedrooms, each with full bath, and a stainless-steel kitchen. Watch breathtaking sunsets painted over the full-service marina from your second-floor balcony, or from the Starbucks-inspired coffee shop's veranda, which turns into a wine bar at night. By day, explore the resort's 18-mi-long shoreline, which is home to more than 20 beaches. For a unique experience, have the staff take you by boat to one of the five nearby, footprint-free islands for the day. Pack a picnic and your seashell bucket and get ready for complete solitude. Barracuda's restaurant is open for private groups and catered events. **Pros:** handsome resort right on the water; professional yet friendly staff; gear rental on-site for water and land excursions (some with fee). **Cons:** isolated from rest of island; two-story town homes are inconvenient for travelers with heavy suitcases or disabilities (there is one ground-floor unit). ☒ *Cape Eleuthera, Powell Point, Rock Sound* ☎ *242/334-8500, 888/270-9642* ⊕ *www. capeeleuthera.com* ⇥ *19 town homes* ♿ *In-room: kitchen, Wi-Fi. In-hotel: restaurant, bar, tennis court, beach, water sports, children's programs, laundry facilities, parking* ⍩ *Multiple meal plans.*

SPORTS AND THE OUTDOORS

Cape Eleuthera Resort and Yacht Club. You can rent kayaks, sailboats, and bicycles here. There are also tennis courts and a dive shop. Reservations must be made for dive trips, which include a variety of destinations such as wall diving. Day trips with picnic lunches are available to nearby deserted islands. ☎ *242/334-8500* ⊕ *www.capeeleuthera.com.*

HARBOUR ISLAND

Updated by
Kevin Kwan

Harbour Island has often been called the Nantucket of the Caribbean and the prettiest of the Out Islands because of its powdery pink-sand beaches (3 mi worth!) and its pastel-color clapboard houses with dormer windows, set among white picket fences, narrow lanes, cute shops, and tropical flowers.

The frequent parade of the fashionable and famous, and the chic small inns that accommodate them, have earned the island another name: the St. Bart's of the Bahamas. But residents have long called it Briland, their faster way of pronouncing "Harbour Island." These inhabitants include families who go back generations to the island's early settlement, as well as a growing number of celebrities, supermodels, and tycoons who feel that Briland is the perfect haven to bask in small-town charm against a stunning oceanscape. Some of the Bahamas' most handsome small hotels, each strikingly distinct, are tucked within the island's 2 square mi. At several, perched on a bluff above the shore, you can fall asleep with the windows open and listen to the waves lapping the beach. Take a walking tour of the narrow streets of **Dunmore Town**, named after the 18th-century royal governor of the Bahamas, Lord Dunmore, who built a summer home here and laid out the town, which served as the first capital of the Bahamas. It's the only town on Harbour Island, and you can take in all its attractions during a 20-minute stroll.

6

GETTING HERE AND AROUND

Access Harbour Island via a 10-minute ferry ride from the North Eleuthera dock. Fares are $5 per person in a boat of two or more, plus an extra dollar to be dropped off at the private Romora Bay Club docks and for nighttime rides.

The best way to get around the island is to rent a golf cart or bike, or hire a taxi, since climbing the island's hills can be strenuous in the midday heat. If you plan to stay in Dunmore Town, you'll be able to walk everywhere.

EXPLORING

Lone Tree. If you stroll to the end of Bay Street and follow the curve to the western edge of the island, you'll find the Lone Tree, one of the most photographed icons of Harbour Island. This enormous piece of driftwood is said to have washed up on shore after a bad storm and anchored itself on the shallow sandbar in a picturesque upright position, providing the perfect photo op for countless tourists.

Loyalist Cottage. The most photographed house on the island is the pretty turquoise-and-white Loyalist Cottage, one of the original settlers' homes (circa 1797) on Bay Street. You can't go inside; it's privately owned. Many other old houses are in the area, with gingerbread trim and picket fences. Amusing names include Beside the Point, Up Yonder, and The Royal Termite.

St. John's Anglican Church. The first church built by the Eleutheran Adventurers and the Bahamas' oldest Anglican church was constructed in

1768. It still welcomes churchgoers after almost 250 years. Services are Sunday at 8 am and 7 pm.

Straw Crafts. A row of straw-work stands are on Bay Street next to the water, including Dorothea's, Pat's, and Sarah's, where you'll find straw bags, hats, and T-shirts. Food stands sell conch salad, Kalik beer, coconut water, and fruit juices.

WHERE TO EAT

Note that many Harbour Island hotels and restaurants are closed from September through mid- to late October.

$$$ ✕ **Acquapazza.** Briland's only Italian restaurant offers a change of pace
ITALIAN from the island's standard fare, and a change of scenery, too. It's located on the island's south end at the Harbour Island Marina, with a dockside terrace where you can take in the sunset while sipping one of its exclusively imported Italian wines. Chef and owner Manfredi Mancini's hearty portions of fried calamari and pasta *e fagioli* (with beans) don't disappoint, and the seafood entrées are always a good choice. ⊠ *Harbour Island Marina, south end of island off Queens Hwy.* ☏ *242/333–3240* ⌒ *Reservations essential.*

¢ ✕ **Arthur's Bakery and Cafe.** Bread and pastries are baked every morning
CAFÉ by *White Shadow* screenwriter and local real-estate agent to the stars Robert Arthur and his Trinidadian wife Anna. The friendly café has a quiet garden nook where you can savor your morning brew with an apple turnover, banana pancakes, or any of the daily breakfast offerings. The most popular item to take back is the jalapeño-and-cheese bread. Computers with Internet access are available for a fee. ⊠ *Crown St. and Dunmore St., Dunmore Town* ☏ *242/333–2285* ▤ *No credit cards* ⊘ *Closed Sun. No dinner.*

$ ✕ **Dunmore Deli.** Patrick Tully's exceptional deli satisfies the epicurean
AMERICAN demands of Briland's more finicky residents and visitors, while its shaded wooden porch, filled with hanging plants and bougainvillea, makes this the perfect spot for a lazy breakfast or lunch. Treat yourself to the Briland Bread Toast, the amazingly fluffy take on French toast, or pick up one of the inventive deli sandwiches for a picnic on the beach. While here, you can also stock up on a variety of international coffees, imported cheeses, produce, and other gourmet items you won't find anywhere else on the island. ⊠ *King St., Dunmore Town* ☏ *242/333–2644* ⊘ *Closed Sun. No dinner.*

$$ ✕ **Harbour Lounge.** Owners of the
CONTINENTAL Bubble Room restaurant—a longtime Captiva Island, Florida, favorite—now own this pink building with green shutters across from the government dock. The front deck is a prime spot for people-watching, as well as for sunsets over cocktails.

HEAVENLY MUSIC

The best live music on Harbour Island is at the Lighthouse Church of God on Chapel Street in Dunmore Town on Sunday mornings. Mick Jagger and Lenny Kravitz have dropped by to hear Pastor Samuel Higgs, drummer and bass player, and guitarist Rocky Sanders, both of whom played Europe's clubs for years before settling down on the island.

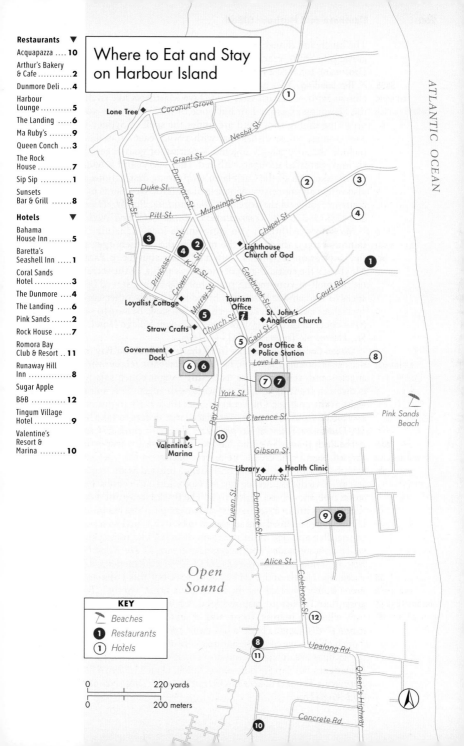

Where to Eat and Stay on Harbour Island

Restaurants ▼

Acquapazza **10**

Arthur's Bakery
& Cafe **2**

Dunmore Deli **4**

Harbour
Lounge **5**

The Landing **6**

Ma Ruby's **9**

Queen Conch **3**

The Rock
House **7**

Sip Sip **1**

Sunsets
Bar & Grill **8**

Hotels ▼

Bahama
House Inn **5**

Baretta's
Seashell Inn **1**

Coral Sands
Hotel **3**

The Dunmore **4**

The Landing **6**

Pink Sands **2**

Rock House **7**

Romora Bay
Club & Resort .. **11**

Runaway Hill
Inn **8**

Sugar Apple
B&B **12**

Tingum Village
Hotel **9**

Valentine's
Resort &
Marina **10**

ATLANTIC OCEAN

Lone Tree

Coconut Grove

Nesbit St.

Grant St.

Duke St.

Bay St.

Pitt St.

Munnings St.

Dunmore St.

Chapel St.

Lighthouse
Church of God

Princess St.

King St.

Crown St.

Murray St.

Colebrook St.

Court Rd.

Loyalist Cottage

Tourism
Office

Church St.

St. John's
Anglican Church

Straw Crafts

Gaol St.

Government
Dock

Post Office &
Police Station

Love La.

York St.

Bay St.

Clarence St.

Pink Sands
Beach

Valentine's
Marina

Gibson St.

Library

Health Clinic

South St.

Queen St.

Dunmore St.

Alice St.

Open
Sound

Colebrook St.

Upalong Rd.

KEY

🏖 *Beaches*

① *Restaurants*

① *Hotels*

0   220 yards

0   200 meters

Queen's Highway

Concrete Rd.

The lunch and dinner fare might include smoked dolphin-fish dip with garlic pita chips, cracked conch, and spicy tequila shrimp. ⊠ *Bay St., Dunmore Town* 🕾 *242/333–2031* ☉ *Closed Mon.*

$$$$ ✕ **The Landing.** You never know which actor or rock star you'll rub
ECLECTIC elbows with—Richard Gere and Dave Matthews like to dine here—at
Fodor'sChoice the Hemingway-esque bar, but none of it matters once you've moved
★ on to the dining room and are under the spell of Sydney-trained chef
Ken Gomes, whose dishes soar with a Southeast Asian flair. Standouts include the surprisingly ingenious pairing of goat-cheese ravioli with shrimp, panfried grouper with red Thai curry, and a banana upside-down cake. One of the Caribbean's top dining destinations, the Landing also offers an impressive wine selection. If the weather is nice, request a romantic table on the porch. ⊠ *The Landing, Bay St., Dunmore Town* 🕾 *242/333–2707* 🍴 *Reservations essential* ☉ *Closed Wed.*

¢ ✕ **Ma Ruby's.** Although you can sample local Bahamian fare at this
BAHAMIAN famous eatery, the star of the menu is the cheeseburger, purportedly
★ the inspiration for Jimmy Buffett's "Cheeseburger in Paradise" song.
Maybe it's the rustic charm of the breezy patio, or the secret seasonings on the melt-in-your-mouth patty, but this burger served between thick slices of homemade Bahamian bread is definitely otherworldly. Dinner specialties include cracked conch and fish stew. Be sure to save room for Ma's coconut tart or key lime pie. ⊠ *Tingum Village Hotel, Colebrooke St., Dunmore Town* 🕾 *242/333–2161.*

¢ ✕ **Queen Conch.** Four blocks from the ferry dock on Bay Street with a
BAHAMIAN deck overlooking the water, Lavaughn Percentie reigns over her colorful
snack stand, renowned for its freshly caught conch salad ($8), which is diced in front of you, mixed with fresh vegetables, and ready to eat right at the counter. On weekends, get there early to put in your order, as visitors from the world over place large orders to take home. ⊠ *Bay St., Dunmore Town* 🕾 *No phone* ▤ *No credit cards* ☉ *Closed Sun.*

$$$ ✕ **The Rock House.** Splendid harbor views and a transporting Mediter-
NEW AMERICAN ranean-loggia vibe create the perfect backdrop for Chef Jennifer Lear-
★ month's California continental menu, infused with tropical accents.
Imaginative dishes include curried Colorado lamb chops and Thai-style stone crab and lobster spring rolls. The Rock House also takes its drinks seriously, with an extensive list showcasing California boutique wines. Dining here is refined and serene, thanks to the flawless service, so linger over coffee and one of the decadent desserts, like rum cake with butter sauce or homemade Pilon espresso ice cream. ⊠ *The Rock House Hotel, Bay St., Dunmore Town* 🕾 *242/333–2053* 🍴 *Reservations essential.*

$$ ✕ **Sip Sip.** Locals and travelers alike seek out this popular snow-cone-
BAHAMIAN green house overlooking the beach for a little "sip sip" (Bahamian for
Fodor'sChoice gossip) and delicious inspired food. Chef and owner Julie Lightbourn
★ uses whatever is fresh, local, and in season to create "Bahamian with
a twist" dishes, so check what daily specials are on the blackboard. Conch chili is one of her signatures; consider yourself lucky if the lobster quesadillas are available, and don't miss the decadent carrot cake with ginger-caramel. Sip Sip only serves lunch, from 11:30 to 4. ⊠ *Court Rd., Dunmore Town* 🕾 *242/333–3316* ☉ *Closed Tues. No dinner. Closed mid-Aug.–Nov.*

Harbour Island tranquillity

$$$ ✕ **Sunsets Bar and Grille.** This waterfront pavilion at the Romora Bay
BAHAMIAN   Club perfectly frames sunsets over Harbour Island, so be sure to get
here in time to snag a good seat for the show. Popular with locals, the
restaurant serves midpriced Bahamian specialties such as conch fritters
for a casual lunch or dinner. The bartender is always happy to create
drinks just to suit your vibe, and be sure to greet Goldie the parrot,
who has held court over the bar for more than 50 years. ✉ *Romora Bay
Club, south end of Dunmore St., Dunmore Town* ☎ *242/333–2325.*

WHERE TO STAY

$ ⊞ **Bahama House Inn.** Originally deeded in 1796 and built by Thomas
★   W. Johnson, Briland's first doctor and justice of the peace, this hand-
some seven-bedroom B&B, in a garden filled with bougainvillea, royal
poincianas, and hibiscus, thrives thanks to the loving preservation work
of genial innkeeper John Hersh. Each guest room is sweetly furnished
with a distinctive array of antiques and local artwork, and overlooks
either the harbor or garden. A favorite is the Harry Potter Room, tucked
under the stairs but much more spacious than you'd imagine with its
vaulted ceiling. Enjoy an alfresco full breakfast every morning on the
verdant deck. **Pros:** central location in the middle of Dunmore Town;
historic house; peaceful garden. **Cons:** not on the beach; limited hotel
services. ✉ *Dunmore St., Dunmore Town* ☎ *242/333–2201* ⊕ *www.
bahamahouseinn.com* ↪ *7 rooms* ⚓ *In-room: a/c, safe, kitchen. In-
hotel: restaurant, bar, laundry facilities, some age restrictions* ⊘ *Closed
July–Oct.* ⑩ *Breakfast.*

$ **Baretta's Seashell Inn.** If all you need is a clean, affordable room that's close to the beach, Baretta's is the place for you. This family-run inn is right next door to the famed Pink Sands Resort and a three-minute walk down a path from the quieter north end of the beach. While the property itself might not impress at first glance with its slightly overgrown yard, its 12 rooms are spotless, surprisingly spacious, and cheerfully decorated with bright pastel bedspreads and comfortable furniture. Two minisuites even have king-size beds and Jacuzzi tubs in the bathrooms. The inn's restaurant is a local haunt that serves authentic Bahamian cuisine. **Pros:** well-maintained rooms; close to the beach; locally owned business. **Cons:** only ocean views are from the second floor over the tops of trees; slightly off-the-beaten-path; limited services. ✉ *Nesbitt St., Dunmore Town* ☎ *242/333–2361* ⊕ *www.barettasseashellinn.com* ⤴ *12 rooms* ⌂ *In-room: a/c, Wi-Fi. In-hotel: restaurant, bar, some pets allowed.*

> **LOCAL FLAVOR**
>
> If you're wondering where the real action is on the weekends, head for Brian's, where barbecue ribs and jerk chicken are expertly grilled on a Dunmore Street front patio every Friday and Saturday night. The barbecue party really heats up after 10 pm and stays packed until the wee hours, because it's where everyone eventually ends up after a night of work or partying.

$$$ **Coral Sands Hotel.** An elegant yet energetic flair accents this 9-acre oceanfront resort, right on the pink-sand beach. The main lobby is a study in British colonial style, while the billiard room off the bar attracts a younger, hipper crowd. Guest rooms are spread out over three buildings, and rooms in the Lucaya building are the largest, with balconies and ocean views. All are decorated in a modern tropical style, with neutral tones, streamlined wood furniture, and flat-screen TVs. Worth the extra splurge is the Beach House, a two-bedroom cottage right on the sand that's closer to the water than any other rental property on the island. At night the lights are dimmed, candles flicker, and Chef Ludovic Jarland serves Caribbean cuisine with a French flair in the Terrace restaurant, where open arches frame views of the lush gardens and the sea beyond. **Pros:** direct ocean access; trendy beach resort vibe; billiard room. **Cons:** rooms vary in quality and style; some rooms feel cramped; only one private cottage. ✉ *Chapel St.* ☎ *242/333–2350, 800/468–2799* ⊕ *www.coralsands.com* ⤴ *32 rooms, 5 cottages, 1 villa* ⌂ *In-room: safe, kitchen, Wi-Fi. In-hotel: restaurant, bar, pool, tennis court, beach, water sports, business center* ⊙ *September.*

$$$ **The Dunmore.** This classic Old Bahamian–style hotel evokes a 1940s private club in the tropics. With its colorfully painted bar, white Chippendale-chaired dining room, and faded paperbacks in the clubhouse library, it's a favorite with the New England yachting set. A guest-to-staff ratio of almost one-to-one services the eight private cottages scattered throughout the grounds, which are done in traditional wicker and floral chintz, with spacious marble bathrooms that have separate sink-vanity areas and stand-alone showers. **Pros:** on the beach with ocean-side bar service; spacious bathrooms; private terraces and lawn chairs

for every cottage. **Cons:** cottages too close for real privacy; small club-house; slightly stuffy vibe. ⊠ *Gaol La., Dunmore Town* ☎ *242/333–2200, 877/891–3100* ⊕ *www.dunmorebeach.com* ⤏ *16 cottages, 1 house* ☾ *In-room: a/c, safe. In-hotel: restaurant, bar, pool, tennis court, gym, beach, water sports* ⊗ *Aug. 15–Nov. 15.*

$$ ⊡ **The Landing.** Spare white walls and crisp white linens evoke a time-
★ less, understated chic at the Landing, which is acclaimed as much for its singular style as for its superb cuisine. Each of its seven intimate guest rooms is simply decorated in a colonial plantation style in the Captain's House, built in 1820, and the main house, built in 1800. Want a memorable harbor view? An antique telescope peers out of a lookout nook from the Attic Room, which also has a gleaming white bathroom complete with a sumptuous white chaise lounge. Soothe yourself in the garden's tranquil pool when you're beached out—and don't miss the sybaritic outdoor shower, cleverly designed around the roots of an ancient fig tree. **Pros:** chic and comfortable rooms; glorious outdoor shower; acclaimed dining. **Cons:** 10 am check-out time; limited hotel services; not on the beach. ⊠ *Bay St.* ☎ *242/333–2707* ⊕ *www. harbourislandlanding.com* ⤏ *13 rooms* ☾ *In-room: no TV, Wi-Fi. In-hotel: restaurant, bar, pool* ⊗ *Closed Aug. 25–Oct. 29.*

$$$$ ⊡ **Pink Sands.** Harbour Island's famed beachfront resort has long been
★ praised by celebrities—Martha Stewart, Nicole Kidman, and Brooke Shields—and honeymooners alike for its 25 private cottages scattered over 20 secluded acres. Biba designer Barbara Hulanicki updated the resort with her eclectic touches, including a cascading mother-of-pearl chandelier that dominates the lobby. The renovations have infused the main house with a sexy, South Beach–Moroccan vibe. With all the creature comforts in the way of luxurious bedding, plasma-screen TVs, and imposing native wood furniture, the newly renovated guest cottages truly feel like an island getaway in paradise. But with two tennis courts, a secluded pool, and the legendary namesake beach just steps away, will you really care? The newly expanded Blue Bar serves Bahamian-infused European cuisine until sunset and has a prime vantage point overlooking the beach. **Pros:** truly private cottages; state-of-the-art media room; discreet and well-trained staff. **Cons:** some cottages quite a walk from the main house and beach (better drive your golf cart on a hot day); resort is a hike from the center of town ⊠ *Chapel St., Dunmore Town* ☎ *242/333–2030* ⊕ *www.pinksandsresort.com* ⤏ *25 cottages* ☾ *In-room: safe, Wi-Fi. In-hotel: restaurant, bar, pool, tennis court, gym, beach, business center* ⊗ *Closed Sept.* ⦿| *Breakfast.*

$$ ⊡ **Rock House.** With a drawing room straight out of a villa on the Amalfi
Fodor's Choice Coast, the Rock House is Harbour Island's most luxurious boutique
★ hotel. Originally a complex of historic harborside buildings, the hotel was designed by the late Wallace Tutt (the builder of Gianni Versace's mansion in Miami) and owner Don Purdy, who attentively orchestrates a pampering, intimate haven for his discriminating international clientele. Fresh orchids fill every room, private cabanas line the heated courtyard pool, and the congenial staff cater to your every need. Guest rooms are a sophisticated mix of contemporary and island furnishings, outfitted with thoughtful amenities like a picnic basket for beach

6

Fresh seafood at the Landing

forays and custom-designed extra-padded mattresses. After feasting at the Rock House's celebrated restaurant, you'll want to take advantage of the island's only fully outfitted gym (exclusively for guest use). **Pros:** heavenly beds; stellar service; best gym on the island. **Cons:** not on the beach; lack of views from some rooms. ⊠ *Bay St., Dunmore Town* ☎ *242/333–2053* ⊕ *www.rockhousebahamas.com* ⤴ *7 rooms, 3 suites* ♿ *In-room: safe, Internet, Wi-Fi. In-hotel: restaurant, bar, pool, gym, business center, some age restrictions* ⊗ *Aug. 1–Nov. 1* ⑩ *Breakfast.*

$$ ⚞ **Romora Bay Club & Resort.** Three pink Adirondack chairs on the dock
Ⓒ welcome you to this colorful and casual resort situated on the bay side of the island. Guest rooms are in cottages with private terraces or balconies, built on sloping grounds, each recently renovated and idiosyncratically decorated (one room might showcase a French armoire and Salvador Dalí prints, while another has a four-poster bed and African tribal masks). Fans of this older property don't mind a little wear and tear, preferring its laid-back character and exceedingly friendly staff. The resort also boasts what is perhaps the island's best sunset view, which you can enjoy while you're splashing around in the infinity pool, lounging in one of the cabanas on the small private beach, or sipping a frosty cocktail at its restaurant Sunsets Bar and Grille. For those arriving by private boat, there's a new 30-slip marina. **Pros:** friendly staff; water views from every room; private bay-side beach. **Cons:** construction on condos ongoing; sloping steps from dock to cottages are a hassle for luggage; main house has been converted into a resort showroom. ⊠ *South end of Dunmore St., Dunmore Town* ☎ *242/333–2325* ⊕ *www.romorabay.com* ⤴ *18 rooms* ♿ *In-room: a/c, safe. In-hotel:*

restaurant, bar, pool, tennis court, beach, business center ☉ *Closed end of Aug.–Nov.*

$$$$ 🏨 **Runaway Hill Inn.** Set on gorgeous rolling grounds, this quiet seaside
★   inn feels far removed from the rest of the island, which is precisely the
point. This is not a place you'll be waited on hand and foot. Rather,
longtime guests appreciate the lived-in quality of this rambling 1938
New England–style beach house, where you have the run of the place
and can be left alone to mix a drink at the honor bar, relax poolside, or
head down the steps to the beach. The lobby and rooms were renovated
in 2009. Guest rooms are simply furnished in a comfortable contemporary style, and bathrooms display colorful tile work and Fresh bath
products. Request Room No. 2, where you can savor the breathtaking
view of the ocean while lying in your bed. At dinnertime, Chef Luc Cas-
tilloux serves French and Bahamian cuisine with modern fusion touches.
Pros: oceanfront location with direct beach access; well-stocked library;
intimate character. **Cons:** limited service; not as chic a vibe as nearby
resorts. ✉ *Colebrooke St., Dunmore Town* 🕾 *242/333–2150* ⊕ *www.
runawayhill.com* 🛏 *11 rooms, 2 villas* ⚹ *In-room: kitchen. In-hotel:
restaurant, bar, pool, beach.*

$ 🏨 **Sugar Apple Bed and Breakfast.** Harbour Island's newest inn has roomy
suites, all with modern full kitchens, handcrafted four-poster beds, and
sitting areas. The two-story motel-style inn is decorated with art and
fabrics from Kenya, where one of the owners is from. The inn is surrounded by a garden of fruit trees and vegetables and guests are free
to pick. This is a great choice for travelers trying to save some money;
it's not as chic as other Harbour Island inns, but not as expensive,
either. **Pros:** Tranquil area; spotless and affordable rooms. **Cons:** a
fairly long walk to beach and town; rent a golf cart. ✉ *Colebrooke St.*
🕾 *242/333–2750* ⊕ *www.sugarapplebb.com* 🛏 *7 suites* ⚹ *In-room:
kitchen.*

¢ 🏨 **Tingum Village Hotel.** Each of the rustic cottages on this property,
☾   owned by the Percentie family, is named after a different island of
the Bahamas. The native theme continues inside the lodgings, where
recently renovated rooms are individually decorated with simple beach
furniture and tropical prints. Larger cottages are ideal for families, with
king-size beds, kitchenettes, and two-person whirlpool tubs. There's no
lobby to speak of, since the room where you check in also doubles as the
famous Ma Ruby's restaurant, but the place is full of local charm and
just a short walk from the pink-sand beach. Juanita Percentie, "Ma"
Ruby's enterprising daughter, also rents a luxurious and tricked-out
five-bedroom beach villa nearby, complete with a romantic rooftop bedroom, gourmet kitchen, and waterfall pool with swim-up bar. **Pros:** family-friendly; local flavor; Ma Ruby's restaurant. **Cons:** no-frills interior
and furnishings; not on beach or harbor; rustic grounds. ✉ *Colebrooke
St* 🕾 *242/333–2161* 🛏 *12 rooms, 7 suites, 2 cottages* ⚹ *In-room:
kitchen. In-hotel: restaurant, bar, spa, water sports, laundry facilities.*

$$$ 🏨 **Valentine's Resort and Marina.** With the largest marina on Harbour
Island, equipped with 51 slips capable of accommodating yachts up to
170 feet, this resort is ideal if you are a self-sufficient traveler or family
that doesn't require many amenities but enjoys spacious condo-style

6

rooms and water-focused activities. Valentine's draws a serious boating crowd with its dockside bar and complete dive shop. Each junior suite or one- and two-bedroom unit is well appointed in a modern colonial style, with rich dark woods and plush beige sofas sharing space with sepia-toned photographs and plasma-screen TVs. Luxurious bathrooms come with soaking tubs, glass shower stalls, and Gilchrist & Soames bath products. For the best marina views, request a room in the Andros building. **Pros:** modern rooms; state-of-the-art marina; large swimming pool. **Cons:** not oceanfront; impersonal condo-style quality; lack of hotel service. ⊠ *Bay St., Dunmore Town* ☎ *242/333–2142* ⊕ *www. valentinesresort.com* ↵ *41 rooms* ✍ *In-room: safe, kitchen, Wi-Fi. In-hotel: restaurant, bar, pool, water sports.*

NIGHTLIFE

Gusty's. Enjoy a brew on the wraparound patio of Gusty's, on Harbour Island's northern point. This lively hot spot has sand floors, a few tables, and patrons shooting pool or watching sports on satellite TV. On weekends, holidays, and in high season, it's an extremely crowded and happening dance spot with a DJ, especially after 10 pm. ⊠ *Coconut Grove Ave.* ☎ *242/333–2165.*

Seagrapes. Enter through the marine life–muraled hallway at Seagrapes to a large nightclub with a raised stage that's home to the local Brilanders band. Seagrapes is usually the last stop in the local club crawl which begins at Gusty's and moves on to the Vic-Hum, before ending up here. ⊠ *Colebrooke and Gibson Sts.*

Vic-Hum Club. Vic-Hum Club, owned by "Ma" Ruby Percentie's son Humphrey, occasionally hosts live Bahamian bands in a room decorated with classic record-album covers; otherwise, you'll find locals playing Ping-Pong and listening and dancing to loud recorded music, from calypso to American pop and R & B. Mick Jagger and other rock stars have dropped by. Look for the largest coconut ever grown in the Bahamas—33 inches in diameter—on the bar's top shelf. ⊠ *Barrack St., Harbour Island* ☎ *242/333–2161.*

SHOPPING

Most small businesses on Harbour Island close for a lunch break between 1 and 3.

Bahamian Shells and Tings. This shop sells island wear, souvenirs, and crafts, many handmade on Harbour Island. ⊠ *Coconut Grove Ave., Dunmore Town* ☎ *242/333–2839* ◷ *Closed Sun.*

Blue Rooster. This is the place to go for festive party dresses, sexy swimwear, fun accessories, and exotic gifts. ⊠ *Dunmore St* ☎ *242/333–2240* ◷ *Closed Sun.*

Briland's Androsia. This shop has a unique selection of clothing, beachwear, bags, and home items handmade from the colorful batik fabric created on the island of Andros. ⊠ *Bay St.* ☎ *242/333–2342* ◷ *Closed Sun.*

Dilly Dally. Here you can find Bahamian-made jewelry, maps, T-shirts, CDs, decorations, and other fun island souvenirs. ⊠ *Dunmore St.* ☎ *242/333–3109* ⊗ *Closed Sun.*

John Bull. This duty-free shop that's part of a Nassau-based chain sells watches, fine jewelry, perfume, cigars, and sunglasses from international brands. ⊠ *Bay St.* ☎ *242/333–2950* ⊗ *Closed Sun.*

Miss Mae's. Miss Mae's sells an exquisite and discerningly curated collection of fashion-forward clothing, accessories, and gifts from international designers and artisans. ⊠ *Dunmore St.* ☎ *242/333–2002* ⊗ *Closed Sun.*

Patricia's Fruits and Vegetables. this is where locals go for homemade candies, jams, and other Bahamian condiments. Her famous hot sauce and native thyme (sold in recycled Bacardi bottles) make memorable gifts. ⊠ *Pitt St., Dunmore Town* ☎ *242/333–2289.*

Pink Sands Gift Shop. This shop offers a trendy selection of swimwear, accessories, casual clothing, and trinkets. ⊠ *Pink Sands Resort* ☎ *242/333–2030.*

Princess Street Gallery. Princess Street Gallery displays original art by local and internationally renowned artists, as well as a diverse selection of illustrated books, home accessories, and locally made crafts. ⊠ *Princess St.* ☎ *242/333–2788* ⊗ *Closed Sun.*

The Shop at Sip Sip. The Shop at Sip Sip sells its own line of T-shirts and a small but stylish selection of handmade jewelry, custom-designed totes, Bahamian straw work, and gifts found by owner Julie Lightbourn on her far-flung travels. ⊠ *Court Rd., Dunmore Town* ☎ *242/333–3316* ⊗ *Closed Tues.*

Sugar Mill. Here you can find a glamorous selection of resort wear, accessories, and gifts from designers around the world. ⊠ *Bay St.* ☎ *242/333–3558* ⊗ *Closed Sun.*

SPORTS AND THE OUTDOORS

BIKING **Michael's Cycles.** Bicycles are a popular way to explore Harbour Island; rent one—or golf carts, motorboats, scooters, Jet Skis, and kayaks—at Michael's Cycles. ⊠ *Colebrooke St.* ☎ *242/333–2384.*

BOATING AND FISHING There's great bonefishing right off Dunmore Town at **Girl's Bank**. Charters cost about $350 for a half day. The Harbour Island Tourist Office can help organize bone- and bottom-fishing excursions, as can all of the major hotels.

SCUBA DIVING AND SNORKELING **Ocean Fox Diving and Deep-sea Fishing Center.** Ocean Fox Diving and Deep-sea Fishing Center provides dive trips. ☎ *242/333–2323.*

Valentine's Dive Center. This dive cetner rents and sells equipment and provides all levels of instruction, certification, and dive trips. ☎ *242/333–2080* ⊕ *www.valentinesdive.com.*

SPANISH WELLS

Off Eleuthera's northern tip lies St. George's Cay, the site of **Spanish Wells**. The Spaniards used this as a safe harbor during the 17th century while they transferred their riches from the New World to the Old. Residents—the few surnames go back generations—live on the island's eastern end in clapboard houses that look as if they've been transported from a New England fishing village. Descendants of the Eleutheran Adventurers continue to sail these waters and bring back to shore fish and lobster (most of the Bahamas' langoustes are caught here), which are prepared and boxed for export in a factory at the dock. So lucrative is the trade in crawfish, the local term for Bahamian lobsters, that the 1,500 inhabitants may be the most prosperous Out Islanders.

GETTING HERE AND AROUND

You can reach Spanish Wells by taking a five-minute ferry ride ($7) from the Gene's Bay dock in North Eleuthera. You can easily explore the area on foot, or rent a golf cart.

WHERE TO STAY

$ **Abner's Rentals.** Abner Pinder's wife, Ruth, keeps these two-bedroom houses as spotless as her own. A tiny, private sand beach overlooking the ocean is just steps from the patio. A house rental includes the discounted use of a golf cart so you can explore the island and pick up groceries at one of the local shops. There's a three-night minimum stay; it's $1,200 per house per week. ⊠ *Between 12th and 13th Sts.* ☎ *242/333–4890, 954/237–6266* ⊕ *www.abnersvacationrentals.com* ⤴ *2 houses* ⚘ *In-room: a/c, kitchen, Internet* ⊟ *No credit cards.*

The Exumas

WORD OF MOUTH

"Although the metaphor of the kid in the candy shop is a well-used one, it's so often used because it is so apt. And so it applies here, except the candy store is the Exuma Cays and the candy is the many varied beaches. Some pocket-sized, some long, some sand-bars. Each cay, each rock, is iced in sugar."

—Callaloo

WELCOME TO THE EXUMAS

TOP REASONS TO GO

★ **Party like a local:** Hot spots include the Fish Fry on weekends for conch salad and fresh fish and Chat 'N' Chill on Stocking Island for Sunday pig roasts.

★ **Island-hop:** You'll want to spend a couple of days boating through the 365 cays (one for every day of the year, as the locals say), most uninhabited, some owned by celebrities. Get ready for iguanas, swimming pigs, and giant starfish.

★ **Enjoy empty beaches:** Beautiful stretches of bleach-white sand are yours to explore, and more often than not you'll be the only person on them, even at noon on a Saturday.

★ **Explore the Land and Sea Park:** Underwater attractions in the 176-square-mi Exuma Land and Sea Park, one of the best snorkel sights in the Bahamas, include queen conchs, starfish, and thriving coral reefs. Keep a lookout for the endangered hawksbill and threatened green and loggerhead turtles.

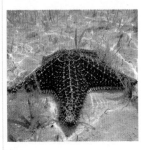

1 Great Exuma. Capital George Town sees most of the action on this mainland, including the 12-day George Town Cruising Regatta and the Bahamian Music and Heritage Festival. But dazzling white beaches and fish fries offering cold Kaliks and conch salad crop up along the coasts of the entire island. Visitors come to fish—especially to stalk the clever bonefish—dive and snorkel, and stay in atmospheric inns and luxurious resorts, where you can find complete solitude or hopping beach parties.

2 Little Exuma. The Tropic of Cancer runs through the chain's second-largest island, which is duly noted on the steps leading to Pelican's Bay Beach, one of the most spectacular on the island. *Pirates of the Caribbean* 2 and 3 were filmed on Sandy Cay, just offshore; stop by Santana's Grill on the beach in historic Williams Town and ask to see

their famous-people photo book while you feast on fresh-cracked lobster.

3 The Exuma Cays. If you're looking for a true escape—a vacation where you're more likely to see giant starfish, wild iguanas, swimming pigs, dolphins, and sharks than other people—boat over to the cays. This is also where celebrities come to buy their own spectacular islands—Johnny Depp, Faith Hill and Tim McGraw, David Copperfield, and Nicholas Cage all have 'em. The renowned Exuma Cays Land and Sea Park, toward the chain's north end, has some of the most gorgeous crystal-clear water and white sand on earth.

Sail Rocks

Ship Channel Cay

Allan's Cays

Highbourne Cay
Highbourne

Long Cay

Norman's Cay

Shroud Cay

Hawksbill Cay

Cistern Cay

Exuma Cays Land and Sea Park **3**

Waderick Wells Cay

Halls Pond Cay

O'Brian's Cay

Bells Cay
Fowl Cay
Compass Cay
Joe Cay
Pipe Creek ◆
Thomas Cay

Sampson Cay

Big Major's Cay
Staniel Cay

Harvey's Cays

○ Black Point

Great Guana Cay

Big Farmer's Cay

Musha Cay
Cave Cay
Rudder Cut Cay

Darby Island
Young Island

Block Cay

Normans Pond Cay
Lee Stocking Island

Brigantine Cays
Barraterre
◆ Starfish Reserve
○ Rolleville
○ Steventon

Great Exuma Island **1**
○ Mt. Thompson
Queen's Hwy.

Exuma Int'l Airport
Moss Town ○
Fish Fry ◆
Elizabeth Harbour
Stocking Island

George Town ○

Channel Cays
Rolle Town Tombs
Rolle Town ○
Forbes Hill
The Hermitage
St. Christopher's **2** ○

Little Exuma Island
Williams Town

GRAND BAHAMA BANK

EXUMA

Exuma Sound

CAYS

GETTING ORIENTED

Thirty-five miles southeast of Nassau, Allan's Cay sits at the top of the Exumas' chain of 365 islands (most uninhabited) that skip like stones for 120 mi south across the Tropic of Cancer. Flanked by the Great Bahama Bank and Exuma Sound, the islands are at the center of the Bahamas. George Town, the Exumas' capital and hub of activity, so to speak, is on Great Exuma, the mainland and largest island, near the bottom of the Exumas' chain. Little Exuma is to the south and connected to the mainland by a bridge. Together, these two islands span 50 mi.

7

0 ⸺ 15 mi

0 ⸺ 15 km

THE EXUMAS PLANNER

When to Go

High season is December through April, when weather is in the 70s (although lows can dip into the 60s). Be warned that hotels will sell out for events such as the George Town Cruising Regatta and the Bahamian Music and Heritage Festival in March, and the National Family Islands Regatta in April.

Summer room rates are cheaper than the winter high season, but fall (late August through November) offers the best deals. That's because it's hurricane season (June–November), with the most chance of a storm from August to November. Weather during this time can be rainy and hot. Some inns close for September and October.

Getting Here

The **Exuma International Airport (GGT)** (☎ 242/345–0002) is 10 mi north of George Town. Taxis wait at the airport for incoming flights; a trip to George Town costs $25 for two people; to Williams Town, $55; to February Point, $27; to Emerald Bay, $20; to Barraterre, $50. Each additional person is $5. Staniel Cay Airport accepts charter flights and private planes.

M/V *Grand Master* travels from Nassau to George Town on Tuesday and returns to Nassau on Friday. The trip's 12 hours and $45 each way. M/V *Captain Sea* leaves Nassau on Tuesday for Staniel Cay, Big Farmer's Cay, Black Point, and Barraterre, returning to Nassau on Saturday. The trip's 14 hours and costs $70. Contact the **Dockmaster's Office** (☎ 242/393–1064). **Bahamas Ferries**' (☎ 242/323–2166). *Sealink* travels from Nassau to George Town Monday and Wednesday, arriving the next day in Exuma on Tuesday and Thursday. The trip's 10 hours and $60 one way, $110 round-trip.

Getting Around

By Boat To reach Stocking Island from George Town, **Club Peace and Plenty Ferry** (☎ 242/336–2551) leaves the hotel at 10 am and 1 pm. It's free for guests and $12 round-trip for nonguests. **Elvis Ferguson** (☎ 242/464–1558 or VHF 16) operates a boat taxi from Government Dock to Chat 'N' Chill on the hour throughout the day. If you plan on leaving the island after 6 pm, tell the captain in advance. If you want to explore the Exuma cays, you'll appreciate the freedom of having your own boat.

By Car If you want to explore Great Exuma and Little Exuma, you'll need to rent a car. Most hotels can arrange car rentals.

By Scooter In George Town, **Prestige Scooter Rental** (☎ 242/524–0066) rents motor scooters for $50 a day.

By Taxi Taxis are plentiful on Great Exuma, and most offer island tours. A half-day tour of George Town and Little Exuma is about $150 for two people.

About the Restaurants

Exuma restaurants are known for terrific Bahamian home cooking—cracked conch, pan-seared snapper caught that morning, coconut fried shrimp, fried chicken served with peas 'n' rice, or macaroni baked with egg and loads of cheese. Try conch salad at the cluster of wooden shacks called the Fish Fry, just north of George Town. Pea soup and dumplings (made with pigeon peas) is a specialty here, and many local restaurants serve it as a weekly lunch special, usually on Wednesday.

Restaurants at larger resorts have upscale dining, including continental twists on local cuisine—fresh snapper with mango salsa—as well as imported steaks, rack of lamb, and gourmet pizzas.

About the Hotels

Accommodations in the Exumas are more wide-ranging than on most Bahamian Out Islands. You can stay in simple stilt cottages, fabulous rooms with butler service, atmospheric old inns, modern condo rentals, all-inclusives, eco-lodges, or bed-and-breakfasts—temporary home-away-from-homes for every taste and price point. Most places have lots of personality and are distinctive in some marvelous way—a great hangout for fishermen, a peaceful place of tranquillity with no distractions, or action-packed resorts with head-spinning activity choices. Meal plans are available at some hotels.

The mainland of Great Exuma has had an energetic growth spurt that includes some of the country's most luxurious hotels: the new Sandals Emerald Bay, which opened in 2010; Grand Isle Resort and Spa; and February Point Resort Estate.

WHAT IT COSTS IN DOLLARS

	¢	$	$$	$$$	$$$$
Restaurants	under $10	$10–$20	$20–$30	$30–$40	over $40
Hotels		under $100	$100–$200	$200–$300	$300–$400	over $400

Restaurant prices are based on the median main course price at dinner, excluding gratuity, typically 15%, which is often automatically added to the bill. Hotel prices are for two people in a standard double room in high season, excluding service and 6%–12% tax.

Essentials

Banks Banks in George Town are open Monday–Thursday 9:30–3 and Friday until 4:30. All have ATMs.

Boat Rentals Minns Water Sports ☎ 242/336–3483, 242/336–2604 ⊕ www.mwsboats.com. **Staniel Cay Yacht Club** ☎ 242/355–2024 ⊕ www.stanielcay.com. **Starfish** ☎ 242/336–3033 ⊕ www.starfishexuma.com.

Car Rentals Airport Rent a Car ✉ George Town Airport ☎ 242/345–0090. **Exuma Transport** ✉ George Town ☎ 242/336–2101. **Thompson's Rentals** ✉ George Town ☎ 242/336–2442.

Emergencies George Town Clinic ✉ Queens Hwy., George Town ☎ 242/336–2088. **Nurse Lydia King-Rolle Health Center** ✉ Queen's Hwy., Steventon ☎ 242/358–0053. **Police** ☎ 911, 242/336–2666 George Town, 242/355–2042 Staniel Cay.

Taxis Exuma Travel and Transportation Limited ☎ 242/345–0232. **Kendal "Dr. K" Nixon** ☎ 242/422–7399. **Leslie Dames Taxi Service** ☎ 242/357–0015. **Luther Rolle Taxi Service** ☎ 242/357–0662.

Visitor Information Exuma Tourist Office ✉ Queen's Hwy., George Town ☎ 242/336–2430 ⊕ www.exuma.bahamas.com. **Out Islands Promotion Board** ⊕ www.myoutisland.com.

7

EXUMA BEACHES

You can't go wrong with the beaches in the Exumas. They're some of the prettiest in the Bahamas—powdery bleach-white sand sharply contrasts the glittery emerald and sapphire waves. You can even stake your umbrella directly on the Tropic of Cancer. And the best part of all? You'll probably be the only one there.

(above) Staniel Cay (upper right) Chat 'N' Chill, Stocking Island

The Exumas are made up of 365 cays, each and every one with pristine white beaches. Some cays are no bigger than a footprintless sandbar. But you won't stay on the sand long; Perrier-clear waters beckon, and each gentle wave brings new treasures—shells, bits of blue-and-green sea glass, and starfish. Beaches won't be hard to find on the tiny cays; on Great Exuma, look for "Beach Access" signs on the Queen's Highway.

PICTURE PERFECT

"My pictures will never show the incredible shades of blue in this water." You're likely to hear this on your vacation, maybe straight from your own mouth. Here are a few tips: shoot early—before 9—on a sunny day, or late in the afternoon. Make sure the sun is behind you. Use a tripod, or hold the camera still. Find a contrasting color—a bright red umbrella or a yellow fishing boat.

THE EXUMAS' BEST BEACHES

CHAT 'N' CHILL, STOCKING ISLAND
The restaurant and 9-acre playground—an amazing white-sand beach—is the Exumas' party central, particularly for the famous all-day-Sunday pig roasts. Play volleyball in the powdery sand, order what's cooking on the outdoor grill—fresh fish, ribs—or chat and chill. There are dances on the beach from January to the end of April, when 200-plus sailboats populate the harbor. The new Conch Bar on the beach serves conch fritters, conch salad, and lobster fritters. The beach is quieter on weekdays, and usually not crowded in summer and fall.

JOLLY HALL BEACH, GREAT EXUMA
Snorkeling, swimming, running; you can do it all on this long beach, a curve of sparkling white sand shaded by casuarina trees, just north of Palm Bay Beach Club. It's quiet, and the shallow azure water makes it a great spot for families or romantics. When it's time for lunch, walk over to Palm Bay, Coconut Cove, or Augusta Bay, three small nearby inns. Watch your bags when high tide comes in; much of the beach is swallowed by the sea. That's the signal for a cold Kalik and a grouper sandwich.

PELICAN'S BAY BEACH, LITTLE EXUMA
This is the beach most visitors come to the Exumas for, although don't be surprised if you're the only one on it

at noon on a Saturday. It's right on the Tropic of Cancer; a helpful line marking the spot on the steps leading down to the sand makes a great photo op. The beach is a white-sand crescent in a protected cove, where the water is usually as calm as a pond. A shady wooden cabana makes a comfortable place to admire the beach and water. *Pirates of the Caribbean* 2 and 3 were filmed on nearby Sandy Cay. Have lunch at the cast's favorite place, the open-air Santana's in Williams Town, a 10-minute drive from the beach.

WARDERICK WELLS CAY, EXUMA CAYS
Next to the park headquarters in Exuma Cays Land and Sea Park is a lovely white beach, but you won't be looking at the sand when you first arrive. The beach is dominated by the stunningly huge skeleton of a sperm whale that died in 1995 because it consumed plastic. The skeleton was fortified in its natural form and makes an emotion-packed statue that no artist could duplicate. Equally striking are the gorgeous blue shades of water and the glistening white sand. Check out the snorkel trail in the park when you've soaked in enough sun.

7

EXUMA CAYS LAND AND SEA PARK

Created by the Bahamas National Trust in 1958, the 176-square-mi Exuma Cays Land and Sea Park was the first of its kind in the world—an enormous open aquarium with pristine reefs, an abundance of marine life, and sandy cays.

(above) Boats anchored in the bay at Warderick Wells Cay, the park's headquarters

The park appeals to divers, who appreciate the vast underworld of limestone, reefs, drop-offs, blue holes, caves, and a multitude of exotic marine life including one of the Bahamas' most impressive stands of rare pillar coral. Since the park is protected and its waters have essentially never been fished, you can see what the ocean looked like before humanity. For landlubbers there are hiking trails and birding sites; stop in the main office for maps. More than 200 bird species have been spotted here. At Shroud Cay, jump into the strong current that creates a natural whirlpool whipping you around a rocky outcropping to a powdery beach. On top of the hill overlooking the beach is Camp Driftwood, made famous by a hermit who dug steps to the top leaving behind pieces of driftwood. ⊠ *Between Conch Cut and Wax Cay Cut* ☎ *242/225–1791 VHF Channel 9 or 16* ⊕ *www.exumapark.info.*

BEST TIME TO GO

In summer the water is as warm as bathwater and usually just as calm. The park has vastly fewer boats than in the busy winter season, when the channel becomes a blue highway for a parade of sailing and motor vessels. Bring insect repellent in summer and fall.

BEST WAYS TO EXPLORE

BOAT

If you rent a boat, you can explore the sandy cays and many islets that are little more than sandbars. Go slow and follow the channels marked on charts; the water is so clear it's hard to determine depths without a depth finder. Some routes are only passable at high tide. Get detailed directions before you go into the park, and be sure to stop by the park headquarters on Warderick Wells Cay for more information. Make sure you have a VHF marine radio on the boat or carry a handheld VHF radio so you can call for help or directions.

HIKE

The park headquarters has a map of hiking trails—most are on Warderick Wells Cay—that range from two-mile walks to two-hour treks. Wear sturdy shoes, because trails are rocky. You'll see red, black, and white mangroves; limestone cliffs; and lots of birds—white-tail tropic birds, green herons, blue herons, black-bellied plovers, royal terns, and ospreys. Take sunscreen and water (you have to bring plastic bottles back with you) and try not to go in the middle of the day; there's very little shade.

KAYAK

Visitors do sometimes take kayak trips from neighboring cays into the park and camp on the beach. The park has two kayaks that can be used free of charge by boaters moored in the park. As you paddle, look for sea turtles, which might pop up beside you.

SNORKEL AND DIVE

You have to go underwater to see the best part of the park—spiny lobsters walking on stilt legs on the sandy floor, sea grass waving in the currents, curious hawksbill turtles (critically endangered), solemn-faced groupers, and the coral reefs that support an astonishing range of sea life. Bring your own equipment.

FUN FACT

The park has one native land mammal—the hutia, a critically endangered rodent that looks similar to a gray squirrel. Thousands roam the park's cays, but are noctunal and seldom seen. The little animals were at one time thought to be extinct, but today flourish in the park.

MAKING A DIFFERENCE

7

How successful has the Exuma Cays Land and Sea Park been at safeguarding marine life? About 74% of the grouper in the northern Exumas' cays come from the park. Crawfish tagged in the park have been found repopulating areas around Cat Island 70 mi away. And the concentration of conch inside the Exuma Park is 31 times higher than the concentration outside the park, according to marine studies. This conservatively provides several million conchs outside the park for fishermen to harvest each year.

Updated by Cheryl Blackerby

The Exumas are known for their gorgeous 365 cays—most uninhibited, some owned by celebrities. Get the wind and sea salt in your hair as you cruise through the pristine 120-mi chain. The water here is some of the prettiest in the world, and comes in every shade of blue and green (you'll grow tired trying to name the exact color); beaches are dazzling white. Combine that with fresh seafood and friendly locals, and you have yourself one of the best vacation destinations in the Bahamas.

Yes, the Exumas are Out Islands in the fullest sense of the word; there isn't a casino or cruise ship in sight. Those who love the remote beauty of the windswept cays keep coming back, people like Jimmy Buffett, who once docked his seaplane behind the historic Club Peace and Plenty and amused islanders by fishing from the cockpit. A vacation here revolves around uncrowded beaches, snorkeling, fishing, and enjoying a freshly caught dinner at an outdoor restaurant by the beach.

In 1783 Englishman Denys Rolle sent 150 slaves to Great Exuma to build a cotton plantation. His son Lord John Rolle later gave all of his 5,000 acres to his freed slaves, and they took the Rolle name. On Great Exuma and Little Exuma you'll still find wild cotton, testaments from plantations first established by Loyalists after the Revolutionary War. But today the Exumas are known as the Bahamas' onion capital, although many of the 3,500 residents earn a living by fishing and farming, and, more recently, tourism.

The Exumas attract outdoorsmen and adventurers, particularly fishermen after bonefish, the feisty breed that prefers the shallow sandy flats that surround these islands. And the healthiest coral reefs and fish populations in the country make for excellent diving and snorkeling. But for those simply seeking secluded beaches, starry skies, and a couple of new friends, the Exumas won't disappoint.

GREAT ITINERARIES

IF YOU HAVE 3 DAYS

Fly into **George Town**, relax on the beach or at the pool, and if it's a Friday-night drive to the Fish Fry, a collection of outdoor fish shacks and bars just north of George Town; eat your dinner on a picnic table next to the beach. Finish the night at Club Peace and Plenty, the heart of George Town for more than 50 years. On Day 2, pick an activity: golfing at Sandals Emerald Bay; diving, snorkeling, or kayaking (make arrangements the night before at your resort); bonefishing; or drive to a beautiful secluded beach. Get gussied up (sun dresses and linen shirts) for a nice dinner in town. On Day 3, head out to **Stocking Island** for some beach volleyball and that it's-five-o'clock-somewhere cocktail. Stay for dinner and sunset. If it's Sunday, a pig roast at noon brings all the islanders over.

IF YOU HAVE 5 DAYS

On Day 4, head to the **Exuma Cays** for some island-hopping: snorkel in Thunderball Grotto, feed swimming pigs and the rare Bahamian iguanas, or find your own secluded sand bar. Spend the night at Staniel Cay Yacht Club, and enjoy a festive dinner at the bar. On Day 5, head to the Exuma Cays Land and Sea Park, and spend the day snorkeling, hiking, and beach snoozing.

IF YOU HAVE 7 DAYS

For the last two days, on your way back from the cays, relocate to Grand Isle or Sandals Emerald Bay for a luxurious end to your vacation. Relax on the beach, go to the spa, and enjoy that gorgeous blue water one last time. Eat at some of the finer restaurants on the island, or at beach shacks off the resort property.

7

GREAT EXUMA

George Town is the capital and largest town on the mainland, a lovely seaside community with darling pink government buildings overlooking Elizabeth Harbour. The white-pillared, colonial-style Government Administration Building was modeled on Nassau's Government House and houses the commissioner's office, police headquarters, courts, and a jail. Atop a hill across from it is the whitewashed St. Andrew's Anglican Church, originally built around 1802. Behind the church is the small, saltwater Lake Victoria. It was once used for soaking sisal used for making baskets and ropes. The straw market, a half-dozen outdoor shops shaded by a huge African fig tree, is a short walk from town. You can bargain with fishermen for some of the day's catch at the Government Dock, where the mail boat comes in.

Small settlements make up the rest of the island. **Rolle Town,** a typical Exuma village devoid of tourist trappings, sits atop a hill overlooking the ocean 5 mi south of George Town. Some of the buildings are 100 years old. **Rolleville** overlooks a harbor 20 mi north of George Town. Its old slave quarters have been transformed into livable cottages. The Hilltop Tavern, a seafood restaurant and bar, is guarded by an ancient cannon.

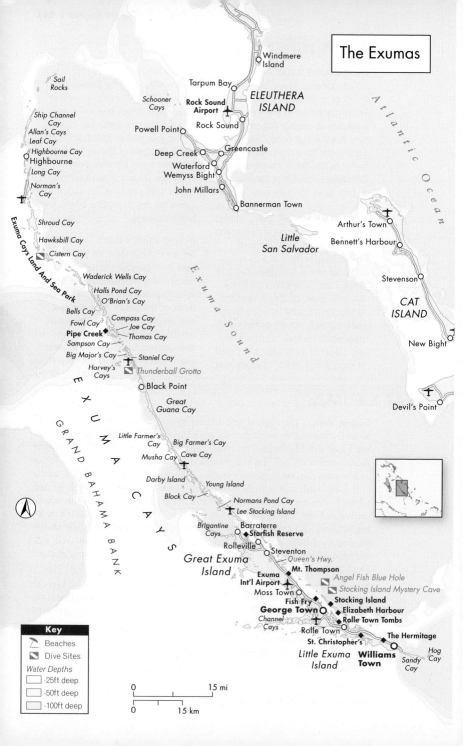

GETTING AROUND

If you are going to sightsee on your own and plan to eat at restaurants and visit beaches outside your resort, you should rent a car, since taxis can get expensive. If you plan to stay at your resort most of your vacation, you can use taxis.

EXPLORING

★ **Fish Fry.** Fish Fry is the name given to a jumble of one-room beachside structures, such as Charlie's and Honeydew, about 2 mi north of George Town. They're favored by locals for made-to-order fish and barbecue. Some shacks are open weekends only, but most are open nightly until at least 11 pm. There's live Rake 'n' Scrape Monday nights and DJs on Friday and Saturday. Eat at picnic tables by the water and watch the fishing boats come into the harbor. This is a popular after-work meeting place on Friday nights, and a sports bar attracts locals and expats for American basketball and football games.

Mt. Thompson. From the top of Mt. Thompson, rising from the Three Sisters Beach, there is a pleasing view of the **Three Sisters Rocks** jutting above the water just offshore. Legend has it that the rocks were formed when three sisters, all unwittingly in love with the same English sailor, waded out into deep water upon his departure, drowned, and turned into stone. If you look carefully next to each "sister" you'll see smaller boulders—the children with which the fickle sailor left them. Mt. Thompson is about 12 mi north of George Town, past Moss Town.

Rolle Town Tombs. Seek out the three Rolle Town Tombs, which date back to Loyalists. The largest tomb bears this poignant inscription: "Within this tomb interred the body of Ann McKay, the wife of Alexander McKay who departed this life on the 8th November 1792. Age twenty-six years and their infant child." The tombs are off the main road; look for a sign. The settlement has brightly painted buildings, several more than 100 years old.

Fodor'sChoice ★ **Stocking Island.** Slightly more than a mile off George Town's shore lies Stocking Island. The 4-mi-long island has only 10 inhabitants, the upscale Hotel Higgins Landing, lots of walking trails, a gorgeous white beach rich in seashells and popular with surfers on the ocean side, and plenty of good snorkeling sites. Jacques Cousteau's team is said to have traveled some 1,700 feet into Mystery Cave, a blue-hole grotto 70 feet beneath the island. Don't miss Chat 'N' Chill, a lively open-air restaurant and bar right on the point. Volleyball games, board games under the trees, and the new Conch Bar make for fun in the sun. The restaurant picks up guests at Government Dock on the hour. Club Peace and Plenty's ferry runs over to Stocking Island twice daily at 10 am and 1 pm, and charges $12 for nonguests. Near the Stocking Island pier, Peace

---

DID YOU KNOW?

Folks are friendly in the Exumas and will readily hail you on the street to chat. Understand that when a man greets a woman as "baby," it doesn't have a derogatory context; it's a term of endearment that women also use when addressing other women.

and Plenty Beach Club provides changing rooms (with plumbing) and operates a lunch spot where Dora's hamburgers and famous conch burgers are the eats of choice. Stocking Island is the headquarters for the wildly popular George Town Cruising Regatta.

WHERE TO EAT

¢   ✕ **Big D's Conch Shack.** For the freshest—and according to locals, best—
BAHAMIAN   conch salad and the coldest beer, look for the splatter-painted seaside shack a stone's throw from Grand Isle Resort, where Big D does the fishing every day. You can't get a better water view, and the beach is great; bring a swimsuit. ⊠ *Queen's Hwy., Steventon* 🕾 *No phone* ⊟ *No credit cards* ☉ *Closed Mondays.*

$ ✕ **Chat 'N' Chill.** Yacht folks, locals, and visitors alike rub shoulders
BAHAMIAN   at Kenneth Bowe's funky open-air beach bar on the point at Stock-
Fodor'sChoice   ing Island. All of the food is grilled over an open fire; awesome conch
★   burgers with secret spices and grilled fish with onions and potatoes attract diners from all over Great Exuma. Dances and bonfires on the beach during the winter season are famous island-wide. Sunday pig roasts, which start around noon, are legendary, but call first to make sure it's scheduled. Most guests arrive by sailboat but you can get here by water taxi (🕾 *242/336–2700; or call Capt. Elvis Ferguson on VHF radio channel 16*) from the Government Dock, which leaves on the hour during the day. ⊠ *Stocking Island* 🕾 *242/336–2700* ⊕ *www.chatnchill. com* ⊟ *No credit cards.*

$ ✕ **Cheater's Restaurant and Bar.** Disregard the lacking ambience, this pop-
BAHAMIAN   ular restaurant serves some of the best food on the island. Fresh fish and fried chicken dinners are the house specialties. Free transportation is available to those staying at hotels within 4 mi of the restaurant. ⊠ *Queen's Hwy., 1½ mi south of George Town* 🕾 *242/336–2535* ⊟ *No credit cards* ☉ *Closed Sun. and Mon.*

$$ ✕ **Club Peace and Plenty.** The legendary hotel's restaurant has a fabulous
CONTINENTAL   view of the pool and harbor, along with traditional Bahamian spe- cialties including cracked conch and grilled fish, and a 12-ounce New York strip steak. This is one of the nicer places to dine on the island, perfect for a romantic dinner or family celebration. For breakfast, start your day with boiled snap- per and johnnycakes or an omelet. ⊠ *Queen's Hwy., George Town* 🕾 *242/336–2551.*

$$ ✕ **Coconut Cove Hotel.** This restau-
ITALIAN   rant, a local institution for 20 years, has a menu that includes continen- tal and Italian cuisine. The delicious pizzas are hugely popular, as well as Bahamian specialties including fresh fish and shrimp. The most popular dish may be grilled lob- ster. It's all served at the bar or by the fireplace, with sliding glass

> **KEEP AN EYE OUT**
>
> During your walks, you might glimpse peacocks on Great Exuma. Originally, a peacock and a pea- hen were brought to the island as pets by a man named Shorty Johnson, but when he left to work in Nassau he abandoned the birds, which gradually proliferated into a colony. The birds used to roam the streets, but development has forced them into the bush, so they are rarer sights these days.

DID YOU KNOW?

The Tropic of Cancer cuts through Little Exuma. A helpful line marking the spot on the steps leading down to Pelican's Bay Beach makes a great photo op.

doors open to ocean breezes. The restaurant is in a small inn in a scenic grove of coconut palms by the beach. Don't miss bartender Fuzz's rum drinks. ⊠ *Queen's Hwy., George Town* ☎ *242/336–2659.*

$ ✕ **Eddie's Edgewater.** Fried chicken,
BAHAMIAN lobster, T-bone steak, and cracked conch are the delicious reasons people eat at this modest lakeside establishment. ⊠ *Charlotte St., George Town* ☎ *242/336–2050.*

$ ✕ **Iva Bowe's Central Highway Inn.** About 10 mi from George Town,
BAHAMIAN close to the airport, this hole-in-the-wall lunch and dinner spot has an island-wide reputation for having the best native food. Try one of the delectable shrimp dishes—coconut beer shrimp, spicy Cajun shrimp, or scampi, all for around $15. ⊠ *Queen's Hwy., Ramsey 9* ⊟ *No credit cards* ⊘ *Closed Sun.*

$ ✕ **Pallappa Pool Bar and Grill at Grand Isle Resort.** This poolside restaurant
CONTINENTAL serves three meals a day. The extensive menu equally features American
★ classics and Bahamian specialties. Dinner highlights include ahi tuna steak, shrimp pasta, prime rib eye, and baby back ribs. A fun drink list including many frozen concoctions complements the food. ⊠ *Queen's Hwy., Emerald Bay* ☎ *242/358–5000.*

$ ✕ **Splash Bar & Grill at Palm Bay Beach Club.** Restaurant highlights for
BAHAMIAN lunch are fish burgers, conch burgers, and regular burgers. Dinner specialties include grilled grouper, cracked conch, and pizza. The restaurant circles a lively bar, a popular hangout for locals as well as guests who enjoy the view of the harbor and Stocking Island. ⊠ *Queen's Hwy., George Town* ☎ *242/336–2787.*

$ ✕ **Towne Café.** This George Town restaurant serves breakfast (especially
BAHAMIAN popular on Saturday)—consider trying the stew' fish or chicken souse—and lunches of grilled fish or seafood sandwiches with three sides. It's open until 3 pm. Don't miss the baked goods, especially the giant cinnamon rolls. ⊠ *Marshall Complex, George Town* ☎ *242/336–2194* ⊟ *No credit cards* ⊘ *Closed Sun. No dinner.*

WHERE TO STAY

$$ ⊞ **Augusta Bay Bahamas.** The perfect balance of luxury and casual chic,
Fodor'sChoice without the megaresort feel, this 16-room resort on 300 feet of narrow
★ beach is a mile north of George Town. The resort underwent a fabulous $2 million renovation in 2008 and another refurbishing in 2009 that includes luxurious dark colonial-style furniture, woven jute beds, and lush red drapes and bedspreads. Pillow-top queen- and king-size beds, 400-thread-count linens, feather-down comforters, stone floors, and marble baths with glass-enclosed rain showers with double vanity sinks round out the opulence. French doors open onto private patios or balconies that overlook the pool and a gorgeous white-sand beach. Marvel at the lodge's tiered, stained-pine cathedral ceiling. The resort provides snorkeling and sea kayaking. **Pros:** luxurious rooms; great

> **THE GOLDEN TICKET**
>
> The new Sandals restaurants aren't open to nonguests, unless you buy a $150 pass that includes all you can eat and drink from 6 pm to 2 am, a $180 pass for 10 am to 6 pm, or an all day pass for $310

Emerald Bay, Great Exuma

water views; friendly service. **Cons:** beach almost disappears at high tide; need a car to drive to town and shops. ✉ *Queen's Hwy., George Town* ☎ *242/336–2250, 954/636–1300* ⊕ *www.augustabaybahamas. com* ⇆ *16 rooms* ⚤ *In-room: safe, Wi-Fi. In-hotel: restaurant, bar, pool, beach, water sports, laundry facilities.*

$ ★ 🖵 **Club Peace and Plenty.** The first Exumas' hotel and granddaddy of the island's omnipresent Peace and Plenty empire, this pink, two-story lodge is in the heart of the action in George Town. Rooms have private balconies overlooking the pool or ocean. There's no on-property beach, but its Beach Club on Stocking Island is a five-minute ferry shuttle away (free for guests). Lermon "Doc" Rolle has held court at the poolside bar since the '70s. The indoor bar, which was once a slave kitchen, attracts locals and a yachting crowd, especially during the Family Islands Regatta. **Pros:** guests are in middle of the George Town action; friendly staff; ocean-view balconies in some rooms. **Cons:** no beach; have to take a water taxi to Stocking Island. ✉ *Queen's Hwy., George Town* ☎ *242/336–2551, 800/525–2210* ⊕ *www.peaceandplenty.com* ⇆ *32 rooms* ⚤ *In-hotel: restaurant, bar, pool, water sports, laundry facilities, business center* ☯ *Closed end of Aug.–Nov.*

$ 🖵 **Coconut Cove Hotel.** This cozy boutique inn has a loyal following. Rooms have queen-size beds, tile floors, and scenic views from private terraces. Bathrobes and fresh-daily floral arrangements add an elegant touch. The Paradise Suite has its own private terrace, a king-size bed, walk-in closet, and an immense bathroom with a black-marble Jacuzzi. **Pros:** nice beach; great for swimming and water sports. **Cons:** need a car to go to George Town. ✉ *Queen's Hwy., north of George Town* ☎ *242/336–2659* ⊕ *www.exumabahamas.com/coconutcove.html*

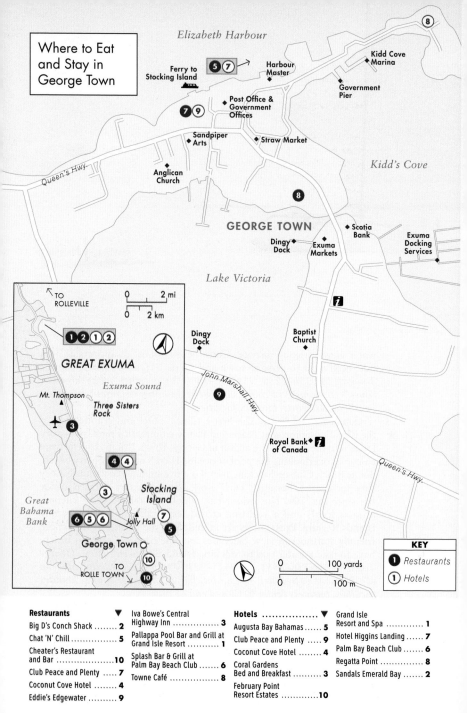

Where to Eat and Stay in George Town

Elizabeth Harbour

Ferry to Stocking Island

⑤ ⑦

Harbour Master

Kidd Cove Marina

Post Office & Government Offices

❼ ❾

Government Pier

Sandpiper Arts

Straw Market

Queen's Hwy.

Anglican Church

Kidd's Cove

GEORGE TOWN

❽

Dingy Dock

Exuma Markets

Scotia Bank

Exuma Docking Services

Lake Victoria

Dingy Dock

Baptist Church

🛈

TO ROLLEVILLE

0 — 2 mi
0 — 2 km

❶❷①②

GREAT EXUMA

Exuma Sound

Mt. Thompson

Three Sisters Rock

❸

❹④

❸

Great Bahama Bank

❻⑤⑥

Jolly Hall

⑦

⑤

Stocking Island

George Town ○

TO ROLLE TOWN

⑩

⑩

John Marshall Hwy.

❾

Royal Bank of Canada 🛈

Queen's Hwy.

0 — 100 yards
0 — 100 m

KEY
❶ *Restaurants*
① *Hotels*

Restaurants ▼

Big D's Conch Shack **2**

Chat 'N' Chill **5**

Cheater's Restaurant and Bar **10**

Club Peace and Plenty **7**

Coconut Cove Hotel **4**

Eddie's Edgewater **9**

Iva Bowe's Central Highway Inn **3**

Pallappa Pool Bar and Grill at Grand Isle Resort **1**

Splash Bar & Grill at Palm Bay Beach Club **6**

Towne Café **8**

Hotels .... ▼

Augusta Bay Bahamas **5**

Club Peace and Plenty **9**

Coconut Cove Hotel **4**

Coral Gardens Bed and Breakfast **3**

February Point Resort Estates **10**

Grand Isle Resort and Spa **1**

Hotel Higgins Landing **7**

Palm Bay Beach Club **6**

Regatta Point **8**

Sandals Emerald Bay **2**

⌐10 *rooms, including 1 suite* ⌂ *In-hotel: restaurant, bar, pool, beach* ☺ *September-October.*

¢ ⌐ **Coral Gardens Bed and Breakfast.** Extremely popular with Brits and Europeans, the sprawling two-story B&B, owned and run by British expats Betty and Peter Oxley, is on a hilltop with an inviting veranda. Three tidy guest rooms with private baths are upstairs, and two spacious apartments with kitchens are downstairs. Furnishings are modest but comfy. It's an extremely good value. **Pros:** superb hilltop view of water in the distance; peaceful location; friendly hosts. **Cons:** not on the beach; need a car to go to George Town and the beach. ✉ *Off Queen's Hwy. 3 mi north of George Town* ☎ *242/336–2880,* ⊕ *www. coralgardensbahamas.com* ⌐*3 rooms, 2 apartments* ⌂ *In-room: kitchen, Wi-Fi* ❖*Breakfast.*

$$$$ ⌐ **February Point Resort Estates.** This gated residential community and resort has 42 villas, including privately owned homes, and 20 villas available as guest accommodations. The two-story villas painted in pastel colors have magnificent harbor views of Elizabeth Harbour, and range from two to six bedrooms. Luxuriously decorated, the villas are serviced by housekeepers every other day. Guests may use the community's fitness center, tennis courts, and infinity pool. The waterfront restaurant serves Bahamian and international cuisine. **Pros:** elegant accommodations that feel like an ultraluxurious home away from home. **Cons:** more like a gated community than a resort. ✉ *Queen's Hwy., 1 mi from George Town* ☎ *242/327–1567, 877/839–4253* ⊕ *www.februarypoint.com* ⌐*20 villas* ⌂ *In-room: kitchen, Wi-Fi. In-hotel: pool, tennis court, gym, beach, water sports, children's programs, laundry facilities.*

$$$$ ⌐ **Grand Isle Resort and Spa.** This luxurious 78-villa complex boasts one

Fodor'sChoice of the island's few spas, an infinity pool overlooking the ocean, and a

★ poolside patio restaurant. A secluded patch of Emerald Bay Beach is right off the pool, and guests can use kayaks and snorkel equipment. Rooms are elaborate, and vary from one-bedroom garden-view villas to four-bedroom penthouses. All have fully loaded kitchens, private patios, and washers and dryers, and come with your own golf cart. **Pros:** the ultimate in luxury accommodations; friendly staff; on-site spa and restaurant. **Cons:** 20-minute drive from Georgetown and not much to do near the resort. ✉ *Off Queens Hwy., Emerald Bay* ☎ *242/358– 5000* ⊕ *www.grandisleresort.com* ⌐*78 villas* ⌂ *In-room: safe, kitchen, Wi-Fi. In-hotel: restaurant, bar, pool, gym, spa, beach, water sports, children's programs, laundry facilities, business center, parking.*

$$$$ ⌐ **Hotel Higgins Landing.** Laid out on undeveloped Stocking Island is

★ this eco-hotel that is 100% solar powered—though everything still works when the weather's overcast. Wood cottages have louvered jalousie windows with dark-green shutters and private spacious decks with ocean views. Interiors have antiques, queen-size beds, tile floors, and folksy Americana furnishings. By day the bar is an alfresco living room where you can play checkers or darts, or read books from the hotel's library. Colorful blossoms and tropical birds abound. Rates in one-bedroom cottages include an outstanding dinner for two; two-bedroom cottage rates include dinner for four. **Pros:** the ultimate in

7

The Straw Market in George Town features handmade crafts.

luxury for the eco-minded; plenty of walking trails and great beaches; nonmotorized water sports. **Cons:** have to take a water taxi to George Town; maybe too rustic for those thinking of luxury lodging. ⊠ *Stocking Island* 🕿 *242/357–0008* ⊕ *www.higginslanding.com* ⛴ *4 cottages* ⛐ *In-room: kitchen. In-hotel: restaurant, bar, gym, beach, water sports* ☉ *July-October* ⏐◎⏐ *Some meals.*

$ ⬛ **Palm Bay Beach Club.** Palm Bay, one of George Town's most modern
☺ accommodations, is all about light and color. The bungalows have
★ brightly painted, gingerbread-trim exteriors (like turquoise with hibiscus pink) and cheerfully sunny interiors with one or two bedrooms. There are five two-bedroom oceanfront villas, renting for $655 per night, for those wanting to splurge. Clustered on oleander-lined boardwalk paths along a lovely sand beach, the indulgence can definitely be justified. Each unit has a patio and a kitchenette or kitchen. Kayaks and paddleboats are available at no charge to guests. The huge circular poolside bar and patio attracts what seems like everybody on the island. **Pros:** luxurious, roomy accommodations; friendly young staff. **Cons:** beach all but disappears at high tide. ⊠ *Queen's Hwy., 1 mi from George Town* 🕿 *888/396–0606, 242/336–2787* ⊕ *www. palmbaybeachclub.com* ⛴ *40 units* ⛐ *In-room: safe, kitchen. In-hotel: restaurant, bar, pool, water sports* ☉ *September.*

$ ⬛ **Regatta Point.** Soft pink with hunter-green shutters, this handsome two-story guesthouse overlooks Kidd Cove from its own petite island. Connected to George Town by a short causeway, the property is only a five-minute walk from town but far enough from the fray to have a secret hideaway's charm. Rooms have superb views of Elizabeth

Harbour, large vaulted ceilings, and porches. Leave the louvered windows open to be lulled to sleep by the waves. The hotel has no restaurant, but units come with modern full-size kitchens, and maid service is included. Dock usage is free to guests, and rental boats are available. **Pros:** in George Town but has the feel of a private island; has beach and fantastic harbor views. **Cons:** water at the beach doesn't look clean; no restaurant. ⊠ *Kidd Cove, George Town* ☎ *242/336–2206, 800/688–0309, 888/720-0011* ⊕ *www.regattapointbahamas.com* ⤳ *6 suites* ⚐ *In-room: kitchen. In-hotel: beach, water sports* ⊟ *No credit cards.*

$$$$
ALL-INCLUSIVE **Sandals Emerald Bay.** The former luxurious Four Seasons is now the even more luxurious Sandals Emerald Bay, an all-inclusive resort of pink and aqua buildings facing a 1-mi-long stretch of powdery white sand. The resort, which opened in 2010, has "all-butler" suites, which means guests have their own butler to tend to their vacation needs. The room rate includes all food at the resort's five restaurants (except the caviar and vodka bar) and all nonmotorized water sports. The 7,000-yard, par-72 Greg Norman–designed championship Sandals Emerald Reef Golf Course is the only one on the island. A deepwater marina with 150 slips, three pools including the largest pool—at over half an acre—in the Bahamas and Caribbean, the largest Jacuzzi in the region, and a huge spa with 17 treatment rooms round out the amenities. The resort complex includes the three-bedroom, two-story house with private pool that Celine Dion rented when she was on the island. **Pros:** all-inclusive; magnificent beach and swimming pools; great water sports. **Cons:** the resort is isolated. ⊠ *Queen's Hwy., Emerald Bay* ☎ *242/336–6800, 800/SANDALS* ⊕ *www.sandals.com* ⤳ *183 suites* ⚐ *In-room: safe, Wi-Fi. In-hotel: restaurant, bar, golf course, pool, tennis court, gym, spa, beach, water sports* ⦙◯⦙ *All-inclusive.*

NIGHTLIFE

Club Peace and Plenty. In season, the poolside bashes at Club Peace and Plenty, fueled by live bands, keep Bahamians and vacationers on the dance floor Friday nights. ☎ *242/336–2551.*

Eddie's Edgewater. On Monday, head to Eddie's Edgewater for rousing Rake 'n' Scrape music. The front porch and the game room behind the restaurant are popular spots where locals hang out all week long, especially come Friday night, when a DJ plays. ☎ *242/336–2050.*

Fish Fry. There's always something going on at the Fish Fry, a cluster of shacks 2 mi north of George Town. On Monday nights there's a Rake 'n' Scrape band; a DJ is usually there on Friday and Saturday.

Two Turtles Inn. Two Turtles Inn is the other hot spot on Friday, when everyone comes to town to celebrate the end of the work week. 2T, as it's known, puts on a barbecue with live music. A week is too long to wait, so the celebration is repeated on Tuesday nights. ☎ *242/336–2545.*

TOP FESTIVALS

WINTER

The Exumas' **Junkanoo Parade** on Boxing Day (Dec. 26) starts around 3 pm in George Town, ending at Regatta Park. Dancing, barbecues, and music happen before and after the parade.

The **Annual New Year's Day Cruising Regatta** at the Staniel Cay Yacht Club marks the finale of a five-day celebration.

The **George Town Cruising Regatta** in March is 12 days of festivities including sailing, a conch-blowing contest, dance, food and entertainment, and sports competitions.

March's **Bahamian Music and Heritage Festival** brings local and nationally known musicians to George Town, along with arts and crafts, Bahamas sloop exhibitions, storytelling, singing, poetry reading, and gospel music.

SPRING

In April the **National Family Islands Regatta** is the Bahamas' most important yachting event. Starting the race in Elizabeth Harbour in George Town, island-made wooden sloops compete for trophies. Onshore, the town is a three-day riot of Junkanoo parades, Goombay music, and arts-and-crafts fairs.

SUMMER

The **Junkanoo Summer Festival** in June and July is held beachside at the Fish Fry in George Town, and features local and visiting bands, kids' sunfish sailing, arts and crafts, and boatbuilding displays. It takes place Saturdays at noon.

FALL

The annual **Bahamas Sunfish Festival** in October at Little Farmer's Cay features exciting races to prepare young sailors for international competition.

SHOPPING

Exuma Markets. At Exuma Markets yachties tie up at the skiff docks in the rear, on Lake Victoria. FedEx, emergency e-mail, and faxes for visitors are accepted here. ⊠ *Across from Scotia Bank, George Town* 📞 *242/336–2033.*

Sandpiper Arts & Crafts. Here you can find upscale souvenirs, from high-quality cards and books to batik clothing and art. ⊠ *Queen's Hwy., George Town* 📞 *242/336–2084.*

Straw Market. The Straw Market offers a wide range of Bahamian straw bags, hats, and beachwear at a half-dozen open-air shops under a huge African fig tree. Prices are negotiable. ⊠ *George Town.*

SPORTS AND THE OUTDOORS

BOATING   Because of its wealth of safe harbors and regatta events, the Exumas are a favorite spot for yachtsmen. Renting a boat allows you to explore the cays near George Town and beyond, and a number of area hotels allow guests to tie up rental boats at their docks. For those who want to take a water jaunt through Stocking Island's hurricane holes, sailboats are ideal.

FISHING Exuma is a fishing haven, a great place to hunt the elusive bonefish (in season year-round and highly prized among fly fishermen). Most hotels can arrange for local guides, and a list is available from the Exuma Tourist Office.

Fish Rowe Charters. This charter company has a 40-foot Hatteras that holds up to four fishermen. Deepwater charters run $800 for a half day, $1,600 for a full day. ☎ 242/357–0870 ⊕ www.fishrowecharters.com.

Garth Thompson. Fisherman and boat owner Garth Thompson will help you hook big game as well as feisty bonefish. ⊕ www.exumabonefish.com.

BONEFISH ARE THE LURE

In the shallow flats off Exuma's windward coast the elusive bonefish, the "ghosts of the sea," roam. Patient fishermen put featherweight thumbnail-size flies on the lines, calculate the tides and currents, and cast out about 50 feet in hope of catching one. For sure success, avid fishermen pay guides about $300 a day to help them outsmart the skinny gray fish that streak through crystal water.

GOLF **Sandals Emerald Bay.** Golf legend Greg Norman designed the 18-hole, par-72 championship course, featuring six ocean-side holes, at Sandals Emerald Bay, the island's only golf course. There are preferred tee times for hotel guests, who pay $175, including golf cart; the fee for nonguests is the same. ☎ 242/336–6882.

KAYAKING **Starfish.** Starfish has guided half-day kayak trips to Starfish Beach and Moriah Cay National Park in sturdy, flat-bottom, oceangoing kayaks. Adults pay $55–$70, children pay $40–$55 for four-hour excursions. Kayak lessons are free with rentals, which start at $50 for a full day in a single. Deliveries are available on rentals of three days or longer. ☎ 541/359–1496, 242/336–3033 ⊕ www.starfishexuma.com.

SCUBA DIVING **Angel Fish Blue Hole.** This popular dive site, just minutes from George Town, is filled with angelfish, spotted rays, snapper, and the occasional reef shark.

Dive Exuma. Dive Exuma provides dive instruction, certification courses, and scuba trips. Two-tank dives are $175; blue-hole one-tank dives are $125. ☎ 242/357–0313 ⊕ www.dive-exuma.com.

Stocking Island Mystery Cave. This site is full of mesmerizing schools of colorful fish, but is for experienced divers only.

SNORKELING **Starfish.** You can rent snorkel equipment by the day or week here. ☎ 877/398–6222, 242/336–3033 ⊕ www.starfishexuma.com.

TENNIS **February Point.** Nonguests can use the two Laykold cushion–surfaced courts at February Point for $35 a day; use of the adjacent fitness center is $20. ☎ 242/336–2693, 877/839–4253.

7

Swimming near Staniel Cay

LITTLE EXUMA

Scenes from two *Pirates of the Caribbean* movies were filmed on the southern end of Little Exuma—only 12 square mi—and on one of the little cays just offshore. The movies' stars, Johnny Depp and Orlando Bloom, often roamed around the island and ate at Santana's open-air beach shack, the island's best-known restaurant. But that's just one of the reasons people are drawn to this lovely island connected to Great Exuma to the north by a narrow bridge. Rolling green hills, purple morning glories spilling over fences, small settlements with only a dozen houses, and glistening white beaches make a romantic afternoon escape. Near **Williams Town** is an eerie salt lake, still and ghostly, where salt was once scooped up and shipped away. You can hike old footpaths and look for ruins of old plantation buildings built in the 1700s near the Hermitage, but you'll have to look beneath the bushes and vines to find them. Little Exuma's best beach is Pelican's Bay Beach, also known as Tropic of Cancer Beach. It is a thrill to stand on the line that marks the spot. You're officially in the tropics now.

GETTING HERE AND AROUND
You need a car or a scooter to explore Little Exuma. It's possible to walk or ride a bike around the island, but it's hot and there's very little shade.

EXPLORING

Hermitage. The Hermitage estate ruins are testaments to the cotton plantation days. The small settlement was built by the Ferguson family from the Carolinas who settled here after the American Revolutionary War.

Visitors can see the foundations of the main house and tombs that date back to the 1700s. The tombs hold George Butler (1759–1822), Henderson Ferguson (1772–1825), and Constance McDonald (1755–1759). A grave is believed to be that of an unnamed slave. ⊠ *Williams Town.*

St. Christopher's Anglican. This is the island's smallest church, built in 1939 when the parish priest Father Marshall heard that a schooner loaded with timber from the Abacos had wrecked off Long Island. He visited the local Fitzgerald family and suggested they use the timber to build a church, which they did. Visitors can see the church and pews, all built of salvaged wood. ⊠ *Ferry.*

IN THE KNOW

People-to-People Program. To get to know Exuma islanders better, hook up with the People-to-People Program. The group hosts a tea the last Friday of the month where visitors can learn about bush medicine and other aspects of local life. ☎ 242/336–2430 ⊕ www.peopletopeople.bahamas. com.

WHERE TO EAT AND STAY

$ ✕ **Santana's Grill Pit.** This seaside open-air restaurant—you can't miss
BAHAMIAN the orange-and-yellow building—is the hot spot in Little Exuma, and the closest restaurant to the Pelican's Bay Beach. Dinner highlights include cracked lobster, cracked conch, shrimp, and grilled grouper, all served with peas 'n' rice or baked macaroni and cheese. Ask to see the photo book of celebrities who have eaten here; it was popular with the *Pirates of the Caribbean* cast and crew. ⊠ *Queen's Hwy., Williams Town* ☎ *242/345–4102* ▭ *No credit cards* ⊘ *Closed Sun.*

THE EXUMA CAYS

A band of cays—with names like **Rudder Cut, Big Farmer's, Great Guana,** and **Leaf**—stretches northwest from Great Exuma. It will take you a full day to boat through all 365 cays, most uninhabited, some owned by celebrities (Faith Hill and Tim McGraw on Goat Cay, Johnny Depp on Halls Pond Cay, and David Copperfield on Musha Cay). Along the way you'll find giant starfish, wild iguanas, swimming pigs, dolphins, sharks, and picture-perfect, footprintless sandbars. The Land and Sea Park, towards the northern end of the chain, is world renowned.

GETTING HERE AND AROUND

Most people visit the cays with their own boats; you'll need one to island-hop, although you can fly into Staniel Cay. The channels are confusing for inexperienced boaters, especially at low tide, and high tide can hide reefs and sand bars just underneath the surface. If this sounds nerve-racking, look into booking a boat tour. Once on a cay, most are small enough to walk. Golf carts are popular on Staniel Cay.

7

Island of the Stars

The Bahamas have served as a source of inspiration for countless artists, writers, and directors. The country's movie legacy dates back to the era of silent films, including the now-legendary original black-and-white version of **Jules Verne**'s *20,000 Leagues Under the Sea,* which was filmed here in 1907. Since the birth of color film, the draw has only increased—directors are lured by the possibility of using the islands' characteristic white sands and luminous turquoise waters as a backdrop. Among the more famous movies shot in the Bahamas are *Jaws: The Revenge,* the cult favorite whose killer shark has terrified viewers for more than three decades; *Flipper,* the family classic about a boy and a porpoise; *Splash,* whose main character is a mermaid who becomes human; and *Cocoon,* about a group of elderly friends who discover an extraterrestrial secret to immortality. Most recently, parts of the two sequels to *Pirates of the Caribbean, Dead Man's Chest,* and *At World's End,* were shot on location in the Exumas. *Thunderball* and *Never Say Never Again* were both shot on location in Staniel Cay, one of the northernmost islands of the Exumas' chain.

Ernest Hemingway wrote about the Bahamas as well. He visited Bimini regularly in the 1930s, dubbing it the "Sportsfishing Capital of the World." His hangout was the Compleat Angler, a bar that housed a small Hemingway museum until it burned down in January 2006. Among the items the museum displayed were Hemingway's drawings for *The Old Man and the Sea*—rumor has it that the protagonist looks suspiciously like one of the Angler's former bartenders.

The Bahamas not only seem to spark the imaginations of artists, but have also become a playground for the rich and famous. **Lenny Kravitz** and **Patti LaBelle** own homes in Eleuthera, while the stars of *Cocoon,* the late **Hume Cronyn** and **Jessica Tandy,** were regular visitors to Goat Cay, a private island just offshore from George Town, Exuma. **Johnny Depp** purchased a cay in the Exumas after filming on location for *Pirates of the Caribbean,* and **Nicolas Cage** and **Faith Hill** and **Tim MacGraw** own private islands in the area as well. Many world-famous celebrities and athletes hide out at **Musha Cay,** an exclusive retreat in the northern part of the Exumas, where a week's stay sets you back $24,750 for the entire island. **David Copperfield** bought Musha and its five houses in July 2006 for $50 million, renaming it Copperfield Cay. Although the cay won't name its guests, the all-knowing taxi drivers at the George Town airport mention **Oprah Winfrey** and **Michael Jordan** as a couple of the esteemed visitors.

EXPLORING

Sights start just north of Great Exuma, going northwest through the chain.

★ **Starfish Reserve.** Just off the mainland of Great Exuma, locals call the water surrounding the first few cays the Starfish Reserve, where tons of giant starfish dot the shallow ocean floor. As long as you don't keep them out of the water for too long, it's okay to pick them up.

Swimming pigs, Big Major's Cay

Little Farmer's Cay. If you're looking for a little civilization, stop off at Little Farmer's Cay, the first inhabited cay in the chain, about 40 minutes (18 mi) from Great Exuma. The island has a restaurant and a small grocery store where locals gather to play dominoes. But don't expect too big a party; just 70 people live on the island. A walk up the hill will reward you with fantastic island views.

★ **Staniel Cay.** Staniel Cay is the hub of activity in the cays, and a favorite destination of yachters. That's thanks to the Staniel Cay Yacht Club, the only full-service marina in the cays. Shack up in one of the cotton candy–color cottages, some perched on stilts right in the water. The club's restaurant is the place to be for lunch, dinner, and nightlife. The island has an airstrip, two hotels, and one paved road. Virtually everything is within walking distance. Oddly enough, as you stroll past brightly painted houses and sandy shores, you are as likely to see a satellite dish as a woman pulling a bucket of water from a roadside well. At one of three grocery stores, boat owners can replenish their supplies. The friendly village also has a small red-roof church, a post office, and a straw vendor. Staniel Cay is a great home base for visiting the Exuma Cays Land and Sea Park.

Thunderball Grotto. Just across the water from the Staniel Cay Yacht Club is one of the Bahamas' most unforgettable attractions: Thunderball Grotto, a lovely marine cave that snorkelers (at low tide) and experienced scuba divers can explore. In the central cavern shimmering shafts of sunlight pour through holes in the soaring ceiling and illuminate the glass-clear water. You'll see right away why this cave was chosen as

Staniel Cay Yacht Club

an exotic setting for such movies as 007's *Thunderball* and *Never Say Never Again,* and the mermaid tale *Splash.*

Big Major's Cay. Just north of Staniel Cay, Big Major's Cay is home to the famous swimming pigs. These guys aren't shy; as you pull up to the island they'll dive in and swim out to greet you. Don't forget to bring some scraps; Staniel Cay restaurant gives guests bags before they depart.

Pipe Creek. Boaters will want to explore the waterways known as Pipe Creek, a winding passage through the tiny islands between Staniel and Compass cays. There are great spots for shelling, snorkeling, diving, and bonefishing. The Sampson Cay Yacht Club at the creek's halfway point is a good place for lunch or dinner.

Compass Cay. Compass Cay has a small convenience store stocked with snacks and beverages. Sit on the dock and watch the sharks swim below. Don't worry, they're harmless nurse sharks. Explore the many paths on the island, which is 1½ mi long and 1 mi wide. There are four houses for rent on the island; all come with a 13- or 15-foot Boston Whaler.

⇨ *For information on the Exuma Cays Land and Sea Park, see the feature at the front of the chapter.*

Norman's Cay. North of the Exuma Cays Land and Sea Park is Norman's Cay, an island with 10 mi of rarely trod white beaches, which attracts an occasional yachter. It was once the private domain of Colombian drug smuggler Carlos Lehder. It's now owned by the Bahamian government. Stop by Norman's Cay Beach Club at MacDuff's for lunch or an early dinner and that it's-5-o'clock-somewhere beach cocktail.

★ **Allan's Cays.** Allan's Cays are at the Exumas' northernmost tip and home to the rare Bahamian iguana. Bring along some grapes and a stick to put them on, and these little guys will quickly become your new best friends.

WHERE TO EAT AND STAY

$ ✕ **Norman's Cay Beach Club at MacDuff's.** The outdoor patio strung with
BAHAMIAN Christmas lights gives this beach bar a lost-island vibe. Inside the screened patio, the restaurant's most famous dish is the curry conch chowder. At dinner you have a choice of three entrées: grilled chicken, grilled fish, or cracked conch. For lunch there are burgers, grilled fish sandwiches or wraps, and salads. Meals are washed down with tasty cocktails from the full bar; enjoy them out on the patio with a backdrop of the glorious ocean. If you're coming for dinner, you must call by 3:30. ✉ *Norman's Cay* ☎ *242/357–8846* ⊕ *www.ncbcmacduffs.com* ⚜ *Reservations essential.*

$$ ✕ **Sampson Cay Yacht Club.** A favorite of boaters passing through the
BAHAMIAN cays, the restaurant has American classics for breakfast, burgers and fish sandwiches for lunch, and shrimp, rack of lamb, grilled chicken, conch, and lobster for dinner. Save room for dessert—pineapple upside-down cake, coconut cake, and chocolate cake. Breakfast is served 8 to 10:30 am, and lunch and dinner noon to 8 pm. Call for dinner reservations. ✉ *Sampson Cay* ☎ *242/355–2034, 877/633–0305* ⊕ *www.sampsoncayclub.com* ⚜ *Reservations essential.*

$$ ✕ **Staniel Cay Yacht Club.** Hand-painted tablecloths cover the tables in
BAHAMIAN the screened-in dining room that serves Bahamian specialties such as cracked conch, fresh grouper, snapper, and grilled lobster with homemade bread. Many of the vegetables come from the restaurant's garden. Don't miss the key lime pie for dessert. A dinner bell rings when dinner is ready and diners move from the bar to the dining room. You must place your dinner order by 5 pm. Three meals are served daily. ✉ *Staniel Cay* ☎ *242/355–2024.*

$$$$ ⌂ **Compass Cay.** Four spacious houses on the island, which is 1½ mi long and 1 mi wide, are so far apart and separated by lush palm and hardwood hammocks that you feel you have the island to yourself. Houses all have spectacular 360-degree water views from atop the limestone hilltops and come with 13- or 15-foot Boston Whalers. There is no restaurant or bar, only a small store selling drinks and snacks, and hotdogs and hamburgers for lunch during high season. Guests are advised to bring groceries with them. **Pros:** remote tranquillity; boat included. **Cons:** Expensive to get to; no restaurant. ✉ *Compass Cay* ☎ *242/355–2137*

TOUR OPERATORS

BOAT TOURS
Charter World ☎ *954/603–7830* ⊕ *www.charterworld.com.* **Exuma Cays Adventures** ☎ *242/357–0390.* **Exuma Water Sports** ☎ *242/336–3422* ⊕ *www.exumawatersports.com.***Four C's Adventures** ☎ *242/464–1720* ⊕ *exumawatertours.com.*

ISLAND TOURS
Exuma Travel and Transportation Limited ☎ *242/334–0232.* **Kendal "Dr. K" Nixon** ☎ *242/422–7399.* **Luther Rolle** ☎ *242/357–0662.*

7

⊕ *www.compasscay.com/* ↩ *4 houses* ♿ *In-room: kitchen. In-hotel: laundry facilities.*

$$ 🔝 **Norman's Cay Beach Club at MacDuff's.** There might be some rust on the refrigerator, but these four pastel cottages are adorable, and just what you need for a true Out Island vacation. Each cottage has one bedroom, a spacious living room, and can accommodate up to five people. Two cottages overlook the ocean. **Pros:** Out Island tranquillity; close to park; good restaurant on-site. **Cons:** expensive to get there; rooms somewhat worn. ✉ *Norman's Cay* ☎ *242/357–8846* ⊕ *www.ncbcmacduffs.com* ↩ *4 cottages* ♿ *In-room: no TV. In-hotel: restaurant, bar, water sports.*

$
ALL-INCLUSIVE
Fodor's Choice
★

🔝 **Staniel Cay Yacht Club.** The club once drew such luminaries as Malcolm Forbes and Robert Mitchum. It's now a low-key getaway for yachties and escapists. The cotton candy–color cottages, perched on stilts along a rocky bank, have broad ocean vistas and dramatic sunsets, which you can treasure from a chaise longue on your spacious private balcony. Take a tour of the cay in one of the club's golf carts. All-inclusive packages are available. **Pros:** simple cottages that give an authentic Bahamian experience; great restaurant. **Cons:** expensive to get to if you don't have your own boat or plane. ✉ *Staniel Cay* ☎ *242/355–2024, 954/467–8920* ⊕ *www.stanielcay.com* ↩ *9 cottages* ♿ *In-room: no TV, Wi-Fi. In-hotel: restaurant, bar, pool, tennis court, beach, water sports* ⵏ◯ *All-inclusive.*

SPORTS AND THE OUTDOORS

BOATING AND
FISHING

Staniel Cay Yacht Club. Staniel Cay Yacht Club rents 13-foot Whalers and arranges fishing guides. ☎ *242/355–2024.*

SCUBA
DIVING AND
SNORKELING

Exuma Cays Land and Sea Park and **Thunderball Grotto** are excellent snorkeling and dive sites.

Staniel Cay Yacht Club. Staniel Cay Yacht Club rents masks and fins for snorkeling and fills tanks from its compressor. ☎ *242/355–2024.*

The Southern Out Islands

WORD OF MOUTH

"In the Out Islands you are visiting one of the world's great destinations. They are a world apart from Nassau, and most of the world's impression of the Bahamas is Nassau. Which is great because that means that most of the world gives the Bahamas a miss as being tacky, thus leaving the relatively secret Out Islands to us!!!"
— markrosy

WELCOME TO THE SOUTHERN OUT ISLANDS

TOP REASONS TO GO

★ **Stage a disappearing act:** Discover your inner castaway on islands way off the trampled tourist track. Pink or white sand, calm azure coves, or rolling ocean waves—you'll have your pick.

★ **Tell your own tall fishing tale:** Whether deep-sea fishing past the Wall off southern Inagua or bonefishing in the crystal-clear shallows on Cat Island's east coast, your fish-capades will be ones to remember.

★ **Explore historic lighthouses:** Surrounded by treacherous shoals and reefs, the southern Out Islands have the country's most famous 19th-century lighthouses, most of which you can climb for stunning views.

★ **Set sail:** Sailing regattas are huge here at the gateway to the Caribbean. It's thrilling to watch the first boats come into view and race across the horizon in full sail.

1 Cat Island. Stunning pink and white beaches, the highest hilltop in the country (the 206-foot Mt. Alvernia), 200-year-old deserted stone cottages, and a cuisine all its own (spicy grits and crab, anyone?) attract loyal visitors. A half dozen small resorts offer low-key luxury for those who want an Out Island experience with creature comforts.

2 San Salvador. Located on one of the largest reefs in the world, the tiny island's crystal-clear waters are a scuba diver's dream. The beach at Club Med is gorgeous, with soft white sand and blinding turquoise water.

3 Long Island. Ringed with stunning natural beaches that reach out into the Bahamas Banks and dip easterly into the deep Atlantic, this island is off the beaten path, yet an adequate infrastructure allows visitors to traverse from one end of the island to the other. It boasts a rich history and is populated by friendly, accommodating people.

4 Crooked and Acklins islands. These islands make great outposts for the self-sufficient adventurer. Fishing and more fishing are the reasons to come here,

except when you take the day off to dive and snorkel. The Wall, a famed dive site about 50 yards off Crooked Island's coast, drops from 45 feet to thousands.

Arthur's Town

Cat Island
1

New Bight
Mt. Alvernia
Port Howe

Exuma Sound

Conception Cay

Stella Maris

Great Exuma Island

Deadman's Cay

Ragged Island Range

GETTING ORIENTED

The southernmost Bahamas islands are remote, exposed to the open Atlantic, and ruggedly dramatic. One hundred and thirty miles southeast of Nassau, Cat Island lies to the west of diminutive San Salvador, about the size of Manhattan. Long Island, which is indeed long, stretches 80 mi across the Tropic of Cancer,

due south of Cat Island. Windswept Crooked and Acklins islands, each with about 400 residents, are southeast of Long Island. And way down at the southernmost point of the country is Inagua, only 55 mi northeast of Cuba and 60 mi north of Haiti.

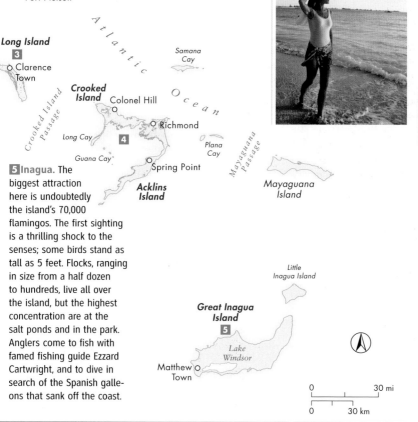

San Salvador
Cockburn Town
2

Rum Cay
Port Nelson

Long Island
3
Clarence Town

Atlantic Ocean

Samana Cay

Crooked Island   Colonel Hill
4
Richmond

Crooked Island Passage

Long Cay

Guana Cay

Plana Cay

Mayaguana Passage

Mayaguana Island

5 Inagua. The biggest attraction here is undoubtedly the island's 70,000 flamingos. The first sighting is a thrilling shock to the senses; some birds stand as tall as 5 feet. Flocks, ranging in size from a half dozen to hundreds, live all over the island, but the highest concentration are at the salt ponds and in the park. Anglers come to fish with famed fishing guide Ezzard Cartwright, and to dive in search of the Spanish galleons that sank off the coast.

Spring Point

Acklins Island

Little Inagua Island

Great Inagua Island
5
Lake Windsor

Matthew Town

0   30 mi

0   30 km

8

THE SOUTHERN OUT ISLANDS PLANNER

When to Go

Few visitors make it to these southern islands, but those who do come at different times. Europeans tend to arrive in summer and stay for a month or longer. Sailors come through on their way to the Caribbean in fall and return to the Bahamas in spring on trips back to the United States. Fishermen arrive all year and divers like the calm seas in summer. Those looking for a winter warm-up visit from December to April, when temperatures are in the 70s. These months have the lowest rainfall of the year, but the ocean is chilly and rough for divers and boaters. Christmas and New Year's are usually booked, so reserve rooms months in advance.

Many inns and resorts are closed September and October for hurricane season, which technically runs from June through November. Mosquito repellent is usually needed year-round, but is imperative in summer and fall. The southern islands are generally warmer than Nassau, but you may need a windbreaker in winter, particularly on a boat. If possible, time your visit for Junkanoo, sailing regattas, and special events such as the Cat Island's Rake 'N' Scrape Festival.

Top Festivals

Winter Inagua puts on a spirited **Junkanoo** parade on Boxing Day, December 26, and New Year's Day. Parades start at 4:30 am; you have to make the decision to stay up all night or get up early. There's food at the Fish Fry at Kiwanis Park in the center of town, where the parades end.

Summer The annual **Long Island Sailing Regatta,** featuring Bahamian-made boats, is a three-day event the first weekend of June. Held in Salt Pond, the regatta is the island's biggest event, attracting contestants from all over the islands. Booths featuring handmade crafts and Bahamian food and drink dot the site and local bands provide lively entertainment beginning at sundown. Salt Pond is 10 mi south of Simms. The **Cat Island Rake 'N' Scrape Festival** in June celebrates the Bahamas' indigenous Rake 'n' Scrape music, and includes food, crafts, and entertainment. The annual **Cat Island Regatta** in August has parties, live music, games, dancing, and lots of island cooking. The annual **Inagua Regatta** in August includes Bahamian-built sailboat races, food, and music.

Fall San Salvador's annual **Discovery Day Festival** in October celebrates Christopher Columbus's discovery of the Americas (the island is his reputed landing place). The festival is held at Graham's Harbour at the small settlement of United States. There are live music, games, food, church services, and a sloop regatta sail.

Tour Operators

Cruises and Water Tours Bahamas Discovery Quest ⊠ *Long Island* ☎ *242/472–2605* ⊕ *www. bahamasdiscoveryquest.com.* **San Salvador Funtimes** ☎ *242/331–2000.*

Island Tours Fernander Tours ⊠ *San Salvador* ☎ *242/331–2676, 242/427–8198.* **Great Inagua Tours** ☎ *242/453–0429.* **Lagoon Tours** ⊠ *San Salvador* ☎ *242/452–0102, 242/452–0506* ⊕ *www.lagoontours-bahamas.com.* **Long Island Ministry of Tourism** ☎ *242/338–8668.* **Nat Walker's Island Adventures** ⊠ *San Salvador* ☎ *242/331–2111.* **Omar Daily** ⊠ *Long Island* ☎ *242/338–2031.*

About the Restaurants

Out Island restaurants are often family-run and focus on home-style dishes. You'll probably eat most of your meals at your hotel, since there aren't many other places. If you want to dine at a restaurant or another inn, it's crucial to call ahead. Dinner choices largely depend on what the fishermen and mail boats bring in; be prepared for few choices.

Don't expect gourmet food, but do anticipate fresh fish, lobster, conch, fresh-baked bread, and coconut tarts. Cat Island is known for its spicy coarse yellow grits cooked with crab, and grits and peas with onions and tomatoes. (Call chef Sherman Russell at the Bridge Inn in New Bight and he will make some for you.) Don't miss "flour cakes," another Cat Island specialty, which taste similar to large vanilla wafers. A good bet for Friday or Saturday nights is an outdoor fish fry at a colorful beach shack, such as Regatta Beach on Cat Island or Kiwanis Park on Inagua.

About the Hotels

The inns in the southern Out Islands are small and intimate, and usually cater to a specific crowd such as anglers, divers, or those who just want a quiet beach experience. Club Med–Columbus Isle, an upscale resort on San Salvador, is the exception, with 236 rooms and a wide range of activities.

Most inns are on the beach, and many have one- and two-bedroom cottages with private verandas. Most inns offer three meals a day for their guests, kayaks, and bikes, and will pick you up at the airport, arrange car rentals, fishing guides, and dive trips. Off-season rates usually begin in May, with some of the best deals available in October, November, and early December. Club Med–Columbus Isle offers early-bird booking bonuses and runs pricing promotions year-round.

WHAT IT COSTS IN DOLLARS

	¢	$	$$	$$$	$$$$
Restaurants	under $10	$10–$20	$20–$30	$30–$40	over $40
Hotels	under $100	$100–$200	$200–$300	$300–$400	over $400

Restaurant prices are based on the median main course price at dinner, excluding gratuity, typically 15%, which is often automatically added to the bill. Hotel prices are for two people in a standard double room in high season, excluding service and 6%–12% tax.

Essentials

Banks Banks are generally open half days (9-2) Monday through Thursday and 9 to 5 on Fridays. There are no banks on Crooked and Acklins islands.

Emergencies AAPI Air Ambulance Services ✉ *Fort Lauderdale* ☎ *954/491–0555, 800/752–4195.* **Acklins Island Clinics** ☎ *242/344–3539 Mason's Bay, 242/344–3673 Salina Point, 242/344–3172 Spring Point.* **Acklins Island Police** ☎ *242/344–3126 Salina Point, 242/344–3666 Spring Point.* **Cat Island Clinics** ☎ *242/342–4049 Old Bight, 242/354–4050 Orange Creek, 242/342–3026 Smith Town.* **Cat Island Police** ☎ *242/354–2046 Arthur's Town, 242/342–3039 New Bight.* **Crooked Island Clinics** ☎ *242/344–2166 Landrail Point, 242/344–2350 Colonel Hill.* **Crooked Island Police** ☎ *242/344–2599.* **Inagua Hospital** ☎ *242/339–1249.* **Inagua Police** ☎ *242/339–1263.* **Long Island Clinics** ☎ *242/338–8488 Simms, 242/337–1222 Deadman's Cay.* **Long Island Police** ☎ *242/337–3919 Clarence Town, 242/337–0999 Deadman's Cay, 242/338–8555 Simms, 242/338–2222 Stella Maris.* **San Salvador Clinic** ☎ *207, 242/331–2105.* **San Salvador Police** ☎ *242/331–2010.*

Visitor Information Bahamas Out Islands ⊕ *www.myoutislands.com.* **Bahamas Tourist Office** ☎ *242/322–7500* ⊕ *www.bahamas.com.*

8

THE SOUTHERN OUT ISLANDS' BEST BEACHES

Beach connoisseurs come to the southern Out Islands to walk luscious pink and sparkling white-sand beaches that have no footprints but their own, and maybe a heron's odd step— three toes facing forward, one backward. These are the things you notice when there's no one on the beach but you.

(above) Cape Santa Maria Beach, Long Island (upper right) Fernandez Bay Beach, Cat Island (lower bottom) Greenwood Beach, Cat Island

Shells tumble in on gentle waves in a rhythmic splash that becomes the sound track for your vacation. Beach lovers sit cross-legged around bonfires at night, entertained by Rake 'n' Scrape musicians; mesmerized by the starry sky (hello, no light pollution!); and curl up on lounge chairs to watch the pale pink rays of the morning sun peek over the horizon, then later set in the west in fiery reds and oranges. You can swim in water as clear and soothing as a pool, or relax in the shade of a coconut tree with a cold Kalik in sybaritic bliss.

HISTORIC LIGHTHOUSES

Since the 19th century, sailors' lives have depended on the lighthouse beacons that rotate over the southern islands and the treacherous reefs that surround them. But for landlubbers, these lighthouses also offer bird's-eye vantage points. Visit the 115-foot Bird Rock Lighthouse on Crooked Island; the Castle Island Lighthouse on Acklins Island; the Inagua Lighthouse; and San Salvador's Dixon Hill Lighthouse.

THE SOUTHERN OUT ISLANDS' BEST BEACHES

BONEFISH BAY, SAN SALVADOR

The 3-mi beach in front of Club Med has bright white sand as fine as talcum powder, and calm water such a neon shade of turquoise it seems to glow. It might possibly be the most gorgeous water you ever lay eyes on. There are activities, such as waterskiing and snorkeling, in front of Club Med, but the beach is long enough that you'll be able to find an isolated spot.

CAPE SANTA MARIA BEACH, LONG ISLAND

Located on the leeward side of the island in the north at Cape Santa Maria Resort, the water colors here range from pale blue to aqua to shades of turquoise. The 4-mi stretch of soft white sand beckons you to stroll, build sand castles, or sun worship. The resort has a beachside restaurant and lounge chairs for guests, but there's also plenty of sand to find a secluded stretch all your own.

FERNANDEZ BAY BEACH, CAT ISLAND

Imagine the perfect calm cove in the tropics—a 1-mi stretch of glistening, pristine white sand, inviting shade under coconut palms and sea grape trees, and a couple of boutique resorts with cottages and verandas facing the spectacular sand and azure water. You'll never want to leave; restaurants and bars built on

decks overlooking the water are a blessing. The beach is often deserted, so dinner for two might really mean just that.

GALLOWAY LANDING, LONG ISLAND

This remarkable beach south of Clarence Town is known only by the locals, but no one will mind if you come. Swim and sun at the first beach, or walk a short distance south to an even more wonderful and secluded stretch of sand. Here canals carved into the limestone hills by the now defunct Diamond Salt Mine are filled with the palest blue ocean water and are home to small marine life. It's a wonderful area to kayak, snorkel, and swim. A bit farther south, a narrow bridge leads to beyond-stunning lagoons and ocean flats.

GREENWOOD BEACH, CAT ISLAND

An 8-mi stretch of pink sand makes this one of the most spectacular beaches in the Bahamas. It is by far the best pink-sand beach on the island. Hypnotized by the beauty, most visitors walk the entire beach, some even farther to an adjoining sandy cove accessible only on foot. After such a long walk, a dip in the shallows of the turquoise ocean is pure bliss. The beach is on the remote southeastern end of the island and has just one resort; stay here for a heavenly escape, but nonguests are welcome on the sand, too.

8

INAGUA NATIONAL PARK

(lower right) Green sea turtle, Union Creek Reserve

Nothing quite prepares you for your first glimpse of the West Indian flamingos that nest in Inagua National Park: brilliant crimson-pink, up to 5 feet tall, with black-tipped wings. A dozen flamingos suddenly fly across a pond, intermixed with fantastic pink roseate spoonbills.

It's a moving experience, and yet because of the island's remote location, only about 50 people witnessed it in 2009. In 1952, Inagua's flamingos dwindled to about 5,000. The gorgeous birds were hunted for their meat, especially the tongue, and for their feathers. The government established the 287-square-mi park in 1963, and today 70,000 flamingos nest on the island, the world's largest breeding colony of West Indian flamingos. The birds like the many salt ponds on Inagua that supply their favorite meal—brine shrimp.

You must contact the **Bahamas National Trust**'s office (☎ 242/393–1317 ⊕ *www.bnt.bs*) or **Warden Henry Nixon** (☎ 242/225–0977) to make reservations for your visit. All visits to the park are by special arrangement. ⊠ *10 mi west of Matthew Town.*

BEST TIME TO GO

Flamingos are on the island year-round, but for the greatest concentration, visit during nesting season, from the end of February through June. Early morning and late afternoon are the best times to come. If you visit right after their hatching, the flocks of fuzzy, gray baby flamingos—they can't fly until they're older—are entertaining.

BEST WAYS TO EXPLORE

GUIDED TOUR

Warden Henry Nixon leads all tours into Inagua National Park and to Union Creek Reserve. Nixon is also a certified birding tour guide. He'll drive you by small flocks of flamingos in the salt ponds and answer questions. Nixon is difficult to reach by phone, so you have to be persistent; your best chance is in the early evening.

KAYAK

You can't kayak in the park's salt ponds because they're too shallow, but you can in Lake Windsor, also called Lake Rosa, a huge inland lake. Its eastern half is in the park. Because of badly washed-out dirt roads, a truck is necessary to reach the lake.

WALK

You can't drive around the park without the warden, and you wouldn't want to because the washed-out roads remain badly damaged from 2008's Hurricane Ike. The best way to see flamingos up close is by parking the car and walking, or sitting quietly for a while in a thicket of mangroves. Flamingos are skittish and easily spooked. Although the ponds and mangroves look a lot like the Florida Everglades, there are no alligators or poisonous snakes here. Make sure you have insect repellent on before you take off; mosquitoes are brutal.

UNION CREEK RESERVE

On the northwest side of the park, **Union Creek Reserve** hosts the University of Florida's Archie Carr Center for Sea Turtle Research. The 7-square-mi site is home to green and hawksbill sea turtles; visitors can prearrange a visit to see the big guys up close and talk with the staff.

FLAMINGO FACTS

■ Flamingos are the country's national bird, and they're protected from hunters by law.

■ Female flamingos lay one egg a year, and both parents take turns sitting on it for 28 days. Both parents also produce milk in the crop at the base of the neck for the chick, for three months. The parents' feathers turn white while they feed the chick because they lose carotene.

■ Flamingos are monogamous and usually mate for life, but are extremely social birds that like to live in groups.

■ Their "knees," which look like they are bent backward, are not knees but ankles. Their knees are tucked under their feathers. What looks like the leg is actually the foot extending from the ankle, so the birds are walking on their toes.

■ Standing on one leg is the most comfortable position for a flamingo.

■ Brine shrimp, the flamingo's main source of food, which is added to Morton Salt Co.'s salt ponds, is what gives the mature bird its brilliant deep pink.

8

RAKE 'N' SCRAPE

HAVE A LISTEN

International recording artist and Cat Island native **Tony McKay**, who went by the stage name Exuma, incorporated Rake 'n' Scrape into his music. He paid homage to the style with the song "Goin' to Cat Island."

George Symonette's "Don't Touch Me Tomato" gained infamy in a recent television commercial for Cable Bahamas. Symonette is associated with Goombay, a music style popular in Nassau in the 1950s. Goombay soon died out, giving way to closely related Rake 'n' Scrape.

Comprised of six Harbour Island natives, **the Brilanders** have toured with Jimmy Buffet. Their hit song "Backyard Party" is a soundtrack standard at just about any Bahamian party.

There's something about Rake 'n' Scrape music that makes you want to dance. The contagious, unique cadence accompanied by the "chink-chink," "kalik-kalik," "scratch-scratch" sound created by the unique instruments, made mostly from recycled objects, brings on a particularly strong urge to get up and shake it.

Most closely linked in sound, rhythm, and composition to zydeco music out of New Orleans, Rake 'n' Scrape is folk music at its best. It's unclear just where Rake 'n' Scrape originated, but most believe it has roots in Africa, made the voyage to the Bahamas with slaves, and was adapted over the years. Today's Rake 'n' Scrape was cultivated on remote Cat Island. Lacking money for and access to modern things, the resourceful locals made use of whatever supplies were available. Years later, many of these musicians could have their pick of shiny, finely tuned instruments, but they stick with what they know makes beautiful music.

INSTRUMENTS

An authentic Rake 'n' Scrape band uses recycled objects to make music. An ordinary saw held in a musician's lap, then bent and scraped, becomes an instrument. A piece of wood, some fishing line, and a tin washtub is a good stand-in for the brass section. Plastic juice bottles are filled with pigeon peas, painted in bright colors, and turned into maracas. Add a goatskin drum, and you have all you need for a Rake 'n' Scrape ensemble, although many bands now add a concertina, guitar, or saxophone.

WHERE TO HEAR RAKE 'N' SCRAPE

Rake 'n' Scrape in its authentic form is a dying art. The handful of groups scattered throughout the Bahamas are comprised of older men, as younger Bahamians prefer more modern sounds. Today **Ophie and the Websites, The Brilanders**, and **Thomas Cartwright** are among the few groups still performing old style Rake 'n' Scrape. Other modern Bahamian musicians, such as **K.B., Phil Stubbs,** and **Ronnie Butler** work the sound and rhythm into their own signature styles.

The popular **Rake 'N' Scrape Festival** each June on Cat Island hosts dozens of bands from all over the Bahamas and the Caribbean. The ·four-day festival also features native food and handmade local crafts.

In Nassau, July's **Junkanoo Summer Festival** showcases notable Rake 'n' Scrape

bands alongside current headliners, who thrill the crowds with their own modern renditions of old favorites. If you happen to see a crowd of locals and tourists dancing on the side of the Cable Beach strip, that means you've found **Curly's** (☎ *242/327–4583*). This tiny bar east of Sandals comes alive on weekend nights; when it's time for Rake 'n' Scrape, owner Curly picks up his saw or the goatskin drums and joins in.

On Harbour Island, **Gusty's** and **Vic-Hum Club** usually work at least one night of Rake 'n' Scrape into the weekly live music schedule. **The Brilanders** often play at **Seagrapes**.

DANCE LIKE A LOCAL

The Rake 'n' Scrape rhythm is so captivating that even the most rhythmically challenged will be hard-pressed to stand still. As the first beats are played, look around and see what the old folk do. It's not unusual to see a man stick his leg out (whether he's sitting or standing), lift his pants leg a bit, and let his footwork get fancy.

At festivals, schoolchildren usually dance the quadrille or heel-toe polka to Rake 'n' Scrape music. Most Bahamians will give you a strange look if you request a demonstration, but ask them to show you how to "mash de roach" or dance "the conch style" and they'll jump up and put on a show.

8

Updated by Cheryl Blackerby, Ramona Settle, and Sharon Williams

Wild and windswept, the southern Bahamian islands are idyllic Edens for those adventurers who want to battle a tarpon, dive a "wall" that drops thousands of feet, photograph the world's largest group of West Indian flamingos, or just sprawl on a sun-splashed beach with no sign of life—except maybe for a Bahama parrot pelting seeds from a guinep tree.

The quiet, simpler way of life on the southern Out Islands is startlingly different from Nassau's fast-paced glitz and glamour, and even more secluded than the northern Out Islands. You won't find huge resorts, casinos, or fast-food restaurants here, not to mention stoplights. Instead, you'll be rewarded with a serene vacation that will make your blood pressure drop faster than a fisherman's hook and sinker.

Sportsmen are drawn to the southern islands to outsmart the swift bonefish, and fish for marlin, black and blue fin tuna, wahoo, and swordfish. Yachties roam these islands on their way to the Caribbean, and vacationers rent Hobie Cats and kayaks. Divers and snorkelers come to see healthy reefs and abundant underwater wildlife. Romantics and honeymooners head south for the glorious sunsets viewed from the verandas of beachside cottages, and for the lovely pink beaches. Bird-watchers arrive with binoculars in hand to see the green and red Bahama parrots, the Bahama woodstar hummingbirds, Bahama pintails, tricolored and crested night herons, and, of course, flamingos.

The friendliness of residents is well known, but visitors are often taken aback by their instant inclusion in the community. You can't walk 100 feet without someone offering a welcome ride on a hot day. Ask an islander where a certain restaurant is and they will walk with you until you see it. Express any disappointment such as not seeing a flamingo up close, and the person standing behind you at the store will get on their cell phone. (There's a big flock now at the Town Pond!) The scenery is gorgeous, but this genuine rapport is what brings regulars back time and again to these tiny communities.

GREAT ITINERARIES

Note: If you don't have a boat, island-hopping is difficult in these parts, as there are no flights that fly directly between the islands (you must transfer back in Nassau). Most visitors choose one island to base themselves on, but if you're feeling ambitious, the following schedule should start on a Tuesday so you can head to Long Island Friday on a 2:15 pm flight from Nassau. It's the only afternoon flight of the week; all other days you'll have to overnight in Nassau in order to make an early morning connection.

IF YOU HAVE 3 DAYS

Fly into **The Bight** on Cat Island and catch what's left of the day on a gorgeous beach, then enjoy a dinner of lobster or fresh fish at your inn's outdoor restaurant. Spend Day 2 **diving** with Greenwood Beach Resort or Hawk's Nest dive staffs and reserve dinner at one of those resorts. The third day, climb to the top of the 206-foot **Mt. Alvernia** and see the Hermitage, the little abbey on top of the hill which is a great place for a picnic. Spend the afternoon **snorkeling**, or with a **fishing** guide, either bonefishing or deep-sea fishing. Have dinner at the Bridge Inn. Call ahead, preferably the day before, and ask chef Sherman Russell to make a dinner of fresh fish or cracked conch and the island specialty of grits and peas or grits and crab.

IF YOU HAVE 5 DAYS

When you arrive on Long Island in the afternoon, head to the beach for some last-chance sun or **snorkeling**. Have an outdoor fresh fish or barbecued chicken dinner, and relax in the bar or on the veranda. On Day 5 pack an ice chest, rent a car, put on your swimsuit, and head south to **Dean's Blue Hole**, the world's deepest, and explore. Spelunkers might want to stop at **Cartwright's Cave** on the way. Leaving the Blue Hole, head to **Clarence Town** and grab a fish sandwich at the Outer Edge at the Flying Fish Marina. Then head to **Galloway Landing** and explore its beaches, canals, lagoons, and ocean flats. Stop by Max's Conch Bar, right on Queen's Highway in **Deadman's Cay**, and enjoy good food, good drink, and good company.

IF YOU HAVE 7 DAYS

On Day 6, head north to the **Columbus Monument**. It's a long and sometimes impassable road, but with four-wheel drive you can make it. From the top of the hill, where the monument stands, is one of the most spectacular views you will ever see. Afterwards, head back to the Queen's Highway and continue north until the road stops at the ocean; this is beautiful **Newton Cay**. Walk across the small crumbling bridge to **Columbus Cove**, where Columbus made landfall. For the more adventurous, follow the beach to the left to find magnificent sea glass or great snorkeling. Stop at **Cape Santa Maria** for lunch or dinner, and feast your eyes on one of the most superb beaches in the world. On your final day, relax on a beach, squeeze in another day of **fishing**, or take a tour with Bahamas Discovery Quest.

8

CAT ISLAND

Updated
by Cheryl
Blackerby

You'll be purring on Cat Island's exquisite pink-sand beaches and sparkling white-sand-ringed coves, as calm and clear as a spa pool. Largely undeveloped, Cat Island has the tallest hill in the Bahamas, a dizzying 206 feet high, with a tiny stone abbey on top, a lovely spot for meditation or a picnic. The two-lane, potholed Queen's Highway runs the 48-mi length of the island from north to south along a gorgeous sandy coastline, through adorable seaside settlements and past hundreds of eerie abandoned stone cottages; some are 200-year-old slave houses, crumbling testaments to cotton and sisal plantation days. Trees and vines twist through spaces that used to be windows and roofs and the deep-blue ocean can be seen through missing walls. In 1938 the island had 5,000 residents and today only about 1,500. Many of the inhabitants left the cottages long ago out of necessity, to find work in Nassau and Florida, but the houses remain because they still mark family land.

Cat Island was named after a frequent visitor, the notorious pirate Arthur Catt, a contemporary of Edward "Blackbeard" Teach. Another famous islander is Sir Sidney Poitier, who grew up here before leaving to become an Academy Award–winning movie actor and director. His daughter Ann lives here and spearheads the annual Rake 'N' Scrape Festival held in June.

GETTING HERE AND AROUND

AIR TRAVEL

Cat Island has two airports: Arthur's Town (ATC) in the north and the Bight (TBI) mid-island. Flights are cheaper and more frequent to the Bight. Cat Island Air flies daily to the Bight from Nassau and is the best and cheapest service to the southern part of the island. Southern Air flies from Nassau to Arthur's Town, and is the best service for the northern portion of the island. Bahamasair flies from Nassau to Arthur's Town or the Bight three times a week. Sky Bahamas Air also flies from Nassau to the Bight. Florida Coastal Air and Continental Connection fly into the Bight from Fort Lauderdale. If you are going to Fernandez Bay Village, Island HoppInn, Greenwood Beach Resort, or Hawk's Nest Resort, fly into the Bight. If you are going to Pigeon Cay or Sammy T's, fly to Arthur's Town.

Airport Information Arthur's Town Airport ☎ *242/342–2016.* **The Bight Airport** ☎ *242/342–2016.*

BOAT TRAVEL

Mail boats that bring supplies to the island each week make an adventurous mode of transportation. You'll ride with groceries, large and small appliances, automobiles, and sometimes even livestock. All boats depart from Potter's Cay in Nassau. Schedules change frequently. The *East Wind* leaves Tuesday for Smith Bay and Old and New Bight, returning Thursday (10 hours; $60 one way).

Boat and Ferry Information Dockmaster's Office ☎ *242/393–1064.*

CAR TRAVEL

The New Bight Service Station rents cars and can pick you up from the Bight airport. You can rent a car from Gilbert's Food Market, also in New Bight, which also picks up from the airport. Greenwood Beach Resort, Sammy T's Beach Resort, Fernandez Bay Village, Island

HoppInn, and Hawk's Nest Resort will all arrange car rentals for guests. Rates depend on the number of days you're renting, but $75 per day is average.

The best way to enjoy the overall Cat Island experience is to rent a car, at least for one day, and do some exploring on your own. You'll need one if you want to check out various settlements, as they're not within walking distance. The two-lane, potholed Queen's Highway runs the 48-mi length of the island from north to south. You can also hire a driver through your hotel.

Car-Rental Contacts Gilbert's Food Market ☎ *242/342–3011.* **New Bight Service Station** ☎ *242/342–3014.*

TAXI TRAVEL Taxis wait for incoming flights at the Bight and Arthur's Town airports, but be warned that fares can be expensive, starting at about $20 for the 10-minute trip from the Bight Airport to the community of New Bight. Most inns and resorts will make arrangements for airport transfers, often complimentary.

ARTHUR'S TOWN AND BENNETT'S HARBOUR

Arthur's Town's claim to fame is that it was the boyhood home of actor Sidney Poitier, who wrote about growing up here in his autobiography. His parents and relatives were farmers. The village has a BaTelCo station, a few stores, and Pat Rolle's **Cookie House Bakery** (☎ *242/354– 2027*)—an island institution that serves lunch and dinner by the order, so call ahead. Or just stop by to say hello, as Pat is a wealth of island knowledge and more than happy to bend your ear.

When you drive south from Arthur's Town, which is nearly at the island's northernmost tip, you'll wind along a road that passes through small villages and past bays where fishing boats are tied up. Fifteen miles south of Arthur's Town is Bennett's Harbour, one of the island's oldest settlements. Fresh-baked breads and fruit are sometimes sold at makeshift stands at the government dock, and there is good bonefishing in the creek.

WHERE TO EAT AND STAY

$$$
BAHAMIAN
Fodor's Choice
★

✕ **Sammy T's Restaurant and Bar.** Score a seat outside on the wooden deck, overlooking a gorgeous white-sand beach. At breakfast try one of the huge omelets with cheese, tomatoes, and peppers. At lunch the salads are fresh and served with Sammy T's secret dressing, or savor the grilled conch or panfried grouper. Want a burger? They're big and tasty. Afternoon snacks of all things conch are served in the bar and on the deck. The evening delights include grouper Parmesan, stuffed lobster tail, fresh grilled or baked catch of the day, plus chicken, pork, and steaks prepared differently each night. Call ahead, because the restaurant closes if business is slow. The bar stays open after dinner as demand indicates, and the fresh-fruit rum drinks are not to be missed. ✉ *Sammy T's Beach Resort, Bennett's Harbour* ☎ *242/354–6009* ✹ *Closed Sept.*

$

🛏 **Pigeon Cay Beach Club.** In a wide bay a half mile off the main road just south of Alligator Point, this club has ten deluxe cottages perched steps away from a 3-mi stretch of sugary white beach. The native stone

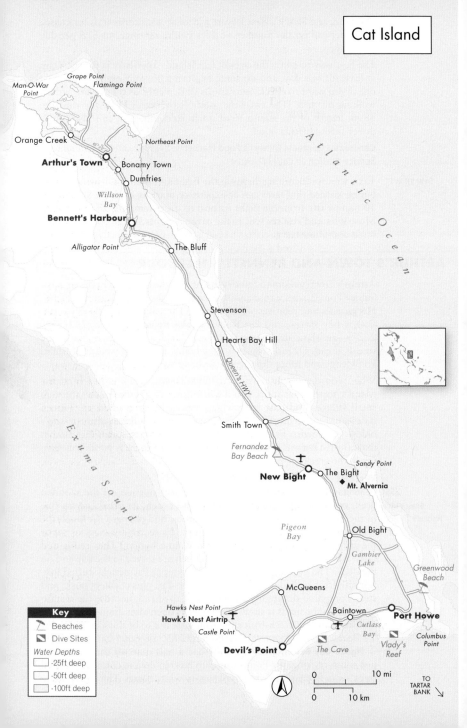

and stucco cottages have wood and tile floors, colorful island furniture, complete kitchenware, and ceiling fans. You can cook yourself or the club chef can prepare breakfast, lunch, and dinner for you. Either way, staff will stock your cottage before your arrival (just send your grocery list). Snorkel, kayak, canoe, fish, swim, or lie on the beach. **Pros:** pristine beachfront location; do-it-yourself private retreat to get away from it all. **Cons:** no TV; don't forget your insect repellent. ⊠ *Rokers* 🕾🕾 *242/354–5084* ⊕ *www.pigeoncaybahamas.com* ⤳ *10 cottages* ⚐ *In-room: kitchen, no TV, Wi-Fi. In-hotel: restaurant, bar, beach, water sports.*

$ ▦ **Sammy T's Beach Resort.** Tucked away in a small cove on a dream
★   beach, this tranquil boutique resort has seven one- and two-bedroom villas. Each villa has rattan furnishings with plush white cushions and fabrics, wooden floors, island art, high-beamed ceilings, and verandas with views of the beach. The restaurant serves three delicious meals a day, plus the bar serves afternoon goodies like conch fritters and conch chowder that go great with a cold Kalik. Sammy T and his staff provide personalized service and can arrange activities from fishing to snorkeling to island tours. Guests play billiards at the bar, which has a great view of the beach. They also arrange your airport ground transfers to and from the resort. **Pros:** a small, private Out Island experience; welcoming personalized service; on-site restaurant with excellent fresh seafood. **Cons:** not close to a big settlement. ⊠ *Bennett's Harbour* 🕾 *242/354–6009* ⊕ *www.catislandbeachresort.com* ⤳ *7 villas* ⚐ *In-hotel: restaurant, bar, beach, water sports, some age restrictions* ⊘ *Closed Sept.*

$ ▦ **Shannas Cove Resort.** This new beachside resort (opened in November 2009) is on the lovely pink sand of Shannas Cove. On the northernmost point of the island in a secluded tropical setting, guests experience total solitude. There are five cottages with porches and a restaurant that serves three meals a day. Activities include fishing, snorkeling, and diving. **Pros:** a gorgeous beach; roomy cottages; a real Out Island experience. **Cons:** isolated from the rest of the island. ⊠ *Orange Creek* 🕾 *242/354–4249* ⊕ *www.shannas-cove.com* ⤳ *5 villas* ⚐ *In-hotel: restaurant, bar, beach, water sports* ⊘ *Closed Sept.*

SPORTS AND THE OUTDOORS

SCUBA DIVING   Coral Reefs teeming with fish and mysterious shipwrecks, make great diving off the north end of the island, where visibility ranges from 165 to 200 feet thanks to a natural filtering system of limestone and rich fauna. The dive sites are a 10- to 15-minute boat ride from Shannas Cove Resort.

Shannas Cove Resort Dive Center. This dive center at Orange Creek on the northernmost tip of Cat Island has a dive school and a 22-foot catamaran for dive trips. Equipment is available. 🕾 *242/354–4249.*

NEW BIGHT

Yachts large and small anchor off the coast of Regatta Beach, and boaters dingy in to the Custom House, located in a small collection of government buildings, in this pretty little community, the largest town on the island. Houses face the Queen's Highway, which twists through green hills. Yachties and visitors stock up at the small grocery store and a bakery. There's a gas station that rents cars, and the Bridge Inn is near the airport, south of Fernandez Bay Village. The island's most iconic sight is **Mt. Alvernia**, which is crowned with a little abbey. There's also a colorful **Fish Fry**, a collection of fish shacks on Regatta Beach that's a lively hangout on weekends, lovely old churches, and eerie abandoned stone cottages whose residents left long ago to find jobs in Nassau and Florida. The town sits along the calm white beaches of the west coast, and has peaceful saltwater estuaries that are nesting areas for great blue herons, egrets, and pelicans. The main hotel in town is the Bridge Inn and Restaurant, where locals catch up on news.

EXPLORING

Fodor's Choice
★

Hermitage. At the top of 206-foot Mt. Alvernia, the Hermitage is the final resting place of Father Jerome. Born John Hawes, he was an architect who traveled the world and eventually settled in the Bahamas. An Anglican who converted to Roman Catholicism, he built two churches, St. Paul's and St. Peter's, in Clarence Town, Long Island, as well as the St. Augustine Monastery in Nassau. He retired to Cat Island to live out his last dozen years as a hermit, and his final, supreme act of religious dedication was to carve the steps up to the top of Mt. Alvernia. Along the way, he also carved the Stations of the Cross. At the summit, he built an abbey with a small chapel, a conical bell tower, and living quarters comprising three closet-size rooms. He died in 1956 at the age of 80 and was supposedly buried with his arms outstretched, in a pose resembling that of the crucified Christ.

The pilgrimage to the Hermitage begins next to the commissioner's office at New Bight, at a dirt path that leads to the foot of Mt. Alvernia. Try not to miss the slightly laborious experience of climbing to the top. The Hermitage provides a perfect inspired place to pause for quiet contemplation. It also has glorious views of the ocean on both sides of the island. A caretaker clears the weeds around the tomb—which islanders regard as a shrine—and lights a candle in Father Jerome's memory.

WHERE TO EAT

$$
✕ **Bridge Inn Restaurant.** Owned by the large, gregarious Russell family, you will usually find at least some of them eating Sherman's delicious Cat Island specialties, including grits and crab cakes, cracked conch, pan-seared whole snapper, barbecued ribs, conch salad, conch chowder, and lobster with peas 'n' rice. Most of the vegetables are grown on the Russells' farm, and the fish comes right off that day's boat. It's best to call ahead and place your order, and also a good

BAHAMIAN
★

ISLAND SPECIALTIES

Cat Island is known for its tasty dishes, most notably spicy grits and crab cakes, and grits and peas, both cooked with tomatoes, onions, lima beans, and okra, depending on the cook's preferences. The island's distinctive coarse yellow grits, made from guinea corn, was originally brought from Africa. Many visitors take a bag with them when they leave the island. Island cooks are also known for their "flour cakes," similar in taste to vanilla wafers.

The Hermitage, Mt. Alvernia

idea to follow Sherman's excellent dinner suggestions. The large restaurant has a big room for meetings and special occasions. ✉ *1 block off Queen's Hwy., look for the sign* ☎ *242/342–3013.*

$$$$ ✕ **Fernandez Bay Village Restaurant.** Meals are served in the Clubhouse at
BAHAMIAN Fernandez Bay Village, and outside on the beach terrace. The breakfast buffet is loaded; you can pile on sweet rolls, croissants, bacon, sausage, grits, and fruit, or order the daily specials of French toast, omelets, or eggs Benedict. Grilled cheese, tuna, turkey, and ham sandwiches, conch chowder, and conch burgers are just a sampling of lunch options. The sumptuous dinner buffet can include lobster in white sauce, grouper almandine, conch fritter, filet mignon, lobster tail, grilled catch of the day along with scalloped potatoes, salads, and fresh baked breads. Spice apple cake goes great with an after-dinner drink from the bar. ✉ *Fernandez Bay Village, 1 mi west of New Bight airport* ☎ *242/342–3043* ⊕ *www.fernandezbayvillage.com* ⊘ *Closed Sept. and Oct., but call to confirm.*

$$ ✕ **Island HoppInn Tiki Bar and Restaurant.** This authentic, island-style,
BAHAMIAN open-air tiki hut restaurant and bar is right on the beach, just steps away from the tranquil lapping waters of Fernandez Bay. The 24-seat eatery has a barbecue grill for cooking up fresh fish of the day, shrimp, lobster, steaks, and ribs. Owner-chef Cathy Bencin is renowned for her conch chowder, fish and vegetable stews, fresh-baked breads, and killer desserts. Guests staying at the inn, which has a bed-and-breakfast casualness, mix in by cooking their own dinners at times. The service is good, the crowd, when there is one, a lot of fun, and the tropical rum drinks are a mellowing delight. ✉ *Island HoppInn, Fernandez Bay* ☎ *242/342–2100* ▬ *No credit cards.*

Tiki bar at Fernandez Bay Village

WHERE TO STAY

Bridge Inn and Restaurant. Atmospheric rooms with walls built of local stone and wood and high wood ceilings and private patios have modern bathrooms and flat-screen TVs. It's not on the beach, but backs up to the pretty Fountain Bay creek, a saltwater estuary great for fishing, and it's a five-minute walk to the white-sand Fountain Bay beach. Use this friendly, family-run motel and apartment property as a base for exploring the island on your own. The apartments, which overlook the creek, have two bedrooms, 1½ baths, cable TV, and a full kitchen. The inn's restaurant will pack you a picnic lunch. Special rates are available if you stay five nights or more. **Pros:** economical, comfortable accommodations in a central location for exploring the island; friendly people. **Cons:** not directly on the beach and no beach views. ⊠ *1 block off Queen's Hwy.* ☎ *242/342–3013* ⊕ *www.bridgeinncatisland.com* ⤴ *12 rooms, 6 apartments* ⌂ *In-room: kitchen. In-hotel: restaurant.*

$$
Fodor's Choice
★

Fernandez Bay Village. This is one of the best kick-back retreats in the islands. Brick-and-stone villas and cottages with verandas facing the water are spread along a dazzling, horseshoe-shape white-sand beach shaded by casuarina pines and coconut palms. Villas have kitchens, private gardens, and accommodations for four to six people. Cottages are for two people, and have private stone patios and garden baths. Canoes, Sunfish sailboats, and kayaks are free to use. Boats and guides can be hired for fishing or snorkeling expeditions. Savory native dishes, including lobster, conch, and prime steaks, are served in the lodge dining room and on the beachside patio, and can be part of an all-inclusive package. **Pros:** a "wow" beachfront location; private spacious accommodations; friendly staff can arrange all water-sports activities. **Cons:**

no TVs; you need insect repellent for outside evening dining. ✉ *1 mi north of the Bight airport* ☎ *242/342–3043, 800/940–1905* ⊕ *www. fernandezbayvillage.com* ↗ *6 villas, 9 cottages* ♿ *In-room: kitchen, no TV. In-hotel: restaurant, bar, beach, water sports, business center.*

$$ 🛏 **Island HoppInn.** The resort's four suites are perched oceanside overlooking magical Fernandez Bay. Step off your private porch and you're on the beach. The roomy yet cozy suites have rattan furnishings, tropical decor, modern kitchens, and outdoor garden showers. In the inn's great room, or on the adjoining beach deck, meals and cocktails are served family style; everything from fresh-baked breads to conch fritters, grilled fish, and delectable desserts. The owners emphasize personal service for each guest, and can arrange activities from fishing to snorkeling and diving, car rentals, or a romantic dinner served in your suite. **Pros:** small private resort on the perfect white-sand beach; you can cook on the outside grill or have meals included in your package; on-site owner-managers go the extra mile to provide exceptional service. **Cons:** don't forget your insect repellent for evenings outside. ✉ *Fernandez Bay* ☎ *242/342–2100, 216/337–8800* ⊕ *www.islandhoppinn.com* ↗ *4 suites* ♿ *In-room: kitchen, no TV, Wi-Fi. In-hotel: restaurant, bar, beach, water sports, laundry facilities* ▭ *No credit cards.*

NIGHTLIFE

Regatta Beach Fish Fry. Don't miss Regatta Beach Fish Fry on Regatta Beach, just south of the government buildings in the town center on Saturday nights. The half dozen fish shacks, including Blue Marlin Take Away (*242/342–3259*), open in the afternoon, and the DJs start playing music around 9 pm. It's a great place for sunset-watching. A few of the shacks are open other days.

SHOPPING

Pam's Boutique. This boutique at Fernandez Bay Village Resort has reasonably priced resort wear, logo hats, and T-shirts. This is one of your few chances to get a Cat Island T-shirt. ☎ *242/342–3043.*

SPORTS AND THE OUTDOORS

FISHING   **Mark Keasler.** Mark Keasler offers deep-sea fishing and bonefishing off the coast of New Bight. ☎ *242/342–3043.*

PORT HOWE

At the conch shell–lined traffic roundabout at the southernmost end of the Queen's Highway, you must turn either east or west; head east out toward Port Howe, believed by many to be Cat Island's oldest settlement. Nearby lie the ruins of the **Deveaux Mansion**, a stark two-story, whitewashed building overrun with vegetation and pretty much unexplorable. Once it was a grand house on a cotton plantation, owned by Captain Andrew Deveaux of the British Navy, who was given thousands of acres of Cat Island property as a reward for his daring raid that recaptured Nassau from the Spaniards in 1783. Just beyond the mansion ruin is the entrance road to the Greenwood Beach Resort, which sits on an 8-mi stretch of unblemished, velvet pink-sand beach.

8

WHERE TO STAY

$ 🗦 **Greenwood Beach Resort.** Set on an 8-mi stretch of pink shell-strewn sand, this remote resort is about 35 minutes from the Bight airport. The resort has a dive shop, one of only two on the island. Divers can go out on the resort's boat or dive at the reef just offshore. Owned by the Illing family from Germany, the resort is popular with Europeans. The large clubhouse, with its yellow-and-white walls and vivid tropical paintings, is the center of activity. You can relax at the attractive stone-work bar or on the veranda, which has open vistas of the violet-blue Atlantic; or catch some rays at the pool or beach. Rooms are bright and cheerfully decorated with colorful fish stencils and rattan furnishings. Breakfast and dinner are served family style. Picnic lunches are prepared for day excursions. This is an ideal location for vacationers looking for beachfront tranquillity. **Pros:** private Atlantic beach location; great snorkeling on coral heads in front of resort; good on-site restaurant. **Cons:** long drive to explore other parts of the island; if you want an air-conditioned room you need to reserve in advance. ⊠ *Ocean Dr. off Queen's Hwy.* ☎ *242/342–3053* ⊕ *www.greenwoodbeachresort. com* 🛏 *16 rooms* ⅛ *In-room: no a/c, no TV. In-hotel: restaurant, bar, pool, beach, water sports, business center.*

SPORTS AND THE OUTDOORS

SCUBA DIVING   **Cat Island Dive Center.** With this full-service center divers can take trips on the 30-foot dive boat or go diving at a coral reef just off the beach. Beginners can take an $80 crash course, and experienced divers can plunge deep with spectacular wall diving. You can also take half-day guided snorkeling trips. ⊠ *Greenwood Beach Resort* ☎ *242/342–3053.*

DEVIL'S POINT

The small village of Devil's Point, with its pastel-color, thatch-roof houses, lies about 10 mi west of the Queen's Highway. Beachcombers will find great shelling on the pristine beach; keep an eye out for dolphins, which are common in these waters. From Devil's Point, drive north through the arid southwest corner of the island to **McQueens,** then west to the area's biggest resort, Hawk's Nest Resort, which has an airstrip, restaurant, and bar next to a gorgeous white-sand beach. This resort is well known to serious anglers and divers, who often fly in to the resort's private airstrip and stay a week doing little else. The southwest end of the island also has good diving spots, such as **Tartar Bank** and **Vlady's Reef,** both teeming with an abundance of marine life and coral heads.

EXPLORING

Richman Hill-Newfield Plantation. Richman Hill-Newfield Plantation shows what plantation days on the island looked like. Look for the slave quarters near the bigger stone buildings. Take photos from the path, but be careful exploring these crumbling buildings.

Fernandez Bay Beach

WHERE TO EAT AND STAY

$$ ✕ **Hawk's Nest Resort Restaurant and Bar.** High-beamed ceilings, tiled
ECLECTIC floors, blue-and-lime-green walls, and blue ceramic-topped tables cre-
★ ate a cheerful vibe to go with the Bahamian comfort-food menu. Start
your day with fresh juices and a full breakfast. For lunch and dinner
there are burgers and Bahamian basics such as cracked conch, lobster,
and fresh fish. You can eat on the terrace or inside and have a great
view of the ocean. ⊠ *Hawk's Nest Resort and Marina, turn right when
Queen's Hwy. ends* ☎ *242/342–7050* ✆ *Closed mid-Sept.–Nov. 1.*

$ ⛺ **Hawk's Nest Resort and Marina.** At Cat Island's southwestern tip, this
★ waterfront resort, just yards from a long sandy beach, has its own
3,100-foot runway and a 28-slip full-service marina with PADI dive
center. The patios of the guest rooms, the dining room, and the lounge
overlook the pool and the aquamarine Exuma Sound. With cheerful
pastel-color walls and bright bedspreads, rooms have either one king-
size or two queen-size beds with baths that have both tubs and show-
ers. The personal service is outstanding, and staff can arrange island
excursions, refer you to bonefishing guides, or set up diving adventures.
Pros: best marina in this area of the Bahamas for blue-water fishing;
quality accommodations and food; best location for diving southern
Cat Island. **Cons:** if you want to explore the rest of Cat Island, it's a
long drive. ⊠ *Turn right when Queen's Hwy. ends* ☎ *242/342–7050*
⊕ *www.hawks-nest.com* ✆ *10 rooms, 3 houses* ⛫ *In-hotel: restaurant,
bar, pool, beach, water sports* ✆ *Closed mid-Sept.–Nov. 1.* ⊚ *Breakfast.*

8

SPORTS AND THE OUTDOORS

FISHING   **Hawk's Nest Marina.** Blue-water angling boat owners make a point of using Hawk's Nest Marina to access the dynamite offshore fishing. Look for wahoo, yellowfin tuna, dolphin, and white and blue marlin along the Exuma Sound drop-offs, Devil's Point, Tartar Bank, and Columbus Point. March through July is prime time, though winter fishing, December through February, is also prime for wahoo. You can arrange bonefishing through the marina with top guide Nathaniel Gilbert; just call him Top Cat. ☎ *242/342–7050.*

SCUBA DIVING   **The Cave.** The Cave has a big channel with several exits to deeper ocean. Reef sharks, barracudas, and other tropical fish are frequently seen here.

Tartar Bank. This offshore site is known for its abundant sea life, including sharks, triggerfish, turtles, eagle rays, and barracuda.

Vlady's Reef. This site, also known as "The Chimney," is near the Guana Cays. Coral heads have created numerous canyons, chimneys, and swim-throughs. You're likely to catch a glimpse of large stingrays.

Dive Cat Island. Dive Cat Island at Hawk's Nest Marina is PADI certified and conducts daily guided diving adventures, rents diving and snorkeling gear, and has equipment and sundries for sale. The running time to dive sites off the southern tip of the island is 15 to 30 minutes in the shop's 27-foot Panga, outfitted with VHF and GPS. ☎ *242/342–7050.*

SAN SALVADOR

Updated by
Ramona Settle

On October 12, 1492, Christopher Columbus disrupted the lives of the peaceful Lucayan Indians when he landed on the island of Guanahani, which he renamed San Salvador. Apparently he knelt on the beach and claimed the land for Spain. (Skeptics of this story point to a study published in a 1986 *National Geographic* article in which Samana Cay, 60 mi southeast, is identified as the exact point of the weary explorer's landing.) Three monuments on the island commemorate Columbus's arrival, and the 500th anniversary of the event was officially celebrated here.

The island is 12 mi long—roughly the length of Manhattan—and about 5 mi wide, with a lake-filled interior. Some of the most dazzling deserted beaches in the country are here, and most visitors come for the peaceful isolation and the diving; there are about 950 residents and more than 50 dive sites. There's also world-renowned offshore fishing and good bonefishing.

GETTING HERE AND AROUND

AIR TRAVEL   The island has one airport, in Cockburn Town (ZSA). Air Sunshine flies from Fort Lauderdale on demand. American Eagle flies from Miami on the weekends. Bahamasair flies from Nassau daily and also offers direct service from Miami three days a week, though this is subject to change. Spirit Airlines flies from Fort Lauderdale on Saturday only. Club Med has packages that include air charters. Riding Rock Resort and Marina can arrange charters.

Airport Information San Salvador Cockburn Town Airport ☎ *242/331–2131.*

BOAT TRAVEL   Mail boats that bring supplies to the island each week make an adventurous mode of transportation. You'll ride with groceries, large and small appliances, automobiles, and sometimes even livestock. All boats depart from Potter's Cay in Nassau. Schedules change frequently. M/V *Lady Francis* leaves Tuesday for San Salvador and Rum Cay, returning Friday (12 hours; $60 one way).

Boat and Ferry Information Dockmaster's Office ☎ *242/393–1064.*

BIKE TRAVEL   For a short visit to Columbus Cross or the lighthouse, a bike is a sufficient mode of transportation. Bike rentals are $15 a day at Club Med.

CAR TRAVEL   If you want to see the entire island, rent a car. Queen's Highway forms an oval that skirts the island's coastline, and road conditions are excellent. Car rentals are about $85 a day.

Car-Rental Contacts C&S Car Rental ☎ *242/331–2631.* **Riding Rock Resort and Marina** ☎ *800/272–1492, 242/331–2631.*

SCOOTER TRAVEL   Scooters are a convenient way to get around the entire island.

Scooter-Rental Contacts K's Scooter Rentals ☎ *242/331–2125* ⊕ *www.bahamas.com/vendors.*

TAXI TRAVEL   Taxis meet arriving planes at the airport. Club Med meets all guests at the airport, and transfers are included if you bought a package including air. Your account is charged $10 for the three-minute transfer if your package from Club Med did not include airfare. Riding Rock, five minutes away, provides complimentary transportation for guests. If you want to take your own taxi, it's approximately $10 to either resort.

Taxi Contacts Fernander Tours ☎ *242/331–2676, 242/427–8198.* **Nat Walker's Island Adventures** ☎ *242/331–2111.*

FERNANDEZ BAY TO RIDING ROCK POINT

In 1492 the inspiring sight that greeted Christopher Columbus by moonlight at 2 am was a terrain of gleaming beaches and far-reaching forest. The peripatetic traveler and his crews—"men from Heaven," the locals called them—steered the *Niña, Pinta,* and *Santa María* warily among the coral reefs and anchored, so it's recorded, in **Fernandez Bay.** A cross erected in 1956 by Columbus scholar Ruth C. Durlacher Wolper Malvin stands at his approximate landing spot. An underwater monument marks the place where the *Santa María* anchored. Nearby, another monument commemorates the Olympic flame's passage on its journey from Greece to Mexico City in 1968.

Fernandez Bay is just south of what is now the main community of **Cockburn Town,** midisland on the western shore. This is where the airport is, and where the weekly mail boat docks. This small village's narrow streets contain two churches, a commissioner's office, a police station, a courthouse, a library, a clinic, a drugstore, and a telephone station.

From Cockburn Town to Club Med you'll pass **Riding Rock Point.** All fish excursions leave from the marina. Riding Rock Resort makes a good spot to stop for a drink, meet locals and divers, and buy a local T-shirt.

8

These settlements are all most visitors explore of San Salvador. You'll base yourself here, as there aren't any hotels and restaurants outside of this area.

WHERE TO EAT AND STAY

$$$$ ✕ **Christopher's, Berimbau, and Watling's at Club Med.** The buffet changes
BUFFET themes nightly, so even after a week it doesn't get boring. Caribbean Night has local fare, such as conch and fresh fish. Carving stations and European pastries and breads are impossible to deny. Don't forget the chocolate-chip bread—so good you'll order some loaves to bring back with you. If you're not staying at Club Med, you must buy the $92 "evening pass," which includes dinner, a show, disco, and all you can drink. ⊠ *Club Med, 3 mi north of Riding Rock Point* ☎ *242/331–2000* ⊕ *www.clubmed.com* ♣ *Reservations essential.*

$ ✕ **Paradis Restaurant and Bar.** A typical Bahamian restaurant, Paradis has
BAHAMIAN a daily changing menu written on a chalkboard. Home-cooked food such as conch, ribs, and the fresh catch of the day are simply prepared. The restaurant is popular with both locals and visitors, and there's free Wi-Fi. ⊠ *Island Plaza, 3 mi from Cockburn Town, across the street from the airport* ☎ *242/331–2400.*

$$ ✕ **Riding Rock Seafront Restaurant and Driftwood Bar.** Eat inside the 60-seat
BAHAMIAN restaurant, or take a table on the patio by the pool. Androsia-print tablecloths create a colorful tropical ambience. Fruit, fresh-baked breads, pancakes, and eggs any style with bacon and grits are daily starters. Burgers, sandwiches, conch chowder, and cracked conch are lunch favorites. The just-off-the-boat catch of the day—wahoo, mahimahi, tuna, grouper, snapper—grilled with lemon and butter or baked with tomatoes and spices, is the dinner specialty. Broiled or stuffed lobster (in season), barbecue shrimp, steaks, and chicken round out the choices, though all are not available each evening, as the menu changes based on availability. ⊠ *Riding Rock Resort and Marina, Riding Rock Point* ☎ *242/331–2631.*

$$$$ 🏨 **Club Med–Columbus Isle.** The 89-acre oceanfront village is one of
ALL-INCLUSIVE Club Med's most luxurious resorts, with state-of-the-art dive facilities,
ⓒ including three custom-made 45-foot catamarans and a decompres-
★ sion chamber. Rooms are in colorful buildings, and all have patios or balconies and handcrafted furniture. Expect the usual Club Med activities: water aerobics, sports tournaments, dance lessons, and theater shows. Guided bike tours introduce vacationers to island life. The resort is sprawling, so you can partake in activities or find secluded spots to yourself. The dining room is set up with both shared tables to mingle, and private tables for more romance. Rates include everything from two daily boat snorkel trips to waterskiing, but charge addition-ally for spa treatments and dives. This resort caters primarily to

> **PRETEND YOU LIVE HERE**
>
> Vacation Rentals by Owners (VRBO) has four homes on the island. Two are near Club Med, making it easy to access its restaurants and activities, yet providing peace and quiet for relaxing. The other two are on the opposite end of the island for that all-to-yourself feeling. ⊕ *www.vrbo.com.*

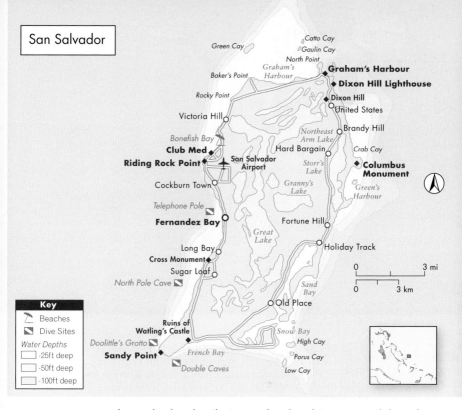

San Salvador

Catto Cay
Gaulin Cay
Green Cay
North Point
Graham's Harbour
Graham's Harbour
Baker's Point
Dixon Hill Lighthouse
Rocky Point
Dixon Hill
United States
Victoria Hill
Brandy Hill
Bonefish Bay
Northeast Arm Lake
Club Med
Hard Bargain
Crab Cay
Riding Rock Point
San Salvador Airport
Storr's Lake
Columbus Monument
Cockburn Town
Granny's Lake
Green's Harbour
Telephone Pole
Fernandez Bay
Fortune Hill
Great Lake
Long Bay
Cross Monument
Holiday Track
Sugar Loaf
Sand Bay
North Pole Cave
Old Place

0   3 mi
0   3 km

Key
Beaches
Dive Sites
Water Depths
-25ft deep
-50ft deep
-100ft deep

Ruins of Watling's Castle
Snow Bay
High Cay
Doolittle's Grotto
French Bay
Porus Cay
Sandy Point
Double Caves
Low Cay

upscale couples, but the vibe is more low-key than at most Club Meds, and is one of the most recommended by Club Med fanatics. Nonguests can also enjoy the property with a day pass ($72), evening pass ($92), or an all-day pass ($140). Passes include meals, all you can drink, and all the activities including the shows and snorkel trips. **Pros:** gorgeous beachfront location; activities galore. **Cons:** pool so heavily chlorinated that white clothes turn green; many members of the customer-service staff are French and speak only passable English; outlying rooms require a lot of walking. ⊠ *3 mi north of Riding Rock Point* ☎ *888/932–2582, 242/331–2000* ⊕ *www.clubmed.com* ➪ *236 rooms* ☐ *In-room: safe, Wi-Fi. In-hotel: restaurant, bar, pool, tennis court, gym, spa, beach, water sports* ⏐◯⏐ *All-inclusive.*

$ 🏨 **Riding Rock Resort and Marina.** A diver's dream, this motel-style resort offers three dives per day to pristine offshore reefs and a drop-off wall teeming with life. It's also the only place to stay on San Salvador if you want to manage your own activities. The resort's three buildings have rooms facing either the ocean or the freshwater pool. All rooms have fresh paint, new tropical curtains and bedspreads, washed-oak or wicker furniture, and a sitting area with a table and chairs; some ocean-side rooms have refrigerators and queen-size beds. The restaurant serves grilled wahoo and tuna right off the boat as well as hearty pancake breakfasts. There's good bonefishing you can do on your own

San Salvador has several popular diving sites.

north of Club Med and in Pigeon Creek. You should rent a car or a bike at least one day and explore the island. **Pros:** some of the best diving in the world; the marina is in a unique location for boaters to access the virgin offshore fishing for marlin, wahoo, tuna, and dolphin. **Cons:** food and fuel supplies can run low at times; not all boats are available for fishing during slow/hurricane season. ⊠ *Riding Rock Point* ☎ *800/272–1492, 242/331–2631* ⊕ *www.ridingrock.com* ⇝ *42 rooms* ⌂ *In-hotel: restaurant, bar, pool, water sports.*

NIGHTLIFE

Club Med. Evening passes to Club Med include themed dinners, shows, a disco, and all you can drink. ☎ *888/932–2582, 242/331–2000* ⊠ *$92.*

Driftwood Bar & Lounge. Friday nights fishermen and scuba divers gather at the Driftwood Bar & Lounge to tell tall tales. ⊠ *Riding Rock Resort, San Salvador Island* ☎ *242/331–2631.*

SHOPPING

Club Med. Club Med has a small boutique with souvenirs, Roxy brand clothes, swimsuits, and sunglasses. ☎ *242/331–2000.*

Shoe's N'Things. The tiny Island Plaza between Club Med and the airport has a Shoe's N'Things which sells local T-shirts, sunglasses, and souvenirs. ☎ *242/331–2778.*

SPORTS AND THE OUTDOORS

Telephone Pole. This is a stimulating wall dive where you can watch stingrays, grouper, snapper, and turtles in action.

Club Med. There are dive boats and a decompression chamber here. There's also tennis, sailing, waterskiing, and windsurfing, among other sports. ☎ *242/331–2000.*

Riding Rock Divers. This dive compnay, which is part of the Riding Rock Resort and Marina, uses mostly buoyed sites to avoid damaging the marine environment by dropping anchor. The 42- and 46-foot dive boats are spacious and comfortable. Resort and certification courses are offered, and a modern underwater photographic facility is available to guests. All new computerized dive gear and camera gear are on-site for guest rental. Complete dive packages, including meals and accommodations, are available through Riding Rock Resort and Marina. Riding Rock also rents bicycles and snorkeling gear and can arrange reef, inshore, and offshore fishing trips ($500 for a half day and $800 for a full day). The offshore waters hold tuna, blue marlin, dorado, and, in winter, wahoo. ☎ *800/272–1492.*

ELSEWHERE ON SAN SALVADOR

Sometimes you just don't want to stay put at the resort. San Salvador's off-the-beaten path places require some work, but make interesting sightseeing. The Bahamian Field Station and the lighthouse are not difficult to get to, but the "other" Columbus monument requires an ATV or a really long beach walk.

EXPLORING

Note: These sights are organized by location, going clockwise around the island.

Graham's Harbour. Columbus describes Graham's Harbour in his diaries as large enough "to hold all the ships of Christendom." A complex of buildings near the harbor houses the **Bahamian Field Station**, a biological and geological research institution that attracts scientists and students from all over the world.

Dixon Hill Lighthouse. A couple of miles south of Graham's Harbour stands Dixon Hill Lighthouse. Built around 1856, it's still hand-operated. The lighthouse keeper must wind the apparatus that projects the light, which beams out to sea every 15 seconds to a maximum distance of 19 mi, depending on visibility. A climb to the top of the 160-foot landmark provides a fabulous view of the island, which includes a series of inland lakes. The keeper is present 24 hours a day. Knock on his door, and he'll take you up to the top and explain the machinery. Drop $1 in the box when you sign the guest book on the way out.

Columbus Monument. No road leads to the Columbus Monument on Crab Cay; you have to make your way along a bushy path. This initial tribute to the explorer was erected by the *Chicago Herald* newspaper in 1892, far from the presumed site of Columbus's landing. A series of little villages—Polly Hill, Hard Bargain, Fortune Hill, Holiday Track—winds south of here for several miles along Storr's Lake. You can still see the ruins of several plantations, and the deserted white-sand beaches on this eastern shore are some of the most spectacular in the islands. A little farther along is Pigeon Creek, which is a prime spot for bonefishing.

8

Sandy Point. Sandy Point anchors the island's southwestern end, overlooking French Bay. Here, on a hill, you'll find the ruins of **Watling's Castle,** named after the 17th-century pirate. The ruins are more likely the remains of a Loyalist plantation house than a castle from buccaneering days. A 5- to 10-minute walk from Queen's Highway will take you to see what's left of the ruins, which are now engulfed in vegetation.

SPORTS AND THE OUTDOORS

SCUBA DIVING *For more information about these and other sites, contact the Riding Rock Resort and Marina.*

Doolittle's Grotto. This is a popular site featuring a sandy slope down to 140 feet. There are lots of tunnels and crevices for exploring, and usually a large school of horse-eye jacks to keep you company.

Double Caves. As the name implies, Double Caves has two parallel caves leading out to a wall at 115 feet. There's typically quite a lot of fish activity along the top of the wall.

North Pole Cave. North Pole Cave has a wall that drops sharply from 40 feet to more than 150 feet. Coral growth is extensive, and you might see a hammerhead or two.

LONG ISLAND

By Sharon Williams

Long Island lives up to its name—80 gorgeous miles are available for you to explore. The Queen's Highway traverses its length, through the Tropic of Cancer and many diverse settlements and farming communities. The island is 4 mi at its widest, so at hilly vantage points you can view both the white cliffs and the raging Atlantic on the east side, and the gentle surf coming to you like a shy child on the Caribbean side. It is truly spectacular.

Long Island was the third island discovered by Christopher Columbus, and a monument to him stands on the north end. Loyalist families came to the island in support of the crown, and to this day there are crown properties all over the island, deeded by the king of England. Fleeing the Revolution, their attempt at re-creating life in America was short-lived. The soil and lack of rainfall did not support their crops, cotton being their mainstay. Today you can see wild cotton growing in patches up and down the island, along with the ruins of the plantations.

Fishing and tourism support the 3,000 residents of Long Island. Farms growing bananas, mangoes, papaya, and limes also dot the landscape. Boatbuilding is a natural art here, and in the south you can always see a boat in progress as you travel the Queen's Highway.

Progress has come to the island slowly. There is now high-speed Internet and cell-phone service, but shops and modern forms of entertainment are still limited. People who come to Long Island don't seem to mind; they're here for the beauty, tranquillity, and the friendly people. Deep-sea fishing and diving are readily available, and bonefishing flats attract sport fishermen from all over the world. The beaches provide breathtaking views, shelling, exploring, and magnificent pieces of sea glass. The laid-back lifestyle is reminiscent of a slower gentler time.

French Bay, San Salvador

GETTING HERE AND AROUND

AIR TRAVEL Long Island has two airports: Deadman's Cay (LGI) in the south and Stella Maris Airport (SML) in the north. Three airlines provide daily service from Nassau to Stella Maris and Deadman's Cay airports. There are also charter services from Nassau, Fort Lauderdale, and the Exumas.

Guests staying at Cape Santa Maria or Stella Maris Resort should fly into Stella Maris airport. Chez Pierre Bahamas' guests can fly into either airport, although the Stella Maris airport is a bit closer. All others should fly into Deadman's Cay airport. Flying into the wrong airport will cost you not only an hour's drive, but also $100 or more in taxi fare. Listen carefully to the arrival announcement when you approach Long Island; most commercial airlines stop at both airports.

Airport Information Deadman's Cay Airport ☎ *242/337–1777.* **Stella Maris Airport** ☎ *242/338–2006.*

BOAT TRAVEL Mail boats that bring supplies to the island each week make an adventurous mode of transportation. You'll ride with groceries, large and small appliances, automobiles, and sometimes even livestock. All boats depart from Potter's Cay in Nassau. Schedules change frequently. M/V *Mia Dean* leaves Tuesday for Clarence Town and returns Thursday (18 hours; $60 one way). The *Island Link*, a fast boat, leaves Tuesday with stops in Salt Pond, Deadman's Cay, and Seymour's, returning Thursday (eight hours; $70 one way).

Boat and Ferry Information Dockmaster's Office ☎ *242/393–1064.*

CAR TRAVEL If you want to explore the entire island, a car is necessary. The Queen's Highway curls like a ribbon from north to south, ending abruptly at the ocean in the north and at a stop sign in the south. It's narrow, with no marked center line, which makes bikes and scooters dangerous modes of transportation. The highway is easily traversed, but some off roads require four-wheel drive, such as the road to the Columbus Monument, which is treacherous. The roads to Adderley's Plantation and Chez Pierre's are rough, but passable.

Most hotels will arrange car rentals, and can have your car waiting on-site. Rentals range from $60 to $85. Some include gas; all have a limited number of vehicles.

Keep your gas tank full; while there are service stations along the highway, hours can be irregular and some take only cash.

Car-Rental Contacts Taylor's Rentals ☎ *242/338–7001.* **Williams Car Rental** ☎ *242/338–5002.*

TAXI TRAVEL   Taxis meet incoming flights at both airports. From the Stella Maris airport, the fare to Stella Maris Resort is $10 per couple; to Cape Santa Maria, the fare is $30 per couple. Guests staying at Chez Pierre Bahamas pay $40 from the Stella Maris airport and $60 from Deadman's Cay. From the Deadman's Cay airport to Gems of Paradise, the fare is $50. Ellen's Inn and Winter Haven provide free transportation from the DC airport. A full-day tour of the island by taxi would cost about $350, and a half-day tour would be about $120. However, all taxis are privately owned, so rates can be negotiated.

Taxi Contacts Leonard Darville ☎ *242/472–0024.* **Omar Daily** ☎ *242/357–1043.* **Scoffield Miller** ☎ *242/338–8970.*

NORTH LONG ISLAND: CAPE SANTA MARIA TO GRAY'S

In the far north you will find two large resort communities: **Cape Santa Maria** and **Stella Maris**. Scattered between are the small settlements of **Seymour's, Glinton's,** and **Burnt Ground**. Columbus originally named the island's northern tip Cape Santa Maria after the largest of his three ships. The beach here is gorgeous, full of private homes and resort villas, and a restaurant, bar, and gift shop that are open to the public. North of the Cape Santa Maria Resort are the **Columbus Monument**, commemorating Columbus's landing on Long Island, and **Columbus Cove**, where he made landfall. Twelve miles south of the Cape, Stella Maris, which means Star of the Sea, is home to the so-named resort. The Stella Maris airport sits on the property, along with private homes, restaurants and bars, the magnificent **Love Beaches**, a full-service marina, and a tackle and gift shop; all open to the public. Just north of Stella Maris, off Queen's Highway, are the ruins of the 19th-century **Adderley's Plantation**.

Traveling south about 8 mi, you'll come to **Simms**, one of Long Island's oldest settlements. The Tropic of Cancer cuts through the island close to here, dividing the subtropics from the tropics.

Farther south are the idyllic communities of **Thompson Bay** and **Salt Pond**; both providing safe harbors for those who visit by sailboat. Salt Pond, a hilly bustling settlement so named for its many salt ponds, hosts the annual Long Island Regatta. Continuing south, you will pass the settlements of **the Bight** and **Gray's** before reaching **Deadman's Cay.**

EXPLORING

Adderley's Plantation. Just north of the Stella Maris Resort are the ruins of 19th-century Adderley's Plantation. Clearly marked, the road is marginally passable by car. It is about a 1-mi drive and then a fairly long walk. The walking path is marked by conch shells, and leads to the cotton plantation ruins. Seven buildings are practically intact. For historians, it is well worth the time.

Columbus Monument. Two miles north of Cape Santa Maria is the Columbus Monument, commemorating Columbus's landing on Long Island. The road to the monument is off the Queen's Highway, and while the sign is often not visible, any Long Islander will gladly give you directions. The 3-mi treacherous road is too rough for vehicles without four-wheel drive, and is an extremely long hike. Check around to make sure the road is passable before heading out, as heavy rains can cause sections to wash out.

At the end of the road is a steep hill, called Columbus Point, and a climb to the summit affords one of the most spectacular vistas you will ever see. This is the highest point on Long Island, and the second highest in the Bahamas. Farther north on Queen's Highway is Columbus Harbor, on Newton's Cay. Columbus made landfall in this cove, protected by limestone outcroppings. The more adventurous can follow the beach to the left, where a rough walking path leads to three other coves; each one a delight. Two coves up you will find sea glass scattered on the beach like sparkling jewels, and by climbing through limestone formations you will discover another cove perfect for snorkeling.

WHERE TO EAT

After a period of rain, the mosquitoes and no-see-ums come out, so bring mosquito repellant with you when dining or playing outdoors.

$$
SEAFOOD

✕ **Cape Santa Maria Beach House Restaurant and Bar.** Upstairs in the Cape Santa Maria Beach House, guests can enjoy sweeping vistas of the turquoise bay during the day and bobbing boat lights in the evening along with the gentle sounds of the sea. Breakfast can be light, with yogurt parfait and a seasonal fruit medley, or splurge with banana-bread French toast or Bahamian-style eggs Benedict. Sit under an umbrella on the oceanfront deck, soak up the mood, and enjoy the lunch favorites, which include the Great Cape burger, the clubhouse sandwich, salads, and soups. For dinner, delight in the Caribbean coconut shrimp, the fresh Island Bahamian grouper, or the Bahamian lobster tail (in season). Steaks, chicken dishes, and vegetarian specialties are also available. Ask about their secret desserts and freshly baked pies, which will satisfy your sweet tooth. Full bar service is available in the Oceanside Bar, on the beachfront deck, and in the restaurant. ⊠ *Cape Santa Maria Beach Resort and Villas, Galliot Cay off Seymour's* ☎ *242/338–5273* ♙ *Reservations essential* ☉ *Closed Sept. and Oct.*

$$
CONTINENTAL
Fodor's Choice
★

✕ **Chez Pierre's.** At this oceanfront tropical restaurant a few steps from the beach, Chef Pierre has spent the last nine years creating his sumptuous continental and Bahamian cuisine. Specialties include pasta dishes with shrimp and scallops, fresh fish, and veal that melt in your mouth.

Cape Santa Maria Beach House Restaurant

Bahamian lobster, steaks, and chicken, along with vegetarian dishes, are also available. Pierre uses island-grown produce and fresh fish from the local waters. A full bar is available, which on busy nights is on the honor system. To get here, watch for the sign on Queen's Highway between the settlements of Weymss and Miller's. ⊠ *Miller's Bay* ☎ *242/338–8809* ⚑ *Reservations essential.*

$
CONTINENTAL
✕ **Long Island Breeze Restaurant.** Overlooking the Salt Pond harbor, this upscale restaurant serves everything from native dishes to continental cuisine, along with steaks, lamb chops, chicken, and the freshest of fish. You can dine inside or on the balcony overlooking the lovely harbor; both provide views of magnificent sunsets. The restaurant is only open for dinner, but the **Pool Patio Bar and Grill** is open Tuesday–Saturday for lunch and early dinner, and serves more casual Bahamian fare. Full bar service is available in the restaurant and the grill. Local bands play on some weekends. Dinghy and motorboat dockage are available. ⊠ *Long Island Breeze Resort, Salt Pond* ☎ *242/338–0170* ⚑ *Reservations essential* ▭ *No credit cards* ☉ *Closed July–Oct. and Sun. and Mon.*

$$
CONTINENTAL
✕ **Stella Maris Restaurant and Bar.** Fresh fruit and home-baked muffins highlight the breakfast buffet, or you can order French toast or a full breakfast from the menu. The lunch menu includes conch chowder, club sandwiches, burgers, and salads. You can have lunch in the dining room or out on the stone terrace, where you can relax under an umbrella and delight in the views of the Atlantic. Chef Bruno continues to prepare the freshest fish with different treatments, along with his Bahamian lobster tail, seafood platter, and cracked conch, an island favorite. Steaks, pasta, chicken, hamburgers, and vegetarian dishes are

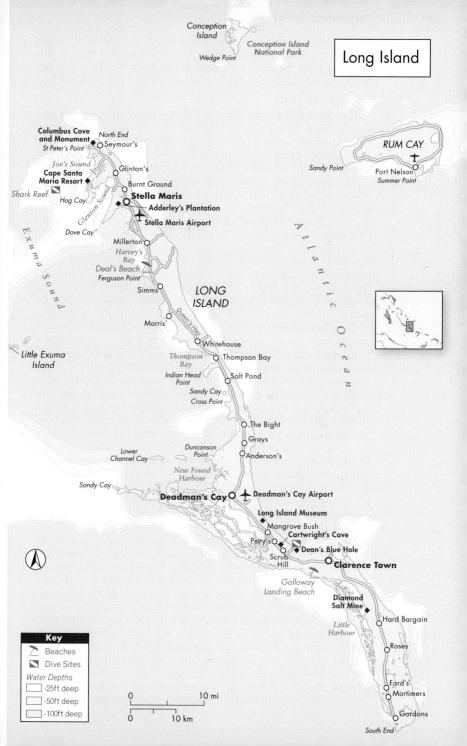

also available. Grilled lamb chops can be special ordered ahead of time. Fresh fruit and ice cream make for a great hot-weather dessert. You can order from the bar menu until 9 pm. ⊠ *Stella Maris Resort Club, Stella Maris* ☎ *242/338–2050* ⚑ *Reservations essential* ⊗ *Closed Sept.*

WHERE TO STAY

$$ 🏨 **Cape Santa Maria Beach Resort and Villas.** This lovely resort sits on a
Fodor's Choice 4-mi gorgeous beach. Overlooking turquoise waters are spacious one-
★ or two-bedroom colonial-style cottages, each with a furnished screened porch. Fifteen luxury villas, completed in 2009, have 1,800 square feet of total comfort, including Wi-Fi, fully equipped entertainment centers, jetted tubs, and full kitchens. The reception building has a small fitness area, gift shop, library, and television room. The activities office arranges Hobie Cat sailing, snorkeling, and deep-sea, reef, or bonefishing trips, along with island excursions and car rentals. Upstairs is the cozy restaurant. The beachfront bar has the best view of the golden to magenta sunsets. **Pros:** a great place to spend your time doing nothing; many amenities. **Cons:** located on the northernmost end so you must rent a car to explore the island. ⊠ *Galliot Cay off Seymour's* ☎ *242/338–5273, 800/663–7090* ⊕ *www.capesantamaria.com* ⊲⊃ *20 bungalows, 15 villas* ⚒ *In-room: safe. In-hotel: restaurant, bar, gym, beach, water sports* ⊗ *Closed Sept. and Oct.* ⓘⓄⓘ *Multiple meal plans.*

$ 🏨 **Chez Pierre Bahamas.** Lining lovely Miller's Bay beach is this rustic and remote resort. Sitting on stilts are six cabins with generous bedrooms, bathrooms, and airy screened porches. Located halfway between Stella Maris and Deadman's Cay, this is a real "get-away-from-it-all" place, and guests should be self-sufficient and adventurous. Chef Pierre whips up innovative dishes, using island-grown produce and fresh fish from the local waters, served in the relaxing oceanfront restaurant. The room rate includes two meals daily. Explore nearby cays in sea kayaks, wade the adjacent flats for bonefish, or schedule a diving adventure. Fishing guides, diving, car rentals, and airport transfers can be arranged. **Pros:** private beachfront location; easy access to fishing and water sports; excellent restaurant. **Cons:** road to resort is rough; must rent a car to explore the island. ⊠ *Miller's Bay* ☎ *242/338–8809* ⊕ *www. chezpierrebahamas.com* ⊲⊃ *6 cottages* ⚒ *In-room: no a/c, no TV. In-hotel: restaurant, bar, beach, water sports, business center* ⓘⓄⓘ *Some meals.*

$ 🏨 **Grotto Bay Bahamas.** In the settlement of Salt Pond is this small private hideaway. Owners Kris and Jean built three lovely guest rooms with sweeping decks on the lower level of their home. Facing the ocean, the rooms are spacious and comfortable, each with a microwave, refrigerator, and coffeemaker. This is a perfect place for water sports enthusiasts to stay, as the owners are professional divers, and can arrange all sorts of great experiences for their guests. Both have worked on underwater scenes in movies such as *Sphere.* Guests also have exclusive use of the beach, hammocks, horseshoe pit, beach volleyball, Windsurfer, sailboat, kayaks, and snorkeling equipment. Grotto Bay practically sits on top of the Salt Pond Cave, one of the largest dry caves in the Bahamas, with two enormous chambers featuring stalagmites and stalactites and six documented species of bats. A restaurant and a burger bar are close by,

Cape Santa Maria Beach Resort

as is the Long Island Regatta site. On-site scuba rentals, including equipment, tank rentals and refills, and scuba instruction, are available; also inquire about waterskiing. **Pros:** great place for water sports; centrally located for exploring north and south; personalized service. **Cons:** no in-house restaurant, bar, or meals; you need to rent a car to explore the island. ⊠ *Salt Pond* ☎ *242/338–0011* ⊕ *www.grottobaybahamas. com* ⊋ *3 rooms* ⚲ *In-hotel: beach, water sports, business center* ▭ *No credit cards.*

$ 🔝 **Long Island Breeze Resort.** Overlooking Salt Pond harbor is this delightful resort. Owners Mike and Jackie are constantly making improvements to the property, such as the dinghy and motorboat floating dock. The resort has choice accommodations including king and double suites and a one-bedroom apartment, each with a phone for incoming calls. The location is ideal for exploring sights, both north and south, and only steps away from the Long Island Regatta site. Upstairs in the main building is a formal restaurant serving a mix of Bahamian and continental cuisine; a downstairs Pool Patio Bar serves burgers and pizza. Both overlook the harbor. The main building has a sitting area with a television and small library. Dances are held many weekends on the lower deck around the pool, with music provided by local bands. The staff can arrange picnics, fishing, diving, snorkeling, bicycles, and car rental. **Pros:** good central location to rent a car and explore the island both north and south. **Cons:** TVs in the rooms are for DVDs only (no reception). ⊠ *Salt Pond* ☎ *242/338–0170* ⊕ *www.longislandbreezeresort. com* ⊋ *7 suites, 1 apartment* ⚲ *In-hotel: restaurant, bar, pool, beach, water sports, laundry facilities* ▭ *No credit cards* ☽ *Closed July–Oct.*

8

$ ⊞ **Stella Maris Resort Club.** Stella Maris is more than a resort; it is a community, with private homes built by people from all over the world. There are many accommodation choices, including spacious one- and two-bedroom cottages steps away from the lodge-restaurant, all with an ocean view or balcony. Lovely beach homes, some with pools, are also available for rent. Sitting atop a hilly ridge overlooking the Atlantic, this sprawling resort has a range of daily activities that make it a Bahamian classic. Swim in three freshwater pools, lounge on a series of private beaches, or explore sandy coves with excellent snorkeling. Free morning and afternoon activity programs include beach trips, sailing at Deal's Beach, boat cruises with snorkeling, and kayaking. The resort can also arrange all sorts of excursions, such as deep-sea fishing, bonefishing, and scuba diving. South of the resort, just off Queen's Highway is the Stella Maris Marina, a full-service marina with showers and changing rooms. Fresh seafood is the highlight of the main restaurant's rotating menus. There is a weekly rum-punch pool party, a cave party, weekly barbecues, and other lively events. **Pros:** perfect location to relax; top-quality scuba diving and bonefishing; outstanding service. **Cons:** the property is so vast that you will need a car or a bicycle to get around. ⊠ *Stella Maris* ☎ *800/426–0466* ⊕ *www.stellamarisresort.com* ⤴ *16 rooms, 4 cottages, 6 houses* ⌂ *In-room: no TV. In-hotel: restaurant, bar, pool, tennis court, gym, beach, water sports* ⍭ *Multiple meal plans.*

NIGHTLIFE

Long Island Breeze Resort. There are weekend dances and local bands on the pool deck here. Admission is $10. ☎ *242/338–0170.*

Stella Maris Resort. This resort often has local bands on Friday or Saturday nights. Admission is $10. Every Thursday night is their Rum Punch Party, which includes rum punch, conch fritters, and dinner. Cost is $55 for nonguests. Call ahead to make reservations. ☎ *242/338–2050.*

SHOPPING

Bonafide Bonefishing. This is actually a tackle shop, but it also sells fresh-brewed coffee, cold drinks and snacks, apparel, and jewelry. ⊠ *Stella Maris Resort* ☎ *242/338–2025.*

Cape Santa Maria Resort. There is a small gift shop here with clothes, swimsuits, native straw works, island books, souvenirs, and sundries. ☎ *242/338–5273.*

Harding's Supply Center. Harding's Supply Center is well stocked and sells food, toiletries, and supplies. ⊠ *Salt Pond* ☎ *242/338–0042.*

Hillside Supply. Here you can find food, toiletries, and supplies. In the back of the store you will find just about anything, from snorkeling gear and ice chests to towels. ⊠ *Salt Pond* ☎ *242/338–0022.*

Tingums. Tingums is Bahamian for "I don't know what to call it." This cute gift shop sells clothing, books, and toiletries. ⊠ *Stella Maris Resort* ☎ *242/338–2050.*

SPORTS AND THE OUTDOORS

DIVING AND SNORKELING **Conception Island Wall** is an excellent wall dive, with hard and soft coral, plus interesting sponge formations. The **M/V *Comberbach*,** a 103-foot British freighter built in 1948, sank off Cape Santa Maria in 1984, and was scuttled by the Stella Maris Resort in 1986 to create an artificial reef and excellent dive site. Take a guided diving excursion to **Shark's Reef** and watch a scuba master safely feed dozens of sharks.

Cape Santa Maria Resort. Cape Santa Maria Resort uses expert divers and guides for water-sport adventures. ☎ *242/338–5273.*

Stella Maris Resort. This resort offers diving and snorkeling trips. ☎ *242/338–2050.*

FISHING **Cape Santa Maria Resort.** Cape Santa Maria Resort arranges deep-sea fishing and bonefishing. ☎ *242/338–5273.*

James "Docky" Smith. Bonafide Bonefishing's James "Docky" Smith is highly regarded as one of the best bonefishing guides in the Bahamas. He does full- and half-day bonefishing excursions, as well as reef-fishing trips. He is also an expert fly-casting instructor. Book well in advance. His operation is based out of the Bonafide tackle shop at Stella Maris, which rents conventional and fly-fishing gear, prepares snacks and box lunches, and sells a range of tackle, clothing, and flies. ☎ *242/338–2025* ⊕ *www.bonafidebonefishing.com.*

Stella Maris Resort. Stella Maris Resort arranges deep-sea fishing trips with well-trained guides. ☎ *242/338–2050.*

SOUTH LONG ISLAND: DEADMAN'S CAY TO GORDON'S

The most populated area on the island is **Deadman's Cay**. This umbrella central settlement covers all the communities stretching from **Gray's** to the north to **Scrub Hill**, and is the social, economic, and educational center of the island. The Deadman's Cay airport is in Lower Deadman's Cay and the infamous Max's Conch Bar is only a short distance to the south. Shops, restaurants, and bars dot this area, along with amazing views of the Bahamas Banks.

Past Scrub Hill is **Dean's Blue Hole**, the deepest blue hole in the world. Free-diving contests, without use of any breathing apparatus, are held here each year, and divers come from all over the world to challenge the record. Fantastic snorkeling can be had around the blue hole's edges.

Clarence Town is the capital of Long Island and home to the Flying Fish Marina in one of the prettiest and safest harbors in the Out Islands. Situated at the top of the highest hills in town are the twin-towered Moorish style churches of **St. Paul's** and **St. Peter's**, designed by Father Jerome. Clarence Town is the last large settlement on the south end of the island.

South of Clarence Town you will find **Galloway Landing**, a long stretch of amazing beaches and saltwater canals dug into the limestone hills by the now defunct Diamond Salt Mine. From here to **Gordon's** is the most undeveloped stretch of the island. Plantation ruins are at **Dunmone's**, secluded beaches at **Ford's**, and the incredible pink flamingos at Gordon's.

EXPLORING

Cartwright's Cave. Cartwright's Cave features stalactites and stalagmites in a large cave system that eventually leads to the sea. The cave has never been completely explored, although Arawak drawings were found on one wall. For guided cave tours, contact Leonard Cartwright. Leonard will customize a tour to suit your needs, although he is often difficult to reach by phone, so be persistent. ⊠ *Hamilton's* ☎ *242/337–0235.*

Fodor's Choice
★
Dean's Blue Hole. Dean's Blue Hole is the most amazing sight on the island. It is the deepest blue hole in the world (663 feet) and is surrounded by hills and a superb beach. The shallows at the edge of the hole are perfect for snorkeling, and tropical fish of all varieties can be spotted. Diving contests, without use of any breathing apparatus, are held here each year, and divers come from all over the world to challenge the record.

To find the Blue Hole, watch for the well-labeled white walls on your left (east) after passing through Scrub Hill. Go through the entrance and drive over a steep hill. At the bottom you will find two dirt roads going to the right. Both will lead to the site, but take the second one, which is sandier and the easiest to follow. If you end up at a gazebo, this is not the place. Get back on the sandy road; you are just about there.

The Long Island Museum and Library. The Long Island Museum and Library is housed in a beautiful little pink cottage with native trees in front. Patty will share the history of Long Island and show you artifacts. You don't need to stay long, but it is worth a short stop. Native wares and books on Long Island are for sale, along with note cards and a Bahamian calendar created by locals. ⊠ *Buckley's* ☎ *242/337–0500* 🖼 *$3* ⊙ *Closed Sun. and holidays.*

St. Paul's. The twin, towered Moorish churches of St. Paul's (Anglican) and St. Peter's (Catholic) are two of the island's most celebrated landmarks. Father Jerome, often referred to as the hermit of Cat Island, built St. Paul's when he was Anglican; later, after converting to Catholicism, he built St. Peter's. The architecture of the two churches is similar to the Spanish missions in California. The churches are open sporadically, but tours are available through the ministry of tourism.

WHERE TO EAT

¢
BAHAMIAN
★
✕ **Max's Conch Bar and Grill.** This island treasure is known up and down the island by locals and visitors alike. You can sit all day on a stool at this colorful roadside gazebo, nursing beers and nibbling on conch salad prepared right before your eyes, and become a veritable expert on Long Island and its people. Such is the draw of this laid-back watering hole. Be sure to try the conch fritters, steamed snapper, and bean soup, or any of the daily specials such as pot roast and stuffed breadfruit. ⊠ *Deadman's Cay* ☎ *242/337–0056* ⊕ *www.maxconchbar.com.*

$
SEAFOOD
Fodor's Choice
★
✕ **Rowdy Boys Bar and Grill.** Don't let the name scare you—it's named after the Knowles family's well-known construction company. Locals and visitors congregate here for the good food and lively scene. Breakfast, lunch, and dinner feature authentic Bahamian and American fare. The restaurant overlooks the roaring Atlantic, with a pool and bar on the large outside deck. ⊠ *Clarence Town* ☎ *242/337–3062.*

$
BAHAMIAN
✕ **Seaside Village at Jerry Wells.** Located at the end of Jerry Wells Road, this cozy little restaurant sits on the ocean and offers friendly service and good food. Seafood specialties include lobster, grouper, and conch. Dine inside or around the Mango Tree Bar for ocean views. ⊠ *Deadman's Cay* ☎ *242/337–0119* ▭ *No credit cards.*

A gray shark circles a boat off Long Island.

WHERE TO STAY

$ **Ellen's Inn.** Right on Queen's Highway in Deadman's Cay, this small B&B is just a few minutes from the airport. The air-conditioned rooms are small but clean and comfortable, and the location is convenient for exploring the island; shops and restaurants are within walking distance. The lounge is always open with an adjacent kitchen where you can prepare coffee or food, and breakfast is included in the price of the room. Manager Olivia Turnquest will pick you up at the airport and can arrange a rental car for $65 per day; fishing trips can be arranged. Because of its location, divers from all over the world often stay here to compete in the free-diving competition at Dean's Blue Hole. **Pros:** friendly and accommodating service; great value; convenient location. **Cons:** right on Queen's Highway; no beach. ⊠ *Deadman's Cay* ☏ *242/337–1086* ⟿ *9 rooms* ⟁ *In-hotel: laundry facilities.*

$ **Gems at Paradise.** Situated on 16 acres of pink-sand beachfront property overlooking the low-lying Clem Cay and the Atlantic Ocean as far as the eye can see, this resort occupies a rare and superb site. Owner and manager Shavonne Darville has created a quality resort with lovely furnishings and special features. All balcony rooms and condos are sea-view, and have either king, queen, or two twin beds. The condos have full kitchens. Diving, kayaks, and deep-sea, reef, and bonefishing are available. It is highly recommended that you rent a car if you stay here. **Pros:** drop-dead-gorgeous location and views; easy access to fishing and water sports; car rentals available on-site. **Cons:** many rooms have stairs; no on-site restaurant. ⊠ *Clarence Town* ☏ *242/337–3016* ⊕ *www.gemsatparadise.com* ⟿ *8 rooms, 2 condos* ⟁ *In-room: kitchen. In-hotel: bar, beach, water sports* ⫧⊙⫧ *All meals.*

8

DID YOU KNOW?

"The sand is Bora Bora soft. The water is so warm and so shallow, I can walk a hundred yards from the shore. It's gorgeous." —DavefromCA

$ 🛏 **Winter Haven.** This small inn overlooks the dark-blue waters of the lively Atlantic in Clarence Town. The colorful little two-story houses have eight rooms, six with king beds and two with two doubles. There are no kitchen facilities in the rooms, but a restaurant, serving three meals a day, is just steps away. The Flying Fish Marina and its Outer Edge Grill is nearby. Transportation to and from the Deadman's Cay airport is provided, and a rental car can be arranged, along with boat rental and guides for fly-fishing, bonefishing, or excursions. **Pros:** great location; on-site restaurant. **Cons:** need to go to nearby BatelCo to make long-distance calls; you must rent a car for exploring. ⊠ *Clarence Town* 🕾 *242/337–3062, 866/348–5935* ⊕ *www.winterhavenbahamas. com* ⤳ *8 rooms* ⚘ *In-room: no TV. In-hotel: restaurant, pool, beach.*

NIGHTLIFE

Midway Bar and Restaurant. Midway Bar and Restaurant has erratic hours, but is open Tuesday through Saturday. Visit on Friday for happy hour; Saturday is for karaoke, which is a hoot. The entertainment starts after 9 pm. ⊠ *Off Queen's Hwy., The Bight* 🕾 *242/337–7345* ⊙ *Tues.–Sat.*

SHOPPING

Sea Winds Super Mart and Supplies. This is one of the largest grocery stores on the island, and has everything you need for a picnic or to stock your vacation kitchen. Toiletries and other supplies are available. There are several other shops in this "strip mall," including Yukon Jack's Wholesale and Retail Liquor. ⊠ *Off Queen's Hwy., Petty's* 🕾 *242/337–0212.*

Under the Sun. Under the Sun has just about everything its name suggests, from a coffee shop with used books, to fishing and boating equipment. ⊠ *Off Queen's Hwy., Mangrove Bush* 🕾 *242/337–0199.*

SPORTS AND THE OUTDOORS

FISHING **Samuel Knowles Bonefish Adventures.** For more than 10 years Samuel
★ Knowles Bonefish Adventures has drawn a loyal following of saltwater anglers from around the globe, and they have earned a reputation as one of the most popular bonefishing programs in the islands. The main attraction is their expert guides, who are Long Island natives, fourth- and fifth-generation bonefishermen, and champions of four of the five Bahamas bonefishing tournaments. Their location at the center of Long Island's pristine shoreline, with unique landlocked flats, creates an unforgettable fishing adventure for all ages and experience levels. ⊠ *Deadman's Cay* 🕾 *242/337–0246* ⊕ *www.deadmansbones.com.*

Winter Haven/The Rowdy Boys Bar and Grill. Winter Haven/The Rowdy Boys Bar and Grill organizes fishing and boating adventures. 🕾 *242/337–3062.*

SCUBA DIVING **Dean's Blue Hole.** This is lauded by locals as the world's deepest ocean hole. It's surrounded by a powder-beach cove.

SNORKELING **Bahamas Discovery Quest.** Bahamas Discovery Quest at Deadman's Cay offers full- and half-day snorkeling trips, along with many others (sponging, crabbing, cruising, hiking, beaching and shelling, deep-sea fishing, deep drop, and reef fishing). 🕾 *242/472–2605* ⊕ *www. bahamasdiscoveryquest.com.*

CROOKED AND ACKLINS ISLANDS

Updated
by Cheryl
Blackerby

Crooked Island is 30 mi long and surrounded by 45 mi of barrier reefs that are ideal for diving and fishing. They slope from 4 feet to 50 feet, then plunge to 3,600 feet in the **Crooked Island Passage**, once one of the most important sea roads for ships following the southerly route from the West Indies to the Old World. If you drive up to **the Cove** settlement, you get an uninterrupted view of the region all the way to the narrow passage at **Lovely Bay** between Crooked Island and Acklins Island. Two lighthouses alert mariners that they are nearing the islands.

The tepid controversy continues today over whether Columbus actually set foot on Crooked Island and its southern neighbor, Acklins Island. What's known for sure is that Columbus sailed close enough to Crooked Island to get a whiff of its native herbs. Soon after, the two islands became known as the "Fragrant Islands." Today Crooked and Acklins islands are known as remote and unspoiled destinations for fishermen, divers, and sailors who value solitude. Here phone service can be intermittent, Internet connections can be hard to find, and some residents depend on generators for electricity. Even credit-card use is a relatively new development. The first known settlers didn't arrive until the late 18th century, when Loyalists brought slaves from the United States to work on cotton plantations. About 400 people, mostly fishermen and farmers, live on each island today. Two plantation-era sites are preserved by the Bahamas National Trust on Crooked Island's northern end, which overlooks Crooked Island Passage that separates the cay from Long Island. Spanish guns have been discovered at one ruin, **Marine Farm**, which may have been used as a fortification. An old structure, **Hope Great House**, has orchards and gardens.

8

GETTING HERE AND AROUND

AIR TRAVEL

Crooked and Acklins have one airport each: Colonel Hill Airport (CRI) on Crooked Island and Spring Point Airport (AXP) on Acklins Island. Bahamasair flies from Nassau to Crooked and Acklins islands twice a week. Crooked Island Lodge picks up its guests flying into Colonel Hill with prior arrangement. The private 3,500-foot airstrip at Crooked Island Lodge is complimentary for hotel guests. Nonguests pay landing and parking fees. This airstrip is most convenient for private and charter flights if you're staying in the area of Pittstown and Landrail Point. Ask your hotel to make arrangements for picking you up at the airport in case there are no taxis.

Hotels will arrange airport transportation. Generally someone from even the smallest hotel will meet you at the airport, but taxis are usually waiting on flights.

Airport Information Acklins Island Spring Point Airport ☎ *242/344–3666.* **Crooked Island Colonel Hill Airport** ☎ *242/344–2599.*

BOAT TRAVEL

Mail boats that bring supplies to the island each week make an adventurous mode of transportation. You'll ride with groceries, large and small appliances, automobiles, and sometimes even livestock. All boats depart from Potter's Cay in Nassau. Schedules change frequently. M/V

Vi Nais sails Wednesday to Acklins Island, Crooked Island, and Long Cay, returning Sunday (30 hours; $90 one way).

Ferry service between Cove Landing, Crooked Island, and Lovely Bay, Acklins Island usually operates twice daily on varying schedules between 9 and 4.

Boat and Ferry Information Dockmaster's Office ☎ *242/393–1064.*

CAR TRAVEL Reserve a car through your hotel prior to your arrival, but even with a reservation be prepared for the possibility of not having one. Gas is also not always available on the island, as it's delivered by mail boat, which are sometimes delayed. Fortunately, it's easy to get a ride to most places with locals.

EXPLORING

Bird Rock Lighthouse. The sparkling white Bird Rock Lighthouse (built in 1872) in the north once guarded the Crooked Island Passage. The rotating flash from its 115-foot tower still welcomes pilots and sailors to the Crooked Island Lodge, currently the islands' best lodging facility.

Castle Island Lighthouse. The Castle Island Lighthouse (built in 1867), at Acklins Island's southern tip, formerly served as a beacon for pirates who used to retreat there after attacking ships.

WHERE TO STAY

$ **Casuarina Villas.** Five modern cottages sit on a ½-mi stretch of white-sand beach between Landrail Point and Pittstown Point Landings. Each has a full kitchen, satellite TV, and a western-facing deck for watching the magnificent sunsets. A local market, gas station, and two restaurants are 2 mi away in Landrail Point, and transportation can be provided. The management will treat you like family. It can arrange meals in your cottage with advance notice, find you a rental car, or set up a diving excursion. It can also book you with the top fly-fishing guides on the island. **Pros:** beachfront location; spacious economical accommodations; great place to hang out, fish, and relax. **Cons:** you need to arrange transportation to do anything; take plenty of insect repellent. ⊠ *Landrail Point, Crooked Island* ☎ *242/344–2197* ⊕ *www.crookedisland.biz* ⤶ *5 cottages* ⟨ *In-room: kitchen. In-hotel: beach, water sports.*

$$ **Crooked Island Lodge at Pittstown Point.** A true anglers' paradise, this is one of the best flats, inshore, and offshore fishing destinations in the Bahamas and Caribbean. Shaded by coconut palms, the remote property on Crooked Island's northwestern tip has miles of open beach at its doorstep and unobstructed views of the emerald water surrounding Bird Rock Lighthouse. Rooms, renovated in 2009, are motel-style units; ask for an ocean view. The main lodge—which has a restaurant, bar, and library—once housed the Bahamas' first post office. Captain Robbie Gibson leads snorkeling, diving, reef, and offshore fishing adventures. All-inclusive bonefishing and offshore fishing packages are available with top guides ranging from $1,350 for four-day packages to $3,000 for a week. **Pros:** mind-bending ocean and beachfront location; good on-site restaurant and bar; private airstrip on the property for easy access. **Cons:** take a lot of insect repellent and have it on when you step out of the plane; don't go unless you want remote, private, and

DID YOU KNOW?

Crooked and Acklins islands each have a lighthouse. Bird Rock Lighthouse (pictured) is the newer of the two, built in 1872.

nothing to do but fish and relax. ⊠ *Portland Harbour, Pittstown Point Landings, Crooked Island* ☎ *242/344–2430* ⊕ *www.pittstownpoint. com* ⇆ *12 rooms* ⌂ *In-room: no TV. In-hotel: restaurant, bar, beach, water sports, business center.*

SPORTS AND THE OUTDOORS

FISHING   Crooked Island has a number of highly regarded bonefishing guides with quality boats and fly-fishing tackle. Most can be booked through the Crooked Island Lodge, but the guides also take direct bookings. Be aware that telephone service to and from Crooked and Acklins islands is not always operational.

You can stalk the elusive and swift bonefish in the shallows, or go deep-sea fishing for wahoo, sailfish, and amberjack.

Michael Carroll (☎ *242/344–2037*), **Derrick Ingraham** (☎ *242/344–2023*), **Elton "Bonefish Shakey" McKinney** (☎ *242/344–2038*), **Randy McKinney** (☎ *242/344–2326*), **Jeff Moss** (☎ *242/344–2029*), and **Clinton** and **Kenneth "The Earlybird" Scavalla** (☎ *242/344–2011 or 242/422–3596*) are all knowledgeable professional guides. **Captain Robbie Gibson** (☎ *242/344– 2007*) has a 30-foot Century boat and is the most experienced reef and offshore fishing captain on Crooked Island, where astounding fishing in virgin waters is the rule. Many wahoo weighing more than 100 pounds are landed each season with his assistance. Robbie's personal best wahoo is a whopping 180 pounds. He's also a skilled guide for anglers pursuing tuna, marlin, sharks, barracuda, jacks, snapper, and grouper.

SCUBA DIVING   **The Wall.** The Wall starts at around 45 feet deep and goes down thousands more. It's about 50 yards off Crooked Island's coast and follows the shoreline for many miles.

Captain Robbie Gibson. Captain Robbie Gibson offers scuba diving, snorkeling, and day tours. ☎ *242/344–2007.*

INAGUA

Updated by Cheryl Blackerby

Inagua does indeed feel like the southernmost island in the Bahamas' 700 mi-long chain. Just 50 mi from Cuba, it's not easy to get to—only three flights a week from Nassau, and you must overnight there to catch the 9 am flight.

At night the lonely beacon of the **Inagua Lighthouse** sweeps the sky over the southern part of the island and the only community, **Matthew Town**, as it has since 1870. The coastline is rocky and rugged, with little coves of golden sand. The terrain is mostly flat and covered with palmetto palms, wind-stunted buttonwoods, and mangroves ringing ponds and a huge inland saltwater lake. Parts of it look very much like the Florida Everglades, only without the alligators and poisonous snakes.

Matthew Town feels like the Wild West, with sun-faded wooden buildings and vintage and modern trucks usually parked in front. It's obviously not a tourist mecca, but it's a shame that more people don't make it here. They are missing one of the great spectacles of the western hemisphere: the 70,000-some West Indian pink-scarlet flamingos that nest here alongside rare Bahama parrots and roseate spoonbills. If you're not a bird lover, there's extraordinary diving and fishing off the virgin reefs.

Although there are few tourists, this remote island is prosperous. An unusual climate of little rainfall and continual trade winds creates rich salt ponds. The Morton Salt Company harvests a million tons of salt annually at its Matthew Town factory, where most of the 1,000 Inaguans work.

GETTING HERE AND AROUND

AIR TRAVEL Inagua has one airport: Matthew Town Airport (IGA). Bahamasair has flights on Monday, Wednesday, and Friday from Nassau. Hotels will arrange airport transportation. Generally someone from even the smallest hotel will meet you at the airport, but taxis sometimes meet incoming flights.

Airport Information Inagua Matthew Town Airport ☎ *242/339–1680, 242/339–1415.*

BOAT TRAVEL Mail boats that bring supplies to the island each week make an adventurous mode of transportation. You'll ride with groceries, large and small appliances, automobiles, and sometimes even livestock. All boats depart from Potter's Cay in Nassau. Schedules change frequently. The *Lady Matilda,* which rotates with the *Rosalind,* leaves Tuesday and returns Sunday (36 hours; $100 one way).

Boat and Ferry Information Dockmaster's Office ☎ *242/393–1064.*

CAR TRAVEL You can rent a car for about $80 a day, but there are few rental cars on the island, so call in advance. If you are driving outside Matthew Town, you will need an SUV or truck to navigate dirt roads. If you plan to stay in Matthew Town, you can easily walk everywhere.

Car-Rental Contact Ingraham Rent-A-Car ☎ *242/339–1677.*

EXPLORING

Erickson Museum and Library. The Erickson Museum and Library is a welcome part of the community, particularly the surprisingly well-stocked, well-equipped library. The Morton Company built the complex in the former home of the Erickson family, who came to Inagua in 1934 to run the salt giant. The museum displays the island's history, to which the company is inextricably tied. The posted hours are not always that regular. The Bahamas National Trust office and the office of the Inagua National Park are also here, but hours are unpredictable. ⊠ *Gregory St. on the northern edge of town across from the police station* ☎ *242/339– 1863* 🖅 *Free* ☉ *Weekdays 9–1 and 3–6, Sat. 9–1.*

Inagua Lighthouse. From Southwest Point, a mile or so south of Matthew Town, you can see Cuba's coast—slightly more than 50 mi west—on a clear day from atop Inagua Lighthouse, built in 1870 in response to the number of shipwrecks on offshore reefs. It's a grueling climb—the last 10 feet are on a ladder—but the view of the rugged coastline and Matthew Town is worth the effort. Look to the west to see the hazy mountains of Cuba. Be sure to sign the guest book just inside the door to the lighthouse. ⊠ *Gregory St., 1 mi south of Matthew Town* 🖀 *No phone.*

Morton Salt Company. Marveling at the salt process lures few visitors to Inagua, but the Morton Salt Company is omnipresent on the island: it

Deep sea fishing in the Southern Out Islands

has more than 47 square mi of crystallizing ponds and reservoirs. More than a million tons of salt are produced every year for such industrial uses as salting icy streets. (More is produced when the northeastern United States has a bad winter.) Even if you decide not to tour the facility, you can see the mountains of salt, locally called the Salt Alps, glistening in the sun from the plane. In an unusual case of industry assisting its environment, the crystallizers provide a feeding ground for the flamingos. As the water evaporates, the concentration of brine shrimp in the ponds increases, and the flamingos feed on these animals. Free tours are available by reservation at the salt plant in Matthew Town. ☎ *242/339–1300*.

WHERE TO EAT AND STAY

¢ ✕ **Cozy Corner.** Cheerful and loud, this lunch spot—locals just call it
BAHAMIAN Cozy's—is the best on the island. It has a pool table and a large seating area with a bar. Stop in for a chat with locals over a Kalik and a Bahamian conch burger. Cozy's also serves excellent island-style dinners on request—steamed crawfish, grilled snapper, baked chicken and fries, homemade slaw, macaroni and cheese, and fresh johnnycake. If it's not open when you stop by, you might still be able to get food and a drink if you ask. ⊠ *Matthew Town* ☎ *242/339–1440* ▭ *No credit cards* ☉ *Closed Sun.*

¢ ▥ **Enrika's Inn.** Opened in August 2009, this inn is a small complex of two two-story Bahamian-colonial-style buildings with inviting verandas leading to five guest rooms in each building. One building has a full kitchen shared by guests, so if you need a kitchen, request that one; the other has a meeting room. Rooms are spacious and modern and exceptionally tidy with modern bathrooms and flat-screen TVs. Manager Evamae Palacious picks up guests at the airport. **Pros:** inexpensive; efficient and friendly service; walking distance to town and across the street from Champ's Chicken takeout and RJ's convenience store. **Cons:** no pool or beach views. ⊠ *Victoria St., Matthew Town* ☎ *242/339–2127* ⟿ *15 rooms* ⬨ *In-room: kitchen* ⊟ *No credit cards.*

¢ ⛶ **The Main House.** The Morton Salt Company operates this small, affordable guesthouse. On the second of two floors, air-conditioned rooms share a sitting area with couches and a telephone. Rooms are spotless and spacious with dark-wood furnishings, Masonite-paneled walls, and floral-print drapes and spreads. The green-and-white hotel is right in Matthew Town, behind the grocery store and directly across the street from the island's power plant. There is a dining room, which may be the only restaurant that serves breakfast on the island. **Pros:** inexpensive; clean; walking distance to a couple of bars and restaurants. **Cons:** no Internet service; power plant can be noisy. ⊠ *Kortwright St., Matthew Town* ☎ *242/339–1266* ⊕ *www.inaguamainhouse.com* ⟿ *6 rooms* ⬨ *In-hotel: restaurant* ⊟ *No credit cards.*

$ ⛶ **Sunset Apartments.** This is your only option for a room with a water view, and a great place to watch sunsets. The two spacious apartments sit next to a rocky shoreline on Matthew Town's southern side. The cement units all have modern Caribbean-style terra-cotta-tile floors, rattan furniture, small terraces, a picnic area, and a gas grill. At low tide there's a nice sandy beach next to the apartments, and about a five-minute walk away is a small secluded beach called the Swimming Hole. Ezzard Cartwright, the owner, is the only fly-fishing guide on the island. He's usually out working, so calling after 7 pm Bahamas time is the best chance to reach him. The apartments are usually fully booked October to June, so reserve early. **Pros:** great place for bonefishing; Ezzard is a wonderful host and a top fly-fishing guide. **Cons:** no Internet service; nothing to do but fish and bird-watch; you need to pay in cash. ⊠ *Matthew Town* ☎ *242/339–1362* ⟿ *2 apartments* ⬨ *In-room: kitchen. In-hotel: beach* ⊟ *No credit cards.*

NIGHTLIFE

After Work Bar. This bar on Gregory Street (the main street) next to Kiwanis Park is the most popular hangout in town and a good place to meet the mayor and other town notables. There's food such as fried chicken and sandwiches on weekends.

The Fish Fry. A collection of fish shacks next to the water is open on weekends, with DJs occasionally in the covered pavilion next door.

SPORTS AND THE OUTDOORS

FISHING **Ezzard Cartwright.** Inagua has one bonefishing and deep-sea fishing guide and he's legendary—Ezzard Cartwright, who has been featured in outdoors and fishing magazines and on ESPN Outdoors shows. Call him if you're a hard-core fisherman who wants to fish for eight hours a day. He's usually booked from January to June for bonefishing, so reserve early. ☎ *242/453–1475.*

8

Turks and Caicos Islands

WORD OF MOUTH

"If you like a gorgeous 12 mile beach, beautiful condo resorts, and the most amazing turquoise water—then check out Turks and Caicos and the main island of Providenciales. You can do great snorkeling right from the beach or take an excursion to other reefs, and even explore some of the other islands by boat."

—sunblockstock

WELCOME TO TURKS AND CAICOS ISLANDS

TOP REASONS TO GO

★ **Get away from it all:** Even on well-developed Provo, there are still miles of deserted beaches without any footprints or beach umbrellas in sight.

★ **Explore under the sea:** A large coral reef system is among the world's top dive sites.

★ **Go back in time:** Island-hopping beyond the beaten path will give you a feel for the past in the present.

★ **Star-gaze:** Destination spas, penthouse suites, and exclusive villas and resorts make celebrity-spotting a popular sport.

★ **Go fish:** The island chain offers excellent fishing and boating opportunities among its uninhabited coves and cays.

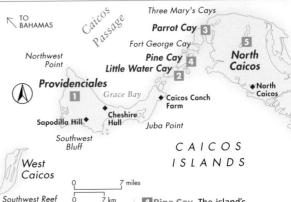

1 Providenciales. A major offshore banking center, Provo is the most developed island in the chain. Land-based pursuits don't get much more taxing than teeing off at the Provo Golf and Country Club or sunset-watching from the seaside terrace of a laid-back resort.

2 Little Water Cay. This small, uninhabited cay is a protected area under the Turks & Caicos National Trust. On these 150 acres are two trails, small lakes, red mangroves, and an abundance of native plants.

3 Parrot Cay. Once said to be a hideout for pirate Calico Jack Rackham and his lady cohorts Mary Read and Anne Bonny, the 1,000-acre cay is now the site of an ultra-exclusive hideaway resort.

4 Pine Cay. The island's 2½-mi-long (4-km-long) beach is among the most beautiful in the archipelago. The 800-acre private island is home to a secluded resort and around 37 private residences.

5 North Caicos. Thanks to abundant rainfall, this 41-square-mi (106-square-km) island is the lushest of the Turks and Caicos. Bird lovers can see a large flock of flamingos here, anglers can find shallow creeks full of bonefish, and history buffs can visit the ruins of a Loyalist plantation.

6 Middle Caicos. At 48 square mi (124 square km) and with fewer than 300 residents, this is the largest and least developed of the inhabited islands. A limestone ridge runs to about 125 feet above sea level, creating dramatic cliffs on the north shore and a cave system farther inland.

ATLANTIC OCEAN

Spanish Point

Highas Cay
Juniper
Hole   Platico
        Point
Haulover Point

6
Middle Caicos
       Middle
       Caicos
Ocean   Hole   Drum Point
Vine   Toll Crawl   East Caicos
Point   Point
Long Bay
Joe Grant Cay

Big Southern
Bush
Big   Middle Creek
Cameron Cay   Cay
Sail Rock Island
Horse Cay   7
South Caicos ◆   **South Caicos**
                 High Point   Columbus Passage
Six Hill
Cays   Long Cay

Fish Cays

Little Ambergris   Big Ambergris Cay
Cay
        AMBERGRIS CAYS

        SEAL CAYS
White Cay   Bush Cay
              Shot Cay

**Grand Turk
Island**

8
                    ◆Grand Turk
                      Gibb's Cay
**TURKS   Cotton   Long Cay
ISLANDS**   Cay
                           East Cay
        9
Salt Cay   Toney Rock
South Point

                Mouchoir Passage

Big Sand
Cay

9

GETTING ORIENTED

Only 10 of these 40 islands between the Bahamas and Haiti are inhabited. From developed Provo to sleepy Grand Turk to sleepier South Caicos, the islands offer miles of undeveloped beaches, crystal-clear water, and laid-back luxury resorts.

7 South Caicos. This 8½-square-mi (21-square-km) island was once an important salt producer; today it's the heart of the fishing industry. Nature prevails, with long, white beaches, jagged bluffs, quiet backwater bays, and salt flats.

8 Grand Turk. Just 7 mi (11 km) long and a little more than 1 mi (1½ km) wide, this island, the capital and seat of the Turks and Caicos government, has been a longtime favorite destination for divers.

9 Salt Cay. Fewer than 100 people live on this 2½-square-mi (6-square-km) dot of land, bordered by beaches where weathered green and blue sea glass and pretty shells often wash ashore.

TURKS AND CAICOS ISLANDS PLANNER

Logistics

Getting to the Turks and Caicos: Several major airlines fly nonstop to Providenciales from the United States. If you're going to one of the smaller islands, you'll usually need to make a connection in Provo. All international flights arrive at Providenciales International Airport (PLS), but you can hop over to the other islands from there.

Hassle Factor: Low–high, depending on the island and your home airport.

On the Ground: You can find taxis at the airports, and most resorts provide pick-up service as well. Taxi fares are fairly reasonable on Provo and Grand Turk; on the smaller islands transfers can cost more, since gas is much more expensive.

Getting Around on the Island: If you are staying on Provo, you may find it useful to have a car, since the island is so large and the resorts so far-flung, if only for a few days of exploring or to get away from your hotel for dinner. On Grand Turk you can rent a car, but you probably won't need to.

Getting to the Turks and Caicos

Nonstop Flights: You can fly nonstop from Atlanta (Delta), Boston (American and JetBlue), Charlotte (US Airways), Miami (American), New York–JFK (American and JetBlue), Newark–EWR(Continental), and Philadelphia (US Airways).

Other Flights: Although carriers and schedules can vary seasonally, there are also several connecting flights to Providenciales as well as flights from other parts of the Caribbean on Air Turks & Caicos, which flies to some of the smaller islands in the chain from Providenciales. There are also flights from Nassau on Bahamas Air.

Local Airline Contacts: Air Turks & Caicos (☎ 649/941–5481 ⊕ www.airturksandcaicos.com). **American Airlines** (☎ 649/946–4948 or 800/433–7300). **Bahamas Air** (☎ 242/377–5505 in Nassau, 800/222–4262 ⊕ up.bahamasair.com). **Caicos Express** (☎ 649/243–0237). **Continental Airlines** (☎ 800/231–0856 ⊕ www.Continental.com). **Delta** (☎ 800/241–4141). **JetBlue** (☎ 800/Jetblue [538–2583] ⊕ www.JetBlue.com). **US Airways** (☎ 800/622–1015).

Airports: The main gateways into the Turks and Caicos Islands are Providenciales International Airport (PLS) and Grand Turk International Airport (GDT). There are smaller airports on Grand Turk (GDT), North Caicos (NCS), Middle Caicos (MDS), South Caicos (XSC), and Salt Cay (SLX). All have paved runways in good condition. Even if you are going on to other islands in the chain, you will probably stop in Provo first for customs, then take a domestic flight onward.

Ferries: Daily scheduled ferry service from **Caribbean Cruisin'** (✉ Walkin Marina, Leeward, Providenciales ☎ 649/946–5406 or 649/231–4191 ⊕ tcimall.tc/northcaicos/images/ferryservice.pdf) began in 2007 between Provo and North Caicos, with several departures from Walkin Marina in Leeward. **Salt Cay Ferry** (☎ 649/946–6909 ⊕ www.turksandcaicoswhalewatching.com) offers a twice-weekly ferry from Salt Cay to Grand Turk (weather permitting).

Getting Around the Turks and Caicos

Driving: Driving here is on the left side of the road, British-style; when pulling out into traffic, remember to look to your right. Give way to anyone entering a roundabout, as roundabouts are still a relatively new concept in the Turks and Caicos; stop even if you are on what appears to be the primary road. The maximum speed is 40 mph (64 kph), 20 mph (30 kph) through settlements, and limits, as well as the use of seat belts, are enforced.

Car Rentals: If you are staying on Provo, you may find it useful to have a car, since the island is so large and the resorts are so far-flung, if only for a few days of exploring or to get away from your hotel for dinner. On Grand Turk you can rent a car, but you probably won't need to. Car- and jeep-rental rates average $39 to $80 per day on Provo, plus a $15 surcharge per rental as a government tax. Reserve well ahead of time during the peak winter season. Most agencies offer free mileage and airport pickup service. Avis and Budget have offices on the islands. You might also try local agencies such as Grace Bay Car Rentals, Rent a Buggy, and Tropical Auto Rentals in Provo. Pelican Car Rentals is on North Caicos.

Car-Rental Agencies: Avis (✉ *Providenciales* ☎ *649/946–4705* ⊕ *www.avis.tc*). **Budget** (✉ *Providenciales* ☎ *649/946–4079* ⊕ *www.provo.net/Budget/*). **Grace Bay Car Rentals** (✉ *Providenciales* ☎ *649/941–8500* ⊕ *www.gracebaycarrentals.com*). **Pelican Car Rentals** (✉ *North Caicos* ☎ *649/241–8275*). **Rent a Buggy** (✉ *Providenciales* ☎ *649/946–4158* ⊕ *www.rentabuggy.tc*). **Scooter Bob's** (✉ *Turtle Cove, Providenciales* ☎ *649/946–4684* ⊕ *www.provo.net/Scooter/*). **Tony's Car Rental** (✉ *Grand Turk* ☎ *649/946–1879* ⊕ *www.tonyscarrental.com*). **Tropical Auto Rentals** (✉ *Providenciales* ☎ *649/946–5300* ⊕ *www.tropicalautorentaltci.com*).

Taxis: You can find taxis at the airports, and most resorts provide pickup service as well. A trip between Provo's airport and most major hotels runs about $12 per person. On Grand Turk a trip from the airport to Cockburn Town is about $8; it's $8 to $15 to hotels outside town on Grand Turk. Transfers can cost more on the smaller islands, where gas is much more expensive. Taxis (actually large vans) in Providenciales are metered, and rates are regulated by the government at $2 per person per mile traveled.

Taxi Companies: In Provo, call the **Provo Taxi & Bus Group** (☎ *649/946–5481*) for more information. In the family islands, taxis may not be metered, so it's usually best to try to negotiate a cost for your trip in advance.

Guided Tours

Nell's Taxi (☎ *649/231–0051*) offers taxi tours of Provo, priced between $25 and $30 for the first hour and $25 for each additional hour.

You can independently arrange day trips to Grand Turk any day of the week on **Air Turks & Caicos** (☎ *649/946–5481 or 649/946–4181* ⊕ *www.airturksandcaicos.com*), and on Friday to Salt Cay.

Island Activities

The vast majority of people come to the Turks and Caicos to relax and enjoy the clear, **turquoise water**.

The Turks and Caicos Islands are known for **luxurious hotels**

Provo has excellent **beaches,** particularly the long, soft beach along Grace Bay. If you can believe it, some of the smaller, more isolated islands have even better beaches.

Reefs are plentiful and are often close to shore, making **snorkeling** excellent. The **reef and wall diving** are among the best in the Caribbean.

The same reefs that draw colorful tropical fish draw big-game fish, so **deep-sea fishing** is also very good.

9

TURKS AND CAICOS ISLANDS PLANNER

Fast Facts	Essentials

Fast Facts

Banks and Exchange Services: The official currency on the islands is U.S. dollars. On Provo there are ATMs at all bank branches (Scotiabank and First Caribbean), at the Graceway IGA Supermarket Gourmet, and at Ports of Call shopping center. There are also Scotiabank and First Caribbean branches on Grand Turk.

Electricity: Current is suitable for all U.S. appliances (120/240 volts, 60 Hz).

Emergencies: Emergency numbers in the Turks and Caicos are ☎999 or 911.

Passport Requirements: A valid passport is required to travel by air to the Turks and Caicos. Everyone must have an ongoing or return ticket.

Weddings: The residency requirement is 24 hours, after which you can apply for a marriage license to the registrar in Grand Turk. You must present a passport, original birth certificate, and proof of current marital status, as well as a letter stating both parties' occupations, ages, addresses, and fathers' full names. No blood tests are required. License fee is $50.

Contacts: Nila Destinations Wedding Planning (☎ 649/941–4375 ⊕ www. nilavacations.com).

Essentials

Mail: There is a post office in downtown Provo at the corner of Airport Road. Stamp collectors will be interested in the wide selection of stamps sold by the **Philatelic Bureau** (☎ 649/946–1534). You'll pay 50¢ to send a postcard to the United States; letters, per half ounce, cost 60¢ to the United States. When sending a letter to the Turks and Caicos Islands, be sure to include the specific island name and "Turks and Caicos Islands, BWI" (British West Indies). There is no home delivery of mail; everyone has a post-office box. Expect postcards to take a month to get to your friends and neighbors, if they get there at all. There's a **FedEx** (☎ 649/946–4682) service on Provo.

Taxes: The departure tax is $35, and is usually included in the cost of your airline ticket. If not, it's payable only in cash or traveler's checks. Restaurants and hotels add an 11% government tax. Hotels also typically add 11% to 15% for service.

Telephones: The country code for the Turks and Caicos is 649. To call the Turks and Caicos from the United States, dial 1 plus the 10-digit number, which includes 649. Be aware that this is an international call. Calls from the islands are expensive, and many hotels add steep surcharges for long distance.

Visitor Information: The tourist offices on Grand Turk and Providenciales are open daily from 9 to 5.

Contacts: Turks & Caicos Islands Tourist Board (☎ 954/568–6588 in Fort Lauderdale, 800/241–0824 ⊕ www.turksandcaicostourism.com). **Turks & Caicos Islands Tourist Board** (✉ Front St., Cockburn Town, Grand Turk ☎ 649/946–2321 ✉ Stubbs Diamond Plaza, The Bight, Providenciales ☎ 649/946–4970 ⊕ www. turksandcaicostourism.com).

Where to Stay

The Turks and Caicos can be a fairly expensive destination. Most hotels on Providenciales are pricey, but there are some moderately priced options; most accommodations are condo-style, but not all resorts are family-friendly. You'll find several upscale properties on the outer islands—including the famous Parrot Cay—but the majority of places are smaller inns. What you give up in luxury, however, you gain back tenfold in island charm. Though the smaller islands are relatively isolated, that's arguably what makes them so attractive in the first place.

Resorts: Most of the resorts on Provo are upscale; many are condo-style, so at least you will have a well-furnished kitchen for breakfast and a few quick lunches. There are two all-inclusive resorts on Provo. A handful of other luxury resorts are on the smaller islands.

Small Inns: Aside from the exclusive luxury resorts, most of the places on the outlying islands are smaller, modest inns with relatively few amenities. Some are devoted to diving.

Villas and Condos: Villas and condos are plentiful, particularly on Provo, and usually represent a good value for families. However, you need to plan a few months in advance to get one of the better choices, less if you want to stay in a more developed condo complex.

HOTEL AND RESTAURANT PRICES

Restaurant prices are for a main course at dinner and include any taxes or service charges. Hotel prices are per night for a double room in high season, excluding taxes, service charges, and meal plans (except at all-inclusives).

WHAT IT COSTS IN U.S. DOLLARS

	¢	$	$$	$$$	$$$$
Restaurants	under $8	$8–$12	$12–$20	$20–$30	over $30
Hotels	under $150	$151–$275	$276–$375	$376–$475	over $475

When to Go

High season in Turks and Caicos runs roughly from January through March, with the usual extra-high rates during the Christmas and New Year's holiday period. Several hotels on Provo offer shoulder-season rates in April and May. During the off-season, rates are reduced substantially, as much as 40%. With bad world economies, you can find specials even during peak seasons or call resorts directly to negotiate.

There are two major festivals in the Turks and Caicos. At the end of November the **Turks & Caicos Conch Festival** offers local boat races, live music, and conch recipe competitions.

At the end of December there is the annual **Maskanoo**, which offers live bands, street vendors, fireworks, and Junkanoo parades.

9

TURKS AND CAICOS BEACHES

If you're on a quest for the world's best beaches, then Turks and Caicos is your destination. They are blessed with stunning strands and shallow waters protected by outer reefs, a combination that makes for the most amazing turquoise water.

(Above) Beach palapas on Grace Bay, Providenciales. (Opposite page bottom) Half Moon Bay at Donna Cay, off Providenciales. (Opposite page top) Sapodilla Bay, Providenciales.

Grace Bay Beach in Providenciales has the best of the best, and most of the island's resorts are clustered here. On the rare occasions that storms bring seaweed, it is quickly raked and buried. The water is protected by an outer reef, so it's often as still as glass. There is never an undertow or litter, and there are no beach vendors, so the opportunities for relaxation are optimal. Grand Turk is spoiled for choices when it comes to beach options: sunset strolls along miles of deserted beaches, picnics in secluded coves, beachcombing on the coralline sands, snorkeling around shallow coral heads close to shore, and admiring the impossibly turquoise-blue waters. There are also great beaches on several other less visited islands.

BEACH LOGISTICS

Although there is no charge for parking at any beach, come prepared. Umbrellas are provided by resorts for guests only, and resorts generally don't share with nonguests, even for a price. Grace Bay has the busiest sections of beachfront, especially at Beaches Resort and Club Med, but there are still plenty of secluded areas if you wish to explore beyond your own resort.

All the beaches of Turks and Caicos have bright white sand that's soft like baby powder. An added bonus is that no matter how hot the sun gets, your feet never burn. The sand is soft and clean, even in the water, so there is no fear of stepping on rocks or corals. Even the beach areas with corals for snorkeling have clear, clean sand for entry until you reach them.

THE CAICOS

PROVIDENCIALES

Grace Bay. Fodor's Choice The 12-mi (18-km) sweeping stretch of ivory-white, powder-soft sand on Provo's north coast is simply breathtaking, and home to migrating starfish as well as shallow snorkeling trails. The majority of Provo's beachfront resorts are along this shore, and it's the primary reason the Turks and Caicos is a world-class destination. ⊠ *Grace Bay Rd., on the north shore, Grace Bay.*

Half Moon Bay. A natural ribbon of sand linking two uninhabited cays is only inches above the sparkling turquoise waters and one of the most gorgeous beaches on the island. There are limestone cliffs to explore as well as small, private sand coves; there's even a small wreck offshore for snorkeling. It's only a short boat ride away from Provo, and most of the island's tour companies run excursions

here or simply offer a beach drop-off. These companies include Silverdeep and Caicos Dream Tours (⇨ *Boating and Sailing, in Sports and Activities*). ⊠ *15 mins from Leeward Marina, between Pine Cay and Water Cay, accessible only by boat, Big Water Cay.*

Malcolm's Beach. It's one of the most stunning beaches you'll ever see, but you'll need a high-clearance vehicle to reach it. Bring your own food and drinks, because it doesn't have any facilities or food service unless you have made a reservation with Amanyara to eat at the resort. ⊠ *Malcolm's Beach Rd., keep straight after passing the Amanyara turnoff.*

Sapodilla Bay. The best of the many secluded beaches and pristine sands around Provo can be found at this peaceful quarter-mile cove protected by Sapodilla Hill, with its soft strand lapped by calm waves, where yachts and small boats move with the gentle tide. ⊠ *North of South Dock, at end of South Dock Rd., Sapodilla Bay.*

NORTH CAICOS

The beaches of North Caicos are superb for shallow snorkeling and sunset strolls, and the waters offshore have excellent scuba diving. **Horse Stable Beach** is the main beach for annual events and beach parties. **Whitby Beach** usually has a gentle tide, and its thin strip of sand is bordered by palmetto plants and taller trees.

9

Pillory Beach, Grand Turk.

SOUTH CAICOS

The beaches at **Belle Sound** on South Caicos will take your breath away, with lagoonlike waters. Expect the beach to be natural and rustic—after storms you will see some seaweed. Due south of South Caicos is **Little Ambergris Cay**, an uninhabited cay about 14 mi (23 km) beyond the Fish Cays, with excellent bonefishing on the second-largest sandbar in the world. On the opposite side of the ridge from Belle Sound, **Long Bay** is an endless stretch of beach, but it can be susceptible to rough surf; however, on calmer days, you'll feel like you're on a deserted island.

THE TURKS

GRAND TURK

Governor's Beach. A beautiful crescent of powder-soft sand and shallow, calm turquoise waters front the official British governor's residence, called Waterloo, framed by tall casuarina trees that provide plenty of natural shade. To have it all to yourself, go on a day when cruise ships are not in port. On days when ships are in port, the beach is lined with lounge chairs.

Pillory Beach. With sparkling neon turquoise water, this is the prettiest beach on Grand Turk; it also has great off-the-beach snorkeling.

SALT CAY

Big Sand Cay. Accessible by boat with the on-island tour operators, Big Sand Cay, 7 mi (11 km) south of Salt Cay, is tiny and totally uninhabited; it's also known for its long, unspoiled stretches of open sand.

North Beach. The north coast of Salt Cay has superb beaches, with tiny, pretty shells and weathered sea glass, but North Beach is the reason to visit Salt Cay; it might be the finest beach in Turks and Caicos, if not the world. Part of the beauty lies not just in the soft, powdery sand and bright blue water, but in its isolation; it's very likely that you will have this lovely beach all to yourself.

By Ramona Settle

With water so turquoise that it glows, you may find it difficult to stray far from the beach in the Turks and Caicos. You may find no need for museums, and no desire to see ruins or even to read books. You may find yourself hypnotized by the water's many neon hues. And since the beaches are among the most incredible you will ever see, don't be surprised if you wake up on your last morning and realize that you didn't find a lot of time for anything else.

Although ivory-white, soft sandy beaches and breathtaking turquoise waters are shared among all the islands, the landscapes are a series of contrasts, from the dry, arid bush and scrub on the flat, coral islands of Grand Turk, Salt Cay, South Caicos, and Providenciales to the greener, foliage-rich undulating landscapes of Middle Caicos, North Caicos, Parrot Cay, and Pine Cay.

A much-disputed legend has it that Columbus first discovered these islands in 1492. Despite being on the map for longer than most other island groups, the Turks and Caicos Islands (pronounced *kay*-kos) still remain part of the less-discovered Caribbean. More than 40 islands—only eight inhabited—make up this self-governing British overseas territory that lies just 575 mi (925 km) southeast of Miami on the third-largest coral-reef system in the world.

The political and historical capital island of the country is Grand Turk, but most of the tourism development, which consists primarily of boutique hotels and condo resorts, has occurred in Providenciales, thanks to the 12-mi (18-km) stretch of ivory sand that is Grace Bay. Once home to a population of around 500 people plus a few donkey carts, Provo has become a hub of activity, resorts, spas, restaurants, and water sports, with a population of around 25,000. It's the temporary home for the majority of visitors who come to the Turks and Caicos.

Despite the fact that most visitors land and stay in Provo, the Turks & Caicos National Museum is in the nation's administrative capital,

Grand Turk. The museum tells the history of the islands that have all, at one time or another, been claimed by the French, Spanish, and British as well as many pirates, long before the predominately North American visitors discovered its shores.

Marks of the country's colonial past can be found in the wood and stone, Bermudian-style clapboard houses—often wrapped in deep-red bougainvillea—that line the streets on the quiet islands of Grand Turk, Salt Cay, and South Caicos. Donkeys roam free in and around the salt ponds, which are a legacy from a time when residents of these island communities worked hard as both slaves and then laborers to rake salt (then known as "white gold") bound for the United States and Canada. In Salt Cay the remains of wooden windmills are now home to large osprey nests. In Grand Turk and South Caicos the crystal-edge tidal ponds are regularly visited by flocks of rose-pink flamingos hungry for the shrimp to be found in the shallow, briny waters.

> ### WHERE WHEN HOW
>
> Check out ⊕ *www.wherewhenhow. com*, a terrific source with links to every place to stay, all the restaurants, excursions, and transportation. You can pick up the printed version of the magazine all around the island, or subscribe before you go so you know what do while in the Turks and Caicos.

Sea Island cotton, believed to be the highest quality, was produced on the Loyalist plantations in the Caicos Islands from the 1700s. The native cotton plants can still be seen dotted among the stone remains of former plantation houses in the more fertile soils of Middle Caicos and North Caicos. Here communities in tiny settlements have retained age-old skills using fanner grasses, silver palms, and sisal to create exceptional straw baskets, bags, mats, and hats.

In all, only 25,000 people live in the Turks and Caicos Islands; more than half are "Belongers," the term for the native population, mainly descended from African and Bermudian slaves who settled here beginning in the 1600s. The majority of residents work in tourism, fishing, and offshore finance, as the country is a haven for the overtaxed. Indeed, for residents and visitors, life in "TCI" is anything but taxing. But even though most visitors come to do nothing—a specialty in the islands—it does not mean there's nothing to do.

THE CAICOS

PROVIDENCIALES

Passengers typically become oddly silent when their plane starts its descent, mesmerized by the shallow, crystal-clear turquoise waters of Chalk Sound National Park. This island, nicknamed Provo, was once called Blue Hills after the name of its first settlement. Just south of the airport and downtown area, Blue Hills still remains the closest thing you can get to a more typical Caicos island settlement on this, the most developed of the islands in the chain. Most of the modern resorts, exquisite spas, water-sports operators, shops, business plazas, restaurants, bars, cafés, and the championship golf course are on or close by the 12-mi (18-km) stretch of Grace Bay beach. In spite of the ever-increasing number of taller and grander condominium resorts—either completed or under construction—it's still possible to find deserted stretches on this priceless, ivory-white shoreline. For guaranteed seclusion, rent a car and go explore the southern shores and western tip of the island, or set sail for a private island getaway on one of the many deserted cays nearby.

Progress and beauty come at a price: there is considerable construction on the island. No worry here—it does not take away from the gorgeous beaches and wonderful dinners. Although you may start to believe that every road leads to a construction site (or is under construction itself), there are, happily, plenty of sections of beach where you can escape the din.

Although you may be kept quite content enjoying the beachscape and top-notch amenities of Provo itself, it's also a great starting point for island-hopping tours by sea or by air as well as fishing and diving trips. Resurfaced roads should help you get around and make the most of the main tourism and sightseeing spots.

EXPLORING PROVIDENCIALES

Cheshire Hall. Standing eerily just west of downtown Provo are the remains of a circa-1700 cotton plantation owned by Loyalist Thomas Stubbs. A trail weaves through the ruins, where a few inadequate interpretive signs tell the story of the island's doomed cotton industry with very little information about the plantation itself. A variety of local plants are also identified. To visit, you must arrange for a tour through the Turks & Caicos National Trust. The lack of context can be disappointing for history buffs; a visit to North Caicos Wades Green plantation or the Turks & Caicos National Museum could well prove a better fit. ⊠ *Leeward Hwy., behind Ace Hardware* ☎ *649/941–5710 for National Trust* ⊕ *www.tcinationaltrust.org* ⊠ *$5* ☉ *Daily, by appointment.*

Sapodilla Hill. On this cliff overlooking the secluded Sapodilla Bay, you can discover rocks carved with the names of shipwrecked sailors and dignitaries from TCI's maritime and colonial past. There are carvings on the rocks that some claim are secret codes and maps to hidden treasures; many have tried in vain to find these treasures. The hill is known by two other names, Osprey Rock and Splitting Rock. The less adventurous can see molds of the carvings at Provo's International Airport. ⊠ *Off South Dock Rd., west of South Dock.*

WHERE TO EAT

There are more than 50 restaurants on Provo, from casual to elegant, with cuisine from Asian to European (and everything in between). You can spot the islands' own Caribbean influence no matter where you go, exhibited in fresh seafood specials, colorful presentations, and a tangy dose of spice. Pick up a free copy of *Where When How's Dining Guide* magazine, which you will find all over the island; it contains menus, Web sites, and pictures of all the restaurants.

Providenciales

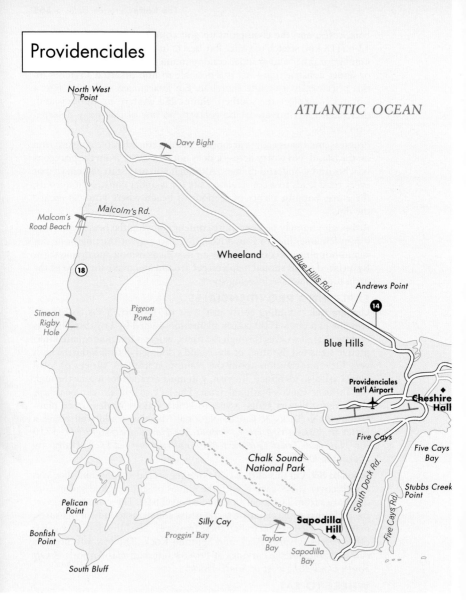

ATLANTIC OCEAN

North West Point

Davy Bight

Malcolm's Rd.

Malcom's Road Beach

Wheeland

Blue Hills Rd.

Andrews Point

(18)

Simeon Rigby Hole

Pigeon Pond

Blue Hills

(14)

Providenciales Int'l Airport

Cheshire Hall

Five Cays

Five Cays Bay

Chalk Sound National Park

South Dock Rd.

Stubbs Creek Point

Pelican Point

Silly Cay

Five Cays Rd.

Sapodilla Hill

Bonfish Point

Proggin' Bay

Taylor Bay

Sapodilla Bay

South Bluff

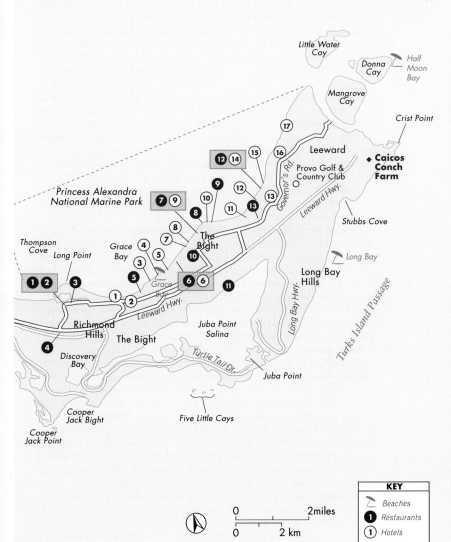

Water Cay

Little Water Cay

Donna Cay

Half Moon Bay

Mangrove Cay

Crist Point

17

Leeward

◆ **Caicos Conch Farm**

12 **14**

15

16

Provo Golf & Country Club

Princess Alexandra National Marine Park

9

12

Stubbs Cove

7 **9**

10

13

Governor's Rd.

8

11

13

Leeward Hwy.

8

Long Bay

7

The Bight

Thompson Cove

Grace Bay

4

10

Long Bay Hills

Long Point

3

5

Long Bay Hwy.

1 **2**

3

5

Grace Bay

6 **6**

11

Turks Island Passage

1

2

Leeward Hwy.

Richmond Hills

Juba Point Salina

4

The Bight

Discovery Bay

Turtle Tail Dr.

Juba Point

Cooper Jack Bight

Five Little Cays

Cooper Jack Point

KEY

~ Beaches
1 Restaurants
1 Hotels

0   2miles
0   2 km

$$$$ ✕ **Anacaona**. At the Grace Bay Club, this palapa-shaded (thatch-roof)
ECLECTIC   restaurant has become a favorite of the country's chief minister. But
despite the regular presence of government bigwigs, the restaurant
continues to offer a memorable dining experience minus the tie, the
air-conditioning, and the attitude. Start with a bottle of fine wine;
then enjoy the light and healthful Mediterranean-influenced cuisine.
The kitchen uses the island's bountiful seafood and fresh produce. Oil
lamps on the tables, gently revolving ceiling fans, and the murmur of
the trade winds add to the Edenic environment. The entrancing ocean
view and the careful service make it an ideal choice when you want
to be pampered. It's a good thing the setting is amazing; portions are
tiny, so you're paying for ambience. Check out the world's first infinity bar, which seems to spill right into the ocean. The lighted menus
are a huge plus—no more squinting in the dark to read—yet they do
not take away from the romantic experience. Children under 12 are
not allowed. Long pants and collared shirts are required. ⊠ *Grace
Bay Club, Grace Bay* ☎ *649/946–5050* ⊕ *www.gracebayresorts.com*
⌖ *Reservations essential.*

$ ✕ **Angela's Top o' the Cove New York Style Delicatessen**. Order deli sand-
AMERICAN   wiches, salads, enticingly rich desserts, and freshly baked pastries at this
island institution on Leeward Highway, just south of Turtle Cove. From
the deli case you can buy the fixings for a picnic; the shelves are stocked
with an eclectic selection of fancy foodstuffs, as well as beer and wine.
It's open at 6:30 am for a busy trade in coffees and cappuccinos. This
is a cheesesteak comparable to what you get in Philly, but the location
isn't where most tourists stay—it's worth the drive, though. ⊠ *Leeward
Hwy., Turtle Cove* ☎ *649/946–4694* ⊙ *No dinner.*

$$$ ✕ **Baci Ristorante**. Aromas redolent of the Mediterranean waft from the
ITALIAN   open kitchen as you enter this intimate eatery east of Turtle Cove.
Outdoor seating is on a romantic canal-front patio, one of the love-
lier settings on Provo. The menu offers a small but varied selection of
Italian dishes. Veal is prominent on the menu, but main courses also
include pasta, chicken, fish, and brick-oven pizzas. You'll never see red-
der tomatoes than those in the tomato-and-mozzarella Caprese salad; a
standout entrée is the chicken with vodka-cream sauce. House wines are
personally selected by the owners and complement the tasteful wine list.
Try tiramisu for dessert with a flavored coffee drink. Wear bug spray at
night. ⊠ *Harbour Town, Turtle Cove* ☎ *649/941–3044.*

$$$$ ✕ **Bay Bistro**. You simply can't eat any closer to the beach than here,
ECLECTIC   the only restaurant in all of Provo that is built directly on the sand.
☾   Although service can be slow, the food and setting are excellent. You
dine on a covered porch surrounded by palm trees and the sound of lap-
ping waves. The spring-roll appetizer is delicious, and the oven-roasted
chicken is the best on the island. Junior, one of Provo's top bartend-
ers, might bring your drink balanced on the top of his head. Brunch
on weekends includes such favorites as eggs Benedict with mimosas
(included) and is very popular; lines can be long if you don't have a
reservation. ⊠ *Sibonné, Princess Dr., Grace Bay* ☎ *649/946–5396* ⊕ *si-
bonne.com/grace-bay-bistro/* ⊙ *No dinner Mon.*

$$$
ECLECTIC

✕ **Caicos Café**. New owners have also brought a new menu focusing on island food with an Italian twist. The bruschetta that everyone gets at the start of the meal is delicious enough that you may ask for seconds, and the bread is baked fresh every day at the bakery next door. Blackened fish and jerk chicken on top of pasta are popular with the locals. Ravioli with cream sauce is the tastiest dish. On windy nights, the inland setting offers protection from the breezes. Be sure to wear bug spray at night. ✉ *Caicos Café Plaza, Grace Bay Rd., Grace Bay* ☎ *649/946–5278* ⊘ *Closed Sun.*

$$$$
ECLECTIC
★

✕ **Coco Bistro**. With tables under palm trees, Coco Bistro has a divine setting, and the food is just as good. Though not directly on the beach, the location under the tropical tree grove still reminds you that you are on vacation. Main courses are complemented by both French flourishes (served au poivre, for example) and West Indian (such as with mango chutney) and are accompanied by fried plantains and mango slaw to maintain a Caribbean flair. Consider conch soup, soft-shell-crab tempura, and sun-dried tomato pasta from the internationally influenced menu. This is one of the better restaurants on Provo. ✉ *Grace Bay Rd., Grace Bay* ☎ *649/946–5369* ⊕ *www.CocoBistro.tc* ⚓ *Reservations essential* ⊘ *Closed Mon. No lunch.*

$$$$
ECLECTIC
Fodor's Choice
★

✕ **Coyaba Restaurant**. Directly behind Grace Bay Club and next to Caribbean Paradise Inn, this posh eatery serves nostalgic favorites with tempting twists in conversation-piece crockery and in a palm-fringed setting. Chef Paul Newman uses his culinary expertise for the daily-changing main courses, which include exquisitely presented dishes such as crispy whole yellow snapper fried in Thai spices. One standout is lobster thermidor in a Dijon-mushroom cream sauce. Try several different appetizers instead of a single more expensive entrée for dinner; guava-and-tamarind barbecue ribs and coconut-shrimp tempura are two good choices if you go that route. If you enjoy creative menus, this is the place for you. Chef Paul keeps the resident expat crowd happy with traditional favorites such as lemon meringue pie, albeit with his own tropical twist. Don't skip dessert; Paul makes the most incredible chocolate fondant you will ever have. The service here is seamless. ✉ *Off Grace Bay Rd., beside Caribbean Paradise Inn, Grace Bay* ☐ *Box 459, Providenciales* ☎ *649/946–5186* ⊕ *www.coyabarestaurant.com* ⚓ *Reservations essential* ⊘ *Closed Tues. No lunch.*

$$
CARIBBEAN

✕ **Da Conch Shack**. An institution in Provo for many years, this brightly colored beach shack is justifiably famous for its conch and seafood. The legendary specialty, conch, is fished fresh out of the shallows and broiled, spiced, cracked, or fried to absolute perfection. On Friday night you can dance in the sand after dinner. This is the freshest conch anywhere on the island, as the staff dive for it only after you've placed your order, but if you don't like seafood, there is chicken on the menu. Thursday night, start rocking while you eat and mingle with the locals; live bands have just been added as headliners to sing songs that make everybody happy. ✉ *Blue Hills Rd., Blue Hills* ☎ *No phone* ⊕ *www.conchshack.tc/* ☐ *No credit cards* ⊘ *No lunch.*

$$$$
ECLECTIC

✕ **Grace's Cottage**. At one of the prettiest dining settings on Provo, tables are artfully set under wrought-iron cottage-style gazebos and around

9

the wraparound verandah, which skirts the gingerbread-covered main building. In addition to such tangy and exciting entrées as panfried red snapper with roasted-pepper sauce or melt-in-your-mouth grilled beef tenderloin with truffle-scented mashed potatoes, the soufflés are well worth the 15-minute wait and the top-tier price tag. Portions are small, but the quality is amazing. Service is impeccable (ladies are given a small stool so that their purses do not touch the ground). ⊠ *Point Grace, Grace Bay* ☎ *649/946–5096* ⚱ *Reservations essential* ⊘ *No lunch.*

$$$ ✕ **Hemingway's.** A casual and gorgeous setting, with a patio and deck
AMERICAN   offering views of Grace Bay, makes this one of the most popular restaurants that cater to tourists. At lunch, do not miss the best fish tacos with mango chutney. For dinner there is an excellent kids' menu and something for everyone, including vegetarians. Order the popular "Old Man of the Sea," which features the freshest fish of the day. It's known for great sauces such as the wine reduction for the filet mignon, the creole for fish dishes, and a delicious curry for chicken. If you're on a budget, go right before 6 pm, when you can still order the less expensive lunch menu items. Go on Thursday night when Quentin Dean plays Caribbean versions of popular songs. ⊠ *The Sands Resort, Grace Bay* ☎ *649/946–5199 Ext. 150* ⊕ *www.thesandsresort.com.*

$$$ ✕ **Magnolia Wine Bar and Restaurant.** Restaurateurs since the early 1990s,
ECLECTIC   hands-on owners Gianni and Tracey Caporuscio make success seem
★   simple. Expect well-prepared, uncomplicated choices that range from European to Asian to Caribbean. You can construct an excellent meal from the outstanding appetizers; do not miss the spring rolls and the grilled-vegetable-and-fresh-mozzarella stack. Finish your meal with the mouthwatering molten chocolate cake. The atmosphere is romantic, the presentations are attractive, and the service is careful. It's easy to see why the Caporuscios have a loyal following. The adjoining wine bar includes a handpicked list of specialty wines, which can be ordered by the glass. The marine setting is a great place to watch the sunset. ⊠ *Miramar Resort, Turtle Cove* ☎ *649/941–5108* ⊘ *Closed Mon. No lunch.*

$$$$ ✕ **O'Soleil.** Located at the Somerset, this is one of Provo's few indoor,
ECLECTIC   air-conditioned restaurants, though you can also eat outside on the
★   terrace. White-on-white decor under vaulted ceilings gives it a Miami-chic ambience. The executive chef mixes international styles, including influences from the Caribbean, Asia, and Europe. Some of the standouts include the best sea bass on the island, served with balsamic cherry tomatoes; roasted Australian rack of lamb; and excellent risotto. You can also order from the tapas menu—the presentations are as creative as the food. Check out the conch spring rolls and shrimp tempura, each with its own dipping sauce. Eat on a couch under the stars during Friday-night happy hour while listening to live music from 7 until 10. Ask for simpler off-the-menu options for the children. ⊠ *The Somerset, Princess Dr., Grace Bay* ☎ *649/946–5900* ⊕ *www.thesomerset.com.*

$$$ ✕ **Tiki Hut.** From its location overlooking the marina, the ever-popular Tiki
AMERICAN   Hut continues to serve consistently tasty, value-priced meals in a fun atmo-
☺   sphere. Locals take advantage of the Wednesday night $13 chicken-and-rib special, and the lively bar is a good place to sample local Turks Head brew. There's a special family-style menu (the best kids' menu in Provo) and kids'

seating. Don't miss pizzas made with the signature white sauce, or the jerk wings, coated in a secret barbecue sauce and then grilled—they're out of this world! The restaurant can be busy, with long waits for a table, and you can reserve only with five people or more. ⊠ *Turtle Cove Marina, Turtle Cove* ☎ *649/941–5341* ⊕ *www.tikihuttci.com/.*

WHERE TO STAY

Most of the resorts on Providenciales are on Grace Bay, but a few are more isolated or even off the beach.

PRIVATE VILLA RENTALS

A popular option on Provo is renting a self-catering villa or private home. For the best villa selection, plan to make your reservations three to six months in advance.

REQUESTING ROOMS

Most of the resorts on Provo are composed of privately owned condos placed into the resort's rental pool when the owners are not present. Unlike at chain hotels and resorts, you cannot request a particular building, floor, or room unless you are a repeat visitor. If you fall in love with the condo, you can probably purchase it, or one that's similar. There are no taxes in T&C except for a onetime Stamp Duty tax—no property tax and no rental tax—which makes owning your own piece of paradise even more tempting.

Prestigious Properties (⊕ *Prestige Pl., Grace Bay* ☎ *649/946–5355* ⊕ *www.prestigiousproperties.com*) offers a wide selection of modest to magnificent villas in the Leeward, Grace Bay, and Turtle Cove areas of Providenciales. **T.C. Safari** (☎ *649/941–5043* ⊕ *www.tcsafari.tc*) has exclusive oceanfront properties in the beautiful and tranquil Sapodilla Bay–Chalk Sound neighborhood on Provo's southwest shores.

The following reviews have been condensed for this book. Please go to Fodors.com for expanded reviews of each property.

$$$–$$$$
RESORT
🕙

The Alexandra Resort. Situated on the most popular stretch of Grace Bay Beach, the Alexandra is within walking distance of shops, Coral Garden's snorkeling, and excellent restaurants. **Pros:** luxury for less; all rooms have ocean views. **Cons:** lots of construction in the vicinity; temporary reception gives a bad first impression; although most resorts have king beds, this one has only queens. ⊠ *Princess Dr., Grace Bay, Providenciales, Turks and Caicos Islands, BWI* ☎ *649/946–5807 or 800/704–9424* ⊕ *www.alexandraresort.com* ⬎ *88 rooms* 🗝 *In-room: a/c, kitchen (some), Wi-Fi. In-hotel: restaurant, tennis courts, bar, pool, gym, laundry facilities, beach, water sports* ❣️ *No meals.*

$$$$
RESORT

Amanyara. If you seek seclusion, peace, and tranquillity in a Zenlike atmosphere, this is your place. **Pros:** on one of the best beaches on Provo; resort is quiet and secluded. **Cons:** isolated; far from restaurants, excursions, and other beaches. ⊠ *Northwest Point, Providenciales, Turks and Caicos Islands, BWI* ☎ *649/941–8133* ⊕ *www.amanresorts.com* ⬎ *40 pavilions* 🗝 *In-room: a/c. In-hotel: restaurants, tennis courts, bar, pool, gym, spa, beach, water sports* ❣️ *No meals.*

$$$$
ALL-INCLUSIVE
🕙
★

Beaches Turks and Caicos Resort and Spa. The largest resort in the Turks and Caicos Islands can satisfy families as eager to spend time apart as together. **Pros:** great place for families; all-inclusive. **Cons:** with an all-inclusive plan you miss out on the island's other great restaurants;

9

CLOSE UP

Best Spas in Provo and Beyond

A Turks Island Salt Glow, where the island's sea salt is mixed with gentle oils to exfoliate, smooth, and moisturize the skin, is just one of the treatments you can enjoy in one of the island spas. Being pampered spa-style has become as much a part of a Turks and Caicos vacation as sunning on the beach. Marine-based ingredients fit well with the Grace Bay backdrop at the Thalasso Spa at **Point Grace,** where massages take place in two simple, bleached-white cottages standing on the dune line, which means you have a spectacular view of the sea-blue hues—if you manage to keep your eyes open. The Regent Spa at the **Regent Palms** offers individual treatments, with a water feature by day, a fire feature at night. The signature body scrub uses hand-crushed local conch shells to smooth

the skin. But the widest choice of Asian-inspired treatments (and the most unforgettable scenery) can be found at the 6,000-square-foot Como Shambhala Spa at the **Parrot Cay Resort,** which has outdoor whirlpools and a central beech-wood lounge overlooking the shallow turquoise waters and mangroves. Provo also has a noteworthy day spa that's not in one of the Grace Bay resorts. Manager Terri Tapper of **Spa Tropique** (⊠ *Ports of Call, Grace Bay Rd., Grace Bay* ☎ *649/941–5720* ⊕ *www.spatropique. com*) blends Swedish, therapeutic, and reflexology massage techniques using oils made from natural plants and products produced locally and within the Caribbean region. The Turks Island Salt Glow has become one of her most popular treatments.

construction next door to the east side of the property. ⊠ *Lower Bight Rd., Grace Bay, Providenciales, Turks and Caicos Islands, BWI* ☎ *649/946–8000 or 800/726–3257* ⊕ *www.beaches.com* ↻ *359 rooms, 103 suites* ⚘ *In-room: a/c, Internet. In-hotel: restaurants, tennis courts, bars, children's programs, pools, gym, spa, beach, business center, water sports* ⓘ◯� ⱷ *All-inclusive.*

$$$

ALL-INCLUSIVE

⊞ **Club Med Turkoise.** Guests still fly in from the United States, Europe, and Canada to enjoy the scuba diving, windsurfing, and waterskiing on the turquoise waters at the doorsteps of the area's first major resort. **Pros:** all-inclusive; active. **Cons:** although the rooms have been updated, the grounds are showing their age. ⊠ *Grace Bay, Providenciales, Turks and Caicos Islands, BWI* ☎ *649/946–5500 or 888/932–2582* ⊕ *www. clubmed.com* ↻ *293 rooms* ⚘ *In-room: a/c, Wi-Fi. In-hotel: restaurants, tennis courts, bars, pool, gym, beach, business center, water sports* ⓘ◯ⱷ *All-inclusive.*

$$$$

RESORT

⊞ **Gansevoort Turks and Caicos, A Wymara Resort.** South Beach Miami chic meets island time at this gorgeous new resort with modern, comfortable furnishings. **Pros:** service is pleasant and eager to please; gorgeous heated pool and beautiful rooms; great ambience. **Cons:** since this is one of Provo's few nightlife venues, Friday and Saturday nights can get a little too lively. ⊠ *Lower Bight Rd., Grace Bay, Providenciales, Turks and Caicos Islands, BWI* ☎ *649/941–7555* ⊕ *www. GansevoortTurksandCaicos.com* ↻ *55 rooms, 32 suites, 4 penthouses*

What Is a Potcake?

Potcakes are indigenous dogs of the Bahamas and Turks and Caicos Islands. Traditionally, the stray dogs would be fed from the leftover scraps of food that formed at the bottom of the pot; this is how they got their name. Much is being done these days to control the stray dog population. The TCSPCA and Potcake Place are two agencies working to adopt out the puppies. You can "travel with a cause" by adopting one of these gorgeous pups; they come with all the shots and all the papers required to bring them back home to the United States. Even if you don't adopt, you can help by volunteering as a carrier—bringing one back to its adopted family. Customs in the States is actually easier when you are bringing back a potcake! For more information on how you can help, check out the Web site for Potcake Place (⊕ *www.potcakeplace.com*).

⚐ *In-room: a/c, kitchen, Internet, Wi-Fi. In-hotel: restaurants, bars, children's programs, pool, gym, laundry facilities, spa, beach, parking, some pets allowed* ⦿| *Breakfast.*

$$$$
RESORT
☾
★

▦ **Grace Bay Club, Villas at Grace Bay Club, and the Estate at Grace Bay Club.** This stylish resort retains a loyal following because of its helpful, attentive staff and unpretentious elegance. **Pros:** gorgeous pool and restaurant lounge areas with outdoor couches, daybeds, and fire pits; all guests receive a cell phone to use on the island. **Cons:** no children allowed at Anacaona restaurant; construction in front of the properties. ⊠ *Grace Bay Rd., behind Grace Bay Court, Grace Bay* ☎ *649/946–5050 or 800/946–5757* ⊕ *www.gracebayclub.com* ⬑ *59 suites* ⚐ *In-room: a/c, kitchen, Internet, Wi-Fi. In-hotel: restaurants, tennis courts, bar, pools, laundry facilities, spa, beach, business center, water sports* ⦿| *Breakfast.*

$$$–$$$$
RESORT
☾
★

▦ **Ocean Club Resorts.** Enormous, locally painted pictures of hibiscus make a striking first impression as you enter the reception area at one of the island's most well-established condominium resorts. **Pros:** family-friendly resort with shuttles between the two shared properties; screened balconies and porches allow a respite from incessant air-conditioning. **Cons:** both resorts are showing their age. ⬠ *Box 240, Grace Bay* ☎ *649/946–5880 or 800/457–8787* ⊕ *www.oceanclubresorts.com* ⬑ *174 suites: 86 at Ocean Club East, 88 at Ocean Club West* ⚐ *In-room: a/c, kitchen (some), Wi-Fi. In-hotel: restaurants, tennis court, bars, pools, gym, laundry facilities, spa, beach, business center, water sports* ⦿| *No meals.*

$$$$
RESORT

▦ **Point Grace.** Asian-influenced rooftop domes blend with Romanesque stone pillars and wide stairways in this plush resort, which offers spacious beachfront suites and romantic cottages surrounding the centerpiece: a turquoise infinity pool with perfect views of the beach. **Pros:** relaxing environment; beautiful pool. **Cons:** can be stuffy (signs around the pool remind you to be quiet). ⬠ *Box 700, Grace Bay* ☎ *649/946–5096 or 888/924–7223* ⊕ *www.pointgrace.com* ⬑ *23 suites, 9 cottage suites, 2 villas* ⚐ *In-room: a/c, kitchen. In-hotel: restaurants, bars, pool, spa, beach, business center, water sports* ☉ *Closed Sept.* ⦿| *Breakfast.*

9

$$$$
RESORT
⊙

Regent Palms. High on luxury and glitz, this is a place to see and be seen. **Pros:** great people-watching; lively atmosphere; one of the best spas in the Caribbean. **Cons:** some would say busy not lively; a little formal and stuffy (cover-ups are required when you go to the pool). ⊠ *Grace Bay, Providenciales, Turks and Caicos Islands, BWI* ☎ *649/946–8666* ⊕ *www.regenthotels.com* ➽ *72 suites* ⅋ *In-room: a/c, kitchen (some), Wi-Fi. In-hotel: restaurants, tennis court, bar, children's programs, pool, gym, laundry facilities, spa, beach, water sports* ⦿| *Breakfast.*

$$$–$$$$
RESORT
★

Royal West Indies Resort. With a contemporary take on colonial architecture and the outdoor feel of a botanical garden, this unpretentious resort has plenty of garden-view and beachfront studios and suites for moderate self-catering budgets. **Pros:** the best bang for the buck on Provo; on one of the widest stretches of Grace Bay Beach. **Cons:** Club Med next door can be noisy. ⬠ *Box 482, Grace Bay* ☎ *649/946–5004 or 800/332–4203* ⊕ *www.royalwestindies.com* ➽ *99 suites* ⅋ *In-room: a/c, kitchen, Internet. In-hotel: restaurant, bar, pools, laundry facilities, beach, water sports* ⦿| *No meals.*

$$$–$$$$
RESORT
⊙

Sands at Grace Bay. Spacious gardens and winding pools set the tone for one of Provo's most popular family resorts. **Pros:** one of the best places for families; central to shops and numerous restaurants; screened balconies and porches give an escape from incessant air-conditioning. **Cons:** a new wooden pool deck can cause splinters, so keep an eye on the kids; avoid courtyard rooms, which are not worth the price. ⬠ *Box 681, Grace Bay* ☎ *649/941–5199 or 877/777–2637* ⊕ *www. thesandsresort.com* ➽ *118 suites* ⅋ *In-room: a/c, kitchen (some), Internet, Wi-Fi. In-hotel: restaurant, tennis court, bar, pools, gym, laundry facilities, spa, beach, business center, water sports, some pets allowed* ⦿| *No meals.*

$$$–$$$$
RESORT

Seven Stars. The tallest property on the island is matched by the pure luxury it offers. **Pros:** gorgeous property in the center of the Grace Bay "hub" is walking distance to everything; terrific deck bar by the beach. **Cons:** some feel the proportions of the resort are too big for the rest of the island. ⊠ *Grace Bay Rd.* ☎ *649/941–7777* ⊕ *www. SevenStarsGraceBay.com* ➽ *113 rooms* ⅋ *In-room: a/c, kitchen (some), Internet, Wi-Fi. In-hotel: restaurants, bars, tennis court, pool, gym, spa, beach, water sports, children's programs, laundry facilities, business center, parking* ⦿| *No meals.*

$–$$
HOTEL

Sibonné. Dwarfed by most of the nearby resorts, the smallest hotel on Grace Bay Beach has snug (by Provo's spacious standards) but pleasant rooms with Bermuda-style balconies and a completely circular but tiny pool. **Pros:** closest property to the beach; the island's best bargain directly on the beach. **Cons:** pool is small and dated. ⊠ *Princess Dr., Box 144, Grace Bay, Providenciales, Turks and Caicos Islands, BWI* ☎ *649/946–5547 or 800/528–1905* ⊕ *www.sibonne.com* ➽ *29 rooms, 1 apartment* ⅋ *In-room: a/c. In-hotel: restaurant, bar, pool, beach, water sports* ⦿| *Breakfast.*

$$$$
RESORT
Fodor's Choice
★

The Somerset. This luxury resort has the "wow" factor, starting with the architecture, followed by the service, and ending in your luxuriously appointed suite. **Pros:** the most beautiful architecture on Provo; terrific service; Wednesday movie nights out on the lawn. **Cons:** the cheapest

West Bay Club.

lock-out rooms are not worth the cost; can get noisy. ⊠ *Princess Dr., Grace Bay, Providenciales, Turks and Caicos Islands, BWI* ☎ *649/946– 5900* ⊕ *www.thesomerset.com* ↯ *53 suites* ⌂ *In-room: a/c, kitchen, Wi-Fi. In-hotel: restaurant, bar, children's programs, pool, gym, laundry facilities, beach, water sports* ¶◎¶ *Breakfast.*

$$$–$$$$
RESORT
★

🏨 **Turks and Caicos Club.** On the quieter, western end of Grace Bay, this intimate all-suites hotel has a unique Caribbean bed-and-breakfast aura. The buildings are colonial-style with lovely gingerbread trim. **Pros:** incredible, lush grounds; on one of the best stretches of Grace Bay Beach; great snorkeling from the beach. **Cons:** small bathrooms. ⊠ *West Grace Bay Beach, Box 687, West Grace Bay, Providenciales, Turks and Caicos Islands, BWI* ☎ *649/946–5800 or 888/482–2582* ⊕ *www.turksandcaicosclub.com* ↯ *21 suites* ⌂ *In-room: a/c, kitchen, Wi-Fi. In-hotel: restaurant, bar, pool, gym, laundry facilities, beach, water sports* ⊘ *Closed Sept.* ¶◎¶ *Breakfast.*

$$$$
RENTAL

🏨 **The Tuscany.** This self-catering, quiet, upscale resort is the place for independent travelers to unwind around one of the prettiest pools on Provo. **Pros:** luxurious; all condos have ocean views; beautiful pool. **Cons:** no restaurant and far from the best restaurants; very expensive for self-catering. ⌂ *Box 623, Grace Bay* ☎ *649/941–4667* ⊕ *www. thetuscanyresort.com* ↯ *30 condos* ⌂ *In-room: a/c, no safe, kitchen, Wi-Fi. In-hotel: tennis court, pool, gym, beach* ¶◎¶ *No meals.*

$$$$
ALL-INCLUSIVE

🏨 **Veranda Resort.** And now for something completely different for Provo: an upscale, quiet, ultraluxury, all-inclusive resort. **Pros:** excellent service; top-shelf spirits included; unique clapboard architecture. **Cons:** included meals mean you may miss out on excellent independent restaurants; only two restaurants can mean a wait for a table at

9

prime times. ✉ *Princess Dr.* ☎ *649/339–5050* ⊕ *www.VerandaTCI.com* ↩ *168 rooms* ⚴ *In-room: a/c, kitchen, Wi-Fi. In-hotel: restaurants, bar, tennis court, pools, gym, spa, beach, water sports, children's programs, laundry facilities, business center, parking* ⑩ *All-inclusive.*

$$$$
RENTAL

⌂ **Villa Renaissance.** Modeled after a Tuscan villa, this luxury property is for the self-catering tourist. **Pros:** luxury for less; one of the prettiest courtyards in Provo. **Cons:** no restaurant; not full-service resort. ⌂ *Box 592, Grace Bay* ☎ *649/941–5300 or 877/285–8764* ⊕ *www.villarenaissance.com* ↩ *20 suites* ⚴ *In-room: a/c, kitchen. In-hotel: bar, pool, laundry facilities, spa, beach* ⑩ *No meals.*

$$$–$$$$
RESORT
Fodor's Choice
★

⌂ **West Bay Club.** One of Provo's newest resorts has a prime location on a pristine stretch of Grace Bay Beach just steps away from the best off-the-beach snorkeling. **Pros:** all rooms have a beach view; new, clean, and sparkling; contemporary architecture makes it stand out from other resorts. **Cons:** a car is needed to go shopping and to the best restaurants. ✉ *Lower Bight Rd., Lower Bight* ☎ *649/946–8550* ⊕ *www.TheWestBayClub.com* ↩ *46 suites* ⚴ *In-room: a/c, kitchen, Internet, Wi-Fi. In-hotel: restaurant, bar, pool, gym, laundry facilities, spa, beach, water sports, parking* ⑩ *No meals.*

$$$–$$$$
RESORT
Fodor's Choice
★

⌂ **Windsong Resort.** On a gorgeous beach lined with several appealing resorts, Windsong stands out for two reasons: an active Snuba program and a magnificent pool. **Pros:** the pool is the coolest; great Snuba program; gorgeous new resort. **Cons:** resort is experiencing some growing pains, so service can be lacking; studios have only a refrigerator and microwave; thinner stretch of beachfront here. ✉ *Stubbs Rd., Lower Bight, Providenciales, Turks and Caicos Islands, BWI* ☎ *649/941–7700* ⊕ *www.windsongresort.com* ↩ *16 studios, 30 suites* ⚴ *In-room: a/c, kitchen (some), Wi-Fi. In-hotel: restaurant, bars, children's programs, pool, gym, laundry facilities, beach, business center, water sports, parking* ⑩ *No meals.*

NIGHTLIFE

Although Provo is not known for its nightlife, there's still some fun to be found after dark. The best ambience can be found with live music from NaDa, a French-Canadian duo, so ask around to find out where they are playing and go! Normally, they appear Tuesday nights at Mango Reef, at Wednesday-night dinners at Parallel 23, and at fun "deck" parties on Thursday nights at The Deck at Seven Stars.

Thursday night through Saturday night, Danny Buoy's is a hot spot, as is Calico Jacks; both places usually have live bands. Somewhere On The Beach Restaurant has live bands—usually reggae and local music—on Tuesday, Thursday, and Saturday. There are live bands on Thursday nights at Da Conch Shack and Hemingway's. On Friday nights there is live music at O'Soleil and Anocaona. On Saturday nights Bagatelle at Gansevoort hosts live bands and DJs. Any night, you can also buy a pass to Club Med, which includes all your drinks, passes to the show, and the disco.

Keep abreast of events and specials by checking **TCI eNews** (⊕ *www.tcienews.com*).

Bagatelle. Bringing South Beach Miami chic to the beach, this is one of the few places that are "happening" on a Saturday night. Live bands, DJs, and celebrity sightings make the action. ⊠ *Gansevoort Wymara Resort, The Bight* ☎ *649/941–7555* ⊕ *www.gansevoortturksandcaicos. com/gansevoort-bagatelle-bistrot-beach-club.php.*

Calico Jack's Restaurant & Bar. On Friday night you can find a local band and lively crowd at this popular bar. ⊠ *Ports of Call, Grace Bay* ☎ *649/946–5129.*

Casablanca Casino. This casino has brought slots, blackjack, American roulette, poker, craps, and baccarat back to Provo. Open from 7 pm until 4 am, this is the last stop for the night. Grace Bay Club has introduced the infinity bar, the only one of its kind in the world, which gives the impression that it goes directly into the ocean. ⊠ *Grace Bay Rd., Grace Bay* ☎ *649/941–3737.*

Danny Buoy's. A popular Irish pub, Danny Buoy's has pool tables, darts, and big-screen TVs. It's a great place to watch sports from anywhere in the world. ⊠ *Grace Bay Rd., across from Carpe Diem Residences, Grace Bay* ☎ *649/946–5921.*

Somewhere . . . On The Beach. A Tex-Mex alternative that gives the wallet a break from fine dining becomes the hot spot on Thursday nights with live music. Three levels of outdoor decks add to the fun. ⊠ *Coral Gardens on Grace Bay, The Bight* ☎ *649/231–0590.*

SHOPPING

Handwoven straw baskets and hats, polished conch-shell crafts, paintings, wood carvings, model sailboats, handmade dolls, and metalwork are crafts native to the islands and nearby Haiti. The natural surroundings have inspired local and international artists to paint, sculpt, print, craft, and photograph; most of their creations are on sale in Providenciales.

★ **Anna's Art Gallery and Studio.** Anna's sells original artworks, silk-screen paintings, sculptures, and handmade sea-glass jewelry. ⊠ *The Saltmills, Grace Bay* ☎ *449/231–3293.*

ArtProvo. ArtProvo is the island's largest gallery of designer wall art; also shown are native crafts, jewelry, handblown glass, candles, and other gift items. Featured artists include Trevor Morgan, from Salt Cay, and Dwight Outten. ⊠ *Regent Village, Grace Bay* ☎ *649/941–4545.*

Caicos Wear Boutique. This store is filled with casual resort wear, including Caribbean-print shirts, swimsuits from Brazil, sandals, beach jewelry, and gifts. ⊠ *Regent Village, Grace Bay Rd., Grace Bay* ☎ *649/941–3346.*

Graceway IGA Supermarket Gourmet. With a large fresh-produce section, bakery, gourmet deli, and extensive meat counter, Provo's largest supermarket is likely to have what you're looking for, and it's the most consistently well-stocked store on the island. It's got a good selection of prepared foods, including rotisserie chicken, pizza, and potato salad. But prices can be much higher than at home. ⊠ *Grace Bay Rd., Grace Bay* ☎ *649/941–5000.*

Greensleeves. This boutique offers paintings and pottery by local artists, baskets, jewelry, and sisal mats and bags. The proceeds from sales of works in the Potcake Corner help fund the Potcake Place rescue center for the islands' stray dogs. ⊠ *Central Sq., Leeward Hwy., Turtle Cove* ☎ *649/946–4147.*

Royal Jewels. This store sells gold and other jewelry, designer watches, perfumes, fine leather goods, and cameras—all duty-free—at several outlets. ⊠ *Providenciales International Airport* ☎ *649/941–4513* ⊠ *Arch Plaza* ☎ *649/946–4699* ⊠ *Beaches Turks & Caicos Resort & Spa, Grace Bay* ☎ *649/946–8285* ⊠ *Club Med Turkoise, Grace Bay* ☎ *649/946–5602.*

☾ ★ **Unicorn Bookstore.** If you need to supplement your beach-reading stock or are looking for island-specific materials, visit the Unicorn for a wide assortment of books and magazines, lots of information and guides about the Turks and Caicos Islands and the Caribbean, and a large children's section with crafts, games, and art supplies. ⊠ *In front of Graceway IGA Mall, Leeward Hwy., Discovery Bay* ☎ *649/941–5458.*

The Wine Cellar. This store has the best prices for alcohol and beer on the island. It's open Monday through Saturday from 8 to 6 (but closed Sunday and public holidays, when liquor sales aren't allowed). ⊠ *Leeward Hwy.* ☎ *649/946–4536* ⊕ *www.WineCellar.tc.*

SPORTS AND ACTIVITIES

BOATING AND SAILING

Provo's calm, reef-protected seas combine with constant easterly trade winds for excellent sailing conditions. Several multihull vessels offer charters with snorkeling stops, food and beverage service, and sunset vistas. Prices range from $39 per person for group trips to $600 or more for private charters.

For sightseeing below the waves, try the semisubmarine operated by **Caicos Tours** (⊠ *Turtle Cove Marina, Turtle Cove* ☎ *649/231–0006* ⊕ *www.caicostours.com*). You can stay dry within the small, lower observatory as it glides along on a one-hour tour of the reef, with large viewing windows on either side. The trip costs $39.

Sail Provo (☎ *649/946–4783* ⊕ *www.sailprovo.com*) runs 52-foot and 48-foot catamarans on scheduled half-day, full-day, sunset, and kid-friendly glowworm cruises, where underwater creatures light up the sea's surface for several days after each full moon.

Silverdeep (☎ *649/946–5612* ⊕ *www.silverdeep.com*) sailing trips include time for snorkeling and beachcombing at a secluded beach.

DIVING AND SNORKELING

Fodor's Choice ★ The island's many shallow reefs offer excellent and exciting snorkeling relatively close to shore. Try **Smith's Reef,** over Bridge Road east of Turtle Cove.

Scuba diving in the crystalline waters surrounding the islands ranks among the best in the Caribbean. The reef and wall drop-offs thrive with bright, unbroken coral formations and lavish numbers of fish and marine life. Mimicking the idyllic climate, waters are warm all year, averaging 76°F to 78°F in winter and 82°F to 84°F in summer. With

Diving with stingrays.

minimal rainfall and soil runoff, visibility is usually good and frequently superb, ranging from 60 feet to more than 150 feet. An extensive system of marine national parks and boat moorings, combined with an ecoconscious mind-set among dive operators, contributes to an uncommonly pristine underwater environment.

Dive operators in Provo regularly visit sites at **Grace Bay** and **Pine Cay** for spur-and-groove coral formations and bustling reef diving. They make the longer journey to the dramatic walls at **North West Point** and **West Caicos** depending on weather conditions. Instruction from the major diving agencies is available for all levels and certifications, even Technical diving. An average one-tank dive costs $45; a two-tank dive, $90. There are also two live-aboard dive boats available for charter working out of Provo.

🌀 **Big Blue Unlimited** (⊠ *Leeward Marina, Leeward, Providenciales* ☎ *649/946–5034* ⊕ *www.bigblue.tc*) has taken ecotouring to a whole new level with educational ecotours, including three-hour kayak trips and land-focused guided journeys around the family islands. Its Coastal Ecology and Wildlife tour is a kayak adventure through red mangroves to bird habitats, rock iguana hideaways, and natural fish nurseries. The Middle Caicos Bicycle Adventure gets you on a bike to explore the island, touring limestone caves in Conch Bar with a break for lunch with the Forbes family in the village of Bambarra. Packages are $255 for adults. No children under 12 are allowed.

Caicos Adventures (⊠ *La Petite Pl., Grace Bay* ☎☎ *649/941–3346* ⊕ *www.tcidiving.com*), run by friendly Frenchman Fifi Kuntz, offers daily trips to West Caicos, French Cay, and Molasses Reef.

CLOSE UP

Diving the Turks and Caicos Islands

Scuba diving was the original water sport to draw visitors to the Turks and Caicos Islands in the 1970s. Aficionados are still drawn by the abundant marine life, including humpback whales in winter, sparkling clean waters, warm and calm seas, and the coral walls and reefs around the islands. Diving in the Turks and Caicos—especially off Grand Turk, South Caicos, and Salt Cay—is still considered among the best in the world.

Off Providenciales, dive sites are along the north shore's barrier reef. Most sites can be reached in anywhere from 10 minutes to 1½ hours. Dive sites feature spur-and-groove coral formations atop a coral-covered slope. Popular stops like **Aquarium, Pinnacles,** and **Grouper Hole** have large schools of fish, turtles, nurse sharks, and gray reef sharks. From the south side dive boats go to **French Cay, West Caicos, South West Reef,** and **Northwest Point.** Known for typically calm conditions and clear water, the West Caicos Marine National Park is a favorite stop. The area has dramatic walls and marine life, including sharks, eagle rays, and octopus, with large stands of pillar coral and huge barrel sponges.

Off Grand Turk, the 7,000-foot coral wall **drop-off** is actually within swimming distance of the beach. Buoyed sites along the wall have swim-through tunnels, cascading sand chutes, imposing coral pinnacles, dizzying vertical drops, and undercuts where the wall goes beyond the vertical and fades beneath the reef.

Caicos Dream Tours (☎ 649/243–3560 ⊕ www.caicosdreamtours.com), at the Alexandra Resort, offers several snorkeling trips, including one that has you diving for conch before lunch on a gorgeous beach. The company also offers private charters.

Dive Provo (✉ Ports of Call, Grace Bay ☎ 649/946–5040 or 800/234–7768 ⊕ www.diveprovo.com) is a PADI five-star operation that runs daily one- and two-tank dives to popular Grace Bay sites.

Provo Turtle Divers (✉ Turtle Cove Marina, Turtle Cove ☎ 649/946–4232 or 800/833–1341 ⊕ www.provoturtledivers.com), which also operates satellite locations at the Ocean Club East and Ocean Club West, has been on Provo since the 1970s. The staff is friendly, knowledgeable, and unpretentious.

FISHING

The islands' fertile waters are great for angling—anything from bottom- and reef-fishing (most likely to produce plenty of bites and a large catch) to bonefishing and deep-sea fishing (among the finest in the Caribbean). Each July the Caicos Classic Catch & Release Tournament attracts anglers from across the islands and the United States who compete to catch the biggest Atlantic blue marlin, tuna, or wahoo. For any fishing activity, you are required to purchase a $15 visitor's fishing license; operators generally furnish all equipment, drinks, and snacks. Prices range from $100 to $375, depending on the length of trip and size of boat. For deep-sea fishing trips in search of marlin, sailfish, wahoo, tuna, barracuda, and shark, look up **Grandslam Fishing Charters** (✉ *Turtle Cove Marina, Turtle Cove* ☎ *649/231–4420* ⊕ *www.GSFishing.com*).

Captain Arthur Dean at **Silverdeep** (✉ *Leeward Marina, Leeward* ☎ *649/946–5612* ⊕ *www.silverdeep.com*) is said to be among the Caribbean's finest bonefishing guides.

GOLF

Fodor's Choice
★
The par-72, 18-hole championship course at **Provo Golf and Country Club** (✉ *Governor's Rd., Grace Bay* ☎ *649/946–5991* ⊕ *www.provogolfclub.com*) is a combination of lush greens and fairways, rugged limestone outcroppings, and freshwater lakes, and is ranked among the Caribbean's top courses. Fees are $160 for 18 holes with shared cart. Premium golf clubs are available.

Turks & Caicos Miniature Golf (✉ *Long Bay Rd., Leeward* ☎ *649/231–4653*) is open every day and offers free shuttle service to most Grace Bay hotels. A round costs $15, and there is an on-site bar and grill where you can eat after your game.

HORSEBACK RIDING

Provo's long beaches and secluded lanes are ideal for trail rides on horseback. **Provo Ponies** (☎ *649/946–5252* ⊕ *www.provoponies.com*) offers morning and afternoon rides for all levels. A 45-minute ride costs $45; an 80-minute ride is $65. The rates include transportation from all major hotels.

PARASAILING

A 15-minute parasailing flight over Grace Bay is available for $70 (single) or $120 (tandem) from **Captain Marvin's Watersports** (☎ *649/231–0643*), who will pick you up at your hotel for your flight. The views as you soar over the bite-shaped Grace Bay area, with spectacular views of the barrier reef, are truly unforgettable.

TENNIS

You can rent tennis equipment at **Provo Golf and Country Club** (✉ *Grace Bay* ☎ *649/946–5991* ⊕ *www.provogolfclub.com*) and play on the two lighted courts, which are among the island's best. Nonmembers can play until 5 pm for $10 per hour (reservation required).

WATERSKIING AND KITESURFING

Nautique Sports (✉ *Ventura House West 101, Grace Bay Rd.* ☎ *649/941–7544* ⊕ *www.nautiquesports.com*) offers a water-sports dream. What better place to learn to ski than on the calm, crystal-clear waters of Providenciales. A great company for beginners, Nautique offers private instruction and will have you skiing in no time. Experts can try barefoot skiing. The company also rents kitesurfing equipment.

LITTLE WATER CAY

☺
★
This small, uninhabited cay is a protected area under the Turks & Caicos National Trust. On these 150 acres are two trails, small lakes, red mangroves, and an abundance of native plants. Boardwalks protect the ground, and interpretive signs explain the habitat. The cay is home to about 2,000 rare, endangered rock iguanas. Experts say the iguanas

are shy, but these creatures actually seem rather curious. They waddle right up to you, as if posing for a picture. Several water-sports operators from Provo and North Caicos include a stop on the island as a part of their snorkeling or sailing excursions (it's usually called "Iguana Island"). There's a $5 fee for a permit to visit the cay, and the proceeds go toward conservation in the islands.

PARROT CAY

Once said to be a hideout for pirate Calico Jack Rackham and his lady cohorts Mary Read and Anne Bonny, the 1,000-acre cay, between Fort George Cay and North Caicos, is now the site of an ultraexclusive hideaway resort.

WHERE TO STAY

$$$$
RESORT
Fodor's Choice
★

Parrot Cay Resort. This private paradise, on its own island, combines minimalist tranquillity with the best service in Turks and Caicos. **Pros:** impeccable service; gorgeous, secluded beach; the spa is considered one of the best in the world. **Cons:** only two restaurants on the entire island; it can be costly to get back and forth to Provo for excursions, as there is only private ferry service. ⊠ *Parrot Cay* ✆ *Box 164, Providenciales* ☎ *649/946–7788* ⊕ *www.parrotcay.como.bz* ⇨ *42 rooms, 4 suites, 14 villas* ⚐ *In-room: a/c, kitchen (some), Wi-Fi. In-hotel: restaurants, tennis courts, bars, pool, gym, spa, beach, business center, water sports* ¶⊙ *Breakfast.*

PINE CAY

Pine Cay's 2½-mi-long (4-km-long) beach is among the most beautiful in the archipelago. The 800-acre private island is home to a secluded resort and around 37 private residences.

WHERE TO STAY

$$$$
ALL-INCLUSIVE
Fodor's Choice
★

Meridian Club. A private club atmosphere on the prettiest beach in Turks and Caicos is *the* place to de-stress, with no phones, no TVs, no a/c, no worries. **Pros:** the finest beach in Turks and Caicos; rates include some of the best food in the Turks and Caicos as well as snorkeling trips. **Cons:** no TVs or phones, so you are really unplugged here; costly to get back to Provo for shopping or other Provo-based excursions or activities. ⊠ *Pine Cay, Turks and Caicos, BWI* ☎ *649/946–7758 or 866/746–3229* ⊕ *www.meridianclub.com* ⇨ *12 rooms, 1 cottage, 7 villas* ⚐ *In-room: no a/c, no phone, no safe, no TV. In-hotel: restaurant, tennis court, bar, pool, beach, business center, water sports, some age restrictions* ☺ *Closed Aug.–Oct.* ¶⊙ *All-inclusive.*

NORTH CAICOS

Thanks to abundant rainfall, this 41-square-mi (106-square-km) island is the lushest of the Turks and Caicos. Bird lovers can see a large flock of flamingos here, anglers can find shallow creeks full of bonefish, and history buffs can visit the ruins of a Loyalist plantation. Although there's no traffic, almost all the roads are paved, so bicycling is an excellent way

Parrot Cay Resort.

to sightsee. The island is predicted to become one of the next tourism hot spots, and foundations have been laid for condo resorts on Horse Stable Beach and Sandy Point. Even though it's a quiet place, you can find some small eateries around the airport and in Whitby, giving you a chance to try local and seafood specialties, sometimes served with homegrown okra or corn.

You can now reach North Caicos from Provo with a daily ferry from Walkin Marina in Leeward; the trip takes about 30 minutes. If you rent a car on North Caicos, you can even drive on the new causeway to Middle Caicos, a great day trip from Provo.

EXPLORING NORTH CAICOS

Flamingo Pond. This is a regular nesting place for the beautiful pink birds. They tend to wander out into the middle of the pond, so bring binoculars to get a better look.

Kew. This settlement has a small post office, a school, a church, and ruins of old plantations—all set among lush tropical trees bearing limes, papayas, and custard apples. Visiting Kew will give you a better understanding of the daily life of many islanders.

Wades Green. Visitors can view well-preserved ruins of the greathouse, overseer's house, and surrounding walls of one of the most successful plantations of the Loyalist era. A lookout tower provides views for miles. Contact the National Trust for tour details. ⊠ *Kew* 🕾 *649/941–5710 for National Trust* 🖅 *$5* ⊗ *Daily, by appointment only.*

CLOSE UP

Local Souvenirs

What should you bring home after a fabulous vacation in the Turks and Caicos Islands? Here are a few suggestions, some of which are free!

If you comb Pelican Beach or go on a conch-diving excursion, bring two conch shells (the maximum number allowed) home. Remember, only the shell, no living thing, is allowed.

The Middle Caicos Coop shop in Blue Hills sells carved wooden boats from Middle Caicos, and local straw hats and bags. You'll find locally made ceramics at Art Provo and at Turks & Caicos National Trust (at Town Center Mall or next to Island Scoop Ice Cream).

There are two cultural centers, one between Ocean Club East and Club Med, and the other next to Beaches Resort (there's a third one under

construction between Aquamarine Beach Houses and Gansevoort). Here you'll find batik clothing and locally made jewelry. Custom-made pieces can be ordered.

The Conch Farm sells beautiful, affordable jewelry made from conch shells and freshwater pearls.

One of the best souvenirs is the hardcover coffee-table cookbook from the Red Cross. Not only is it gorgeous, featuring recipes from all the great chefs of the Turks and Caicos, but the proceeds help the Red Cross.

The best free souvenir—besides your phenomenal tan—is a potcake puppy. The puppy you adopt comes with carrier, papers, and all the shots—and will remind you year after year of your terrific vacation.

WHERE TO STAY

$–$$
RENTAL
🏨 **Caicos Beach Condos.** On Whitby Beach, this horseshoe-shape, two-story, solar-paneled hotel offers ocean views, comfortable and neatly furnished apartments, and a freshwater pool at quite reasonable rates. **Pros:** on the best beach of North Caicos; has the best restaurant on the island. **Cons:** you need a car to get anywhere on North Caicos; property is starting to age and could use some TLC. ⊠ *Whitby, North Caicos, Turks and Caicos, BWI* ☎ *649/946–7113 or 800/710–5204, 905/690–3817 in Canada* ⊕ *www.CaicosBeachCondos.com* 🛏 *10 suites* 🛎 *In-room: a/c, kitchen (some), no safe, no TV (some). In-hotel: restaurant, bar, pool, beach, business center, diving, water sports* ⊗ *Closed June 15–Oct. 15* � *No meals.*

¢
HOTEL
🏨 **Pelican Beach Hotel.** North Caicos islanders Susan and Clifford Gardiner built this small, palmetto-fringed hotel in the 1980s on the quiet, mostly deserted Whitby Beach. **Pros:** the beach is just outside your room. **Cons:** location may be too remote and sleepy for some people; beach is in a "natural" state, meaning seaweed and pine needles. ⊠ *Whitby, North Caicos, Turks and Caicos, BWI* ☎ *649/946–7112* ⊕ *www.pelicanbeach.tc* 🛏 *14 rooms, 2 suites* 🛎 *In-room: a/c, no phone, no safe, no TV. In-hotel: restaurant, bar, beach, water sports* ⊗ *Closed Aug. 15–Sept. 15* � *Some meals.*

MIDDLE CAICOS

At 48 square mi (124 square km) and with fewer than 300 residents, this is the largest and least developed of the inhabited islands in the Turks and Caicos chain. A limestone ridge runs to about 125 feet above sea level, creating dramatic cliffs on the north shore and a cave system farther inland. Middle Caicos has rambling trails along the coast; the **Crossing Place Trail**, maintained by the National Trust, follows the path used by the early settlers to go between the islands. Inland are quiet settlements with friendly residents. North Caicos and Middle Caicos are linked by a causeway; since they are now linked by a road, it's possible to take a ferry from Provo to North Caicos, rent a car, and explore both North Caicos and Middle Caicos.

EXPLORING MIDDLE CAICOS

Conch Bar Caves. These limestone caves have eerie underground lakes and milky-white stalactites and stalagmites. Archaeologists have discovered Lucayan Indian artifacts in the caves and the surrounding area. The caves are inhabited by some harmless bats. If you visit, don't worry—they don't bother visitors. It's best to get a guide. If you tour the caves, be sure to wear sturdy shoes, not sandals.

CAVE TOURS

Taxi driver and fisherman **Cardinal Arthur** (☎ 649/946–6107) can give you a good cave tour.

Local cave specialist and taxi driver **Ernest Forbes** (☎ 649/946–6140) can give you a cave tour and may even arrange for you to have a prix-fixe lunch at his house afterward if you ask nicely.

WHERE TO STAY

$–$$ ▣ **Blue Horizon Resort.** At this property, undulating cliffs skirt one of
RESORT the most dramatic beaches in the Turks and Caicos. **Pros:** breathtaking views of Mudjin Harbor from the rooms; lack of amenities and development make you feel like you're away from it all. **Cons:** lack of amenities and development; may be too isolated for some. ⊠ *Mudjin Harbor, Conch Bar, Middle Caicos, Turks and Caicos, BWI* ☎ *649/946–6141* ⊕ *www.bhresort.com* ↝ *5 cottages, 2 villas* ⚷ *In-room: a/c, no phone (some), kitchen (some), no safe, no TV (some). In-hotel: beach, water sports* ⊙ *No meals.*

SOUTH CAICOS

This 8½-square-mi (21-square-km) island was once an important salt producer; today it's the heart of the fishing industry. Nature prevails, with long, white beaches, jagged bluffs, quiet backwater bays, and salt flats. Diving and snorkeling on the pristine wall and reefs are a treat enjoyed by only a few.

In September 2008 Hurricanes Hanna and Ike gave South Caicos a one-two punch, and many of the buildings at Cockburn Harbour received substantial damage; island residents had to wait more than a month to have power restored. The dive sights are fine, but the dive shops are gone, so you have to be an independent diver or take a diving excursion from another island. Also, there are four places to eat (with two of them open only occasionally for dinner).

EXPLORING SOUTH CAICOS

At the northern end of the island are fine white-sand beaches; the south coast is great for scuba diving along the drop-off; and there's excellent snorkeling off the windward (east) coast, where large stands of elkhorn and staghorn coral shelter several varieties of small tropical fish. A huge, sunken plane broken in pieces makes an excellent site. Spiny lobster and queen conch are found in the shallow Caicos Bank to the west and are harvested for export by local processing plants. The bonefishing here is some of the best in the West Indies.

Cockburn Harbour. The best natural harbor in the Caicos chain hosts the South Caicos Regatta, held each year in May.

THE TURKS

GRAND TURK

Just 7 mi (11 km) long and a little more than 1 mi (1½ km) wide, this island, the capital and seat of the Turks and Caicos government, has been a longtime favorite destination for divers eager to explore the 7,000-foot-deep pristine coral walls that drop down only 300 yards out to sea. On shore, the tiny, quiet island is home to white-sand beaches, the National Museum, and a small population of wild horses and donkeys, which leisurely meander past the white-walled courtyards, pretty churches, and bougainvillea-covered colonial inns on their daily commute into town. A cruise-ship complex that opened at the southern end of the island in 2006 brings about 300,000 visitors per year. Despite the dramatic changes this could make to this peaceful tourist spot, the dock is self-contained and is about 3 mi (5 km) from the tranquil, small hotels of Cockburn Town, Pillory Beach, and the Ridge, and far from most of the western-shore dive sites. The influx has also pushed Grand Turk to open up a few new historic sites, including Grand Turk's Old Prison and the Lighthouse.

EXPLORING GRAND TURK

Pristine beaches with vistas of turquoise waters, small local settlements, historic ruins, and native flora and fauna are among the sights on Grand Turk. Fewer than 5,000 people live on this 7½-square-mi (19-square-km) island, and it's hard to get lost, as there aren't many roads.

COCKBURN TOWN

The buildings in the colony's capital and seat of government reflect a 19th-century Bermudian style. Narrow streets are lined with low stone walls and old street lamps, which are now powered by electricity. The once-vital *salinas* (natural salt pans, where the sea leaves a film of salt) have been restored, and covered benches along the sluices offer shady spots for observing wading birds, including flamingos that frequent the shallows. Be sure to pick up a copy of the tourist board's *Heritage Walk* guide to discover Grand Turk's rich architecture.

All in the Family

Belongers, from the taxi driver meeting you to the chef feeding you, are often connected. "Oh, him?" you will hear. "He my cousin!" As development has been mercifully slow, such family connections, as well as crafts, bush medicine, ripsaw music, storytelling, and even recipes, have remained constant. But where do such traditions come from? Recently, researchers came closer to finding out. Many Belongers had claimed that their great-great-grandparents told them their forebears came directly from Africa. For decades their stories were ignored. Indeed, most experts believed that Belongers were descendants of mostly second-generation Bermudian and Caribbean slaves.

In 2005 museum researchers continued their search for a lost slave ship called *Trouvadore*. The ship, which wrecked off East Caicos in 1841, carried a cargo of 193 Africans, captured to be sold into slavery, almost all of whom miraculously survived the wreck. As slavery had been abolished in this British territory at the time, all the Africans were found and freed in the Turks and Caicos Islands. Since there were only a few thousand inhabitants in the islands at the time, these first-generation African survivors were a measurable minority (about 7% of the population then). Researchers have concluded that all the existing Belongers may be linked by blood or marriage to this one incident.

During one expedition divers found a wrecked ship of the right time period. If these remains are *Trouvadore*, the Belongers may finally have a physical link to their past, to go with their more intangible cultural traditions. So while you're in the islands, look closely at the intricately woven baskets, listen carefully to the African rhythms in the ripsaw music, and savor the stories you hear. They may very well be the legacy of *Trouvadore* speaking to you from the past. For more information, check out the Web site ⊕ www.trouvadore.org.

9

Her Majesty's Prison. This prison was built in the 19th century to house runaway slaves and slaves who survived the wreck of the *Trouvadore* in 1841. After the slaves were granted freedom, the prison housed criminals and even modern-day drug runners until it closed in the 1990s. The last hanging here was in 1960. Now you can see the cells, solitary-confinement area, and exercise patio. The prison is open only when there is a cruise ship at the port. ⊠ *Pond St., Cockburn Town* 🕾 *No phone.*

⏱ ★ **Turks and Caicos National Museum.** In one of the oldest stone buildings on the islands, the national museum houses the Molasses Reef wreck, the earliest shipwreck—dating to the early 1500s—discovered in the Americas. The natural-history exhibits include artifacts left by Taíno, African, North American, Bermudian, French, and Latin American settlers. The museum has a 3-D coral reef exhibit, a walk-in Lucayan cave with wooden artifacts, and a gallery dedicated to Grand Turk's little-known involvement in the Space Race (John Glenn made landfall here after being the first American to orbit the Earth). An interactive children's gallery keeps knee-high visitors "edutained." The museum also claims that Grand Turk was where Columbus first landed in the New World.

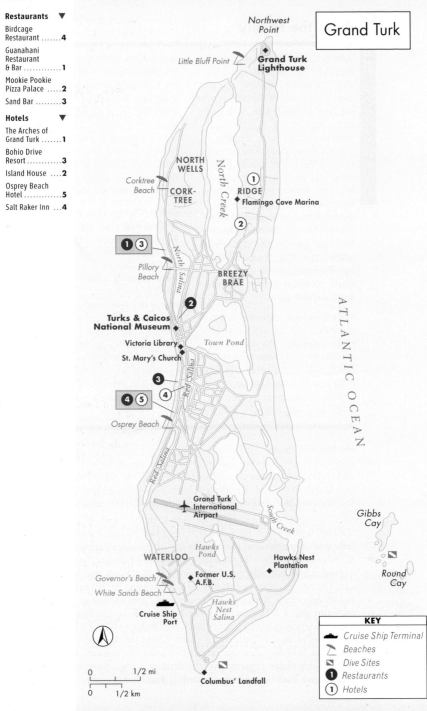

Grand Turk

Northwest
Point

Little Bluff Point

**Grand Turk
Lighthouse**

North Creek

**NORTH
WELLS**

Corktree
Beach

**CORK-
TREE**

RIDGE ①

● Flamingo Cove Marina

②

① ③

North Salina

Pillory
Beach

**BREEZY
BRAE**

②

**Turks & Caicos
National Museum** ●

Victoria Library ●

St. Mary's Church ●

Town Pond

③

④

④ ⑤

Osprey Beach

Red Salina

**Grand Turk
International
Airport** ✈

South Creek

A T L A N T I C   O C E A N

Gibbs
Cay

WATERLOO

Hawks
Pond

**Hawks Nest
Plantation** ●

Round
Cay

Governor's Beach

White Sands Beach

● **Former U.S.
A.F.B.**

Hawks
Nest
Salina

**Cruise Ship
Port**

Columbus' Landfall

0 ——— 1/2 mi

0 ——— 1/2 km

KEY

⛴ Cruise Ship Terminal

◿ Beaches

◼ Dive Sites

① Restaurants

① Hotels

The most original display is a collection of messages in bottles that have washed ashore from all over the world. ⊠ *Duke St., Cockburn Town* ☎ *649/946–2160* ⊕ *www.tcmuseum.org* 🎫 *$5* ⊙ *Mon., Tues., Thurs., and Fri. 9–4, Wed. 9–5, Sat. 9–1.*

BEYOND COCKBURN TOWN

Grand Turk Lighthouse. More than 150 years old, the lighthouse, built in the United Kingdom and transported piece by piece to the island, used to protect ships in danger of wrecking on the northern reefs. Use this panoramic landmark as a starting point for a breezy cliff-top walk by following the donkey trails to the deserted eastern beach. ⊠ *Lighthouse Rd., North Ridge.*

WHERE TO EAT

Conch in every shape and form, fresh grouper, and lobster (in season) are the favorite dishes at the laid-back restaurants that line Duke Street. Away from these more touristy areas, smaller and less expensive eateries serve chicken and ribs, curried goat, peas and rice, and other native island specialties. Prices are more expensive than in the United States, as most of the produce has to be imported.

$$$
CARIBBEAN
★
✕ **Birdcage Restaurant.** At the top of Duke Street, this has become the place to be on Sunday and Wednesday nights, when a sizzling barbecue of ribs, chicken, and lobster combines with live Rake 'n' Scrape music from a local group called High Tide to draw an appreciative crowd. Arrive before 8 pm to secure beachside tables and an unrestricted view of the band; the location around the Osprey pool is lovely. The rest of the week, enjoy more elegant and eclectic fare accompanied by an increasingly impressive wine list. ⊠ *Osprey Beach Hotel, Duke St., Cockburn Town* ☎ *649/946–2666* ⊕ *www.ospreybeachhotel.com/dining/.*

$$$
ECLECTIC
★
✕ **Guanahani Restaurant and Bar.** Off the town's main drag, this restaurant sits on a stunning but quiet stretch of beach. The food goes beyond the usual Grand Turk fare, thanks to the talents of Canadian-born chef Zev Beck, who takes care of the evening meals. His pecan-crusted mahimahi and crispy sushi rolls are to die for. For lunch, Middle Caicos native Miss Leotha makes juicy jerk chicken to keep the crowd happy. The menu changes daily. The food is some of the best in Grand Turk. ⊠ *Bohio Dive Resort & Spa, Pillory Beach* ☎ *649/946–2135* ⊕ *www.bohioresort.com.*

$
ECLECTIC
✕ **Mookie Pookie Pizza Palace.** Local husband-and-wife team "Mookie" and "Pookie" have created a wonderful backstreet parlor that has gained well-deserved popularity over the years as much more than a pizza place. At lunchtime the tiny eatery is packed with locals ordering specials such as steamed beef, curried chicken, and curried goat. You can also get burgers and omelets, but stick to the specials if you want fast service, and dine in if you want to get a true taste of island living. By night the place becomes Grand Turk's one and only pizza take-out and delivery service, so if you're renting a villa or condo, put this spot on speed dial. ⊠ *Hospital Rd., Cockburn Town* ☎ *649/946–1538* ▭ *No credit cards* ⊙ *Closed Sun.*

$$
AMERICAN
✕ **Sand Bar.** Run by two Canadian sisters, this popular beachside bar is a good value, though the menu is limited to fish-and-chips, quesadillas,

9

and similarly basic bar fare. The tented wooden terrace jutting out onto the beach provides shade during the day, making it an ideal lunch spot, but it's also a great place to watch the sunset. The service is friendly, and the local crowd often spills into the street. ⊠ *Duke St., Cockburn Town* ☎ *No phone.*

WHERE TO STAY

Accommodations include original Bermudian inns, more modern but small beachfront hotels, and very basic to well-equipped self-catering suites and apartments. Almost all hotels offer dive packages, which are an excellent value.

The following reviews have been condensed for this book. Please go to Fodors.com for expanded reviews of each property.

$ **Bohio Dive Resort and Spa.** Completely restored after two hurricanes

RESORT   in September 2008, this basic yet comfortable hotel is the choice of divers. **Pros:** has the best restaurant in Grand Turk; on a gorgeous beach; steps away from awesome snorkeling. **Cons:** three-night minimum doesn't allow for quick getaways from Provo. ⊠ *Pillory Beach, Grand Turk, Turks and Caicos, BWI* ☎ *649/946–2135* ⊕ *www.bohioresort. com* ⇨ *12 rooms, 4 suites* △ *In-room: a/c, no phone, no safe, kitchen (some). In-hotel: restaurant, bars, pool, spa, beach, business center, water sports* ⇨ *3-night minimum* ⊚ *No meals.*

$ **Island House.** Years of business-travel experience have helped Colin

RENTAL   Brooker create the comfortable, peaceful suites that overlook North

☾   Creek. **Pros:** full condo units feel like a home away from home. **Cons:** not on the beach; you need a car to get around. ⊠ *Lighthouse Rd., Box 36, Grand Turk, Turks and Caicos, BWI* ☎ *649/946–1519* ⊕ *www. islandhouse.tc* ⇨ *8 suites* △ *In-room: a/c, kitchen, no safe, Wi-Fi. In-hotel: pool, laundry facilities, water sports, some pets allowed* ⇨ *2-night minimum* ⊚ *No meals.*

¢–$ **Osprey Beach Hotel.** Grand Turk veteran hotelier Jenny Smith has

HOTEL   transformed this two-story oceanfront hotel with her artistic touches:

Fodor's Choice   palms, frangipani, and deep green azaleas frame it like a painting. **Pros:**

★   renovated in 2007; best hotel on Grand Turk; walking distance to Front Street, restaurants, and excursions. **Cons:** three-night minimum; rocky beachfront. ⊠ *Duke St., Cockburn Town, Grand Turk, Turks and Caicos, BWI* ☎ *649/946–2666* ⊕ *www.ospreybeachhotel.com* ⇨ *11 rooms, 16 suites* △ *In-room: a/c, kitchen (some), no safe, Wi-Fi (some). In-hotel: restaurant, bar, pool, beach, water sports, some pets allowed* ⇨ *3-night minimum* ⊚ *No meals.*

¢–$ **Salt Raker Inn.** A large anchor on the sun-dappled pathway marks the

B&B/INN   entrance to this 19th-century house, which is now an unpretentious inn. **Pros:** excellent location that is an easy walk to Front Street, restaurants, and excursions. **Cons:** no no-smoking rooms. ⊠ *Duke St., Box 1, Cockburn Town, Grand Turk, Turks and Caicos, BWI* ☎ *649/946–2260* ⊕ *www.hotelsaltraker.com* ⇨ *10 rooms, 3 suites* △ *In-room: a/c, no safe, Wi-Fi. In-hotel: restaurant, bar, some pets allowed* ⊚ *No meals.*

Cockburn Town, Grand Turk.

NIGHTLIFE

Grand Turk is a quiet place where you come to relax and unwind, so most of the nightlife consists of little more than happy hour at sunset, so you have a chance to glimpse the elusive green flash. Most restaurants turn into gathering places where you can talk with the new friends you have made that day, but there a few more nightlife-oriented places that will keep you busy after dark. On some evenings you'll be able to catch Mitch Rollings of Blue Water Divers; he often headlines the entertainment at the island's different restaurants.

Nookie Hill Club. On weekends and holidays the younger crowd heads over to the Nookie Hill Club for late-night drinking and dancing. ⊠ *Nookie Hill* ☏ *No phone.*

Osprey Beach Hotel. Every Wednesday and Sunday there's lively Rake 'n' Scrape music at the Osprey Beach Hotel. ⊠ *Duke St., Cockburn Town* ☏ *649/946–2666.*

Salt Raker Inn. On Friday, Rake 'n' Scrape bands play at the Salt Raker Inn. ⊠ *Duke St., Cockburn Town* ☏ *649/946–2260.*

SPORTS AND ACTIVITIES

BICYCLING

The island's mostly flat terrain isn't very taxing, and most roads have hard surfaces. Take water with you: there are few places to stop for refreshments. Most hotels have bicycles available, but you can also rent them for $10 to $15 a day from **Oasis Divers** (⊠ *Duke St., Cockburn Town* ☏☏ *649/946–1128* ⊕ *www.oasisdivers.com*).

DIVING AND SNORKELING

★ In these waters you can find undersea cathedrals, coral gardens, and countless tunnels, but note that you must carry and present a valid certificate card before you'll be allowed to dive. As its name suggests, the **Black Forest** offers staggering black-coral formations as well as the occasional black-tip shark. In the **Library** you can study fish galore, including large numbers of yellowtail snapper. At the Columbus Passage separating South Caicos from Grand Turk, each side of a 22-mi-wide (35-km-wide) channel drops more than 7,000 feet. From January through March, thousands of Atlantic humpback whales swim through en route to their winter breeding grounds. **Gibb's Cay,** a small cay a couple of miles off of Grand Turk where you can swim with stingrays, makes for a great excursion.

Blue Water Divers (✉ *Duke St., Cockburn Town, Grand Turk* ☎649/946-2432 ⊕ *www.grandturkscuba.com*) has been in operation on Grand Turk since 1983 and is the only PADI Gold Palm five-star dive center on the island. Owner Mitch will undoubtedly put some of your underwater adventures to music in the evenings when he plays at the Osprey Beach Hotel or Salt Raker Inn. **Oasis Divers** (✉ *Duke St., Cockburn Town* ☎649/946-1128 ⊕ *www.oasisdivers.com*) specializes in complete gear handling and pampering treatment. It also supplies Nitrox and rebreathers.

SALT CAY

Fewer than 100 people live on this 2½-square-mi (6-square-km) dot of land, maintaining an unassuming lifestyle against a backdrop of stucco cottages, stone ruins, and weathered wooden windmills standing sentry in the abandoned salinas. The beautifully preserved island is bordered by beaches where weathered green and blue sea glass and pretty shells often wash ashore. Beneath the waves, 10 dive sites are minutes from shore.

There are big plans for Salt Cay, which will change the small island forever, though probably not for several years. Gone will be the donkeys and chickens roaming the streets; in their place will be a luxurious resort and new golf course. If you want to see how the Caribbean was when it was laid-back, sleepy, and colorful, visit the island now before it changes.

EXPLORING SALT CAY

Salt sheds and salinas are silent reminders of the days when the island was a leading producer of salt. Now the salt ponds attract abundant birdlife. Island tours are often conducted by motorized golf carts. From January through April humpback whales pass by on the way to their winter breeding grounds.

What little development there is on Salt Cay is found in its main community, Balfour Town. It's home to several small hotels and a few cozy stores, as well as the main dock and the Coral Reef Bar & Grill, where locals hang out with tourists to watch the sunset and drink a beer.

White House. The grand stone house, which once belonged to a wealthy salt merchant, is testimony to the heyday of Salt Cay's eponymous industry. Still privately owned by the descendants of the original family, it's sometimes opened up for tours. It's worth asking your guesthouse or hotel owner—or any local passerby—if Salt Cay islander "Uncle Lionel" is on-island, as he may give you a personal tour to see the still-intact, original furnishings, books, and medicine cabinet that date back to the early 1800s. ⊠ *Victoria St., Balfour Town.*

WHERE TO EAT

$$$
ECLECTIC
★

✕**Island Thyme Bistro.** Owner Porter Williams serves potent alcoholic creations as well as fairly sophisticated local and international cuisine. Try steamed, freshly caught snapper in a pepper-wine sauce with peas and rice, or spicy-hot chicken curry served with tangy chutneys. Don't forget to order the "Porter" house steak. You can take cooking lessons from the chef, enjoy the nightly Filipino fusion tapas during happy hour, and join the gang for Friday-night pizza. This is a great place to make friends and the best place to catch up on island gossip. The airy, trellis-covered spot overlooks the salinas. There's a small shop with gifts and tourist information; you can also get a manicure or pedicure here. ⊠ *North District* ☎ *649/946–6977* ⊕ *www.islandthyme.tc/* ⟲ *Reservations essential* ☉ *Closed Wed. mid-May–June and Sept.–late Oct.*

$$
CARIBBEAN

✕**Pat's Place.** Island native Pat Simmons can give you a lesson in the medicinal qualities of her garden plants and periwinkle flowers, as well as provide excellent native cuisine for a very reasonable price in her typical Salt Cay home. Home cooking doesn't get any closer to home than this. Try conch fritters for lunch and steamed grouper with okra rice for dinner. Be sure to call ahead, as she cooks only when there's someone to cook for. Pat also has a small grocery shop selling staples. ⊠ *South District* ☎ *649/946–6919* ⟲ *Reservations essential* ⊟ *No credit cards.*

WHERE TO STAY

$
HOTEL

⛱**Pirates Hideaway and Blackbeard's Quarters.** Owner Candy Herwin— true to her self-proclaimed pirate status—has smuggled artistic treasures across the ocean and created her own masterpieces to deck out this lair. **Pros:** artist workshops are offered during peak season. **Cons:** rocky beachfront. ⊠ *Victoria St., South District, Salt Cay, Turks and Caicos, BWI* ☎ *649/946–6909* ⊕ *www.saltcay.tc* ↷ *2 suites, 1 house* ⟲ *In-room: no a/c, no phone, kitchen (some), no safe. In-hotel: beach, water sports* ⎟◎⎟ *No meals.*

$
RENTAL

⛱**Tradewinds Guest Suites.** Yards away from Dean's Dock, a grove of whispering casuarina trees surrounds these five single-story, basic apartments, which offer a moderate-budget option on Salt Cay with the option of dive packages. **Pros:** walking distance to diving, fishing, dining, and dancing. **Cons:** a/c costs extra; some may feel isolated with few nighttime activities and no TV. ⊠ *Victoria St., Balfour Town, Salt Cay, Turks and Caicos, BWI* ☎ *649/946–6906* ⊕ *www.tradewinds.tc* ↷ *5 apartments* ⟲ *In-room: no phone, kitchen (some), no TV, no safe. In-hotel: beach, water sports* ⎟◎⎟ *No meals.*

$$–$$$
RENTAL

⛱**Villas of Salt Cay.** One of the nicest and newest places to stay in Salt Cay is centrally located on Victoria Street, in the middle of everything.

Pros: bedrooms are set up for extra privacy; on Victoria Street within walking distance of everything; on a private stretch of beach. **Cons:** not all rooms have a/c; cabanas don't have kitchens; shared pool. ⊠ *Victoria St., Balfour Town, Salt Cay, Turks and Caicos, Islands, BWI* ☏ *649/946–6909* ⊕ *www.villasofsaltcay.com* ⥲ *1 2-bedroom villa, 1 1-bedroom cottage, 3 cabanas* ⚇ *In-room: no a/c (some), kitchen (some), no safe, Wi-Fi. In-hotel: pool, beach* ◯| *No meals.*

SPORTS AND ACTIVITIES

DIVING AND SNORKELING

Scuba divers can explore the wreck of the *Endymion,* a 140-foot wooden-hull British warship that sank in 1790; you can swim through the hull and spot cannons and anchors. It's off the southern point of Salt Cay.

Salt Cay Divers (⊠ *Balfour Town* ☏ *649/946–6906* ⊕ *www.saltcaydivers. tc*) conducts daily dive trips and rents all the necessary equipment. You'll pay around $80 for a two-tank dive.

WHALE-WATCHING

During the winter months (January through April), Salt Cay is a center for whale-watching, when some 2,500 humpback whales pass close to shore. Whale-watching trips can most easily be organized through your inn or guesthouse.

Travel Smart
Bahamas

WORD OF MOUTH

"FYI—most of the Bahamas Islands are fairly far north in the Atlantic and can be 'cool' in February, in some cases it could be too cool for swimming."
—Roams Around

"February—March is still peak season in Caribbean and Bahamas. If you are on a budget, you may want to hold off until May, when prices drop."
—BLamona

GETTING HERE AND AROUND

▌ AIR TRAVEL

Most international flights to the Bahamas connect through airports in Florida, New York, Charlotte, or Atlanta. The busiest airport in the Bahamas is in Nassau, which has the most connections to the more remote Out Islands. If you're traveling to these more remote islands, you might have to make a connection in both Florida and Nassau—and you still may have to take a ferry or a water taxi to your final destination.

A direct flight from New York City to Nassau takes approximately three hours. The flight from Charlotte to Nassau is two hours, and the flight from Miami to Nassau takes about an hour. Most flights between the islands of the Bahamas take less than an hour. You'll probably spend more time on the ground waiting than in the air.

Airline Security Issues Transportation Security Administration (⊕ *www.tsa.gov*).

AIRPORTS

The major gateways to the Bahamas include Lynden Pindling International Airport (NAS) on New Providence Island, and Freeport Grand Bahama International Airport (FPO) on Grand Bahama Island. There are no hotels near either airport. *For more airports, ⇨ see individual chapters.*

Airport Information Grand Bahama International Airport (☎ *242/352–6020*). **Lynden Pindling International Airport** (☎ *242/377–0209*).

FLIGHTS

Air service to the Bahamas varies seasonally, with the biggest choice of flights usually available in the Christmas to Easter window.

Local carriers come and go, especially in the Out Islands, which are served mostly by smaller commuter and charter operations. Schedules change frequently. The smallest cays may have scheduled service only a few days a week. In the Out Islands, ask your hotel for flight recommendations, as they are likely to have the most up-to-date information on carriers and schedules; some can even help you book air travel.

Airline Contacts American Airlines (☎ *800/433–7300*). **Continental Airlines** (☎ *800/231–0856*). **Delta Airlines** (☎ *800/221–1212*). **JetBlue** (☎ *800/538–2583*). **Spirit Airlines** (☎ *800/772–7117*). **US Airways** (☎ *800/428–4322*).

Smaller Airlines Air Sunshine (☎ *954/434–8900 or 800/327–8900* ⊕ *www.airsunshine. com*). **Bahamasair** (☎ *242/702–4140 or 800/222–4262* ⊕ *www.bahamasair.com*). **Cat Island Air** (☎ *242/377–3318* ⊕ *www.flycatislandair.com*). **Cherokee Air** (☎ *242/367–1900 or 866/920–9970* ⊕ *www.cherokeeair. com*). **Gulfstream International Airways** (☎ *800/231–0856* ⊕ *www.gulfstreamair.com*). **Florida Coastal Air** (☎ *954/990–1700* ⊕ *fly-fca.net*). **Island Air** (☎ *800/444–9904* ⊕ *www. islandaircharters.com*). **LeAir** (☎ *242/377–2356* ⊕ *www.leaircharters.com*). **Performance Air** (☎ *242/341–3281* ⊕ *www.performance-air. com*). **Pineapple Air** (☎ *242/377–0412* ⊕ *www. pineappleair.com*). **Regional Air** (☎ *800/598–8660* ⊕ *www.goregionalair.com*). **Sky Bahamas Air** (☎ *242/300–0294* ⊕ *skybahamas.net*). **Southern Air** (☎ *242/377–2014* ⊕ *www. southernaircharter.com*). **Twin Air Calypso** (☎ *954/359–8266* ⊕ *www.flytwinair.com*). **Yellow Air Taxi** (☎ *888/935–5694* ⊕ *www.flyyellowairtaxi.com*). **Western Air** (☎ *242/377–2222* ⊕ *www.westernairbahamas.com*).

Within the Turks and Caicos Air Turks and Caicos (☎ *649/946–4999 or 954/323–4949* ⊕ *www.airturksandcaicos.com*). **Lynx Air International** (☎ *888/596–9247*).

▮ BOAT TRAVEL

BOATS AND FERRIES

If you're adventurous and have time to spare, take a ferry or one of the traditional mail boats that regularly leave Nassau from Potter's Cay, under the Paradise Island Bridge. Although fast, modern, air-conditioned boats now make some of the trips, certain remote destinations are still served by slow, old-fashioned craft. Especially if you choose the mail-boat route, you may even find yourself sharing company with goats or chickens, and making your way on deck through piles of lumber and crates of cargo; on these lumbering mail boats, expect to spend 5 to 12 or more hours slowly making your way between island outposts. These boats operate on Bahamian time, which is a casual unpredictable measure, and the schedules can be thrown off by bad weather. Mail boats cannot generally be booked in advance, and services are limited. In Nassau, check details with the dockmaster's office at Potter's Cay. One-way trips can cost from $35 to $100.

Within the Bahamas, Bahamas Ferries has the most, and most comfortable, options for island-hopping, with air-conditioned boats that offer food and beverages served by cabin attendants. Schedules do change rather frequently; if you're planning to ferry back to an island to catch a flight, check and double-check the departure times, and build in extra time in case the weather's bad or the boat inexplicably doesn't make the trip you'd planned on. Ferries serve most of the major tourist destinations from Nassau, including Spanish Wells, Governor's Harbour, Harbour Island, Abaco, Exuma, and Andros. The high-speed ferry that runs between Nassau and Spanish Wells, Governor's Harbour, and Harbour Island costs $65 one way, and takes about two hours each way.

Local ferries in the Out Islands transport islanders and visitors from the main island to smaller cays. Usually, these ferries make several round-trips daily, and keep a more punctual schedule than the longer-haul ferry.

If you're setting sail yourself, note that cruising boats must clear customs at the nearest port of entry before beginning any diving or fishing. The fee is $150 for boats 35 feet and under and $300 for boats 36 feet and longer, which includes fishing permits and departure tax for up to four persons. Each additional person above the age of four will be charged the $15 departure tax. Stays of longer than 12 months must be arranged with Bahamas customs and immigration officials.

Boat and Ferry Contacts Bahamas Ferries (☎ 242/323–2166 ⊕ www.bahamasferries. com). **Potter's Cay Dockmaster** (☎ 242/393–1064).

CRUISES

A cruise can be one of the most pleasurable ways to see the islands. A multi-island excursion allows for plenty of land time because of the short travel times between destinations. Be sure to shop around before booking.

From Florida, the Discovery Cruise Line departs for Grand Bahama Island at 9:30 am daily, except Wednesday, with its 1,100-passenger *Discovery Sun*, complete with swimming pool, casino, live entertainment, disco, and buffets. Passengers can make it a day trip, arriving in the Bahamas by 1:30 pm and departing at 5:15 pm, or they can stay on the island for a few days. Round-trip fares, including two buffets and drinks, start at about $80, plus a surcharge of $35 per person to cover fees and taxes.

Cruise Lines Carnival Cruise Line (☎ 800/227–6482). **Celebrity Cruises** (☎ 800/647–2251). **Costa Cruises** (☎ 800/ 462–6782). **Discovery Cruise Line** (☎ 800/259–1579). **Disney Cruise Line** (☎ 800/951–3532). **Holland America Line** (☎ 877/932–4259). **Norwegian Cruise Line** (☎ 866/234–7350). **Princess Cruises** (☎ 800/774–6237). **Regent Seven Seas Cruises** (☎ 800/505–5370). **Royal Caribbean International** (☎ 800/327–6700).

▌ CAR TRAVEL

International rental agencies are generally in Nassau, and you will rent from privately owned companies on the small islands. Be warned that you might have to settle for a rusty heap that doesn't have working seat belts. Check it out thoroughly before you leave. And assume that companies won't have car seats—bring your own.

To rent a car, you must be 21 years of age or older in both the Bahamas and the Turks and Caicos, the latter of which charges a flat tax of $15 on all rentals.

It's common to hire a driver with a van, and prices are negotiable. Most drivers charge by the half day or full day, and prices depend on the stops and distance, although half-day tours are generally $50 to $100 for one to four people. Full-day tours are $100 to $200. It's customary to pay for the driver's lunch. All tour guides in the Bahamas are required to take a tourism course, pass a test to be a guide, and are required to get a special license to operate a taxi.

GASOLINE

The cost of fuel in the Bahamas is usually at least twice that in the United States, and prepare to pay in cash. Stations may be few and far between on the Out Islands. Keep the car full. You can ask for a handwritten receipt if printed ones are not available. Gas stations may be closed Sunday.

PARKING

There are few parking meters in the Bahamas, none in downtown Nassau. Police are lenient with visitors' rental cars parked illegally and will generally just ask the driver to move it. Parking spaces are hard to find in Nassau, so be prepared to park on a side street and walk. Most hotels offer off-street parking for guests. There are few parking lots not associated with hotels.

ROADSIDE EMERGENCIES

In case of a road emergency, stay in your vehicle with your emergency flashers engaged and wait for help, especially after dark. If someone stops to help, relay information through a small opening in the window. If it's daylight and help does not arrive, walk to the nearest phone and call for help. In the Bahamas, motorists readily stop to help drivers in distress.

Ask for emergency numbers at the rental office when you pick up your car. These numbers vary from island to island. On smaller islands the owner of the company may want you to call him at his home.

RULES OF THE ROAD

Remember, like the British, islanders drive on the left side of the road, which can be confusing because most cars are American with the steering wheel on the left. It is illegal, however, to make a left-hand turn on a red light. Many streets in downtown Nassau are one-way. Roundabouts pose further confusion to Americans. Remember to keep left and yield to oncoming traffic as you enter the roundabout and at "Give Way" signs.

▌ TAXI TRAVEL

There are taxis waiting at every airport and outside all of the main hotels and cruise-ship docks. Beware of "hackers"—drivers who don't display their license (and may not have one). Sometimes you can negotiate a fare, but you must do so before you enter the taxi.

You'll find that Bahamian taxi drivers are more talkative than their U.S. counterparts. When you take a taxi to dinner or to town, it's common for the driver to wait and take you back, which doesn't cost more. A 15% tip is suggested.

ESSENTIALS

▮ ACCOMMODATIONS

The lodgings we list are the cream of the crop in each price category. We always list the facilities that are available—but we don't specify whether they cost extra: when pricing accommodations, always ask what's included.

⇨ *For lodging price categories, consult the price charts found near the beginning of each chapter.*

▮TIP➔ Assume that hotels operate on the European Plan (**EP**, no meals) unless we specify that they use the Breakfast Plan (**BP**, with full breakfast), Continental Plan (**CP**, continental breakfast), Full American Plan (**FAP**, all meals), or Modified American Plan (**MAP**, breakfast and dinner), or are all-inclusive (**AI**, all meals and most activities).

APARTMENT AND HOUSE RENTALS

Contacts **Bahamas Home Rentals** (☎ 888/881–2867 ⊕ www.bahamasweb.com). **Bahamas Vacation Homes** (☎ 242/333–4080 ⊕ www.bahamasvacationhomes.com). **Hope Town Hideaways** (☎ 242/366–0224 ⊕ www.hopetown.com). **Villas & Apartments Abroad** (☎ 212/213–6435 ⊕ www.vaanyc.com). **Villas International** (☎ 800/221–2260 ⊕ www.villasintl.com). **Villas of Distinction** (☎ 800/289–0900 ⊕ www.villasofdistinction.com). **Wimco** (☎ 800/449–1553 ⊕ www.wimco.com).

BED-AND-BREAKFASTS

Contacts **BedandBreakfast.com** (☎ 512/322–2710 or 800/462–2632 ⊕ www.bedandbreakfast.com).

HOME EXCHANGES

With a direct home exchange you stay in someone else's home while they stay in yours. Some outfits also deal with vacation homes, so you're not actually staying in someone's full-time residence, just their vacant weekend place.

Contacts **Home Exchange.com** (☎ 800/877–8723 ⊕ www.homeexchange.com). **HomeLink**

International (☎ 800/638–3841 ⊕ www.homelink.org). **Intervac U.S.** (☎ 800/756–4663 ⊕ www.intervacus.com).

▮ COMMUNICATIONS

INTERNET

Wireless Internet service is becoming more available throughout the islands, but there are still pockets where service is impossible or difficult to get, and it's likely to be slower than you may be accustomed to. If Internet is important, ask your hotel representative about service before traveling.

If you're carrying a laptop into the Bahamas, you must fill out a Declaration of Value form upon arrival, noting make, model, and serial number. The Bahamian electrical current is compatible with U.S. computers.

Contacts **Cybercafes** (⊕ www.cybercafes.com).

PHONES

Bahamas Telecommunications Company (BTC) is the phone company in the Bahamas. Pay phones accept Bahamas Direct Prepaid cards purchased from BTC at vending machines, stores, and BTC offices. You can use these cards to call within the country or to the United States.

Check with your calling-card provider before traveling to see if your card will work in the islands (on the smaller cays it almost certainly won't) and to see about surcharges. Always ask at your hotel desk about what charges will apply when you make card calls from your room. There's usually a charge for making toll-free calls to the United States. To place a call from a public phone using your own calling card, dial 0 for the operator, who will then place the call using your card number.

When you're calling the Bahamas, the country code is 242. The country code for the Turks and Caicos is 649. You can dial either number from the United States as you would make an interstate call.

CALLING WITHIN THE BAHAMAS

Within the Bahamas, to make a local call from your hotel room, dial 9, then the number. If your party doesn't answer before the fifth ring, hang up or you'll be charged for the call. Some 800 and 888 numbers—particularly airline and credit card numbers—can be called from the Bahamas. Others can be reached by substituting an 880 prefix and paying for the call.

Dial 916 for directory information and 0 for operator assistance.

CALLING OUTSIDE THE BAHAMAS

In big resorts instructions are given by the room phones on how to make international calls and the costs, which differ from resort to resort. In small inns, especially those in the Out Islands, you may not be able to get an AT&T, Sprint, or other operator or international operator, but the hotel front desk can usually do it for you.

The country code is 1 for the United States.

Access Codes AT&T USADirect (☎ *800/872-2881*). **MCI Call USA** (☎ *800/888-8000*). **Sprint** (☎ *800/389-2111*).

Phone Company BTC (☎ *242/225-5282* ⊕ *www.btcbahamas.com*).

MOBILE PHONES

Some U.S. cell phones work in the Bahamas; check with your provider before your trip. The BTC has roaming agreements with many U.S. companies,

including AT&T, T-Mobile, and Sprint Nextel. Roaming rates are $3 per day and $1.19 per minute.

In Nassau you can rent phones from BTC on a variety of packages. Or purchase a SIM card for about $15 at any BTC office; this will allow you to use your own cell phone while in the Bahamas. (You'll also need a BTC prepaid minutes card, but these cards can be purchased for as little as $10.) You can rent GMS cellular phones from companies such as Cellular Abroad, which charges $1.14 to $1.32 a minute on calls to the United States plus the rental of the phone, starting at $69 for a week or less. Service is improving, but is still spotty, and on the Out Islands, cell phones may not work at all.

▌ CUSTOMS AND DUTIES

Customs allows you to bring in 1 liter of wine or liquor and five cartons of cigarettes in addition to personal effects, purchases up to $100, and all the money you wish.

Certain types of personal belongings may get a raised eyebrow—an extensive collection of DVDs, for instance—if they suspect you may be planning to sell them while in the country. However, real hassles at immigration are rare, since officials realize tourists are the lifeblood of the economy.

You would be well advised to leave pets at home, unless you're considering a prolonged stay in the islands. An import permit is required from the Ministry of Agriculture and Fisheries for all animals brought into the Bahamas. The animal must be more than six months old. You'll also need a veterinary health certificate issued by a licensed vet. The permit is good for one year from the date of issue, costs $10, and the process must be completed immediately before departure.

U.S. residents who have been out of the country for at least 48 hours may bring home $800 worth of foreign goods duty-free, as long as they have not used the

$800 allowance or any part of it in the past 30 days.

Contacts Ministry of Agriculture and Fisheries (☎ *242/325-7502*). **U.S. Customs and Border Protection** (⊕ *www.cbp.gov*). **U.S. Embassy** (☎ *242/322-1181*).

▌EATING OUT

The restaurants we list are the cream of the crop in each price category. You'll find all types, from cosmopolitan to the most casual restaurants, serving all types of cuisine. Unless otherwise noted, the restaurants listed in this guide are open daily for lunch and dinner.

⇨ *For information on food-related health issues, see Health below. For dining price categories, consult the price charts found near the beginning of each chapter. For guidelines on tipping, see Tipping below.*

PAYING
The U.S. dollar is on par with the Bahamian dollar and both currencies are accepted in restaurants. Most credit cards are also accepted in most restaurants. Typically, you will have to ask for your check when you are finished.

RESERVATIONS AND DRESS
Reservations are sometimes necessary in Nassau and on the more remote islands, where restaurants may close early if no one shows up or says they're coming. We mention dress only when men are required to wear a jacket or a jacket and tie. Otherwise, you can assume that dining out is a casual affair.

WINES, BEER, AND SPIRITS
Kalik and Sands beer are brewed in the Bahamas and are available at most restaurants for lunch and dinner.

▌ELECTRICITY

Electricity is 120 volts/60 cycles AC, which is compatible with all U.S. appliances.

▌EMERGENCIES

The emergency telephone number in the Bahamas is 919 or 911. Pharmacies usually close at 6 pm. Emergency medicine after hours is available only at hospitals, or, on remote Out Islands, at clinics.

⇨ *For health-care contacts, please see the numbers listed at the front of each chapter.*

Emergency Contacts Bahamas Air Sea Rescue Association (☎ *242/325-8864 Nassau, 242/352-2628 Grand Bahama, 242/367-2226 Marsh Harbour*). **United States Embassy** (☎ *242/322-1181*).

▌HEALTH

FOOD AND WATER
The major health risk in the Bahamas is traveler's diarrhea. This is most often caused by ingesting fruits, shellfish, and drinks to which your body is unaccustomed. Go easy at first on new foods such as mangoes, conch, and rum punch. There are rare cases of contaminated fruit, vegetables, or drinking water.

If you're susceptible to digestive problems, avoid ice, uncooked food, and unpasteurized milk and milk products, and stick to bottled water, or water that has been boiled for several minutes, even when brushing your teeth.

Drink plenty of purified water or tea; chamomile is a good folk remedy. In severe cases, rehydrate yourself with a salt-sugar solution (½ teaspoon salt and 4 tablespoons sugar per quart of water).

DIVING
Do not fly within 24 hours of scuba diving. Always know where your nearest decompression chamber is *before* you embark on a dive expedition, and how you would get there in an emergency. The only chambers in the Bahamas are in Nassau and San Salvador, and emergency cases are often sent to Miami.

Decompression Chamber Bahamas Hyperbaric Centre (☎ *242/362-5765*).

LOCAL DO'S AND TABOOS

CUSTOMS OF THE COUNTRY

Humor is a wonderful way to relate to the islanders, but don't force it. Don't try to talk their dialect unless you are adept at it. Though most Bahamians are too polite to show it, you may offend them if you make a bad attempt at local lingo. Church is central in the lives of the Bahamians. They dress up in their fanciest finery; it's a sight to behold on Saturday evening and Sunday morning. To show respect, dress accordingly if you plan to attend religious ceremonies. No doubt you'll be outdone, but do dress up regardless.

GREETINGS

Bahamians greet people with a proper British "good morning," "good afternoon," or "good evening." When approaching an islander to ask directions or information, preface your request with such a greeting, and ask "how are you?" Smile, and don't rush into a conversation, even if you're running late.

LANGUAGE

Islanders speak English with a lilt influenced by their British and/or African ancestry. When locals talk among themselves in local dialect, it's virtually impossible for the unaccustomed to understand them. They take all sorts of shortcuts and pepper the language with words all their own. When islanders speak to visitors, they will use standard English.

OUT ON THE TOWN

When you hail a waiter, say Sir or Miss. Your check usually will not be brought until you ask for it. Bahamians do not like drunkenness, and, regrettably, frequently have to put up with drunken Americans. Bahamians generally are not smokers, so smokers should choose outdoor cafés and terraces at restaurants. And all you honeymooners, save the displays of affection for the hotel. PDAs are not accepted here—although Americans will blush at the way Bahamians dance, even the middle-aged, which is pelvis to pelvis. Bahamians love to dress up and will wear Sunday suits and dresses to dinner at nice restaurants and clubs.

SIGHTSEEING

Visitors should dress conservatively when going to houses of worship. Bahamians love hats, and you will see quite a parade of fancy hats at church even on small islands. You should not wear swimsuits into stores and restaurants, even those on the beach. There are very few homeless Bahamians, and on the few occasions when people ask for money, just shake your head and keep walking. Polite children in school uniforms will often have fund-raisers in tourist areas, and parents and teachers will be there. Donations are greatly appreciated and help local schools. A decade ago, drug dealers frequently approached visitors on Nassau's streets, but police have cracked down, especially in tourist areas. Most likely you'll only be asked if you want your hair braided. It's customary to address people by Mr., Miss, and Mrs. in business situations, and with taxi drivers, concierges, hotel managers, guides, and tour-desk operators. Bahamians are more formal than Americans, and they value good manners; always remember your pleases and thank-yous.

TIME

Bahamians tend to have a more casual attitude about time than visitors may be used to, which islanders say is because they've long lived a good life in a land where nature provided just about every need for housing, food, and livelihood. Bahamians believe there is always time to worry about the bad things tomorrow. Don't take it personally; things DO get done, though perhaps not at the rate you'd expect. Asking a Bahamian to hurry, especially if done rudely, however, may just slow things down. Stay polite, keep your humor, and try to slow down yourself—you'll have a better island experience.

INSECTS

No-see-ums (sand fleas) and mosquitoes can be bothersome. Some travelers have allergies to sand-flea bites, and the itching can be extremely annoying. To prevent the bites, use a recommended bug repellent. To ease the itching, rub alcohol on the bites. Some Out Island hotels provide sprays or repellents but it's a good idea to bring your own.

SUNBURN

Basking in the sun is one of the great pleasures of a Bahamian vacation, but because the sun is closer to Earth the farther south you go, it will burn your skin more quickly, so take precautions against sunburn and sunstroke.

On a sunny day, even people who are not normally bothered by strong sun should cover up with a long-sleeve shirt, a hat, and pants or a beach wrap while on a boat or midday at the beach. Carry UVA/UVB sunblock (with an SPF of at least 15) for your face and other sensitive areas. If you're engaging in water sports, be sure the sunscreen is waterproof.

Wear sunglasses, because eyes are particularly vulnerable to direct sun and reflected rays. Drink enough liquids—water or fruit juice preferably—and avoid coffee, tea, and alcohol. Above all, limit your sun time for the first few days until you become accustomed to the rays. Do not be fooled by an overcast day. The safest hours for sunbathing are 4–6 pm, but even then it's wise to limit initial exposure.

MEDICAL INSURANCE AND ASSISTANCE

The most serious accidents and illnesses may require an airlift to the United States—most likely to a hospital in Florida. The costs of a medical evacuation can quickly run into the thousands of dollars, and your personal health insurance may not cover such costs. If you plan to pursue inherently risky activities, such as scuba diving, or if you have an existing medical condition, check your policy to see what's covered.

Consider buying trip insurance with medical-only coverage. Neither Medicare nor some private insurers cover medical expenses anywhere outside the United States. Medical-only policies typically reimburse you for medical care (excluding that related to preexisting conditions) and hospitalization abroad, and provide for evacuation. You still have to pay the bills and await reimbursement from the insurer, though.

Another option is to sign up with a medical-evacuation assistance company. A membership in one of these companies gets you doctor referrals, emergency evacuation or repatriation, 24-hour hotlines for medical consultation, and other assistance. International SOS Assistance Emergency and AirMed International provide evacuation services and medical referrals. MedjetAssist offers medical evacuation.

Medical Assistance Companies AirMed International (⊕ www.airmed.com). **International SOS Assistance Emergency** (⊕ www.internationalsos.com). **MedjetAssist** (⊕ www.medjetassist.com).

Medical-Only Insurers International Medical Group (☎ 800/628–4664 ⊕ www.imglobal.com). **International SOS** (⊕ www.internationalsos.com). **Wallach & Company** (☎ 800/237–6615 ⊕ www.wallach.com).

OVER-THE-COUNTER REMEDIES

Pharmacies carry most of the same pain-relief products you find in the United States, but often at a higher price, so pack any over-the-counter medications you regularly use. They also sell a product called 2-2-2, which is equal parts aspirin, caffeine, and codeine. It's an effective pain-killer but can cause upset stomach.

Travelers prone to travel-related stomach disorders who are comfortable with alternative medicine might pick up some *po chai* tablets from a doctor of Eastern medicine or an Asian pharmacy—it's a great stomach cure-all.

▋ HOURS OF OPERATION

Banks are generally open Monday–Thursday 9 or 9:30 to 3 or 4 and Friday 9 to 5. However, on the Out Islands banks may keep shorter hours—on the smallest cays, they may be open only a day or two each week. Most Bahamian offices observe bank hours.

Hours for attractions vary. Most open between 9 and 10 and close around 5.

Though most drugstores typically abide by normal store hours, some stay open 24 hours.

Most stores, with the exception of straw markets and malls, close on Sunday.

HOLIDAYS
The grandest holiday of all is Junkanoo, a carnival that came from slaves who made elaborate costumes and instruments such as goatskin drums. Junkanoo is celebrated on Boxing Day, the day after Christmas, and New Year's Day (the bands compete in all-night parades that start in the wee hours). Don't expect to conduct any business the day after the festivities.

During other legal holidays, most offices close, and some may extend the holiday by keeping earlier (or no) hours the day before or after.

In the Bahamas official holidays include New Year's Day, Good Friday, Easter, Easter Monday, Whit Monday (last Mon. in May), Labour Day (1st Mon. in June), Independence Day (July 10), Emancipation Day (1st Mon. in Aug.), National Heroes Day (Oct. 12), Christmas Day, and Boxing Day (Dec. 26). In Turks and Caicos, islanders also celebrate Commonwealth Day (Mar.), Easter Monday, National Heroes Day (May), the Queen's Birthday (June), National Youth Day (Sept.), and International Human Rights Day (Oct.). They celebrate Emancipation Day (Aug. 1), but do not celebrate Whit Monday, Labour Day, or Independence Day.

▋ MAIL

Regardless of whether the term "snail mail" was coined in the Bahamas, you're likely to arrive home long before your postcards do—it's not unheard of for letters to take two to four weeks to reach their destinations. No postal (zip) codes are used in the Bahamas—all mail is collected from local area post-office boxes.

First-class mail from the Bahamas to the United States is 65¢ per half ounce; you'll pay 50¢ to mail a postcard. In Turks and Caicos prices are comparable. Postcard stamps good for foreign destinations are usually sold at shops selling postcards, so you don't have to make a special trip.

From the United States a postcard or a letter sent to the Bahamas costs 98¢.

SHIPPING PACKAGES
If you want to ship purchases home, take the same precautions you take in the United States—don't pack valuables or fragile items.

Express Services Copimaxx (☎ 242/328–2679). **FedEx** (☎ *242/352–3402 Freeport, 242/322–5656 Nassau, 242/367–2817 Abaco, 242/368–2540 Andros, 242/332–2720 Eleuthera, 242/337–6786 Long Island, 649/946–2542 Grand Turk, 649/946–4682 Providenciales, 800/247–4747 U.S. international customer service*). **Mail Boxes Etc.** (☎ *242/394–1508*).

▋ MONEY

Generally, prices in the Bahamas are slightly higher than in the United States. Businesses usually don't care whether you pay in U.S. dollars or Bahamian dollars, since they're the same value. In the Out Islands you'll notice that meals and simple goods can be expensive; prices are high due to the remoteness of the islands and the costs of importing.

ATMs are widely available, except on the most remote islands, but often the currency dispensed is Bahamian. If you have any left at the end of your stay, you can exchange it at the airport.

ITEM	AVERAGE COST
Cup of Coffee	$2
Glass of Wine	$7
Glass of Beer	$5
Sandwich	$8
Five-Mile Taxi Ride in Capital City	$12
Museum Admission	$5

Prices throughout this guide are given for adults. Substantially reduced fees are almost always available for children, students, and senior citizens.

ATMS AND BANKS

There are ATMs at banks, malls, resorts, and shops throughout the major islands. For excursions to remote locations, bring plenty of cash; there are few or no ATMs on some small cays, and on weekends or holidays, those that exist may run out of cash.

Banks are generally open Monday–Thursday 9 or 9:30 to 3 or 4 and Friday 9 to 5. However, on the Out Islands, banks may keep shorter hours—on the smallest cays, they may be open only a day or two each week.

■TIP➔ PINs with more than four digits are not recognized at ATMs in the Bahamas. If yours has five or more, remember to change it before you leave.

ATM Locations MasterCard/Cirrus (🖃 800/307–7309). **Visa/Plus** (🖃 800/847–2911).

CREDIT CARDS

When you book your hotel accommodations, be sure to ask if credit cards are accepted; some smaller hotels in the islands do not take plastic.

It's a good idea to inform your credit-card company before you travel, especially if you don't travel internationally very often. Otherwise, the credit-card company might put a hold on your card owing to unusual activity—not a good thing halfway through your trip.

Although it's usually cheaper (and safer) to use a credit card abroad for large purchases (so you can cancel payments or be reimbursed if there's a problem), note that some credit-card companies *and* the banks that issue them add substantial percentages to all foreign transactions, whether they're in a foreign currency or not. Check on these fees before leaving home, so there won't be any surprises when you get the bill.

CURRENCY AND EXCHANGE

The U.S. dollar is on par with the Bahamian dollar and is accepted all over the Bahamas. Bahamian money runs in bills of $1, $5, $10, $20, $50, and $100. The U.S. dollar is the currency of the Turks and Caicos. Since the U.S. currency is accepted everywhere, there really is no need to change to Bahamian. Also, you won't incur any transaction fees for currency exchange, or worry about getting stuck with unspent Bahamian dollars. Carry small bills when bargaining at straw markets.

▌PACKING

Aside from your bathing suit, which will be your favorite uniform, take lightweight clothing (short-sleeve shirts, T-shirts, cotton slacks, lightweight jackets for evening wear for men; light dresses, shorts, and T-shirts for women). If you're going during high season, between mid-December and April, toss in a sweater for the occasional cool evening. Cover up in public places and downtown shopping expeditions, and save that skimpy bathing suit for the beach at your hotel.

Some of the more sophisticated hotels require jackets for men and dresses for women at dinner. The Bahamas' casinos do not have dress codes.

PASSPORTS AND VISAS

U.S. citizens need a valid passport when entering and returning from the Bahamas, but do not need a visa.

U.S. Passport Information U.S. Department of State (☎ 877/487-2778 ⊕ travel.state.gov/passport).

SAFETY

Since 2009 there has been a significant spike in violent crime in Nassau, especially near the cruise-ship dock and in off-the-beaten-path locations. Exercise caution in these areas: be aware of your wallet or handbag at all times, and keep your jewelry in the hotel safe. Be especially wary in remote areas, always lock your rental vehicle, and don't keep any valuables in the car, even in the locked trunk.

Women traveling alone should not go out walking unescorted at night in Nassau or in remote areas. To avoid unwanted attention, dress conservatively and cover up swimsuits off the beach.

General Information and Warnings U.S. Department of State (⊕ www.travel.state.gov/travel).

TAXES

There's no sales tax in the Bahamas; the $15 departure tax is usually included in the price of commercial airline tickets. The departure tax from Turks and Caicos is $30 for persons older than age 12. It will probably be included in your airfare, but you may need to pay it in cash at the airport.

Tax on your hotel room is 6%–12%, depending on the island visited; at some resorts, a small service charge of up to 5% may be added to cover housekeeping and bellman service.

TIME

The Bahamas and the Turks and Caicos lie within the Eastern Standard Time (EST) Zone, which means that it's 7 am in the Bahamas (or New York) when it's noon in London and 10 pm in Sydney. In summer the islands switch to Eastern Daylight Time (EDT).

TIPPING

The usual tip for service from a taxi driver or waiter is 15% and $1–$2 a bag for porters. Many hotels and restaurants automatically add a 15% gratuity to your bill.

TIPPING GUIDELINES FOR THE BAHAMAS	
Bartender	$1–$2 per drink
Bellhop	$1–$5 per bag, depending on the level of the hotel
Coat Check	$1–$2 per item checked unless there is a fee, then nothing
Hotel Concierge	$5 or more, if he or she performs a service for you
Hotel Doorman	$1–$2 if he helps you get a cab
Hotel Maid	$1–$3 a day (either daily or at the end of your stay, in cash)
Hotel Room-Service Waiter	$1–$2 per delivery, even if a service charge has been added
Porter at Airport or Train Station	$1 per bag
Restroom Attendant	Small change or $1 in more expensive restaurants
Skycap at Airport	$1–$3 per bag checked
Taxi Driver	15%–20%, but round up the total to the next dollar amount
Tour Guide	10% of the cost of the tour

TIPPING GUIDELINES FOR THE BAHAMAS	
Valet Parking Attendant	$1–$2, but only when you get your car
Waiter	15%–20%, with 20% being the norm at high-end restaurants

▮ TRIP INSURANCE

Comprehensive trip insurance is valuable if you're booking a considerably expensive or complicated trip (particularly to an isolated region) or if you're booking far in advance. Comprehensive policies typically cover trip cancellation and interruption, letting you cancel or cut your trip short because of illness, or, in some cases, acts of terrorism in your destination. Such policies might also cover evacuation and medical care. (For trips abroad you should have at least medical-only coverage. ⇨ See *Medical Insurance and Assistance under Health.*) Some also cover you for trip delays because of bad weather or mechanical problems as well as for lost or delayed luggage.

Another type of coverage to consider is financial default—that is, when your trip is disrupted because a tour operator, airline, or cruise line goes out of business. Generally you must buy this when you book your trip or shortly thereafter, and it's available to you only if your operator isn't on a list of excluded companies.

Always read the fine print of your policy to make sure that you're covered for the risks that most concern you. Compare several polices to be sure you're getting the best price and range of coverage available.

Insurance Comparison Info Insure My Trip (☏ 800/487–4722 ⊕ www.insuremytrip.com). **Square Mouth** (☏ 800/240–0369 ⊕ www.squaremouth.com).

Comprehensive Insurers Access America (☏ 800/284–8300 ⊕ www.accessamerica.com). **AIG Travel Guard** (☏ 800/826–4919 ⊕ www.travelguard.com). **CSA Travel Protection** (☏ 800/711–1197 ⊕ www.csatravelprotection.com). **HTH Worldwide** (☏ 610/254–8700 ⊕ www.hthworldwide.com). **Travelex Insurance** (☏ 800/228–9792 ⊕ www.travelex-insurance.com). **Travel Insured International** (☏ 800/243–3174 ⊕ www.travelinsured.com).

▮ VISITOR INFORMATION

Contacts Bahamas Ministry of Tourism (☏ 800/224–2627 ⊕ www.bahamas.com). **Bahamas Out Islands Promotion Board** (☏ 954/475–8315 ⊕ www.myoutislands.com). **Caribbean Tourism Organization** (☏ 212/635–9530 ⊕ www.doitcaribbean.com). **Grand Bahama Island Tourism Board** (☏ 800/545–1300 ⊕ www.grandbahamavacations.com). **Harbour Island Tourism** (⊕ www.harbourislandguide.com). **Nassau/Paradise Island Promotion Board** (☏ 888/627–7281 ⊕ www.nassauparadiseisland.com). **Turks and Caicos Islands Tourist Board** (☏ 800/241–0824 ⊕ www.turksandcaicostourism.com).

BahamasGateway.com (⊕ www.bahamasgateway.com). **BahamasIslands.com** (⊕ www.the-bahamas-islands.com). **Bahamasnet.com** (⊕ www.bahamasnet.com). **Bahamas-Travel.info** (⊕ www.bahamas-travel.info). **FishingtheBahamian.com** (⊕ www.fishing.thebahamian.com). **Friends of the Bahamas** (⊕ www.friendsofthebahamas.com). **Nassau Guardian** (⊕ www.thenassauguardian.com). **Bahamas Visitors Guide** (www.bahamasvisitorsguide.com).

INDEX

A

35 (all), The Bahamas Ministry of Tourism. 36, frantisekhojdysz/Shutterstock. 38, Ray Wadia/The Bahamas Ministry of Tourism. 39 (both), 40, and 41 (top left and bottom left), The Bahamas Ministry of Tourism. 41 (right), Ray Wadia/The Bahamas Ministry of Tourism. 42, The Bahamas Ministry of Tourism. Chapter 2: New Providence and Paradise Islands: 43, DEA/A VERGANI/age fotostock. 44 (top), Roland Rose. 44 (bottom right), Lijuan Guo/Shutterstock. 45, Macduff Everton/Atlantis. 48, Firecrest Pictures/age fotostock. 49 (top), Dolphin Encounters Limited/wikipedia.org. 49 (bottom), Ramona Settle. 50, Daniel Korzeniewski/iStockphoto. 52, The Bahamas Ministry of Tourism. 56, Laurin Johnson/iStockphoto. 58, Macduff Everton/Atlantis. 59 (bottom left), Richard Riley/Atlantis. 59 (top right), Macduff Everton/Atlantis. 59 (center right), livingonimpulse/Flickr. 59 (bottom right), Seth Browarnik. 60, Tim Aylen/Atlantis. 61 (top left), Ron Starr/Atlantis. 61 (top center), Jeffrey Brown/Tallgrass Pictures LLC/Atlantis. 61 (top right), Jeffrey Brown/Atlantis. 61 (bottom), Macduff Everton/Atlantis. 62 (left), Fred Hsu/wikipedia.org. 62 (right), Ron Starr/Atlantis. 67, Meazza/IML/age fotostock. 72, Francis Janisch. 76, Graycliff Hotel. 81, Bruce Wolf. 87, Ramona Settle. 91, Walter Bibikow/age fotostock. 92 (left), biskuit/Flickr. 92 (right), Jef Nickerson/Flickr. 93 (top), Bahamas Ministry of Tourism. 93 (bottom), Peter Adams/age fotostock. 94, Shane Pinder/Alamy. 95 (top), JTB Photo/photolibrary.com. 95 (bottom), Shane Pinder/Alamy. 100-101, Remedios Valls Lopez/age fotostock. 102, Lars Topelmann/The Bahamas Ministry of Tourism. Chapter 3: Grand Bahama Island: 105, Walter Bibikow/age fotostock. 106 (left), Thomas Lorenz/Shutterstock. 106 (right) and 107 (top), The Bahamas Ministry of Tourism. 107 (bottom), Denis Jr. Tangney/iStockphoto. 110, Alvaro leiva/age fotostock. 111 (top), Ramona Settle. 111 (bottom), Letizia Spanò/Shutterstock. 112, The Bahamas Ministry of Tourism. 113 (top), Thomas Lorenz/Shutterstock. 113 (bottom) and 114, The Bahamas Ministry of Tourism. 116, FLPA/Michael Gore/age fotostock. 121, The Bahamas Ministry of Tourism. 122, Robert Holmes/Alamy. 127, Our Lucaya Beach and Golf Resort. 132, The Bahamas Ministry of Tourism. 135, Davis James/age fotostock. 139, Dirscherl Reinhard/age fotostock. 142, The Bahamas Ministry of Tourism. Chapter 4: The Abacos: 145, SuperStock/age fotostock. 146, Island Effects/iStockphoto. 150, DEA/A VERGANI/age fotostock. 151 (top and bottom), The Bahamas Ministry of Tourism. 152, FLPA/age fotostock. 153 (top), flickerized/Flickr. 153 (bottom), Kate Philips/iStockphoto. 154, The Bahamas Ministry of Tourism. 159, Danita Delimont/Alamy. 164, Sunpix Marine/Alamy. 170, Mathew Lodge/lodgephoto.com/Alamy. 177, Imagestate/age fotostock. 180, keithwright.com. 182, Ramona Settle. Chapter 5: Andros, Bimini, and the Berry Islands: 191, Greg Johnston/age fotostock. 192 (left), The Bahamas Ministry of Tourism. 192 (right), andydidyk/iStockphoto. 193 (top and bottom), Lars Topelmann/The Bahamas Ministry of Tourism. 196 Gregory Pelt/Shutterstock. 197 (top), Mangrove Mike/Flickr. 197 (bottom), Knumina/Shutterstock. 198, Lars Topelmann/The Bahamas Ministry of Tourism. 201, Juliet Coombe/age fotostock. 206, Greg Johnston/age fotostock. 213, Tiamo Resort. 216, BARBAGALLO Franco / age fotostock. 219, Mark Conlin/Alamy. 222, Larry Larsen / Alamy. 227, Amy Strycula / Alamy. Chapter 6: Eleuthera and Harbour Island: 229, John Webster / age fotostock. 230 (left), Cookie Kincaid. 230 (center), pics721/Shutterstock. 230 (right), Jon Beard/Shutterstock. 234, Ellen Rooney / age fotostock. 235 (top), Lars Topelmann/The Bahamas Ministry of Tourism. 235 (bottom) and 236, The Bahamas Ministry of Tourism. 237 (top), Cookie Kincaid. 237 (bottom), The Bahamas Ministry of Tourism. 238, Trevor Bauer/iStockphoto. 244, Cheryl Blackerby. 247, Greg Johnston/age fotostock. 251, Cheryl Blackerby. 254-55, The Bahamas Ministry of Tourism. 256, Greg Johnston/The Bahamas Tourist Office. 261, Alvaro Leiva/ age fotostock. 264, Cookie Kincaid. 268-69, Ian Cumming/age fotostock. Chapter 7: The Exumas: 271, ARCO/F Schneider / age fotostock. 272 (all) and 273 (top), Staniel Cay Yacht Club. 273 (bottom), The Bahamas Ministry of Tourism. 276 and 277 (bottom), Staniel Cay Yacht Club. 277 (top), Ramona Settle. 278 and 279 (bottom), The Bahamas Ministry of Tourism. 279 (top), Ray Wadia/The Bahamas Ministry of Tourism. 280, The Bahamas Ministry of Tourism. 285, Cheryl Blackerby. 287, Ramona Settle. 290, Cheryl Blackerby. 294, Staniel Cay Yacht Club. 297, Cheryl Blackerby. 298, Staniel Cay Yacht Club. Chapter 8: The Southern Out Islands: 301, Greg Johnston/age fotostock. 302 (top), The Bahamas Ministry of Tourism. 302 (bottom), Ray Wadia/The Bahamas Ministry of Tourism. 303 (left), Nina Henry/iStockphoto. 303 (right), The Bahamas Ministry of Tourism. 306, Greg Johnston/Cape Santa Maria Beach Resort. 307 (top), The Bahamas Ministry of Tourism. 307 (bottom), Ray Wadia/The Bahamas Ministry of Tourism. 308, Cheryl Blackerby. 309 (top), Patrick Swint/Flickr. 309 (bottom), stephan kerkhofs/Shutterstock. 310, Jeff Greenberg / Alamy. 311 (top), Cheryl Blackerby. 311 (bottom), mweichse/Shutterstock. 312, Greg Johnston/Cape Santa Maria Beach Resort. 319, Michael DeFreitas / age fotostock. 320, Ray Wadia/The Bahamas Ministry of Tourism. 323, Greg Johnston/age fotostock. 328, The Bahamas Ministry of Tourism. 331, Greg Johnston/age fotostock. 334 and 337, Greg Johnston/Cape Santa Maria Beach Resort. 341 and 342-43, BARBAGALLO Franco / age fotostock. 347, Greg Johnston/age fotostock. 350, Greg Johnston/Cape Santa Maria Beach Resort. Chapter 9: Turks and Caicos Islands: 353, Takaji Ochi – VWPICS/age fotostock. 354 (left), Angelo Cavalli/age fotostock. 354 (right) and 355, Turks & Caicos Tourism. 359, Joaquin Palting/iStockphoto. 360-63, Ramona Settle. 375, West Bay Club. 379, Turks & Caicos Tourist Office. 383, COMO Hotels and Resorts. 391, Ian Cumming/age fotostock.

ABOUT OUR WRITERS

Cheryl Blackerby has written for *The New York Times, The Chicago Tribune, The Miami Herald,* and was the travel editor at *The Palm Beach Post.* She lives in Florida, just 56 miles from the Bahamas, her favorite home-away-from-home. She spent plenty of time there this year, updating our Eleuthera, Exumas, and Southern Out Islands chapters.

Born and raised in Nassau, Justin Higgs now resides in the Abacos with his wife, his daughter, and his dog. They enjoy the many outdoor adventures that the island offers and can often be found anchored off a beach or kayaking a creek. Justin runs a small kayak company and teaches at a local primary school. He also wrote our Great Water Adventures feature.

Chelle Koster Walton admits she's a "fairweather writer"—her specialty is travel to Florida and the Caribbean. She has written for such publications as *FamilyFun, Bridal Guide, The St. Petersburg Times, National Geographic Traveler,* and the *Miami Herald.* For us, she updated the Grand Bahama Island and Andros, Bimini, and the Berry Islands chapters. A resident of Sanibel Island, Florida, for 25 years, she is the author of several Florida guidebooks, including *Sarasota, Sanibel Island & Naples, Fun with the Family in Florida,* and *Adventure Guide to Tampa Bay & Florida's West Coast.*

Kevin Kwan, our Harbour Island guru, is a writer, photographer, and creative consultant who considers himself a perpetual islander. Born on the island of Singapore, he is now based on the island of Manhattan, but spends as much time as he can discovering other islands around the globe. Books he's authored include *I Was Cuba* and *Luck: The Essential Guide.*

Born in England and bred in the Bahamas, Jessica Robertson has traveled the world for work and play but calls Nassau home. Our New Providence expert has visited just about all of the populated islands in the Bahamas, as well as some occupied only by hermit crabs and seagulls, and works as the online editor for *The Tribune,* the country's daily newspaper. Jessica also wrote our Experience chapter, and the beautiful features on Bahamas beaches, Atlantis, Junkanoo, and Rake 'n' Scrape.

Patricia Rodriguez Terrell lived in the Caribbean for nearly three years, including a stretch on a tiny cay in the Abacos, where everyone got around by golf cart or fishing boat and where she developed a deep love of grouper burgers and cracked conch. She, her husband (a chef), and their young son—who learned how to walk on the soft beaches of the Bahamas—now live in Texas, where she works as a writer and editor. Patricia updated our Bahamas Travel Smart section.

On a quest to find the best beaches in the world, Ramona Settle chose Providenciales in the Turks and Caicos Islands—where each beach has more beautiful turquoise water than the last—to be her second home. She also updated our San Salvador coverage.

After years of traveling all over the United States, Europe, and twenty-six Caribbean islands, Sharon Williams and her husband decided to make Long Island, Bahamas, their second home. They divide their time between the island and Little Rock, Arkansas. A former newspaper columnist, Sharon has had articles published in magazines such as *International Living.*